Contributors

Brian W. Beeley, *Pahlavi University (Shiraz, Iran)*

The Christian Science Monitor, **John K. Cooley**

Richard H. Dekmejian, *State University of New York, Binghamton*

Pennsylvania State University, **Arthur E. Goldschmidt, Jr.**

George H. Gardner, *Alfred University*

Eastern Michigan University, **Benjamin T. Hourani**

Norman F. Howard, *Washington, D.C.*

State University of New York, Stony Brook, **Eliyahu Kanovsky**

Robert G. Landen, *University of South Carolina*

U.S. Department of State, **David E. Long**

James B. Mayfield, *University of Utah*

U.S. Department of State, **David Wm. McClintock**

John G. Merriam, *Bowling Green State University*

Bowling Green State University, **Kathleen H. Merriam**

Gholam H. Razi, *University of Houston*

Wisconsin State University, Oshkosh, **Farouk A. Sankari**

Frank Tachau, *University of Illinois, Chicago*

New College, **Majid Tehranian**

The Middle East: Its Governments and Politics

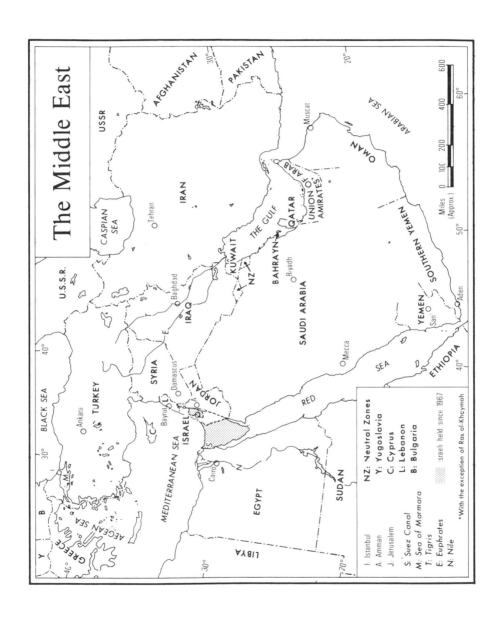

The Middle East

I. Istanbul
A. Amman
J. Jerusalem
S. Suez Canal
M. Sea of Marmara
T. Tigris
E. Euphrates
N. Nile

NZ: Neutral Zones
Y: Yugoslavia
C: Cyprus
L: Lebanon
B: Bulgaria

Israeli held since 1967

*With the exception of Ras al-Khaymah

Miles
(Approx)
0   100   200   400   600

The Middle East: Its Governments and Politics

by
Abid A. Al-Marayati
Professor of Political Science
The University of Toledo
and others

Foreword by John S. Badeau

Duxbury Press
A Division of Wadsworth Publishing Company, Inc., Belmont, California

Dedication

To
Gordon W. Allport
and
C. Worth Howard
and
all who by their interest and support
have assisted
the people of the Middle East
through humanitarian endeavors

Duxbury Press

A Division of Wadsworth Publishing Company, Inc.

L.C. Cat. Card No.: 72-75342   ISBN: 0-87872-016-2

Printed in the United States of America
1 2 3 4 5 6 7 8 9 10–76 75 74 73 72

Contents

Maps

Foreword

A century ago Muhammad Abdu, the Egyptian reformer, complained that "verily, politics corrupts everything." Without subscribing to this cynical view (born out of the frustrations of a liberal amidst a conservative society) we can say that "verily, politics *infects* everything." For as the ancients well knew, "man is a political animal," and almost everything he does is colored by political behavior. Only religion has had a deeper and more pervasive effect—and religion often has a political dimension, as Islam clearly shows.

This obvious point is made only because it is sometimes forgotten. With the myriad new approaches to human behavior, politics may be seen as only secondary or derivative, the more basic place being assigned to economics or sociology. Even when the role of politics is admitted, it may be undervalued as being the exclusive preserve of the elite and thus irrelevant to the bulk of Middle Eastern society.

A practical refutation of this point of view came when the Anglo-Iranian Oil Company and the Iranian government moved toward their final confrontation in 1951. It was then argued that Iran would never cut off its economic nose to spite its political face; oil revenues were too basic to the Iranian economy to be sacrificed to the political demands of nationalism, which paid no bills. But the sacrifice was made just the same; when the cards were down Iran chose its political amour propre rather than a balanced budget. This is a value judgment many other Middle Eastern countries have made and will continue to make.

Thus politics—its institutions, operations, popular manifestations, ideologies, and policies—is an unusually revealing area for the study of the Middle East. Hence this book, designed in part as a general introduction to the area, chooses as its focus and organizing principle the political dimension of the contemporary Middle East.

But how is that dimension to be appraised and understood? One method is to use the theoretician's approach and to construct a model of political development in the Middle East during modern times. This might begin with the traditional "Oriental despotisms" with which the Middle East emerged from the medieval period, then note the introduction of modern, Western political institutions (constitutions, parliaments, cabinets, political parties) under the impact of contact with and penetration by Western powers. Both the modernizing Middle Eastern elite and the liberal European imperialist seemed to agree that "a little dose of constitutionalism would cure all ills" (to quote an Egyptian friend).

But the dose was either too little or the prescription inappropriate, for constitutionalism in the liberal Western pattern has not been a notable success in most Middle Eastern countries. With the slackening of colonial controls, the attainment of full sovereignty, and the pressure of swelling social discontent after the war, many Middle Eastern states abandoned their Western political patterns and adopted some form of radical, authoritarian government. Kemalism in Turkey, Nasserism in Egypt, and the Baath party program for the Arab world are examples of this trend, which some analysts see as the wave of the future in the Middle East's political development.

But such theoretical models, useful as they are in providing an overview of the political development of the area, are inadequate as descriptions of the political process. For one thing, they neglect the inherent differences which characterize the states and societies that make up that misleading concept *the Middle East*. Excluding North Africa west of Egypt, there are twelve major political units in the region, each of which has its own ethnic composition, social patterns, economic forms, and national interests. Inevitably these differences affect political behavior and are elements in the particular path of political development the nation follows. That the throne in Egypt toppled before the first serious challenge of social discontent, whereas the monarchy in Iran has proved remarkably resilient amid the turmoil of popular pressures, is no accident. Iran and Egypt are different countries with different traditions; it is not to be assumed that they will act alike.

Moreover, although the modern political development of the Middle East bears the impact of foreign institutions and ideas (conservative, liberal, and radical) it is shot through with its own traditions and practices. What appeared to many as a copy of European statism (Marxist or Fascist) in the recent wave of radical political developments is in fact partly the reemergence of an indigenous pattern of absolutism and military rule that was native to the area long before the rise of Communist Russia or Nazi Germany.

The Middle East: Its Governments and Politics is concerned with just such diffuse and diverse elements in the political life of the contemporary Middle East. Its object is not to supply the student with a theoretical analysis of political behavior or the structure of political systems but to place him 'inside" the scene, viewing it "from the bottom," where all the tangled skeins of political influences hang loose. This is why the book, politically oriented as it is, will be such a useful general introduction to the modern scene. "Pull out one brick and the whole house falls down," says an Arab proverb; having started with politics we find ourselves quickly involved in almost every other aspect of Middle Eastern life.

It follows that the treatment of the Middle East is necessarily interdisplinary in character. In addition to political science, history, geography, economics, and sociology, diplomacy and the experience of a foreign correspondent are brought to bear on the study. This provides a multidimensional framework within which the political characteristics of the area are appraised. To this diversity of disciplines is added a careful balance between the area as a whole and the various distinct countries which are included in it. The interdisciplinary emphasis is found chiefly in the first section of the book, where the Middle East as a region is considered. In the following section each country is given separate treatment, which provides both illustrations of and variances from regional characteristics.

Such treatment could result in little more than a potpourri of general information, especially when it is the work of a panel of authors, but it does not in this book. The central theme of politics and the editor's coordination of his authors results in a well-articulated presentation. Politics has not corrupted this book, but it does infect everything– which is one reason the book will be a useful addition to our study of the region.

Georgetown University   John S. Badeau
Washington, D.C.

Preface

It is difficult to understand a political system merely by studying its constitution or its government organization. History, cultural milieu, social structure, economic conditions, and other factors also affect political processes and must be taken into account. *The Middle East: Its Governments and Politics* attempts to pursue such an interdisciplinary course in an effort to offer the reader a balanced, thorough picture of the Middle Eastern political scene. Because no one specialist could know the entire region—an area of great complexity and diversity—a group of authors collaborated on the book. The group includes representatives from such academic disciplines as history, sociology, economics, geography, and political science—as well as a journalist and two diplomats.

Due to many limitations it was not possible to include contributions from some disciplines that could further aid the study of political processes—psychology and anthropology, for example—which is unfortunate because efforts at policy planning can be frustrated if psychological and cultural factors are ignored.

Each author assumes sole responsibility for his work and does not necessarily agree with the other points of view expressed in the book. The reader should be aware of these conflicting attitudes regarding the Middle East and should note the different opinions and interpretations.

The transliterations adopted in this text do not pursue a single system. The spellings adhere as closely as possible to the pronunciations of the original language, but names that are familiar—Gamal Abdul Nasser, for example—are usually given their popular spelling as a convenience to the reader.

In executing this project I have had help and advice from persons too numerous to mention by name. However, I would like to express my particular thanks to the group whose cooperation made this study possible. Frank Tachau, Arthur Goldschmidt, Jr., Brian Beeley, Robert Landen, John and Kathleen Merriam, Norman Howard, and Eliyahu Kanovsky provided advice and comments that facilitated the coordination of the project. John Merriam also assisted in the preparation of the list of foreign names and words. Dr. Beeley initiated work on the glossary and prepared all maps except the map of the Gulf states, which was provided by Robert Landen.

Special thanks are due Abbas Alnasrawi, Robert Cunningham, Joseph Ben-Dak, Samir Abu Absi, Nabil Sukkar, J. van Wijk, Basil A. Collins, and Betty Steele for their suggestions. I am also grateful to my students Timothy Leonard, Arthur Marquardt, and Charles Grossman, who as prospective readers contributed valuable advice. I appreciate the work of Peter K. Bechtold, Dwight J. Simpson, and Stanford J. Shaw, who provided thoughtful comments that helped the group revise their chapters and who assisted in coordinating the project.

Thanks are also due to Constance Sherman and Stephen Hammalian, initial editors, and to Sandra Craig, who edited the final manuscript. And special thanks are due to Betty Lampert, Doris Taube, Elaine Welling, Barbara Rendahl, and Patricia Wiczynski for their typing.

Last, but not least, my apologies to Ghazi and Connie for the neglect that resulted from my involvement in this project.

Toledo, Ohio, January 1972   Abid A. Al-Marayati

1

Introduction

Spreading into three continents, the Middle East defies description by one or even a few criteria. Neither the Islamic religion nor the Arabic language characterizes the region. Whereas most Americans know that the Middle East holds more than half the world's known petroleum reserves, few are familiar either with Islam or with the political and cultural variety of the mosaic of independent states. Instead, the stereotypical camel-riding bedouin crossing desert wastes looms large in Western eyes, even though most Middle Easterners are as far removed from this tradition as Americans from the life of the Old West.

Strategic considerations have figured prominently in the big powers' view of the Middle East ever since Marco Polo traveled to the Far East, the Ottomans sat astride the Mediterranean, and the British in more recent times considered it the lifeline of their empire. Today the ships of the Soviet Union cruise the waterways of the region alongside those of the United States, perhaps signaling the beginning of a new era in the region's politics. If this is the case, long-held stereotypes associated with the area and its peoples will be a poor substitute for a more sophisticated understanding of the region.

The birthplace of human civilization and of Judaism, Christianity, and Islam, the Middle East is also a center of cultural, political, and economic conflict. In its widely varied population, in living conditions that range from abject poverty to the most sumptuous riches, in fierce domestic and national rivalries, and in its crucial position amid the world's great power blocs, the area mirrors the complex struggles in the rest of the world.

There are, in fact, perhaps as many sources of conflict and rivalry among the Middle Eastern states as bases for unity and cooperation. Islam provides a common cultural heritage for the Muslim states (all of the Middle East except Israel and half of Lebanon); oil has encouraged some cooperation among the major petroleum exporting countries (Iran, Iraq, Kuwait, Saudi Arabia, and some of the Gulf states); and Arab nationalism is a source of unity for the Arab states of the region. At the same time, however, nationalism is a source of rivalry between the Arab and the Zionist, between the parochial Arab and the pan-Arab. Conflicts of ideology (e.g., monarchic versus republican, neutralist versus aligned, nationalist versus Communist) also cut across religious and national loyalties.

Middle Eastern countries also differ in a variety of other ways. No two states have identical government structures. Each has its own traditions and its own political, religious, linguistic, and economic groupings. Some countries have meager resources; others are rich in oil.

Despite the diversity, regional trends can be discerned and valid comparisons can be made. The Middle Eastern states are all searching for a "modern" political community, a community based on "modern" as opposed to "traditional" structures and belief systems. This political modernization process involves adapting man's belief systems and political structures to cope with new environmental challenges. The precise nature of that modern community and the progress toward it differ from state to state and must be understood in terms of each state's heritage, present cultural development, and specific objectives.

Traditionalism and modernity are not "bad" or "good" per se; rather, these terms are the social scientist's shorthand for describing change in the socioeconomic and political life of a state. Nor is this transition uniquely Middle Eastern; it is worldwide in the twentieth century. Despite the agonies of change, the problems it creates, and the sacrifices it demands, it is sought by most leaderships.

This transition has proceeded further in some Middle Eastern countries than in others. Israel has a high proportion of modern trained and oriented personnel and is in several respects a modern state, in government as in war. Turkey and Egypt, which initiated comprehensive reform programs in the nineteenth century, have advanced further than Iran, which did not do so until the middle of the twentieth century. Since World War II immense oil export revenues have accelerated the development of Iran, Iraq, Kuwait, Saudi Arabia, and the Gulf states. In some countries special local factors, such as the power of Israel's and Lebanon's religious establishments and the barriers to communication between different parts of Iran, impede the transition to modernity. The social strain caused by transition may also erupt in internal strife and lead to unstable governments, as in Syria and Iraq, and possibly to dictatorial regimes that suppress liberty to restore order. Foreign political control, in Egypt, for instance, may hasten economic and political development but may also aggravate social divisions and delay the assumption of self-government.

The major instruments of modernization available to the Middle Eastern states have been the army, the bureaucracy, the political party, and voluntary associations in the form of interest groups. Charismatic leaders have been effective catalysts for change but have found it necessary to institutionalize their rule through one or more of the modernizing instruments.

Thus the Middle East is far more complex than popular stereotypes would suggest. Partly because of the Arab-Israeli conflict, the Middle East has become the arena for clashes of the big powers and conflicts between and within states that may well dominate the remainder of the twentieth century. These main conflicts, however, should not be allowed to obscure the many other important processes and problems in the area.

This volume covers the non-Arab states of Iran, Israel, and Turkey and the Arab states of Egypt, Iraq, Syria, Lebanon, Jordan, Saudi Arabia, Kuwait, the Gulf states (Bahrayn, Qatar, Abu Dhabi, Dubai, Sharjah, Ajman, Umm al-Qaywayn, Ras al-Khaymah, Al-Fujayrah, Oman),* Yemen, and the People's Democratic Republic of Yemen (see table 1), and attempts to examine this core area comprehensively. It is concerned with the area's political systems at the national, regional, and international levels as they interact with its social and economic systems. It emphasizes a political perspective on the region and recognizes political change as a dynamic process requiring an understanding of the historical and environmental patterns.

Part 1 of this book studies the geography, history, economic conditions, and sociocultural factors in the region as a whole; there is also an introduction to contemporary political thought and the challenge of political modernization. It is hoped that the reader can proceed "inside" the region via these interdisciplinary chapters and keep this vantage point as he examines the area country by country in part 2. The chapters provide a brief introduction to the history, economics, culture, and social structure of each country, and analyze each state's political structure and processes and foreign policy, with particular emphasis on events since World War II. Part 3 shows how internal social, economic, and political change in a strategic area like the Middle East is affected by external and regional forces and examines the region's international relations. Because of its regional and international significance, the emergence of Palestinian nationalism is especially emphasized.

In general this book concentrates on what is happening in the Middle East and why. Thus, each chapter in part 2 asks these fundamental questions: What are the problems facing this country? What institutions have been developed to solve these problems? What processes of political decision making are emerging, and to what extent have they been successful in solving their problems and achieving their goals?

Although the chapters analyze the development and organization of the country's formal political institutions, these formal

---

*Six of these states—Abu Dhabi, Dubai, Sharjah, Ajman, Umm al-Qaywayn, and Al-Fujayrah—formed the Union of Arab Amirates in December 1971. Ras al-Khaymah (who with the six made up the former Trucial States) elected to remain out of the union.

institutions are examined in terms of what they really do—not what they are supposed to do. In other words, the function they perform in the political process must be identified, and students must be able to distinguish between a legislature that actually makes laws and one that merely rubber-stamps a decision made by someone else. This is often more difficult than it may seem. These chapters seek to make the distinctions by emphasizing the dynamics of political decision making, focusing on the ideology, group behavior, and leadership styles of the various political elites. A beginning student of Middle Eastern politics who understands this complex interaction of formal and informal processes will have a fuller awareness of the problems and prospects faced by the nations of this troubled area.

Table 1
Political Data

Country[a]	Form of Government[b]	Capital	Arab League	Other Membership	Colonial Influence[c]
Egypt[d]	Republic	Cairo	Yes		U.K., 1882-1954; Ottoman, 1517-1914
Iraq[e]	Republic	Baghdad	Yes	OPEC	U.K., 1918-32; Ottoman, 1638-1918
Syria[f]	Republic	Damascus	Yes		France, 1918-46; Ottoman, 1516-1918
Lebanon	Republic	Beirut	Yes		France, 1918-46; Ottoman, 1516-1918
Jordan[g]	Monarchy	Amman	Yes	Sterling area	U.K., 1918-46; Ottoman, 1516-1918
Saudi Arabia[e,h]	Monarchy	Riyadh	Yes	OPEC	(Hijaz) Ottoman, 1517-1916
Kuwait[h]	Amirate (monarchy)	Kuwait	Yes	OPEC	U.K., 1899-1961; Ottoman, 1871-1914
Bahrayn	Amirate	Manama	Yes		U.K., 1880-1971
Qatar	Amirate	Doha	Yes	OPEC	U.K., 1916-71
Trucial States[i]	Amirates	Dubai	No		U.K., 1853-1971
Oman	Sultanate	Muscat	Yes		U.K., 1798-1971
Yemen	Republic	Sanaa	Yes		Ottoman, 1568-1630, 1849-1918

Table 1 (Continued)

Country[a]	Form of Government[b]	Capital	Arab League	Other Membership	Colonial Influence[c]
People's Democratic Republic of Yemen	Republic	Aden	Yes		U.K., 1839-1967
Israel[j]	Republic	Tel Aviv[k] Jerusalem	No[l]		(Palestine) U.K., 1918-48; Ottoman, 1516-1918
Turkey	Republic	Ankara	No	NATO, CENTO, EEC (assoc.)	
Iran	Monarchy	Tehran	No	OPEC, CENTO	

[a]This list only includes countries considered in this book. Arab countries excluded are Libya, Tunisia, Algeria, Morocco, and the Sudan; non-Arab countries such as Cyprus, Afghanistan, and Pakistan are also excluded.

[b]The form of government is based mainly on the constitutional enactments of the states.

[c]"Colonial influence" implies either political or military presence; brief occupations (such as wartime occupations of parts of Turkey and Iran) are not covered.

[d]From 1949 to 1967 Egypt also administered the Gaza Strip (Palestine). Since 1967 part of Egypt (Sinai) has been under Israeli occupation.

[e]Plus a share in the Iraq-Saudi Arabia Neutral Zone.

[f]Since 1967 the Golan Heights area of Syria has been under Israeli occupation.

[g]From 1949 to 1967 Jordan also administered the West Bank (Palestine), now under Israeli occupation.

[h]Plus a share in the Kuwait-Saudi Arabia Neutral Zone.

[i]Dubai, Abu Dhabi, Sharjah, Al-Fujayrah, Ajman, and Umm al-Qaywayn formed the Union of Arab Amirates in December 1971; Ras al-Khaymah was the only one of the Trucial States that did not join the union.

[j]The territory within the 1949 Armistice lines; since 1967 the West Bank, the Gaza Strip, the Golan Heights (Syria), and the Sinai (Egypt) have also been under Israeli rule.

[k]Israel considers Jerusalem its capital; other countries recognize Tel Aviv.

[l]The Palestine Liberation Organization is associated with the Arab League.

The Land and The People

The Land

Physical Setting

In the physical setting of the Middle East, concentrations of population and political action are separated from one another. To begin with, several major waterways fragment the region. In the west, the Mediterranean separates Arab North Africa from Europe, although an arm of that sea, the Aegean, provides a link through the Sea of Marmara and the Bosporus with the Black Sea. South of the Suez Canal, the Red Sea extends to the Indian Ocean. The Gulf (known also as the Persian or the Arabian Gulf) lies between the Arabian peninsula and Iran, which also has a northern coast on the Caspian, the world's largest inland sea. These land-sea divisions helped create the region's historical and societal variety, as did the contrast between upland and lowland. In terms of geologic structure, there are folded mountain ranges in Turkey and Iran, and to their south, a basement of hard rock split by the east African Rift Valley and its northerly extension up through the Red Sea and the Jordan valley.

Thus, for most of the Arab world, nature has provided a lowland zone interrupted by seas and by arid desert rather than by great mountain ranges. One could consider the spread of Arab culture through this southern zone or study the persistence of Byzantine power in Anatolia until it was eventually subordinated to Turkic penetration from central Asia. Much of the cultural variety of the northern uplands can be understood in terms of its topographic variety, which has facilitated the survival of many ways of life. In the past, some peoples were oriented to the sea. The Phoenicians, for instance, spread their maritime commerce from their base in the Levant through the Mediterranean and beyond. Others—the Hittites, Assyrians, Sumerians, and many more—were landlocked. The open spaces of the Middle East have invited penetration, except where they were too dry; thus, the Arab move into North Africa was rapid and overwhelming outside the arid mountains of the Maghrib and the desert. Similarly, Kurds, Armenians, Nestorians, and other small groups have preserved minority identities in the upland fringes of the Fertile Crescent and the Caucasus.

Strategy and Communications

The Middle East is the crossroads of the Old World. It lies across the water route from the southern Ukraine to the Mediterranean, and between that sea and the Indian Ocean. Since the domestication of the camel, men have been crossing the deserts, and many invaders and traders have entered the Middle East from central Asia, Europe, and Africa. Rarely in the past four thousand years has the Middle East known a respite from outside pressures and influences.

A hundred years ago British policy was concerned with the imperial lifeline to India and aimed at curtailing Russian and other outside influence in the region. Today the United States sees the Middle East in terms of the containment of communism and has formed pacts (NATO, CENTO) linking the "key" countries into a defensive rim around the Eurasian heartland. The Soviet Union is pushing into the Arab world—a traditional Russian objective—at the same time, setting its sights on expansion into Africa and the Indian Ocean. Meanwhile, mainland China is beginning to extend its influence into the region from the east. All of this has had an effect on the political processes of the states of the modern Middle East.

The principal outside rivals now are the United States and the USSR. Although neither superpower aims to carve out dependent colonies, each is anxious to secure influence over those parts of the region considered important to its strategic, economic, and other interests. The countries and politicized groups of the Middle East therefore tend to fall into pro-West, pro-Soviet, or neutral categories.

A number of locations are crucial points of international concern. The most important are the waterways—the Suez Canal, the Bab al-Mandab at the southern end of the Red Sea, and the Bosporus between Europe and Asia. Today the USSR, along with the United Kingdom and other Western European powers, would like to see the Suez reopened, which has been denied since Israel's 1967 advance. Access through Suez, however, would mean little if the Bab al-Mandab were blockaded. Both Egypt and Israel wish to dominate the entrance to the Gulf of Aqabah, for it controls shipping into and out of the Israeli port of Eilat. The Bosporus is internationalized under the Convention of Constantinople so that the USSR can use the waterway (now being bridged) for moving south out of the Black Sea.

Rivers are also objects of political concern, especially where several countries are involved. Egypt and the Sudan are bound by their common dependence on the Nile as a source of water and as a communications artery. Dam construction on the Euphrates in Turkey directly involves Syria and Iraq, whose approval must be sought. The Jordan is a military front line as well as a vital source of water to Israel and to neighboring Arab states, and the Euphrates and the Tigris join to form the Shatt al-Arab, a crucial accessway for both Iran and Iraq.

Land routes have also figured in communications and in strategy in the Middle East. Here again movement is channeled into key locations and routes. The link through the Fertile Crescent from the Gulf to Sinai has existed since Abraham followed this route. The isthmus at Suez is both a waterway and a land link between Sinai and the Egyptian corner of Africa and is at the moment closed by Israeli forces, a situation that has obvious political implications. Long-established land routes also exist along the Mediterranean coast of Africa, through Anatolia and Iran. Others cross the desert hinterland of the Middle East, linking oases to larger settlements and even to trans-Saharan destinations.

Mineral Resources

The distribution of oil and other minerals has important political implications. Several countries in the region have vast reserves of petroleum; in Kuwait, Saudi Arabia, Libya, and the oil-rich amirates of the Gulf petroleum is overwhelmingly the main source of government income.

Collectively, the Middle East has known reserves of some 480 billion barrels of oil, compared to only 40 billion in the United States. It is also endowed with vast quantities of natural gas, increasingly used both as fuel and as a raw material. To date, however, the emphasis remains on oil production. Although it has about one-third of the world's output of oil, the Middle East itself annually consumes only about 2 percent of the total. Thus, at least for the foreseeable future, it is dependent on outside markets and to a large extent on foreign companies for exploration and extraction.

Moreover, the unequal distribution of petroleum within the region is a divisive factor. Two of the larger states, Turkey and Egypt, have only limited oil reserves—although both hope for spectacular discoveries. On the other hand, Kuwait, with only 733,000 people, can finance substantial development projects in other Arab countries from its petroleum revenues and thus commands an influence it otherwise would lack. A large Arab state such as Egypt may thus have to achieve an accommodation with its oil-rich neighbors despite underlying divisions in political philosophy. At the same time, some states without significant oil reserves—Syria, for example—control transit pipelines through their territories, giving them power on the international scene that they could not otherwise claim. This uneven pattern of oil reserves

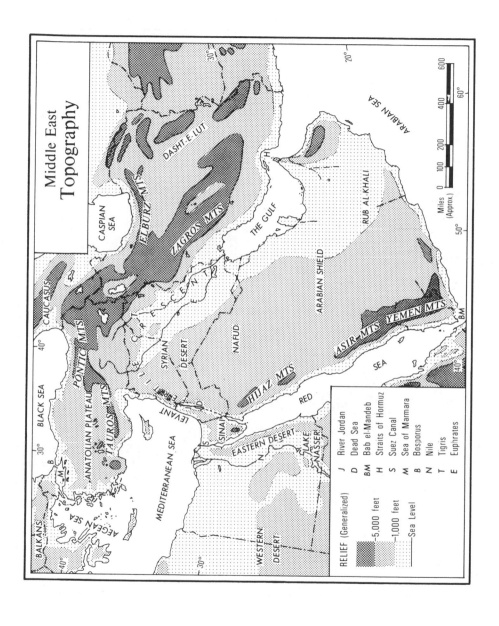

Middle East
Topography

BALKANS

BLACK SEA

CAUCASUS

CASPIAN SEA

PONTIC MTS

ANATOLIAN PLATEAU

TAUROS MTS

ELBURZ MTS

ZAGROS MTS

DASHT-E LUT

AEGEAN SEA

MEDITERRANEAN SEA

LEVANT

CRESCENT

SYRIAN DESERT

NAFUD

THE GULF

ARABIAN SHIELD

RUB AL-KHALI

WESTERN DESERT

SINAI

EASTERN DESERT

LAKE NASSER

HIJAZ MTS

RED SEA

ASIR MTS

YEMEN MTS

ARABIAN SEA

20°

60°

50°

40°

30°

40°

30°

30°

40°

RELIEF (Generalized)

5,000 feet

1,000 feet

Sea Level

J   River Jordan
D   Dead Sea
BM Bab el-Mandeb
H   Straits of Hormuz
S   Suez Canal
M   Sea of Marmara
B   Bosporus
N   Nile
T   Tigris
E   Euphrates

Miles (Approx.)

0   100 200   400   600

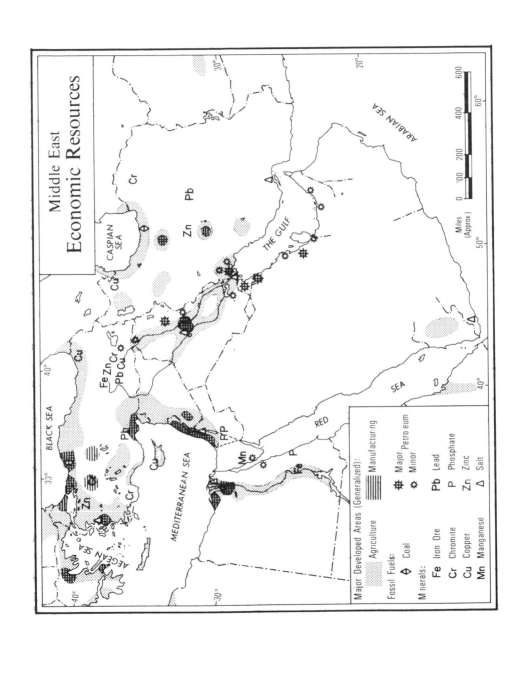

Middle East
Economic Resources

Major Developed Areas (Generalized):

Agriculture   Manufacturing

Fossil Fuels:

◇ Coal   ✳ Major Petroleum   Pb Lead   P Phosphate
                     ✳ Minor   Zn Zinc   △ Salt
Minerals:

Fe Iron Ore   Cr Chromite   Cu Copper   Mn Manganese

BLACK SEA

CASPIAN SEA

AEGEAN SEA

MEDITERRANEAN SEA

RED SEA

THE GULF

ARABIAN SEA

Miles (Approx.)

0   100   200   400   600

30°   40°   50°   60°

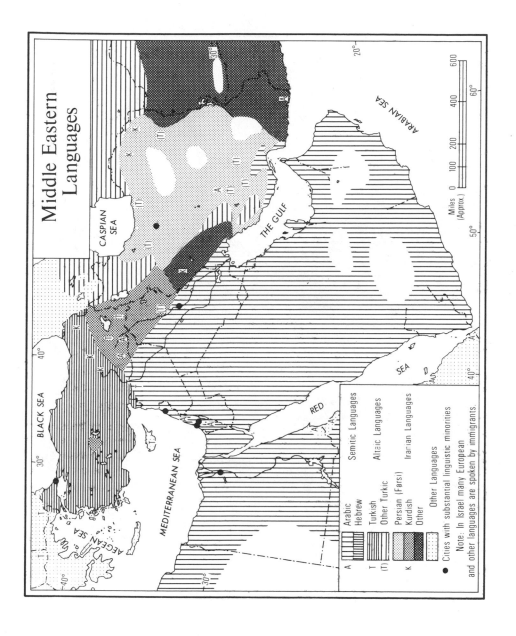

Middle Eastern Languages

CASPIAN SEA

BLACK SEA

MEDITERRANEAN SEA

AEGEAN SEA

CASPIAN SEA

THE GULF

RED SEA

ARABIAN SEA

		Semitic Languages
A	Arabic	
	Hebrew	
		Altaic Languages
T	Turkish	
(T)	Other Turkic	
		Iranian Languages
	Persian (Farsi)	
K	Kurdish	
	Other	
		Other Languages

● Cities with substantial linguistic minorities

Note: In Israel many European
and other languages are spoken by immigrants.

Miles (Approx.)

0   100   200   400   600

20°

60°

50°

40°

40°

30°

30°

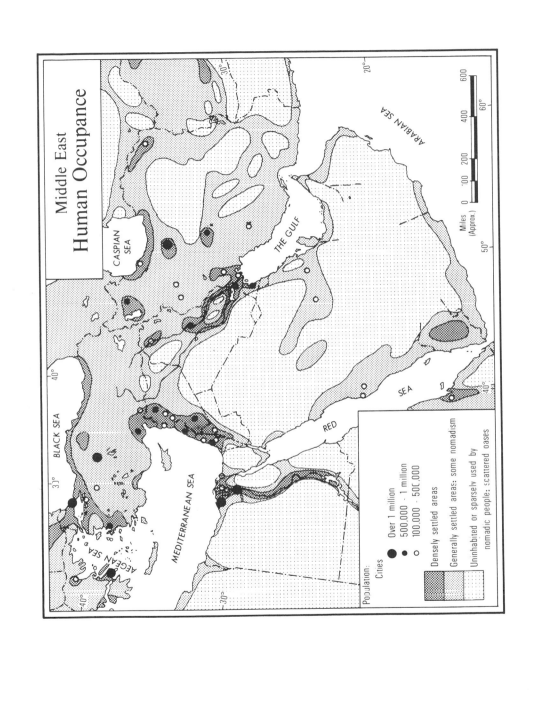

Middle East
Human Occupance

CASPIAN SEA

BLACK SEA

AEGEAN SEA

MEDITERRANEAN SEA

THE GULF

RED SEA

ARABIAN SEA

Population:

Cities
● Over 1 million
● 500.000 - 1 million
○ 100.000 - 50C.000

Densely settled areas

Generally settled areas: some nomadism

Uninhabited or sparsely used by
nomadic people: scattered oases

Miles
(Approx.)

0   100 200   400   600

20°

30°

40°

30°

40°

30°

20°

40°

50°

60°

is also making it difficult for the Gulf states to form a federation, because some of the constituent amirates are as poor in petroleum as others are rich.

Turkey is the richest of the Middle Eastern countries in minerals other than petroleum, having major deposits of chromite, copper, lead, and zinc in addition to the important Zonguldak coalfield. Iran has fewer known mineral reserves. There is a manganese deposit in the Sinai; phosphates are found in Jordan and in eastern Egypt, potash in the vicinity of the Dead Sea, and salt in many parts of the region, although most of the Arabian peninsula lacks even this. However, mineral exploration is far from complete.

Climate Pattern

Nature, which endows the Middle East with an unusually generous reservoir of oil, is also responsible for giving much of the region a modified version of the Mediterranean type of climate, with rain in winter and desert conditions in summer. Crops that call for moisture in summer months can survive only with irrigation. The pattern of agriculture and settlement reflects the climate, because people concentrate in "islands" around available water, separated from one another by dry areas, and the separation of population concentrations has led to the emergence of local identities and variants of political practice.

The annual seesaw contest between "Mediterranean" winds coming from the west and the monsoon coming from the Indian Ocean basically determines the Middle Eastern climate, but intrusive winds from Asia and Africa cause important breaks in the pattern. Topography, orientation and alignment of hills and valleys, and the location of water account for much local climatic variety. The high plateau country of eastern Anatolia, for example, annually experiences an average of 120 days of snow cover, whereas the long, hot summers south of the mountain uplands of Turkey and Iran produce temperatures often higher than at the equator. The irregular pattern of land and sea also affects the climate; a wind dessicating one area may become extremely moist after crossing even a narrow body of water. Thus a combination of climatic and topographic factors accounts for the variety in this landscape of pronounced areal, seasonal, and even diurnal contrasts.

Water

Most of the region is arid. Outside the uplands of Turkey, Iran, and the eastern shore of the Mediterranean, water-rich areas seem to be islands in a sea of sand. Some of these are large and of persistent historical importance, especially Egypt's delta, along the valley of the Nile, and along the Euphrates and the Tigris in Mesopotamia (Iraq).

Other well-watered areas are the Jebel al-Akhdar in eastern Libya and the monsoon-fed highlands of Yemen. Oases large and small, fed by underground water, dot the rest of the region.

Although precipitation partly depends on altitude and location, it is mainly controlled by the seasonal rhythm of summer drought and winter rain. The exceptions are northern Turkey and the neighboring parts of Iran, Yemen, and Southern Yemen, which receive summer rain.

Outside such comparatively wet areas, surface water consists of temporary stream (*wadi*) drainage, except where rivers are fed from the highlands. Thus the Nile, which is supplied from eastern Africa, flows through a desert to the Mediterranean. The twin rivers of Mesopotamia depend on eastern Turkey and not on tributaries in Iraq for their existence. Apart from man-made lakes behind dams on these rivers, such as Lake Nasser on the Nile, the major lakes of the Middle East are formed by interior drainage and therefore tend to have a high salt content (the salt is trapped when much of the water is lost by evaporation). The Dead Sea, at 1,286 feet below sea level, is the best known. On a map these lakes may appear to have some potential for irrigation, but their high mineral content makes them unsuitable for agriculture.

So important is water that elaborate attempts are made to collect it. A common sight in many parts of the dry Middle East and North Africa is the modern water-drilling rig. Long before such equipment was available, however, some Middle Easterners had dug intricate systems of tunnels, some several miles in length, to drain ground water down to artificial springs for irrigation or for human consumption. In recent years technical improvements have drastically lowered the cost of desalinization of sea water, but it is still too costly for irrigation. Kuwait, however, is using such water for municipal and industrial consumption, and within another decade or two distilled sea water may revolutionize the pattern of agriculture and settlement in the Middle East.

Meanwhile, the most reliance will be placed on the dams and man-made lakes that are now changing the Middle East. The best known, at Aswan in Egypt, provides both water for irrigating new farmland and electric power. Lake Nasser behind the dam straddles the border between Egypt and the Sudan, which also stands to benefit. Financing such huge projects almost inevitably requires outside aid—sometimes with political strings attached. Political problems could also emerge as the salt content and temperature of the eastern Mediterranean are raised by the Aswan High Dam, which has cut off the annual Nile flood. Already Egypt's sardine fisheries have been severely hit, and neighboring countries will feel a variety of adverse effects. Another great dam rising at Keban on the Turkish section of the Euphrates also involves more than a single country; it is hoped that this dam will stimulate economic development over a wide area of eastern Anatolia, and as with Aswan, it can only succeed with international agreement. Schemes involving water such as these become the objects of political rivalry and lobbying at the interprovincial level and even at the village level within a state.

Sand, Soil, and Vegetation

The word *Sahara* evokes a picture of the desert. Nearly two-thirds of the Middle East and North Africa are covered by sand or gravel; no other area of similar size has so much desert surface. Deserts limit settlement and movement, and historically some parts of the Middle East's sea of sand have been a more effective barrier to movement than the oceans.

Despite the scarcity of vegetation in the desert, the dry zones of the Middle East can be drastically changed with water. Some of the now dry parts, moreover, reflect a humid past. Rock carvings and paintings, for instance, show that the central Sahara once supported man as well as large animals, and remains of Roman dams in the Libyan Desert suggest that the environment was wetter there as recently as two thousand years ago. The spread of aridity in the past may have greatly affected the pattern of civilization and the political character of the Middle East, and today's political relationships may change if large-scale irrigation profoundly alters the settlement pattern in the future.

Middle Eastern soils would have some deficiencies even if water were available, although water could make some areas quite productive. The soils are generally low in humus (organic matter) both because the high temperatures tend to promote its decay and because the little water will not support much natural vegetation. Salinity is another major problem and is related to the desert's heat and high evaporation rates; for example, the salt content of the Euphrates and Tigris doubles in the desert region between the Turkish border and the Shatt al-Arab in Iraq. In swamp areas, where soils are poorly drained, irrigation may lead to the spread of malaria and other diseases. In the past, cities such as Side in southern Anatolia have in fact been destroyed by malaria produced by the presence of excess water.

Vegetation in the Middle East reflects the pattern of topography, aridity, and high temperatures. In much of the region vegetation, whether natural or cultivated, must be able to survive the summer drought. Where water is available in all seasons, however, such as along the Nile, several crops may be grown in one year. Further, in the highlands of Turkey, Iran, and the Levant moist conditions support natural forests, and in the highest areas the vegetation resembles that of the Alps; vegetation, like climate, is a function of elevation as well as latitude.

For a very long time man has changed the natural vegetation of the Middle East. In many areas inferior scrub and heath and erosion have replaced forest and woodland, which may lower the water table. Governments and development agencies are now attempting to restrict the spread of aridity and to increase the cultivable area. Farms on the desert fringes strive to hold back the encroaching sand, and governments are intensely concerned with overgrazing and excessive tree cutting. Huge dams such as Keban and Aswan provide water to irrigate acreage further into the desert. Yet some authorities' efforts to settle nomads in sedentary farming or even in urban areas increase the pressure on the available farmland and raise questions about who will use the drier parts of the Middle East in the future.

The Pattern of Occupance

Despite generalizations about the physical setting of the Middle East, the area has tremendous variety. There is a sharp ecological distinction between Turkey and parts of Iran and the drier countries to the south. Yet even the dry Arab lands contain areas where enough water is available to support heavy concentrations of people, areas which resemble an archipelago of islands of settlement in a sea of aridity. Some concentrations—the Nile valley, Mesopotamia, the Levant, and the uplands of Yemen, for instance—support millions. Others are smaller and closer to the oasis stereotype. These core areas of settlement have figured as social and political centers throughout the history of the Middle East. The earliest powers were located in Mesopotamia (e.g., the Sumerians) and on the Nile (the Egyptians), and the Queen of Sheba is believed to have ruled in the fertile highlands of Yemen. The Hittites and other Anatolian peoples were able to develop their civilizations within the northern zone, where the dry lands are not separated from the wet in the same discontinuous way in which the Arabian peninsula, North Africa, and much of Iran are divided.

Archeological and climatic evidence suggests that the pattern of settlement and activity has not remained constant, although certain core areas have remained predominant. Today the "oil oasis" has added a new pattern in which the lure of an exploitable petroleum reserve attracts people and development much as water and the prospect of agriculture have done for centuries. Thus, a country such as Kuwait, which is ecologically an arid waste, appears today as a new core of activity and wealth, and a few countries, such as Turkey, have a resource base (coal, iron, etc.) that puts them in a strong position for conventional industrialization.

In several areas huge projects promise irrigation and power that could push settlement into hitherto dry areas. Yet even the most spectacular of these, on the Nile, is said to be merely keeping pace with the rising population along the river. Meanwhile, those people who have traditionally lived a nomadic life in the dry hinterland of the Middle East are moving in increasing numbers into the already crowded settled areas. The traditional peoples of the region have had answers to some of these difficulties, but today new methods and techniques permit developments that were impossible a short while ago. Development is not steady progress, however; the Sumerians and the Romans were experts in irrigation and water management, and the nomadic bedouin has long been able to survive in arid areas.

The People

The pattern of activity in the Middle East today is the result of the interaction of man and environment over many centuries. To assess the political character of Middle Eastern states and peoples, it is necessary to see that there are differences as well as similarities among different parts of the region. One must avoid misleading simplifications such as "the Arab view" or "the Egyptian position" and indicate what is referred to in each case, whether government pronouncements or the feelings of a minority or majority of a population. This section briefly outlines the demographic, cultural, and socioeconomic patterns of contemporary life in the Middle East.

Demographic Patterns and Trends

About 130 million people live in the countries considered in this book. They are very unevenly distributed across the 2.5 million square miles shared by twenty-two republics, monarchies, and amirates (see table 2[2]). Many are concentrated in Cairo, Istanbul, Tehran, and the other great cities, and millions more live in the hundreds of regional centers and smaller towns. Most are villagers, however, whether in the fertile Nile delta or in some inhospitable upland valley in the southern Caucasus. Very few still follow a nomadic way of life. The eastern borders of the Mediterranean in Israel, Lebanon, and Syria also have heavy concentrations of population, as do the wetter parts of Yemen. Elsewhere in the Arab Middle East scattered oases interrupt the desert. Some support settlements; others have water enough for little more than temporary use. In Turkey and in western and northern Iran settled areas are more widely dispersed, and some areas are sparsely inhabited at most.

In common with most of the developing world, the Middle East is experiencing rapid population growth (see table 2[3,4]). Several countries show annual population increase of over 3 percent, and the growth rates of some are further swollen by an influx of refugees (Jordan) or other migrants (Kuwait). In recent decades mortality rates have dropped markedly; infant mortality in particular is no longer as high as it was only a generation ago. Since birth rates remain high as life expectancy increases, the population of most Middle Eastern countries will double in twenty-five years or less. The growth rate promises to be even more rapid in the urban areas of the region as incoming rural people add to the already high rate of natural increase. Greater Cairo, for instance, could well pass the ten million mark in little more than a decade.

Governments are concerned with the pressure of population on their limited arable land and production capacity, and some countries have recently initiated programs of family planning. Others have encouraged greater populations: Israeli authorities are encouraging large families among Jewish settlers and are strenuously exhorting Jews in other parts of the world to move to Israel, and other Middle Eastern countries have accepted large numbers of refugees and other immigrants (Turkey has received several hundred thousand from Europe and the Soviet Union in recent decades, and Kuwait's 1970 census shows that more than half its inhabitants are recent arrivals).

As mentioned before, one consequence of population growth is the movement out of the villages and rural areas into the towns and cities. This migration results in part from the push of growing village populations and increasing pressure on limited land and in part from hope for a better job, greater security, and an easier life in the city. However, the towns are unable to absorb great numbers of rural people, many of whom lack the education, skills, and familiarity with urban society necessary to adapt to urban life. Most of these migrants become unemployed or underemployed burdens in cities where meaningful jobs are already scarce.

Nevertheless, millions of villagers now live on the fringes of cities and towns, often in hastily built huts without running water, electricity, or adequate sanitation. In many cases groups of villagers (perhaps an extended family or even a whole village) set themselves up as a communal group in their new urban location to preserve some of the village functions, such as mutual security, in an urban context. Sometimes ties with the home village are so strong that the village continues to supply village-grown food to the exiles in the city.

These settlements pose a dilemma for governments and planning agencies. Should they do nothing to improve the conditions of squatter life on the urban fringes, should they discontinue the village development programs, which help stimulate the rural-urban exodus by decreasing the number of farming jobs, or should they accept the flight from the villages as inevitable and do everything possible to improve conditions in the town, thereby encouraging still further movement? It is not an easy problem.

Apart from interregional and rural-urban movements of people, hundreds of thousands of Middle Easterners are attracted on a temporary basis to Germany and other European countries where well-paid employment is available. Wages sent home to relatives in Turkey are that country's major source of hard currency for foreign exchange, and an additional benefit is the skills acquired in European factories by returned workers. At the same time, of course, the foreign work experience may also result in dissatisfaction with conditions at home. Professionals in particular are sometimes reluctant to return home to much lower pay rates and inferior working conditions, and the Middle East feels the impact of the "brain drain" to economically more advanced countries.

Ethnic and Cultural Contrasts

Much confusion arises from the misuse of terms in this region. *Arabic*, a language, is sometimes used for *Arab*, a culture. Arabic, like

Hebrew, is a Semitic tongue, although *Semite* is often inappropriately used to connote race. Many Muslim and Christian Arabs share a common biologically determined ethnic origin with many Jews in Israel and the Arab states, but Judaism and Islam are religions which, like languages, can be acquired by an individual. Iran and Turkey are not Arab states, though they share a common religion with the Arabs. The Farsi language of Iran is, like Kurdish, a member of the Indo-European group, and Turkish is a Ural-Altaic tongue with linguistic relatives in central Asia. The imperial histories of Iran and Turkey have further nurtured their distinctiveness from the Arab world.

Race: Characteristically Middle Eastern is the long-headed Armenoid racial type found in its purest form in the highlands of eastern Anatolia and in the Zagros Mountains of Iran. In western Anatolia this stock is clearly mixed with the round-headed Mediterranean type. The Mongoloid element within Turkey is very limited, because incoming groups from central Asia were numerically inadequate to substantially affect the Anatolian racial stock. The Armenoid type (not to be confused with the Armenians) is also evident in eastern and southern Arabia and the Gulf, where it is mixed, as in western Anatolia, with Mediterranean types. South of the Fertile Crescent and in inner Arabia, Mediterranean is the dominant strain; it is also evident in northeast Africa, although in the crowded lower Nile valley Armenoid and other types, such as brown-skinned Hamitic peoples, have combined with it to product a heterogeneous racial mix. In Iran an Indo-Aryan element is intermixed with the Armenoid and Mediterranean strains in the west and northwest, and in the northern parts of the country the genetic contribution of Turki and other Mongoloid invaders is clear. Israel's present Jewish population presents a particularly heterogeneous mixture of Armenoid types characteristic of many Middle Eastern Jews and a variety of racial strains among the European and other settlers. European characteristics also appear in other parts of the Levant, and the Negroid and Nilotic contribution is evident in northern Africa and in the Arabian peninsula.

Only in a few areas of the Middle East are there largely unmixed racial types. In general, the intermixture of various Caucasoid strains with Mongoloid and Negroid types has produced a population reflecting the crossroads character of the Middle East. Such is the degree of heterogeneity that race per se takes second place to cultural traits such as religion and language in differentiating groups within the region.

Language: Today Arabic predominates in the Middle East (see table 2 [6,7]). Turkish is the majority tongue of Turkey itself, while the Osmanli form of the language is spoken in parts of Iran, Syria, and Cyprus. Farsi, or Persian, is official in both Iran and Afghanistan. All three languages show marked differences from place to place. Speakers of Arabic, the language of the Quran and thus of special significance to Muslims, make a clear distinction between the classical form and the various colloquial dialects. Kurdish, spoken by nearly six million people in several countries, ranks second to Arabic in Iraq and is now recognized as one of the state's two official languages.

Aramaic, the language of Jesus, is still spoken in a few villages in Syria and Iraq. Greek and Armenian are heard in Cairo, Beirut, Istanbul, and other urban centers, as are English and French. Nowhere is the linguistic variety greater than in Israel, where settlers have in recent decades brought several dozen languages, including Yiddish, based on German, and Ladino, based on Spanish. Ladino is also spoken within the Jewish community in Turkey, whose members brought it as refugees from Spain five centuries ago. Many Israeli Jews continue to speak Arabic, although Israel has successfully revived Hebrew as the principal spoken national tongue after its long confinement to religious use. Iran has been less successful in developing national unity through Farsi, which 30 percent of the population does not speak.

Religion: In many respects the Middle East can be considered a crossroads absorbing outside influences, but in this one its role has been reversed (see table 2 [8,9]). Several religions, including Christianity and Islam, which now claim hundreds of millions of adherents, have been exported from the region. Zoroastrianism and Judaism were early monotheistic faiths, the former strong in Persia until the rise of Islam, although Zoroastrians are now only a tiny minority in Iran. Judaism developed in the latter part of the second millennium B.C., when a Jewish-ruled state was established in the highlands of Judea. First by the Assyrians and later by the Romans, Jews were dispersed to many parts of Europe and the Middle East, where they absorbed cultural and racial traits characteristic of the areas in which they settled.

Christianity, an outgrowth of the Judaic tradition, emerged in Palestine, spread, and later became the official religion of the Roman Empire. Regional differences soon fragmented the church, however, and four of the leading cities of the day came to be identified with different versions of the Christian tradition. Rome became the center for the Latin language and culture; Constantinople incorporated Greek traditions and was the center for the Byzantine culture of the Eastern Roman Empire. (The patriarch of the Greek Orthodox church still resides in Constantinople, today Istanbul.) The thriving cities of Antioch and Alexandria also represented special regional interests and cultural backgrounds and from them developed, respectively, the Syrian, or Jacobite, and the Coptic churches. Later, further regional divisions emerged to give rise to the Armenian (Gregorian), Nestorian, Maronite, and other Christian churches, which still survive in the Middle East.

After A.D. 622 Islam spread from its Arabian base into North Africa and Persia and soon displaced Christianity as the predominant religion in the Middle East. In the north, however, Byzantine power preserved Christian predominance until Turkish tribes brought Islam some centuries later.

Sectarian differences appeared in Islam as they had in Christianity. Today Shiite Muslims are numerous in Iran, Iraq, and parts of Lebanon and Yemen and account for about 10 percent of all Muslims. Most other Muslims are Sunni, but numerous sects, smaller than the

Shiites, add further variety. Some sects are notably regional in character, such as the Senussi movement in eastern Libya and the Wahhabi following in Saudi Arabia, both of which adhere rigidly to Islam. Groups that have developed forms of Islam incorporating features of other religions are the Druze (in Lebanon, Syria, and Israel), the Ismaili Shiites in eastern Africa, India, and the Middle East, and the Alawi sect in Syria and Lebanon, which has grafted Christian and pagan practices onto its Shiite origins.

A religion influences the way in which people react to their environment and to each other. It may affect the way they live, eat, build houses, and group their settlements. Religious conflict may explain rifts between people, although it is rarely the sole reason for conflict. (Arab opposition to Israel is not based on religion, for instance.) Some countries, such as Saudi Arabia, are said to be more conservative or "traditional" because they pattern their way of life strictly on Islamic teaching; other Middle Eastern countries have sharply separated church and state. Turkey, for example, has made this separation, has accepted Westernization, and with modernizing zeal has legislated the introduction of the Latin alphabet, the Christian calendar, European legal codes, Western dress, Sunday as the official weekly holiday, and the like. A tourist in the Middle East cannot fail to be impressed by the contrasts between town and country and between economic classes regarding the place of religion in social life. Whereas short skirts, alcohol, and "dating" are now accepted in sections of the big cities, they are still totally rejected—ultimately because of religion—in remote rural areas.

Social and Economic Change

We now briefly review the distribution of and changes in socioeconomic activity, which provides the setting for political processes.

Traditionally the middle class accounted for only a small part of the Middle East's total population; outside the cities it was scarcely evident at all. At the top of the socioeconomic hierarchy was the elite, also small but possessing economic and political power; the working class was by far the largest section of society in both town and countryside. It is still larger than the middle and upper classes combined, but the proportion is shrinking in the face of the emerging urban middle class, which is progressively taking power from the privileged elite. The transition is far from even. At one end of the spectrum stand Oman and some of the Gulf states, where power and leadership are concentrated in the hands of small ruling elites and where there is as yet only an embryonic middle class. By contrast, in Turkey, Lebanon, and elsewhere the substantial middle class and increasingly the rural people are directly involved in the political system. Such changes in the socioeconomic structure involve profound changes in the two principal components of Middle Eastern life, the village and the town.

The Village: Today the Middle Eastern village is changing from a largely self-sufficient (or peasant) society—one in which each family supported itself and money played little, if any, part—to a "modern" cash-conscious society that is increasingly involved with a regional, national, and even an international market economy. With the income from his surplus produce, the villager today is able to satisfy many more material demands than previously. Within the village more diverse activities are evident; shopkeepers, teachers, health officials, policemen, and others appear in communities that were traditionally composed almost entirely of farming families. Age and lineage have given way to wealth and education as a basis for social stratification. Villagers may also be integrated into a "national unit" by military service. Clearly such changes are not emerging at the same pace or in quite the same fashion throughout the Middle East.

Land is basic to village life. A major problem is the need to change the relationship of man to his land so that he may be able to function as an entrepreneur in the modern market economy. Plots have become fragmented within a single family farm unit because of the social and economic demands made by subsistence society on the land. Today, however, many states require more efficient and larger scale operations, and land consolidation is a major emphasis in most Middle Eastern countries, many of which have initiated substantial land-reform programs.

The village is growing in importance in the Middle East and North Africa, and nomadism and pastoralism are declining. Indeed, very few true nomads remain. Some settle down as villagers; others move straight into urban life and have even less chance of success than the average villager who makes the same move. Nomads have been of traditional importance, however; they have been—and are—able to live in areas where nature offers only a narrow range of choices.

The Town: Towns have long dominated political life in the region and are centers of trade and cultural change. In the history of the Middle East, one political authority after another based its power on control of strategic cities and towns, bringing together national and local treasuries, merchants, tax collectors, absentee landlords, wholesaling, retailing, and artisan skills and trades.

Governmental and economic influences penetrate the rural hinterlands through the cities. Nevertheless, cities and villages have frequently differed considerably in such characteristics as religion and language from the rural areas around them. Such contrasts are being reduced, but the urban Middle East retains its distinctiveness. Cities are adapting to Western communications, technology, and attitudes toward life—including attitudes about the political structure and the functioning of society. Modern factories and stores are becoming the centers of economic activity in place of the ancient bazaars where traders and skilled craftsmen were concentrated. An American tourist sees a great deal with which he can identify in the cities of the region; in the rural areas he sees more of the traditional way of life, which is unfamiliar, even "quaint." In fact, the gulf between Istanbul and rural Turkey is greater than that between Istanbul and any European or North American city.

The association between development initiative and the city is certainly not new. Most of the great cities of the region are located on the coasts, in the river valleys, or along established trade routes from which they have always influenced their hinterlands. Today many cities are capitals of countries striving for social and economic progress in their rural areas. Government agencies prepare and implement plans designed to integrate the nation and to bring to all its inhabitants the benefits hitherto largely confined to the cities. Political decisions are no longer made exclusively in the cities, which are becoming merely focal points from which the rural Middle Easterner can become increasingly involved in his government.

The villages are responding to the urban stimulus not only in terms of social and economic change but also demographically. Most Middle Eastern cities and towns now have large populations of rural people in search of jobs and other benefits of modernization. Figures about the urbanized population have to be treated with some caution. The figure ranges from more than 80 percent in Israel (where international rather than internal migration has been prominent) to 45 percent in nearly Lebanon and 30 percent in Iran. As in the United States, the proportion of urban people is likely to grow rapidly in most parts of the Middle East.

Conclusion

The present Middle Eastern states can be characterized in terms of a series of human variables, some tending to unify and some to divide the nations. To these must be added the physical diversity of the region, the contrasts between settled and empty lands, between land and sea, between upland and plain. Within this mosaic of human society, the variable with perhaps the most important implications for political action is a nation's resources, both human and physical. In political terms a strategic location or an important waterway is a resource as much as is petroleum or irrigable land, and ways of life and technical capabilities are as much human resources as numbers of people. Both kinds of resources are irregularly spread across the Middle East, and they greatly influence political processes and actions.

Table 2
People and Resources[a]

Country	Population Estimate (Millions)	Annual Birth Rate (Per 1,000)	Annual Population Growth (%)	Literacy (% of Pop.)	Language		Religion		Resources	
					Arabic (%)	Other (%)	Muslim (%)	Other (%)	Area (100 sq. miles)	Main Source of Revenue
[1]	[2]	[3]	[4]	[5]	[6]	[7]	[8]	[9]	[10]	[11]
Egypt	32.5	43	2.9	40	99[b]		92	Coptic (7)	387[c]	Agriculture (cotton)
Iraq	9.4	48	3.2	30	80[b]	Kurdish (15) Farsi (2) Turkish (2) Aramaic	96[d]	Christian (3) Yazidi Sabaean Jewish	168	Oil agriculture
Syria	6.0		2.9	50	86[b]	Kurdish (9) Turkish Armenian Aramaic	68	Christian (21) Alawi Druze (2) Jewish	72[e]	Agriculture
Lebanon	2.8		2.5	70	99[b]	French	48	Maronite (30) Greek Orth. (10) Greek Cath. (6) Druze (5) Jewish	4	Agriculture tourism commerce
Jordan	2.3[f]	47	4.1	50	100[b]	Circassian	90	Christian (10)	37[g]	Agriculture mining tourism
Saudi Arabia	4.7		2.3	10	100[b]		98		873	Oil
Kuwait	0.7	52	7.6	60	100[b]		98		6	Oil
Gulf states[h]	1.3			10	96[b]	Farsi (3) Urdu	99		118	Oil
Yemen	5.7		2.8	10	100[b]		100[d]		75	Agriculture
People's Democratic Republic of Yemen	1.2	37	2.2		100[b]		100		112	Agriculture commerce

Table 2 (Continued)

Country [1]	Population Estimate (Millions) [2]	Annual Birth Rate (Per 1,000) [3]	Annual Population Growth (%) [4]	Literacy (% of Pop.) [5]	Language		Religion		Resources	
					Arabic (%) [6]	Other (%) [7]	Muslim (%) [8]	Other (%) [9]	Area (100 sq. miles) [10]	Main Source of Revenue [11]
Israel[i]	2.8	25	2.9	88	14[j]	Hebrew[b] Yiddish etc.	11	Jewish (86) Christian (2) Druze	8	U.S. funds diamonds citrus textiles tourism
Turkey	34.4	46	2.5	50	1	Turkish[b] (90) Kurdish (7)	98	Greek Orth. Arme- nian Jewish (1.5)	296	Agriculture mining
Iran	27.9	50	3.1	20	1.5	Farsi[b] (70) Turkish (19) Other Turkic (3) Kurdish (6)	99[d]	Christian Jewish Zoroastrian Bahai	636	Oil

[a] Many of the figures in this table are the latest available estimates.

[b] Official language.

[c] Less Sinai (since 1967).

[d] Shia sect of Islam prominent.

[e] Less Golan Heights (since 1967).

[f] About half are Palestinian refugees.

[g] Less the West Bank (since 1967).

[h] Bahrayn, Qatar, the Union of Arab Amirates (Dubai, Abu Dhabi, Sharjah, Al-Fujayrah, Ajman, Umm al-Qaywayn), Ras al-Khaymah, and Oman.

[i] Data for Israel as of early 1967 (1949 Armistice lines); the present population under Israeli rule is 3.9 million, of whom some 66 percent are Jewish.

[j] Excluding Arabic-speaking Israeli Jews.

Selected Bibliography

Arberry, A. J., ed. *Religion in the Middle East.* 2 vols. New York: Cambridge University Press, 1969.

An examination of Middle Eastern Islam, Christianity, and Judaism over the past hundred years, with emphasis on the interactions of the three and on ethnic, economic, political, social, and cultural factors.

Atlas of the Arab World and the Middle East. Amsterdam: Djambatan, 1960.

Contains forty pages of maps, twenty pages of photographs and accompanying text, and an index.

Cressey, George B. *Crossroads: Land and Life in Southwest Asia.* Philadelphia: J. B. Lippincott Co., 1960.

A geographical survey and assessment of the human and physical patterns of the region.

Economist Intelligence Unit. *Oxford Regional Economic Atlas: The Middle East and North Africa.* Prepared by the Economist Intelligence Unit and the Cartographic Department of the Clarendon Press. London: Oxford University Press, 1960.

Includes sixty-four pages of maps and fifty-three pages of economic statistics.

El-Badry, M. A. "Trends in the Components of Population Growth in the Arab Countries of the Middle East: A Survey of Present Information." *Demography* 2 (1965): 140-86.

Detailed assessment of the components of population growth in Egypt, Jordan, Syria, Lebanon, Iraq, and Kuwait.

English, Paul Ward. "Urbanites, Peasants, and Nomads: The Middle Eastern Ecological Trilogy." *Journal of Geography* 66, no. 2 (February 1967): 54-59.

Examines the city, the village, and the tribe as specialized ways of life which combine to produce the equilibrium in Middle Eastern society now undergoing change.

Fisher, W. B. *The Middle East: A Physical, Social, and Regional Geography.* New York: E. P. Dutton & Co., 1961.

A standard text on the countries covered in this volume plus Libya and Cyprus; first published in 1950.

Gulick, John, ed. "Dimensions of Cultural Change in the Middle East." *Human Organization* 24, no. 1 (Spring 1965).

Fifteen selected articles, mostly on individual countries, covering spatial and structural aspects of the process of modernization and chance.

Hourani, Albert H. *Minorities in the Arab World.* London: Oxford University Press, 1947.

Lerner, Daniel. *The Passing of Traditional Society: Modernizing the Middle East.* New York: Free Press, 1958.

Covers Egypt, Iran, Jordan, Lebanon, Syria, and Turkey, and includes a general statement of the process of cultural change.

Longrigg, Stephen H. *The Middle East: A Social Geography.* Chicago: Aldine Publishing Co., 1963.

The human patterns of the region with emphasis on recent decades.

The Middle East and North Africa, 1969-70. 16th ed. New York: International Publications Service, October 1970.

Published annually for the countries of the Middle East and North Africa (including the countries of the Sahara). Part 1: general; part 2: country sections; part 3: who's who, bibliography, etc.

The Middle East and North Africa, 1968-69: Survey and Directory. London: Europa Publications, 1968.

A standard survey and guide, with introductory statements, country statements, bibliographies, and statistical data. See especially, "The Middle East: An Outline of Its Physical and Social Geography."

Riess, Richard O. " 'The Middle East': The Problem of Geographic Terminology." *Journal of Geography* 68, no. 1 (January 1969): 34-40.

Roolvink, Roelof. *Historical Atlas of the Muslim Peoples.* Amsterdam: Djambatan, 1957.

U. S. Department of the Army. *Middle East: Tricontinental Hub: A Bibliographic Survey.* Vol. 2. Washington, D.C.: U.S. Department of the Army, 1968.

Includes regional and country maps, annotated bibliography, and background notes published by the Department of State on each country in the Middle East and North Africa.

Historical Perspectives

History is the systematic study of man's recorded past. Since writing and the preservation of records were both Middle Eastern inventions, it should come as no surprise that the Middle East has a longer recorded history than any other part of the world. It was here that most staple food crops were first cultivated, most farm animals were first domesticated, and the earliest agricultural villages were founded. Here too were the world's oldest cities, the first governments, and the earliest great religious and ethical systems. As a crossroads of ideas and men, the Middle East has undergone many fundamental changes, yet there is much continuity in its history, and even today ancient traditions and time-tested beliefs shape the course of events.

What are the elements of continuity in Middle Eastern history? And what factors have caused changes to occur? At times the area has constituted a single political or cultural system; at others it has split into competing fragments. During the periods of internal cohesion and power Middle Easterners ruled over remote parts of Europe and Asia. During the times of dissension and weakness they fell under the domination of Europeans or Asians. Middle Easterners made important contributions to civilization, but they also borrowed from their rulers and their subjects, often reshaping foreign ideas and institutions to fit their needs.

The political power of Middle Easterners has risen and fallen many times. They have seen many invaders and conquerors come, and when they have not been able to drive their invaders away, they have adjusted to them and subtly made their rulers adapt to them. The interplay between invasion and accommodation is characteristic of the Middle Eastern history. This chapter provides a chronological summary of that history: the ancient empires, the rise of Islam, and the region's subordination to European control. Later chapters will show how the

Middle Eastern countries have tried to regain their independence in the
twentieth century.

The Ancient Middle East

Environment has shaped much of the Middle East's history.
When the polar icecaps retreated, rainfall declined in North Africa and
southwest Asia, and hunting and food-gathering men had to learn how
to control their sources of sustenance. Hunting and gathering as a way
of life seem to have died out in the Middle East some five thousand
years ago. Some men learned how to move up and down mountains or
between desert oases to find forage for their sheep and goats, their
donkeys, and later their camels. Innovations such as the domestication
of animals and the building of huts were followed by reliance on
agriculture instead of on wild foods. The rainfall is not adequate or
regular enough in most areas to support settled agriculture, but the
world's oldest agricultural villages have been discovered in northeastern
Africa and in the highlands of Anatolia. Many others migrated into the
valleys of the Nile, the Tigris, and the Euphrates and learned how to
tame the annual river floods to water their fields.

As grain cultivation spread there were significant improvements
in pottery and implements. Peasants came to need governments to
organize the building of dams, dykes, and canals for large-scale
irrigation, to regulate the distribution of river waters, and often to
protect them from wandering herdsmen. Meanwhile, although the
nomads sometimes served the settled peoples as merchants and soldiers,
they also pillaged their cities and farms. Despite the tension between
the sedentary peasant and the nomadic herdsman, personified in Cain
and Abel, they needed each other. Without both groups, cities, states,
and civilizations would not have come into being.

The earliest known governments arose in the first agrarian
societies, Egypt and Sumer. Beginning in the third millennium before
Christ, however, the people of the ancient Middle East submitted to
invasion and conquest, acquired new ideas and institutions, and
eventually either absorbed or expelled their conquerors. The result was
a succession of ecumenical states that combined the cultures of the
rulers and the various subject peoples, culminating in the Roman
Empire.

River States

The first states based on settled agriculture were the kingdoms
of the Upper and Lower Nile, which combined around 3000 B.C. to
form Egypt, and the kingdom of Sumer, which arose somewhat earlier
in Mesopotamia, the land between the Tigris and the Euphrates rivers.
Both developed strong monarchies supported by elaborate bureaucracies, codes of conduct, and religious doctrines, which integrated the

political system into a cosmological order. Their governments marshaled large work forces to protect the lands from floods and invaders, and a complex division of labor made possible the development of writing, calculation, architecture, metallurgy, and hydraulic engineering.

Semitic and Indo-European Invasions

The river states were disrupted and partially transformed by outside infiltrators and invaders. Sumer was conquered successively by the Akkadians and the Amorites, both of whom spoke Semitic languages. The resulting synthesis produced Babylonia, which reached its height during the reign of the lawgiver Hammurabi (1792-50 B.C.). Meanwhile, Indo-European invaders from the north mixed with local peoples in Anatolia and Iran and created new nations— the Hittites, the Kassites, and the Hurrians—which harassed (and also horsed) the Mesopotamians. The introduction of the horse chariot in fact enabled another Semitic people, the Hyksos, to occupy the Nile delta from 1720 to 1570 B.C. Whereas the Babylonians absorbed their invaders, the Egyptians drove out the Hyksos and then established an empire in Syria, a pattern followed by many later rulers of Egypt.

Internal dissensions and external pressures finally weakened Egypt and Babylonia. The period that followed, around 1000 B.C., was a chaotic one, characterized by a bewildering succession of invasions and new states. New Indo-European tribes, invading Greece and Anatolia from the north, introduced iron tools and weapons. Many historians believe that the climate of the Middle East was becoming drier, forcing more Semitic peoples to migrate from the Arabian desert into the better-watered lands of Syria and Mesopotamia. Among these Semites were the Aramaeans, the Philistines, the Phoenicians, and the Hebrews. The Aramaeans formed several states in Syria; their language, Aramaic, served as the Middle East's common tongue for religion and trade for a thousand years. The Philistines gave their name, but little else, to southern Syria, which became known as Palestine (*Filistin* in modern Arabic). The Phoenicians of the Syrian coast became the great traders, seafarers, and colonizers of the ancient world. One of their lasting contributions was the phonetic alphabet. During the reign of King David (1000-969 B.C.) the Hebrews established a kingdom in Palestine with its capital at Jerusalem; it later split and fell to powerful conquerors. The Hebrews developed a faith in one god, Yahweh, who, according to the Bible, revealed himself to Moses on Sinai and later to the prophets, setting a high standard of belief and behavior for them. Elements of this ethical monotheism had existed in earlier Middle Eastern religions, but the ideas of the Hebrews, crystallized in Judaism, profoundly influenced the intellectual history of both the Middle East and the West.

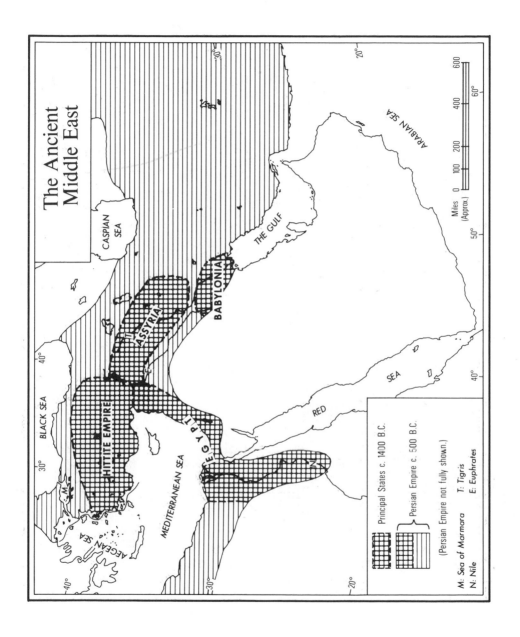

The Ancient
Middle East

CASPIAN SEA

BLACK SEA

ASSYRIA

BABYLONIA

HITTITE EMPIRE

EGYPT

MEDITERRANEAN SEA

AEGEAN SEA

ARABIAN SEA

THE GULF

RED SEA

40°

30°

40°

40°

30°

20°

50°

60°

20°

30°

20°

Miles
(Approx.)

0   100   200   400   600

Principal States c. 1400 B.C.

Persian Empire c. 500 B.C.

(Persian Empire not fully shown.)

M: Sea of Marmara   T: Tigris
N: Nile   E: Euphrates

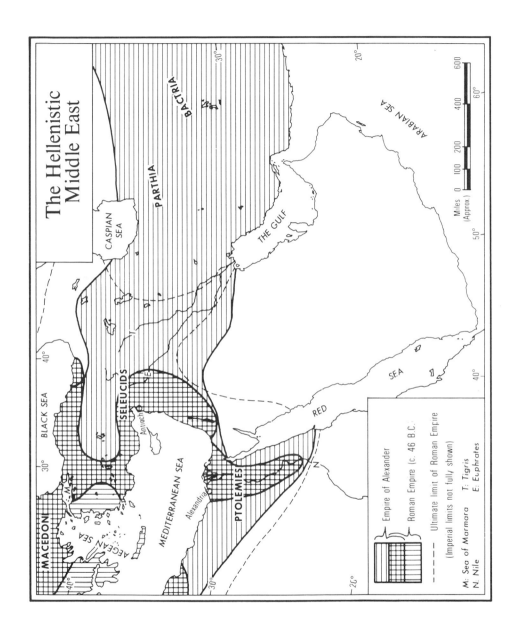

The Hellenistic
Middle East

CASPIAN
SEA

BACTRIA

PARTHIA

THE GULF

ARABIAN SEA

BLACK SEA

40°

30°

SELEUCIDS

Antioch

MACEDONI

AEGEAN SEA

MEDITERRANEAN SEA

Alexandria

PTOLEMIES

RED   SEA

40°

30°

20°

20°

30°

40°

50°

60°

Miles   0 100 200   400   600
(Approx.)

Empire of Alexander

Roman Empire (c. 46 B.C.)

Ultimate limit of Roman Empire
(Imperial limits not fully shown)

M: Sea of Marmara   T: Tigris
N: Nile   E: Euphrates

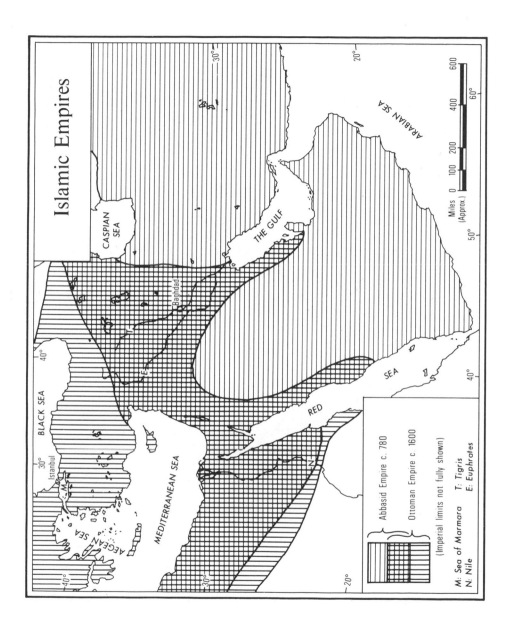

Islamic Empires

CASPIAN SEA

THE GULF

ARABIAN SEA

BLACK SEA

Istanbul

Baghdad

AEGEAN SEA

MEDITERRANEAN SEA

RED SEA

Miles 0 100 200 400 600
(Approx.)

Abbasid Empire c. 780

Ottoman Empire c. 1600

(Imperial limits not fully shown)

M: Sea of Marmara   T: Tigris

N: Nile   E: Euphrates

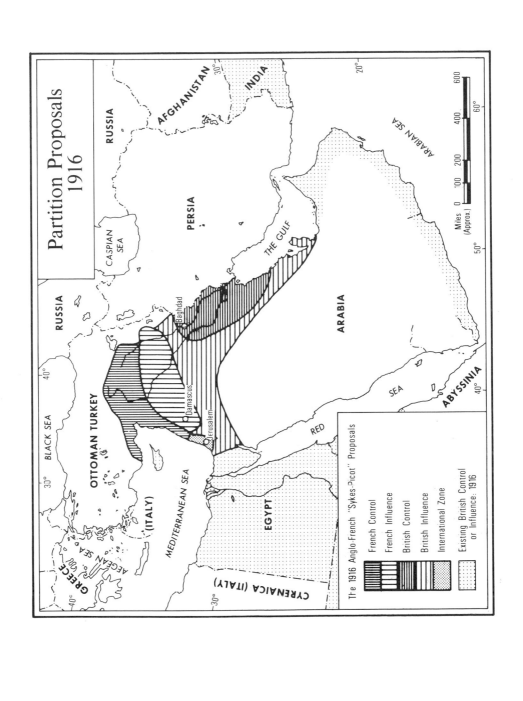

Partition Proposals
1916

The 1916 Anglo-French "Sykes-Picot" Proposals

French Control
French Influence
British Control
British Influence
International Zone

Existing British Control
or Influence: 1916

Miles
(Approx.)

0   100   200   400   600

RUSSIA

BLACK SEA

OTTOMAN TURKEY

GREECE

AEGEAN SEA

(ITALY)

MEDITERRANEAN SEA

CYRENAICA (ITALY)

EGYPT

RED SEA

ABYSSINIA

ARABIA

Jerusalem
Damascus
Baghdad

THE GULF

PERSIA

CASPIAN SEA

RUSSIA

AFGHANISTAN

INDIA

ARABIAN SEA

Iron Age Empires

The introduction of cheap and effective means of manufacturing iron tools and weapons led to the emergence of larger and longer lasting empires. About 1350 B.C. Babylonia gave way to the powerful Assyrian empire, an amalgam in northern Mesopotamia of the Semitic and Indo-European cultures. This first Iron Age empire went through several cycles of rise and decline; at its height (c. 700 B.C.), Assyria ruled Syria and even Egypt. Its Semitic rivals and inheritors, the Chaldeans, maintained the glory of Babylon for another century. Then Mesopotamia and eventually the entire Middle East were conquered by King Cyrus of Persia (550-29 B.C.).

From the time of King Cyrus until modern times, the political history of the Middle East has been that of the rise and fall of successive multinational empires: Persia, Greece, Rome, the Arabs, the Seljuk Turks, the Mongols, and the Ottoman Turks. Like Babylon, most of these empires were created by outside invasions. The rule of the invaders, however, invariably unleashed forces of local resistance that finally sapped the invaders' strength and paved the way for political fragmentation and new invasions. Often the conquerors adopted the institutions and beliefs of their Middle Eastern subjects; rarely did they succeed in uniformly imposing their own.

The Persian empire of Cyrus and his successors, the Achaemenid dynasty, was the prototype of this multinational system. Sprawling from the Indus valley to the Nile, this empire could not impose uniformity on its subjects. Instead, it tolerated their beliefs and practices so long as they were obedient, paid their taxes, and sent men to the Persian army. The provincial governors were given broad civil, judicial, and fiscal powers and even some diplomatic and military autonomy by the Persian emperor, and a feudal system of land tenure ensured the loyalty of local aristocracies. A postal system and a network of roads (and spies), along with a uniform coinage, calendar, and administrative language, helped further unite the empire. Thus, much cultural blending took place; the architectural remains of Achaemenid Persia, for instance, show both Babylonian and Egyptian influences.

The state religion, Zoroastrianism, was original to Persia, however. It stressed the dualism of good and evil, man's responsibility to choose between them in this life, and his duty to bear the consequences in the afterlife. Zoroastrianism and its offshoot, Mithraism, were widely practiced in the ancient world and left their imprint on Christianity and Islam. Achaemenid Persia weathered political crises for two centuries before it succumbed to internal dissension and the military genius of Alexander the Great.

Hellenistic Culture and Rule

Alexander's whirlwind conquest of the Middle East between 332 and 323 B.C. marks a critical juncture in the history of the area.

For the next millennium the Middle East was part of the Hellenistic world, and long afterward it shared with the West the cultural heritage of the Classical Age. Surviving artifacts of Greek and Roman rule, such as buildings, roads, and coins, testify to the two cultures' presence in the Middle East. Even some of their words remain in use, such as the Arabic names of two common coins, the *dirham* (Greek *drachma*) and the *dinar* (Latin *dinarius*).

Alexander wanted to fuse Greek culture with that of the ancient Middle East, adopting ideas, institutions, and talented administrators from the Egyptians, Mesopotamians, and Persians. This fusion did not occur in his lifetime, nor was it ever complete; but from Alexander to Muhammad the entire Mediterranean shared a common civilization, of which the Middle East was a part. The coastal cities, the greatest of which was Alexandria (named for its founder), were the main centers of this cultural blending; Alexandria, although mainly a Greek city, harbored many Middle Easterners. Alexander's successors in Egypt, the Ptolemies, ruled the country like pharaohs. They erected magnificent public buildings, such as the Alexandria Lighthouse, one of the seven wonders of the ancient world, and the Museum, or academy of scholars, which housed the greatest library of ancient times. Astronomy, mathematics, physics, and medicine flourished.

Southern Anatolia, Syria, and Mesopotamia were ruled for two centuries by the Seleucids; descendants of one of Alexander's generals, but their capital, Antioch, was culturally and economically inferior to Alexandria. In the third century B.C. the Seleucids lost control of the eastern parts of Alexander's empire, Bactria (in what is now Afghanistan and West Pakistan), to a separate dynasty descended in part from Alexander's soldiers, and Persia to a Hellenized Turkish dynasty, the Parthians.

The Roman Empire and Its Decline

Meanwhile, a new state, Rome, rose to power in the western Mediterranean. Having taken Carthage, Macedonia, and Greece by 100 B.C., the Roman legions marched eastward, conquering Asia Minor, Syria, and Egypt. Once again most of the Middle East was united in an ecumenical empire; only Iran and part of Mesopotamia lay under the unsubdued Parthians. As in previous empires, the conquerors absorbed much from their Middle Eastern subjects, including several religions and mystery cults, two of which, Mithraism, an offshoot of Zoroastrianism, and Christianity, vied for popular favor throughout the Roman Empire. Christianity finally triumphed. After his conversion, the Emperor Constantine (306-37) moved the imperial capital—and with it Rome's economic and cultural center—to Byzantium, which he renamed Constantinople. The city nevertheless gave its old name to Rome's successor state, the Byzantine Empire. Even now Arabs, Turks, and Persians say *Rum* to mean the Byzantine Empire, its lands (especially Anatolia), and also its Orthodox Christianity and its believers.

Under Roman rule commercial cities flourished, and Syrian and Egyptian merchants grew rich from the trade between Europe, Asia, and eastern Africa. Arab camel nomads, or bedouin, prospered as carriers of cloth and spices. Other Middle Easterners learned to navigate the Red Sea, the Persian Gulf, and the Indian Ocean. But Roman rule also meant supporting a large army of occupation, and Syria and Egypt, the granaries of the ancient world, were taxed heavily. If an urbane tolerance of other peoples' beliefs and customs was the hallmark of a Roman gentleman, it was often honored only in the breach; Roman soldiers destroyed the Jewish Temple in Jerusalem, and many of Jesus' early followers suffered martyrdom for their beliefs. Christian Rome was even less tolerant. Many Christians in North Africa and Egypt espoused heterodox beliefs which the emperors regarded as treasonous, and Roman and Byzantine efforts to suppress heresy alienated many of their Middle Eastern subjects.

Rome and later Byzantium had one major rival, Persia. The Parthians had given way in the third century to the Sassanid dynasty. Bolstered by a strong military aristocracy and the resources of many Hellenized religious refugees from Byzantium, Sassanid Persia included Iran, Mesopotamia, and central Asia. With their bedouin allies in Arabia, the Sassanids threatened Byzantine rule in the Middle East and early in the seventh century briefly overran Syria, Palestine, and Egypt. The Hellenistic era of Middle Eastern history was coming to an end.

The Islamic Middle East as an Autonomous System

The revelation of Islam to an unlettered Meccan merchant in the early seventh century, the unification of hitherto feuding Arab tribes under this new religion, their rapid conquest of the Middle East and North Africa, the conversion of millions of Asians and Africans to Islam, and the development of Arabic-Islamic civilization under a succession of mighty empires marked a new epoch in Middle Eastern history. Egyptians, Syrians, and Persians influenced the beliefs of their Arab conquerors, just as they had transformed and absorbed earlier invaders. Yet the rise of Islam created new ideas and institutions, monuments and memories, which still affect the peoples of the Middle East.

The Arabs before Islam

After the domestication of the camel around 1000 B.C., bands of men roamed the arid wastes of the Arabian peninsula in search of water and forage for their camels, sheep, and goats. Milk and dates—rarely meat and bread—were their diet. They augmented their income by raiding or protecting the commercial caravans between Syria and the Indian Ocean and by serving as auxiliaries in the Persian and Roman armies. Sometimes these Arabs moved into more fertile areas and built cities, such as Petra in Jordan, and established states, especially in relatively well watered Yemen.

If these pre-Islamic Arabs lacked the refinement of the Romans and the Persians, they were not uncivilized barbarians. They were warlike and often aggressive, to be sure, and their nomadic existence gave them little chance to develop architecture, sculpture, or painting. But they did compose poetry that embodied their code of values— bravery in battle, patience in misfortune, persistence in revenge (the only form of justice where there is no government), protection of the weak, defiance of the strong, loyalty to the tribe, hospitality to the guest, generosity to the needy, and fidelity to their promises. These were the virtues men needed to survive in the desert. Their poems, recited from memory, expressed the joys and tribulations of nomadic life, extolled the bravery of their heroes, lauded the virtues of their tribes, and lampooned the faults of their rivals. This poetry still influences the thoughts and behavior, the language and literature of modern Arabs.

In Roman times the southern Arabs were economically and culturally more advanced; they developed Yemen, colonized Ethiopia, and traded across the Indian Ocean. The northern Arabs, unless they fought for the Byzantines or the Sassanids, were relatively isolated. Some adopted Christianity or Judaism, but most adhered to primitive forms of animism or ancestor worship. One of the northern tribes, the Quraysh, built a religious shrine, the *kaabah*, at a small city, Mecca, situated on the main trade route between Syria and the Yemen. Mecca became a great commercial and religious center. Once a year the pagan tribes of northwestern Arabia suspended their quarrels to make pilgrimages to the kaabah, and some Meccans grew wealthy on the proceeds of the caravan and pilgrimage trade.

Muhammad

In this prosperous desert city Muhammad, one of the world's greatest religious leaders, was born about 570 to an impoverished branch of the Quraysh. Orphaned at an early age, Muhammad was raised by an uncle and became the agent for a rich merchant widow, Khadijah, whom he married. Until he was forty, Muhammad was nothing more than a Meccan merchant distinguished mainly by his honesty. However, he seems to have been troubled by the widening disparity between the accepted Arab virtures of bravery and generosity and the blatantly acquisitive practices of Mecca's commercial leaders. He probably knew of the Jews' and Christians' belief in one God and of the high moral standards imposed on them by their sacred scriptures. Frequently he went to one of the hills near Mecca to meditate.

One day in the Arab month of Ramadan Muhammad heard a voice exhorting him to recite. In awe and terror Muhammad cried, "I cannot recite." The voice replied:

> Recite in the name of thy Lord, the Creator
> who created man of a blood-clot.
> Recite, for thy Lord most generous
> who taught by the pen,
> taught man what he knew not.

Fearing that he had gone mad, Muhammad rushed home and asked Khadijah to cover him. Again the voice sounded:

> O thou enshrouded in thy mantle
> rise and warn!
> Thy Lord magnify,
> thy raiment purify
> and from evil flee!

Reassured by his wife, Muhammad accepted the voice as God's command to proclaim His existence to the Arabs and to warn them of an imminent judgment day when all men would be called to account for their good and evil deeds. In the ensuing years he received more revelations and attracted a few followers, mostly Meccans of modest means and social standing. Those who accepted Muhammad's divine message called themselves Muslims and their religion Islam, meaning submission to the will of God (Arabic *Allah*), the creator and sustainer of all being.

Muhammad's public recitations of these revelations disturbed the Meccan leaders. Did their wealth and power mean nothing in this new scale of values? If the pagan Arab tribes accepted Islam, would they stop their annual pilgrimages to the kaabah, so lucrative to the Meccan merchants? If there was one God, why did he choose to reveal his message to Muhammad, rather than to one of the Quraysh leaders? The pagan Meccans began to revile and to persecute the Muslims, and after Muhammad's uncle and protector died, life in Mecca became intolerable for Muslims. Finally the Arabs of Medina, a city north of Mecca, asked Muhammad to arbitrate their tribal disputes and accepted Islam as the condition for his coming.

The *hijrah*, or emigration, of Muhammad and his followers from Mecca is for Muslims the most significant event in their history. The Muslim calendar begins in the year it occurred, A.D. 622. For it was in Medina that Muhammad founded the Islamic *ummah*, or community, a state governed by a divine plan, which was revealed to him gradually. Politics and religion were not separated in Islam; God, speaking to men through Muhammad, was the supreme legislator. Thus the Prophet was a political leader and when the Meccans tried to destroy the ummah, a military commander as well. Buttressed by their faith, the Muslims of Medina vanquished Meccan armies larger and stronger than their own, converted most of the pagan Arab tribes, and finally brought Mecca into the fold of Islam. In 630 Muhammad made a triumphal pilgrimage to the kaabah, destroyed its pagan idols, and declared it a Muslim shrine. Two years later, having united most of Arabia under the banner of Islam, he died.

Islamic Beliefs and Institutions

Muslims believe that there is one God, who is all powerful and all knowing, who has no partner and no offspring. He has revealed himself to man, not by sending a son, but by speaking to a succession of human messengers or prophets, the last of whom was Muhammad. To the Jewish prophets he revealed the Torah and to Jesus and his followers the Gospels. Muslims believe that the Jews and the Christians later corrupted their scriptures, and thus God sent his perfect revelation, the Quran (Arabic for "recitation"), to Muhammad. Muslims are not intolerant of Jews and Christians, however; rather, they view the Quran as a more genuine revelation than the Bible in its present form, and a Muslim may not reject any of God's prophets, including Abraham, Moses, and Jesus. Muslims believe also in a final day of judgment, when God will judge all men and send them to heaven or to hell.

Although it is simple to understand, Islam makes heavy demands on its followers. These are usually summarized as "the five pillars of Islam": acknowledgment of belief in one God and in Muhammad as his prophet; prayer five times daily; fasting in the daylight hours of the Muslim month of Ramadan; payment of a share of one's income (called *zakat*) to provide for the needy; and the pilgrimage (*hajj*) to Mecca. Muslims must also abstain from drinking alcoholic beverages, gambling, and all forms of licentious and dishonest behavior. Muslim standards of sexual morality are strict, and contacts between unmarried men and women are limited. Even today marriages in Muslim countries are usually arranged by parents, and dating is uncommon. On the other hand, Muslims do not believe in original sin. They ascribe man's misdeeds to ignorance or forgetfulness and see God as forgiving those who sincerely repent.

Islam is more than a religion; it is a way of life. It dictates man's relationship to his fellowman as well as to God. Muhammad's ummah was an attempt to provide the ideal earthly setting in which believers could prepare for the day of judgment. In the centuries following Muhammad's death, Muslim scholars (*ulama*) developed an elaborate law code, the Shariah ("holy law") to regulate all aspects of human behavior. The Shariah was derived from the Quran, the sayings and actions of the Prophet (or those actions of his followers sanctioned by Muhammad), the consensus of the ummah, legal analogy, and judicial opinion. In principle, all Muslims were bound together in one community; in fact, dynastic and doctrinal schisms would later divide the ummah. But the authority of the Shariah, upheld by the ulama, united Muslims of various races, cultures, geographical areas, and political allegiances. Muslim rulers always in principle and usually in practice (or at least appearance) either upheld the Shariah or forfeited the loyalty of their subjects.

**Muhammad's Successors and the
Arab Conquests**

When Muhammad died his followers had to act quickly to choose a successor. No one could succeed Muhammad as God's prophet, but someone had to lead the ummah, for many of the Arab tribes were renouncing Islam and rebelling against Medina's rule. Abu Bakr, one of Muhammad's most trusted companions, was chosen as his successor, the first caliph. During his caliphate the Muslims won back the rebellious Arab tribesmen and deflected the Arabs' energies outward against Byzantium and Persia. Under Umar, the second caliph, these Arabs defeated armies far stronger than themselves, wresting Palestine, Syria, and Egypt from Byzantine control and completely absorbing Sassanid Persia.

The Arab conquests were almost fantastic. This small army of bedouin tribesmen imbued with religious zeal conquered most of the Middle East in a generation and much of the Old World in a century. These conquests did not mean the extermination of the conquered peoples. Indeed, many Syrians, Egyptians, and Persians welcomed Arab rule as a respite from Byzantine intolerance and Sassanid exploitation; they were neither forced to speak Arabic nor to become Muslims, although some did so voluntarily.

Generally the new Arab rulers retained local administrative customs and languages and even the administrators themselves; the Arabs had neither the numbers nor the political experience necessary to govern their large empire unaided. All they demanded was that every non-Muslim pay a head tax in return for exemption from military service. In fact, it was several centuries before most people living in lands under Islamic rule were actually Muslims; some Muslim rulers even discouraged conversions to Islam to prevent a loss of tax revenues. Jerusalem under Arab rule remained a religious center and pilgrimage site for Jews and Christians, but now it became a holy city for Muslims as well; two of their oldest and most venerated mosques, the Dome of the Rock and al-Aksa, were built on the site of the Jewish Temple.

Jerusalem remains important to Muslims. After a 1969 fire destroyed part of the al-Aksa mosque, situated in the part of Jerusalem annexed by Israel after the 1967 War, an Islamic summit conference met in Rabat, Morocco, and demanded the return of the holy places to Muslim control.

Although Arab toleration of local customs maintained stability in the empire, the conquests put a heavy strain on the Islamic ummah itself. The caliphs in Medina set aside some of the captured booty for charitable or communal use and put the troops on a payroll, but the sudden influx of wealth corrupted some Arabs and made others increasingly restive. In 656 the third caliph, Uthman, was murdered. Many of Uthman's supporters suspected his successor, Ali, the Prophet's son-in-law, of complicity in the assassination. Thus, Uthman's cousin, Muawiya, the governor of Syria, demanded revenge and fought Ali's followers in a battle that ended in an arbitration favoring Muawiya. Ali's supporters began to drift away. A group called the Kharijites rebelled against Ali, and one of them killed him in 661. Muawiya named himself caliph, moved the capital to Damascus, pacified the dissident Muslims, and finally made the caliphate hereditary in his own family, the Umayyad branch of the Quraysh, replacing the earlier elective system.

The Umayyad rulers tended to be more political than pious. They crushed their opponents and presided over the spread of Arab rule to North Africa and Spain, to central Asia, and to northwestern India (but not, much to their sorrow, to Constantinople). The period of Umayyad rule remains bright in the memory of Arab nationalists, especially in modern Syria, but many Muslims of that period hated the Umayyads. One of those the Umayyads destroyed was the Prophet's grandson, Husayn, who led a revolt at Kerbala, Iraq, in 680. Husayn's martyrdom led to a political and religious opposition movement known as Shiism (from the Arabic *shiat Ali*, "the party of Ali"). Even now a split remains between the Shiis, who accept only Ali and his descendants as legitimate leaders of the ummah, and the Sunnis (orthodox Muslims), who recognize the caliphs that actually ruled. Today Sunnis outnumber Shiis in most parts of the Muslim world, but Shiism is the state religion of Iran and differentiates the Persians from other Middle Eastern peoples. There are also some Shiite Arabs. A majority of Iraq's Arab Muslims, for instance, are Shiis, and this contributes to political fragmentation in Iraq. The politics of modern Lebanon, Syria, and Yemen are also affected by the presence of Shiite communities. Compared with the divisions within Christianity, however, sectarian differences among Sunnis, Shiis, and Kharijites are minor.

The Arab Empire

The Umayyads' power rested on their main fighting force, the Arab tribesmen. The Arabs received preferential treatment, even after many non-Arabs converted to Islam, and some non-Arab Muslims turned to revolutionary movements, often with Shiite undertones, in opposition to Umayyad rule. One such movement, led by the Abbasid family, overthrew the Umayyads in 750 and established its own caliphate at Baghdad in Iraq, basing its authority on public adherence to orthodox Islam rather than on Arab supremacy, as the Umayyads had done. At this point the formal unity of the ummah ended, since the Umayyads retained control of Spain. The Berber provinces of North Africa broke away from Abbasid control, and ambitious local governors, warlords, and religious leaders began to carve out their own states.

The two sons of the renowned caliph Harun al-Rashid (786-809) fought each other in a civil war that symbolized the struggle between the Arabs and the Persians. The Persian-backed contestant won. Increasingly the Arabs either reverted to nomadism or intermarried with the peoples they had conquered, many of whom were now Arabized in language and culture.

Once the Abbasid caliphs ceased to rely on Arab tribesmen, they needed a new source of fighting men. Like their Greek and Roman predecessors, they preferred to recruit mercenaries rather than conscript their own subjects. For a time they hired Persians; later they imported Turkish slaves from central Asia. Converted to Islam and schooled in the arts of government and war, the Turks were more reliable than the caliphs' other Muslim subjects, and these pliable servants soon dominated the administration and the army. The Turks took over whole provinces and finally made the caliph their hostage. Revolts by gypsies, African slaves, and bedouin and Byzantine conquests in Syria punctuated the Abbasid decline in the ninth and tenth centuries, and Shiite dynasties took over in North Africa, Egypt, Syria, and even Baghdad, the seat of the Abbasids. Thus the institution of the caliphate, which was born out of the need of Muhammad's followers for some supreme leadership, developed into a hereditary monarchy buttressed first by Arab supremacy, then by Muslim orthodoxy, and it was finally reduced to a powerless figurehead position.

Despite its turbulent politics, the Abbasid era was one of agricultural and commercial prosperity. As industry and trade flourished, so did science and letters. Individual rulers and dynasties vied with one another in patronizing the translation of scientific and philosophical works from Greek into Arabic, supporting court poets and historians, building mosques and palaces, and sponsoring astronomical and medical research. Thus the Muslims preserved and added to their classical patrimony and later passed it along to medieval Europe to help spark the Renaissance.

Turkish Invasions: Ghaznavids and Seljuks

It used to be common for both Muslims and Westerners to ascribe the decline of the Middle East to the Turkish incursions. Turks were depicted as nomadic barbarians, destroyers of cities and civilizations, and autocratic rulers. The fact is that the influx of Turks from central Asia was neither sudden nor devastating. Just as the Arabs who served in Roman or Persian armies helped unintentionally to prepare local peoples for the seventh century Arab conquests, so Turkish slave soldiers and bureaucrats paved the way for the eleventh century Turkish invasions. From the ninth century on, some central Asian Turkish tribes converted to Islam and served the Abbasids or local Muslim rulers as frontier guards against non-Muslim Turks farther east.

These *ghazis* (literally "raiders," or military adventurers) often rose to positions of power.

One Turkish family serving a Persian dynasty received a fief—a piece of land given in return for military or administrative service to the government—in Ghazna (in what is now Afghanistan). This family, the Ghaznavids, parlayed their fief into an immense empire encompassing eastern Iran, Afghanistan, and parts of India never before under Muslim rule. The Ghaznavids, like their Persian predecessors, gave fiefs of land to Turkish clans from central Asia. One of their fiefholders, the Seljuks, embarked on a similar course of conquest that carried them westward across Iran and Mesopotamia and into Anatolia, most of which they took from the Byzantines after 1071. The military success of these families attracted other Turks to serve as ghazis and opened the way for large-scale immigration of Turkish nomadic tribes with their horses, sheep, and goats. In a few generations, Azarbayjan (northwestern Persia), northern Iraq, and much of Anatolia, upland areas which had never been conquered by the Arabs, had become predominantly Turkish. By 1100 most of the Middle East was under Turkish rule.

The Turks did not destroy Islamic civilization. Devout Muslims themselves, they built new cities and refurbished old ones. They rescued the Abbasid caliph from his Shiite captors and restored his authority, although not his power. For several generations the caliph ruled in Baghdad beside a Seljuk sultan (a title meaning "holder of power"). The Turks strengthened Sunni Muslim legal and educational institutions, but they also encouraged trends that would later fossilize Islam, such as sufism (organized Islamic mysticism), and banned reinterpretations of the Shariah. Sufism gave Muslims a sense of greater involvement in their faith, but it also caused them to withdraw from worldly activities into contemplation, and once the Shariah became immutable for Sunni Muslims, changing social needs caused rulers and subjects to circumvent it, and practices diverged ever further from Islamic precepts.

The Crusades

As the Turkish nomads poured in from the East, lured by land, wealth, and opportunities for power, a different group of invaders came from the West. In 1096 the pope proclaimed a crusade to regain the Holy Land for Christianity. Muslims had ruled Jerusalem for over four centuries without harming Christian interests, but the Turkish invasion of Anatolia under the Seljuks had seriously weakened the Byzantine Empire and had endangered the Christian pilgrimage routes to the Holy City. The European Crusaders helped the Byzantines to stem the Seljuk tide and then went on to capture western Syria and Palestine from divided and weak Muslim rulers. For almost a century Jerusalem, purged of its Muslim and Jewish inhabitants, was the capital of a European Christian kingdom. Three lesser crusading states shared control over the Syrian coast with the Latin Kingdom of Jerusalem.

Both Westerners and Muslims tend to exaggerate the importance of the Crusades, partly because of the tempting historical parallels with modern colonialism in the area. Actually the Crusaders did not commonly uproot the local inhabitants, and they never captured the major power centers: Cairo, Damascus, Aleppo, and Mosul. Once Egypt and Syria were united under a strong Sunni Muslim ruler, Salah al-Din, the Crusaders' threat to these large cities dimmed, and the Muslims recaptured Jerusalem in 1187. The Crusaders held part of the Syrian coast for another century and twice invaded the Egyptian delta, but Saladin's descendants, the Ayyubids, kept them in check.

Mongol Invasions and Mamluk Resistance

Far more serious in their effects on Islam were the continued invasions from central Asia, especially those of the Mongols. Taking advantage of the power vacuum created in eastern Iran by the destruction of the Khorezmian Turks, Mongol armies led by Genghis Khan (1206-27) conquered Muslim central Asia, eastern Iran, and Azarbayjan. His grandson, Hulagu, pressed farther into Persia and Mesopotamia and in 1258 took Baghdad and terminated the Abbasid caliphate.

The Mongols were not Muslims. Horse nomads accustomed to vast grassy steppes, they saw no need for cities or the peasant cultivators who supported them, and thus they destroyed irrigation works in Persia, Mesopotamia, and Syria, impoverishing the land and its people. Many Muslim rulers, such as the Seljuks of Anatolia, were reduced to vassalage. However, in 1260 the Mongols failed to capture Palestine and Egypt, where the Ayyubids had been overthrown in 1250 by their well-organized corps of Turkish soldiers, the Mamluks, and the Mamluks thus saved Islamic Africa from the fate of Asia. The Mamluks built a prosperous empire in Egypt and Syria, the bulwark of Muslim power until its conquest by the Ottoman Turks in 1516-17. Mongol dynasties in Persia and Mesopotamia soon adopted Islam, accepted Persian culture, and restored much of what they had earlier destroyed. Their immense mosques, decorated with colorful glazed tilework, still grace many Iranian cities.

The harnessing of gunpowder in Europe during the fourteenth century profoundly affected the relationship of Europe with the rest of the world. The invention was used initially to destroy fortifications and only later to kill men and animals. Gunpowder weapons and long-distance sailing ships soon enabled Europeans to explore and conquer distant lands and finally to encircle the Muslim world.

Gunpowder-using states require large, disciplined infantries rather than the feudal cavalries of medieval times. Thus, the gunpowder revolution in Europe—together with the secularism of the Renaissance— sparked the development of strong, monarchical states, a commercial middle class, and the industrial revolution, all at the expense of the feudal aristocracy and the clergy. In the Middle East some Muslim states learned how to use gunpowder weapons on land and sea; others never did. The gunpowder revolution weakened the aristocracy there also but failed to stimulate economic and social modernization on the European pattern.

The Ottoman Empire

The Ottoman Empire was the archetypal Muslim state built on the use of gunpowder. From their humble beginnings in the late thirteenth century as Turkish ghazis for the Seljuks, the Ottomans (or Osmanlis, the descendants and followers of Osman, the founder of the Ottoman dynasty) expanded their landholdings into a mighty empire that stretched from central Europe to the Persian Gulf and from Algeria to Azarbayjan. Like most ghazis, the Ottomans began as horse soldiers raiding peasant lands. During the fourteenth and fifteenth centuries, however, they developed a disciplined corps of foot soldiers, the famous janissaries (Turkish *yeni cheri,* "new troops"), who could use siege cannon and lighter firearms against the Europeans. The janissaries were taken from the Christian peasants under Ottoman rule by a periodic levy against adolescent boys. They were converted to Islam, taught Turkish and Arabic, and trained as soldiers (or in a few cases as administrators). Regarded as slaves of the Ottoman sultan, the janissaries were forbidden to marry or to own land (they were paid salaries, not given fiefs like the cavalry) and had to live in barracks in order to be ready to fight whenever needed. This system of recruitment was called *devshirme,* as were the group of Ottoman soldiers and administrators it produced.

With powerful, well-equipped armies and loyal, competent administrators, the Ottoman sultans conquered the Christian peoples of the Balkans, where no Muslim army had ever gone before, and surrounded Constantinople. In 1453 they captured the city and terminated the thousand-year-old Byzantine Empire. Once the greatest Christian city, Constantinople (Istanbul today) became a major Islamic center. In the following century the Ottomans subjugated most of their Muslim neighbors, including the Mamluks of Egypt and Syria. Only Persia, ruled after 1501 by another gunpowder-using dynasty, the Safavids, withstood the Ottoman onslaught.

Ottoman power rested on two practices: (1) the power of the ruling class was balanced between the traditional aristocracy and the devshirme soldiers and administrators; and (2) the subject peoples were organized into confessional communities, called *millets,* which had autonomous control over their laws, education, and general welfare. These internal divisions were a source of strength for the sultan. So long as he could play the aristocracy off against the devshirme class, both ruling groups had to perform their tasks as defenders and managers of the Ottoman Empire. The subject peoples, divided into Jewish and various Christian and Muslim communities, were largely self-sufficient but scattered geographically and could not easily combine against their Ottoman overlords. These subjects relied on their religious leaders— rabbis, priests, and ulama—appointed by and responsible to the sultan, to serve as their intermediaries with the government. Thus, until recently the political and social identity for the average Middle Easterner has been his religion, or millet, not his nationality.

Of the many factors that caused the decline of the Ottoman Empire, the most significant was the triumph of the devshirme administrators and the janissaries over the aristocracy, which paradoxically occurred during the reign of the most illustrious Ottoman sultan, Suleyman the Magnificent (1520-66). Unchecked by the less competent succeeding sultans or by the aristocracy, these one-time slaves corrupted the Ottoman government to serve their own material interests. Janissaries married, bought property, and eventually enrolled their sons in the corps. They stopped training and degenerated into a hereditary, privileged caste. Military ineptitude and maladministration ensued. Taxes rose, especially for the peasants, who were the least able to avoid paying them. Agricultural and commercial prosperity diminished, partly because the trade routes between Europe and Asia shifted away from the Middle East. Many formerly loyal subjects rebelled against Ottoman misrule. By the end of the seventeenth century, the Ottoman Empire was no longer the scourge of Christian Europe. The power relationship between the Middle East and the West was turning again.

The Subordination of the Middle East to the West

Since the early eighteenth century the West has achieved military, political, and economic superiority over the people of the Middle East, who had been accustomed to view the West with contempt. Whereas Middle Easterners once controlled the trade routes between Europe and Asia and traded with both as equals, by 1700 Europe sold its manufactured goods to the Middle East in exchange for raw materials and agricultural products. Europeans in Muslim lands were exempted from local taxes and legal jurisdiction; in the Ottoman Empire this exemption was guaranteed by treaties called the Capitulations. Whereas once the Mediterranean Sea and the Indian Ocean were controlled by Muslim navies, now European sailing ships dominated the high seas. Whereas once the Ottoman sultan could choose the time and place for an attack on Christian Europe and could dictate the terms of peace, now his armies were at the mercy of the stronger forces of Hapsburg Austria and the Russian czars. In 1683 the Ottomans failed to take Vienna; in 1699 they surrendered Hungary to the Hapsburgs and parts of Greece and the Adriatic coast to the Venetians in the humiliating Treaty of Karlowitz; in 1718 they signed away more of their European lands at Passarowitz; in 1774 they lost the Crimea and acknowledged Russia's right to intervene on behalf of the Ottoman Empire's Orthodox Christian subjects; in 1798 Napoleon occupied Egypt and marched on Palestine.

Early Ottoman Reform

As early as the seventeenth century some Ottoman sultans and their ministers saw the need for internal reform. At first they regarded reform as the restoration of the institutions and practices that had made the Ottomans strong in the fifteenth and sixteenth centuries. Military defeat at the hands of Western armies taught them that conditions had changed, however, necessitating even more drastic transformations. It is not surprising, then, that the first attempts at modernization occurred in the military; Sultan Selim III (1789-1807) tried to establish a new army corps, trained and equipped in the European fashion. The janissaries, however, fearing the loss of their power, destroyed the new corps and deposed Selim.

In any case the deeply ingrained conservatism of the ulama and other vested interest groups blocked reform in other aspects of Ottoman life. Even the introduction of printing was long delayed by the opposition of the ulama and the scribes, one fearing an innovation contrary to Islam, the other fearing unemployment. Muslim rulers had to learn that reform could not occur only in the military, divorced from the other institutions of society.

Nineteenth Century Reform

The failure of early Ottoman reform taught the Muslim rulers that defense against European expansionism required concentration of power in the state. Thus, in the nineteenth century Middle East political reform meant autocracy, not democracy. Three reforming rulers can serve as examples: Muhammad Ali (1805-49) of Egypt, Mahmud II (1808-39) of the Ottoman Empire, and Nasser al-Din Shah (1848-96) of Persia. Each tried to concentrate power in his own hands, and each found himself hamstrung by European actions taken to serve European interests.

The ablest of these reformers was Muhammad Ali, an Ottoman officer in charge of an Albanian regiment. He gained control of Egypt after the evacuation of Napoleon's forces and proceeded to eliminate every rival power in the country. He massacred the Mamluks and weakened the ulama, who had enjoyed special power and prestige in Egypt, by exploiting their internecine rivalries and confiscating the Muslim endowments (Arabic *waqf*). Furthermore, he subordinated the rural aristocracy to the state by taking control of the agricultural land. He developed the strongest military force in the Middle East, supported by a centrally directed program of administrative, economic, and educational modernization. Not only did he become the main land-owner in Egypt but he also decided what crops the peasants might grow; he supplied them with seed, fertilizer, and tools, purchased their entire harvests, and sold them at a profit. He conscripted peasants to build roads, barge canals, and irrigation systems.

Under his reign Egypt became the first Middle Eastern country to make the transition from subsistence to market agriculture. Tobacco, sugar, indigo, and cotton became Egypt's cash crops, earning the revenue for Muhammad Ali's ambitious projects for industrial and military development. The first non-Western ruler to grasp the significance of the industrial revolution, he built textile mills and munitions factories with the help of European advisers. He sent hundreds of Turks (most of Egypt's aristocracy was Turkish by origin and language) and Egyptians to Europe for technical and military training and imported European instructors to start schools in Egypt. He was the first ruler of Egypt since ancient times to use Egyptian peasants as soldiers. Officered by Turks, they became such a potent force that Muhammad Ali's son, Ibrahim, conquered Syria in 1832 and might have captured the whole Ottoman Empire in 1839 if the European powers had not intervened to protect it. Despite Ottoman recognition of Egypt's autonomy in 1840, Muhammad Ali felt that his ambitions had been thwarted and let his reforms lapse. His heirs ruled Egypt with almost no Ottoman control.

Muhammad Ali's Ottoman contemporary, Sultan Mahmud II, also tried to reform his state by a policy of centralization but with less immediate success. Remembering the lesson of Selim III, he waited until he was strong enough to destroy the janissary corps, the main obstacle to change. Then he reorganized the army, abolished feudalism, and began to reform finances, education, and provincial government. But Mahmud's efforts were hampered by the diversity and extent of his domains, the lack of a loyal and trained bureaucracy, the successful Greek war for independence, and European interference. When Abdul Mejid succeeded him in 1839, Mejid issued a reform proclamation called the Hatt-i Sherif of Gulhane, which ushered in the era of the Tanzimat (reorganization), a period of more intensive centralization and modernization of the Ottoman Empire. The Tanzimat reforms worked better than those of Mahmud, but they did not strengthen the Ottoman Empire enough to stop Russian imperialism in the Balkans, so Britain and France had to help the Turks fight Russia in the Crimean War (1853-56). The victorious Western powers then forced their Ottoman ally to issue another reform decree, which gave Christians and Jews legal equality with Muslims in the Ottoman Empire.

Persia was the only Middle Eastern country that never fell under Ottoman rule. From the fifteenth century a succession of Turkish dynasties ruled that sprawling and heterogeneous country, either in uneasy alliance or open contention with the nomadic tribes, feudal landlords, and urban merchants. The rulers' revival of ancient Persian imperial customs preserved a feeling of national identity, reinforced by their adherence to Shiism, in contrast with the prevalence of Sunni Islam in the Ottoman Empire. In the sixteenth and seventeenth centuries Persia flourished under the Safavid shahs, who built their magnificent capital at Isfahan and formed commercial and diplomatic ties with European countries, seeking an ally against the Ottoman Empire.

In the eighteenth century Nadir Shah, a military adventurer, extended Persian rule far into Asia and drove the Ottomans from Azarbayjan. But Persia too declined. The Qajar dynasty (1794-1925) halfheartedly resisted decay and dissolution from within and Russian and British encroachments from without. During the first three years of the reign of Nasser al-Din Shah, Persia witnessed a series of military, financial, and educational reforms instituted by his energetic chief minister. In 1851, however, the shah executed his minister, and the country became embroiled in a war with Britain and in tribal and religious uprisings. Later in his reign Nasser al-Din began selling concessions to British investors and hiring Russian officers to train his army. Thus, instead of using reform to protect Persia from foreigners, the shah encouraged them to take control. His policies became increasingly unpopular; a nationwide tobacco boycott forced him to cancel one of his most lucrative concessions, and he was finally assassinated. The later Qajar shahs were even less reform-minded than Nasser al-Din and even more subservient to British and Russian influence.

European Policies in the Middle East

If the power of the Europeans stimulated reforms in the Middle East, their policies and actions often hindered them as well. European states preserved peace among themselves during the nine-teenth century by maintaining a balance of power. This meant that neither Britain nor Russia could let the other become supreme in the Middle East. Since a partition of the Ottoman Empire was likely to give Russia control of the Balkans and the straits connecting the Black Sea with the Aegean, Britain usually tried to uphold Ottoman territorial integrity. Thus Britain led the European powers in opposing Muham-mad Ali's threat (backed by France) to the Ottoman Empire in 1839, Russia's occupation of the Rumanian principalities in 1853 (leading to the Crimean War), and Russia's efforts to exploit rising nationalism in the Balkans.

Britain backed reforms that seemed likely to help the Ottoman government resist Russia, especially those during the Tanzimat era that promised equality to non-Muslims. But Britain also made sure that Middle Eastern markets for her manufactured goods were kept open, using a tariff treaty that effectively prevented the Ottoman government from protecting local manufacturers from European competition. Russia's territorial ambitions, her claim to protect Orthodox Christians in the Ottoman Empire, and later her sponsorship of Slavic nationalism in the Balkans—to say nothing of her periodic wars against the empire—undermined Ottoman reform efforts.

Because she needed to guard her route to India, Britain vied with France for power in the eastern Mediterranean; she fought to expel Napoleon from Egypt and later to remove Muhammad Ali from Syria. Britain signed treaties with Persian Gulf rulers and occupied

Aden in order to outflank Muhammad Ali and France. It was a British company that started steamship navigation on the Euphrates in the 1830s; another built the first railroad from Alexandria to Cairo in 1852. On the other hand, a French engineer, Ferdinand de Lesseps, gained a concession from the Egyptian government to cut a canal across the Isthmus of Suez, joining the Red Sea to the Mediterranean and further reducing the travel time between Europe and the Far East. Britain initially tried to block this largely French project, but she became the principal user of the Suez Canal soon after it was opened in 1869.

The Middle Eastern Reaction to the West

By the 1860s many Middle Easterners were beginning to wonder if Westernization had gone too far. In the Ottoman Empire many Muslims espoused Pan-Islam to counter external threats and the divisive nationalist movements of non-Muslim subjects in the Balkans. In one sense this merely reaffirmed the tradition of Muslim unity to defend the ummah, but the new doctrine had more activist connotations: the Ottoman sultan claimed for himself the caliphate, hence the political allegiance of all Muslim peoples, regardless of who actually ruled them. Since Britain, France, and Russia all had Muslim subjects, they quickly saw the revolutionary threat in Pan-Islam, although they often exaggerated it.

Pan-Islam was only one manifestation of the intellectual changes that were taking place in the Middle East. The Ottoman and Egyptian reform programs were creating a new elite which had acquired Western technical skills. As Middle Easterners studying in European universities, mission schools, or Ottoman and Egyptian state institutions learned how to act like Europeans, they also began to think like them. They learned that bad governments could be altered or overthrown, that individuals had rights and freedoms, and that they belonged to political communities based on race, language, culture, and shared historical experience, called "nations." In the late nineteenth century these liberal and nationalist ideas gave birth to new movements: the Nationalist party in Egypt, the New Ottomans and later the Young Turks in Ottoman Turkey, the Arab secret societies in Beirut and Damascus, and the Constitutionalists in Persia. Each of these groups rebelled against the centralization of power by its rulers and tried to establish a constitutional form of government. Not one was wholly successful.

Egyptian Nationalism

Muhammad Ali's grandson, Ismail (1863-79), resumed the Westernization of Egypt. He secured Egypt's financial and administrative independence from the Ottoman Empire. He sent explorers to find the sources of the Nile and military expeditions to conquer the southern Sudan. He transformed Cairo and Alexandria with great mansions, wide boulevards, and public gardens. Factories and public works improved the economy as a cotton boom, the growing availability of European capital, and the construction of the Suez Canal made Egypt an attractive field for investment.

Egypt developed rapidly, but so did Ismail's problems. In 1866 he created a representative assembly to advise his government and raise revenue. Timid at first but later incited by a press that expressed the views of the Egyptian elite, this new body gradually began to demand constitutional government. Ismail borrowed vast sums from foreign bankers to cover his extravagant expenditures. Unable to pay his debts, Ismail had to sell his government's Suez Canal shares to Britain, then to accept British and French control over Egypt's finances, and finally to admit representatives of these two creditor nations into his cabinet. The Egyptians reacted strongly. The representative assembly demanded the right to supervise the government's internal and financial affairs. It called for a cabinet constitutionally responsible to the assembly and devoid of its European members, whose restrictions on government expenditures were harming many Egyptians. Following an Egyptian officers' uprising, Ismail dismissed his "European cabinet" and appointed one that supported the assembly's demand for constitutional government. At this point the European powers pressured the Ottoman sultan to replace Ismail with his son, Tawfiq.

Obedient to his European advisers, Tawfiq (1879-92) removed the dissidents from his government and tried to pay some of his father's debts. But many Egyptians resented European control and called for national independence. Three groups made up this first Egyptian nationalist movement: the Constitutionalists, who wanted to end absolute rule and to establish a representative government committed to reform; the religious leaders, who wished to reform Egyptian society on Islamic principles; and the Egyptian army officers, led by Colonel Ahmad Urabi, who demanded an end to the subordination of Egyptians to Turks and Europeans. In 1881 Urabi's men surrounded Tawfiq's palace and demanded a new cabinet responsible to an elected parliament. Tawfiq acquiesced, and soon Egypt got its first democratic constitution. The triumph of Egyptian nationalism was short-lived; the leaders quarreled among themselves, Britain and France threatened to intervene, and Tawfiq turned against the nationalists. Britain landed troops at Alexandria in July 1882. Two months later Urabi surrendered and the first constitutional experiment came to an end. Today Egyptians regard Urabi's movement as a precursor to the 1952 revolution that brought Nasser to power.

When Britain occupied Egypt she promised to leave as soon as she had restored order to the country. It was easy to defeat the nationalists and prop Tawfiq back on his throne, but it was harder to remedy the causes of Egypt's disorder—huge debts, a peasantry impoverished by heavy taxes, and a rebellion in the Sudan. The longer Britain stayed to tackle Egypt's problems, the harder it was to leave. A talented administrator, Lord Cromer, came to Egypt in 1883 to serve as Britain's chief political representative. Tactful but determined, Cromer reformed the finances and administration of Egypt and gradually emerged as ruler in all but name.

Although the country prospered, British advisers sapped the authority and initiative of the Egyptian ministers. The British claimed that they were preparing Egyptians for self-rule, but in fact Egypt became a training ground for British administrators, paid by the Egyptian government. They often forgot that Egypt was not a colony but rather an autonomous Ottoman province temporarily occupied by Britain. The extension of irrigation under British rule was not paralleled by improved education or industrial development. Cromer became autocratic and spiteful in undermining the authority of Tawfiq's son, Abbas II (1892-1914). Remote from politically articulate Egyptians, Cromer did not sympathize with their demands for independence and constitutional reforms.

A decade after Urabi's defeat a new nationalist movement arose. When Abbas succeeded Tawfiq in 1892, he attracted a group of young Egyptians to help him in reducing Cromer's power. Their chief spokesman, an articulate lawyer named Mustafa Kamil, founded the Nationalist party. The Nationalists urged Britain to withdraw her forces from Egypt and later called for a constitution. Cromer ignored them, but his successor promised administrative changes to hasten Egypt's progress toward self-rule. Unfortunately for the Nationalists, Mustafa Kamil died prematurely in 1908, and his followers split. A more repressive British policy forced many of the Nationalists into exile, and their party disintegrated into an ineffectual debating society. At the outbreak of World War I the British declared Egypt a protectorate and severed her last ties with the Ottoman Empire. A nationwide revolt in 1919 gained for the Egyptians the shadow, but not the substance, of national independence from Britain.

Turkish Liberalism and Arab Nationalism

Within the Ottoman Empire a group of Westernized intellectuals called the New Ottomans agitated for the liberalization of the regime. In 1876, amid Balkan revolts, growing indebtedness to Europe, and the threat of Russian intervention, a military coup brought a liberal sultan to the throne. He had to be replaced shortly by Abdul Hamid II, who issued a constitution in December 1876 to forestall the Russians and the possible partition of the empire. For about a year the Ottoman Empire had a democratically elected parliament, but as Russia advanced on Istanbul, Abdul Hamid adjourned it and suspended the constitution. For thirty years the sultan ruled as a dictator, further centralizing Ottoman control and suppressing nationalist and liberal opposition movements.

A group of Westernized students and army officers, convinced that the Ottoman Empire could only be saved by restoring the 1876 constitution, formed the Committee of Union and Progress, or the Young Turks. In 1908 they forced the sultan to restore the constitution and hold free elections; in 1909, after an abortive countercoup, they deposed him. But the rule of the Young Turks soon turned into a new dictatorship controlled by three army officers, Enver, Talat, and Jemal. As Balkan revolts and European imperialism sheared off one Ottoman province after another between 1908 and 1914, they turned increasingly to a policy of Turkish nationalism.

The policies of the Young Turks alienated their non-Turkish subjects, most of whom spoke Arabic. Long divided by local, sectarian, or family rivalries, the people of Syria, Mesopotamia, and Arabia began to think of themselves as one nation. Arabic-speaking lawyers, journalists, students, and military officers formed nationalist societies in the main cities of the Ottoman Empire. Some asked for internal autonomy and equality of status as Ottoman subjects; others demanded Arab independence from Turkish rule. Christian and Muslim emigrés in Egypt, Europe, and America contributed to the literary and political renaissance of the Arabs. There was even talk of restoring the caliphate, usurped by the Ottomans, to an Arab ruler. Although Arab nationalism attracted little foreign attention before 1914, its ideas helped to spark the Arab revolt during World War I.

Persian Constitutionalism

The Persian Constitutionalists rose to power because the Qajar shahs were autocratic and ineffectual. They could not protect the peasants and townsmen from nomadic tribes, nor could they stop Russian military incursions and the commercial ascendancy of the British and other Europeans. The Constitutionalists included three main groups—the merchants, the Shiite ulama, and the liberal intellectuals. The merchants resented the shahs' concessions to foreign companies, a practice that undermined their livelihood; the ulama feared that the Western cultural impact would undermine Islam generally and their influence in particular; and the intellectuals, influenced by Western liberal and nationalist ideas, regarded the shah, backed by foreign advisers and money, as an obstacle to their hopes for reforming Persia.

United by nationalist and anti-imperialist feelings, these diverse groups engineered a tobacco boycott in 1891-92 and a national revolution in 1905-6. In 1906 the shah granted a constitution providing for a popularly elected parliament, or Majlis; but in the following year his successor called in Russian troops to suppress the Majlis and its revolutionary supporters. Outside the capital, however, the Constitutionalists continued their struggle. In 1909 they regained control of Tehran and replaced the shah with a more docile relative.

Having attained power, the Constitutionalists failed to implement their program for national reform and revival. Their political revolution did not transform social and economic conditions; they were politically inexperienced and tended to divide into factions; and foreign

attitudes added more problems. Western liberals hailed the Persian
Constitutionalists (just as they greeted the 1908 Young Turk uprising)
for bringing liberty to a backward country long blighted by corrupt and
autocratic rulers. An American banker's well-meaning efforts to reform
the finances of the Persian government foundered on Russian opposition, British acquiescence, and Persian weakness. The British government sometimes encouraged the Constitutionalists but first wished to
protect commerce and to defend India. In addition, a British company
had gained a concession to explore southern Persia for oil. The first
major discovery came in 1908; the Anglo-Persian Oil Company was
formed the next year, and Persia's new role as an oil producer made her
even more important to Britain.

Britain and Russia agreed in 1907 to define spheres of influence
for themselves. Russia's sphere covered the northern third of the
country, including Tehran. Britain, whose sphere bordered on northwestern India, did not oppose Russian efforts to increase her control
over the Persian government before and during World War I. Even the
Bolshevik Revolution in 1917 and the consequent withdrawal of
Russian troops and advisers provided only a brief lull in the
Anglo-Russian contest to control Persia.

World War I

World War I completed the subordination of the peoples of the
Middle East to Western political control, but European domination was
already a fait accompli by 1914. Since the eighteenth century Russia
had won control over the lands north and west of the Black Sea, most
of the Caspian coast, and vast stretches of Muslim central Asia. Persia
was almost a Russian protectorate, and the czarist regime expected to
gain Istanbul and the Straits in the war. Britain held Egypt, the strategic
island of Cyprus in the Mediterranean, and Aden at the southern
entrance to the Red Sea, and she had treaties making her the protector
of most of the Persian Gulf states. British and French capitalists had
immense sums invested in Middle Eastern land, buildings, factories,
railroads, and public utilities. By 1914 Germany seemed likely to
become the protector of what remained of the Ottoman Empire.

Turkey's entry into World War I as Germany's ally sealed the
doom of the Ottoman Empire. The Ottoman proclamation of holy war
failed, as few Muslims under Allied control rallied to Turkey's support.
As Britain repulsed Turkish attacks on the Suez Canal and sent
expeditionary forces into Mesopotamia (Iraq) and Palestine, the Arabs'
loyalty to their Ottoman rulers waned. Husayn, the sharif (governor) of
Mecca and leader of the prestigious Hashimite family, negotiated
secretly with Sir Henry McMahon, the British high commissioner in
Egypt, who pledged his government's support for an independent Arab
state if Husayn would launch an Arab revolt against the Turks.
However, Britain reserved the provinces of Baghdad and Basrah for
separate administration and excluded Mersina, Alexandretta, and

"portions of Syria lying to the west of the districts of Damascus, Homs, Hama, and Aleppo," and the terms thus fell short of the Arab nationalists' dream of complete independence for all Arabic-speaking Ottoman territories. Husayn was disappointed, but the repression of the Arabs in Syria by the Ottoman government angered him and led him to declare an Arab revolt in 1916. Together the Arabs and the British drove the Turks out of Palestine and Syria. The Ottoman Empire formally surrendered to the Allies in October 1918.

The Postwar Peace Settlement

Since the Arabs constituted the majority in Palestine, Syria, and Mesopotamia (Iraq), their leaders expected Britain to grant them their independence. President Wilson had urged autonomy for these former Ottoman lands in the twelfth of his Fourteen Points, which Britain and France accepted as the basis for the postwar peace settlement. As well, under the terms of the Husayn-McMahon correspondence, confirmed in 1918 by several British and French assurances to the Arabs, the Fertile Crescent and the Hijaz were to be ruled by Sharif Husayn's family, the Hashimites.

But during the war Britain had made conflicting commitments to other parties interested in the Middle East. In a series of secret agreements, the Allies had agreed that the Straits and eastern Anatolia were to go to czarist Russia, portions of western Anatolia to the Greeks and the Italians, and the Arab lands to Britain and France. The Sykes-Picot Treaty (1916) designated part of the Syrian coast for direct French control and a larger zone of French influence in the Syrian interior as far east as Mosul. Britain was to control lower Iraq directly and to have a sphere of influence covering the rest of Iraq and Palestine, except that the Christian holy places were to be under international administration. Only in the desert were the Arabs to be free from Western rule.

Meanwhile, another group, the Jewish nationalists, or Zionists, were pressing both Britain and Germany for recognition of their claim to Palestine. Since their dispersion by the Romans, the Jews had never ceased to hope that they might someday return to Palestine. With the nineteenth century rise of nationalism in Eastern Europe, where most Jews lived, there was also an upsurge of officially condoned persecution. Many Jews escaped to Western Europe or America and became partially assimilated. Some leaders, however, such as Theodor Herzl and Chaim Weizmann, argued that the Jews should not lose their identity and should try to form their own national state, preferably in Palestine.

Thus, before World War I groups of European Jews settled in Palestine, which was under Ottoman rule and inhabited mainly by Arabs. During the war Chaim Weizmann gained the attention of the British cabinet; in 1917 the foreign secretary, Sir Arthur Balfour, declared his government's support for the establishment in Palestine of a national home for the Jewish people. He cautiously added that nothing was to be done to prejudice the rights of its non-Jewish inhabitants, who then constituted over nine-tenths of Palestine's population. The Balfour Declaration was a major triumph for the nascent Zionist movement, which aspired, Weizmann stated, to make "Palestine as Jewish as England is English."

All these commitments were aired at the postwar Paris Peace Conference. Sharif Husayn's son, Faysal, spoke on behalf of the Arab provisional government established in Damascus. In order to discover the views of the Arabs in Syria and Palestine, President Wilson sent the King-Crane Commission, which found that the Arabs opposed French rule and Zionist colonization. The report was ignored. The British let the French occupy Beirut and eventually acceded to French control over Syria, including Lebanon but not Palestine. The nationalists in Damascus declared Syria's independence in March 1920, proclaimed Faysal "king of the Arabs," and vowed to resist; but the French defeated their forces in July and overthrew the Arab provisional government.

By this time the Allies had agreed on the division and administration of the conquered Ottoman provinces. In deference to Wilson's principle of self-determination, Britain and France did not annex them to their empires, as earlier conquerors had done. Under Article 22 of the League of Nations Covenant, territories taken from Turkey as a result of the war were designated as mandated Class A territories—territories that had reached a stage of development where their independence could be provisionally recognized subject to foreign tutelage. Accordingly, the Allies designated France as the mandatory power in Syria and Lebanon and Britain in Iraq and Palestine. In principle, the mandatory powers were to administer their mandates for the benefit of the inhabitants and to prepare them for self-rule. To ensure that this tutelary relationship would not become exploitative, the League Council set up the Permanent Mandates Commission to supervise their administration. In practice, the mandates were resented by the inhabitants and were beneficial chiefly to the mandatory powers.

France tried to divide Syria into smaller and weaker administrative units, but this embittered the nationalists. Faysal, ousted from Damascus, was crowned instead in Baghdad as the British tried to suppress a nationwide revolt. For Faysal's brother, who had hoped to rule Iraq, the British carved out of Palestine the amirate of Transjordan. Britain's mandate over Palestine west of the Jordan River specifically called for the implementation of the Balfour Declaration by allowing Jewish immigration and settlement in the country. Palestine's Arab leaders, fearful that their majority would eventually be submerged in a Jewish state, vowed resistance. Thus the seeds of enmity between Arabs and Jews and between Arabs and the West were sown in the aftermath of World War I, and future generations would reap a bitter harvest.

Selected Bibliography

Anderson, M. S. *The Eastern Question, 1774-1923*. New York: St. Martin's Press, 1966.
A thorough, detailed account of the diplomatic and military struggle among the European powers to control the Balkans and the Middle East.

Armajani, Yahya. *Middle East: Past and Present*. Englewood Cliffs, N.J.: Prentice-Hall, 1970.
The most comprehensive introduction to Middle Eastern history now available.

Brockelmann, Carl. *History of the Islamic Peoples*. New York: G. P. Putnam's Sons, 1944.
A detailed history suitable for advanced students.

Coles, Paul, *The Ottoman Impact on Europe*. New York: Harcourt Brace Jovanovich, 1968.
An attractive introduction to Ottoman culture and society.

Collins, Robert, and Tignor, Robert. *Egypt and the Sudan*. Englewood Cliffs, N.J.: Prentice-Hall, 1967.
A concise historical survey of the Nile valley from prehistoric to modern times.

Covensky, Milton. *The Ancient Near Eastern Tradition*. New York: Harper & Row, Publishers, 1966.
An important introduction to the role of myth and religion in pre-Hellenistic Near Eastern societies.

Davsion, Roderic. *Turkey*. Englewood Cliffs, N.J.: Prentice-Hall, 1968.
A short history of the Turks from their central Asian origins to the present.

Fisher, Sydney N. *The Middle East: A History*. New York: Alfred A. Knopf, 1968.
A well-written introduction to Middle Eastern history.

Frye, Richard N. *The Heritage of Persia*. Cleveland, Ohio: World Publishing Co., 1963.
A good introduction to pre-Islamic Persia.

Gabrieli, Francesco. *Muhammad and the Conquests of Islam*. New York: McGraw-Hill Book Co., 1968.
An attractive introduction to the life of the Prophet and the rise of the Arabs.

Gibb, Sir Hamilton. *Mohammedanism: An Historical Survey*. New York: Oxford University Press, 1962.
A discerning study of the development of Islamic beliefs and institutions.

von Grunebaum, Gustave E. *Classical Islam: A History, 600-1258*. London: George Allen and Unwin, 1970.
An interpretive survey of Islamic history, incorporating many new findings.

Hitti, Philip K. *History of the Arabs*. New York: St. Martin's Press, 1970.
A detailed account of Arab history to Ottoman times.

Holt, Peter M. *Egypt and the Fertile Crescent, 1516-1922*. Ithaca, N.Y.:
Cornell University Press, 1966.
A detailed history of the Arabs under Ottoman rule.

Holt, Peter M.; Lambton, Ann K. S.; and Lewis, Bernard, eds. *The
Cambridge History of Islam*. 2 vols. Cambridge: Cambridge University
Press, 1970.
A collaboratively written, detailed survey of Islamic history.

Landen, Robert G. *The Emergence of the Modern Middle East*. New
York: Van Nostrand Reinhold, 1970.
An anthology of speeches and writings with editorial notes, illustrating the process of Middle
Eastern modernization since the late eighteenth century.

Lewis, Bernard. *The Arabs in History*. New York: Harper & Row,
Publishers, 1967.
A concise history of the Arabs.

————. *The Middle East and the West*. Bloomington, Ind.: Indiana
University Press, 1964.
A series of lectures exploring the Western impact on Middle Eastern politics, society, and
culture.

Saunders, J. J. *A History of Medieval Islam*. New York: Barnes &
Noble, 1965.
A well-written survey of Islamic history to the Mongol invasions.

Setton, Kenneth M., ed. *A History of the Crusades*. 2 vols. to date.
Philadelphia: University of Pennsylvania Press, 1955 and 1962. Reprint.
Madison, Wis.: University of Wisconsin Press, 1969.
A collection of studies of Middle Eastern states, both Christian and Muslim, for the eleventh
to the fifteenth centuries.

Stavrianos, L. S. *The Balkans since 1453*. New York: Holt, Rinehart
and Winston, 1958.
Includes an introduction to the efflorescence and decline of the Ottoman Empire.

Watt, W. Montgomery. *Muhammad: Prophet and Statesman*. New
York: Oxford University Press, 1961.
An introduction to Muhammad's life and teachings within their social and cultural
environment.

Sociocultural Determinants

This chapter probes the dynamics of Middle Eastern politics from a sociological perspective. The material explores the proposition that because he lives in a particular geographical environment and has a particular history, Middle Eastern man has developed characteristic social relations, ways of life, cultural habits, and personality traits that are significant factors, or *determinants*, for both Middle Eastern society in general and its political behavior in particular.

In other words, this approach aims at probing beneath what seems to be strictly political behavior for the social factors that might explain that behavior. It looks at four major kinds of determinants: cultural, environmental, psychological, and social processes. Each determinant both restricts and offers opportunities. Culture is a kind of bondage as well as man's primary tool of expression; environment provides the limited raw materials, human and physical; personality colors a man's responses; and social processes regulate the ways in which he relates to his fellowmen.

Cultural Determinants

Culture largely accounts for what people do, within the limitations set by environment, personality, and social process. It encompasses the system of meanings that motivate and specify action. These meanings include value judgments of the actions—whether they are good or bad, forbidden or required, recommended or of no particular importance. Because decision making, including political decision making, involves choosing between two or more alternatives, the politics of any society cannot be understood unless the underlying value system of its culture, which affects those choices, is understood.

Meanings and values operate at several levels; some are ephemeral, others habitual. At the deepest level lie the more absolute values, which sanction and maintain a society's distributive order. It is here—at this deep personal level—that the real battle is being fought between traditionalism and modernity in contemporary Middle Eastern society. One aspect of the controversy, for example, involves the discrimination between what is modern and what is merely Western. Inherited values and meanings ultimately determine what choices people make, which changes they will accept. Thus, if Middle Eastern leaders wish to create a political system that can cope in the contemporary world, they must ask what basic value premises have to be taken into account.

A useful, comprehensive concept here is that of *core culture*— that is, the persistent ultimate values that lie at the heart of a people's way of life. A useful analogy is the nature of personality. For example, although an individual may participate in change or may himself grow through experience, once his basic personality has crystallized it will change very little thereafter. His stance toward the outer world will remain relatively stable, and in addition, he will become anxious if anything threatens his inner personality. The core culture of a society is very similar to the inner personality of the individual.

In the 1840s Alexis de Tocqueville (in *Democracy in America*) perceived fundamental characteristics that we identify today as "the American way." The influence of core culture can be easily shown in Middle Eastern history. When the Muslims first made contact with the Byzantines and Persians, the Muslims welcomed with enthusiasm the sophisticated, rational modes of Byzantine and Persian thought and their philosophy, science, and art. The result was a rich flowering of complex civilization during the Umayyad and Abbasid empires. Toward the end of this brilliant period (during the eleventh and twelfth centuries), however, Muslim leaders began to perceive Greek thought as a threat to the religion-oriented core culture of Islamic society (for a description of Islamic core culture see p. 32). The fundamental Greek attitude was rationalist and individualistic, secularist and scientific; it appealed to man and his reason. Thus, it was destructive of the traditional Islamic attitudes of mind and structure of society. The Muslim community drew back, sensing clearly the danger of *shirk* ("making equal with God") and the anarchy of *hubris* ("arrogance"). It perceived the threat posed by the subtle infidelities of pure rationalism, with its inclination to divide.

As a result, the Muslim rejected this Greek sense of man and society, a rejection so complete that creative thought among Muslims ceased almost completely. The Muslim Middle East withdrew into itself until modern times, a period of some five hundred years. This same process of enthusiastically welcoming Western culture and then suddenly drawing back, perhaps even rejecting it, was repeated in the nineteenth century and continues today among Arabs, Iranians, and even Turks. Western culture, the child of Greek civilization, is still perceived as the major threat to the Muslim core culture. Even in Israel, so dominantly Western, this same core culture contest goes on between the Liberal and the Orthodox and between the Ashkenazic Jews, steeped for centuries in European civilization, and the Sephardic Jews of North Africa, the Middle East, and Asia.

What, then, are the features of this basic culture of Middle Eastern society? To begin with, the Middle East (together with North Africa) comprises a *culture area*; one can travel throughout with a sense of being in a familiar world where one knows the rules and the foods. Middle Eastern culture is strongest in Egypt, in the Fertile Crescent, and in Saudi Arabia; in the peripheral regions of Upper Egypt, Iran, Turkey, and Israel the culture of the Middle East shades into that of other areas, including Africa south of the Sahara, India, Russia, and Europe.

As one surveys the Middle East one sees ways of life that have remained nearly unchanged for seven thousand years—the wooden plow, the circular threshing floor, the sun-dried-brick houses, the broken flail stick and winnowing fork, the water wheels and water screws, the tents and flocks of the nomads, the babble of the open markets. Yet at close range one finds ways of life that require up-to-date equipment and modern techniques—high-rise steel and concrete buildings, automobiles, television, oil refineries, steel mills, textile factories.

The Middle East has been a bridge between Asia, Europe, and Africa over which Muslims, Arabs, Seljuk Turks, European Crusaders, Mamluks, Mongols, Ottoman Turks, French, British, and European Jews have traveled. An immense variety of languages and subcultures are thus found in juxtaposition, and the topographic contrasts of the area have helped to preserve these differences, giving rise to a complex web of group rivalries and conflicts. A deep sense of protective in-group loyalties has developed, resulting in a failure to evolve any sense of broad community identification. In the villages around Cairo, for example, where Arabs from the Arabian peninsula have been living side by side with the native Nile valley fellaheen for centuries, the Arabs are still considered foreigners. And so they are to the Nile villager, who has been on this land for five thousand years. The Arab villagers, on their part, maintain a proud consciousness of their ancestry and look with displeasure on marriages between their daughters and fellaheen men. A similar situation characterizes the Greeks, who have resided throughout the Middle East since the time of Alexander. Crossbreeding has taken place, but cultural "melting" has occurred only in a few areas.

Religion provides a further example of variety. The Arabian peninsula and its environs have always been peculiarly fertile in the development of religious concepts. The Judaic-Christian-Muslim concepts of the one God, the personal God, the revealed God, and the Christian incarnate God first emerged here. Different prophets and teachers, various efforts to work out the implications and systems of these concepts, attempts to reconcile them with Greek philosophy, pagan nature-worship, and other powerful religious systems, such as Persian Zoroastrianism, have led to a great diversity of faiths. The same intensity of affirmation and denial that caused this diversity also ensured that each faith should find adherents throughout the generations.

Yet, as in a mosaic, the diverse pieces together form a general design. More than half of the inhabitants of this region speak one language—Arabic. Two other large blocs speak Turkish and Persian, and the people of Israel speak Hebrew. There is even some evidence that under the influence of nationalism Arabic-speaking people are learning a renewed appreciation of their shared culture, which could break down some of the barriers that separate them. Further, the people of the Middle East are seeking to know the same God, and thus they possess a common reference system of shared meanings and ultimate values. And in spite of deep regional rifts and the divisiveness of foreign power rivalries, they have shared a brilliant, highly productive civilization during several long periods of world history.

Capturing the personal, intimate aspects of this traditional way of life—the core culture of the Middle East—so that a Westerner can comprehend it is difficult. However, the American small-town society before World War I was similar, not in its details but rather in the "feel" of the way of life.

American small-town society was a stable, decorous, orderly, provincial, family-oriented community life. Families were large and they participated in relatively simple, closely interwoven activities and interests with each other and with close friends. Time moved at a leisurely pace and religion was important. Families were strongly patriarchal and the father received a considerable degree of formal deference from the members of the household. Hospitality was generous, manners were important, and sex was veiled with modesty and governed by a double standard for men and women. Women were homemakers and carefully modest in dress. Businesses tended to be small and family-run. The "great" were very great, possessing fabulous wealth and power, but they were few in number. Authoritarianism and paternalism were strongly approved. There was a wide difference between city and village life, and industrial labor was often cruelly exploited.

The traditional Middle Eastern way of life possesses many of these characteristics and several other important traits in addition. First, the presence of the tribal, or extended, family, almost entirely atrophied in Western society, intensifies the already authoritarian bonds that hold the Middle Eastern family together. Marriages are usually arranged by parents; first-cousin mates are preferred. Young couples remain closely tied to their parents' families, and young men tend to make their way in the world through nepotism. Second, formal secular schooling has only recently been emphasized, and illiteracy in the area still averages 60 to 70 percent and reaches well above 90 percent in most rural areas. Third, the pervasive religious life of the area values submissiveness under the all-powerful hand of God and acceptance as means of coping with the vicissitudes of life. The hard-driving, acquisitive Westerner finds this quality of mind particularly incomprehensible. Fourth, the nomads, the bedouin, have made an immense impact on the ideas and values of neighboring peoples in villages and towns. Finally, because of the strong emphasis on in-group loyalties, epitomized by the phrases *our people* and *one of us*, the individual has little sense of responsibility to a larger community beyond the family. These facets of Middle Eastern life are reflected in political decision making.[1]

To pursue the argument further, we assume that the underlying world view of a political system plays a decisive role in its development. For example, the Muslim world view dominates everywhere in the Middle East except, of course, in Israel and possibly in Turkey, although the secularism of modern Turkey is too recent for us to assess its depth. (After all, for many centuries the Turks were the fierce defenders and propagators of the Sunni Muslim faith.)

In the world view of Islamic society,[2] the sacred and the secular are joined together, although the sacred is dominant, providing the ultimate value system, and the secular is the application of the sacred. Islam rejects the principle of the separation between spiritual and temporal; to the Muslim believer religion and life, faith and politics are inseparable. Islam is therefore more than a formal religion; it is a pervasive way of life, guiding thought and action to a degree without parallel in the modern Western world. (It was Iranian dualistic monotheism that in one form or another became the foundation of Western religious and philosophical thought.[3]) The supreme motive of the Islamic way of life is the quest for the correct life, an emphasis on deed rather than idea, on doing what God has willed. Law is the epitome of the Islamic spirit. For the Greek, law was the product of men's minds; for the Muslim, law is the will of God.

This centuries-long emphasis on correctness as the basic purpose of life has led to much authoritarianism and legalism and thus to a rigid social system. Initiative and inventiveness have been inhibited, not because they are bad in themselves—although inventiveness easily leads to the ultimate sin of *shirk*—but because the correct way for man has already been defined. Man's task is to discover God's will, and this axiom forms a framework within which the Muslim builds his social relations, including his political system.

Because Islam is permeated by a sense of the autocracy of God and Muslims place a high value on acceptance and contentment as ways to cope with problems, they have developed a rather limited concept of political authority. In the community of believers, the ummah, resides the ultimate power and wisdom, expressed over time through the working of *ijmaa*, or consensus. Thus, the major function of formal state machinery is limited to ensuring the order and security necessary for the exercise of the religious life of the community. As the modern political leaders of Islamic countries wrestle with problems of political reorganization, they will find in Islam both a guardian of the old ways and an important ally for their efforts to create new and viable political institutions. For instance, Islam is being linked to socialism to distinguish the latter from communism and to give it legitimacy.

The ethnocentric factor, that one's own way of life is to be preferred to all others, is another important cultural determinant in the political process. In each of the four subcultures of the Middle East—the Arab world, Iran, Turkey, and Israel—sensitivity over basic core values has generated controversies that have influenced behavior at the political level, causing public violence, party splits, and interregional tensions and affecting election results and foreign relations. For example, the religious factor has played an important role in the tensions between Shiite Iran and her Sunni neighbors, particularly Turkey and the Persian Gulf states. In Turkey there are deep divisions over how to build a Turkish society that can retain its authentic traditional culture and yet achieve secular modernity. In Israel the pioneering communal idealism of the kibbutznics, who provided the power to create the state, vies with the encroaching capitalism of the urban dwellers of the successful Israeli state.

In the Arab world the urubah-shuubiyyah controversy, which is twelve hundred years old,[4] finds modern expression in the present-day insistence upon a distinction between socialism and communism. *Urubah* denotes Arabism, Arab self-awareness, Arab identity, Arab communal consciousness. It is strongly ethnocentric and partly nationalistic, but as Middle Eastern culture ignores political boundaries, so urubah is a larger concept than the nationalism of particular Arab states. *Shuubiyyah*, which has no single English equivalent, denotes "belonging to the people." It denigrates the making of ethnic distinctions such as Arab, Persian, Turkish, Egyptian, and thus negates ethnocentric attitudes and values.

Shuubiyyah has an evil connotation in Arab history because it refers to the many attempts to play down the contributions of the Arabs to Middle Eastern society and thus represents a threat to Arab self-identity. The term originated during the early centuries of Islam between 657 and 960 A.D., when the *mawali*, or non-Arab Muslims, especially the Iranians, began to dominate the Abbasid empire. Later we find the opprobrious (from the Arab point of view) term *shuubi* being applied to the Ottoman Turks, who attempted during the late nineteenth and early twentieth centuries to Ottomanize all of their minorities and who thus denounced the Arabs. Today Arabs have again resurrected this term to differentiate between Arab socialism and international communism. For instance, Nikita Khrushchev's remarks were labeled *shuubi* when during the Aswan Dam celebrations (May 16, 1964) he was moved to say, "I hear you, colleagues, appealing in your speeches, 'Arabs unite!' What about us, the Russians, who are not Arabs? Shall we go home? Lenin did not call for unity in this way. His slogan was 'unity of peoples,' not on the basis of nationalism, but on the basis of work."[5]

The general acceptance of socialism in the Middle East provides another example of culture as a determinant. Although it may be seen entirely as a response to a current ideological fashion or as a form of rebellion against Western capitalist imperialism or as due to the prestige and the active machinations of the Soviets, there is a deeper reason. The adoption of socialism can be related to central Middle Eastern cultural values, to their sense of community and beliefs about how men are and should be related. This basic social philosophy can be sensed in the use of such concepts as *falah*, the "good," in the Muslim call to prayer; in *zakat*, "sharing," in the five pillars of Islam; and in *ijmaa*, consensus of the authorities.

Environmental Determinants

The environment provides the raw materials, human and nonhuman, that offer both restrictions and opportunities for society. The physical scene is one factor; the combination of culture and geography is another; and the demographic characteristics of the people is a third. These elements have been outlined in chapter 1; here they will be examined as determinants of political behavior.

The countries of southwest Asia and northeast Africa—from Iran and Turkey to Egypt and Libya—are situated on the bridge that connects the Eurasian and African land masses. In truth, this area is "mid-land, mid-sea, and mid-air," where three continents merge and three oceans meet. There the four elements of classical mythology— earth, water, air, and fire (oil)—have consolidated into a unique geographical unit that is decisive for peace and war.[6] As an ancient Sumerian text puts it, "Man was created at the navel of the earth."

It would be difficult to substantiate exact cause-and-effect relationships between this pivotal position and the consequences, but the historical reality is that in this geographical area mankind was stimulated to begin the process of constructing the complex system that is human society. In our own day the Middle East has clearly lost none of its geostrategic importance. This relatively small land area has an almost incredible power to embroil not only the people who live in and around it, but the rest of the world as well. One is reminded of Rudyard Kipling's story of the King's Ankus; men were led to kill each other in order to possess it. For example, behind the deadly conflict between the Israelis and the Palestinian Arabs for the future of Palestine lie world Zionism and Arab nationalism, and behind these, again in confrontation, stand the Euro-American powers and the Communist world.

In addition to the Middle East's pivotal physical position, a second geographical factor—the existence of *ethnemes*—functions as a determinant for political behavior.[7] The phenomenon of ethnemes has not received the attention it deserves, although it points to a profound and continuing influence on political processes. The concept is borrowed from linguistics, in which *phoneme* refers to a basic unit of language. An ethneme is a basic ethnic unit, a complex of human interrelations that has crystallized from the sharing of geographical position, ways of life, and historical experience. It makes itself felt through patterns of solidarity or conflict under conditions of strain.

The border areas dividing ethnemes can be conceived of as *shatter zones*, to borrow a geological term. That is, these are the places where cracks appear under stress. To change metaphors, if Middle Eastern society were compared to a fabric, *ethneme* would indicate the varying capacities for absorption of dyes of different parts of the material. An illustration is the varying acceptance accorded to the culture of the Muslim Arabs as they spread throughout the Middle East.

The area under discussion in this book could be roughly divided into seven ethnemes: Turkey; Iran and Shiite Iraq; Israel; Lebanon; Syria, Jordan, and Sunnite Iraq; the Arabian penisula; and Egypt, Cyrenaica, and North Sudan. The ethneme concept may explain the continuing failure of the Arabs to achieve unity despite their general acceptance of the idea. To succeed, nationalism needs a strong ethnic foundation, because nationalism tends to degenerate to empty posturing unless shared cultural understandings are present. This nationalism-ethnic combination seems to be effective for modern Turkey, Iran, and Israel and possibly for the Arabs of Palestine and the Kurds. Arab nationalism does not draw the Arab world together, however, because of the weakness of the ethnic factor. The ethnemic factor is surely one of the reasons why the Arab unity movement germinated in Iraq, but flowered in Egypt, for instance. It is also important in the 1961 failure of the Egypt-Syria federation after less than four years, a failure that has occurred twice before, in the time of Salah al-Din and of Muhammad Ali. The ethnemic factor partially explains the comparative indifference of Iran toward the affairs of Palestine and Turkey. Another historical example is the conquering Muslim Arabs, who brought from the desert a religion, a language, and a culture. The Byzantines accepted none of these; the Egyptians, all three; and the Persians and the Turks absorbed the religion but rejected the language and the culture. The current effort of Egypt, Libya, and the Sudan toward federation is interesting because the northeast corner of Africa has distinct ethnemic characteristics.

A third type of environmental determinant is *gross population characteristics*. There seems to be a significant relationship between the characteristics of a society's population and its government structures and political processes. For example, one may contrast the political process in a predominantly mobile, literate, urban population with that in a population that is largely illiterate, village-oriented, and familistic.

With the exception of the Ashkenazic Jewish population of Israel, the countries under examination in this book fall demographically into the transition stage—that is, they are moving from the relatively stable situation of high birth and high death rates into the stage at which birth rates remain high while death rates rapidly decline as a result of better nutrition and medical care. Thus the general rate of increase for the Middle East is about 2.5 percent per year. This skyrocketing population is rather a new phenomenon—it began in earnest after 1945. Such a population tends to outstrip all efforts at economic and social development and political reform. The problem is made even more difficult by the fact that this rising population is accompanied by rising expectations. As more people want more, the pressure on government authorities increases.[8] Field reports from the area provide evidence that among the newly awakened masses in the Arab world there is a growing restiveness against the whole present ruling establishment because of its failure to bring about promised political, economic, and social improvements.

The high Middle Eastern rate of increase lowers the average age and results in increasing pressures from the demanding young segment of the population. This "youth power"* often seriously affects political behavior, a phenomenon with which Americans have become familiar during the 1960s. The 1952 Egyptian revolution, for example, was brought about by young men, and young men turned out King Idris of Libya in September 1969. In Arab countries that have remained moderate or neutral regarding the Arab-Israeli conflict—Morocco, Tunisia, Libya before 1969, and Saudi Arabia—the youth are generating considerable pressure for their countries to become actively involved. In the spring of 1960 student demonstrations in Istanbul and Ankara and public indignation at the government's handling of them sparked the overthrow of Turkey's Menderes regime. The Palestine Arab guerrilla movement is essentially a youth movement also. And in Israel in April 1969 five thousand members of the Hashomer Hatzair youth movement adopted a resolution stating that Palestine was the common homeland of two nations, Arabs and Jews, and that each had the right to an independent national life in it.

The proportion of the population of a nation that is urban and literate is another important determinant of political behavior. The urbanization of the Middle East is explosive politically for three reasons: urbanization is recent—it has occurred largely since World War II; it is massive—some cities have doubled their populations; and it is concentrated—most of the growth has been in only one or two major centers, usually including the capital.

The low literacy situation in the Middle East generates serious obstacles for communication, which raises problems for modernization in general and political development in particular. People who can neither read nor write tend to be parochial in their interests, limited in empathic capacity, and hampered in participation in the wider society. Modern political organization demands a constituency that is both literate and participant.

Personality Determinants

A man's personality selects the way in which he perceives incoming stimuli and the manner in which he responds to them.

*Youth power means not just a high proportion of young in the population, a familiar phenomenon in all areas that have a high birth rate and a short life expectancy, but especially a high proportion of young who are aware and politically active. This phenomenon is associated particularly with the spread of higher education.

Because a particular culture tends to cause a certain kind of child training, life experience, and the like, a culture tends to create, however tentatively, particular kinds of personalities. This is not to say that the full range of personalities does not occur in every society but rather that certain characteristics appear more frequently in some cultures than in others, and dominant personality characteristics are significant for political behavior.

To illustrate, there are notable character differences between the urbanized, technology-oriented Israeli and his more traditional, family-oriented Arab neighbor. The differences have become sharply defined, especially in Jerusalem, where Israelis and Arabs meet daily with both the desire and necessity of communicating. The problem is not just one of hostility between the two; rather, their expectations are different; they do not perceive or respond in the same way; they are operating on different "wavelengths."

Similar differences separate the Oriental Sephardic Jews from the Occidental Ashkenazic Jews of Israel. In the rest of the Middle East there are wide personality differences between the nomad, the villager, and the urbanite. Americans also experience frustrations and failures when they talk with Middle Easterners. It therefore becomes important to ask what kind of person the Arab, the Israeli, the Turk, the Iranian is.

Let us take one example, the Arab. The Arab seems to harbor two major contradictory impulses: egotism and conformity.[9] The first is shown in his extreme self-assertiveness before others and in his pride and sensitivity to criticism. The second is reflected in his obedience to certain group norms, which may frequently be resented, and in his inability to assert his independence confidently. Egotism and conformity are deeply rooted in the child-rearing practices of traditional Arab society. Boys are trained to be aggressive and combative with their peers; they are laughed at and shamed if they do not fight back. The purpose is partly to maintain the honor of the family and to take vengeance when that honor is besmirched. Conformity reflects another central value, the importance of respect. Lack of respect is a dreadful thing to the Arab and is also related to his demand for conformity in manners. Motivated by both loyalty and shame, the individual is taught reticence and submissiveness in the presence of those who are older, wiser, or superior.

The Arab manifests his egotism in his unique sense of self-esteem, in his need to assert his differences, in his lack of civic responsibility, in his unruly spirit, and in his lack of cooperation with and trust in others. Arab life is filled with interpersonal rivalry—tribal feuding in the desert, family and village feuding in the settled areas, and intergroup hostility in the towns—which furthers an attitude of secretiveness and mistrust. Arab political writers never tire of stressing Arab contentiousness, perhaps partly caused by poverty and frustration, which are so pervasive that there is a great deal of what is called free-floating hostility. Arab social interrelationships are brittle, difficult, hidden, and marked by aggressiveness.

And yet there is a degree of loyalty, warmth, and responsiveness among Arabs that is seldom matched among frank and pragmatic Americans. The Arab is extremely sociable, but he is not given to irresponsible hedonism. He can be obstinate to the point of self-destruction, but he has a keen sense of humor. He shows great flexibility in difficult situations. Arabs hold the deep conviction that "everything is in the hands of God" and have learned to take life as it is and to accept the inevitability of hardship and deprivation. Thus they have developed endurance; resistance to suffering has become a challenge by necessity.

One further illustrative characteristic of the Arab personality—his love of and talent for words[10]—is significant for the politics of the Middle East and the region's relations with the rest of the world. The Arab speaks powerfully and eloquently, but he does not always mean literally what he says, and it is a serious error to take him at his exact words. In anger his aggression tends to be spoken rather than physical. The Arabic language, with its phonetic beauty, richness of synonym, imagery, rhythm, and majesty, arouses the passion of the people. The Persian language shares this emotional power, but by contrast, modern Hebrew and Turkish are direct and utilitarian. Part of the communication problem between the Arabs and the Israelis is thus caused by their differing uses of language.

Social Processes as Determinants

Social processes—which include conflict, competition, accommodation, and assimilation—may also determine political behavior. Through them men implement decisions and achieve adaptations to situations. Culture systems vary widely in tension, tempo, and color, depending on which of the various social processes are emphasized. The combination depends largely on what relationships a sociocultural system needs to function successfully. For example, a relatively mobile and secular society, such as Western capitalist democracy, which is oriented to performance and the consumer, both engenders and requires one combination; whereas a relatively closed, traditional society that is compartmentalized and familistic like Middle Eastern society is characterized by a different combination. A society's political behavior will conform in general to the social processes emphasized in that society and may be conflicting, competitive, accommodative, or assimilative.

Traditional Middle Eastern society is a system of relatively closed but interlocking ethnic groups, religious sects, craft organizations, village-nomad-urban complexes, desert-town systems, and specialized product regions.[11] Here the predominant social style is accommodative despite the presence of bitter conflict and intense competition. For a people who live in a lean environment and maintain rigid cultural barriers, accommodation, including tolerance, humor, and live-and-let-live attitudes, was, and is, the most efficient way of relating to each other. Differences are valued and jealously guarded; in-group loyalties are strong. "Mechanical" solidarity provides the social cement that ties the individual parts together, as contrasted with the "organic" solidarity found in the rational or planned organization typified by industrial or bureaucratic society.[1][2]

The persistence of this ancient accommodative system in modern technological mass society accounts for many of the political problems that are associated with the contemporary Middle East. Attempts to develop Western-style democracy, with its principle of equality for all, for example, are continually subverted by traditional loyalties (religious, ethnic, family, etc.). The workings of the delicately balanced sectarian political system of the Lebanon provides an almost perfect example (see the chapter on Lebanon). In Iran the shah is trying to respond to pressures for modernization and yet to retain his traditional autocratic monarchy.

Accommodation is thus presented as the dominant relationship in a society of interdependent but rigidly separated units. Accommodation is a social process essentially oriented to the status quo, inward-looking, defensive, and traditionalist; change is suspect. The function of government in such a society is to keep the peace, leaving the different groups to regulate their own affairs. Interunit relations are negotiated through intermediaries. In the modern nation-state, on the other hand, political processes seem to require a high degree of extensive and flexible communication among a population that is characterized by considerable sociocultural assimilation, a situation yet to be achieved in the Middle East except in Israel.

Conflict and competition reflect the structural divisions, basic values, and scarce resources distinctive of the Middle East as set forth in this and other chapters. As a special case, in the family-oriented Middle East, the Arabic concept *asabiyyah*, or "group feeling," is used to identify the winning relationship in conflict and competition. Where group feeling is strongest, there is power, vitality, creativity; where group feeling is loose, there is weakness, inefficiency, decay, the withdrawal of consent by the governed. Stable power in a traditional society rests on asabiyyah. In Rosenthal's summary description of Ibn Khaldun's argument:

> Preponderance of *asabiyyah*, or group feelings, renders one group superior to others; it also determines leadership within a given group. The leading or ruling element within one or more groups will be that person, or, more frequently, that family, the importance and ramifications of whose blood relationships give them the strongest and most natural claim to control of the available *asabiyyah*. And no group can retain its preponderance, nor any leader his dominant position in the group, when their former *asabiyyah* is no longer there to support them.[13]

There is little doubt, for example, that the late Gamal Abdul Nasser's astonishing capacity to survive as the dominant figure in modern Egypt was determined not only by masterful strategy, good fortune, and a charismatic personality but also by the continuing presence of this asabiyyah factor in Egyptian society. The rise and disintegration of the Islamic empire followed this pattern.

In contrast to accommodation, the fourth major social process, assimilation, is change-oriented, outward-looking, receptive, participatory, and empathic; change is welcomed. In short, assimilation must be a dominant social process for any society that seeks modernization, but in the Middle East only Israel has achieved a high degree of assimilation. The function of government here is to facilitate and innovate, to unite the people in a common effort, to ensure equal opportunities, and to raise standards of living.

In the tension between accommodation and assimilation, the contemporary Middle Eastern society seeks to evolve political systems that will not only enable it to survive but also to attain a sense of personal meaningfulness. This dilemma is not a new one; history casts a long shadow. As was mentioned earlier, seventh to twelfth century Muslim society showed an enormous and avid capacity to assimilate the high culture of the classical Mediterranean world, and it modernized with remarkable success. But the protective, accommodative reaction set in; Muslim society moved from offense to defense, withdrawing into itself. Modernization, as then defined, was repudiated as destructive of the ultimate traditional values, and government became repressive. Only time can tell whether assimilation will succeed in the contemporary Middle East. The old order is no longer tenable; a growing number of Middle Easterners realize that they must help construct a new society, a new way of life that involves more assimilation.

Two developments show this activism strongly. First, the Middle Eastern woman now participates economically and politically in her society, often against strong opposition from her male counterparts. Because this new woman is strong and ambitious, the old image of the retiring female who is submissive and unreliable is no longer tolerable. Although they are not feminists in the narrow sense of that word, Middle Eastern women are nevertheless demanding more alternatives through which to exercise their talents. A witty Arab male has described woman as society's second lung, insisting that complete health can be achieved only when both lungs are fully active. Middle Eastern educational and occupational statistics show a steadily increasing proportion of females.

Second, after ages of feuds and rivalries the major groups—Arabs, Turks, Iranians, and Jews—are achieving new national self-awareness enhanced by sufficient skills, manpower, money, and cultural sophistication to guarantee that they will be taken seriously by the rest of the world and by each other. In addition, they are aware of possessing two priceless trumps—geographical position and massive oil resources—to be bargained with in the international market. All does not go smoothly, however. In their political behavior both among themselves and with outsiders Middle Easterners are still unpredictable. Although they value a long and proud history, they bear the scars of foreign colonial rule, domination, and minority status, and at times they overcompensate in speech and action.

Both the Muslim majorities and the Christian minorities must work out the implications of modern ideas, particularly Western ones, for their traditional world views. Even in Israel there is conflict between the Orthodox and the Liberal, between the religious and the secular, although Israel may have solved this dilemma best, having been formed *de novo* by settlers from the West. Among the indigenous peoples the Turks seem to have reached the most stable compromise because they are closest to and most involved with Europe and the West. Arab civilization is so completely a product of its religion that its reaction to the secular modernity of the West is in terms of the reaction of Islam to Western civilization. The crisis in Iran is even more complex; because it has lived within itself longest, some elements of its civilization antedate the Judeo-Christian-Muslim tradition.

The materials of this chapter and the chapters on geography and history will provide a useful foundation for the study of the economy of the Middle East that follows. Economic development is dependent on political stability, and this discussion has outlined some of the sociocultural factors that determine stability. Economic progress is also dependent on the development of human resources, including a population that possesses adequate literacy and physical health. These are closely interwoven with attitudes rooted in the traditional, essentially religious, culture. Finally, modern economic development depends heavily on a culture that respects work, time, and money, yet the basic value system of most of Middle East society relates to a vastly different way of life, in which money is treated circumspectly, work is little honored for its own sake, and time is not an urgent matter.

Footnotes*

[1] See Morroe Berger, *Bureaucracy and Society in Modern Egypt* (Princeton, N.J.: Princeton University Press, 1957); Charles Gallagher's chapter, "Language, Culture, and Society: The Arab World," in *Expectant Peoples,* ed. K. H. Silvert (New York: Random House, 1963); K. H. Silvert, ed., *Churches and States* (New York: American Universities Field Staff, 1967), particularly section 3 on Islam; or Hanna and Gardner, *Arab Socialism.*

[2] The material of this section follows closely the discussion of von Grunebaum, *Islam,* the chapter "The Profile of Muslim Civilization."

[3] Anshen, *Mid-East,* p. 19.

[4] Treated in some detail in chapter 4 of Hanna and Gardner, *Arab Socialism,* and in Faris and Husayn, *Crescent in Crisis,* pp. 134ff.

[5] Quoted from translation in *Mideast Mirror,* May 23, 1964.

[6] Adapted from Ernest Jackh, "Mid-Land, Mid-Sea, Mid-Air," in Anshen, *Mid-East,* p. 89.

[7] E. A. Speiser, "Cultural Factors in Social Dynamics in the Near East," in *Social Forces in the Middle East,* ed. S. N. Fisher (Ithaca, N.Y.: Cornell University Press, 1955).

[8] For an excellent summary discussion of these pressures and their consequences see J. C. Hurewitz, "The Politics of Rapid Population Growth in the Middle East," in *Modernization of the Arab World,* ed. J. H. Thompson and R. D. Reischauer, pp. 87-101 (New York: Van Nostrand Co., 1966).

[9] The material of this section follows in part the discussion of Berger, *Arab World Today,* the chapter "Personality and Values."

[10] For a full statement consult Hamady, *Temperament and Character of the Arabs*, the chapter "The Arab Mind."

[11] Coon, *Caravan*, is organized around this mosaic structure.

[12] For a full discussion of the differences between these two concepts refer to Emil Durkheim, *The Division of Labor in Society* (New York: Free Press, 1933).

[13] Franz Rosenthal, Introduction to Ibn Khaldun, *The Muqaddimah*.

*Throughout the book, footnote references which are duplicated in the Selected Bibliography have been abbreviated. Complete information is included in the bibliography.

Selected Bibliography

Anshen, Ruth A., ed. *Mid-East: World Center*. New York: Harper & Row, Publishers, 1956.

Attempts to analyze man's widening conceptual framework as it applies to the Middle East and explains the interrelation of Middle Eastern man and the universe, the individual and society.

Berger, Morroe. *The Arab World Today*. New York: Doubleday & Co., 1962.

A sociologist's attempt to get away from the Arabs of the newspaper headlines to see how they worship, live, work, and think.

Coon, Carleton S. *Caravan: Story of the Middle East*. New York: Holt, Rinehart and Winston, 1964.

A source book about preindustrial, traditional Middle Eastern civilization. Documents the mosaic concept as applied to Middle Eastern society.

Cragg, Kenneth. *The Call of the Minaret*. New York: Oxford University Press, 1956.

The Muslim concept of human society explained through a detailed analysis of the background and implications of each phrase in the Muslim call to prayer.

Eisenstadt, S. N. *Israeli Society*. New York: Basic Books, 1967.

An analysis of the changes in Jewish society brought about by the establishment of the state of Israel; a case study of nationalization and modernization.

Faris, Nabih A., and Husayn, Mohammed T. *The Crescent in Crisis*. Lawrence, Kan.: University of Kansas Press, 1955.

A study of the unifying and disruptive forces in the modern Arab world written from the Arab point of view. Discusses political, economic, social, and cultural problems in relation to nationalism.

Fisher, Sydney N., ed. *Social Forces in the Middle East*. Ithaca, N.Y.: Cornell University Press, 1955.

The perceptions, problems, and possible contributions of intellectuals, clergy, nomads, villagers, merchants, political leaders, army officers, minorities, entrepreneurs, workers, planners, farmers, and refugees.

Gibb, H. A. R. "Social Reform: Factor X." In *The Middle East in Transition*, edited by W. Z. Laqueur. New York: Frederick A. Praeger, 1958.

A brief but remarkably stimulating statement of the dilemma posed by modernization of traditional Middle Eastern society.

Goitein, S. D. *Jews and Arabs: Their Contacts through the Ages*. New York: Schocken Books, 1955.

Deals with social and cultural relationships, not political and military issues.

von Grunebaum, Gustave E. *Islam: Essays in the Nature and Growth of a Cultural Tradition*. London: Routledge and Kegan Paul, 1955.

Deals with three fundamental problems in Islamic civilization: the growth among Muslims of a consciousness of belonging to a culture; the unity of Muslim civilization as expressed in literature, political thought, attitude to science, and urban structure; and the interaction of Islam with other civilizations.

Hamady, Sania. *Temperament and Character of the Arabs*. New York: Twayne Publishers, 1960.

A study of Arab (mostly Egyptian) personality.

Hanna, Sami A., and Gardner, George H. *Arab Socialism*. Leiden, Holland: E. J. Brill, 1969.

An exploration of the hypothesis that Arab socialism is a cultural phenomenon that has deep roots in Middle Eastern history and society.

Ibn Khaldun. *The Muqaddimah*. Translated by Franz Rosenthal. New York: Bollingen Foundation, 1958.

One of the most famous examples of Arab historiography; written in 1377 and recognized by modern social scientists as contributing much to the understanding of social processes.

Polk, W. R., and Chambers, R. L., eds. *Beginnings of Modernization in the Middle East: The Nineteenth Century*. Chicago: University of Chicago Press, 1968.

Emphasizes the interrelationship of linguistic and geographical components but gives the regional variables due recognition.

Rivlin, B., and Szyliowicz, J. D., eds. *The Contemporary Middle East*. New York: Random House, 1965.

Deals with the process of change, organized around an analytical scheme—the transition from traditionalism to modernity.

Shiloh, Ailon, ed. *Peoples and Cultures of the Middle East*. New York: Random House, 1969.

A comprehensive approach; includes articles that integrate political, historical, economic, demographic, and health data into the study of culture and behavior.

Economic Development

This chapter is concerned with recent economic developments, primarily in the 1950s and 1960s, but many of the current economic problems stem in part from the legacy of foreign domination and misrule. Economic success is crucially dependent on political stability, high levels of education and health, and proper economic policies and their effective implementation, and the colonial powers did little to advance these goals.

Most Middle Eastern countries attained their political independence during the period following the Second World War. Their socioeconomic characteristics are in many respects similar to those commonly found in other underdeveloped countries: low per capita income; agriculture predominant, at least in terms of employment and exports; a high rate of population growth; and low education and health levels. Similarly, they universally desire to attain the economic position of the developed countries as soon as possible. However, their methods vary, ranging from rigorous government controls and the socialization of many economic sectors (particularly finance, industry, foreign trade, transport, and communications) to laissez faire; Lebanon's system is probably as nearly laissez faire as that of any nation, whereas Egypt, Syria, Iraq, and Algeria have adopted rigorous controls and large-scale socialization.

Most of the countries in the intermediate category also control their economies to a degree not commonly found in the West, regulating foreign trade, finance, prices, and investment, giving special treatment to certain sectors (e.g., industry), and adopting other legal and quasi-legal measures to direct economic development. In many of these countries various economic enterprises are state owned. In Israel, for example, about one-fifth of the net domestic product comes from the public sector;* in Turkey, about one-third of industrial production is accounted for by state-owned enterprises. Iran favors private enterprise, both domestic and foreign, but since the government commands large and growing resources from its oil royalties, it is the primary source of investment capital. In 1963 Iran's government accounted for 35 percent of the country's gross investment; the 1968-73 plan calls for the state to undertake 55 percent of investment.

Also in common with many other developing countries, almost all the Middle Eastern states engage in economic planning, at least on paper. However, an economic plan (for instance, a five-year plan) can take a wide variety of forms. Some are similar to the Soviet model; others are based on the French and Dutch plans, which rely primarily on indirect controls and incentives rather than on direct state supervision and management. Most of the plans view rapid industrialization as the panacea for economic ills, to the detriment of agriculture and the economy as a whole; lacking the necessary skills and even more important, the managerial ability to plan and efficiently operate large industrial firms, the states inevitably make costly errors.

On the other hand, the Middle East as a whole possesses advantages that many other developing countries lack. Probably of greatest importance are the region's enormous petroleum reserves. Its proximity to Europe provides a large and growing market for oil and other products and also job opportunities. The area's mild climate has been exploited to attract European and other tourists. However, political instability and internal and international conflict have diverted resources from economic development to the military.

The Record of Economic Growth

Economic growth is tremendously important to developing countries. A nation that can maintain a relatively steady record of high per capita economic growth can allocate the increased resources toward more investment and further growth, toward higher living standards, or toward a combination of the two. By diverting an increasing share of its resources to savings, private or governmental, a nation can finance internally a larger proportion of the necessary investment, thereby decreasing its dependence on foreign aid. This assumes, however, that the country is not allocating a larger share of these resources to defense.

The most commonly used measure of economic growth is changes in the gross national product (GNP) in real terms (corrected for price changes), preferably on a per capita basis. For growth to occur, capital that can be used for investment must be available. Some Middle Eastern countries have ample revenues from oil royalties for investment; others must depend on internal savings, foreign aid, or a

*Another fifth is owned by the Histadrut, the labor federation that owns and operates many enterprises. About three-fifths of production is by the private sector.

combination of both. But capital resources by no means ensure economic growth. Political stability, effective leadership, appropriate economic policies and their efficient implementation, and improvements in human resources—health, education, and skills—are also vital. Natural resources such as petroleum, minerals, agricultural land, water, geographical position, and climate play an important role, but in the Middle East and elsewhere human resources have been crucial. The clearest example is Japan. Although she is relatively poor in natural resources, by use of her skilled manpower Japan has developed a modern economy with a rate of economic growth that is the envy of the world.

In the Middle East economic growth varies greatly. Over time the difference between growth rates of, for example, 5 and 7 percent is substantial, and taking broad regional averages is as meaningless as combining the incomes of a millionaire and a pauper and arguing that "on average" both are well off. Table 3 makes clear that some countries have had a very good record of growth, whereas others have lagged. Why have some countries succeeded and others have not?

Oil revenues have transformed Kuwait and Saudi Arabia from underdeveloped countries into modern states with rapidly growing economies and world influence. Iran's 1969 oil revenues were quite high, but her large population (28 million) made her per capita income far less than that of some Middle Eastern states. However, Iran has allocated an increasing share of her oil income (about 80 percent) to investment, has borrowed from abroad, and has invited foreign companies to invest, and since the 1960s she has been successfully developing other resources, mainly agriculture and minerals. Iraq, which has abundant natural resources in addition to oil and which has a relatively small population (9 million in 1969), has been adversely affected by serious political instability and the civil war with the Kurdish minority. Iraq has spent less than 50 percent of her oil revenues on economic growth, and the proportion has declined since 1958. Actual development expenditures (compared with those planned) have been especially low in agriculture (about 25 percent of planned investment) and in industry (about 40 percent).[1]

Israel's rate of economic growth has been unusually high, averaging 11 percent between 1950 and 1965 despite a serious recession in 1952 and 1953. Another recession in 1966 and 1967 was followed by a sharp postwar upsurge in 1968 and 1969, and GNP increased by 13 percent annually. Israel's per capita income, living standards, and technological level approach those of the Western European countries. Israel had many development advantages; the most important was that prior to independence in 1948 the education level of her population was extraordinarily high, second only to the United States. Large amounts of foreign economic aid during the 1950s were of crucial importance also. But she has had disadvantages as well. Between 1948 and 1951 Israel absorbed a mass of destitute and relatively unskilled and uneducated immigrants from the European refugee camps and Asian and African countries, which virtually doubled her population[2] and caused widespread unemployment and underemployment. Since 1952 immigration has been much more moderate but with natural increase has caused a high rate of population growth. Israel's mineral and oil resources are meager, and both her direct and indirect costs of defense have been unusually high.

Israel has laid great emphasis on education and skills. She has steadily moved away from rigid controls and socialism toward liberalization and the encouragement of both public and private enterprise, giving increasingly liberal inducements to investors, both local and foreign. Israel initially emphasized agriculture, which differed from the policy of most Middle Eastern countries, but the appearance of many agricultural surpluses in the late 1950s and a drive to increase exports caused her to gradually shift toward industry. However, although the growth rates of the various economic sectors have differed from each other at times, there has been overall balanced economic development. The data on productivity indicates that these achievements are attributable in part to education and skill levels—over and above the increase in capital and labor resources.

Turkey's economic development has fluctuated greatly, mainly because of her dependence on largely unirrigated agriculture, but partly as a result of her changing political and economic policies. From 1950 to 1969 her GNP grew at a good rate, averaging 5.8 percent annually or 3.0 percent on a per capita basis. From 1963 to 1969 her growth rate was even higher, averaging about 6.6 percent, or 3.0 percent per capita, which is close to the 7 percent target set by the First Five-Year Plan (1963-67) and the second plan (1968-72). During the 1950s Turkey overwhelmingly emphasized the expansion of industrial capacity, largely ignoring problems such as high production costs and the lack of foreign currency to import raw materials, spare parts, and the like, but she changed this policy in the late 1950s. Nonetheless, industrial production (including mining) rose rapidly in the 1960s and has assumed an increasingly important role in the economy, although agriculture remains dominant, accounting for two-thirds of employment, one-third of GNP, and most of the exports. Turkey's Second Five-Year Plan stressed private enterprise, and the large-scale economic aid she has received from the United States and in more recent years from a consortium of Western countries has been of crucial importance to her development.

Jordan's GNP grew at a rate of 9.5 percent annually between 1954 and 1967, an impressive gain. The economy is based on largely unirrigated agriculture and, like Turkey's, is therefore subject to wide annual fluctuations. However, irrigation and the introduction of modern methods has reduced—though far from eliminated—these variations. Industry has expanded even more rapidly, but unlike many Middle Eastern countries, Jordan has not built up industry at the expense of agriculture. Following the Arab-Israeli War of 1948, about 350,000 Palestinian refugees entered Jordan.[3] Jordan also annexed the West Bank, causing the kingdom serious internal political problems. However, the Palestinians were far more advanced than the

Transjordanians, both economically and educationally, and the uniting of the two peoples strongly stimulated economic development. Also, Jordan has put greater emphasis on education than most of the countries in the area (see table 4), which accounts in part for its impressive rate of economic growth. Thus, Jordan succeeded in reducing both unemployment and underemployment, and according to one estimate, almost two-thirds of the refugees had been fully absorbed into the economy by 1964, and many of the others had part-time employment.[4] It can be assumed that the number of unemployed refugees continued to fall between 1964 and 1967 as a result of Jordan's high rates of growth.

Other sources also stimulated Jordan's growth. Between 1960 and 1967 tourism grew rapidly. Many Jordanians found work abroad, mostly in the Persian Gulf area, and sent remittances home to their families; these remittances became a source of foreign currency earnings almost equal to tourism. Substantial foreign aid from the United States, the United Kingdom, some other Western countries, and international organizations such as the United Nations Relief and Works Agency and charitable organizations was of importance during this period. Aid from the Arab states began in 1964 and has been of primary importance since 1967. This foreign aid was the source of virtually all the gross investment in the economy before the 1967 War; in other words, gross national saving approximated zero.* Jordan plans to reduce its dependence on foreign aid, but there has been little evidence of progress in this respect.

Lebanon has one of the highest levels of per capita income in the region. Although agriculture occupies about one-half of its labor force, it accounted for only 11 to 12 percent of her gross domestic product from 1964 to 1967. By Middle Eastern standards Lebanon's industry is well developed, and it accounts for another 13 percent of her gross domestic product.† The economy depends mainly on services. The country's political and economic freedom make it a haven for much of the capital escaping restrictions and nationalization in other Arab countries, and its developed financial institutions attract funds from the oil-rich Persian Gulf area. Many large Western companies, both industrial and financial, have located their regional headquarters there, and the trading abilities of the Lebanese have enabled them to reap profits from regional trade. Tourism has also developed rapidly,

---

*Most Middle Eastern countries rely on foreign aid to finance at least part of their investment. Turkey's Second Five-Year Plan (1968-72) calls for an average annual investment of $500 million and anticipates $280 million annually in foreign aid. In Israel, only about one-half of gross investment was financed by national saving from 1964 to 1966. Part of the remainder was financed by foreign aid; the rest, by immigrant transfers, foreign private investment, and other sources.

†The error in the national income data of underdeveloped countries is usually far greater than in the developed countries. In Lebanon the error may well be even higher. No census has been taken since the early 1930s, because it might upset the tenuous political balance between the evenly divided Muslim and Christian sects. Furthermore, illegal transactions and smuggling are known to be significant. See Economist Intelligence Unit, *Annual Supplement*, 1969. See also United Nations, *Studies on Selected Development Problems in Various Countries in the Middle East*, p. 17.

attracting other Arabs as well as Westerners, and has become one of the main props of the economy. All in all, the services—tourist, trading, and financial—account for about half of Lebanon's gross domestic product (GDP). Thus, earnings from these sources, remittances from the many Lebanese living abroad, and the capital inflow from other Arab states balance Lebanon's highly unfavorable trade balance (imports minus exports).[5] However, internal political problems exacerbated by regional conflicts have retarded her growth, particularly in 1958 and 1967, and because the economy is so dependent on trade and services, it is very sensitive to inter-Arab political conflicts and their economic corollaries. Thus, Lebanon's long-term economic growth rate has been moderate, averaging 5 percent between 1957 and 1966.

Syria has far more cultivable land per capita than most countries in the area, as well as the potential for major expansion of irrigation. During the 1950s she made rapid progress in extending irrigation and mechanizing agriculture, but political instability in the 1960s retarded her growth. Concurrent with the political union with Egypt from 1958 to 1961, Syria suffered a period of drought and imposed restrictions on private enterprise. After 1963 she extended nationalization and expanded her land-reform program, redistributing large estates and pressing farmers to join cooperatives. These measures had an adverse impact on the economy; between 1964 and 1967 investment in agriculture declined by 60 percent.[6]

Because 60 percent of Syria's labor force is engaged in farming and accounts for 25 to 28 percent of the national income, the economy is particularly sensitive to the successes and failures of this sector. During the 1960s, when agricultural production annually increased by only 2.8 percent, barely keeping up with population growth (see table 3), the First Five-Year Plan (1960/61-1964/65) fell far short of its target for total growth of 7.2 percent, achieving only about 5 percent. Only 60 to 70 percent of planned investment in the public sector occurred and much less of that planned for the private sector, apparently as a result of government restrictions and the fear of further nationalization. The Second Five-Year Plan (1966-70) also aims at a growth rate of 7.2 percent and appears to have been exceeded during the first three years of the plan.[7] After many years of delay, work was recently begun on the Euphrates Dam, which should greatly increase the irrigated area and provide electric power. In the mid-1970s a major expansion of agricultural production will be initiated also.

The 1952 revolution in Egypt was followed by a number of basic economic and political changes, in particular land reform. After the Suez-Sinai War of 1956 the government announced a policy of "Egyptianization," in which British, French, and Jewish businesses were taken over, and non-Arab Egyptian residents were gradually eliminated from the country's economic life.[8] Large-scale nationalization began in 1960 and was intensified following the secession of Syria from the United Arab Republic in 1961, when banking, insurance, transport, wholesale trade, mining, and most of the manufacturing sector were largely or completely taken over by the state. The land-reform program was made even more stringent, and the remaining private sector was placed under far more severe controls. The First Five-Year Plan (1960/61-1964/65) emphasized industrialization, in particular heavy industry, and Egypt initiated the Aswan Dam project in 1960.

Foreign aid from the East and the West was substantial during the latter half of the 1950s and increased markedly during the first half of the 1960s. However, state planning and control failed to increase efficiency and productivity. Quite the contrary; whereas productive *capacity* in agriculture, industry, and some other sectors increased greatly, *production* rose far less. Shortages of skilled and managerial personnel became more acute, and many new industrial enterprises operated well below capacity, raising the per unit costs of production. Egypt's planners had anticipated that by the end of the plan period (mid-1965) her balance of payments deficits would decline from their initial 1959/60 levels and would turn into surpluses. Instead, they rose precipitously. The country's foreign exchange reserves were steadily depleted, and Egypt's inability to pay for the import of spare parts and raw materials depressed production and incomes.

One major exception was the Suez Canal transit dues, which rose rapidly as a result of Europe's growing oil imports from the Persian Gulf area. The government's 1956 takeover of the canal was highly successful, and it would appear that the authorities had assigned capable administrators to the canal. In 1966 transit dues plus subsidiary trade from the Suez Canal operations brought in close to $300 million in convertible foreign currencies, almost equaling the country's foreign exchange earnings from its major export, cotton. The Aswan Dam project proceeded on schedule and, together with other reclamation projects, steadily increased the productive capacity of agriculture and electric power. However, agricultural production lagged seriously, rising by only 1.6 percent annually during the 1960s; per capita agricultural production from 1967 to 1969 was 9 percent below that of a decade earlier. Because agriculture employs over one-half the labor force and accounts for 30 percent of GDP, the lag in this sector has a depressing effect on the entire economy.

According to official accounts, GDP grew by an annual rate of 4.8 percent and industrial production by 5.3 percent between 1960 and 1967. However, real production—that is, production corrected for price changes—increased at a lower rate (see table 3, note d). The explanation commonly given for Egypt's economic problems is that her productive capacity, primarily in agriculture, lags behind population growth. However, it seems that at least during the 1960s her problem was instead the failure to utilize efficiently the major increase in productive capacity afforded by the Aswan Dam and other reclamation projects and by the industrialization program.

Agriculture

Agriculture is the Middle East's single most important economic sector. In all countries except Israel, Lebanon, and the major oil producers, agriculture accounts for both the largest share of GNP and the bulk of commodity exports. Moreover, industry, commerce, transport, and other sectors are directly and indirectly dependent on farming; in many countries industry is concentrated in the processing of local farm products, such as the textile industry in Egypt, Turkey, and Syria and the food-processing industry in most of the other Middle Eastern countries. Agriculture also employs by far the greatest share of the labor force, accounting for from one-third to three-fourths of those employed except in Israel and in some small Persian Gulf states.

The record for agricultural production during the 1960s is varied. A few countries (Jordan, Israel, and Lebanon) had excellent records (see table 5), whereas Egypt and Iraq showed only small increases, considerably below their population growth. The others either barely managed to keep up with population growth or exceeded it. There are a variety of reasons for these differences. Natural conditions vary from country to country; some are blessed with abundant cultivable land and have at least the potential for expanding irrigation, whereas others are more restricted. Egypt has the smallest amount of agricultural land per capita, but the land is irrigated, and yields are thus far greater than in countries that depend on the vagaries of rain-fed agriculture. In most countries, however, the potential cultivable land far exceeds the land actually used. Irrigation schemes have expanded both the area under cultivation and the yields, but official policies, such as government policies whereby farmers are paid less than market prices for products, often act as deterrents to full and efficient utilization of the nation's agricultural potential. Governments usually view their country's future as lying in industrialization; also, such major projects as the Aswan Dam are not usually accompanied by mundane extension services such as instructing farmers in modern agricultural methods. Egypt during the 1960s is a clear-cut example of failure to utilize agricultural potential; between 1960 and 1967, 784,-000 feddans* were reclaimed, but the tilled area in 1967 was only 92,000 feddans greater than that in 1960.

Many of agriculture's problems stem also from social, traditional, and historical factors. In a number of countries the system of land tenure was such that: (1) Land ownership was concentrated in the hands of the few. (2) Some of the land was held under a system called *mushaa*, in which the lands of a village were held in common, and individual rights were shares of the total rather than specific parcels of

*A feddan is somewhat larger than an acre.

land. This tended to discourage long-term investment and improvement. (3) The continued division of the land among male heirs eventually resulted in fragmentation of ownership, each holder having only small, narrow, scattered strips of land. This had obvious adverse effects on efficiency and productivity. (4) Any farmer wishing to borrow was usually charged usurious rates of interest by the landlord, the merchant, or the money lender. (5) Landlords, merchants, and money lenders also dominated marketing and demanded such exorbitant rentals that the small farmer was left in a state of perpetual poverty that often bordered on feudal bondage.

Land-reform programs have generally embraced provisions for dealing with these problems, including land redistribution, the regularization of disputed or unclear land titles, lowering of rentals or crop shares taken by landlords, and the organization of cooperatives to provide seed, credit, marketing, and other services. Land reform was introduced in Egypt shortly after the 1952 revolution, and government-managed cooperatives have taken over many of the functions previously exercised by landlords. The problem of land fragmentation has proved more intractable, although the newly reclaimed land has been used partly to help consolidate some of the farm units.[9] Generally speaking, the Egyptian land-reform program is considered successful.[10]

The problems of land tenure are particularly severe in Iran, where landownership is extremely concentrated and absentee ownership is widespread. Before land reform the peasant's share of the crop was extremely low (often one-fifth). The shah began to distribute the crown lands in 1951 but did not initiate a comprehensive agrarian reform program until 1960. The land transfers which took place between 1962 and 1966 benefited between one-sixth and one-seventh of the rural population. Thousands of cooperatives were established to deal with such problems as credit and marketing, and the government encouraged the voluntary establishment of farm corporations to eliminate the problems of land fragmentation. New Iranian and foreign agriculture development companies were also encouraged to take over parts of newly irrigated lands made available by the various dam projects.[11]

In Iraq land ownership was highly concentrated for many centuries. Some agrarian reform laws were passed in the early 1950s, but the landowning classes resisted implementing them. Following the 1958 revolution, however, a far more comprehensive land-reform law was passed that included limits on landholdings, the encouragement of cooperatives, redefinition of contracts in favor of the tenant or sharecropper, and various provisions for the protection of the farm laborer. However, the instability of Iraqi governments and the lack of adequate technical personnel have seriously deterred the execution of these laws, and progress in land reform has been slow.[12]

In Middle Eastern countries such as Turkey, Lebanon, and Jordan farms are predominantly owner-operated, but land fragmentation is often critical, seriously depressing efficiency and productivity.

In Turkey, for example, less than one-tenth of the farms are in one contiguous piece, and according to the 1963 census, even smaller farms were split into many pieces.[13] Israeli agriculture is unique in the Middle East and elsewhere. The major kinds of farms are the *moshav*, an integrated cooperative based on family farms; the *kibbutz*, based on collective production and consumption; and private Jewish and Arab farms. The *kibbutzim* (plural of *kibbutz*) have increasingly emphasized the expansion of industrial enterprises, and in a few rural settlements industry has become the primary source of income. To some extent this has helped to stem (but not stop) the flow of population from the country to cities.

In the Middle East land-reform programs are often viewed as essential to economic progress, but there has often been a danger that the programs would reduce, rather than increase, farm production. For instance, breaking up large estates might reduce total production if the new landowner lacked managerial expertise and the necessary investment capital. Some land-reform programs took these difficulties into account and were able to contend with them. The development plans of most Middle Eastern countries include provisions designed to accelerate the shift from subsistence to modern agriculture, to raise productivity, to improve marketing facilities, to provide inexpensive credit, to increase the irrigated area, and to raise farm incomes and living standards. However, the degree of success of implementation of these plans varies, and the gap between rural and urban incomes is often so wide that the movement of population from rural to urban areas has gathered momentum, transferring unemployment and underemployment from rural farms to sprawling urban slums.

Industry

The initial stage of industrial development usually requires labor-intensive industries that need relatively few skilled people and use a relatively simple technology. Often the industries include textiles, building materials, and the processing of agricultural products and local mining products, such as phosphates in Jordan and Morocco, various minerals in Turkey, and oil in most of the countries. At this stage the nations are aiming for import substitution—the substitution of locally produced goods for imported goods—and increased exports. At a later stage other industries will be developed, such as the assembly of motor vehicles and the production of sophisticated consumer durables. Hopefully, technology and skills will then develop to the point at which a nation's industry can itself manufacture the component parts rather than merely assembling them. At this stage poor managerial and technical skills can cause large problems, and the scale of production is usually small, resulting in high per unit costs of production. When the country attempts to advance to an even higher stage—developing industries that are not related to the availability of local raw materials and expanding industrial exports—the problems of production costs and quality standards may become far more acute. These stages overlap considerably, of course, and some countries have attempted to "leapfrog" into stages for which they were technically unprepared, prematurely engaging in steel production, automobile assembly, or other such projects in a search for prestige.

Many countries expected industrialization to improve their balance of payments by providing import substitutions and more exports. However, the reverse has often been true; the need to import raw materials and spare parts for these industries has often caused a deterioration in the balance of payments. Egypt during the 1960s is a prime example, and the same is true to a lesser extent of Turkish industries that depend heavily on imported raw materials. Israel's development of vehicle assembly and steel industries in the mid-1950s were widely acknowledged to be costly errors.

By and large, Israel's industries have grown to very advanced levels, especially during the 1960s. Like Japan, Israel has utilized her highly educated and skilled population to industrialize in spite of the absence of significant natural resources.[14] Between 1958 and 1968 industrial exports increased by 20 percent annually, reaching over $.5 billion in 1968, and over 70 percent of her commodity exports consisted of a wide range of industrial products. Industry employs over one-fourth of Israel's labor force and accounts for about the same share of her national income.

The other countries in which industry has developed are Egypt, Turkey, Lebanon, and more recently Iran. However, national income data often includes mining, crude oil production, and electric power production in the industrial sector, giving an exaggerated view of industrial development. In Jordan, for example, the largest single industry is phosphates, which accounted for over one-third of all commodity exports in 1966, and thus figures for industry do not necessarily indicate the country's stage of industrial development. Nevertheless, it is clear that a number of Middle Eastern countries have advanced beyond the initial stages, and the process is likely to continue.*

Other than the export of oil and mining products, the only significant industrial export of Turkey and Egypt is textiles. Lebanese industrial exports include textiles and a number of other consumer products; industrial exports increased by about 7 percent annually between 1961 and 1968, and the rate of growth has gone up sharply since the 1967 Arab-Israeli War. Manufacturing is thus assuming an increasingly

---

*In Egypt industry accounted for 21 percent of the gross domestic product and employed 11 percent of the labor force. By way of contrast, agriculture accounted for 30 percent of gross domestic product and employed one-half of the labor force. In Turkey the figures for industry were 19 and 13 percent and for agriculture, 33 and 68 percent; in Lebanon, the figures for industry were 13 and 12 percent and for agriculture, 12 percent and one-half the labor force. All the statistics are for the latest available dates and should be taken as approximations. They may include, as noted, mining and quarrying, crude oil production, and electric power production.

important role in Lebanon's economy. Iran is a latecomer to industrialization, but it has vast oil revenues and has given official encouragement to both local and foreign private investors. In consequence, production increased rapidly in the 1960s. Plants have recently been established to manufacture steel, machine tools, chemicals, aluminum, diesel engines, tractors, vehicles, and other products; crude oil is refined on a larger scale than in any other Middle Eastern country; and textiles have become the largest private industry. Many of the new industrial plants are being established by foreign companies, and growth should continue.*

Petroleum

Oil is of overwhelming importance in a few of the Middle Eastern countries, plays a lesser role in others, but directly or indirectly affects almost every country in the Middle East. In 1959 the Middle East accounted for 23 percent of world oil production and one-half of world exports. In the 1960s the discovery and exploitation of Libya's vast oil resources and smaller ones in Algeria raised the Middle East's share in 1969 (including the North African Arab states) to 38.6 percent of world production and 68.6 percent of world exports (see table 6). Furthermore, the governments have exerted strong pressures on foreign oil companies for a larger percentage of profits; whereas the Middle East produced three and one-half times more oil in 1969 than in 1959, government oil revenues increased much more rapidly. The per capita oil income of a number of Persian Gulf states and of Kuwait and Libya is enormous.

Iran was one of the first large-scale oil producers in the region, but because of ineffectual political leadership and the 1951 nationalization of the British oil company, oil production was almost nil until an agreement was reached with a consortium of Western oil companies in 1954. Thereafter production rose steadily, but it was not until the 1967 Arab-Israeli War that Iran regained its regional preeminence. Whereas the Arab countries imposed an oil embargo on the United States, the United Kingdom, and West Germany for a few months after the war, Iran stepped up production and exports. Oil revenues were expected to exceed $1/billion in 1970 and to provide the main source of investment capital for the country's ambitious development program.

Saudi Arabia began to produce oil in the late 1930s, and its proved oil reserves are the largest in the area. A consortium of American oil companies has been instrumental in rapidly increasing

---

*Manufacturing and mining, other than crude oil production, accounted for 11 percent of Iran's gross domestic product in 1968-69, and Iran's share of oil production after deducting payments to foreign companies accounted for an additional 25 percent of gross domestic product. The industrial sector as a whole employed 18 to 19 percent of the labor force; agricultural brought in 21 percent of gross domestic product and employed almost half the labor force.

production. The equal division of profits agreed to by the Saudi government and the oil companies in the early 1950s set the pattern for agreements in other countries; more recently, the governments' share has risen to 60 or even 75 percent.* During the 1950s much of the growing Saudi wealth was squandered, but more effective political leadership in the 1960s has successfully channeled these revenues toward economic development.

Commercial oil production began in Kuwait in 1946 and grew by leaps and bounds until 1967. The Kuwait Oil Company is the joint venture of an American and a British oil company. With her small population and vast oil reserves, Kuwait's per capita GNP in 1967 was second only to that of the United States, although Kuwait's income was distributed far more unequally. More than half of her 733,000 people and two-thirds of her labor force are foreigners. Foreigners are granted only temporary work permits, which can be renewed only at the discretion of authorities, and this overwhelming dependence on a foreign labor force has caused political problems.

A consortium of Western oil companies initiated Iraqi oil production in 1934. However, political instability, deteriorating relations with the Western oil companies during the 1960s, and the Syrian shutdown of the oil pipeline in 1966 have retarded oil production.

Egypt was a small producer of oil for many years, but new discoveries made by Western oil companies in the mid-1960s substantially increased production, even after the loss of the Sinai oil fields in June 1967. However, Egypt was a major beneficiary of Middle Eastern oil mainly through her possession of the Suez Canal. Transit dues plus subsidiary trade in 1966 reached about $300 million, compared with Iran's $600 million in oil revenues. The oil pipeline from Saudi Arabia through Jordan, Syria, and Lebanon carried about one-sixth the 1969 Saudi output and paid transit dues to these countries. About 70 percent of Iraqi oil production in 1968 was carried by the oil pipeline crossing Syria and Lebanon, and Syria in particular was a major beneficiary of transit dues. Syria's settlement with the Iraq Petroleum Company in early 1967 provided her with a substantial increase in transit dues.

In 1970 Israel completed a pipeline from her Red Sea port, Eilat, to Ashkelon, on the Mediterranean. It has a capacity of twenty million tons annually. Additional pumping stations are expected to raise capacity to sixty million tons by 1974, equivalent to about one-third the oil transit through the Suez Canal in 1966. Her sources are apparently Iranian and Sinai oil destined for shipment to Eastern

*The agreement between the Western oil companies and the Persian Gulf oil-producing countries in March 1971 raised both the price for crude oil charged by the governments and the tax rate. Thus, government oil revenues were expected to rise rapidly during the period of the five-year agreement. Negotiations between the Western oil companies and Libya were concluded in April 1971. The Libyans received even higher payments than the Gulf states, based on their geographic advantage. It was assumed that Iraq and Saudi Arabia would also receive higher payments for that part of their oil exports made through their Mediterranean oil pipelines.

Mediterranean countries. Egypt has announced plans for a similar pipeline paralleling the Suez Canal, but no work had begun on this project as of November 1971. Negotiations took place in 1970 for a major pipeline from Iran through Turkey, to avoid the circuitous route around the Cape of Good Hope, which had been necessary since the closure of the Suez Canal in June 1967.

Although the bulk—over 90 percent—of Middle Eastern oil is exported as crude petroleum, there are refineries in many countries, and their number is steadily increasing. The major refineries are in Iran, Kuwait, Saudi Arabia, Bahrayn, and Aden, in that order. Most of the other countries have refineries to provide part or all of the local consumption of oil. Even countries such as Lebanon and Jordan, which have no oil of their own, have easy access to it through the pipeline traversing their territories. Israel has a small exportable surplus of refined oil products ($18 million in 1968) and is expanding its refining capacity. Prior to the 1967 War, Egypt had exported refined oil products worth about $20 million annually. A few countries have developed a petrochemical complex of industries based on oil and gas.

The oil revenues received by the major producers have been used partly as capital to aid the economic development of other countries in the region. Kuwait set up a development fund in 1961 and made loans to various Arab states, in particular Egypt, even before the War of 1967. Since the war Saudi Arabia, Libya, and Kuwait have provided Jordan and Egypt with an annual grant. Additional aid to Jordan has been provided by some of the Persian Gulf amirates.

Middle Eastern oil is centrally important for both the suppliers and their Western customers. Periodic disruptions in oil shipments, especially since the closure of the Suez Canal in June 1967, and the subsequent boycott of the United States, the United Kingdom, and West Germany from June to September 1967 have induced the Western oil companies to expand oil production outside the Middle East. However, the steady increase in Western oil consumption makes it likely that its dependence on Middle Eastern and in particular on Arab oil supplies will continue, although perhaps at a relatively reduced level. Also, most Middle Eastern producers have learned from the Iranian experience of the early 1950s that nationalization can backfire. Further, the ineffectiveness of the 1967 boycott indicated that both producers and consumers have a stake in stability and in normal commercial relations; the only Middle Eastern country that produced less in 1967 than in 1966 was Iraq, primarily as a result of the Syrian shutdown of the pipeline in December 1966 and early 1967. Saudi Arabia, Algeria, Libya, and the Persian Gulf amirates all increased production substantially in 1967, from 8 to 20 percent. Kuwait's oil production was only slightly above 1966 levels, possibly due to the boycott and intense political pressures from its large foreign population, many of whom are Palestinian.

It is noteworthy that Egypt, the leading Arab country, encouraged the Western oil companies to continue their oil operations and explorations in the country during and following the War of 1967.

In an article published in 1968 in *Al Ahram*, the semiofficial Cairo daily newspaper, the oil editor called for the encouragement of foreign oil companies because of finances and because advanced technology is necessary to "thoroughly exploit" Egypt's petroleum resources.[15] This policy has been followed and has resulted in a major expansion of oil production since 1968.

Foreign Trade and the Balance of Payments

In small developed countries foreign trade plays a much greater role than in large countries such as the United States and the Soviet Union. The more advanced the development of the smaller countries, the greater the importance of foreign trade. For the major oil-producing countries foreign trade is obviously crucial. Development plans require large-scale imports of machinery, equipment, spare parts, and often raw materials, and as these plans are implemented, the demand for food and consumer goods rises far more rapidly than population growth. The relative neglect of agriculture adds to the severity of the trade imbalance (exports minus imports), and the result is often a rising demand for imported food and consumer goods, as well as machinery, equipment, spare parts, and raw materials. For the largest oil producers these imports do not present a problem, although even Iran faces balance of payments difficulties because of its rapid growth and development. But for most Middle Eastern countries, paying for these imports necessitates a rapid rise in exports, foreign aid, foreign private investment, or some combination of these.

Other than oil, the Middle East's commodity exports are mainly agricultural and mining products (see table 7). They include cotton from Egypt, Sudan, Turkey, Iran, and Syria; citrus from Israel and Lebanon; tobacco from Turkey; and dates from Iraq. Other products are mainly for regional trade. As noted earlier, Israel is the only country that has succeeded thus far in exporting a wide range of technologically advanced industrial products. Mining products such as phosphates from Jordan and minerals from Turkey and Iran have become significant in the development of these countries.

Often overlooked is the importance of service exports. For Lebanon these exports—tourism, trade, commerce, banking, and transportation—are of far greater importance than commodities. Israel exports such services as tourism, air travel, and shipping and undertakes various projects, mainly irrigation and agricultural development, in developing countries. Israel's exports of services in 1969 totaled $571 million, compared with $747 million in commodity exports. In 1966 Jordanian exports of goods amounted to $29 million; her service exports equaled $76 million, including tourism, remittances, oil transit dues, and income from investments held abroad.

For a number of other countries also remittances from nationals working abroad assume a major role in the balance of payments. Six hundred thousand Turks working in Europe, mainly in West Germany, sent home $141 million to their families in 1969. Total remittances were expected to reach nearly $200 million in 1970; 1969 commodity exports were $537 million. Countries with large incomes from remittances include Jordan and Lebanon (mainly from the Persian Gulf area) and recently Egypt (from the various oil-producing Arab states). In addition, Lebanon in particular receives significant sums from her nationals who have permanently emigrated.* Since the families receiving these remittances must exchange the foreign currency for local currency, the badly needed foreign currency accrues to Middle Eastern treasuries. This system reduces unemployment in the Middle East as well.

The ratio of exports to imports—both goods and services—varies widely from country to country and over time. The more rapid the pace of investment and hence economic development is, the greater the deterioration in the balance of payments usually is.† For example, Iran, which has been developing rapidly, has deficits, whereas Iraq, which has been lagging, has surpluses (see table 7). Jordanian deficits resulted from rising defense expenditures and living standards, which entailed the import of consumer goods, both necessities and so-called luxuries. The deficits were covered by foreign aid, mainly grants. Israeli deficits resulted from high levels of investment, rising living standards, and defense expenditures; her gap is covered by grants from the U.S. and reparations from West Germany, which both ceased in 1965; loans from the U.S. and international sources such as the World Bank; donations to the Jewish Agency; donations to various religious, educational, health, and charitable institutions; Israel bonds sold abroad; immigrant transfers; restitution payments by West Germany to Israeli residents who were victims of Nazi persecution; and commercial loans. In Lebanon the deficits are covered primarily by capital transfers, mainly from the Persian Gulf area.** Turkish deficits are mainly covered by grants and loans from Western countries. Egyptian trade data is incomplete; military aid and much economic aid are excluded from the official trade figures.[16] However, even excluding the importation of military supplies, it would appear that the deficit was far higher than indicated in table 7.

The inability of most of the countries in the region to increase exports rapidly is a serious constraint on their development plans. The curtailment of foreign aid programs in recent years, especially by the United States, has added to the difficulties faced by those who are attempting to accelerate their economic development.

---

*Strictly speaking, the latter are not service exports but private transfer payments.

†The reference here is to the balance on current account, which includes the exports and imports of goods and services.

**Capital transfers in this case refer to deposits in Lebanese banks by Persian Gulf residents and governments, as well as direct doreign investment in Lebanon.

Regional Economic Cooperation

The Middle East is long on discussions and resolutions regarding economic cooperation and short on performance. In 1953 economic agreements signed by the members of the Arab League called for preferential trade and transit and favored treatment for internal capital transfers. In 1958 the league decided to set up a Council of Economic Union, and between 1962 and 1964 seven of the thirteen Arab League members (at that time)—Jordan, Kuwait, Morocco, Syria, Egypt, Yemen, and Iraq—ratified the agreement. Subsequently, it was decided to establish an Arab Common Market, scheduled to come into being on January 1, 1965. The Arab Common Market, modeled along the lines of the European Economic Community (usually known as the European Common Market), included the abolition of tariffs over a ten-year period plus a range of uniform economic policies that would eventually create one large economic unit. Five countries ratified this agreement: Egypt, Syria, Iraq, and Jordan, and, at a later date, Yemen. However, each country listed so many exceptions to its formal adherence to the pact that the market was devoid of meaning.[17] In a 1969 assessment of the efficacy of the Arab Common Market and of the myriad other resolutions and trade pacts, a Beirut economic journal noted, "The list of products affected by the successive [tariff] reductions contains those that are little or not exchanged between member countries. . . . The improvement observed in certain cases [in regional trade] has been of little importance, and cannot be explained by the measures adopted within the framework of the Arab Common Market."[18]

Economic relations are affected by political relations to a far greater extent than is usually the case in Western countries. The union of Egypt and Syria between 1958 and 1961 was accompanied by an almost complete cutoff of trade between Syria and Lebanon, between whom there is traditionally a large volume of trade. Other political and economic disputes, such as the Syrian shutdown of the oil pipelines, the closing of the Syrian-Lebanese border in 1969, and the cessation of trade between Iraq and Kuwait in the early 1960s, have also inhibited attempts at regional economic cooperation. In countries that espouse socialism, foreign trade is usually assigned to a government agency, in which case profit considerations are not paramount and tariff reductions have little effect on trade. Many of the other countries exercise tight controls on foreign trade.

Another regional grouping was established in 1964 and included Iran, Turkey, and Pakistan. The Regional Cooperation for Development, as the group is known, has adopted a policy of undertaking joint projects, particularly in the fields of transportation, communications, and industry, and already has a few tangible achievements, including a joint shipping line, work on a highway linking Ankara, Tehran, and Karachi, and rail connections. Over fifty joint industrial projects have been approved and twenty have reached the implementation stage. Eight are already producing. Afghanistan may also join this regional group.[19]

The experience of underdeveloped countries in general suggests that, in addition to serious political problems, objective economic difficulties impede economic cooperation. By and large both developed and underdeveloped countries conduct most of their trade with the economically advanced countries. The range of industrial goods, and in some cases agricultural products and raw materials, needed for investment, production, and consumption is available primarily in the developed countries, usually at lower cost and of superior quality. Thus, Algeria, Morocco, Tunisia, Israel, and Lebanon already have preferential trade agreements with the European Common Market, and Egypt is negotiating with the European Common Market for an agreement similar to the one concluded with Israel in mid-1970. Turkey has an even closer tie; she is an associate member of the European Common Market.[20]

In addition to intra-Arab political problems, the Arab economic boycott of Israel also impedes regional economic cooperation. The boycott includes blacklisting foreign firms that do business with Israel, although the definition of "doing business" changes from time to time and is applied in varying degrees by different Arab countries. The boycott has spurred Israel to rapid development of a large merchant marine and airline, but it is difficult to determine if Israeli exports would have been greater or if investment might have advanced more rapidly without the boycott. The cutoff of the oil pipeline from Iraq to Israel in 1948 added to Israel's costs of transporting oil until she began to import Iranian oil following the Suez-Sinai War of 1956. The closure of the Suez Canal to Israeli ships and to ships bound for Israel also added to her transportation costs and spurred the development of Israel's Red Sea port of Eilat. On the other hand, the boycott has inflicted economic damage on some sectors in Arab countries,[21] and economic cooperation and trade would certainly benefit all sides.[22]

The Economic Impact of the Six-Day War

Since the War of 1967, the military expenditures of almost all the countries in the region have escalated, particularly Egypt, Israel, and Jordan, the three countries most actively involved in the war and in the postwar hostilities. Although loss of lives and injuries are impossible to measure, some assessment of the economic impact can be made.

Egypt

The closure of the Suez Canal was a blow to the Egyptian economy that may prove to be long-term. The tolls and subsidiary trade related to canal operations covered two-thirds of Egypt's trade deficit in commodities in 1966. Further, these revenues had been rising by about 10 percent annually before the war. The shift to larger supertankers (which cannot traverse the canal) started before the war but has been sharply accelerated since. The longer the canal remains closed, the more international trade will reorient itself toward alternative methods of transportation. It appears that the canal will recapture some of its former business when it reopens, but it will take a long time and huge investments to widen and deepen the channel before it can resume its former role.

Besides the closing of the canal, Israel's possession of the Sinai peninsula means the loss of oil fields that had brought in $40 to $50 million annually. As noted earlier, Egypt's postwar development of the oil fields raised oil production in 1969 to levels much higher than those of 1966. Tourist revenues estimated at $50 to $100 million in 1966 also declined precipitously after the war, mainly as a result of the continuation of hostilities. The postwar fighting also meant the evacuation of over half a million Egyptians from the Suez area and the destruction of oil refineries, other industrial plants, and a number of towns in the region.

War has also escalated Egypt's military expenditures over and above the arms and military aid provided by the Soviets. Western sources believe that the military equipment received by Egypt since the war is worth at least $2 billion. According to a statement made by President Nasser in June 1970, Egypt would begin making payments on its postwar Soviet arms deliveries in 1971. However, it is believed that the Soviets charge only nominal prices, and that even these payments may be canceled if they prove burdensome. Egypt's own military expenditures rose from about $1.2 billion in fiscal year 1969/70 to $1.3 billion in 1970/71—about one-fifth of Egypt's GNP.[23] Economic aid from the Soviet Union, a number of Eastern European countries, and the major Arab oil-producing states has reduced, but not eliminated, the war's impact on the Egyptian economy.

The economic slowdown, which began in Egypt two or three years before the war, accelerated during the immediate postwar period. An upturn was evident in 1969, however, and the growth of GNP approximated the growth of population. For the 1965-69 period as a whole, GNP apparently increased at an average annual rate of 1.4 percent; on a per capita basis this would indicate an average annual decline of about 1.5 percent.[24]

Jordan

The loss of the West Bank during the 1967 War was viewed by almost all observers as a very severe, if not catastrophic, blow to the Jordanian economy, primarily because the West Bank (including East Jerusalem) was the source of most of Jordan's tourist revenues. However, the East Bank's agriculture, industry, transportation, communications, electricity, irrigation projects, trade, commerce, and banking were much more developed. Amman was not only the political capital but also the commercial and financial center, and with neighboring Zarqa was the industrial center as well. Even before the war, a few hundred thousand West Bank residents had moved to the East Bank in response to the latter's much greater rate of development.

In the immediate aftermath of the war a large number of refugees migrated to the East Bank. They are supported by the United Nations Relief and Works Agency and by other international aid programs. Because both Israel and Jordan agreed to continue trade between the East Bank and the West Bank, the postwar recovery was accelerated. Foreign aid increased from $84 million before the war to $135 million in 1968-69 (annual average), and a large part of this increase went toward augmenting the country's foreign exchange reserves, which were far higher at the end of 1970 than four years earlier. Military expenditures rose precipitously to double their prewar level, but so did expenditures on economic development. Agricultural and industrial production and commodity exports have also been far higher than before the war. However, the balance of payments deficit also increased substantially, mainly because of lower tourist revenues and much higher imports. This high level of imports reflects the purchase of military equipment abroad but is mainly due to imports of consumer goods, both necessities and luxuries; raw materials for production; and machinery and equipment for investment. Undoubtedly the war has affected certain economic sectors adversely, but on the whole the economic impact has been far less than is commonly believed. This does not minimize the political impact of the war, which is far more serious.

The rise of the fedayeen groups following the war and the hostilities along the Israel-Jordan cease-fire lines undoubtedly had a negative impact on certain sectors of the economy, but the Jordanian civil war in the fall of 1970 may have inflicted more serious economic harm. However, if the first three postwar years (mid-1967 to mid-1970) are a guide, the initial reports of the economic costs of the civil war were probably exaggerated, and the fundamental strength of the Jordanian economy has probably been underestimated.

Israel

In 1967 the Israeli economy was in the midst of a recession that had begun in late 1965. There were indications of an upturn before the war, but there is no doubt that the war and its aftermath accelerated recovery. The factors accounting for the postwar upsurge include the large financial aid received from Jewish communities abroad in 1967; the psychological impact of the military victory; the rapid rise in local military production (partly as a result of France's postwar arms embargo); a rapid rise in exports; a large increase in tourism; and a substantial increase in immigration, especially from the Western countries. GNP increased by 15 percent in 1968 and 11 percent in 1969, but postwar hostilities and the regional arms race raised military expenditures to unprecedented levels; they absorbed 20 percent of GNP in 1968 and 1969 compared with less than 10 percent in 1966. Arms purchased abroad rose steadily also, from $159 million in 1966 to $423 million in 1969, and contributions from Jewish communities abroad rose sharply in 1967 and then declined in 1968 and 1969, though they were still above their prewar levels.* The result was a serious deterioration in the balance of payments and a sharp decline in foreign exchange reserves.[25]

Syria

Syria's economy was affected only peripherally by the War of 1967 and its aftermath; the loss of the Golan Heights and the flight of seventy-five to one hundred thousand refugees from the area did not have a significant impact on the Syrian economy. A Syrian economic journal list of the economic losses resulting from the war included the shutdown of the oil pipeline, the loss of transit dues between June and September of 1967, and the rising military expenditures, but it ignored the severence of the Golan Heights. Syrian military expenditures have risen from 11 to 12 percent of national income before the war to 13 to 14 percent in 1967-68. How much of the increase stems from internal political problems and how much from hostilities with Israel is difficult to assess.[26]

Lebanon

The war caused a temporary downturn in Lebanon's all-important tourist sector, but she recovered rapidly. In 1968 tourist revenues reached an all-time high, $117 million compared with $104 million in 1966,[27] and tourist revenues rose again in 1969.[28] Lebanon's postwar economy was more seriously affected by the 1966 banking crisis and the rising interest rates in the Western countries, which have attracted capital from Lebanon and from the Persian Gulf area. For some sectors of the Lebanese economy the closure of the Suez Canal has provided a powerful stimulus, particularly in transit trade to Middle Eastern countries that had previously used the canal. Furthermore, industrial exports from Lebanon to these countries have expanded rapidly. Between 1967 and 1969 Lebanese industrial exports,

*Military expenditures totaled $377 million in 1966 and $947 million in 1969, excluding civilian expenditures in the occupied territories and other indirect costs related to defense. Their inclusion might raise defense expenditures to about 25 percent of GNP in 1968-69. Institutional transfers, which include contributions to the Jewish Agency and to a host of educational, religious, health, and welfare institutions, rose from $97 million in 1966 to $181 million in 1969. Receipts from the sale of Israel bonds abroad rose from $11 million in 1966 to $63 million in 1969. See Bank of Israel, *Annual Reports*.

primarily processed foods, textiles, and furniture, increased by 33 percent annually, and the result has been a sharp rise in industrial investment.[29] Invested capital in industry in 1968 was five times the 1958 level, and industrial employment rose more than threefold during the decade. Industrial growth continued in 1969 and 1970, and a Beirut economic journal gave a number of reasons: (1) the closure of the Suez Canal gave Lebanese products an advantage in exporting to Saudi Arabia, Kuwait, Iraq, Jordan, and the Arabian peninsula; (2) the Lebanese improved quality and marketing; (3) the nationalization of industry in other Middle Eastern countries weakened the competitive position of their products in terms of costs and quality.[30]

The economic impact of the conflict with the fedayeen groups in 1969-70, the fighting in southern Lebanon, and the flight of a few thousand Lebanese from the area of conflict are difficult to assess at this time. It will certainly have some adverse impact but appears not to have significantly retarded the growth of the economy as a whole. The closing of the pipeline from Saudi Arabia (through Jordan, Syria, and Lebanon) in 1969 and again in 1970 had more serious consequences.* It would also appear that Syria is attempting to capture some of the transit trade to neighboring Arab countries, which is one of the mainstays of the Lebanese economy.[31]

The war has also affected other countries in the region. The three largest Arab oil-producing states, Libya, Kuwait, and Saudi Arabia, are providing sizable subsidies to Egypt and Jordan† and to some extent to the fedayeen groups. However, the rapid rise in postwar Libyan oil production and revenues is also partly a result of the Suez Canal closure. Iranian and Saudi military expenditures have risen since 1967, but mainly because of the announced withdrawal of British forces from the area and increased tension in the Persian Gulf region.

Conclusion

In an excellent and prescient analysis of the region's economic problems, Charles Issawi, a noted specialist in Middle East economics, stated in 1966: "Economic policies in the Middle East have, of late, been based on certain presuppositions which, on examination, may turn out to be mere myths. One of these is that industry should be given priority over agriculture in economic planning, and another is that in land reform the goal should be collective rather than individual ownership."[32] Countries that pay insufficient attention to agriculture

---

*The regime that took over the government in Syria toward the end of 1970 negotiated a new agreement with the American oil companies that called for higher transit fees and permitted the reopening of the pipeline in January 1971.

†During the September 1970 civil war in Jordan, Kuwait and Libya suspended their subsidies to Jordan. A few months later Kuwait announced a resumption of its subsidy, but as of December 1970 Libya had made no similar announcement. However, it would appear that there will be increased U.S. aid to Jordan.

create inflationary pressures and serious balance of payments difficulties and aggravate rather than solve their unemployment problem.
Even where financial constraints do not exist, such as in the major
oil-producing countries, the emphasis on industry, especially on heavy
industry, creates grave problems of technical know-how, and because
this industry uses more capital than labor, it fails to provide adequate
employment.

Unemployment statistics are even more deficient than other
data in underdeveloped countries, and the Middle East is no exception.
However, even crude estimates show that unemployment is inordinately
high in most Middle Eastern countries, and underemployment is the
rule rather than the exception. To raise national income and to reduce
unemployment, economic growth must significantly exceed the rate of
population growth—usually 2.5 to 3 percent annually—and must be
directed toward sectors that are labor-intensive, such as agriculture,
textiles, food processing, tourism, and public works.

The contrast between Jordan and Egypt—before 1967—is
instructive. Jordan's economy was far less developed than Egypt's in
1950 and suffered from the kingdom's history of serious political
problems. The government then stressed agriculture, irrigation, light
industry, tourism, and job opportunities in the Persian Gulf area,
fostered private enterprise in various ways, and received large-scale
foreign aid, which it utilized with relative efficiency. Thus, Jordan's
national income increased rapidly, unemployment was significantly
reduced, and most of the refugees were absorbed. On the other hand,
since 1952 Egypt has had political stability, large amounts of foreign
aid, and a relatively large number of academically trained people. The
government imposed rigorous controls, stifled private enterprise, and
overwhelmingly stressed industry, especially heavy industry, but it
failed to raise its overall growth rate significantly. To deal with
unemployment, state-owned enterprises and the government bureaucracy were compelled to employ unneeded workers. It is interesting to
note that since the 1967 War there has been some reappraisal of Egypt's
economic policies, and she now provides more incentives to farmers and
to what remains of the private industrial sector.*

Most Middle Eastern governments have made serious efforts to
raise their nation's education standards, which is no doubt a prerequisite for economic success. However, in some cases the growth of the
economy has lagged seriously behind the increase in the number of
academically trained people and is responsible in part for the growing
"brain drain." Some of the countries have been reappraising their
economic policies, laying greater stress on agriculture, incentives to
private enterprise, and the improvement of human resources. The latest
Iraqi development plan (1970-74) gives priority to agriculture, whereas
the previous plan had stressed industry. The adoption of appropriate
economic policies, a reallocation of resources from war to peace, and a

---

*The Sadat government, inaugurated in the fall of 1970, has apparently adopted even more
liberal economic (and political) policies designed to spur economic development.

greater degree of regional and international cooperation and aid will do much to accelerate economic advancement and to improve the living standards of the people of the Middle East.

Table 3

Economic Growth Rates
(Average Annual Percentage Change for Years Indicated)

	Agriculture[a]	Industry[b]	GNP or GDP[c]	GNP or GDP Per Capita[d]
Arab States				
Egypt[d]	1.6	5.3	4.8	2.2
Iraq	1.1	5.4	6.4	3.5
Syria	2.8	8.9	5.5	2.5
Lebanon[e]	5.8	NA	5.0	2.0
Jordan	7.8	13.9	9.0	6.5
Saudi Arabia	NA	NA	10.1	7.5
Non-Arab Middle Eastern States				
Israel	7.2	11.8	8.4	5.1
Turkey	3.0	8.9	5.4	2.8
Iran	3.3	12.4	7.5	4.6
Developed Countries				
United States	1.0	6.1	4.3	3.0
West Germany	2.0	4.8	5.2	4.8
Italy	3.0	6.9	5.5	4.8

Sources: Saudi Arabian Monetary Agency, *Annual Report 1388-89* (Saudi Arabia).

United Nations, *Yearbook of National Accounts Statistics, 1968 and 1969* (New York: United Nations, 1969 and 1970).

U.S. Agency for International Development, *Gross National Product-Growth Rates and Trend Data* (Washington, D.C.: USAID, April 1970).

U.S. Department of Agriculture, *Indices of Agricultural Production 1960-69 in Africa and the Near East* (Washington, D.C.: U.S. Government Printing Office, April 1970).

U.S. Department of Commerce, *Overseas Business Report: Lebanon* (Washington, D.C.: U.S. Government Printing Office, June 1969).

Notes: The growth rates for agricultural production are derived from the U.S. Department of Agriculture data except for the developed countries' rates, which are based on the United Nations *Yearbook of National Accounts Statistics*.

The growth rates for industrial production came from the *Yearbook of National Accounts Statistics*, computed from the industrial origin of gross domestic product at factor cost, in constant prices. The data for Israel is based on its national accounts. The data for Jordan also came from its national accounts but is not corrected for price changes.

Table 3 (Continued)

The industrial sector includes manufacturing, mining, crude oil production, and sometimes electricity, gas, and water. The following are the growth rates for countries that provide separate data for manufacturing: Iraq, 4.6 percent, and Turkey, 9.1 percent (1960-68); Iran, 12.5 percent (1960-67); Israel, 11.7 percent (1958-68).

The growth rates for gross national product (GNP) in constant prices are from the U.S. Agency for International Development for Israel, Turkey, Jordan, Iran, and the developed countries. For Lebanon the estimate is from the U.S. Department of Commerce *Report*. For Saudi Arabia the estimate is from the Saudi Arabian Monetary Agency *Report*, p. 98. For Egypt, Iraq, and Syria the data refers to gross domestic product (GDP) at factor cost, in constant prices. This differs from GNP insofar as it excludes net factor incomes from abroad and the excess of indirect taxes over subsidies. However, the rates of growth of GNP and GDP are usually very similar.

The International Monetary Fund, *Annual Report 1970*, p. 104, provides more recent data for three Middle Eastern countries. For the 1965-69 period average annual growth rates of GNP at constant prices were: Iran, 9.3 percent; Iraq, 4.6 percent; and Egypt 1.4 percent. This would mean that per capita growth rates were: Iran, 6 to 6.5 percent; Iraq, 1.5 to 2.0 percent; and Egypt, minus 1.4 percent.

Kuwait, Yemen, and the People's Democratic Republic of Yemen have been omitted because data is unavailable or of doubtful reliability.

[a]Agricultural growth rates compare the 1967-69 average with the 1957-59 average, except for the developed countries, which give the average rates for 1960-68.

[b]For industry the years indicated are 1960-68, Iraq, Turkey, and the developed countries; 1960-67, Egypt and Iran; 1959-68, Israel and Jordan; 1963-68, Syria.

[c]For GNP or GDP and per capita GNP and GDP the years are 1959-69, Iran, Israel, Turkey, and the developed countries; 1960-67, Egypt; 1960-68, Iraq; 1959-67, Jordan; 1957-66, Lebanon; 1962/63-1968/69, Saudi Arabia.

[d]The Egyptian data is apparently inflated. See, for example, the Economist Intelligence Unit, *Annual Supplement: Egypt and Sudan*, 1969, p. 6, which states that "there seems to be a tendency to exaggerate the economic achievements of the present regime."

[e]The margin of error for Lebanon is probably greater than for most of the countries in the region. (See the footnote on p. 72.)

Table 4

Selected Economic Indicators

	1969 Population (Millions)	Urban Population as Percentage of Total Population	Life Expectancy (Years)	Primary and Secondary Students as Percentage of 5-19 Age Group	Literacy Rate (Percent)	Estimated GNP Per Capita in U.S. Dollars (1967 or 1968)a	Electric Power Production Per Capita (Kilowatt Hours Per Annum in 1968)
North African Arab States							
Egypt	32.5	38	53	43	30	186	205
Algeria	13.4	38	44	34	25-30	239	101
Libya	1.9	25	37	41	27	1,412	165
Morocco	15.1	32	47	27	14	208	105
Sudan	15.2	8	40	11	10-15	110	25
Tunisia	4.8	40	NA	51	30	225	117
Asian Arab States							
Iraq	9.4	44	NA	38	20	257	174
Syria	6.0	37	30-40	43	35	200	131
Lebanon	2.8	45	NA	47	86	491b	377
Jordan	2.3	44	52	54	35-40	283	68
Saudi Arabia	4.7	28	30-40	12	5-15	444c	109
Kuwait	0.7	99	NA	59	47	3,738	3,074
Yemen	5.7	11	30-40	4	10	100d	NA
People's Democratic Republic of Yemen	1.2	NA	NA	13	NA	200d	NA
Non-Arab Middle Eastern States							
Israel	2.8	82	72	66	90	1,460	2,006
Turkey	34.4	34	53	39	48	380	205
Iran	27.9	31	NA	32	15-20	295	178
United States	203.2	70	71	87	98	4,379	7,100

Table 4 (Continued)

Sources: U.S. Agency for International Development, *Economic Growth Trends: Africa, Near East, and South Asia* (Washington, D.C.: USAID, January 1970).

_____, *Gross National Product-Growth Rates and Trend Data* (Washington, D.C.: USAID, April 1970).

United Nations, *Yearbook of National Accounts Statistics, 1969* (New York: United Nations, 1970).

Notes: All data is from the USAID publication except as noted.

The reader should be aware of the fact that the GNP is converted into dollars at the official exchange rates, which are in most cases artificially fixed by the governments and do not necessarily reflect either international or internal purchasing power. Thus, for example, the official devaluation of the Israeli currency in November 1967 reduced its GNP per capita in U.S. dollars. In reality, GNP per capita was at that time rising rapidly in real terms. Similarly, the official devaluation of the Turkish currency in August 1970 meant that its GNP per capita, expressed in U.S. dollars, declined sharply. In real terms, the Turkish GNP per capita apparently increased in 1970. The data on GNP per capita do provide some rough international comparisons, however.

The data for the percent of urban population usually came from the most recent census and is often outdated. In most of the countries there is a strong rural-to-urban trend, and it can be assumed that more recent data would show higher percentages. Similarly, the rapid growth of the student population has probably increased the literacy rates, which are also usually taken from the most recent census.

[a]The data for GNP per capita are for 1968 for the United States, Libya, Morocco, Sudan, Tunisia, Iran, Israel, and Turkey. The estimate is for 1967 for Algeria, Iraq, Jordan, Kuwait, Lebanon, Saudi Arabia, the People's Democratic Republic of Yemen, Syria, and Yemen. The estimate for Egypt is for the fiscal year 1967/68.

[b]The estimate for GNP per capita for Lebanon comes from the United Nations *Yearbook of National Accounts Statistics*; USAID estimates $633. (See the footnote on p. 72.)

[c]The GNP per capita given for Saudi Arabia is the one estimated by USAID. The United Nations *Yearbook of National Accounts Statistics* offers an estimate of $351. The large difference stems from the lack of reasonably accurate population data. See, for example, United Nations, *Studies on Selected Development Problems in Various Countries in the Middle East,* p. 152, and U.S. Department of Labor, *Labor Developments Abroad* (Washington, D.C.: U.S. Government Printing Office, August 1969), p. 1. It would appear that the estimate offered by USAID is more reliable.

[d]The GNP per capita estimates for Yemen and the People's Democratic Republic of Yemen should be taken as very rough approximations.

Table 5

Agriculture

	Agricultural Land Per Capita (Acres)[a]	Percentage of Labor Force in Agriculture[a]	Percentage of National Income or GNP Derived from Agriculture[a]	Index of Agricultural Production[b]	Index of Agricultural Production Per Capita[b]
Arab States					
Egypt	0.2	52	28-30	117	91
Iraq	3.3	48	20	116	87
Syria	4.8	60	25-28	132	99
Lebanon	0.3	55	12	176	135
Jordan	1.5	35	20-25	211	156
Non-Arab Middle Eastern States					
Israel	1.1	12	8-9	200	146
Turkey	3.8	68	32-34	135	104
Iran	1.6	47	21	139	105

Sources: U.S. Agency for International Development, *Economic Growth Trends: Africa, Near East, and South Asia* (Washington, D.C.: USAID, January 1970).

U.S. Department of Agriculture, *Indices of Agricultural Production 1960-69 in Africa and the Near East* (Washington, D.C.: U.S. Government Printing Office, April 1970).

[a]The data for agricultural land per capita, the percentage of the labor force, and the share of national income or gross national product derived from agriculture are for the latest available dates, which are not necessarily the same years. The share of the labor force in agriculture is usually for the latest census date and may be outdated; generally, one can assume that it is somewhat, but not much, lower. It also appears that the high percentage of the labor force in agriculture is partly attributable to the inclusion of part-time and seasonal workers. However, the wide gap between the share of the labor force in agriculture and agriculture's share of national income or GNP reflects the much lower per capita incomes in the agricultural than in other sectors.

[b]1967-69 average as compared with 1957-59 average, defined as equal to 100. Since there are frequently wide fluctuations in agricultural production, three-year periods are used both for the base years and for more recent years.

Table 6

Petroleum

	Production (In Millions of Metric Tons)		Average Annual Growth Rate (Percent)		Share of World Oil Production (Percent)	Oil Revenues in Millions of U.S. Dollars	
	1959	1969	1959-1969	1964-1969	1969	1964	1969
Iran	46	168	13.8	14.5	7.8	475	938
Iraq	42	75	6.0	4.0	3.5	353	483
Saudi Arabia	54	149	10.5	11.5	6.9	561	1,008
Kuwait	70	130	6.5	4.0	6.0	655	812
Algeria	1	45	43.5	11.0	2.1*	140	250
Libya	NA	150	NA	29.5	7.0	197	1,132
Other Middle East and North Africa	19	113	19.5	23	5.3		
Total Middle East and North Africa	233	828	13.5	12.7	38.6		
United States	382	515	3.3	4.3	24.0		
Soviet Union	130	328	9.8	8.0	15.3		
Venezuela	144	189	2.8	1.5	8.8		
World Production	1,012	2,145	7.8	8.0			
World Oil Exports	401	1,123					
Middle East and North African Exports	208	771					

Sources: British Petroleum Company, *Statistical Review of the World Oil Industry, 1969* (London: British Petroleum, 1970).

Economist Intelligence Unit, *Annual Supplement: Middle East Oil, 1969, 1970* (London: *Economist Intelligence Unit,* 1970).

Notes: The other Middle Eastern producers in 1969 were (in millions of metric tons): Abu Dhabi, 29; Neutral Zone, 23; Qatar, 17; Egypt, 15; Tunisia, 3; Turkey, 4; Oman, 16; Bahrayn, 4; Syria, 2. Abu Dhabi received $191 million in oil payments in 1969 and Oman, $74 million.

Other countries in the area derived revenues for pipelines through their territory, and until June 1967 the bulk of Egypt's fees for passage through the Suez Canal was from oil tankers. Egypt received $219 million in 1966. Pipeline transit payments in 1969 were (in millions of dollars): Jordan, 4; Syria, 57; and Lebanon, 13. The latter were lower than in 1968 as a result of the closure of Tapline for about four months in 1969. Tapline was again closed in March 1970, and Syrian authorities refused to permit its reopening until January 1971.

*1965

Table 7

Foreign Trade

	Ratio of Exports to Imports (Percent of Goods and Services)	Principal Exports (Goods and Services)
Arab States		
Egypt (1964/65-1966/67)	81.4	Cotton, cotton textiles, rice (Suez Canal dues and tourism before June 1967)
Iraq (1962-65)	109.9	Oil, dates, cement, other agricultural products
Syria (1963-67)	83.4	Cotton, agricultural products, textiles, oil transit dues
Lebanon (1964-65)	56.2	Fruits and vegetables, industrial products, tourism, financial and trading services
Jordan (1963-67)	59.9	Phosphates, tomatoes, tourism, remittances
Saudi Arabia	NA	Oil, pilgrimage
Kuwait (1963-67)	177.6	Oil, shrimp
Yemen	NA	Coffee, cotton, other agricultural products
People's Democratic Republic of Yemen	NA	Petroleum products (Aden refinery)
Non-Arab Middle Eastern States		
Israel (1963-67)	59.4	Diamonds, various industrial products, citrus and other agricultural products, tourism
Turkey	NA	Cotton, tobacco, various agricultural products, minerals, remittances
Iran (1963-67)	98.8	Oil, minerals, carpets, cotton, various agricultural products

Sources: Economist Intelligence Unit, *Annual Supplements* (London: *Economist Intelligence Unit,* 1969).

International Monetary Fund, *International Financial Statistics* (Washington, D.C.: International Monetary Fund).

United Nations, *Yearbook of National Accounts, 1968* (New York: United Nations, 1969).

U.S. Department of Commerce, *Overseas Business Reports* (Washington, D.C.: U.S. Government Printing Office).

Other government and Central Bank reports.

Footnotes

[1] Economist Intelligence Unit, *Iraq*, no. 1 (London: *Economist Intelligence Unit*, 1970), p. 8.

[2] See Richard A. Easterlin, "Israel's Development: Past Accomplishments and Future Problems," *Quarterly Journal of Economics* 75 (1961):63-86.

[3] International Bank for Reconstruction and Development, *The Economic Development of Jordan* (Baltimore: Johns Hopkins Press, 1957), p. 3.

[4] D. R. Campbell, "Jordan: The Economics of Survival," *International Journal* 23, no. 1 (1967-68):122.

[5] U.S. Department of Commerce, *Overseas Business Report: Lebanon* (Washington, D.C.: U.S. Government Printing Office, June 1969).

[6] United Nations, *Yearbook of National Accounts Statistics, 1968* (New York: United Nations, 1969).

[7] Banque Centrale de Syrie, *Bulletin Périodique*, septième année, numéro 16, 1969, p. 7.

[8] Charles Issawi, *Egypt in Revolution* (New York: Oxford University Press, 1963), p. 55.

[9] U.S. Department of Agriculture, *Agricultural Development and Expansion in the Nile Basin* (Washington, D.C.: U.S. Government Printing Office, October 1968), pp. 41-43.

[10] Economist Intelligence Unit, *Annual Supplement: Egypt and Sudan* (London: *Economist Intelligence Unit*, 1969), p. 8.

[11] Economist Intelligence Unit, *Annual Supplement: Iran* (London: *Economist Intelligence Unit*, 1969), pp. 7-8.

[12] Fuad Baali, "Agrarian Reform in Iraq," *American Journal of Economics and Sociology* 28, no. 1 (January 1969):61-76; John L. Simmons, "Agricultural Development in Iraq: Planning and Management Failures," *Middle East Journal* 19, no. 2 (Spring 1965): 129-40.

[13] U.S. Department of Agriculture, *Turkey's Agricultural Economy in Brief* (Washington, D.C : U.S. Government Printing Office, April 1970), p. 4.

[14] See Orville J. McDiarmid, "Japan and Israel," *Finance and Development,* publication of the International Bank for Reconstruction and Development and the International Monetary Fund, June 1966.

[15] *Middle East Economic Digest,* April 26, 1968, p. 361.

[16] See National Bank of Egypt, *Economic Bulletin* 22, no. 3 (1969), statistical section 3.

[17] For a fuller discussion see Kanovsky, "Arab Economic Unity."

[18] *Middle East Economic Digest,* July 11, 1969, p. 877.

[19] *Middle East Economic Digest,* December 12, 1969, pp. 1525-26, 1546.

[20] For a fuller discussion of the problems of economic integration in developing countries see Yu Min Chou, "Economic Integration in Less Developed Countries: The Case of Small Countries," *Journal of Development Studies,* July 1967.

[21] See *Economist,* December 3, 1966, p. 1060; *Wall Street Journal,* November 15, 1966, p. 4; *Monthly Survey of Arab Economies* (Beirut), January 1960, p. 13.

[22] For a fuller discussion of the Arab economic boycott see the *New York Times,* October 17, 1966, pp. 1, 16; *Business Week*, August 23, 1969, pp. 80, 82.

[23] Economist Intelligence Unit, *Egypt and Sudan* (London: *Economist Intelligence Unit,* July 1970), pp. 5-6.

[24] International Monetary Fund, *Annual Report 1970* (Washington, D.C.: International Monetary Fund, 1970), p. 104.

[25] For a detailed discussion of the impact of the war on these countries see Kanovsky, *Economic Impact of the Six Day War.*

[26] See Eliyahu Kanovsky, "The Economic Aftermath of the Six-Day War: UAR, Jordan, and Syria," *Middle East Journal* 22, nos. 1 and 2 (Spring and Summer 1968).

[27] U.S. Department of Commerce, *International Commerce,* January 13, 1969, p. 51; January 6, 1970, p. 53.

[28] *Middle East Economic Digest,* September 25, 1970, p. 1130.

[29] U.S. Department of Commerce, *International Commerce,* June 29, 1970, p. 50; *Foreign Economic Trends: Lebanon,* September 15, 1969, pp. et 69-116.

[30] *Monthly Survey of Arab Economies* (Beirut), July 1970, pp. 46-50.

[31] Economist Intelligence Unit, *Syria, Lebanon, Cyprus* (London: *Economist Intelligence Unit,* August 1970), pp. 10-11.

[32] Issawi, "The Strategy of Land Problems and Policies in the Economy of the Middle East."

Selected Bibliography

Diab, M. A. *Inter-Arab Economic Cooperation, 1951-60.* Beirut: American University of Beirut, 1963.
A study of the agreements regarding trade and payments, the decisions to establish joint enterprises, and their implementation. See especially the summary chapter, pp. 87-89.

Economist Intelligence Unit. *Quarterly Economic Review* and the *Annual Supplement.* London: *Economist Intelligence Unit.*
Brief political and economic surveys (*Annual Supplements*) and information on current developments (*Quarterly Economic Review*), for various countries, individually or in groups.

Issawi, Charles. "The Strategy of Land Problems and Policies in the Economy of the Middle East." *Middle East Economic Forum* 20, no. 2 (1966):17-25.
An analysis of the socialization and land-reform programs in various Middle Eastern countries.

Kanovsky, Eliyahu. "Arab Economic Unity." *Middle East Journal* 21, no. 2 (Spring 1967).
A study of the prospects for and obstacles to inter-Arab economic cooperation, focusing on the 1965 Arab Common Market.

———. *The Economic Impact of the Six-Day War: Israel and the Occupied Territories, Egypt and Jordan.* New York: Frederick A. Praeger, 1970.
Economic development problems before and after the 1967 War.

Stocking, G. W. *Middle East Oil.* Nashville, Tenn.: Vanderbilt University Press, 1970.
Development of Middle Eastern oil and the changing relationship between Western oil companies and local governments.

United Nations. *Industrial Development in the Arab Countries.* New York: United Nations, 1967.
Selected documents that were presented to the Symposium on Industrial Development in the Arab Countries in Kuwait, March 1966. Focuses on industry in the Asian Arab countries and on inter-Arab cooperation in the industrial sphere.

———. *Studies on Selected Development Problems in Various Countries in the Middle East.* Beirut: United Nations, Department for Economic and Social Affairs, 1970.
Analysis of development plans and socioeconomic problems in the Asian Arab countries; annual since 1967; includes current statistical data.

U.S. Department of Agriculture. *Agricultural Economy in Brief.* Washington, D.C.: U.S. Government Printing Office.
Published annually for individual countries, including most of the Middle Eastern states. Describes the structure and problems of the agricultural sector and provides some current data.

———. *The Africa and West Asia Agricultural Situation.* Washington, D.C.: U.S. Government Printing Office.
Published annually; provides current statistical data for each country and brief explanations.

———. *Economic Progress of Agriculture in Developing Nations, 1950-68.* Washington, D.C.: U.S. Government Printing Office, May 1970.
A study of the progress of fifty-four developing countries in improving agricultural output and productivity during the 1950s and 1960s, including most Middle Eastern states.

U.S. Department of Commerce. *Basic Data on the Economy*. Washington, D.C.: U.S. Government Printing Office.

Published annually for individual countries, including most of the Middle Eastern states. Provides brief surveys of the economy.

U.S. Department of Labor. *Labor Law and Practice*. Washington, D.C.: U.S. Government Printing Office.

Published for most of the Middle Eastern states. Provides good surveys of the economy, including the political background, education and health standards, the labor force, and conditions of employment.

Ward, J. W. "The Long-Run Employment Prospects for Middle East Labor." *Middle East Journal* 24, no. 2 (Spring 1970).

The current employment and unemployment situation in a number of Middle Eastern states, including the territories occupied by Israel in June 1967.

Political Thought

The Search for an Ideology

As in other regions of the world, ideological development in the Middle East is closely related to social and political crises. This chapter traces the emergence of various ideologies in the crisis milieu that has prevailed in the area since late Ottoman times. The chapter treats briefly the role of ideology in political development and focuses on the evolution and content of contemporary Middle Eastern political thought.

In a general sense, a political ideology consists of the norms, values, and beliefs that are inculcated into a particular society. These in turn shape an individual's attitudes toward the external world and equip him with a conceptual medium to help him interpret his environment and his role in the social process. It includes both a plan of action and the means to execute it.

Ideology plays a number of roles in society. To its followers it provides identity and a sense of belonging. It also creates cohesion and solidarity in society. Last, but not least, ideology is used by political elites as a tool to maximize compliance and legitimize their leadership.

Origins of Ideological Ferment

The contemporary ideological ferment in the Middle East can be traced to the erosion of traditional Islam and the concomitant decline in Ottoman imperial power during the last century. The Ottomans' manifest inability to check the growing European ascendancy in the Middle East gave rise to Ottomanism and Pan-Islamism, which were designed to reform the imperial system and its Islamic ideological substructure. This reformist phase was a response to the deep crisis situation in the Ottoman-Islamic realm; it aimed at selectively modernizing the imperial system in order to preserve it.

Ottomanism and Pan-Islamism

Because of the nature of the Ottoman-European confrontation, ideological development within the empire was strongly influenced by the prevailing political thought and practices of the West; in view of the European states' successes in nation building, industrialization, and military affairs, the Western experience constituted a powerful model. Sultans and statesmen sought to selectively adopt those portions of the Western success formula that were compatible with the Islamic social and political reality. At the outset these borrowings consisted only of superficial aspects of the Western experience and resulted in military modernization, the haphazard emulation of constitutional processes, and diplomatic reforms. Subsequently, attention focused on the ideological underpinnings of the Western model, specifically the values and beliefs that made up Western nationalism, and during the nineteenth century nationalism spread infectiously among the Christian minorities of the empire—notably the Greeks and Armenians. Soon nationalism appeared among Muslim Ottomans as well—Egyptians, Turks, Albanians, Arabs, and Kurds. Thus, two main lines of political thought, Ottomanism and Pan-Islamism, emerged as reformist ideologies designed to breathe new life into the faltering empire.

Ottomanism encompassed a political program of Westernization and liberalization that found its expression in the Tanzimat reforms and Midhat Pasha's constitution of 1876. It bore the clear imprint of Western liberal constitutional thought, especially in its focus on equality, judicial reform, and the fair treatment of the non-Muslim minorities. However, the accession of Sultan Abdul Hamid II brought the liberal aspects of the Ottomanist experiment to an abrupt halt, and in the repressive political climate that ensued, the various indigenous nationalisms of the empire found new impetus. Increasingly, Abdul Hamid associated himself with the ideological tenets of Pan-Islamism, a noted proponent of which was Shaykh Jamal al-Din al-Afghani.

Pan-Islamism preached a return to the historic unit of the Islamic community; it aimed at reinvigorating the Islamic ethos through a united movement headed by the sultan-caliph. Ultimately, the Pan-Islamists expected to threaten the British hold on Indian Muslims and to strengthen the position of Abdul Hamid vis-à-vis the European imperialist powers. In terms of modernization, they were primarily interested in emulating the West's scientific and technological achievements rather than its social and political institutions and theories.

The Young Turk revolution of 1908 brought an end to the sultan's despotic rule in the name of liberal Ottomanism. Yet during the three decades of Abdul Hamid's rule, when Ottomanism was in abeyance, a number of significant ideological movements developed (see figure 1), setting the stage for the modern era of Middle Eastern politics.

Pan-Turkism

The rise of minority nationalism, encouraged by the despotism of Hamid's regime, contributed to the gradual emergence of Turkish nationalism during the second half of the nineteenth century. One of its most eloquent proponents was the emigré journalist Ahmet Riza—a follower of August Comte's positivist philosophy and a persistent foe of the sultan's repressive policies. As a humanist, Riza propounded a nationalism devoid of militancy and pursued within the general framework of Ottomanism. Despite the wide respect he enjoyed as a founding member of the Young Turk party, Riza's brand of Turkish nationalism, tempered by positivist constitutionalism, did not prevail in the post revolutionary period. His campaign against the sultan had inspired the 1908 revolution, but the actual takeover of power was the work of a small group of young army officers who did not share Riza's humanistic ideals. Military reverses in Libya and the Balkans and internal instability further strengthened the militarists' hand, and the brief constitutional period after 1908 consequently proved unsuccessful. The Young Turks' promises of reform went unfulfilled.

The militarists' ideology centered on Pan-Turkism (Turanism). By origin, Pan-Turkism was not an indigenously Ottoman doctrine but one imported from Russia. Its first ideologues were the intellectuals of the large Turkish communities in Russia and central Asia, who had begun to resist the political and cultural imperialism of the czars. Their most notable representative was Yusef Akçura (Akçuraoglu), whose writings had great impact on political thought and action in the Ottoman Empire. Based on the historical findings of Hungarian and French Turkologists, the new ideology recreated myths and symbols of past Turkic unity as bases for a future Pan-Turkish state.

In their quest for a counterweight to Russian power, the Pan-Turkists strove to redirect the focus of the Young Turk movement from Ottomanism and Pan-Islamism to Pan-Turkism. Because Pan-Turkism was espoused at a time of crisis and disintegration, it spread rapidly; an early convert was Ziya Gokalp, whose theoretical writings made him the foremost idealogue of Pan-Turkism in official circles. After 1910 the leadership of the Young Turk party was captured by adherents of Pan-Turkism—Enver, Talat, Nazim, Shakir—who subsequently took over the imperial government. The Pan-Turkism of these men was strongly influenced by German nationalism; indeed, the successful German nation-building experience had a powerful impact on the ideology and practice of the entire Young Turk party.

Pan-Turkism was a far cry from Ahmet Riza's peaceful brand of Turkish nationalism. In practice, the new creed meant the Turkification

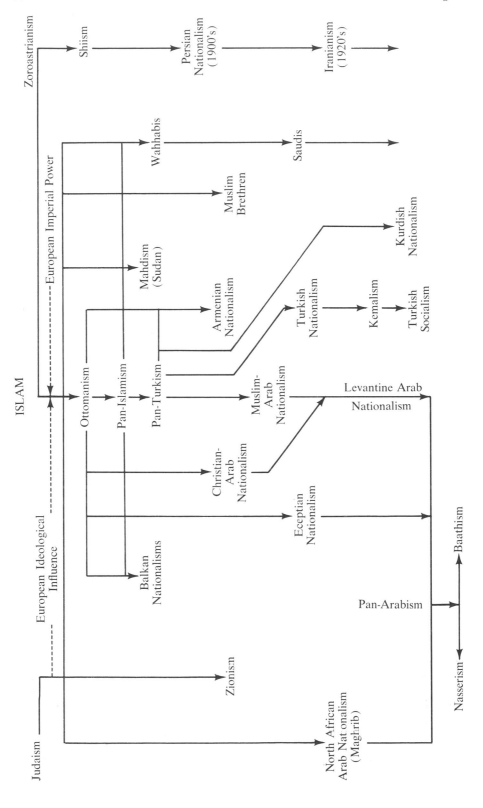

of the language by purging Arabic and Persian terms and a concomitant intellectual concern with the pre-Ottoman Turkish past. The Pan-Turkist leaders imposed a centralized dictatorship by suppressing Turkish liberal groups and ethnic minority movements, and in this context the imperial government began to pursue a policy of Turkification with respect to its non-Turkish subjects, regardless of their religious affiliation. As a direct consequence, three of the main component groups of the empire—the Arabs, Armenians, and Kurds—were permanently alienated. The pervasive German influence among the elite and the anti-Russian orientation of Pan-Turkism caused the Young Turks to enter the war on the German side. During the war years the ideological commitment to Pan-Turkism produced Enver Pasha's abortive Pan-Turanist March against Russia, the liquidation of Christian minorities, and the oppression of the Arabs in Syria and Lebanon.

The Search for Ideology

The dissolution of the Ottoman Empire signaled the beginning of a new phase in the search for ideology. For the Turks themselves, the quest for a new nationalism culminated in the adoption of Kemalism.

Kemalism

The defeat of the German-led Ottoman armies in World War I led to the occupation of the empire by the Allies and the Greek incursion into eastern Anatolia, and the war's aftermath found the Young Turk leaders in flight and their Pan-Turkist ideology discredited. Faced with the prospect of large-scale territorial contraction, a nationalist movement sprang up in the unoccupied Anatolian interior around General Mustafa Kemal Ataturk. One of the few genuine heroes of the war, this former Young Turk officer had been at odds with the ruling Pan-Turkist elites, who had kept him away from the seats of power. Armed with a message of Turkish national survival and with Russian Bolshevik financial and military support, Ataturk was able to defeat both the Greek invasion in the west and the Armenian republic in the east, thereby ensuring Turkish preponderance over all of Anatolia. Soon after victory Ataturk promulgated a comprehensive program of reform in an effort to create a modernized Turkey, and he presided over the decisive reversal from Pan-Turkism to Turkish nationalism.

In contrast to the Pan-Turkists, who dreamed about a central Asian empire, Ataturk's nationalism focused exclusively on Anatolia, which also contributed to the normalization of relations with the Soviet Union. After victory he was concerned primarily with strengthening Turkish ties to the land, reinterpreting Turkish and Middle Eastern history to do it. He identified the Turks with the early inhabitants of Anatolia—the Sumerians and the Hittites—and despite its lack of authenticity, he considered this enterprise politically necessary to provide Turkish nationalism with historical roots.

An inseparable component of Ataturk's Turkish nationalism was reform aimed at establishing a modern nation-state unburdened by the shackles of the Ottoman past. As far as Ataturk was concerned, a clean break was imperative not only from Pan-Turkism but also from the whole archaic complex of Ottoman institutions and processes. He thus abolished the sultanate in favor of populist republicanism and terminated the caliphate to develop a secular state, republicanism and secularism became two basic tenets of the Kemalist ideology. What followed was major reform aimed at the "de-Islamization" and "de-Ottomanization" of society based on the Western model. It included discarding the veil and the fez, reforming the Turkish language, and secularizing education. Kemalism's final component was etatism, only a degree of private enterprise was permitted, and the state was assigned the major role in Turkey's economic development.

These changes were tantamount to disestablishing the traditional Ottoman-Islamic system and eliminating its pervasive influence on education, politics, law and social life. Because of Ataturk's great charismatic appeal and influence, his reformist program became the official ideology of the Turkish state. However, not all of Ataturk's ideological legacy survived his death. Whereas Kemalism remains modern Turkey's official ideology, the advent of the Democratic party in 1950 brought together commercial and capitalist interests, traditionalist landowners, peasants, and religious conservatives. Under the Democratic party's rule the private sector was strengthened and Islam revived against a background of increasing repression. However, the military takeover of May 1960 brought back Kemalist principles amid a freer atmosphere, in which a number of new ideological trends became discernible (see figure 1).

One of the most significant of these ideological movements was the Turkish Left. It included two distinct groupings—the *Yön* group and the Turkish Worker's party. The first group consisted of highly educated intellectuals (such as professors and journalists) who were in search of a socialistic solution to Turkey's serious economic and political problems. The Turkish Worker's party was less elitist and more politically oriented. In addition to advocating state socialism, the Turkish Left preached a policy of neutralism based on withdrawal from NATO and improvement of relations with the Soviet Union.

The Republican People's party of Inonu adopted some aspects of the leftists' ideological program during its brief tenure in the early sixties, but with the electoral victory of the Justice party in 1965 the conservative ideology of the defunct Democratic party was partially revived. Thus, during the late sixties the Left (workers, students, intellectuals) and the Right (students, clerics) appeared ideologically polarized amid bloody clashes and growing anti-American sentiment. The prospects for ideological consensus for the seventies remain unpromising, and the search for a viable ideology will continue in the aftermath of the March 1971 military coup.

Iranian Nationalism

In many ways Ataturk was Reza Shah's model for transforming Iran—a country that fell outside the Ottoman realm. After forcibly uniting the country in the early twenties, he faced the creation of an Iranian national identity among a heterogeneous population of Persians, Azaris, Kurds, and other minorities. In 1925 he established a royal dictatorship by proclaiming himself shah. The name he chose for the new dynasty—Pahlavi, the name of the ancient Zoroastrian language— symbolized Reza's attempts to construct a new ideology embodying the early glories of the Persian civilization. Thus, the new nationalism was given historical anchors and a specific content and was based on the pre-Islamic Parthian and Persian past (the Achaemenids and Sassanids) and the Zoroastrian-Aryan tradition (see figure 1). One of the shah's aims was to use the new ideology to combat the entrenched influence of Shiite Muslim clerics. Iranianism also included a program of modernization, including the discarding of veils and rapid economic development, in keeping with the shah's admiration for the West's economic and technological progress. However, Reza Shah's reformist policies were less successful than Ataturk's because he lacked systematic planning and an able bureaucracy, and the shah's rule was heavy handed. Tribalism and the heterogeneity of the population also impeded modernization.

A number of other ideologies came to the fore after Reza Shah's exile and the Allied occupation in 1941. On the conservative side were various traditionalist groups, notably the Pan-Iranians and the Fedayan-e-Islam. On the extreme left was the once-powerful Tudeh party, which had close affinities to orthodox Marxism and the Soviet Union. (Since its suppression in 1953 it has gone underground.) Moreover, the liberal constitutionalists supported the establishment of a constitutionalist monarchy; Ahmad Kasravi (1890-1946), for instance, advocated anti-imperialist nationalism and liberalism in the context of a Zoroastrian revival. In recent years the younger Reza Shah has pursued a modernization program of his own, a major aspect of which is distribution of land to the peasants. In view of the shah's seriousness in pursuing these goals, agrarian reform might be considered the latest addition to the ideology of Iranianism.

Arab Nationalism

Several main currents and phases are discernible in the chronological study of contemporary Arab nationalist thought. Between the Lebanese crisis of 1861 and Algerian independence in 1962, these diverse components of Arab nationalism began to converge into a single ideological complex known as Arabism or Pan-Arabism, a synthesis that is still in progress.

The earliest nationalist trend emerged among Arab Christian intellectuals in Lebanon, spurred by repressive Ottoman policies,

European intellectual and political thought, and Western schools, especially the Syrian Protestant College (later renamed the American University of Beirut). With the advent of Sultan Abdul Hamid's Pan-Islamism, Arab Christian nationalism intensified and assumed an increasingly pro-French orientation.

Although these Levantine Christian Arabs exercised a lasting influence on subsequent Arab nationalist thought, in terms of political action the nationalist awakening of Muslim Arabs was more significant because of their numerical and political preponderance. The appearance of Muslim Arab nationalism had lagged behind Christian Arab nationalism primarily because of the differing positions of the two groups within the empire. Abdul Hamid's revival of the Pan-Islamic ethos, which alienated the Christians, left the Muslim Arabs relatively satisfied. Not until the rise of Pan-Turkism did Muslim Arabs begin to react; the policy of Turkification ultimately threatened to replace Arabic with Turkish. Perceiving the danger to their national existence, the Muslim Arabs began to identify themselves with the main tenets of Arab nationalism, and Muslims and Christians came together for united action against the Turks. The Young Turk appeal for a *jihad* (holy war) at the outset of World War I therefore failed to rouse the Muslim Arabs, and the Arab revolt—supported by the British—was born amid Jemal Pasha's suppression and hanging of Arab nationalist leaders in Syria and Lebanon.

The ultimate aim of every nationalist ideology is the creation of a sovereign, independent nation-state based on shared traditions, language, and culture, and Arab nationalism was no exception. Christian and Muslim Arabs were united primarily by their opposition to Ottoman rule. Other components of unity included the Arabic language and the past glories of Arab civilization. Dividing the Arabs was religion; Christians were wary of their minority position in a future Arab state dominated by Muslims, and the proclamations of Sharif Husayn, the leader of the Arab revolt who wanted to resurrect an Arab caliphate, did not enjoy wide support among Christian Arabs.

Because Britain, France, and the United States supported the Arabs during the war, Arab nationalist thought evolved in a pro-Western direction. However, postwar Anglo-French reluctance to fulfill their promises of independence to the Arabs caused the reversal of the pro-Western trend. The subsequent establishment of the mandate system, coupled with Anglo-French-American support for the Zionist cause, made anti-Westernism a basic component of contemporary Arab nationalist ideology and practice. Further, the arbitrary division of the Arab East into separate mandates introduced the idea of Arab unity, or Pan-Arabism, into the emerging ideology.

Arab opposition to the Anglo-French imperial system did not at first include the United States. Indeed, President Wilson's policy of self-determination had left a favorable impression on the Arabs, as indicated by the King-Crane Commission reports issued soon after World War I (1919). U.S. support of the establishment of the state of Israel in 1948 marked the reversal of pro-American nationalism, and by the late sixties the U.S. had become a major villain to virtually every branch of the Arab nationalist movement.

Somewhat less enduring was the brief pro-Axis phase of Arab nationalism, which developed in the 1930s. In German and Italian ascendancy the Arabs saw a welcome counterweight to Anglo-French rule and influence. Especially in Egypt, Syria, Iraq, and Palestine the Italian-German appeals against the Allies found receptive audiences. For polities emerging from the despotic-authoritarian structure of the Ottoman state, the philosophies of Fichte, Hegel, and Mazzini were more comprehensible than those of Locke, Montesquieu, and Mill. Also, the successful nation building of the two Axis powers constituted an attractive model for Arabs. Despite such influences, however, Arab nationalist ideology remained singularly void of the racist tendencies of the Nazis.

Egyptian Nationalism

The emergence of Arab nationalism in Syria was accompanied by the parallel development of an indigenous nationalism in the Nile valley (see figure 1). This appearance of nationalism in a land that had been continuously ruled by foreigners since the last pharaoh was destined to have considerable impact on Middle Eastern politics.

Not until the Napoleonic conquest was the Egyptian province of the Ottoman Empire exposed to European influences. With the advent of Muhammad Ali modernization was accelerated, yet he and his descendants constituted a continuation of foreign rule with a military-bureaucratic structure consisting of Turks, Circassians, Armenians, and Europeans. Indigenous opposition assumed a number of configurations. One was the Islamic reformist movement centered on Cairo's Al-Azhar University and led by renowned Pan-Islamists Jamal al-Din al-Afghani and Muhammad Abduh. Another trend was the puritanical fundamentalist Mahdism of the Sudan, the origins of which went back to the Wahhabis of Arabia. So great was the military and religious fervor of the Mahdists that their state survived for almost eighteen years before a combined British and Egyptian force under Sir Herbert Kitchener subdued it. Finally, there was the nationalism of Egyptian soldiers and intellectuals led by Ahmad Urabi Pasha, which culminated in the revolution of 1882.

Urabi Pasha's seizure of power symbolized Egyptian opposition to the foreign military and political elites of the Muhammad Ali dynasty and the pervasive influence of Europeans in Egypt. His diverse supporters did not possess a cohesive, well-defined ideology beyond the general tenets of Pan-Islamism, yet the subsequent Egyptian defeat, which ushered in the long British occupation, crystallized the nascent nationalist movement. Under Mustafa Kamil (1874-1908) Egyptian nationalism began to manifest strong secular fervor independent of Pan-Islamism.

The search for ideology, for a new system of values and beliefs, begins when the existing value system of a society begins to erode. This search is essentially a quest by individuals and groups for identity—an identity that reflects present conditions and values to replace the identity lost by the erosion of traditional values. During the late nineteenth and early twentieth centuries, the Egyptians awakened from long lethargy and initiated a tortuous search for identity that culminated in the advent of Nasserism.

Initially, the Egyptian intellectual knew only that he was born in Egypt. In the alien world of competing nation-states, the reidentification with a cross-national Islamic community that Pan-Islamism offered seemed increasingly irrelevant, and as European intellectual, political, and economic influences intensified in the face of declining Islam, the question of personal and national identity became acute. Egyptians had to decide whether they were Ottomans, Arabs, or pharaonics—a question that remained unanswered until the new intellectual elite rediscovered the Egyptian past and related it to the Egyptian present.

Because of the powerful French and British intellectual influences, the early phase of Egyptian nationalist thought assumed a Western, liberal-rational orientation. However, the rationalist, secular nature of the European nation-state model brought the proponents of Westernization into conflict with Islam. Therefore, if an Egyptian nationality was to be created, the historical concept of the Muslim ummah would have to be revised and the Islamic religion separated from the state. The thinkers who initiated this significant transformation included Ali Abd al-Raziq, Ahmad Amin, Abbas Mahmud al-Acqad, Taha Husayn, and Tawfiq al-Hakim. They argued that Islam had been used by the Umayyad and Abbasid rulers as an ideology of conquest to impose unity upon the newly Islamized lands. In a radical rejection of Egypt's Arab past, these intellectuals regarded the Arabs as subjugators of the Egyptian people. As a consequence of the dissociation of Egyptian reality from its traditional Arabist moorings, a new Egyptian national identity emerged. Under the intellectual leadership of Lutfi al-Sayyid, Egyptian nationalism was given a specific cultural personality with the revival of the pharaonic past and the Greco-Roman and Coptic-Christian heritage.

The pharaonic trends in Egyptian nationalism soon began to recede under the impact of conditions emerging in the thirties and forties, which included the growing alienation of Egypt's intelligentsia from the West European model of social and political development. The Egyptian experience with the constitutionalist-royalist regime after 1923 had been particularly disappointing in the context of the persistent struggle between the palace, the dominant Wafd party, and the British residency. The resulting reaction to the Westernist-pharaonic phase was a reversion to the reformist Islamic precepts of al-Afghani, Abduh, and Rashid Rida. Led by Muhammad Husayn Haykal—a former Westernist intellectual the anti-Westernists opposed secularism and rejected virtually everything Western except science and technology.

However, Haykal's Pan-Islamic notion of a divinely ordained unity did not constitute a viable ideological formulation. Indeed, no great sentiment to unite for the common cause existed among non-Arab Muslims. Only in the Arab realm could one detect the beginnings of a genuine Islamic revivalism that could reinforce the religious ties between Egyptians and other Arabic-speaking peoples in the Levant and North Africa. In this sense the Islamic revivalism of the thirties and forties worked against Egypt's exclusivism and isolationism from the Arabs and thereby strengthened the bonds among the Arab states in preparation for the subsequent phase of ideological development—Arab unity, or Pan-Arabism. At the level of the masses the strength of the revivalist movement was manifested in the emergence of the Ikhwan al-Muslimin—the Muslim Brotherhood—who advocated a fundamentalist, puritanical Islamic doctrine in the realm of politics.

The economic aspects of Egyptian liberal democracy also came under attack. The misery of the masses was blamed on the large landowners and emerging capitalists, who were identified with the existing power structure. The Western model of capitalist development was considered too materialistic, and the atheistic aspect of Marxism rendered it an unacceptable alternative. Under these circumstances, Shaykh Muhammad al-Ghazzali proposed a theory of Islamic socialism based on a reapplication of early Muslim social and economic practices. Essentially, this concept represented the Muslim Brotherhood's ideological position regarding the socioeconomic reorganization of Egyptian society.

Pan-Arabism: Nasserism and Baathism

On the eve of the 1952 revolution ideological evolution had not reached its culmination; the revolution carried out in the name of Egyptian nationalism lacked a detailed philosophy. The revolutionary officers came from diverse ideological backgrounds reflecting the variety of intellectual currents in mid-twentieth century Egypt. Thus, despite the takeover of power, the crisis among intellectuals continued without a consensus on a social and political philosophy. Only in the late fifties, after seventy years of intellectual, social, and political ferment, were the beginnings of an ideology discernible. Significantly, the culminators of this search were neither the ulama nor the intellectuals but young army officers led by Gamal Abdul Nasser.

Because of Nasser's primary role in the formation of Egyptian ideology, the new ideological complex is often referred to as Nasserism. One of its major components is Pan-Arabism, which was first propounded by the Syria-based Baath party. Nasser's commitment to Pan-Arabism and his leading role in that movement have had wide repercussions in Egypt and the entire Arab world.

Egyptian nationalism had developed independently of the Arab nationalism of the Levantine provinces. Identification with the Arab ethos had been opposed by the Western-oriented intellectuals of the

pharaonic era and by the political leadership under Prime Minister Saad
Zaghlul. Arab nationalist intellectual trends made their appearance in
Egypt only in the thirties. During the forties politicians such as Azzam
Pasha and Nahhas Pasha manifested a pro-Arab orientation, yet Egypt's
adherence to the Arab League in 1945 was not the result of widespread
grass-roots pressure from the Egyptian people; rather, it was due to
diplomatic and security considerations. Similarly, Egypt's involvement
in the 1948 Palestine War was prompted by security calculations
coupled with the king's desire to redirect popular attention away from
the prevailing domestic turmoil. With the defeat of Egyptian arms,
reidentification with Egyptianism emerged amid vociferous demands to
withdraw from the Arab League.

During the first three years of the military regime, Arabizing
trends reemerged as competitors to Egyptian nationalism. In *Egypt's
Liberation: The Philosophy of the Revolution,* Nasser placed emphasis
on "the Arab Circle," indicating the singular role of the 1948
Palestine defeat as the crystallizer of Arabist sentiments among
Egyptian officers. However, it was not until the events of 1955 and
1956 that firm commitment to Arab nationalism emerged. The West's
attempt to isolate Egypt from the Arab orbit through the Baghdad Pact
(February 1955) motivated Nasser to seek closer identification with
other Arab countries, and his rejection of the pact was consistent with
the deep anti-Western sentiment of the Arab masses.

Nasser emerged as a world figure at the Bandung Conference of
nonaligned states (April 1955), and in September he broke the West's
arms embargo by purchasing weapons from the Soviet bloc. These acts
of defiance, coupled with his sudden nationalization of the Suez Canal
Company, propelled him into an unrivaled position of Arab leadership.
His contribution to the building of ideology was thus pragmatic; it
resulted from his successful performance as a leader. Because of
tremendous mass support from the entire Arab realm, the emerging
leader's message could be none other than Pan-Arabism, and the
ultimate goal, the creation of a Pan-Arab state from the Atlantic to the
Indian Ocean. Nasser's commitment to Pan-Arabism marked the formal
transformation of Egyptian nationalism into Arab nationalism; the
process of Arabization (*istirab*) of the Nile valley, which started with
the Arab conquest, had reached its culmination.

Nasserite Pan-Arabism is similar to that propounded by the
Baath ("renaissance") party, but Nasserite ideologues do not agree with
the Baath's leading ideologue and founder, Michel Aflaq, that Arab
nationalism is a matter of feeling and emotion. The ex-Baathist writer
Abdullah al-Rimawi sees Aflaq's intuitive approach as unscientific and
romantic. Rimawi, a rationalist, believes that the romantic stage of the
Arab nationalist movement has passed and that contemporary Arabism
is a rational and pragmatic movement derived from the realities of Arab
existence. The empirical, pragmatic approach of Rimawi and other
Nasserite ideologues is a distinctive feature of Arab Egyptian thought.
All revolutionary endeavor is described as experimental; thus, the only
valid guide to action is Arab national experience. In Nasser's thinking,

the common historical experiences of the Arabs—especially in times of crisis—and the realities of the present are sufficient grounds to unite the Arab future. Similar sentiments have been expressed by others, especially Sati al-Husari. Special emphasis is placed on the unifying role of classical Arabic, Islamic traditions, and the Arab's cultural heritage. In a world of superpowers and power blocs, Arab unity is viewed as imperative for economic, political, and especially military reasons.

The desire for unity is virtually universal among Arabs, but there is disagreement about the methods by which final unity should be achieved. The initiator of Pan-Arabism, the Baath party, aspired to be the unifier of the Arabs, yet its first leaders—Michel Aflaq and Salah al-Bitar—lacked support from the masses, and their military successors in Syria and Iraq were unknown in most Arab countries. Indeed, the Baathist idea of Arab unity remained dormant until its propagation by Nasser. The Egyptian president's most important contribution to Pan-Arabist ideology was the conversion of a generally dormant sentiment into one possessing psychological and political presence among the Arab masses. His political performance on the world stage—defiance of the West, acquisition of arms, proclamation of positive neutralism, support of the North African Arabs' struggle against the French—was in line with mass Arab sentiment, and so Arab loyalties began to transcend local rulers and boundaries to focus on Abdul Nasser and Egypt.

In *Philosophy of the Revolution* Nasser speaks of a double role—that of an Arab hero leader and an Arab state—to lead the Arabs to unity. Because of mass Arab support generated for him after the midfifties, it seemed natural for the Egyptian president to fill the role of unifier of Arabs; and by extension, Egypt became the base country, or the "nucleus state," of the Pan-Arab movement. Although the Egyptian assumption of leadership has been frequently attacked by other Arab leaders, to the Nasserites it represented a natural historical development based on objective realities: no previous Arab leader had been able to command the wide respect and loyalty that Nasser possessed; and Egypt has a unique position and resources, which include size, population, economic wealth, internal stability, military potential, political experience, and intellectual and religious leadership of the Arab world. Nasser himself wrote that "the role of the base is not domination but service," and the United Arab Republic Charter declares that "unity cannot be imposed." These declarations do not mean that Egypt will refrain from supporting pro-Nasser unionist elements in other Arab lands; indeed, the Nasserite call to Arab unity was not directed primarily at governments but at every Arab citizen, as stated in the charter: "The UAR, firmly convinced that she is an integral part of the Arab Nation, must propagate her call for unity so that it would be at the disposal of every Arab citizen, without hesitating for one minute before the outworn argument that this would be considered an interference in the affairs of others."

Despite Nasser's initial hesitation, the United Arab Republic was established in February 1958 with the union of Egypt and Syria.

What Pan-Arabist ideologues had regarded as an inevitable historical process became reality for a brief period. Syria's secession in September 1961 caused an ideological crisis among Nasserites everywhere, and changes were introduced into the ideology. "The lesson of Syria" prompted caution and reluctance to engage in premature unity experiments. It is now recognized that the path of ultimate union is composed of at least three stages: formation of Arab nationalist governments "representing the will of the people" (which is perceived as desiring Arab unity); preparation of the people for future unity by the initiation of social transformation according to the ideological maxims of Arab socialism; and finally, union.

The fundamental issue that now divides the Nasserites and the Baathists is the location of the base country of the Pan-Arabist movement. Although the Syrian Baathists initially accepted a Cairo-based union, since their resumption of power in 1963 they have been reluctant to rejoin Egypt. Others who have contested Egypt's role as nucleus state include Saudi Arabia, Tunisia, Lebanon, and more recently Iraq and Algeria.

Arab Socialism

During the first half of the twentieth century the Arab world was exposed to a wide variety of socialist doctrines, but none left a deep impression on the Arabs because the teachings of Islam were contrary to the atheistic nature of communism and because of the predominance of non-Muslim and non-Arab minorities in early Communist parties.

The situation changed after World War II. The Arabs were faced with the establishment of viable political systems capable of meeting new challenges, which included the persistence of Western imperial influence, the rise of the Israeli state, and an unprecedented revolution of rising expectations among the Arab masses. In such times of crisis the old tenets of nationalism were clearly inadequate. In order to effect comprehensive and rapid social and economic development, Arab nationalism and Pan-Arabism had to be supplemented by ideological constructs aimed specifically at the transformation of Arab society. Hence the search for a new ideology.

The Arab quest for an ideology of change was limited by the fact that most Arab ideologues agreed that the wholesale adoption of any foreign ideology was not desirable; it was considered imperative that new ideological norms be related to the Arabs' traditions and existing milieu. Thus, borrowing from the major ideologies of the East or the West would have to be highly selective. Other determinants were the contents of the existing ideological models and the Arabs' evaluation of the success of these models.

The Arabs could not fail to be impressed by the advances of communism in the USSR and China, yet most were unwilling to make the massive human and spiritual sacrifices that Stalinism or Maoism required. The shortcomings of the Western ideological model became equally apparent, and the early Arab admiration for it began to wane during the forties. The initial successes of the Germans in World War II in rapidly conquering most of the West European democracies seemed to have demonstrated the weaknesses of the latter. Meanwhile, Arab experience with modified versions of liberal constitutionalism in Egypt, Syria, and Iraq had been singularly unsuccessful. The success of the American and West German mixed capitalist systems could not escape the Arabs' attention, but the semifeudal structure of landownership and the absence of a large middle class meant that the Western capitalist model could not be a viable alternative. Finally, the growing Arab antagonism to the United States generated by the Arab-Israeli conflict precluded any attempt to follow the American social and political experience.

Within these parameters of ideological choice, an Arab socialism was developed by Nasserite, Baathist, and Algerian thinkers during the early sixties. As radicalization of the Arab world accelerated after the 1967 War, extremist ideologies—militant communism, Castroism, Maoism—began to emerge, especially among displaced Palestinian Arabs. Of the leftist creeds, only Arab socialism has been adopted by a significant number of Arab governments—Egypt, the Baathist states of Syria and Iraq, and the leftist regimes of Yemen and the People's Democratic Republic of Yemen. Since mid-1961 Egypt has taken the lead in developing and implementing Arab socialism, establishing ideological precedents for other Arab states.

To create an indigenously Arab socialist creed and to gain its popular acceptance, Egyptian and Arab ideologues attempted to find historically legitimate bases for their doctrine, invoking aspects of the Islamic tradition that include references to the Quran and the hadith and the social and political practices followed in the early days of the Islamic ummah. Thus, the Islamic way of life is regarded as inherently socialistic, particularly in the following aspects: (1) equality—Islam dictates equality among the Muslim faithful; (2) social justice—based on the Muslim religious duty to help the poor by paying the alms tax (*zakat*). Reference is made to the Prophet Muhammad's practice of sharing booty and taxing the rich to help the poor; (3) prevention of monopoly—based on the illegality of usury in Islam and on the opinions handed down by the *fuqaha* (jurists) condemning the centralization of wealth in the hands of the few. In the modern context this is interpreted to mean that the necessities of life and the means of production are to be publicly owned; (4) the limited right to property—the right to property is limited by the interests of the ummah as outlined in the Quran.

Relating Arab socialism to Islamic principles and practices neutralizes criticism from traditionalists, who tend to equate socialism with atheism and communism. Further, because the Islamic past is considered identical with the Arab past, Arab socialism is said to be derived from the experience of the early Arabs, and it thus constitutes a distinctly Arab ideology. The common historical roots of Arab nationalism and Arab socialism unite them into a single ideology to guide modern Arab political, social, and economic activity.

Arab socialism is considered distinct from and preferable to other leftist creeds, not only because it is Arab but also because it is considered more moral and humanistic than either communism or capitalism. The stress placed on the humanistic content of Arab socialism in the UAR Charter and in other ideological treatises indicates Arab reluctance to divorce contemporary political thought from their religious heritage. They hold that the infusion of the spiritual values into Arab socialism has given that doctrine an inner strength that other ideologies lack. Capitalism and communism are thus rejected because of their singular commitment to materialism and concomitant lack of spiritual values, and Arab socialism stresses both material progress and spiritual fulfillment as two seemingly antithetical forces that need to be harmonized. Capitalism is also criticized for its stress on private ownership and individual interest, and Marxist society is castigated for its suppression of individual liberty and religion and confiscation of property. In contrast, Arab socialism endeavors to create a society characterized by individual freedom reinforced by economic well-being.

Two other factors that work against Arab adherence to Marxism or capitalism are the eclecticism and pragmatism of the Arab approach to ideological development. Although it rejects wholesale ideological borrowing, the UAR Charter considers the selective incorporation of specific foreign theories and methods a legitimate and prudent endeavor so long as these fit the Arab situation. Whatever is borrowed is accorded experimental status without rigid commitment to an inflexible doctrine. Therefore, ready-made ideologies such as Marxism are rejected because they impose "a predetermined path" of development without reference to differing national realities.

Arab socialist thinkers owe perhaps the heaviest intellectual debt to orthodox Marxism in their view of the unity of the political and economic realms. The UAR Charter adopts a view of economic determinism, stating that "the political system in any state is . . . a direct reflection of the prevailing economic state of affairs." Those who control the economic substructure will thus ultimately shape the political superstructure. The political system of prerevolutionary Egypt is therefore viewed as one controlled by an alliance of "feudalist landowners and exploiting capitalists." After the Syrian secession from the UAR a third category of "people's enemies" was identified, and the "exploiting bourgeoisie" joined landowners and capitalists in opposition to the evolution toward socialism. The noted writer Abdullah al-Rimawi equates the people's enemies with "national reactionism:"

National reactionism =
capitalists + feudalists + exploiting bourgeoisie + imperialist inspiration

According to Egyptian idealogues, the mere overthrow of the monarchy was insufficient to change Egypt's political structure; indeed, the economic substructure had to be radically transformed by crushing

the classes representing national reactionism. Nasserite socialists therefore agree with Marxists on the necessity of transforming the economic
substructure, but disagree with the Communists in their view of the
nature of the transformation. Arab theorists accept only a limited class
struggle devoid of large-scale violence. The Marxist idea of a classless
society dominated by the proletariat is rejected; instead, Arab socialist
society includes within a framework of national unity all exploited
classes of people—farmers, workers, small businessmen, intellectuals,
professionals, nonexploiting proprietors, and soldiers. The idea of a
class struggle among these "productive" classes is unacceptable, because
these legitimate sectors of society would cooperate for the national
good in the context of a single political organism—the Arab Socialist
Union. The only class struggle that is expected to develop is between
the exploited classes and their former exploiters.

In virtually all of the Arab countries previously identified as
socialistic, the major means of production have been progressively
nationalized to the extent that the public sectors of their economies are
preponderant. In practice, Arab socialism has meant the establishment
of etatism in which the state has emerged as the supreme capitalist,
guiding development through comprehensive planning and supervision.
The implementation of the Socialist Laws of 1961 has radically
transformed Egypt's ownership structure. Three main types of property
are identified: (1) public property—outright state ownership, commonly called national capital; (2) cooperative property—lands and
buildings jointly owned by members of cooperatives; (3) private
property—certain types of individually owned property legally protected from expropriation so long as the owners are nonexploiting.

In Egypt, landownership is limited to fifty feddans, and
indications point to further lowering of that limit. Small private
enterprise is still permitted, as is the ownership of buildings, which are
subject to taxation and rent controls. However, private property can be
nationalized if the public interest requires it. In one important
sector—agriculture—private ownership by the fellaheen is officially
encouraged by the agrarian reform acts of 1952 and 1961. In their
attempts to create landowners of the peasants by giving them land,
Egyptian revolutionaries proceeded along a path diametrically opposed
to that of the Soviets and the Chinese, who resorted to forced
collectivization. In addition to destroying the old feudal landowning
class, the distribution of land has brought the peasants into the political
process for the first time in history—an act of major long-range
significance.

The Arab Socialist Man

In the context of social justice and equality of opportunity, the
state is expected to guarantee to the individual freedom of speech and
belief, the right to a job that is in harmony with the individual's
interests and abilities, medical care and old-age benefits, and free

education. In return, the individual is expected to contribute fully to the building of a "cooperative socialist and democratic" society. In the tradition of Kant and Hegel, Egyptian and other Arab ideologues stress each citizen's specific roles and duties within the total program of the state. He is constantly reminded of the "sanctity of productive work" and is taught to regard labor as an honor. Arab socialism also defines the function in society of intellectuals and artists: they are to express popular sentiments and aspirations. The acquisition of knowledge for its own sake and the idea of art for art's sake are rejected. All citizens are urged to compare themselves to the objective realities perceived through Arab socialist ideology, which is a "scientific" tool to discern and analyze reality. Finally, the Arab man is invited "to impose his will on life," without being bound by fatalism or the idea of predestination. Arab socialism has thus settled the age-old conflict in Islam between fatalism and free will in favor of free will.

Nevertheless, a major problem concerning Islam remains unresolved on both the theoretical and the pragmatic levels. Most Arab socialists overwhelmingly oppose any attempt to de-Islamize Arab society. Baathists and Nasserites alike reiterate the singular role of Islam in recasting Arab society along progressive lines, and the Baath's Christian cofounder, Michel Aflaq, goes as far as to regard Islam as the national culture of the Arabs. Yet the relationship between Arab socialism and Islam and its institutions is uneasy, especially concerning secularization. To be sure, Nasserites and Baathists are confirmed secularizers; not only have they made the Islamic institutions subject to secular state power in their respective countries but they envisage political and social change in secular terms, as opposed to such fundamentalist Islamists as the Muslim Brotherhood and King Faysal of Saudi Arabia.

Zionism

The rise of Zionism influenced the direction and content of Arab nationalism more than any other single factor, yet in origin and development Zionist ideology bore little relationship to the Arabs and Arab nationalism. Most of its founders had never been in contact with Arabs. Zionism was European in inception; it represented a Jewish nationalist reaction to the increasingly hostile milieu of the Christian states of Europe.

Centuries of subjugation as a minority in the diaspora had created a Jewish collectivity distinguished by an attitude of subservience. Not until the half century preceding 1948 did a value transformation begin to take place among European Jewry. With the advent of nationalism in Europe, the situation of Jews became more intolerable than during previous centuries. The indigenous nationalisms of the European nation-states by their very nature could not accommodate religious-ethnic minorities, especially the Jews. The Dreyfus Affair in France, the pogroms in Russia, and the Hitlerite massacres in Germany were manifestations of the new nationalist milieu.

Three choices were open to European Jewry: (1) acculturation or dissolution of the Jewish identity into the majority culture (e.g., the Mendelsohns, the Marxes); (2) Jewish identification with leftist international movements, including communism, with the hope of finding a haven in a "denationalized" new world community (e.g., Trotski, Deutscher); (3) the adoption of an indigenous nationalism based on a repoliticization of the Jewish heritage with a territorial focus on Palestine. An overwhelming number of Jews chose the last alternative because of the inadequacy and unworkability of the first two alternatives.

Acculturation and assimilation can be extremely taxing experiences psychologically; for many Jews it was not a viable alternative. And ironically, those who chose assimilation were often rejected by the majority culture; the Nazi extermination policy did not discriminate between Jews and fully assimilated ex-Jews or even the non-Jewish descendants of Jews. The second alternative—leftist internationalism— lost its appeal after the Russification of the Marxist movement and the progressive purging of Jewish Bolsheviks under Stalin. The Birobidzhan scheme for an autonomous Soviet Jewish concentration in Siberia was also a failure. In a world of nation-states, the Zionist goal of a Jewish nation-state was perceived as the only alternative, a perception powerfully reinforced after the mass liquidation of European Jews in the forties. Not all Jews supported the Zionist program, however, and voices of dissent continued even after the 1967 War.

At the outset, Jewish nationalism had no geographical base and there was wide disagreement among Jewish leaders concerning the choice of territory for settlement. Theodore Herzl and other West European leaders favored the British government's offer of a Jewish state in Uganda. However, East European Jewish leaders insisted on Palestine because of Judaism's historical ties to the Holy Land, and this view prevailed at the First Zionist Congress in 1897 in Basel, Switzerland. Meanwhile, the First Aliyah ("immigration") had started (1882), but from the point of view of the emerging Zionist ideology its results were unsatisfactory. By 1904 only 25,000 settlers had joined the Jewish community in Palestine (*Yishuv*), and most became city dwellers rather than farmer-pioneers. This pattern began to change with the Second Aliyah (1904-13), which also signaled important developments in Zionist ideology. The most fundamental of these was the grafting into Zionism of heavy doses of socialist ideology, for many of the new settlers were socialists from Russia.

The nascent socialist Zionism propagated by a small vanguard of the Second Aliyah strove to disrupt traditional modes of Jewish life by stressing the development of a genuine laboring class of workers and peasants. They insisted that a Jewish renaissance in Palestine would have to be based on working the soil of the land and not on bourgeois values. Simultaneously, two other precedent-setting tenets were introduced into the ideological complex: (1) the revival of the long-dormant Hebrew language and (2) the settlers' assumption of the responsibility of defending their own settlements—an act that was expected to heighten self-reliance and self-respect. Their most significant innovation was the *kibbutz*, or collective settlement—the antecedents of which went far back into socialist history. The kibbutz embodied all of Zionism's ideological tenets: self-sacrifice, egalitarianism, voluntarism, collectivism, self-reliance, and militancy, all of which became the basic ingredients of the Israeli political culture.

In the political realm the Yishuv's ideology laid the foundations for a socialistic democracy in which planning and welfare-statism were to prevail. Since independence, however, much of Zionism's pioneering socialistic fervor has been dissipated. The ruling MAPAI party still stresses its labor origins, but its policies have tended to strengthen private enterprise, especially in recent years. Of Israel's political parties only MAPAM and to a lesser extent Ahduth Avodah retain a Marxist orientation; both draw support from the Histadrut (Israeli Federation of Labor) and the kibbutz movement. An advocate of a binational state before 1948, MAPAM still champions the cause of the Arab minority, as do the small Communist parties of Israel. Vehemently opposed to MAPAM's socialism and pro-Arab orientation is the Gahal party (formerly Herut), which represents the extreme right of Israel's ideological spectrum. MAPAI's right wing and Gahal represent the most militant and expansionist elements of the country. Finally, there are the various religious parties, which have a generally theocratic orientation. Nevertheless, the factionalism of the parties has been mostly submerged in the present protracted armed confrontation with the Arabs.

Ideological Trends and Prospects

A number of significant ideological trends have emerged since the 1967 Arab-Israeli War. The shock of defeat produced a great deal of soul-searching among Arabs—a reexamination of the prevailing value system, including the tenets of Arab nationalism itself. Defeat in battle created a profound ideological crisis, the full dimensions of which will become apparent only in time.

In addition, the developments since 1967 have illustrated the weaknesses of the Arab nationalist movement, which failed to achieve a united front against Israel. As a result, the ruling elites of virtually all Arab countries have been discredited among the masses in varying degrees. Failure of the prevailing ideologies and leaders has generated a search for a more productive system of values and for more competent leaders. In ideological terms, the mass alientation from the existing elites and values has given rise to an unprecedented movement of radicalization among Arabs. Radicalization is most intense among Palestinian Arabs, the ones most directly affected, but it has spread to every Arab country, including the Maghrib. At the epicenter of crisis, the Palestinian guerrillas have developed leftist doctrines ranging from orthodox Marxism to Maoism, and they threaten particularly Jordan and Lebanon. They are supported in varying degrees by Algeria, the

Baathist regimes of Syria and Iraq, and Egypt. The process of radicalization was also apparent during the 1969 military coups in Libya and the Sudan, which adhered to Nasserite Arab socialism.

Throughout the Arab world radicalization is accompanied by anti-Americanism that threatens pro-Western regimes in Saudi Arabia, Tunisia, and Lebanon, and ultimately all remaining U.S. influence and interest in the area. American identification with Israel coupled with massive Soviet military and economic aid have undermined the Nasserite-Baathist doctrine of positive neutrality. Even in Egypt itself, where Nasserite influence remains powerful, radical ideological change has been advocated. Indeed, since 1968 some Egyptian Marxists have pressed for a dilution of the bourgeosie's considerable role in the Arab Socialist Union and a concomitant increase in worker-peasant representation, which is now placed at 50 percent. The leadership under Nasser was able to resist leftist proposals, but continuance of Israeli superiority over Egypt may lead to the radicalization of Egyptian society now that the Egyptian president is gone. In such an eventuality, the Soviet military presence in Egypt (and elsewhere in the Arab world) may become a permanent political presence in the midst of Marxist Arab regimes. Another possibility is a partial Egyptian reversion from Levantine Arab nationalism and a reidentification with African Arab nationalism, suggested by the recently concluded unity accords with Libya and the Sudan.

Whatever the immediate outcome of the Arab-Israeli conflict, the search for ideology continues in both the Arab and non-Arab countries of the Middle East. The 1967 defeat acted as the main catalyst to the quest for more viable ideologies in the Arab sphere, but countries such as Turkey, Israel, and Iran are also seeking effective political creeds of social change. Because of the critical role of ideology in nation building, the nature and direction of Middle Eastern ideological evolution will have a decisive influence on political modernization—which is the subject of the next chapter.

Selected Bibliography

Abu Jaber, Kamel S. *The Arab Ba'ath Socialist Party: History, Ideology, and Organization.* Syracuse, N.Y.: Syracuse University Press, 1966.
The only book-length study of the Baath party available in English. Includes a discussion of the ideas of Aflaq, al-Bitar, and Razzaz, and translations of the Baath constitution of 1947.

Ahmed, Jamal M. *The Intellectual Origins of Egyptian Nationalism.* London: Oxford University Press, 1960.
One of the first studies of the backgrounds of Egyptian nationalist thought.

Binder, Leonard. *The Ideological Revolution in the Middle East.* New York: John Wiley and Sons, 1964.
A comprehensive study of various ideological movements in the Arab world, including Egyptian nationalism, Arab nationalism, Nasserism, Baathism, positive neutralism, and Arab socialism. Also includes an in-depth analysis of the interaction between religion and politics in Islam.

Dekmejian, R. H. *Egypt under Nasir: A Study in Political Dynamics*. New York: State University of New York Press, 1971.
A brief discussion of the role of ideology in political modernization included in chapter 5; the process of historical reinterpretation treated in chapter 6. Also includes an analysis of the transformation of Egyptian nationalism to Pan-Arabism and the adoption of Arab socialism.

al-Ghazzali, Muhammad. *Our Beginning in Wisdom*. Washington, D.C.: American Council of Learned Societies, 1953.
Contains the political and social ideas of Shaykh al-Ghazzali, including an analysis of Islamic socialism.

von Grunebaum, Gustave E. *Modern Islam: The Search for Cultural Identity*. New York: Vintage Books, 1962.
A collection of various articles and papers concerning the role of Islam and nationalism in the process of modernization in the Middle East.

Halpern, Ben. *The Idea of the Jewish State*. Cambridge, Mass.: Harvard University Press, 1961.
Essential reading for an understanding of Zionist ideology and practice; religious and political backgrounds of Zionist nationalism presented in detail.

Heyd, Uriel. *Foundations of Turkish Nationalism: The Life and Teachings of Ziya Gokalp*. London: Luzak, 1950.
An analysis of the ideological contributions of Gokalp.

Hourani, Albert. *Arabic Thought in the Liberal Age, 1798-1939*. New York: Oxford University Press, 1962.
A perceptive presentation of the intellectual trends in the Arab world from the Napoleonic conquest of Egypt to World War II.

Hostler, Charles Warren. *Turkism and the Soviets*. New York: Frederick A. Praeger, 1957.
An early work dealing with the origins and evolution of Pan-Turkism in the Ottoman and Russian empires.

Karpat, Kemal H., ed. *Political and Social Thought in the Contemporary Middle East*. New York: Frederick A. Praeger, 1967.
A comprehensive anthology of Arab, Turkish, and Iranian thinkers. Introductory commentaries on ideological trends.

Kerr, Malcolm, *Islamic Reform*. Berkeley and Los Angeles: University of California Press, 1966.
A detailed analysis of Islamic reformist thought with particular focus on the contributions of Muhammad Abduh and Rashid Rida.

Khadduri, Majid. *Political Trends in the Arab World*. Baltimore: Johns Hopkins Press, 1970.
One of the most insightful treatments of the main trends of political thought in the Eastern Arab world, including nationalism, democracy, socialism, Islamic revivalism, and secularism.

Khalid, Khalid M. *From Here We Start*. Washington, D.C.: American Council of Learned Societies, 1953.
A classic work on social reform by one of Egypt's most liberal thinkers.

Nasser, Gamal Abdul. *Egypt's Liberation: The Philosophy of the Revolution*. Washington, D.C.: Public Affairs Press, 1955.
A brief statement of the early political thought of President Nasser.

Ramsaur, Ernest E. *The Young Turks: Prelude to the Revolution of 1908*. Princeton, N.J.: Princeton University Press, 1957.
One of the first studies in English of Young Turk political thought and action prior to the 1908 revolution.

Safran, Nadav. *Egypt in Search of Political Community*. Cambridge, Mass.: Harvard University Press, 1961.
A detailed examination of the divergent belief systems in prerevolutionary Egypt, with special emphasis on Islamic political thought.

Tutsch, Hans E. *Facets of Arab Nationalism*. Detroit, Mich.: Wayne State University Press, 1965.
A brief introduction to the study of Arab nationalism, including a section on the role of religion, language, and history in the development of Arab unity.

Political Modernization*

Most Middle Eastern countries are at a transitional stage—culturally traditional and predominantly agricultural with a measure of industrialization. They are also determined to match the political, economic, and social achievements of the industrialized, or "modern," states, whatever the human and material costs. But what constitutes modernity?

It is not necessary to duplicate the political system of a "great power" to achieve modernity, nor is technological development necessarily an index of the modernity of a government. Rather, as we use the term, *modern* describes a country that has achieved the greatest development (as opposed to mere growth) of political, social, and economic foundations. Stated simply, modern countries have adapted to environmental pressures or challenges by undergoing changes in their structures to cope with or to control these pressures or challenges. Adaptation involves the greater division of labor among new structures or reformed older structures or both, the development by citizens of responsive attitudes to adjust to these changes, and the development of political decision-making processes that are based on the systematic gathering and evaluation of information.

A modern political system needs a high capacity to implement government policies such as welfare services and literacy through such means as tax collection and compulsory education. But to implement policies a government must first secure the active cooperation of its citizens. Sometimes citizen participation in political processes precedes national integration, in which case the regime must translate the demands of this activated populace into policies that maintain the

*For our purposes the terms *political modernization* and *political development* are interchangeable, with no ethnocentric bias intended.

system without alienating the citizen. In other cases a government may have to suppress what are considered illegitimate or destructive demands while generating support for its programs.

Political modernization also requires the rationalization and specialization of government organizations in order to efficiently develop and allocate resources to maintain the system, because modernization increases complexity—people and governments demand more goods and services from each other. Job specialization involves the problems of recruitment and popular participation in the development process. Specialization of function means that more people are involved in the political system and necessitates the application of objective standards (e.g., public examinations for the civil services) as opposed to subjective standards (e.g., family, tribe, or party membership) as a basis for recruitment.

A "participation crisis"[1] may result if a regime controls personnel recruitment by giving political office or favors only to members of a certain party, religion, or region, thereby precluding the participation of others. For instance, if loyalty is used as a basis for recruiting political leaders, well-educated army officers, teachers, and bureaucrats may be excluded and may then demand decision-making roles. The response of the political leadership to these pressures will affect the capability of those in authority to achieve long-range objectives. In Iran's case, for example, economic and some social modernization appear to be taking place under the shah. The political loyalty of the modern bureaucratic and military elites is not fully assured, however, because the shah has depended for political support more on traditional elements than on the trained elites. On the other hand, for implementation of economic reform programs the shah has relied on the modern elites rather than on political parties, trade unions, or interest groups.

It is often difficult for the official leadership to channel new interests and demands to assure some stability and an orderly allocation of available resources without creating alienation. For example, in Turkey the Justice party and the preceding Democratic party relied on a popular political base, especially among previously nonpolitical Anatolian peasants. An attempt to secure support from the traditional peasantry by ill-planned economic expansion resulted in dissatisfaction among the sophisticated urban population and eventually contributed to the downfall of the Menderes regime. In Egypt Gamal Abdul Nasser first sought to mobilize popular support for implementing modernizing plans with the Liberation Rally, and military officers thus became independent of prerevolutionary policy makers. The military cliques that seized power in Syria and Iraq had strong connections with civilian political groups, which used the military to acquire power.

Whatever the means used to achieve popular commitment, many Middle Eastern regimes have embarked upon adventurous industrialization programs without developing political organizations of adequate specialization and without reaching all levels of the citizenry, both of which are essential to modernization. To develop performance capacity, power must be located in an accepted central government and the forces desiring change must be constructively channeled by an accepted official leadership. Otherwise, internal conflict or even civil war will impede modernization. Because the development of performance capacity depends on support from the governed, a primary political objective is a sense of national purpose, which may have been achieved in the struggle for independence from a colonial power (e.g., Egypt) or in the desire to prevent foreign encroachment (e.g., Turkey and Iran). Yet often the departure of the colonial power has caused more struggle as to who would lead than how modernization might be achieved. Moreover, even agreement on who shall provide leadership is not sufficient unless there are recognized political institutions through which the people can provide support and channel demands.

Political modernization in the Middle East is examined in the remainder of this chapter, with particular attention to identifying the environmental challenges to Middle Eastern political systems—mainly Western colonial pressure—and the responses to these challenges, which often suggest what resources are available for the state's further development. The chapter also identifies the major political structures or institutions that are contributing to the adjustment to these environmental pressures and evaluates their roles in the development of the different states. By using selected examples, a framework is suggested within which the student can examine the Middle Eastern states and make some evaluation about which institutions are likely to predominate or to emerge in the maintenance of the political system.

Historical and Contemporary Factors That Affect Political Modernization

---

All the Middle Eastern states felt the influence of European institutions, especially before the post-World War II arrival of the Russians and the Americans. Many, indeed, experienced rule by the technologically advanced French and British: between the two world wars France was master of Syria and Lebanon and Britain controlled Egypt, Palestine (out of which emerged Israel), Transjordan (now Jordan), the People's Democratic Republic of Yemen, and the Gulf states. Without colonial experience were only Saudi Arabia, Iran, Turkey, and Yemen; Turkey was an imperial power in her own right, forming the heart of the Ottoman Empire when it ruled much of the Middle East in the centuries preceding World War I, and Iran has a long history of independence.

The European powers affected the nation-building process in two ways: they inadvertently stimulated the development of nationalism and they aroused the desire for economic and social change not only among the dependent but also among the independent polities.

Yet the political, social, and economic transformations during the interwar period were limited and superficial at best.

Egypt possessed a strong national identity, which provided the foundation for the establishment of political authority. In 1922 the emerging parties and parliaments were able to secure a limited independence from the British, which was broadened in 1936, but they proved ineffective in coping with social and economic change. Further, the failure of these parties and parliaments to deliver the country fully from foreign rule caused their repudiation as instruments of modernization.

With the exception of Egypt and noncolonized Iran and Turkey, no Middle Eastern country had created a national identity prior to the establishment of a national political structure. The prevalent pattern was that of a central government's deliberate attempt to create a sense of national identity among the people. In some former mandated territories, such as Iraq, national uprisings against the occupying power temporarily fostered national identity, but loyalties continued to be fragmented. In a sense, the colonial powers made a negative contribution by providing something against which the citizens of the occupied country could unite. But the net contribution to political development was minimal because the colonial powers prevented the establishment of the kind of indigenous, legitimate political authority essential for a modernizing leadership. They provided education, communications, finance, and military training but stressed maintenance of security rather than modernization.

Nation-Building Formulas

An ideology gives meaning to man's existence and his relationship to society and can contribute to or inhibit political, social, and economic change. Externally imposed and internally developed ideology must therefore be considered in the assessment of the modernization process.

Liberal Nation Builders

The liberal nationalists of the period between the two world wars desired popular sovereignty and constitutionalism, or the establishment of the basic rules of the political game, to limit the power of traditional rulers or to gain popular acceptance for modernizing leaderships. However, most of the states that adopted Western-style constitutions in the post-World War I period did not possess the supportive attitudes necessary for viable liberal nationalist political cultures.

Nevertheless, the liberal parliamentary structures for which these constitutions provided were effective means to national unification and development in the eyes of politically aware Middle Eastern intellectuals. By more or less copying some aspects of Western institutions, Egyptian moderate nationalists, for example, endorsed parliamentarism not only for its own sake but also to prove to the British that Egyptians were capable of self-rule. The negative British attitude was expressed by Lord Cromer, who governed Egypt from 1883 to 1907 and who did not "believe that such education as can be imparted in the schools and colleges will [ever] render the Egyptians capable of complete self-government without some transformation of the national character, which must necessarily be a slow process."[2]

Despite Cromer's imperialist philosophy, parliaments and local councils provided political apprenticeship in countries like Egypt where few had shared in the decision-making process. The small political elite generally owed its strength to other political structures, however, particularly to political parties, which can deeply penetrate society and provide the supporting aspect of a politically informed and articulate public.

Liberal parties and parliaments did not bring about national unification and independence in countries subject to colonial rule, however. Parliaments irritated both the colonial power and the national leadership. Egyptian parliaments, for example, were frequently dissolved during crises, and the dominant nationalist Wafd ("delegation") party, despite repeated electoral victories, behaved more like a counterelite than a legitimate incumbent leadership in its struggles with the British high commissioner and the king. In Iraq, parliaments were poor substitutes for a popularly penetrative party system and were simply overridden by strong cabinets. In fact, quarrelsome deputies representing Iraq's minorities aided Britain's divide-and-rule policy of curtailing strong nationalist leadership. The failure of parliamentary government cannot be entirely blamed on colonial administrations, but imperialism and parliamentarism came to be linked in the minds of the occupied, with the result that both were rejected.

Significantly, parliamentary regimes came into their own in the Middle East only after World War I, when their effectiveness was already being questioned in Europe. Also, parliaments might reflect an accepted political process, but they could not establish that basic process. Nationalist leaderships naively thought that the introduction of European law codes would result in a Western-style political system. Hence, liberal nationalism provided an impetus for political change in the post-World War I period, but its instrumentalities did not provide effective vehicles for modernization because they were not accompanied by the commitment to develop other political, social, and economic aspects of modernization. Neither the modernizing leadership nor the occupying power addressed itself wholeheartedly to the problem of increasing the scope and capacity of the citizenry—through education, for example—to exercise its sovereignty by expressing demands through the parliamentary organization. Clearly these liberal leaders cared more about obtaining national sovereignty than about developing an adequate foundation for the political system.

The result was that if these parliaments were in opposition to the existing government, they were muzzled by the occupying power or the indigenous leadership itself (which feared the consequences of an imperialist reaction). Press censorship and harsh assembly laws impeded nonviolent political expression outside of parliament, and the conspiratorial response became a habit in many Middle Eastern countries. If political interests are not peacefully expressed, changes of government take place not at the polls but by coups d'état, and protests are made not by orderly pickets but by mob action: subversion replaces participation.

Religion

Political claims to legitimacy have often been expressed in religious terms, and the struggle for power has been complicated by the split between religious traditionalists and secular, liberal modernists. In the first group are the ulama, or Muslim religious leaders, who appeal to the predominantly Muslim rural population. The modern group consists of men who have studied European languages and thought—a generation ago they would have been lawyers and journalists; today they are military officers and engineers.

Islam, with its detailed prescription for the well-being of the individual and the community, has played both positive and negative roles in the political modernization process. Religion and religious leaders have aided national integration in countries that did not have serious minority problems. Because Islam is an integral part of traditional Middle Eastern society, it can be used to mobilize the tradition-bound masses for action by political leaders who have the support of the ulama.

Religion has often played a negligible role in changing popular attitudes, however, despite modern reformers such as Muhammad Abduh and Muhammad Rashid Rida. The ulama have generally resisted changes that endangered their political positions, usually because of the ill-planned manner in which reform was advocated combined with traditional rulers' use of the ulama against modernizing political leaders who were challenging the ruler *and* the ulama. Before World War II the ulama lost many of their functions in society to the secular domain of Western-style law codes, courts, and governments because of their resistance to change.

The post-World War II leadership, particularly in the radical Arab socialist states, has recognized the interrelation of Islam and society and has used religion's mass appeal to mobilize the population. At the same time the new leaders seek to alter the traditional framework of Islam by obtaining religious endorsement of governmental policy. Religious leadership has thus either returned to its policy of acquiescence, particularly to the holders of military power, or has become more practical in outlook; for example, a mosque sermon might exhort the people to practice birth control or to profess loyalty to the political leadership.

In nonradical political systems such as those in Saudi Arabia and Yemen, in which the political leaders have depended on religious traditionalists for legitimacy, leaders have only recently expressed interest in modernization. But where nonreligious symbols provided legitimacy for political leaders—as in Turkey, where Mustafa Kemal Ataturk gained popular acceptance because of his role in the war of independence and his use of the Grand National Assembly—there was much less hesitation to break away from religious traditions. For instance, Ataturk abolished the caliphate in 1924 because it did not serve Turkey's modern needs.

Modernization proceeded slowly in Iran under Reza Khan because of opposition from the ulama. Lacking the essential consensus for his modernizing rule, Reza Khan hesitated to press his programs and even assumed the title of shahanshah in deference to traditionalists. To take another example, Egypt's King Fuad followed the retrogressive course of supporting religious traditionalist forces in order to gain enough political power to implement his plans for nation building.

Resistance to modernization also manifested itself in the emergence of religious interest groups, some of which—the Muslim Brotherhood, for example—developed into mass movements. The Brotherhood seeks a return to the fundamentals of Islam, rejects the "demoralizing" aspects of Western civilization, and wants to eliminate foreign languages and customs. This militant movement and similar groups generally favor a return to the Islamic concept of the political community—the caliphate—wherein the subjects would be governed solely by Islamic principles and law. The Muslim Brotherhood does not hesitate to use modern organizational techniques to challenge government authority. It has often joined forces with other groups— sometimes even with the Communists, with whom it is ideologically at odds—against secularist leadership in Egypt and other countries. At the opposite end of the spectrum is a religious movement called the *Mutawwiun* ("those who compel obedience"), which has been organized by the government to serve as a quasi-police organization in traditional Saudi Arabia.

Religious movements could be utilized as socialization agents for national integration, provided everyone agreed on how to blend religious aspects of the culture with secular imports. Such a synthesis has not developed, however, and the result has often been the bypassing of the religious leadership by the more secular political leadership. The search for an effective ideology of modernization therefore continues.

Radical Nation Builders

Although nationalism is limited as a means to modernization, it persists wherever there are unresolved quarrels. Note, for example, the growth of Palestinian nationalism, particularly since the June 1967 War. Before World War II the liberal nation builders attempted to use nationalism as a unifying and liberating force, but this formula was used only by a relatively small group of the intelligentsia, who involved the masses merely in a peripheral sense, asking only that they help to oust the foreign controllers and recognize an indigenous elite. Since World War II, however, Arab nationalism has developed into a supranational effort to resolve differences through a common outlook and to bolster the Arab role in world affairs. The movement asserts independence from the Western-influenced ideologies of the colonial period. Among its protagonists, the Baathists emphasize unity and the Nasserites stress the rapid achievement of modernizing roles through the development of popular commitment to those goals.

Radical Arabs seek to eliminate the economic and political power of the wealthy landed classes because big landowners neglected social and economic reform.[3] These landowners are usually replaced by reform-minded Arabs who are committed to a collectivized economy, industrialization, and improving the economic and social welfare of the peasants and workers. These reformist leaders hope to create a cohesive set of political attitudes that successfully incorporate traditional Islamic values and institutions and a modern universal orientation. The obstacles to success are many. Following the departure of colonial rulers there is apt to be a shortage of skilled entrepreneurs and competent technicians. The indigenous bureaucracies must fill the vacuum and alleviate the distribution crisis by establishing priorities on political, economic, and social goods. Secularization is not necessarily taking place; rather, Islam, at least in some instances, is playing a modernizing role.

Constitutions were put to new purposes by those who assumed power in such countries as Egypt, Syria, and Iraq after World War II. New documents were drafted, to be supplemented by party organizations and the mass media to legitimize and prescribe programs. Whereas under the liberals a constitution was designed to limit a ruler's power, under the radicals it was supposed to build a new political culture to support modernizing regimes.

Arab nationalism, Arab socialism, and modernization are closely interconnected, we maintain. Israeli nation-building efforts, which more closely approximate the continental European model, will be treated under the section on political parties, as they provide the vehicle through which modernization is largely effected in Israel.

Arab socialism may provide the activating force in many countries to translate nationalism into modernization, but they do not always support each other; goals have not been uniformly achieved. The nationalistic, unifying aspects have tended to take precedence; problems between nations, such as the Arab-Israeli conflict, are far from resolution, and plans in the economic and social spheres have been implemented only on a limited basis. Syria, for example, has settled neither its internal politics nor its relations with neighboring Israel, and a preoccupation with holding power has prevented the Baathists from building a modern nation-state. Leaders of Egypt and the Fertile Crescent no doubt want to end exploitation and poverty, but they usually give priority to building more factories. In countries such as

Syria and Iraq, which have fragmented political cultures, the basic power struggle precludes attention to economic and social development or to relations with other nations. It is too early to determine if radical Arab nation builders will be more successful than their liberal predecessors in surmounting the challenge of modernization. Success may depend on the agents of political modernization in both radical socialist and conservative nonsocialist countries.

Agents of Political Modernization

Parliaments did little to develop political capacity, and Western-style parliamentary regimes, with their faction-ridden parties, were repudiated by military coups in many countries after World War II, often with the military assuming leadership.

The Military

Political involvement of the military is traditional and is likely to continue because of persistent regional rivalries and domestic strife. The military can usually maintain a degree of stability, and it tends to be the most modern of institutions, but military skills alone cannot substitute for bureaucratic implementation of government policies or for aggregation and expression of interests by political parties.

The military can play either an initiating or a supporting role in the nation-building process. In the *initiating* role the civilian instrumentalities are controlled by the military. In the *supporting* role, the military is the servant of civilian authorities but may develop considerable autonomy because of the difficulty encountered by fragile civilian institutions in maintaining the political system. Typically the army does not long remain subordinate to civilian rule.

An initiating role in the early post-World War I period in Turkey, in the 1920s in Iran, and in 1952 in Egypt was later supplemented by the use of civilian agencies to maintain legitimacy. Although the Turkish military institution under Mustafa Kemal Ataturk was able to establish legitimacy, unlike most Middle Eastern armies it restricted its role to that of caretaker. Ataturk understood and was committed to modernization, but he was careful to work through the Grand National Assembly. He supported the separation of the military from government and insisted that his officers leave the military if they pursued political careers. Since World War II a viable multiparty system has provided much of the leadership in the modernization process, but the military has intervened when necessary. In early 1971 the Turkish army forced the government of Suleyman Demirel to resign and ordered the creation of a new civilian government to restore order.

In Iran the seizure of power by the soldier-father of the present shah was not sufficient to ensure widespread dedication to modernization. The military dictatorship found it necessary to establish its legitimacy over the years through the use of traditional symbols of authority.

Since Napoleon's invasion in the late eighteenth century, Egypt has not successfully sustained a military tradition, partly because of foreign intervention. Muhammad Ali sought to make Egypt a military and industrial power early in the nineteenth century, but when blocked by British forces supporting the Ottoman Empire, he lost interest in military modernization. Broad modernizing efforts by his grandson, Khedive Ismail, eventually resulted in a military takeover under Urabi, the British occupation in 1882, and a deliberate weakening of the Egyptian army by the British. Not until the 1952 coup d'état did the military resume its aborted leadership role under Gamal Abdul Nasser. However, the assumption of power was not enough to ensure successful modernization: the military regime had to create civilian organizations and to depend on the existing bureaucracy for implementation of national plans.

In Iraq the military has played political roles during 1936-41, the period of the first series of coups d'état. The first coups were the efforts of old-line nationalists in the army who were allied with civilian politicians often more interested in power than in modernization. The second series of military coups, which began in 1958, did aim at revolutionary change, however, starting with the overthrow of the monarchy. Yet the military has not succeeded in consolidating its position and maintaining popular acceptance from the governed for several reasons: the means of seizing power, the junior rank of many of these second-generation military leaders, and Iraq's fragmented political culture.

The military plays a *supportive* role in Jordan, Saudi Arabia, and Israel. Maintaining public order is essentially a task that involves political choices unless civilians have the final say. The military may aid civilian leaders in the exercise of their authority, but too often its involvement in the political process inhibits the development of alternate organizations that could play a constructive part in modernization. Yet, in countries where basic political questions have not been resolved, the military role might be the only alternative to total disruption of the nation-building process. In Jordan, for instance, establishment of the military preceded the creation of the state of Transjordan and served to unify the tribal society. More recently the military has helped maintain loyalty to the monarchy, although at considerable cost. The army has not provided the impetus for thoroughgoing change in the economic, social, and political spheres of Jordanian life, however.

Modern military institutions are somewhat more representative of the population than older armies because they recruit from the middle and lower middle classes rather than from the upper class. But the professional role often becomes more influential than class status, and soldiers tend to become conservative and dogmatic. Further, the military tends to mistrust civilians, civilian institutions, and the civilian skills of cooperation and compromise, so that what may begin as military support of a civilian government often ends in military coercion, which may achieve compliance but at the cost of destroying legitimacy and creating a reservoir of distrust. The military, then, does not usually contribute significantly to political, social, and economic change—in fact, it often prevents modernization—but is useful chiefly as a last-ditch effort to prevent disintegration of the state.

Political Parties

With committed leaders and a dedicated following, the political party can penetrate the society and establish trust among the people more effectively than a government bureaucracy. Political organizations, chiefly the mass-supported single party, are thus needed to secure popular commitment and to review increasing popular demands generated by the new middle-class leadership's promises.

The Western-style parliamentary party that surfaced in the Middle East between the two world wars was typically small in size, it mobilized the people for securing independence rather than for modernization, and it generally did not have a coherent ideology other than nationalism to bind members together. Once independence was achieved, the party leaders maneuvered for political office and lost contact with members and the populace. In the early phases of modernization, political parties in the Middle East tended to support personalities or particular interests; they also did little to aid modernization. In the postwar period of rapid social and political change, however, a new type of party emerged—an instrument of the new, middle-class, radical political leadership (chiefly the military), who sought to create bases of legitimacy and communication.

The political party plays three types of roles in the Middle East today. In the first situation, the party is the creature of a ruling elite, such as the Arab Socialist Union in Egypt, because of its role in the modernization schemes set by the regime. In the second situation, the political party is the instrument of an aspiring elite that lacks full control and shares power with another elite, typically the military. Examples are the Baath organizations in Syria and Iraq. In the third case, the political party has evolved from one-party status and shares power with other parties *because* sufficient progress has been made in modernization. Its status may remain tenuous, depending on whether it performs to the satisfaction of the guardians of modernization, as, for example, in Turkey.

In Egypt, Gamal Abdul Nasser and his military colleagues first created the Liberation Rally, then the National Union, and finally the Arab Socialist Union. Each time they tried to involve the ordinary Egyptian, who has not yet committed himself to modernization. The Arab Socialist Union seeks to recruit village leadership, urban professionals, and technical specialists and attempts to create a general commitment to the political formula of Arab socialism.

The trend in the Middle East, particularly among the other radical countries (Iraq, Syria, Yemen, and the People's Democratic Republic of Yemen), has been toward the single-party system, but power has not been consolidated by any one group. The Baath party emerged as the major ideological party and has become supranational in scope primarily because of its strong Arab nationalist tenets. As a result of factionalist politics in Syria, Iraq, and Jordan and the entrenchment of the bourgeoisie in these countries until a later time than in Egypt, the Baath party organization was a very small elite until its sudden success in merging with other parties in 1954. Its transnational organization prevented the Baath from consolidating control when it seized power in Iraq and Syria, however, and in Iraq ideological intensity also contributed to the party's failure. Despite the Baath party's dedication to social revolution, Egypt's brand of Arab socialism has been more successful at implementing a social program.

In Turkey, Ataturk's Republican People's party (RPP) finally shared the political arena in 1950 when it was challenged by the Democratic party of Adnan Menderes, which was composed largely of dissident Republicans who believed that the RPP had not adequately responded to particular interests. The Menderes leadership provided a real test for the Turkish commitment to modernization. Menderes raised expectations among the Turkish lower-middle classes that he could not meet, and his superficial and unecomonical policies ultimately caused his downfall.

Although the 1960 army-led coup d'état—which dissolved the Democratic party and executed Menderes—apparently boded ill for the multiparty system, the army proved that it wanted only to restore its own neutrality and to curb the repressive tendencies of the Democratic party. The subsequent restoration of power to civilian groups under the leadership of the aging RPP leader Ismet Inonu demonstrated Turkey's commitment to democratic government that would implement social and economic development programs. In 1971 the army again assumed its caretaker role by forcing Prime Minister Suleyman Demirel to resign and by creating the national coalition government under Nihat Erim, another civilian, in order to restore order.

We have discussed the party institution in systems that have undergone political change when governments made verbal and practical commitments to modernization. Other political systems have several functioning political parties, such as Lebanon and Israel, but have manifested different purposes for political parties. In Lebanon, a precarious accommodation exists among the religious minorities that comprise Lebanon's society. This mountainous country has faced the problem of national integration in the face of Pan-Arab pressure from within and without. The political party structure reflects the polycommunalism, or political strength of the religious communities, and the strong influence of a few prominent families within these communities. Parties have not therefore contributed to the economic and social development of Lebanon but have served rather as instruments of sectarian leaders or as instruments of competing ideologies, with little impact on the voter in terms of party identification. The comparatively high economic and social development that has taken place in Lebanon is a product of the polycommunalism, individualism, and competitive spirit that have marked the style of Lebanese party politics.

Israel's multiparty system also mirror's differences in the society, in which even the dominant MAPAI party was unable to constitute a majority because of factional differences. Israel's multiparty system is more structurally differentiated, ideological, and disciplined than its counterpart in Lebanon, reflecting the origins and priorities of Israeli society. The European background of the bulk of the pre-1948 population, the need for integration and accommodation of immigrants of diverse backgrounds, and the pressing question of survival as a state have led to the situation of political parties serving first as quasi governments, then as agents of political socialization. Yet parties reflect the ideological diversity of the Israeli and offer alternate programs to the electorate.

No political parties have developed in such tradition-bound political systems as Saudi Arabia, Kuwait, and the Gulf states, although parties may yet emerge. *Patriarchal rulers*[4] preside over their national families, supported by a host of relatives holding positions according to birth rather than merit. Such modernization as has been achieved is largely a result of skilled foreign manpower exploiting oil reserves. Even without the development of political parties the traditional leadership will be increasingly challenged by the bureaucracy and other skilled indigenous elites, but in the future these elites will probably express interest in developing political parties because of participation crises.

The remaining *palace systems* of Jordan and Iran do not use the party system to effect economic and social change; rather, the traditional rulers have attempted to seize the modernizing initiative from contending factions. In Iran there has been an attempt to establish Western-style parties, but the bulk of the *political effectives,* or modern intelligentsia, have not been impressed by this effort. In Jordan security, stability, and the predominance of displaced Palestinians are the prime issues rather than the development of political party structures. During the mid-1950s, so-called political parties did exist, but they were outlawed by the palace when external forces threatened the stability of the regime.

Thus the political party, where it exists in the Middle East, is either a *manifestation* of a stage of development, recognition of national diversity, or an *instrument* created by a modernizing leadership that is seeking commitment from the citizenry. The performance of parties and of the military may now be compared with that of the bureaucracy.

The Bureaucracy

Bureaucracy is defined as "systematic administration characterized by specialization of functions, objective qualifications for

office, action according to fixed rules, and a hierarchy of authority,"
although many bureaucracies fall short of these criteria and function
reasonably well. Bureaucracies are absolutely essential to modernization, which depends on the administration of development programs.

Traditionally bureaucracies have been the most authoritative
and effective implementers of policy of Middle Eastern political
institutions. Turkey, Egypt, and Iran developed bureaucratic systems
from the rulers' ambitions to control their subjects and—in the cases of
the nineteenth century Ottoman ruler Sultan Mahmud II and Egyptian
viceroy Muhammad Ali—to compete with the more advanced European
powers. Early bureaucracies were frequently oriented to service of the
ruler, not the population, and when not compelled to serve authority
they often served themselves. Foreign control increased the effectiveness of some bureaucrats because colonial powers used a cooperative
indigenous bureaucracy to rule, but colonial administration eventually
retarded development by preempting the most responsible posts.

Independence from colonial powers, internal social pressures,
and the demands of economic development have caused bureaucracies
to burgeon since World War II. But mere bureaucratic proliferation is
insufficient to cope with the complexities of modern budgetary
methods or health programs; development is achieved by increasing the
division of labor. A bureaucratic organization must also recruit
personnel to at least some degree on the basis of ability and
achievement rather than on the ascriptive basis of political favoritism.
Job descriptions and standards and methods of objective testing to
determine applicants' qualifications must therefore be established. Too
often Middle Eastern bureaucracies are top-heavy structures that lack
the capacity to perform modernizing tasks because the middle-range
and lower-range civil servants cannot or do not assume responsibility.
Also, a disparity may exist between ambitious programs and the
amount or accuracy of information on which they are based. The
bureaucracy must therefore develop the means of gathering, organizing,
and evaluating precise, complete information from which successful
programs can be built.

A particularly serious impediment to modernization—the
difficulty in adapting to new conditions—stems from the nature of
bureaucracies rather than from a malfunction of the system. Although
the bureaucracies may have initiated a change—the construction of a
state university, for example—they often remain curiously untouched
by the products of such a change. They are often reluctant to listen to
the new generation, whose ideas may differ from their own, and if the
bureaucracy cannot incorporate the new forces it may try to preempt
their roles.

Another bureaucratic impediment to modernization is
corruption, which persists when salaries that are high by local standards
are inadequate to maintain the European life-styles with which
bureaucrats frequently become familiar. A high volume of petty
corruption generally exists at the lower levels of a bureaucracy, where
fair treatment depends on the citizen's ability to bribe. Higher officials

do not accept small bribes and run considerable risks accepting large ones.[5] Corruption may be a means of getting the job done, but the net result is inefficiency because public resources are diverted into private pockets.

Regimes that are preoccupied with consolidation of political authority may tolerate corruption, and loyalty to the regime may take precedence over expertise as the basis for hiring personnel. Such policies do not always stand in the way of modernization; the United States, for example, managed to modernize despite a flourishing spoils system. But with the establishment of an agreed-upon political system and adequate economic resources, ascriptive recruitment and the inefficiency of which corruption is an example become unnecessary costs. (As a transitional step, the most competent of the politically loyal employees may be chosen.)

If a bureaucracy is to be the agency through which modernization is accomplished, someone or some group must mobilize the generally conservative bureaucracy to perform its demanding new roles. The political party might provide the means by which politically awakened citizens could articulate their demands to the bureaucracy, but historically Middle Eastern parties have not played this role. (It is possible that as the authoritarian, mass-oriented party grows, increasing attention will be given to the mobilizing function.) In some cases the military organization is able to influence bureaucratic action. However, modernizing structures are most likely to function for their designed purpose if there is the kind of catalyst that charismatic leadership can provide.

The Limitations of Charismatic Leadership

Charisma, an overworked term, is sometimes incorrectly equated with mere popularity, but charisma is a special quality for leading others, a kind of superpersonalism that lends itself to amplification in an age of mass communication. Egypt's Nasser had it, as does Israel's Moshe Dayan, but Iraq's less well known General Ahmad Hasan al-Bakr does not. Charismatic leadership operating in conjunction with (but always distinct from) the requisite modernizing structures can provide the sense of commitment that leads to modernization, although neither is likely to prove adequate by itself. The crises[6] identified below emphasize the need for charismatic leadership.

The *crisis of identity* results from the problem of minorities. If they occupy a compact area, as do the Kurds in northern Iraq and Iran, and are distinguished from the majority by language, religion, or custom, a minority may be more interested in autonomy or independence than in identification with the country. The modernizing leadership generally has difficulty persuading groups of similar background to transfer their loyalty from the village or region to the nation;

local tradition and sentiment persist despite the exhortations of the leader and the adulatory cries of responding masses. The charismatic leader, however, may serve as a national focal point to transcend these local loyalties.

The *legitimacy crisis*, the problem of a new regime's acceptance, may be more important at the outset than the nature of the political system. In order to stay in power, modernizing autocrats must appeal to political, religious, and societal elements, and the traditional ruler may have to reestablish his legitimacy on the basis of contemporary ideologies. Charismatic leaders, whether traditional or modernizing, more easily bridge the gap.

The failure of the modernizing leadership to reach the masses may result in a *penetration crisis*. As the leadership increases its demands, the people must be persuaded to report for military service, to pay taxes, or to maintain a regular work schedule. The villager cannot comply if he does not understand what is expected of him, and he may resort to subterfuge if unreasonable pressure is brought to bear by inept bureaucrats. The people may nevertheless continue to support the charismatic leader and may contribute to the general viability of the system.

Rapid change tends to create an *integration crisis* by increasing the gap between traditional and modern patterns. In the Arab socialist countries in particular, the landlords and men of religion formerly had the most contact with the rural people, yet they have been pushed to one side as inimical or irrelevant to the nation's goals and no one has taken their place. Government officials may prefer life in the metropolis and may not give full attention to the agricultural cooperative, school, or health station in the rural area; local leaders may encourage indifference to preserve their power. Charismatic leadership can unite the traditional religious leader, the modern bureaucrat, and the rural masses.

Conclusion: Political Style
For Development

The agents for modernization in the Middle East have been briefly examined. Even the army, with its new elite officer class, cannot easily transform an underdeveloped country into a developed one endowed with the capacity to convert demands into goods and services. Symbolic agents are needed to develop the material and human resources—a political formula to unify and extract commitment from the populace and an organizational apparatus to sell the political formula to the masses. Since World War II socialism has been added to nationalism to produce a distinctly Middle Eastern philosophy of development, but political conflicts have diverted attention from the modernization program for which these political organizations and formulas were created. Nevertheless, the masses have been mobilized, and they will not easily revert to traditional passivity. If their demands are not satisfied, their energies may be directed toward regional or international conflict, which would be counterproductive to modernization.

The possession of resources and the unity to use them do not always go hand in hand. Densely populated Egypt possesses a sense of nationhood and has lent itself to bureaucratic elitist control, but attempts at rapid social mobilization, even with a charismatic political leader like the late Gamal Abdul Nasser, have been only moderately successful because of the problems of overpopulation, extreme poverty, traditional skepticism of the people, and lack of a variety of natural resources. Yet Egypt's attempts at modernization have been relatively more successful than those of other socialist regimes, such as Syria and Iraq, because of the latter's problems of fragmented political culture, the absence of strong charismatic leaders capable of unifying the people, and conflicts coinciding with attempts at rapid social change.

Of the nonsocialist regimes, Turkey and to a lesser extent Iran have made progress in political development. Historical national identity, distance from regional conflict, absence of the complicating factor of supranationalism, and the development of modern bureaucracies have contributed to their success in political modernization. In the case of Israel, a strong national identity and a high proportion of skilled human resources have contributed to success in state building.

The consciously modernizing country will probably be strongly statist like Mussolini's protototalitarian Italy, which some Middle Easterners admired. The people rely on the government to take the initiative, but unlike the frankly antidemocratic fascist ideology, the language of democracy is used for the exploitation of the mobilized populace. The technology-oriented new middle class rule as the national elite, but they rule in the name of the populace, whose commitment to modernizing goals they must have in order to enlarge the capacity of the political system to produce goods and services for its members and to maintain itself.

Footnotes

---

[1] Pye, *Aspects of Political Development,* p. 65.

[2] The Earl of Cromer, *Abbas II* (London: Macmillan & Co., 1915), p. xxiii.

[3] Be'eri, *Army Officers in Arab Politics and Society*, p. 466.

[4] This and the following terms are adapted from Sharabi, *Nationalism and Revolution in the Arab World*, p. 48.

[5] Examples of the exposure of and crackdown on corrupt officials in Egypt may be found in Manfred Halpern, *The Politics of Social Change in the Middle East and North Africa* (Princeton, N.J.: Princeton University Press, 1963), p. 346n.

[6] Pye, pp. 62-67.

Selected Bibliography

Al-Marayati, Abid A. *Middle Eastern Constitutions and Electoral Laws*. New York: Frederick A. Praeger, 1968.
Provides relevant information on constitutions and electoral laws.

Almond, G., and Coleman, J., eds. *The Politics of the Developing Areas*. Princeton, N.J.: Princeton University Press, 1960.
Despite some dated material, provides relevant classifications and generalizations about developing political systems, specifically Dankwart Rustow on the Middle East.

Be'eri, Eliezer. *Army Officers in Arab Politics and Society*. New York: Frederick A. Praeger, 1970.
Awkward translation but comprehensive, rich in source material.

Black, C. E. *The Dynamics of Modernization*. New York: Harper Torchbook, 1967.
Wise, readable, with many profound insights; general typology of political modernization not particularly helpful, however.

Huntington, S. *Political Order in Changing Societies*. New Haven, Conn.: Yale University Press, 1968.
Political stability seen as a test of a system's efficiency in accommodating change while making full use of the nation's human and material resources.

Hurewitz, J. C. *Middle Eastern Politics: The Military Dimension*. New York: Frederick A. Praeger, 1969.
A recent, comprehensive historical overview.

Janowitz, Morris. *The Military in the Political Development of New Nations*. Chicago: University of Chicago Press, 1964.
The general categories of civil-military relations useful, but specific observations on the Middle East not always accurate.

LaPalombara, J., and Weiner, M. *Political Parties and Political Development*. Princeton, N.J.: Princeton University Press, 1966.
Performance of political parties rated according to four demanding criteria under which only Turkey and Israel are examples of Middle Eastern countries that have successful party systems.

Organski, A. *The Stages of Political Development*. New York: Alfred A. Knopf, 1965.
Preoccupied with economic management in a modern nation-state but recognizes the priority of political questions in four stages of political development.

Packenham, Robert A. "Political Development Research." In *Approaches to the Study of Political Science*, edited by Michael Haas and Henry S. Kariel, pp. 169-93. Scranton, Pa.: Chandler Publishing Co., 1970.
Recommended for the serious student.

Pye, Lucian W. *Aspects of Political Development*. Boston: Little, Brown & Co., 1966.
An essential introduction to the literature; has a structural-functional orientation.

Schweinitz, Karl de, Jr., "Growth, Development, and Political Modernization." *World Politics*, July 1970, pp. 518-40.

Systematically presents many of the concepts applied in this chapter.

Sharabi, Hisham B. *Nationalism and Revolution in the Arab World.* Princeton, N.J.: D. Van Nostrand Co., 1966.

A brief but lucid and knowledgeable introductory study of Arab politics.

Ward, R. E., and Rustow, D. A., eds. *Political Modernization in Japan and Turkey.* Princeton, N.J.: Princeton University Press, 1964.

Some rather specialized contributions, but comprehensive and comprehensible introductions and conclusions by the editors.

11

Arab Republic of Egypt

Civilization has existed in the Nile valley since the dawn of recorded history. Blessed with rich soil, abundant water, and a long growing season, Egypt provided fertility from which a large population could live in relative comfort. The Nile proved to be a political and economic unifier, for no part of the pharaonic empire was more than a few miles from this mighty river. The river was also motive power for shipping; current carried vessels northward and the etesian winds of the Mediterranean brought them south again. Fecundity, a line of communication, manpower, and facilities for organization were the essential ingredients for a kingdom, and this mighty Egyptian civilization sowed the seeds of early human progress. The visitor who stands before the great pyramids of Giza or the temples and statues of Karnak and Abu Simbel cannot but wonder how these ancients attained such perfection in the arts and sciences.

Today Egypt, named the United Arab Republic (UAR) in 1958 and the Arab Republic of Egypt in 1971, is caught between the glories of her past and the visions of her future. These glories and visions are blurred by the realities of a society that is torn between the old and the new, between the East and the West, and between clouded desires for peace and the disastrous imperatives of war caused by the protracted Arab-Israeli conflict. To understand modern Egypt one must consider four trends of the past thirty years: (1) the gradual decline of Western colonialism, (2) the emergence of Arab revolutionary regimes, (3) the establishment of the state of Israel, and (4) the penetration of Soviet influence into the Middle East. The politics of Egypt can be perceived as a confluence of these trends in a society faced with the herculean task of social, economic, and political modernization. Egypt is experiencing revolutionary changes, the vast majority of which are spontaneous reactions to the culture diffusion resulting from the transportation and communications revolution penetrating the emerging nations of Asia and Africa.

After the revolution of 1952, President Gamal Abdul Nasser's regime voiced strong commitment to reform and development, and Nasser sought to introduce new processes and institutions through which reform and development could be encouraged. This chapter seeks to analyze the interaction of the historical, cultural, social, and economic factors that shape and mold the political dimensions of Egyptian society.

Historical Background

Egypt has been predominantly Arabic-speaking and Sunni Muslim since its conquest by the Arabs in the seventh century, but until 1952 none of her rulers since the pharaohs had been Egyptian. From 1517 to 1798, for example, Egypt was a province of the Ottoman Empire. Napoleon's invasion in 1798, followed shortly by the modernizing reforms of Muhammad Ali (1805-49), began the Westernization of Egypt, and the development of large-scale cotton growing and the construction of the Suez Canal (completed in 1869) made Egypt a desirable prize for the European powers. Britain, the world's greatest sea power in the nineteenth century, became especially interested in Egypt. Using the excuse of a nationalist revolution, British troops occupied Egypt in 1882, and Britain proceeded to institute many reforms and to consolidate her rule over Egypt.

The outbreak of World War I in 1914 focused the attention of British imperial interests on the strategic importance of Egypt and the Suez Canal. When the Turks aligned with the Central Powers, Britain declared a protectorate over Egypt (1914-22) and the nominal rule of the Ottoman caliphate came to an end. The title *khedive* was abolished and the pro-Turkish ruler Abbas Hilmi (1892-1914) was forced into exile. His uncle, Husayn Kamil, was placed on the throne with the title *sultan*, and upon his death in 1917 he was succeeded by his brother Prince Ahmad Fuad. Egyptian opponents of British rule were temporarily silenced, but when the Allied victory appeared imminent they reemerged, demanding the immediate evacuation of British troops, complete independence, and constitutional government.

As political consciousness began to permeate the society, a new, broadly based political organization, the Wafd al-Misri (the Egyptian delegation), emerged under the leadership of Saad Zaghlul as the most important Egyptian political party—a position it held until the revolution of 1952. The Wafd demanded the right to represent Egypt at the Paris Peace Conference, and after several months of opposition, in March 1919 the British agreed to allow the Wafd to attend the conference but denied Zaghlul permission to accompany it. The other members of the Wafd refused to go without him and Wafd members in the government cabinet resigned. The British, convinced that Zaghlul meant to obstruct the formation of a new government, arrested him and three others and exiled them to Malta.

Egyptian reaction was spontaneous insurrection; violence quickly spread throughout the Nile valley. The British government finally responded to this popular revolt of 1919 by sending a special mission to Egypt under the leadership of Lord Milner. The Milner Commission, impressed by the people's unanimous, intransigent opposition to British rule, proposed a renunciation of the protectorate, a formal declaration of Egyptian independence, and a treaty of alliance. Failing to achieve complete agreement from Egyptian nationalists, in February 1922 the British unilaterally proclaimed Egypt to be an independent constitutional monarchy; however, they reserved liberty of action in four strategically important spheres: (1) imperial communications in Egypt, (2) Egyptian defense needs, (3) protection of foreigners, and (4) continued military and civil rule in the Sudan. In tacit recognition of the declaration, Fuad assumed the title *king* on March 15, 1922.

The Egyptian Constitution of 1923

The promulgation of a new constitution in April 1923 initiated a new era in Egyptian politics, and Egypt's attitudes toward Western political institutions today are colored by this early experience in constitutional government. Britain maintained a large contingent of troops in Egypt and continued to exert considerable influence, but domestic politics became more the prerogative of King Fuad and later his son, Faruq, and the various groups of nationalists, landowners, and aristocracy who dominated the Egyptian economy and society.

The structures of the monarchy, the cabinet, and the legislature appeared consistent with democratic theory, yet in practice the Egyptian political process was still generally dominated by the rich landowning class, as it had been in the past. Thus, although the Egyptian peasants were supposed to have an opportunity to exercise their franchise under the 1923 constitution, in reality the ballot proved to be a myth for the peasants. Al-Hakim, a well-known Egyptian author, describes a village election of the 1930s with this tragicomic anecdote:

"Please believe me. I am a ma'mur [district representative of the Ministry of Interior] with a sense of honour. I'm not the usual sort of ma'mur. I never interfere in the elections and never say 'vote for this man.' Nothing of the kind. My principle is—leave folk alone to vote for whomever they want. . . ." I could not forbear to interrupt with words of approval: "That's really wonderful! But isn't it risky for a man of your position to talk like that? I can see that you're a remarkable person, but . . ." "Well, that's my method with elections," he continued. "Complete freedom. I let people vote as they like-right up to the end of the election. Then I simply take the ballot box and throw it into the river and calmly replace it with the box which we prepare ourselves."[1]

Constitutional government was bringing the people into slightly more contact with the urban political world, but it was hardly educating them to appreciate the value of such government. King Fuad was against constitutional government and the growing power of the Wafd party, both of which were perceived as obstacles to his full prerogative as king. His only recourse against the Wafd was to periodically dissolve its government, with British support or acquiescence, and to permit one of the smaller parties to win by rigging the elections. This bitter struggle between the king and the Wafd party accentuated the national legislature's inability to develop or implement programs to solve the overwhelming economic and social problems of Egypt. Land reform, education, health services, and modernization of the government were often discussed but were generally shelved in this uncompromising struggle for power.

However, all Egyptians did agree that the British must withdraw. In early 1936 the British suggested their willingness to engage in new negotiations, seeking to resolve the conflict with Egyptian leaders in view of Mussolini's menacing advances in North Africa. The Wafd, fresh from a resounding election victory in May, played the key role in the negotiations. Finally in August 1936 the Anglo-Egyptian treaty was signed, the British high commissioner became an ambassador, British troops withdrew from Cairo to the Suez Canal, and Egypt, with virtually complete independence, joined the League of Nations. However, the British retained the right to keep troops in the Suez Canal Zone for twenty years and promised full military assistance if Egypt were invaded.

Despite the outbreak of World War II in 1939, Egypt stayed technically neutral until 1942, although the British and Americans used Cairo as an essential military base for operations throughout the Middle East. It served the Allied purpose for Egypt to remain a "nonfighting ally," but in fact, many leading Egyptians wanted the Axis to win the war, not the British. Although the Egyptian masses often cheered the early victories of Britain's enemies, General Naguib later explained in his book, *Egypt's Destiny*, that "they were not supporting fascism any more than they were opposing democracy. Like the Irish they were simply applauding the powers that promised to rid them of the hated occupation."[2]

The situation became critical when Rommel's Afrika Korps captured Benghazi, Libya, and appeared to be on the verge of invading Egypt. Lord Killearn, British ambassador, recognizing the need for a strong, united, and pro-Allies government, demanded that King Faruq appoint al-Nahhas Pasha, the leader of the Wafd, as the prime minister. When the king hesitated, Lord Killearn had the palace surrounded by a British military escort of troops and tanks and demanded that Faruq appoint al-Nahhas immediately or be deported. The king's capitulation on that February evening in 1942 had a profound impact on a young Egyptian officer, Captain Gamal Abdul Nasser, who vowed that someday the British would no longer control Egypt's destiny.

For nearly thirty years, the Egyptian people had turned to the Wafd party and had been disappointed. Most citizens blamed the British for their problems, yet internal conflicts and jealousies among the party leaders and the aristocracy blocked many major reforms. Western parliamentary democracy in Egypt was shallow and farcical, the whole political system plagued by corruption and irresponsibility, and large numbers of intellectuals, students, and army officers gravitated to extremist groups who promised progress and purposeful leadership.

Yet in the 1950 elections the Egyptian people responded to the Wafd plea for support, and the party achieved a resounding victory, securing 228 out of 319 seats in the national legislature. Wafd leaders sought to revise the treaty of 1936, particularly two points of special grievance: the continuing presence of British troops in the Suez Canal Zone and the British control over the Sudan. But these problems were almost impossible to solve to the satisfaction of both British interests and Egyptian public opinion, and frequent clashes between Egyptian civilians and British soldiers resulted. Both sides refused to compromise, and finally negotiations completely broke down.

In October 1951 Egypt's nationalistic fervor, greatly intensified by the Iranian government's success in challenging British oil interests, encouraged Prime Minister al-Nahhas Pasha to abrogate the 1936 treaty unilaterally, and King Faruq was declared ruler over both Egypt and the Sudan. The British protested that such action was illegal and took such forcible action as was necessary to maintain themselves in the Suez Canal. Sporadic clashes developed into a state of guerrilla warfare, and British troops became a target for sniping and assault. The British retaliated by sending a strong British force, including several tanks, into the nearby provincial capital of Ismailia, and in the ensuing battle, nearly one hundred Egyptians were killed or wounded. The immediate result of this Ismailia incident was widespread commitment to push the British out of Egypt at any cost. On January 26, 1952, a mob formed in central Cairo, and as the police watched, the crowd set fire to many buildings—especially foreign-owned hotels, restaurants, clubs, and business establishments. To this day it is not known for certain who organized this "black Saturday"; in the mob were dissidents from nearly the entire political spectrum—including the Muslim Brotherhood, Communists, nationalists—and thousands of young people who joined spontaneously.

By the early 1950s two of Lenin's three prerequisites for a revolutionary situation already existed in Egypt—widespread discontent and government impotence, the third prerequisite—an organization capable of taking advantage of the first two—had not yet emerged. Extremists of both the Left and the Right had been unable to gather a widespread following; the military establishment had been weakened and humiliated by its disastrous defeat in Palestine; the Wafd party and the monarchy were perceived as totally ineffective in providing leadership. Three alternatives confronted Egypt—reform, repression, or revolution. There seemed to be neither the will nor the means to accomplish the first; the successful accomplishment of the second depended on strengthening the loyalty and efficiency of the army, the police, and the administrative services; and revolution required the emergence of a revolutionary organization, which leads to the story of Nasser.

Nasser and the Revolution of 1952

Gamal Abdul Nasser was born in Alexandria on January 15, 1918, to a postmaster earning less than thirty dollars a month and to the daughter of a local businessman. Nasser's ancestral home was Beni Mor, a village in Upper Egypt, where his grandfather and uncles held small plots of land, living symbols of Nasser's ties to the fellaheen class—the true Egyptian peasant. At the age of eight he was sent to Cairo to be educated, and in the same year his mother, to whom he was strongly attached, died. His loss deeply affected him and increased his natural propensity for privacy and contemplation. He obtained his secondary school certificate from al-Nahdah al-Misriyah School, where he displayed an interest in law and the biographies of great men. While he was still in school Nasser became involved in several student demonstrations, joined the Young Egypt party—an ultranationalistic group—and sought actively to organize his classmates.

Upon graduation his thoughts turned briefly from politics to finding a profession. As a result of the 1936 treaty, the Egyptian government opened the military academy to young men of all classes. Some four hundred applied, but only forty were selected, Nasser among them. As a young cadet, he was noted for exemplary conduct, self-reliance, and a serious outlook, and also for his outspokenness and his hatred of British colonialism. Anwar al-Sadat, a close friend during this time, quotes him: "We must fight imperialism, monarchy, and feudalism because we are opposed to injustice, oppression, and slavery. Every patriot wants to establish a strong and free democracy. This aim will be established by force of arms if need be. The task is urgent because the country has fallen into chaos. Freedom is our national right. The way lies before us."[3]

Nasser graduated as a second lieutenant from the academy and joined the Fifth Battalion at Munqabad in Upper Egypt, where he met several young officers who later became members of the revolutionary government in 1952. Nasser's record during World War II is incomplete, but it is known that he was assigned to al-Alamayn, a key defense point in the Western Desert, during 1941. During this period Nasser quietly and carefully began recruiting members for a clandestine organization later to be called the Free Officers. By 1943 Nasser was a captain and an instructor at the military academy, where he came into contact with hundreds of cadets, many of whom he converted to his secret revolutionary movement.

To Nasser and other Arab leaders the 1948 establishment of a Jewish state in Palestine was the culmination of a long series of attempts by the Western powers to control the Arab world, and the shame of the Palestine defeat stimulated recruitment into the Free Officers movement. The aim of these young officers was the moral regeneration of their country, beginning with a purification of the army. No longer were they primarily concerned with Palestine or the British; the failure of Egypt's dealings with Israel and Britain was seen as the result of corruption and treachery in the national leadership.

During the first half of 1952, one weak, palace-appointed government succeeded another, riots and demonstrations increased throughout the country, and the Free Officers were spurred to overthrow Faruq as soon as possible. On July 23, 1952, this small group of conspirators precipitated a coup d'état that initiated an era of political and social revolution. Under the leadership of Nasser, the Free Officers' executive committee became the Revolutionary Command Council (RCC). Because nearly all of these young officers were from middle-class and lower-class families and their average age was just over thirty years, they invited a respected officer, General Muhammad Naguib, to be the titular head of the Free Officers.

The RCC was forced to make several difficult decisions during its first year in power. After several hours of heated debate, they decided against executing Faruq and allowed him to leave Egypt on his private yacht, the Mahrusa. Initially it was assumed that the constitutional monarchy would be preserved, and a three-man regency was named for Faruq's infant son, Fuad II. Nasser himself indicated that the military rule was temporary until a competent, reform-minded civilian government could be formed. Ali Mahir, a veteran politician, was asked to head the new government. Royal civilian titles *pasha* and *bey* were abolished; Faruq's secret police was disbanded; a general housecleaning of corrupt officials was initiated; and a land-reform program directed against the large landowners was outlined by the RCC.

Nasser's early optimism for the establishment of responsible civilian government was shattered by the realities of postrevolutionary Egypt. He describes his experience seeking advice and support from various parties, groups, and organizations: "Every man we questioned had nothing to recommend except to kill someone else. . . . We were deluged with petitions and complaints by the thousands and hundreds of thousands. . . . If anyone had asked me in those days what I wanted most, I would have answered promptly: to hear an Egyptian speak fairly about another Egyptian."[4]

In December 1952 parliamentary government and the 1923 constitution were suspended, and early in 1953 all political parties were dissolved and their funds confiscated. The RCC declared a three-year transitional period during which the establishment of democratic institutions would be postponed. In June 1953 the RCC abolished the monarchy by proclaiming the Republic of Egypt with Naguib as president. A power struggle between Nasser and Naguib emerged as Naguib began to challenge Nasser's primacy in the RCC, but Nasser maintained his position with the support of the army, and Naguib was forced to resign from all government positions and was placed under house arrest in late 1954. Nasser's claim to leadership was then unchallenged.

Nasser's coup of 1952 precipitated new political institutions, policies, and programs designed specifically to achieve the Free Officers' six basic principles: (1) the eradication of imperialism and its agents, (2) the extinction of feudalism, (3) the eradication of monopolies and control of capitalistic influence over the system of government, (4) the establishment of a strong national army, (5) the establishment of social justice, and (6) the establishment of a sound, democratic life.

Political Environment

The challenges facing Egypt are found in the political environment, which can be most easily understood by an examination of social and economic conditions set in the context of Egypt's political culture.

The People

Social Structure: Traditionally, status and influence have been a function of landownership in Egypt. Before the 1952 revolution the society was composed of three more or less self-contained sections: wealthy landowners, middle-class city dwellers, and rural peasants. The landed and educated clique surrounding the khedive, including members of his family and the old Turkish aristocracy of Egypt, had maintained their high economic and social position, but since the early twentieth century the growing middle class had been gaining in power and position. Modern urban social structures were emerging in Alexandria and Cairo; special-interest guilds and groups of religious scholars were giving way to political parties, labor unions, and business organizations.

In this highly structured society wealth was concentrated in the hands of a few feudal families. Less than 6 percent of landowners controlled nearly 65 percent of the land; some 280 families possessed one-tenth of the total cultivable land. These wealthy were noted for their conspicuous spending and ostentatious display of wealth; they appeared to be totally impervious to the abject poverty and misery of the fellaheen. The July 23 revolution initiated policies designed to divest this older elite of their lands and special privileges.

After the abdication of King Faruq, power and prestige quickly moved to the Free Officers and to civilian administrators who were willing to serve the new regime, and the gradual development of an economy that is controlled and directed by the government has precluded the emergence of a new upper class that is based on a system of entrepreneurial capitalism. Egypt's upper class today is thus largely composed of army officers, high civilian administrators, and persons who have specific technological skills.

The professional and clerical middle class, whose members are prominent in the new political elite of the Arab Socialist Union (Egypt's present single party, originally established by Nasser in 1962), is predominantly an urban group, although some have peasant origins. Indeed, the government has difficulty persuading these newly educated people to live in rural areas, where they are desperately needed. The lowest social level in the urban centers of Cairo and Alexandria comprises persons of limited skills, nonskilled factory workers, domestics, and peddlers. Largely illiterate, desperately poor, and often unemployed, this group is constantly swelled by the influx of people from rural areas.

The social elite in rural areas are still those who own relatively large pieces of property (thirty to fifty acres). Social status is held by families more than by individuals, and status symbols are related to specific families who have traditionally monopolized village leadership positions. Specific rural leadership thus rests mostly on wealth and family connections. Even today some families maintain their status in spite of some dissipation of their wealth through Nasser's land-reform program, and other families have acquired status from the political and educational achievements of their children. Below the top level, social gradations between small landowners, tenant farmers, and agricultural laborers are gradual.

Social Conditions: Few Westerners can comprehend the miserable existence of the average Egyptian peasant, who has a life expectancy of less than fifty years, an annual income of less than two hundred dollars, a diet largely made up of beans, cornmeal bread, and tea, and a high probability of suffering from two or three diseases, including anemia, trachoma, hookworm, rickets, dysentery, bilharziasis, and typhoid. These figures apply largely to the rural population, but nearly six out of every ten Egyptians live in rural areas. To break the vicious cycle of poverty, hunger, malnutrition, disease, and apathy, the Egyptian government must stimulate agricultural and industrial production, offer opportunities for education and technical training, provide sanitation and welfare services, and emancipate the Egyptian peasant from the habits and social structures of past centuries.

Economists have argued for years that labor is the source of all wealth, but a nation's labor force must be trained and organized to be efficiently productive. In an attempt to raise the standards of education and to encourage a greater social awareness, a sense of discipline, national pride, and habits of personal hygiene, a prodigious program of social welfare services has been adopted. Egypt's annual health budget has increased 500 percent since 1952, infant mortality has decreased, potable water is now available in most villages, and the ratio of one doctor per 13,000 citizens in prerevolutionary days has been improved to one physician for every 2,000 persons today. Students in secondary and primary schools have increased by 600 percent, and the number of college students has more than doubled. Thousands of university-trained civil servants (doctors, agronomists, social workers, school teachers, etc.) are sent to the villagers and the urban poor, and community development projects are springing up everywhere.

Economic Conditions

Most economists recognize that Egypt's economic problems result from the interaction of (1) a restricted amount of cultivable land for agricultural production, (2) a population explosion, and (3) a limited amount of foreign currency and investment funds, which are required for a sustained program of industrialization.

Egypt has an area of 386,000 square miles, of which only 2.5 percent is cultivable. In 1897 the total cropped area was 7 million acres, and with a population of only 10 million, the per capita share of harvested land was seven-tenths of one acre. By 1970 the cropped area had reached 10 million acres, yet because of a population increase of over 200 percent, the per capita share had dropped to less than three-tenths of one acre. One of the government's responses has been a comprehensive program of land reclamation, of which the most ambitious project is the Aswan High Dam, completed in 1970. With a storage capacity of 130 billion cubic meters, a height of 350 feet, and a width of nearly 3 miles, the huge Russian-financed dam will back up the world's largest man-made lake (extending nearly 400 miles upstream) and will increase the cultivable land by nearly 30 percent. Additional acres may be available through reclamation programs in the Western Desert regions and by draining large areas of marshland in the delta. Yet this additional arable land provides no long-term solution unless the birth rate decreases.

Because nearly 97 percent of the area is uninhabited desert, Egypt's 33 million people are squeezed into the narrow Nile valley, often resulting in a population density of 2,000 per square mile. Assuming that the present annual growth rate of 2.9 percent (one of the highest in the world) continues, the population will double in less than thirty years. In 1962 President Nasser declared in his new charter: "Population increases constitute the most dangerous obstacle that faces the Egyptian people in their drive towards raising the standard of production. . . . Attempts at family planning deserve the most sincere efforts. . . ." However, the government did not take practical action to disseminate birth control information on a countrywide basis until 1965. Today Egypt has a family planning association that coordinates all efforts related to birth control services, education, and research. Although the present plan includes the establishment of twenty-five hundred new centers for child planning, officials agree that the difficulty is modifying fertility patterns sanctioned by traditional values and social customs.

The agrarian reform laws of 1952 and 1961 sought to restructure the agricultural system to achieve the following goals: (1) compensated requisition of excessive land holdings from families who owned more than 200 acres in 1953, 100 acres in 1961, and 50 acres in 1970; (2) distribution of nearly 800,000 acres of this requisitioned land to over 300,000 peasant farmers between 1954 and 1966; (3) government control to prevent excessive rents and to ensure adequate wages for Egypt's nearly 5 million tenant farmers;

(4) establishment of multipurpose cooperatives; and (5) the prevention of land fragmentation. These agrarian reforms have had some impact on the agricultural sector of the economy, but probably more significantly, they have greatly undermined the political power and the economic position of the Egyptian upper class.

Many in Egypt are convinced that industrialization is the only hope for economic development, and Egypt's five-year plans have projected the extremely ambitious goal of doubling the national income in ten years. Nearly 50 percent of the distribution of investments was earmarked for industry, electricity, transportation, communications, and housing. As a result of the broad program of nationalization in the early 1960s, the Egyptian government now controls the entire infrastructure of roads, public transportation, and public services, most of the heavy and medium industry, all foreign trade, and the banks and insurance companies. Today Egypt manufactures a wide variety of items, including iron and steel products, insecticides, fertilizers, automobiles, refrigerators, and television sets, yet Egypt's future as an industrial power is still threatened by the persistent problems of inadequate management skills, a shortage of technically trained workers, a lack of raw materials, and a foreign currency shortage. Since 1967 Egypt's confrontation with Israel has channeled much of her national budget into military expenditures, hindering for the moment plans for economic development.

Political Culture

The description of the social and economic factors that impinge on Egyptian society sets the stage for a careful analysis of the Egyptian political culture. By political culture is meant the general beliefs, attitudes, and sentiments that give order and meaning to a political process and that provide the underlying assumptions and rules that govern behavior in the political system. Egyptian perceptions of politics are the product of both the collective history of the Egyptian political system and the life histories of the members of that system.

Stable political systems tend to have relatively homogeneous political cultures within which there is general agreement about the proper limits and functions of politics. In such a system each generation is socialized through a common cultural experience that is accepted and strengthened by most agents of the socialization process, such as the family and schools.

One factor that has had a subtle but important impact on Egypt's political processes is the demographic homogeneity of the population. Minority groups in Egypt, including Armenians, Greeks, Nubians, and Turks, have always been small and have generally been integrated into the common cultural milieu. This lack of sharp demographic divisions has encouraged a sense of common identity that is often lacking in many Middle Eastern societies, which are torn by ethnic and religious antagonisms. Yet in spite of this tendency toward uniformity, Egypt, like many emerging nations, is faced with a political culture that is fragmented between traditional and modern concepts of authority and political action, which hindered Nasser's attempt to introduce attitudes, values, and behavioral norms conducive to the achievement of modernization. But as many new symbols of power and legitimacy are accepted and internalized by the Egyptian masses, their support and acceptance of old patterns of power and control will diminish, and Nasser's attempts to introduce the concepts of land reform, social equality, antifeudalism, and government responsibility will gradually encourage citizens to turn to the central government instead of to traditional sources for leadership and guidance.

Influence of Nasser

Probably the greatest influence on Egypt's present political environment is the memory of Nasser, who ruled Egypt for nearly twenty years and who suddenly died of a heart attack on September 29, 1970. Few political leaders have had such a profound impact on their countries. Egyptians identified with this great leader and thus accepted many of the regime's symbols and values, which were validating a new pattern of leadership and legitimacy. Nasser was the undisputed leader of progressive forces in the Arab world. He shifted the balance of power in the Middle East and inspired the Arabs to new superlatives of ferment and energy. Few leaders in the Arab world appealed to the masses as Nasser did. After five days of crushing defeats in the 1967 War, Nasser publicly accepted culpability on June 10, 1967, but his decision to retire to private life was met with a popular demand for his return. The almost hysterical grief at Nasser's funeral dramatized the depths to which the loss of this charismatic leader shook the Arab world.

To understand the popularity of Nasser, we must recognize first that he was a genuine son of the Nile and perhaps the first "true Egyptian" to rule Egypt since the days of the pharaohs. Second, Nasser was a military leader, and in Arab history the legitimate claims of authority and rulership have traditionally rested on a foundation of power and military success. Third, Nasser's charisma rested on a series of successful exploits. He ousted the king and the land-rich pashas, instituted a measure of land reform, established real social and apparent political equality, and attempted to clean up the corruption and squalor that had characterized the government of Egypt for centuries. Nasser negotiated the removal of the British base in the Suez Canal Zone and a final solution for the Anglo-Egyptian condominium in the Sudan. He demonstrated his independence of the West and his determination to deal forcefully with Israel by buying large quantities of arms from the Communist bloc and by nationalizing the Suez Canal in 1956. These successful attempts at defying the old order, though never fully understood by the average Egyptian, verified in their eyes his power and influence; his success proved that "Allah was with him."

Nasser's image did not remain untarnished, however. The illustrious prototype for future united Arab states was nullified in 1961 when Syria withdrew from the United Arab Republic; Nasser's support of Yemeni Republican forces in 1962 (see the chapters "Yemen Arab Republic" and "International Perspectives" for details) failed to recapture the brilliance of his earlier international exploits; the fiasco in June 1967 signaled a most humiliating debasement for Nasser's image; and more recently, student riots in 1968 and 1969, disaffection in the army, and an increasing dependence on the Soviet Union probably lessened his popularity, although they did not weaken his hold on the reins of power.

Today the political environment in Egypt is relatively stable despite Nasser's death. This apparent calm can be misleading, however, for a number of political forces are capable of fomenting unrest and violence. Nasser's attempt to neutralize all groups that were in competition with his rule forced many underground or into exile, and today such groups, including the religious Muslim Brotherhood, the outlawed Communist party, various landowning families, intellectuals, and students, present a potential threat to the new regime. Even within the military and the bureaucracy a maze of divergent groups vacilate among pro-Russian, pro-Western, and neutralist persuasions.

During Nasser's years in power he came to symbolize a pattern of political beliefs that rested or his personality and on an ideological system—Arab socialism. If Nasser's authority and new ideological commitments are to outlive him, the basis for his authority must be transferred to institutions and structures. Nasser's regime recognized this problem, and in recent years had strengthened the civil administration and established a pervasive political party (the Arab Socialist Union) in an attempt to institutionalize the goals and reforms championed by Nasser and to gain popular acceptance of Arab socialism.

Political Structure

Between 1952 and 1956 Egypt was ruled by the Revolutionary Command Council. Although some council members had specific responsibilities, the council as a whole did not share policy-making prerogatives. With the announcement of the republic in 1953, a cabinet composed of military officers and civilians was established, with each member of the RCC assigned to a particular ministry.

Early in the regime Nasser promised a return to civilian government pending the settlement of domestic and international problems. This transition period ended in June 1956, when martial law was terminated, press censorship was formally abolished, political prisoners were released, and the RCC was publicly discontinued. However, members of the RCC, except Major General Amir (minister of defense), retired from the military service and appeared in all government activities as civilians. A general plebiscite on June 23, 1956, formally accepted the new constitution, and on the same date Nasser was elected president, but the Suez Canal crisis of 1956 postponed the election of the National Assembly until July 1957.

Some of the provisions and phrasing of Nasser's new constitution were apparently patterned after the U.S. Constitution; the opening statement begins "We, the Egyptian people." Many of the major policies of the RCC were enunciated in the new constitution: abolishment of feudalism, monopoly, and imperialism. A fairly comprehensive bill of rights was included, and the constitution provided for a 350-member National Assembly, with all candidates to be nominated by Nasser's newly created political party—the National Union. On close analysis, however, the office of president was structured to dominate the entire system, and the National Assembly, with all its members screened for political loyalty to Nasser, readily accepted the legislative program submitted by the chief executive.

The United Arab Republic

In early 1958, Syrian leaders, fearing an internal Communist takeover, pleaded with Nasser to form a union of Egypt and Syria for mutual protection and development. In spite of Nasser's misgivings, the United Arab Republic was proclaimed on February 21, 1958, when the people of Egypt and Syria participated in a plebiscite that approved both the creation of the UAR and the acceptance of Nasser as president. The provisional constitution, which was announced in March, proclaimed the UAR to be a democratic, independent, sovereign state.

The new constitution provided for the creation of a presidential democratic system with the executive authority to be vested in the head of state, who was to be assisted by ministers appointed by him and responsible to him. Nasser appointed four vice-presidents (two Egyptians and two Syrians), a cabinet consisting of fourteen Egyptians and seven Syrians, and a 600-member National Assembly structured to include 400 Egyptians and 200 Syrians. Two regional councils (one for Egypt and one for Syria) were established to provide advice and counsel to the president. These councils were largely ignored, however; President Nasser and his chief lieutenants ruled both areas largely through decrees. Much of this authoritarian rule was deemed appropriate by the Egyptian government, but Syrian military leaders regretted their decision to unite with Egypt and on September 28, 1961, engineered a bloodless coup and seceded from the UAR. Nasser bowed to this regional decision but announced that Egypt would still be known as the United Arab Republic.

The dissolution of the union led to an intensification in Egypt of the drive toward nationalization and the creation of a completely socialist state. Convinced that the Syrian secession was mainly caused by the forces of reaction in Syria itself and in the Arab world generally, Nasser decided that the social revolution he had pursued must be completed to curb the power of capitalists and landowners and to present a stronger appeal to the masses. Nasser thus implemented a widespread policy of sequestration of the property of wealthy families, restricting annual income to less than $20,000 and land holdings to 100 acres.

In May 1962 a newly-elected National Congress of Popular Forces unanimously adopted Nasser's new Charter for Democracy, Socialism, and Arab Unity. Nasser emphasized the need to create a new political organization based on collective leadership and declared that the new constitution must ensure that farmers and workers hold at least half the seats in the national legislature. In March 1964 elections were held, and 1,750 candidates competed for 350 seats in the National Assembly. In accordance with the law, half of those elected were workers or farmers. Shortly after the elections, a new provisonal constitution declared the UAR to be a "democratic socialist state based on an alliance of the working forces of the people." This new constitution of 1964 established the president of the republic as head of state, chief executive, and commander-in-chief of the armed forces. The constitution specifically authorized the president to appoint vice-presidents (usually five or six), to be responsible for specific activities of government, and to select a cabinet (of twenty-five to thirty members), whose major function would be to implement policy and to administer the general affairs of state.

The Al-Sadat Era

When al-Sadat succeeded President Nasser, many dismissed him as a "caretaker" who would soon be replaced by a more powerful leader. One year later al-Sadat was still the leader of Egypt and was running the government with far greater authority and efficiency than most would have believed possible. In early May 1971 Vice-President Ali Sabri, former secretary-general of the Arab Socialist Union and a man known for his pro-Soviet Union tendencies, was caught attempting to overthrow al-Sadat and was subsequently arrested. A new government was announced on May 14, 1971, and several ministers and members of the National Assembly closely aligned to Ali Sabri were also purged.

On May 20, 1971, far-reaching reforms were announced; al-Sadat noted that the ASU would not be abolished, merely reorganized and reformed. He also promised that a new system would be established to ensure more equitable welfare, a strengthened judiciary, and guaranteed social and political freedom for all. New elections for the 5,720 basic units took place July 1, 1971. By the beginning of 1972 Egypt had a new name (Arab Republic of Egypt) and a new constitution and was a member (with Libya and Syria) of the Federation of Arab Republics.

This new constitution, the first permanent constitution since Nasser came to power in 1952, defines Egypt as democratic and socialist and designates Islam as the state religion and the ASU as the sole political party. Executive authority is vested in the president, who may appoint one or more vice-presidents and who appoints all ministers. The president, who must be at least forty years old, is nominated by the People's Assembly and elected for a six-year term by popular referendum. The People's Assembly, made up of at least 350 members elected for five-year terms, is the legislative branch of government and it approves general policy, the budget, and the development plan. Al-Sadat has always claimed continuity, and in most public utterances he claims he is merely following policies formulated by Nasser.

Political Processes

In order to maintain the nation's stability as modern social, cultural, economic, and political structures replaced traditional patterns, the Egyptian government developed a political system based on strong central authority, a system in which communication was most often directed down from those in authority to the people, a system that was generally unwilling to tolerate political autonomy in institutions, groups, or individuals. But in order for traditional attitudes to change completely, social groups must feel that they are part of the political process. And as Nasser's government programs and social services became accepted, as the people began to understand the privileges and responsibilities of citizenship in a modern state, they began to demand the right to participate in decisions that affected their lives. Nasser's solution to this participation crisis was the creation of local government councils and political party organs through which popular demands could be articulated and channeled to the central government.

The Arab Socialist Union

The Arab Socialist Union was Nasser's third attempt to create a mass-based organization. The first two attempts, the Liberation Rally and the National Union, failed because Nasser tried to mobilize the entire nation behind the goals and aspirations of a modernizing elite that still felt compelled to rely on political structures primarily to prevent certain groups from participating in the political process. Little spontaneous support and enthusiasm were allowed to germinate in either the Liberation Rally or the National Union, and undoubtedly the major function of the parties was prevention of the participation of any group opposed to the policies and programs of the ruling elite. Analysis thus suggests that these early experiments in mass mobilization were attempted because of Nasser's fear of the past rather than because of his hope for the future.

One innovation that distinguishes the ASU from Nasser's previous mass parties is the recruitment pattern for all elective units.

The charter states: "The popular and political organizations based on free and direct elections must truly and fairly represent the power forming the majority of the population. . . . It follows then that the new constitution must ensure that its farmers and workmen will get half the seats in political and popular organizations at all levels, including the National Assembly."

Nearly six million members of the ASU are distributed among 7,584 basic units (the lowest organizational unit), each of which elects a ten-member basic unit committee. The membership of each committee must be at least 50 percent workers or peasants. (A worker is defined as one who "works manually or intellectually in industry, agriculture, or services, and lives from the income of this work." A peasant is one who, with his immediate family, "does not possess more than ten feddans of land"; agriculture must be "his source of income and only work" and he must "live in the country-side.") One hundred eighty thousand candidates sought membership on basic unit committees at the June 25, 1968, elections.

The next level of organization is the district, which includes a congress composed of delegates elected by the basic units under its jurisdiction. Each congress in turn elects a twenty-member governing committee from among its members, and the committee selects a secretary and two assistant secretaries from among its members. In each of Egypt's twenty-five governorates, the next level of organization, there is a governorate congress consisting of elected delegates from the district congresses. The number of representatives sent by each district is determined by the size of the district congress, with a maximum of sixteen representatives from one district. A committee of twenty members is elected by each governorate congress from its members.

The National Congress of the ASU includes all members of the governorate congresses, plus the fifty members of the Election Supervision Committee, totaling eighteen to nineteen hundred members. The National Congress elects the highest governing bodies of the ASU from among its members. First of these bodies is the 150-member Central Committee, which in turn elects the Higher Executive Committee of ten men and a chairman, who until his death was President Nasser. It is interesting to note that immediately after Nasser's death, this Higher Executive Committee submitted a formal report to the ASU Central Committee, nominating Anwar al-Sadat, Egypt's chief vice-president under Nasser, to be the new president. On October 15, 1970, 7,143,839 Egyptians participated in the nationwide presidential election that gave al-Sadat 90.04 percent of the total vote.

Far more significant than the ASU's organizational structure is the role this single-party system plays in the Egyptian political process. The struggle for power in Egypt was decided in the early years of the revolution, when all political parties, groups, and individuals opposed to President Nasser's rule were removed. Because it has a monopoly of political power, the ASU fulfills a familiar function of political parties everywhere—recruiting members for positions of political leadership. Also, the ASU serves as an agency of aggregation and integration of popular political demands and as an organization from which programs, platforms, ideological positions, and policies can emerge. Policy formation in Egypt was primarily the result of deliberation among Nasser's close associates in the government and in the Arab Socialist Union. As the responsibility for policy formulation gradually shifts to the party, the ASU will become the arena within which all conflicts of interest in the Egyptian political system must occur. Egyptian leaders must therefore learn to formulate policies that will not disrupt the political system itself; they must steer carefully among the conflicting interests of labor, students, and professional and agricultural groups.

Another important function of the ASU can be described as political communication, which involves different but related tasks. One task is obtaining information from and about various groups in Egyptian society. The ruling elite must keep itself informed about all developments within the entire system that might affect the success or failure of its goals and policies. By delegating to the members of the ASU the supervision of the execution of policies, the government elite can gather much of the information it needs through the ASU hierarchy. But the central government also wants information about the needs and interests of the groups composing Egyptian society, and thus the government needs a communications system that moves up from the masses, enabling the government to gauge public opinion. The second communications task is the downward flow of instructions that control the political, economic, and social policies implemented by the central administrative agencies. Recently it has appeared that local ASU units have been used to check and evaluate the degree to which bureaucratic agencies are implementing the directives and communiqués from Cairo.

Today the ASU is organized as a command structure in which information moves up and policies and directives are handed down. In an attempt to increase its attractiveness and acceptance by society, the ASU has sought to monopolize all symbols of progress, reform, modernity, and prosperity. The local press cooperates to strengthen the ASU's image as the instrument through which change is introduced. The single-party organization in Egypt encourages mass political participation but only within carefully controlled and prescribed limits. Participation is only a means to mobilize the population for modernization.

Egypt's Pattern of Arab Socialism

Because of the tenacity of traditional belief systems, many emerging nations are concerned with developing new ideologies that will neutralize and even replace older systems. The new belief system in Egypt is Arab socialism, and the charter is the written embodiment of this comprehensive national socialist doctrine, outlining the historical dimensions of the modern Egyptian's new identity. The charter places the Egyptian people in the stream of human history, noting that

Egypt's unique role in history has been to defend and preserve the "heritage and wealth of Arab civilization." Egypt's decline is attributed to foreign domination, which saw "the whole area swept by the darkness of the Ottoman invasion." No Egyptian need feel inferior before Western civilization, for "modern science developed by Europe out of the science taken over from other civilizations, foremost among which is the Pharaonic-Arab civilization." Thus the past need not be rejected or vilified, for in reality the greatness of Egypt today rests in part on this "sacred mission" of past generations.

History not only establishes a sense of identity but explains most of the problems facing Egypt today. Nasser, seeking to discover the cause of the present-day Egyptian's apathy and unconcern, lamented: "My soul is torn with grief when I think, as I often do, of that period in our history when a despotic feudalism was formed; a feudalism directed towards bleeding the people and depriving them of their last vestige of power and dignity. We shall have to fight hard and long before we can rid ourselves completely from the deleterious effect of that system."

Although history clarifies Egypt's position and identity in the present, Arab socialism is conceived as the key to realizing a future commensurate with the greatness of Egypt's past. The charter notes that "the socialist solution was a historical inevitability imposed by reality, the broad aspirations of the masses and the changing nature of the world in the second part of the twentieth century." Yet Ali Sabri, a leading figure in Nasser's ASU, has argued that socialism must not be construed as a sharp break with Egypt's past, for "the Charter has established religion as the foundation of our surge forward as the substance of social revolution, for the prophets always constituted a revolutionary force for social justice and against the exploitation of man by man. Consequently, all revealed religion constituted a principal factor in our socialist ideology."

In Nasser's view, socialism is compatible with Egypt's past, but more importantly, it implies a rejuvenation of a past Arab characteristic—interest in science and the scientific method as a tool for man to use in an attempt to free himself from the restrictions of his environment. Nasser continually sought to emphasize that "scientific socialism" is the key to progress. Arab socialism must not be seen as springing from Western or Marxist teachings, for its concepts and beliefs originated in the Arab and Islamic tradition. It accepts private property, sees human competition as a necessary process for growth and development, and denies the Communist concepts of class war, atheism, and the dictatorship of the proletariate. Finally, Arab socialism seeks to bring about social, economic, and political equality among all citizens.

Foreign Policy

Egypt's foreign policy is determined by its geographic location, Islamic and Arab affiliations, and most significantly at the present time, by the four-cornered confrontation of Egypt, Israel, the Soviet Union, and the United States.

Until the summer of 1955 U.S.-Egyptian diplomatic relations were characterized by friendship and optimism for the future. The American government had appropriated over $40 million for economic development between 1952 and 1955, and hundreds of technicians had been sent to train Egyptian workers and peasants. During this period the United States also acted several times as the mediator between Britain and Egypt in solving their differences regarding the Sudan and the stationing of British troops in the Suez Canal Zone.

Relations between the U.S. and Egypt became strained during 1955 and 1956, however. The establishment of the Western-sponsored Baghdad Pact in early 1955 was greatly resented by President Nasser, who perceived it as an attempt to divide the Arab world and to force Arab leaders into a defense agreement at the very time when the Middle East was seeking autonomy and independence from Western colonialism. Increased pressures and intrusions into Israel by Palestinian refugees in late 1954 and the subsequent Israeli retaliatory raids galvanized the Egyptian government into seeking military aid. The refusal of the United States to furnish Nasser with arms resulted in the famous Czechoslovakian arms deal of September 1955, in which Nasser received a substantial quantity of military equipment in exchange for Egyptian agricultural produce. This blow to Western prestige, coupled with Nasser's later recognition of Red China, provoked John Foster Dulles to withdraw an earlier offer to finance the much-needed Aswan High Dam. Nasser's reaction to this "Western affront" was the nationalization of the Suez Canal in July 1956; he argued that Egypt did not need Western aid and that Egypt would finance the Aswan Dam through the proceeds of the Suez Canal.

Israel was deeply concerned over Nasser's increased influence and military capability (which was demonstrated by Egyptian commando raids into Israel), and in late October 1956 Israel suddenly invaded Egypt, quickly destroyed the Egyptian forces in Sinai, and moved to the edge of the Suez Canal. Britain and France issued an ultimatum that both Egyptian and Israeli forces must withdraw at least ten miles from the Suez Canal so that joint Anglo-French control over the canal could be established. When Nasser rejected these demands, French and British forces moved against Egypt. Immediate reaction from both the United States and the Soviet Union plus widespread opposition at home and abroad forced the French and British to terminate their military operations in Egypt. Nasser emerged a national hero and his reputation rapidly spread throughout the Arab world.

Egypt's foreign policy gradually crystallized after the 1956 Suez Canal crisis, based on Nasser's political insight, his pragmatic evaluation of Egypt's national interest, and his desire to focus world attention on Arab goals. The fundamentals of Egypt's foreign policy came to include (1) a commitment to Arab nationalism, including the eventual unity and development of the Arab world, (2) a desire to see Egypt emerge as a power whose voice will be heard in the councils of world leadership, and (3) the acceptance of neutralism as the basis on which relations with other states will be established.

Of specific concern to the United States has been Egypt's gradual shift to an anti-American position and her concomitant identification with the Soviet Union and acceptance of Soviet aid— results mainly of Nasser's commitment to socialism, the withdrawal of American aid, the establishment and growth of the state of Israel, and the long-range goals of Russian foreign policy. To place the anti-American stance of Arab nationalism in context, we must see the revolutionary forces of the Middle East as directed against the status quo as both an internal social order and an external relationship with the Western powers. Although the U.S. encouraged withdrawal of British troops from Egypt's Canal Zone, cold war preoccupations led to American identification with the British and French colonial powers, and as the leading Western power, the United States has emerged as the main bulwark of this status quo.

Significantly, this status quo has also been under attack from the Soviet Union since the Bolshevik Revolution of 1917. Thus Egypt, like so many of the newer nations, found herself tactically united with the Communists, while the United States, with commitments to NATO, Middle East oil interests, and friendship with traditional oligarchies, emerged as anti-Communist and also antinationalist. The Soviet Union was far ahead of the United States in recognizing the advantages of encouraging instead of obstructing the growth of neutralism in the Arab world, at least in part because the self-extrication of Arab countries from special politicomilitary ties with Western powers represented a net loss for the West, whereas it entailed no loss of established positions to the Soviet Union. Whatever the reasons, the fact remains that the Soviet Union began in the early 1950s to extend aid and encouragement to the nationalism sweeping the Middle East precisely at the time when the United States was becoming more militant in its efforts to force the Arab states into Western military alliances. From the long-range point of view, it appears that this contrast between Eastern and Western policies augmented the original causes of Arab distrust of the West. Gradually the Soviet Union has come to identify with Arab nationalism as a means of weakening Western influence in the Arab world, of achieving access to the warm-water ports, and eventually of denying Middle Eastern petroleum reserves to NATO allies. These trends have been deeply reinforced by the Arab-Israeli conflict.

During the first week of June 1967 the Arab world suffered one of its most disastrous defeats. Nasser announced his resignation and took full responsibility for the defeat, in which 15,000 Arab soldiers were killed, nearly $2 billion worth of Arab military equipment was lost, and 26,000 square miles of Arab soil was occupied. Within three years after the Israeli victory, however, the USSR had refurnished the Egyptian armed forces with warplanes, tanks, and missiles and with 8,000 Russian advisers, pilots, and technicians to provide technical support.

Today President al-Sadat, like his predecessor, insists that Egypt would accept a political settlement with Israel if it were based on the

U.N. Security Council resolution (November 22, 1967), which requires "withdrawal of Israeli armed forces from territories occupied in the recent conflict; termination of all claims or states of belligerency and respect for and acknowledgement of the sovereignty, territorial integrity, and political independence of every State in the area and their right to live in peace within secure and recognized boundaries free from threats or acts of force; guaranteeing freedom of navigation through international waterways in the area; achieving a just settlement of the refugee problem; and guaranteeing the territorial inviolability and political independence of every State in the area, through measures including the establishment of demilitarized zones." Although an uneasy cease-fire was adopted in August 1970 by President Nasser and the Israeli government, the Arab-Israeli conflict remains unresolved.

Political Prospects

Egypt's prospects must be interpreted largely in terms of her past. Following centuries of political apathy, foreign domination, and centralized government control, the Egyptian masses were slow to harken to Nasser's call for modernization and development. The programs of the central ministries, the ASU party activities, and the local government institutions developing in the rural provinces of Egypt were heralded as positive proof of Nasser's concern for the Egyptian masses, and his personal integrity and devotion to Egypt's growth and development should not be doubted. But if Nasser's policies, programs, and institutions are to permanently influence Egyptian leaders and citizens, his charismatic authority must be institutionalized into government structures, procedures, and organizations that will survive him.

Today Egyptian leaders appear committed to pursuing the programs and policies for national development initiated by President Nasser. Armed with the powerful memory of Nasser's goals, the new regime must seek to channel this memory into policies that will stimulate development and reform. Recent events suggest, however, that Egypt is on the threshold of a completely new political identity. In March 1971 Egypt and Syria placed their armies under a single military command, and on September 1, 1971, Egypt, Libya, and Syria formed the Federation of Arab Republics. Sudan has also expressed a desire to join. A united Libya, Sudan, Egypt, and Syria would have a total population of 55 million (becoming the fourteenth most populous state in the world) and a land area of just over 2 million square miles (the seventh largest in the world). The economies of the four countries are broadly complementary: Libya has substantial mineral resources, and oil could bring in $2 billion in foreign currency in 1972 (based on the 1970 level of production). Sudan and Syria have vast expanses of cultivable land; and Egypt has a substantial surplus of human resources, skilled and unskilled.

Nasser's death provides a break in Egypt's drive for modernization and allows a brief pause for reflection. The new rulers of Egypt must analyze what Nasser accomplished, and perhaps more important, what he did not accomplish, because although his accomplishments were great, his unfulfilled dreams were even greater. This, then, is the challenge facing Egypt's present leadership.

Footnotes

[1] Tawfiq al-Hakim, *Maze of Justice*, trans. A. S. Eban (London: Harvill Press, 1947), p. 99.
[2] Neguib, *Egypt's Destiny*, p. 85.
[3] El-Sadat, *Revolt on the Nile*, p. 12.
[4] Gamal Abdul Nasser, *Egypt's Liberation: The Philosophy of the Revolution* (Washington, D.C.: Public Affairs Press, 1955), pp. 34-35.

Selected Bibliography

Copeland, Miles. *The Game of Nations*. New York: Simon and Schuster, 1969.
Detailed description of Nasser's foreign policies and the role of various foreign powers in shaping events in the Middle East by an ex-CIA agent.

Cremeans, Charles. *The Arabs and the World: Nasser's Arab Nationalist Policy*. New York: Frederick A. Praeger, 1963.
An excellent attempt to describe the political and ideological foundations of Nasser's foreign policy.

Cromer, Earl of. *Modern Egypt*. 2 vols. New York: Macmillan Co., 1908.
A personal account of Lord Cromer's rule over Egypt during the latter part of the nineteenth century.

Issawi, Charles. *Egypt in Revolution: An Economic Analysis*. London: Royal Institute of International Affairs, 1963.
A detailed analysis of Nasser's economic progress and developments, with special emphasis on Egypt's socialist policies.

Lacouture, Jean, and Lacouture, Simonne. *Egypt in Transition*. New York: Criterion Books, 1958.
One of the earliest and most complete analyses of the Nasser regime in the 1950s; a detailed survey of economic, social, and political changes.

Mansfield, Peter. *Nasser's Egypt*. London: Penguin Books, 1965.
Description of the problems facing Egypt and an objective analysis of Nasser's programs and policies by an English journalist.

Mayfield, James B. *The Politics of Rural Egypt: Nasser's Quest for Legitimacy*. Austin, Texas: University of Texas Press, 1971.
An in-depth analysis of Nasser's attempt to introduce reform and modernization into the rural areas of Egypt. Emphasis on the role of village councils, the Arab Socialist Union, and Egyptian rural bureaucracy in solving the problems of the Egyptian fellaheen.

Neguib, Mohammed. *Egypt's Destiny*. New York: Doubleday and Co., 1955.

Personal description of the Egyptian revolution and its goals by the Egyptian general invited to head the Free Officers organization.

El-Sadat, Anwar. *Revolt on the Nile*. New York: John Day Co., 1957.

An inside description of the Free Officers' organization, including several interesting anecdotes about events leading to the 1952 revolution.

Safran, Nadav. *Egypt in Search of Political Community*. Cambridge, Mass.: Harvard University Press, 1961.

An extremely well-written analysis of Egyptian political thought, which largely shaped the modern philosophical and ideological trends of the Egyptian political system.

Tignor, R. L. *Modernization and British Colonial Rule in Egypt, 1882-1914*. Princeton, N.J.: Princeton University Press, 1966.

A well-written analysis of British administration during the British rule in Egypt. Probably one of the most objective and complete studies available on this period.

Vatikiotis, P. J. *The Egyptian Army in Politics*. Bloomington, Ind.: Indiana University Press, 1961.

An American political scientist presents a systematic description of the Egyptian army and its role in the political system of the United Arab Republic.

Vatikiotis, P. J., ed. *Egypt since the Revolution*. New York: Frederick A. Praeger, 1968.

One of the few up-to-date scholarly descriptions of Egypt during the latter 1960s; various scholars on the economic, political, social, and literary developments of the United Arab Republic.

Wheelock, Keith. *Nasser's New Egypt*. New York: Frederick A. Praeger, 1960.

A carefully documented analysis of the Nasser regime, including changes and trends.

Republic of Iraq

The ancient civilization of Iraq, formerly known as Mesopotamia, was as highly developed and as influential as that of ancient
Egypt. Modern Iraq, however, is a developing state that was established
as a result of the dismemberment of the Ottoman Empire following
World War I. Iraq is an artificial creation resulting mainly from
Anglo-French plans to establish a state regardless of ethnic, religious,
social, or political considerations, and it thus lacks a national identity
and other prerequisites for a viable state. The country is beset by
cultural fragmentation, a heterogeneous population structure, and
political cleavages that reflect traditional attitudes. In the countryside
particularly, primary loyalty still belongs to the family or religious
community rather than to the state; indeed, the concept of a
nation-state is foreign to many communities. Political forces in Iraq
contribute to both national integration and disintegration: some of the
Kurds, who constitute an ethnic minority, are attempting to divide
Iraq, Pan-Arabs advocate an allegiance that cuts across political
boundaries of all Arab states; and another group advocates Iraqi
nationalism. Under such conditions the governance of Iraq is indeed a
difficult task.

In 1920 Iraq adopted a monarchical system of government,
which was overthrown in 1958 by army officers led by Abd al-Karim
Qasim, "the sole leader," who proclaimed a republic. During the
republican era, new political groups emerged and the country's policies
changed, but political styles and institutions remained basically intact
and no change occurred in the political culture. Reformists in Iraq
desire to establish a modern state with workable institutions, although
the immediate aim may not be democracy, a system not necessarily
suitable to conditions in Iraq. The formula has not yet been found, and
political experimentation continues, Iraq, an emerging country rich in

natural resources, is thus undergoing recurrent, intense growing pains in her search for identity.

Historical Background

The Sumerians founded city-states in southern Mesopotamia about 3000 B.C. and were followed by the Akkadian, Babylonian, and Assyrian civilizations. The Persians seized the area in 539-38 B.C., and Alexander the Great brought Persian rule to an end between 334 and 327 B.C. In 637 A.D. Iraq was conquered by the Arabs, and in 750 the Abbasids transferred the seat of the Muslim empire from Damascus to Baghdad, which became a center of science, culture, trade, and military and political power. In 1258 the Mongols captured Baghdad and ended Abbasid rule. Mongol devastation was severe in Iraq and included considerable damage to the irrigation system and the destruction of centuries of accomplishments. Commerce was crippled, and the country never recovered. In the sixteenth century the region fell to the Ottoman Turks, under whose rule it remained until World War I.

Establishment of Independent Iraq

Three Ottoman provinces—Mosul, Basrah, and Baghdad—were consolidated into a new state following the Allied defeat of the Ottoman government in 1918, and for two years the area was administered by the commander-in-chief of British forces. The new regime was more modern and efficient than its Turkish predecessor, yet because the regime was alien and non-Muslim it was distrusted by both Muslims of Ottoman loyalty and Iraqi nationalists. At the Paris Peace Conference plans for disposing of non-Turkish former Ottoman provinces were presented, and a compromise between outright annexation and complete independence was reached under Article 22 of the League of Nations Covenant. Accordingly, Iraq was entrusted as a Class A mandate to the United Kingdom on April 25, 1920 (see the Glossary for a description of the mandate system).

The announcement of the mandatory regime spurred nationalist feeling, which had been mounting since the last phase of Ottoman domination. The word *mandate* was immediately discredited as a disguise for colonialism, and efforts were made to abolish the mandate system. Growing tension reached a climax in the revolt of June 1920 and normal administrative control was not completely restored until the spring of 1921.

At a Cairo conference in March 1921 British officials decided to establish an Arab kingdom in Iraq. Instead of proposing an Iraqi as king, however, the British put forth a Hashimite, Amir Faysal (the son of Sharif Husayn, a leader of the Arab revolt against the Ottomans), who had already lost the Syrian throne. He assumed power on August 23, 1921, after an endorsement by a plebiscite described as "politics running on wheels greased with extremely well-melted grease."[1] The regime thus established was unique among the mandated territories. William Rappard observed that Iraq "could be compared to a two-faced Janus—one face, looking towards Geneva, wearing the expression of a mandate, and the other face, looking towards Baghdad, wearing the expression of a treaty. . . . It was quite clear that Iraq was administered under Article 22 of the Covenant."[2] The original text of the mandate was replaced by treaties, subsidiary agreements, and protocols concluded between Iraq and Britain, which were approved by the Council of the League of Nations.

Despite the establishment of an Arab kingdom in Iraq, the British retained extensive control. During the 1920s Iraqi demands for complete independence became more vocal, and intensive Anglo-Iraqi negotiations took place. The United Kingdom was aware of the country's economic and strategic importance and Iraq's aim was complete self-rule; it was therefore difficult to develop a formula ensuring the preservation of mutual interests. Taking into account his experience in Syria, Faysal pursued a moderate approach toward Britain. In April 1930 the countries concluded a compromise that was to last twenty-five years and which terminated the British mandate. The agreement provided for full consultations in foreign affairs and mutual aid in time of war, and British forces maintained two military bases in Iraq. On October 3, 1932, Iraq was admitted to the League of Nations.

In 1939 war swept Europe, and Axis successes strongly impressed Iraqi political circles. Ultranationalists desired German victory as a means to end Anglo-French control over Arab territories. Allied war reverses and anti-British sentiment strengthened neutralist and ultranationalist tendencies and allowed the Axis to make considerable propaganda inroads, and Iraqi leaders became divided about policy toward the big powers. Would Iraq gain more from cooperating with the Axis or by continuing to support Great Britain? In 1941 a coup d'état brought Rashid Ali al-Gaylani to power, and Nuri al-Said, Iraq's "strong man," and regent Abd al-Ilah escaped to Jordan. Differences between British and Iraqi interpretations of treaty obligations, the nonbelligerent attitude of al-Gaylani's cabinet, and Iraq's strategic importance led to the second British occupation in May 1941. Al-Gaylani's government was overthrown, and Nuri al-Said and the palace reassumed political power with even greater influence.

Al-Said had become prominent, but he failed to build a party organization and to attract followers capable of succeeding him in command. He was a competent, if autocratic, politician trained in the tradition of the Ottoman officer corps; he showed skill, leadership, and a capacity for political survival for over forty years. His dominance in the political arena of Iraq was so great that no potential successor could emerge.

Republican Iraq in the Making

After World War II there was intense politicization among the masses; only the army and security forces maintained the power of the oligarchy. The gap between popular expectations and government performance fostered disillusionment with paternalism. Iraqis demanded the abrogation of the 1930 Anglo-Iraqi treaty, pursuance of a policy of positive neutrality, greater political liberties, and land redistribution and other economic reforms. The opposition often resorted to "street power," a traditional Iraqi forum for political expression. In 1948 Iraq and Britain revised the Anglo-Iraqi treaty of 1930 by concluding the Portsmouth Agreement, which sparked intense popular disturbances—the climax is still celebrated as *al-Wathbah*, the "glorious uprising." In 1952, the year in which the monarchy was overthrown in Egypt, opposition parties unsuccessfully demanded the introduction of direct elections and retorted by calling election boycotts. In November a minor student quarrel ignited an already agitated populace, and disturbances swept the capital and other cities. Police stations were attacked, and the United States Information Service was burned. Demonstrators demanded a government headed by an opposition leader, Kamil al-Chadirchi. This time the oligarchy found it necessary to use the army. Chief-of-Staff Nouri al-Din Mahmoud became prime minister; martial law was declared; political parties were dissolved; and opponents were arrested. However, in December a new electoral law was decreed. The attack on Egypt by France, Britain, and Israel in 1956 also had an intense political impact on Iraqis.

Increased oil revenues had enabled Iraq to embark on programs for economic development, but although these piecemeal reforms were basically sound, they failed to gain popular support or to alter significantly the conditions of the peasants. Economic and social transformations should have been accompanied by new forms of political organization; instead, successive governments used communism as a pretext for limiting political expression. The regime had the characteristics of a police state and was incapable of making the adaptations necessitated by the emergence of a middle class. Many Iraqis detested Nuri al-Said and the crown prince; the country's misfortunes, whether real or imaginary, were blamed on feudalism and imperialism, and in Iraqi eyes the regime was an ally of both.

Nuri al-Said and the palace monopolized power but lacked deep popular support. They refused to expand the base of political participation so the new forces were unrepresented in the decision-making processes. The regime was supported by the upper class, the senior civil and military officials, and government protégés, but the majority of the middle and lower classes were in opposition. Although Nuri al-Said was a capable veteran politician, he was in his late sixties and had grown out of touch with the new generation and the political trends in the country. Gamal Abdul Nasser represented a younger and more vigorous generation, most of whom belonged to middle or lower socioeconomic classes. Although party activities were formally outlawed in 1954, a secret group organized in 1957, the National Union Front, represented opposition parties (including the Communists).

All the ingredients for revolutionary change were present in the 1950s. Civilian opposition provided the psychological atmosphere, and the "free officers" in the army, drawn mostly from modest backgrounds, organized into cells and awaited their opportunity. Under Colonel Abd al-Salam Arif, units of the 19th Brigade carried out a predawn coup d'état on July 14, 1958, and within a few hours all safeguards against a revolution collapsed. The Hashimite monarchy was liquidated, a republic was declared, and Brigadier-General Abd al-Karim Qasim assumed the reins of authority.

Political Fragmentation

Many Iraqis expected the destruction of the monarchy and acquisition of national independence to lead to democratic institutions, but this hope proved delusive. The revolution of 1958 accelerated political fervor, released long-suppressed forces, and sharpened old suspicions. Initial republican solidarity was short-lived; once the monarchy had been overthrown, conflicts among factions in the army and among civilian groups were inevitable, since each faction had aims that were incompatible with those of other groups. Thus Iraq plunged into an era of political chaos and crisis.

Abd al-Karim Qasim emerged from obscurity into a position of leadership, and although he had wide popular support, he lacked the intellectual background and experience demanded by his role. He attempted to keep a political balance by playing off one faction against another rather than by following a middle course: "Just as the rope-dancer has to maintain his balance by swinging from side to side, so did Qasim swing from one ideology to another in order to remain in power, but he himself had no leanings towards any particular idealogy."[3]

A key issue—Arab unity—polarized Iraqi politics immediately following the 1958 revolution. The problem was whether Iraq should foster Pan-Arabism or pursue an Iraqi national policy. To resist attempts at union with the UAR, Qasim tried to stimulate Iraqi nationalism, and he suppressed his chief adversaries, the Baathists and pro-Nasser elements. However, he did not organize his own party, insisting that he was above partisanship, and he was thus driven to depend on the Communists and their sympathizers for support. Again political fragmentation was reinforced by traditional cultural patterns reflected in the multigroup character of the country: initially Qasim received support from the Kurds and, to a lesser extent, from the Shiites, because these groups are apprehensive of Iraq's submergence in a larger Arab state dominated by Arab Sunnis.

In September 1958 Colonel Abd al-Salam Arif, who advocated union with the UAR, was relieved of his post as deputy premier and minister of interior. In November he was arrested, accused of plotting against the regime, and condemned to death, but he was later released. On March 8, 1959, an ill-planned revolt with UAR backing erupted in Mosul, but with the aid of Kurdish tribesmen, loyal army units, and the Communists the uprising was crushed, and Mosul became the scene of atrocities. In July disturbances resulting from political and ethnic (Kurd and Turkoman) tensions broke out in Kirkuk and seventy-nine persons were reported killed. Iraq's perennial family and group allegiances have caused hatred and blood feuds that characterize the country's political atmosphere.

These setbacks weakened the Pan-Arabs. The Communists and leftists received increasing support from the masses and the cabinet, but when it appeared that they were seriously competing for political control, Qasim publicly denounced the Communists and encouraged a split among their ranks. Nonetheless, since the Communists lacked an alternative and shared common adversaries with Qasim, they continued to support his regime. By 1963 Qasim had lost the support of many groups, and on both the domestic and international scenes his government became isolated. The regime suffered economic setbacks and seemed unable to control or moderate opposing political currents. Qasim relied mainly on loyal army units and the security forces, but his political allies, the Communists, were weakened. A Kurdish rebellion in the north and a lack of mass support further weakened the regime's authority.

On February 8, 1963, Baathists, Nasserites, and disenchanted army elements executed Qasim and overthrew his regime, and Pan-Arab groups have since dominated the political scene. Abd al-Salam Arif became president and Brigadier Ahmad Hasan al-Bakr, prime minister. The Baathists headed a new wave of terror, imprisoning opponents and meting out instant "justice," and soon estranged moderates and former supporters like the Nasserites. Attempts to settle the Kurdish problem failed, the new privileged position of the National Guard alienated army professionals; Baathists' insistence on playing a dominant role in Syria and Iraq rendered illusory the Arab Union Pact that had been concluded with the United Arab Republic on April 17. The Iraqi Baathists were engulfed by party factionalism, and being inexperienced in the conduct of government administration, they failed to implement party programs. On November 18, 1963, President Abd al-Salam Arif staged another coup with help from the armed forces, crushed Baathist resistance, and established a new government. In April 1966, after President Arif was killed in a helicopter crash, his brother Abd al Rahman Arif became president. Iraq did not acquire stability, but between 1963 and 1968 high-handed measures were avoided, partly a reaction to earlier excesses and partly an adjustment to new conditions. Meanwhile, the regime constantly faced attempted coups and cabinet changes.

As a result of the 1967 War with Israel, Iraqis felt a strong sense of humiliation that compounded disenchantment with the regime. On July 17, 1968, the "white revolution" was staged; Ahmad Hasan al-Bakr became president and the Baath party reemerged. In 1969 the government conducted fruitless negotiations with the Communists, the Democratic party of Kurdistan, the National Democratic party, and the leftist faction of the Baath party (the National Front) in an attempt to expand its political base and to form a new cabinet under its dominance. However, Marxist Aziz Sharif, formerly leader of the People's party, accepted a cabinet post, and following the 1970 agreement with Kurdish rebels, five Kurds joined the government. Although the cabinet formed in April 1970 was dominated by Baathists, its members were drawn from Iraq's main religious and ethnic groups as well as other political factions, and a woman was included. (The first woman cabinet member was appointed in July 1959.)

This new regime has been sustained by a political organization consisting of disciplined members of the army and segments of the population. Sensitive positions in the political and administrative hierarchy are assigned to Baathists and those loyal to the regime. The Baath party is determined to maintain power by resorting to harsh measures against opponents or by assigning political positions to non-Baathist leaders who accept the regime's dominance. At the same time, it seeks to create political cohesion based on doctrinal principles and programs that aim to modernize Iraq's social and economic institutions. A new experiment is in the making; success or failure will be determined by the ability of the regime to foster among Iraqis a measure of consensus and legitimacy. There are many problems: the military era in Iraq inhibited the country's leadership potential; the army and the administrative machinery have suffered recurring purges; insecurity and fear have directed energies away from the establishment of suitable economic and political institutions; and the country has been besieged with a new Kurdish insurgency.

Political Environment

Iraq was subjected to centuries of misrule. The interwar period however, witnessed an intense conflict between traditionalism and modernism. Particularly since World War II and the introduction of modern mass communications, there has been strong interest in foreign and domestic political ideologies. Awareness of modern institutions has contributed to rising expectations, and hence to rising frustrations. Modernists demand the transformation of their country into an industrialized state, but such hopes do not take into account the incapacity of the country to meet accelerating demands. This has been a cause of recurring changes in government.

As in Lebanon, the multigroup character of the Iraqi society makes the impact of modernization rather disparate; groups tend to accept or reject the concept of a nation-state and modernization in varying degrees, which results in a mixture of traditionalism and modernity that compounds political, religious, and ethnic conflicts.

The People

Ethnic and Religious Groups: The heterogeneous social, religious, and ethnic groups in Iraq and in Syria are politically divisive, unlike those in the Arab Republic of Egypt. This multigroup character and traditional tribal characteristics have developed in the Iraqis a sectarian consciousness resulting in fragmented loyalties, which poses a constant threat to political cohesion. Private and public allegiance exists simultaneously but inharmoniously, and regional, religious, and family loyalties take precedence over national orientation.

There is no real majority in Iraq. The main religious communities in the country are the Shiites and the Sunnis. During the Ottoman-Sunni rule discrimination was practiced against the Shiites, and although the Shiites are a majority among Iraqi Arabs, the Sunnis dominate politically, perpetuating the persecution complex of the Shiites. In recent times, however, the politically aware population has, on the whole, become ideologically oriented, and the sectarian conflict is being subordinated to national political affiliation.

The main ethnic groups are the Arabs and the Kurds. During both the monarchical and the republican eras Kurdish rebellions erupted, and the Muslim Kurds, who are ethnically different from the Arabs, still pose the most serious minority problem. Small Kurdish groups live in Syria and the USSR, but the majority, probably some six million, inhabit parts of Turkey, Iran, and Iraq. Iraq has fewer Kurds than Turkey and Iran, but they represent between 15 and 20 percent of the country's population, and in some areas they are an ethnic majority. The Kurds demand autonomy and complain of discrimination and an inequitable share in Iraq's economic development, yet many Kurds have held high-ranking administrative, political, and military positions. Some have served as prime ministers, cabinet members, deputies, senators, and chiefs of the army general staff.

Widespread Kurdish rebellions occurred in 1919, 1927, and during the 1930-32 period. Because the Kurds live in mountainous areas in the north suppression efforts were costly. In 1943 Mullah Mustafa al-Barzani led a new revolt that was suppressed in 1945, but al-Barzani and his followers fled to the USSR and persisted in fostering Kurdish nationalism. To acquire Kurdish support, Prime Minister Abd al-Karim Qasim granted amnesty in 1958, and 855 of the exiles returned.

The 1958 revolution accelerated the growth of Arab nationalism, but it also stimulated Kurdish demands for a separate or autonomous state. In 1961 al-Barzani led another rebellion, demanding local autonomy, among other things. The Iraqi government and some Kurdish supporters attempted a military solution, but indiscriminate bombing of Kurdish villages only strengthened al-Barzani's movement and necessitated long military operations. External support to the rebels was apparently provided, particularly from Iran. The Kurds were able to sustain guerrilla resistance against an army equipped with modern weaponry.

The Iraqi army was not able to subdue the rebels, yet the Kurds could not achieve military victory either. Cease-fires were announced but fighting broke out; settlement programs were adopted but without significant results. A workable definition of *autonomy* has yet to be found; the central Arab government cannot agree to a plan that might be construed as creating a new political entity, but military approaches cannot provide solutions to what are basically political problems.

A major accomplishment of the new Baathist government is its agreement of March 1970 with the Kurdish rebels. The settlement program recognizes that the Iraqi people consist of two main nationalities—Arabs and Kurds—and the Kurdish language has been officially recognized in addition to Arabic in areas where Kurds constitute a majority. One of the vice-presidents will be a Kurd and there will be Kurdish representation in the cabinet. In future legislative assemblies Kurdish representation will be based on the proportion of the Kurdish population.

Intergroup cleavages in Iraq tend to be reinforced by geographical sectionalism. Sunnis live mainly in the center of political power—Baghdad and northward; the Shiites populate areas in the capital city and southward; and most of the Kurds are settled in the mountainous northern areas. These divisions are compounded by intragroup conflicts based on economic class structure, social status, and ideological differences.

Social Structure: A century ago many Iraqis were nomads, but today most bedouin have settled in villages. The majority of the people in Iraq live in small towns, although since the 1950s the expanding economy has caused many villagers to move to the cities, and many cities have more than doubled their populations. The capital has received most of the influx, and today Baghdad and its environs has a population of two million.

During the monarchy, political influence depended to a large extent on wealth and social position, but the power of large landowners and big businessmen has diminished since the 1958 revolution. The expanding national economy and improved educational facilities have enabled the middle class to assert a greater political role. Prime Minister Qasim, the Arif brothers, and President al-Bakr all came from humble social and economic backgrounds, and political decision making at present generally resides with men who have come from obscure towns and from low-income or middle-income families. At least among the technically educated the belief in predestination has been replaced by the belief that he who works hard shall be rewarded, which contributes to intense interpersonal and group competition. As in other Middle Eastern states, the role of women is undergoing considerable change, and now women are assuming administrative, professional, and political positions.

Within less than one generation Iraq has acquired new social patterns, drastically shaking traditionalism and subjecting her inhabitants to conflicting cultures. Despite social and economic improvements, and although many Iraqis are modern in outlook, they continue to exhibit strong bonds of kinship, which constitutes a cohesive factor at the group level but a divisive element on the national level. These cultural conflicts are reflected in the country's political structures and processes.

Social Conditions: Social and economic reforms were initiated under the monarchy, and the republican regime adopted impressive social and economic legislation, emphasizing the redistribution of wealth, industrialization, and direct exploitation of oil resources. However, politically engendered problems contributed to economic stagnation, and improvements proceeded at a slow pace in comparison to demands and needs.

Economic and social changes are evident in the emphasis placed on education. In 1920 a modern educational system was almost nonexistent, and as recently as 1947 less than 9 percent of the population was literate. Since 1955, however, school enrollment has increased nearly threefold, and in 1969 about 30 percent of the population was literate. The economic capacity of the country has been incapable of absorbing many new college graduates, however, and psychologically the technically educated person often suffers from the cultural gap between the home environment and the foreign milieu in which he was trained. Education has also increased the number of discontented "intellectual refugees" who are demanding changes in Iraq's political processes.

Economic Conditions

Economic development in Iraq has promoted a measure of national cohesion as a result of the growth of the administrative bureaucracy, the labor movements, and the middle class, and increasing political awareness among workers and peasants. Iraq is rich in oil deposits and other minerals. Iraq Petroleum Company, with its associated companies, is the main foreign oil concessionnaire (U.S., British, Dutch, and French interests hold 23.75 percent each, and the C. S. Gulbenkian Estate holds 5 percent). Following fruitless negotiations, the government in 1961 restricted the area of prospecting rights by dispossessing the oil companies of 99.5 percent of the area held under original oil agreements. The Iraq National Oil Company formed in 1964, and in 1969 the Soviet Union granted a $142 million loan to assist INOC in exploiting Iraq's oil deposits.

Oil royalties have become an important source of national revenue—in 1969 oil income amounted to about $485 million, and as a result of a new accord with the oil companies, it is expected that oil income will reach $924 million in 1971. In 1950 a development board was established and 70 percent of oil revenues were allocated to development programs, but this amount was reduced to 50 percent after the revolution of 1958, because implementation of many projects became the responsibility of various ministries, and greater emphasis was placed on providing social services.

Because agriculture absorbs 60 percent of the country's employed, no development program would be effective unless it was accompanied by agrarian reform. Under the monarchy a small minority owned immense amounts of land, but in September 1958 Iraq enacted a land-reform measure limiting land holdings to about 620 and 1240 acres. The peasants received approximately 18 or 36 acres, depending on the method of irrigation used. The year 1963 was set as the deadline for completing land seizure and distribution, but implementation proceeded at a much slower rate; by 1970 perhaps no more than 2 million acres had been distributed among some 60,000 peasants. Since 1958 over 500 agricultural cooperatives have been established.

Political Structure

Because Iraqis are members of minority groups, they tend to suspect government authorities, and although the principles of constitutional government have gained general acceptance among the politically aware segments of the population, such a system has yet to become a workable reality in the political life of the country.

In 1925 Iraq adopted a Western-style parliamentary system of government in form but not in substance, and attempts at institutionalizing this system were unsuccessful. Constitutional enactments emphasized equal rights for all Iraqis, the Kurds being "partners" within a "fraternal unity," and declared that Iraq was an independent Muslim state guaranteeing freedom of expression, a hereditary monarchy, and a representative and secular system of government. In practice, however, power was exercised by an oligarchy drawn from Iraq's major ethnic and religious groups (including Kurds, Christians, and Jews). Parliament was not a forum for expressing and harmonizing diverse interests, and cabinets frequently dissolved the chamber because of the deputies' assertiveness, or conversely, their submissiveness to cabinet will. Since segments of the public considered parliaments excessively submissive to the elite, they often resorted to extraparliamentary means, and the cabinet dissolved the parliament to placate popular dissidence. Between 1925 and 1958 Iraq had sixteen chambers, none serving its full term except the ninth and the twelfth. Oligarchic interference in elections paralyzed the parliamentary system and rendered constitutionalism devoid of political significance.

A new constitution enacted after the revolution of July 1958 declared Iraq a sovereign republic, part of the Arab nation, and declared that Islam was the religion of the state. The presidency of the republic was vested in the Presidential Council, which consisted of three members. Membership in both the cabinet and the council was again distributed among Kurds, Shiites, and Sunnis. It was anticipated that a permanent constitution would be promulgated and general elections held; instead, the government of Iraq regressed into a personal dictatorship under General Abd al-Karim Qasim.

Following Qasim's overthrow in February 1963, the new National Council of the Revolutionary Command assumed both legislative and executive powers. On April 24, 1964, a new provisional constitution was announced. Iraq was again declared part of the Arab nation and a democratic, socialist state that derived its principles from Arab heritage and from Islam. During a transitional period not to exceed three years, a permanent constitution was to be promulgated by "parliament or the rising of [a] state of unity." Neither parliament nor the state of unity has yet been acquired. Although a republican form of government was established in 1958, power was merely transferred to another elite group; regardless of constitutional enactments, traditionalists were replaced by another group dominated by the army.

Political Processes

Iraq's modern political history has been characterized by conflict between the forces of change and those who are endeavoring to maintain the status quo. Coups and countercoups have impeded harmonious political interaction. Government positions in Iraq offer comparatively high financial rewards and social status, and the loss of political tenure drastically reduces personal status. High personal risks therefore contribute to intense competition and extremism among politicians. Iraq has endured continual tension as one faction after another has dominated its political processes.

The Traditional Leadership

A traditional leadership emerged with the establishment of the Hashimite monarchy; centered around the palace, it represented city notables, political clusters, army officers, high administrative officials, and tribal and religious leaders. This oligarchy legitimatized its rule through an impotent parliament unrepresentative of Iraq's economic and political groups.

Iraqi cabinets, whose prominence was enforced by constitutional enactments, exerted a dominating role as the ruling elite made cabinets the focus and the instrument for political control. Cabinet members customarily included Kurds and Shiites, although only five Shiites became prime minister during the fifty-nine cabinets established under the monarchy. Although cabinets changed frequently, ministerial positions have been the monopoly of a small circle. The same prime ministers and ministers appeared again and again, sometimes performing different roles. Between 1920 and 1958 twelve prime ministers formed forty-five cabinets, and the same twelve men held a total of 123 ministerial posts.[4] As prime minister, Nuri al-Said formed fourteen cabinets that lasted for eleven and a half years, and he participated in fifteen others, serving mainly as foreign minister, minister of interior, and minister of defense. Even when not in office he remained a dominant figure. "With a small pack of cards, you must shuffle them often,"[5] he once told Wendell Willkie.

With the establishment of a republic in 1958 two groups emerged on the political scene, political parties and the military, with the latter assuming a dominant position. The role of the traditional leadership diminished after the 1958 revolution.

Political Parties

Political parties in Iraq reflect the fragmented culture of this transitional society. These groups, which are arbitrarily classified below, range from the exclusively ethnic Kurdish to internationalists such as the Communists, who have highly developed ideologies. It should be noted, however, that the party system has failed for several reasons: absence of political freedom, suppression by the oligarchy, use of parties to support the regime in power, individual persecution, personal and factional allegiances, and lack of organizational leadership.

The *personalistic* type of party includes groups limited to followers of a leading political personality such as Nuri al-Said, who in 1949 created the Constitutional Union. That same year the Reform party was organized, which later merged with the People's Socialist, established in 1951 by former prime minister Salih Jabr. The word *socialist*, equated in Iraqi thinking with *progress*, was a misnomer. Except for personal allegiances, Jabr's faction could hardly be differentiated from al-Said's. Traditional politicians joined either group, depending on their private interests.

Associations of political leaders who were attempting to acquire political control and who were advocating a moderate reform program with limited popular appeal can be classified as *pragmatic* parties. In 1946 the Liberal party, including many ex-ministers, was licensed. Following the death or resignation of its leading members, the party disintegrated. The United Popular Front, composed mainly of members of the Chamber of Deputies, was formed in 1951 and provided moderate opposition to the regime's internal and external policies.

Kurdish associations represent the *communal* type of party. The Democratic party of Kurdistan, which advocated Kurdish autonomy, was licensed in 1960 but outlawed in September 1961. In 1964 the Kurdish Revolutionary Command, consisting of the Democratic party of Kurdistan and Kurdish tribal leaders, was established. This coalition directed the struggle against the central government during the 1960s and advocates Kurdish autonomy within an Iraqi republic.

Fundamentalist groups advocate the establishment of an Islamic state with the Quran as the constitutional basis. Such associations have always existed in Iraq, but their political influence has been minimal. In April 1960 an Islamic party advocating policies based on the "spirit of Islam" and demanding the enforcement of Muslim religious codes was licensed, but in March 1961 it was suppressed.

For the purpose of this classification, *nationalist* refers to groups that appeal to many segments of the population, crossing ethnic and religious factions. These groups advocate plans for Arab unification but emphasize a reformed Iraqi state as the immediate aim.

Al-Ahali ("populace") group was formed in the 1930s by men who advocated moderate socialist measures but emphasized democracy. Members of this group organized the National Democratic party in 1946, but due to government suppression its activities were suspended in 1948. In 1960 it was again officially recognized under the leadership of Kamil al-Chadirchi and Muhammad Hadid. This party has suffered many rifts, disagreements erupted over the extent of cooperation with the Communists and Prime Minister Qasim, and party policies toward the new military rule. In 1960 al-Chadirichi insisted that the military regime did not deserve party support, but Hadid objected. These intraparty disagreements weakened the party and its influence declined.

Following his split with the National Democrats, Muhammad Hadid and his faction established the National Progressive party, which was licensed in July 1961. Originally this group supported Qasim, but lack of constitutional progress led the party to criticize his government. Farther to the left were the National Union and the People's parties, both licensed in 1946 but suppressed in 1948. The former stressed socialism and democracy and the latter emphasized Marxist-Leninist socialism. In 1960 a leftist faction led by members from both parties petitioned unsuccessfully for official recognition. The ideas of democracy and socialism, with varying interpretations, appeal to segments of the population, and political organizations persist in advocating these principles regardless of the attitude of the elite in power.

Among the *internationalist* parties are the Communists, who form a worldwide movement. During the 1940s the Communist party emerged, though clandestinely, as a small but well-organized, disciplined group. As a Communist front, the National Liberation party attempted without success to acquire official recognition. The Communist party again failed to acquire official approval following the establishment of the republic; instead, the Iraq Communist party, a splinter group supported by Prime Minister Qasim, was legalized in 1960. Like the transnational Baath party, the Communists emerged as a potent political force following the 1958 revolution. Although Iraqi Communists suffer from disagreements reflecting the ideological fragmentations of international communism flavored by Iraqi conditions, and despite setbacks and repressions, they have endured as a well-organized political group.

The *transnational* type of party includes groups emphasizing Pan-Arabism. The Independence party, advocating a strong Arab nationalist program with domestic reforms, was recognized in 1946.

The main supporters of Egypt's President Nasser came from the Arab nationalist movement, which advocated union with the United Arab Republic. This group, with the Arab Socialist party, the Social Unionist movement, and the Democratic Social Unionists, formed the Arab Socialist Union in 1964. Patterned on its Egyptian counterpart, the ASU functioned as the only legal political party during the Arifs' era. This association was intended as a mobilization organization, but its members had differing interests, and the experiment was a failure.

The Baath party, currently in power, bears the motto "unity, freedom, and socialism." It emerged clandestinely during the 1950s as a small but disciplined group, and despite its limited membership, its organizational structure and penetration among army officers enabled it to become a major political force in 1958. In 1963 the Baath became the only officially recognized party because of the role it played in overthrowing the Qasim regime, and following the 1968 coup d'état, it again became the ruling party. As in Syria, Iraqi Baathists have suffered factional disputes over its programs, particularly in the interpretation of socialism and Arab unity. One group insists that socialism should be based on Arab heritage, while the leftist faction insists on Marxist interpretations. Currently the moderate faction is the ruling party in Iraq, and the leftists are cooperating with the Communists and other groups that challenge the government. It is yet to be seen if the Iraqi Baathists can reconcile their differences and offer programs that will lead to wide public support.

Political parties in Iraq, as in neighboring Syria and Iran, are not organized mass movements that integrate group interests into action to gain and exercise political power in competition with similar groups. Rather, a political elite has always dominated the country's political processes—under the monarchy the traditional leadership monopolized political power, and since 1958 the army has exercised the decisive role.

The Army in Politics

Under Ottoman rule many Iraqis served in the Turkish army—indeed, it was a primary source of professional careers—and many, including Nuri al-Said, joined Sharif Husayn and his sons in the revolt against the Turks. After the establishment of an Arab kingdom in Iraq, trained personnel were needed, and former officers consequently assumed key positions in the administrative and political apparatus of the country. In fact, during the mandatory regime most prime ministers were former army officers, and between 1936 and 1941 and again since 1958, army officers have assumed the role of arbitrators in the political processes of the country.

The army in Iraq has become a major political force partly because army officers were among the first to be exposed to Western education and were thus more receptive to demands for change. Military involvement in politics may also be attributed to a lack of peaceful means for harmonizing differences, the inability of civilians to maintain control, inexperience in self-rule, reliance on the army by civilian governments to curb internal unrest, and the Palestine problem.

During the British mandate the Iraqi leadership was united by the goal of independence, but after the mandatory regime was terminated, divisions within the oligarchy arose. Also, Turkey and Iran altered their institutions, which gave impetus to Iraqi demands for change. Arab frustrations in Lebanon, Syria, and Palestine and internal conditions generated two movements in Iraq, both calling for a new government. The civilians, among them the al-Ahali group, advocated democracy and moderate socialism, whereas nationalist army officers attempted to establish a military dictatorship. In 1933 Faysal I died and young Ghazi became king, and Faysal's moderating and compromising influence was thus lost. Iraq then experienced internal unrest and tribal uprisings that were instigated to a degree by politicians maneuvering against one another. Rebellions, especially in the south, were suppressed by the military, and as a result of their role in suppressing the Assyrian uprising,* the army and Commander Bakr Sidqi emerged as a political force.

On October 29, 1936, Bakr Sidqi staged the first military coup, which was followed by a series of coups fomented by traditional politicians striving for ascendency until the military influence was crushed after the 1941 Anglo-Iraqi war. Most of these coups were initiated by senior officers, Sunni Arabs and Kurds, who came from major urban centers. Violence was negligible and the monarchy was not eliminated.

The military coups of 1958 to 1970 were mainly initiated by Muslim Arabs, junior officers, many of whom came from obscure towns. The participants were ideologically oriented and were able to eliminate the monarchy. Although civilians collaborated in these conspiracies, officers dominated the cabinets. Since 1958 only one civilian has become prime minister, although many of the officers who assumed cabinet posts relinquished their former military positions. Despite the involvement of Shiites, only one Shiite has headed a government. (Although Qasim had a religious association with both the Shia and Sunni sects because his mother was a Shiite). The fact that more Sunnis than Shiites preferred to join the officer corps in part explains the continued imbalance, although the ratio of the Shiite civilians who became cabinet members is higher, estimated at about 35 percent.[6] During this period the power of the large landowners was almost eliminated, and officers seized complete political control.

Initially military coups were received with varying degrees of popular satisfaction. It was hoped that army officers could change Iraq from a traditional, basically agricultural state into a modern state. Instead, partly because of lack of political sophistication, politics has

---

*Several mountainous tribes revolted against Ottoman rule during World War I and fled to Iraq. When the war ended, Turkey refused to accept their return. In 1932 they demanded an autonomous province in Iraq. A year later a group of them crossed to Syria but France refused to settle them there. When they returned, fighting erupted with an Iraqi force attempting to disarm them, and the Iraqi army suffered casualties. Fighting spread, and in the heat of the uprising atrocities were committed. Assyrians were well trained and armed; their demands were received with apprehension and resentment, particularly in view of Iraq's commitments to resettle them in their original homes or in another country. Hence, the performance of the young army was received with public satisfaction. Between 1932 and 1937 the Council of the League of Nations considered plans for resettlement, but only the Khabur settlement in Syria was organized. The rest of the Assyrians resumed their positions as a minority in Iraq.

been reduced to a struggle among officers; civilians' roles are subordinated to routine administrative functions; and frequent military announcements of a future transfer to civilian control have so far come to naught. Successive military-oriented governments have failed to create political institutions capable of absorbing the participation of new groups, and social and economic changes were not promoted at a rate that would minimize dissatisfaction. Also, legitimacy has not been acquired, and internal security, a basic function of governing, has not been provided. These conditions have intensified intergroup power struggles and political fragmentation, resulting in continual crises. The current political instability in Iraq might be partly attributed to military control; nonetheless, in view of Iraq's transitional stage, it is doubtful if civilian governments can prevent complete chaos. Military coups and military control over government therefore remain the primary methods of political action.

Foreign Policy

Iraq's foreign policy has been determined by its former semicolonial status and eventual emergence as an independent state, its geographic location, its traditional relations with Turkey and Iran, and its Arab affiliations.

As a mandate, Iraq's foreign relations were controlled by Britain. The Hashimite-al-Said regime followed a consistent pro-Western policy, even when Arab interests conflicted with Anglo-American policies, particularly over Palestine.

After World War II Iraqi demands for the abrogation of the 1930 Anglo-Iraqi treaty increased, and the 1948 agreement was abandoned in response to highly inflamed public opinion. In 1955, encouraged by a British-American scheme for a "northern tier" defense plan and in view of its proximity to the USSR, Iraq concluded the Baghdad Pact with Turkey, Britain, Iran, and Pakistan, terminating the 1930 Anglo-Iraqi treaty. The fact that Iraq was the only Arab party in the arrangement contributed to her isolation from the rest of the Arab world. Iraqi nationalists vehemently criticized the pact; they considered Israel, not the Soviet Union, the real threat to the Arabs. In July 1958 republican Iraq declared its adherence to the policy of positive neutrality. Baghdad Pact headquarters were moved to Ankara, and in March 1959 Iraq formally withdrew from this pact, and the British contingents were withdrawn.

Relations with the United States became important only after World War II, as previously American interests had been confined mainly to a share in the Iraq Petroleum Company. From 1946 to 1967 U.S. military and economic grants and loans to Iraq amounted to $96.6 million, although in May 1959 Iraq renounced U.S. military aid agreements. Iraq's current attitude toward the United States stems mainly from the latter's support of Israel. As a result of the Palestine problem, especially following the 1967 Arab-Israeli War, the United States became resented. Iraq broke off diplomatic relations with Washington in June 1967 and increased its cultural, economic, and military cooperation with France and the USSR. Iraqi intellectuals see the United States as supporting conservative monarchical systems in Arab countries. Nationalists equate America with Zionism and consider the United States as obsessed with the destruction of communism, emphasizing military approaches but failing to offer economic and political safeguards against Soviet intrusion.

In view of the country's experiences and goals, the policy of noninvolvement, which has provided advantageous economic ties without strings and the procurement of arms, which are particularly needed in view of Arab setbacks against Israel, has gained general public acceptance.

In July 1958 the new republic received instant support from the Communist bloc. Diplomatic relations with the Soviet Union, severed in 1955, were restored, Communist China was recognized, and in 1969 East Germany was accorded diplomatic recognition. Soviet foreign policy toward Iraq is based on the Kremlin's aim of acquiring a dominant role in the Middle East by pursuing flexible policies in dealing with "national bourgeoisies" and by capitalizing on anti-American sentiments, the perennial Palestine problem, and the desire for neutrality. The Soviet Union presents itself as a champion of Arab nationalism, as anti-imperialistic, and as interested in economic development. In non-Marxist terms, Soviet motivations are based on traditional Russian interests pursued within the context of *Realpolitik*.

Without committing itself to communism, Iraq has established close relations with the USSR and other Communist countries. In 1969 Soviet aid to Iraq amounted to about $1 billion, of which $250 million was in economic credits. Despite Government changes, by 1971 an Iraqi-Soviet community of interests had been created, based on military, political, and economic considerations, with the USSR emerging as a dynamic power in the Middle East. Since 1967 Iraq has been heavily dependent on Soviet arms deliveries, and Soviet naval units have been visiting Iraqi ports.

The peoples of Iraq and Iran share a common historical, cultural, and religious affinity. There are large Iranian communities in Iraq, especially in the holy cities of al-Najaf and Karbala, where the Prophet's son-in-law (Ali) and grandson (Husayn) are buried, respectively. Iraq welcomes and supports the shah's opponents, but the shah has been apprehensive because of the overthrow of the monarchy in Iraq. During 1959 and 1960 and since 1969 there has been a dispute between the two countries regarding jurisdiction over the Shatt al-Arab. In view of Arab preoccupation with Israel, the government of Iran has been attempting to extend her influence over the oil-rich Gulf states. In December 1971, immediately after Britain withdrew from the area, Iran seized on historical grounds the islands of Abu Musa, Big Tunb, and Little Tunb (near the Strait of Hormuz), which were formerly under the jurisdiction of the Arab amirates of Ras al-Kaymah and Sharjah.

This move was accomplished with little bloodshed, but it stirred considerable apprehension in the Arab world, particularly in Iraq, Kuwait, and the Gulf states. Because of this action, Iraq severed diplomatic relations with Iran.

Iraq has also taken an active role in programs for Arab unification. In 1943 Nuri al-Said submitted his plan for a Fertile Crescent unity, but the plan was abandoned because of inter-Arab rivalries, and in 1945 the looser but broader League of Arab States was established.

The polarization of inter-Arab politics between Egypt and Iraq led to intense rivalry between these two major Arab powers both within and outside the league. In 1957 Iraq withheld payment of annual dues to the league, considering it a tool of Egypt's foreign policy. In this power contest Syria served as a theater for Iraqi-Egyptian competition; both intervened in Syria's internal affairs to effect government changes favorable to their policies. Iraq also furthered Arab monarchical alliances. In 1958 Syria and Egypt merged into the United Arab Republic, and in response Iraq federated with Jordan. Nationalists regarded this federation as an imperialistic device, however, and republican Iraq withdrew.

The overthrow of the monarchy was expected to end Egyptian-Iraqi hostilities, but disputes continued. Republican Iraq boycotted Arab League Council meetings between 1959 and 1961, and payments of dues were again withheld. Restive Syria was wooed by Qasim, and following its break with Egypt, Syrian relations with Iraq improved. Egyptian-Iraqi relations were mended during the Baathist regime, but the Nasserite-Baathist rivalry persisted. The Arif regimes, however, had distinct pro-Nasser orientations.

Successive regimes have been interested in effecting union with Kuwait. When Kuwait was proclaimed an independent state in 1961, Abd al-Karim Qasim reiterated Iraq's claims to the territory and appointed the head of state a qaimaqam (district head). In response, British military units landed in Kuwait but were replaced by an Arab League force. In 1963 the new Baathist regime recognized the independence of Kuwait, and relations were further cemented through a Kuwaiti loan to Iraq of $84 million.

Arab questions make an impact on the Iraqi public and governments. As a League of Nations member, in the 1930s Iraq repeatedly demanded independence for Syria, Lebanon, and Palestine and provided aid and support for nationalists in these territories. In 1945 Iraq finally witnessed the independence of Syria and Lebanon. Following World War II successive regimes gave assistance to Libya, Morocco, Tunisia, Algeria, and Southern Yemen (Aden), all of which acquired independent status. The nationalist movement in Oman also received Iraq's support.

Palestine is a different story; in this case Iraq has been unable to achieve its aims. The Iraqi army participated in the 1948 and 1967 Arab-Israeli wars, and moral and financial support is being provided to Palestinian commando organizations. It can be expected that Iraq's direct involvement will increase.

In 1932 Iraq became a member of the League of Nations, where the great powers dominated the conduct of diplomacy. Iraq's potential influence was then minor, but because of the polarization of international politics and the increasing membership of Asian and African states, Iraq has taken an active role in the United Nations. Iraq has been directly involved in disputes considered by both international organizations—controversies over territorial questions, internal problems involving external powers, and self-determination and independence for Arab countries. Because of the frequency and complexity of Middle Eastern problems, Iraq will continue to participate actively in the United Nations.

Political Prospects

Iraq has had four distinct regimes—the monarchy, Qasim, the Arif brothers, and the present Baathist government—but the country continues to suffer from chronic political problems, economic disparities, and factionalism. Like Syria, Iraq is a transitional country that has the potential for transformation into a developed state, but although traditional patterns have been broken, modern political organizations have yet to evolve. The country possesses leadership with experience and organizational abilities reflecting its heterogeneous body politic, but these groups have failed to devise rules for political participation.

Experience and experimentation are characteristics of any program that aims at political change, and any program for the establishment of a nation-state must suffer setbacks and difficulties. The demands of a people for modern political institutions will be pursued largely by trial and error. If political and economic change cannot be achieved by evolution, then resort to revolution can be expected.

Iraq's horizontal and vertical divisions, crisscrossed by ideological diversities, must be considered an important factor in the possible future development of a representative government suitable to Iraqi conditions. Iraq's future political order will depend on the mobilization of political forces in the country and the process of national integration through active political participation.

Footnotes

[1] Lady Florence Bell, ed., *The Letters of Gertrude Bell*, 2 vols. (New York: Boni and Liveright, 1927), 2:533 ff, quoted by George Lenczowski, *The Middle East in World Affairs*, 3d ed. (Ithaca, N.Y.: Cornell University Press, 1962), p. 263.

[2] League of Nations, Permanent Mandates Commission, Seventh Session (1925), p 123.

[3] Interview with Kamil Chadirchi, August 1, 1966, in Khadduri, *Republican Iraq: A Study in Iraqi Politics since the Revolution of 1958*, p. 185.

[4] Abdul H. Raoof, "The Iraqi Political System: 1920-58" (Ph.D. diss., New York University, 1965), pp. 217-19.

[5]Wendell Willkie (without mentioning Nuri by name), *One World* (New York: Simon and Schuster, 1943), p. 19, quoted by Raoof, p. 214.

[6]Phebe Ann Marr, "Iraq's Leadership Dilemma: A Study in Leadership Trends, 1948-68," *Middle East Journal* 24, no. 3 (Summer 1970):289.

Selected Bibliography

Al-Marayati, Abid A. *A Diplomatic History of Modern Iraq*. New York: Robert Speller and Sons, 1961.
Focuses attention on Iraq's relations with the League of Nations in contrast to the United Nations.

Alnasrawi, Abbas. *Financing Economic Development in Iraq: The Role of Oil in a Middle Eastern Economy*. New York: Frederick A. Praeger, 1967.

Arfa, Hassan. *The Kurds: An Historical and Political Study*. London: Oxford University Press, 1966.

Birdwood, Christopher. *Nuri al-Said: A Study in Arab Leadership*. London: Cassell, 1959.
A biography.

Caractacus. *Revolution in Iraq: An Essay in Comparative Public Opinion*. London: Victor Gollancz, 1959.
An account of Iraqi republican temperament preceding the 1958 revolution.

Dann, Uriel. *Iraq under Qassem: A Political History, 1958-63*. New York: Frederick A. Praeger, 1969.

Foster, Henry A. *The Making of Modern Iraq*. Norman, Okla.: University of Oklahoma Press, 1935.
A thorough account of Iraq's emergence as an independent state.

Gallman, Waldemar, Jr. *Iraq under General Nuri*. Baltimore: Johns Hopkins Press, 1964.
Personal recollections by a former U.S. diplomat.

Harris, George. *Iraq: Its People, Its Society, Its Culture*. New Haven, Conn.: HRAF Press, 1958.

International Bank for Reconstruction and Development. *The Economic Development of Iraq*. Baltimore: Johns Hopkins Press, 1952.

Ireland, Philip W. *Iraq: A Study in Political Development*. New York: Macmillan Co., 1938.
Iraq's early development as an independent state.

Khadduri, Majid. *Independent Iraq: A Study in Iraqi Politics from 1932 to 1958*. New York: Oxford University Press, 1960.
A valuable and thorough study.

—————. *Republican Iraq: A Study in Iraqi Politics since the Revolution of 1958*. New York: Oxford University Press, 1969.

Longrigg, Stephen. *Iraq: 1900 to 1950: A Political, Social, and Economic History*. New York: Oxford University Press, 1956.

Syrian Arab Republic

Syria is plagued with unrest, sectionalism, and chronic political instability. Since 1949 Syrian army officers have attempted twenty-odd coups d'état; political jealousies and quarrels have generated innumerable cabinet and government changes; and Syria's constitution has been completely rewritten more than half a dozen times. Many factors contribute to this political instability: (1) Syria's history of conquest, invasion, and more recently the French mandate rule; (2) religious, ethnic, and regional differences; (3) sharp economic and social cleavages between the wandering bedouin, sedentary villagers, and sophisticated urbanites, which have inspired mistrust, jealousy, and questions of political identity; and (4) regional and international problems—the Arab-Israeli problem, the goals of Arab nationalism, and the East-West power struggle in the Middle East.

Even among Middle Eastern states Syria stands out for instability, presenting a crazy quilt pattern of conflicting forces and pressures and a society that is torn and divided. Yet Syrians possess goals and ideals that could provide the basis for a unified and progressive state: modernization, Arab nationalism, and Arab unity, at least among a large section of the population.

Historical Background

Ancient Syria was the home of Amorites, Aramaeans, Phoenicians, and Hebrews. After a succession of invaders that included Assyrians, Babylonians, Egyptians, Hittites, and Persians, the country was unified under Alexander the Great in 331 B.C. It later fell under Roman rule, becoming part of the Byzantine Empire when the Roman Empire was divided between East and West. Following its conquest by the Arabs in the seventh century, Syria became predominantly Arabic-speaking and Muslim. Its chief city, Damascus, served as the capital of the Arab empire of the Umayyads from 661 to 750, when Syria fell under the rule of Muslim dynasties from other regions. After incorporation into the Ottoman Empire in 1516, Syria declined economically, culturally, and politically.

Establishment of Independent Syria

World War I brought Ottoman hegemony over Syria to an end. In 1919 the General Syrian Congress, which was convened by Amir Faysal, adopted a constitution establishing a limited constitutional monarchy with Faysal as king over Greater Syria (including Lebanon, Transjordan, and Palestine). The constitution provided for an elected bicameral legislature and an independent judiciary. The Allies refused to recognize this new Arab state, however, as Great Britain and France had already decided to establish a mandatory regime for the region. The initial confidence that an independent Arab state would be established was shattered when General Gouraud and his French troops seized Damascus on July 24, 1920. In the same year Syria was entrusted as a French mandate territory, an action deeply resented by Arab nationalists.

In 1925 a general insurrection that had begun among Druze tribesmen spread to Damascus and other parts of Syria. In an attempt to keep the Arabs divided, France established an administrative structure designed to separate Syria into five autonomous regions— Lebanon, Damascus, Aleppo, Jabal Druze, and Alawi. Once the insurrection was crushed in the latter part of 1926, France reluctantly introduced political reforms that would allegedly lead to self-government, but it was not until 1928 that France abolished martial law, reintroduced certain civil liberties, and authorized elections for a constituent assembly. The April elections brought an overwhelming victory to the Nationalists, who were dominated by upper-class, Western-educated intellectuals. The constitution of 1930, written by the Constitutional Assembly, was largely patterned after the French model. Legislative power was granted to a Chamber of Deputies to be elected every four years. The chamber was responsible for the election of the president, whose term of office was to be five years. The president, in turn, was given the authority to select a prime minister and cabinet.

Throughout the mandate period of the 1930s, however, the Syrian constitutional system was totally subservient to the French high commissioner. At no time during the period was an elected national assembly able to satisfy the French commissioner, who consistently suspended these assemblies before the end of their regular term. From this system of political sterility emerged two key factors that profoundly affected the Syrian republic: (1) official positions of local leadership were allowed to be monopolized by the traditional families, and (2) these traditional leaders were never given an opportunity to develop the administrative and political skills necessary to solve the problems facing Syria once independence was gained.

In 1941 British forces defeated the Vichy government in Syria, and under an agreement with General de Gaulle, Syrian independence was declared. After pressures from Great Britain, France in 1943 agreed to permit elections. The newly elected Chamber of Deputies, with a majority of Nationalists, elected Shukri al-Quwatli president and Jamil Mardam Bey prime minister. Yet French tutelage remained in various subtle ways, and the French commander still maintained a number of political controls over the newly founded republic. It was not until 1946, after considerable pressure from both the United States and Great Britain, that France finally evacuated all troops from Syria.

For the first time in nearly five hundred years, Syria was suddenly faced with new challenges—political independence, economic development, and governmental effectiveness—which were to interact with Syria's cultural environment. One of the sad ironies of post-World War II Syria was that the Nationalist bloc leaders—who had devoted the larger part of their adult lives to fighting for independence, who had defended the liberal tradition of Western constitutionalism, and who had hoped to set the course of a free Syria—would prove to be so inept, so completely identified with the past and with conservatism, and so easily criticized for inefficient and corrupt administration.

Al-Quwatli's government might have continued in power if the Syrian army had not been soundly defeated in the Palestine War of 1948; the Israeli victory reinforced the general view that al-Quwatli and his aged colleagues were unfit to rule. Far more significant to the constitutional history of Syria was the impact that the Israeli victory had on the army and the younger nationalist leaders. The army felt betrayed and demanded revenge for the ineptitude of the Syrian government. The younger nationalist leaders in the somewhat regimented National Syrian party and the more democratic People's party began calling for unity with the Hashimite kingdoms of Jordan and Iraq as the only legitimate strategy against Israel.

In late March 1949 the interaction of these demands stirred the young Kurdish army chief of staff, Husni al-Zaim, to arrest al-Quwatli, dissolve parliament, and assume dictatorial powers. Obviously the passions of the times motivated al-Zaim's coup d'état, yet the die had now been cast, and future generations of coups and countercoups would look back at this act, which for the first time placed the military in a position of extraconstitutional power.

The life of parliamentary government was not to be snuffed out so easily, however; al-Zaim's military dictatorship lasted less than five months. Syria's second coup, led by Colonel Sami al-Hinnawi, arrested and executed al-Zaim and invited the former president of the republic, Hashim al-Atasi, to form a civilian caretaker government until a new constitution could be written and elections held.

In the general elections of November 1949 for the Constitutional Assembly, the People's party failed to secure a majority of the 114-seat assembly but with forty-two members emerged as the largest political party. Colonel al-Hinnawi, failing to note the opposition of many army officers, sought support from the People's party to establish the Greater Syria scheme (unification of Syria, Iraq, and Jordan). In the third coup of 1949, another colonel, Adib al-Shishakli, deposed al-Hinnawi, officially rejected any plan for unification, and publicly denied any desire to rule Syria himself.

Initially al-Shishakli kept his promise. In September 1950 a new constitution, which was very similar to the earlier 1930 constitution, was adopted. The major innovation was the strengthening of the power of the Chamber of Deputies to prevent the reemergence of a strong executive. The Constitutional Assembly insisted on a detailed enunciation of powers, prerogatives, and procedures. The amending process was extremely complicated and thus new interpretations, changes, and adaptations became difficult to adopt. The rigidity of this new instrument of government soon rendered stability and governmental effectiveness a function of military intervention.

Although a civilian government dominated the political process in 1950 and most of 1951, international and domestic issues exacerbated and reinforced all party rivalries, making compromise and unity in the national Chamber of Deputies impossible. Hasan al-Hakim, who became prime minister in August 1951, staked his political career on a close defense arrangement with the Western powers. By November, opposition to his pro-Western policies had become so pronounced that he was forced to resign. Several weeks of government crisis again invited Colonel al-Shishakli to assume the reins of government in the name of the army.

In his efforts to bring order and stability again to Syria, al-Shishakli dissolved the Chamber of Deputies, declared all political parties outlawed, and placed all government power in the hands of a Supreme Military Council. In July 1953 al-Shishakli, hoping to establish a constitutional system capable of withstanding chaos and political instability, announced the third constitution of Syria, which in many ways was patterned after the American presidential system. Later al-Shishakli was elected president by popular vote in spite of strong opposition by political and religious groups, who felt that their interests would not be protected in an ineffective national parliament.

In an open attempt to consolidate his dictatorial powers, al-Shishakli formed the Arab Liberation Movement, which was designed to replace the corrupt, unstable party system. When his mobilization organization won seventy-two out of eighty-two seats, parliament began to decree controls, including restricted freedom of the press, a ban on student strikes and unauthorized demonstrations, and an emphasis on military prowess, patriotism, and security. Not too surprisingly, al-Shishakli's regime gradually came under attack from practically all the major groups in society. By the end of 1953, students, lawyers, the ulama, and various Socialist and Nationalist party leaders (primarily in the Syrian Social National and Baath parties) were all seeking al-Shishakli's downfall. These popular grumblings were reinforced by a major Druze revolt in Jabal Druze, which in February 1954 precipitated an army rebellion in various parts of the country. Under this pressure al-Shishakli resigned and fled into exile.

Following the overthrow of al-Shishakli's dictatorship, Hashim al-Atasi was reinstated as president; the parliament, dissolved in December 1951, was convened; and the 1950 constitution was readopted. This new commitment to civilian government did not bring stability to Syria, however. Between 1954 and 1957 seven cabinets exercised control. No single group of civilian leaders was able to rally the people or propose the political and economic policies required for modernization and development. Finally, in late 1957 several members of the political and military elite, fearing a leftist takeover, sought unification with Egypt as the only viable alternative to political disintegration. Nasser considered this plan for unification premature, yet he agreed when the Syrians accepted his three demands: (1) a popular plebiscite to confirm the unification, (2) the dissolution of all political parties in Syria, and (3) the withdrawal of the Syrian officer corps from politics.

On February 21, 1958, a provisional constitution was approved by a plebiscite. The government structure of the United Arab Republic of Syria and Egypt placed virtually total control in the hands of President Nasser, who appointed vice-presidents, a cabinet of Egyptians and Syrians, and a 600-member National Assembly structured to include 400 Egyptians and 200 Syrians. By the autumn of 1961, however, Syrian military leaders were resenting Egyptian hegemony, and they instigated a bloodless coup with the support of other factions in Syria and promptly seceded from the union. The military then invited civilian leaders to reestablish a government under the constitution of 1950. However, no single political party gained enough seats in the legislature to ensure a stable coalition government. Constant bickering, denunciations, total lack of compromise and effective decision making again stirred the army to involvement, and civilian rule succumbed to a military coup led by General Abd al-Karim Zahr al-Din within six months of secession from the United Arab Republic.

During the 1960s Syria was plagued with an internal struggle for power. In 1963 the Baathists assumed control of the government, but the various civilian and military factions of the Baath party fomented several coups and countercoups in their struggle for ascendancy. Finally, in November 1970 General Hafiz al-Assad, leader of the moderate elements of the officer corps, gained control of Syria, established relative peace and stability, and in September 1971 joined with the leaders of Egypt and Libya to establish the Federation of Arab Republics.

Political Environment

Like other emerging states, Syria today is an agrarian society in which traditional social and economic status has long dominated the political system. A small number of feudal families have tended to control economic life by their large landholdings or commercial interests in and around the major population centers of Damascus, Homs, Hamah, and Aleppo. Modernization has meant changing traditional behavior to new patterns because of the imposition of modern political institutions and the development of conflicts within the body politic that have proven to be insoluble by older methods. Many of these conflicts are in turn a reflection of the changes occurring in the social and cultural milieu of Syria.

The People

Ethnic Groups: Ethnic divisions in Syria are largely determined by the language spoken, and by this classification scheme nearly 90 percent of the population are considered Arab. In addition to Arabs there are six minor ethnic groups: Armenians, Assyrians, Circassians, Jews, Kurds, and Turkomans.

Armenians in Syria have their own language, religion, and cultural traditions and make up nearly 3 percent of the population. Most of the 170,000 Armenians are descendants of political refugees who fled the Turkish persecution of the mid-1920s, and large numbers eventually settled in Damascus and Aleppo. Armenians today generally reject government pressures to assimilate into the Arab culture and thus remain outside the pale of Arab nationalism.

The Assyrians also have their own language, Neo-Syriac, and their own religion, Nestorianism, and tend to live in isolation in fifteen to twenty villages along the upper Khabur River near the Iraqi border. The poorest ethnic group in Syria, the Assyrians generally engage in small-scale agriculture or sheep raising.

The approximately 50,000 Circassians, like the Armenians, are immigrants to Syria; they were forced to leave the Caucasus region as the Russian army moved south in the late nineteenth century. Although they have gradually been assimilated, their loyalty is still somewhat suspect because they readily served in the French army under the mandate and have periodically demanded political autonomy.

The 260,000 Kurds, who constitute over 4 percent of the population, have generally settled in the foothills of the Taurus Mountains north of Aleppo or in the Jazirah region of northeast Syria. Both the Kurds and the Circassians have their own languages, although most are bilingual and speak Arabic also. Most of the Kurds are villagers who engage in agriculture or manual labor, although socially they retain the outward tribal organization and maintain primary loyalty to their tribe and clan. As in neighboring Iraq, some Kurds favor an independent Kurdistan, but in recent years many Kurds have assumed high positions in the government bureaucracy and military establishment.

The Turkomans are a Turkic-speaking people numbering close to 70,000. Most have settled in the lower Euphrates River basin near the Iraqi border, where they engage in farming and cattle raising. Of all the ethnic groups, the Turkomans have shown the greatest proclivity to assimilate, adopting the Arabic language and customs at a much faster rate than other ethnic groups.

Most distinctions of ethnicity are limited to language and customs, although the Armenians and Assyrians add religious differences as well. The vast majority of these non-Arab groups tends to concentrate in one of two regions: the area north of Aleppo or the al-Jazirah district in the desert plateau region of northeastern Syria. Since Syria gained its independence, the fundamental imperative of Arab nationalism has generated a government policy that deemphasizes ethnicity and encourages all Syrians to consider themselves Arabs. Ethnic differences are gradually weakening, but the government of Syria officially recognizes the sectarian and religious groups that make up the Syrian population, although the present government tends to encourage social relationships on a nonreligious, secularized basis. The emergence of Arab nationalism has produced an overwhelming demand for unity and national integration, yet the existence of many religious communities poses a dilemma that deeply influences attitudes and behavior in the political, economic, and social life in Syria. An understanding of the political environment in Syria necessitates a careful delineation of the religious communities.

Religious Groups: At present approximately 85 percent of the population is Muslim, but far more significant are the divisions within the Muslim and Christian faiths.

The largest group of Muslims are the Sunnis, who constitute over 70 percent of the total population. Because of their large majority they are found in all parts of the country, are represented in all social classes, and tend to support a wide spectrum of political views. They are the majority group in eleven of the thirteen provinces. (The Suwayda province, with a Druze majority, and Latakia, with an Alawi majority, are the exceptions.)

The Alawites, whose religion is a subdividion of Shiism, are the largest (some 650,000) and most politically significant of the religious minorities. Since the 1966 coup, military officers of the Alawite faith have held leadership positions in the army high command and the radical left wing of the Baath party. Socially and economically the average Alawite is below the Sunni, yet because of their majority status in the province of Latakia, located along the only seacoast in Syria, their influence has been greater than their number would justify.

The Druze community is the second largest religious minority group and numbers about 80,000. Jabal Druze, in the southern part of Syria, is an isolated mountain range where persecuted Druzes have gathered for over a hundred years. Concentrated in over one hundred villages, the Druzes have consistently isolated themselves from the Sunni majority. Playing an important role in the internal politics of Syria, Druze leaders have at the most sought autonomy and at the least, a significant voice in the decision-making process of the Syrian government.

Social Structure: The decade of the 1960s must be seen as a decisive period of change for the traditional social structure of Syria. Historically Syrian society consisted of three major groups: the urban elite, the sedentary peasants living in small towns and villages, and the nomadic tribes. Interaction among these communities was generally restricted to simple trading, collection of taxes, and the drafting of men for military service. Most of the wealth was monopolized by a few families living in Damascus and Aleppo. The agricultural lands were largely controlled by absentee landlords, who through their great wealth dominated the positions of power and prestige in the traditional political process. Since World War II a new group of businessmen has emerged as a result of commercial activities, and although the old feudal families tend to regard these nouveaux riches as socially inferior, the 1950s saw the two groups gradually integrate through intermarriage and business ventures.

Syrian urban residents include unskilled laborers and domestics and artisans and shopkeepers, who usually keep their businesses in the extended family or the kin group, training their sons to follow their professions. Before the 1960s ownership of land and Quranic learning were the usual basis for social status; commercial success in the Westernized sector of the economy and participation in the army were secondary avenues to social advancement for a few. Today social status and advancement can be attained by commercial success anywhere, participation in the army, government positions, and secular education.

Most of the rural population—farmers, herders, and share-croppers—live in villages and hamlets ranging in size from a few families to several hundred people and are organized into kin groups within which marriages are made and disputes are settled by councils of elders or arbitration by religious leaders.

Some of the most significant structural changes have been caused by large-scale immigration from rural areas into Damascus, Homs, and Aleppo, with consequent residential overcrowding and aggravation of unemployment problems. Social disorientation is common among the mass of poor people in the cities, where new shantytowns have developed; and the various quarters no longer consist of homogeneous groupings that have common ethnic or regional origins or common occupations.

Over the past several decades bedouin tribesmen have gradually discontinued their nomadic or seminomadic way of life. The present government has sought to integrate these tribal communities, which constitute less than 5 percent of the population, into the villages and small towns of rural Syria. Many tribes are somewhat divided, with portions of the tribal group settling in rural communities while others continue pastoral existence. Most of the tribal leaders have now at least nominally settled in the major urban centers of Syria, and communication between the central government and the tribal units is facilitated through these leaders.

Since World War II the patterns of social relationships based on the kin group, local community, ethnic or religious group, and a comparatively static class system have given way to social and geographical mobility. Particularly important has been the emergence of a class of professionals and military men, many of whom are only a generation or two removed from the village or the urban lower middle class and who represent various ethnic and religious minorities. The growing importance of relationships with persons who are neither kin nor of the same ethnic or religious background has led to strains for many individuals. The old rules of personal conduct are being challenged; new values, behavioral norms, attitudes, and perceptions are conflicting with the traditional cultural values as people seek to adapt to social and economic change.

Social Conditions: In spite of the great emphasis on the military, the Syrian governments of the past two decades have made serious efforts to improve the life and opportunities of the Syrian people, especially in the areas of education, health, and agrarian reform. Education is seen as the key to quick advancement into positions created by changes in the economic and administrative structure of the country, and during the 1960s education was consistently high on the list of priorities, generally second only to defense in budget allocations. Hundreds of tuition-free government schools have been constructed to accommodate children at the primary-grade level, and a broad program of curriculum development and teacher training has been initiated.

Syrian officials have cooperated with the World Health Organization and UNICEF to construct facilities for the production of medical supplies, drugs, and diet supplements. The Ministry of Health has sponsored programs to build hospitals, to establish health centers for the control of malaria and tuberculosis, and to provide free medical service to low-income families.

The limited nature of these programs, however, reflects one of Syria's major dilemmas: the government is deeply committed to reform and modernization, but many of the needed programs must be restricted or postponed because of the lack of funds and trained personnel.

Economic Conditions

Syria is a predominantly agricultural country that is endowed with substantial yet largely undeveloped land and water resources. With a population of nearly six million, the country is not densely populated, and only 38 percent of the arable land is being cultivated. Economic development during the 1960s showed a comparatively satisfactory cumulative annual rate of growth, but Syria's per capita annual income remains a low $200, as agricultural production barely kept up with the growth in population during the 1960s.

Despite considerable diversification of the economy after World War II, Syria still suffers from a heavy dependence on the production of cereals and cotton for its subsistence and for earning the foreign exchange necessary for development. Agricultural output, which accounts for 25 to 28 percent of the country's net domestic product, comes from rain-fed land and is therefore subject to fluctuation from weather variations. In order to reduce dependence on weather conditions and to achieve steady growth, efforts have been made to increase the irrigated area and to diversify the economy through the development of industry.

Land-reform programs during the 1960s have helped to eliminate the abuses of a tenancy system in which landowners were free to evict peasants without notice and to charge extremely high rents, and in which they seldom invested money to increase productivity on their lands. Since 1958 landownership has been limited to 200 acres of irrigated land or 740 acres of dry-farmed land. All holdings in excess of these limits have been expropriated and are being distributed to the landless peasants.

Industry has been growing steadily in recent years and accounts for about 15 percent of the national output. Prior to 1960 planning was limited in scope and purpose and was undertaken mainly with the specific objective of rationalizing the investment efforts of the public sector. The country's first real venture into comprehensive planning started when Syria became part of the United Arab Republic. After the establishment of a Ministry of Planning in 1958, the First Five-Year Plan (1961-65) was initiated with the hope of doubling the national income by 1970.

Syria's socioeconomic infrastructure has undergone tremendous change in the past decade. In addition to the program of land distribution, banks and insurance companies were nationalized, and by 1965 most of the manufacturing industries and the export-import trade were taken over by the government. Because most of the public utilities, such as railways, airlines, electricity, petroleum refining, and mineral wealth, were already state-owned, the public sector had by 1965 replaced private enterprise as the mainspring of economic activity. Moreover, in June 1968 Syria reorganized its planning apparatus, substituting for the Ministry of Planning the Supreme Planning Board, which seeks a totally integrated economy structured to meet the demands of a military-oriented economy.

In early 1971 Syria's President al-Assad announced the Third Five-Year Plan, which seeks to ensure an annual income increase of over 8 percent. Efforts are being made to relax some restrictions on travel and foreign trade. The liberalizing trend in Syria today should have a profound impact on the Syrian economy, as attempts are made to encourage foreign investments, to revitalize the long-idle private sector, and to integrate Syria's market into the full potentialities of the newly formed Federation of Arab Republics.

The commitment to industrialization, national planning, and economic progress has introduced a catalyst into Syrian society that is having a significant impact on the political environment. The concept of political culture provides a framework for examining the character of these changes and for weaving the relevant strands of Syrian life into a political order.

Political Culture

The concept *political culture* seeks to analyze the psychological makeup of a nation's people and their inherited patterns of behavior and to show how these factors influence political action—the ways in which people respond to authority, the political roles they play, and their degree of participation in political affairs. An examination of Syrian society reveals the highly personal and reciprocal nature of authority, a tendency to form relationships that will be useful, the use of manipulative language, and the traditional practice of using middlemen in sensitive negotiations.

For centuries Syrian society remained relatively static, although since World War II attitudes and values have undergone an impressive transformation. Traditionally, man's relationship with his society was determined by his religion, his customs, and his values. The importance of the family group (as opposed to the individual), respect for older male authority, and mutual aid among members of the kin group were stressed, as were overt piety, acceptance of the exigencies of fate, education in the religious scriptures, and the restriction of women in affairs outside the home. It was believed that Islam defined the role of the individual, the good life, and rules of social conduct. The good man was equated with the pious man, he who follows the will of God, and it was also praiseworthy to follow men believed to be the elect of God or those endowed with spiritual or political power (*baraka*).

The Syrian political environment is deeply colored by Islam. In many rural areas, poor climatic conditions and low agricultural potential have helped to underscore a consciousness of dependence on forces beyond the control of men, and value is therefore placed on calm patience and acceptance of the hazards of existence and the decrees of God that determine them. Resignation to fate has a profound impact on the Syrian people and their relationship to their political leaders. Loyalty to leaders can be somewhat ephemeral, and the one who has lost support is regarded as chastised by God.

A Syrian's love of language and eloquence and hypersensitivity to reflections on his reputation are the bases for political relationships. Syrians are aware of the risks in personal interaction outside the family and have traditionally sought to avoid potential conflict by ritual means. This fear of conflict is related to the perception of all human relationships as power struggles that are potentially dangerous to one's image in society, and unwillingness to make open commitments and a tendency to rely on implicit cues and social obligations are the results. But the necessity for dealing with strangers is indispensable, especially as urbanization, communications, and transportation expand; hence, some means for dealing with those for whom social obligations and family status have less meaning must be found.

In modern societies a well-developed system of functional roles removes much of the inherent personality conflict and threats to personal identity from personal relationships. A man's action as an administrator, for example, is governed by a widely accepted norms that include objectivity, equality, and adherence to established rules. Such an objective system would be totally unacceptable to a Syrian accustomed to the warmth, security, and intimacy of human relations based on personal commitments.

In Syria, as in other transitional societies, the boundaries between the political system and other subsystems are poorly defined. Nor do Syrians usually distinguish between the man and his job. Any action involves a personal commitment, and Syrians expect that personal obligations and desires will dominate everyone's behavior. The government official is expected to treat citizens in accordance with their relationship to him; he is expected to help his relatives and those to whom he has an obligation. When the Syrian deals with government offices or private business, he attempts to use his network of personal relationships.

This behavior makes common interest difficult to establish and to articulate, and it thwarts attempts to establish modern group relationships and mutually beneficial institutions. Thus Syria's major political problem is the lack of political institutions and processes that are considered legitimate and proper. Institutionalization of the political system will require new political values, orientations, and aspirations that go beyond the family, the ethnic group, and the religious community. The description of the environment places in focus some of the pressures evolving from the confrontation of change and traditionalism and sets the stage for a study of the political structures now developing in Syria.

Political Structure

Government structure in Syria today is a military-dominated organization; although a provisional constitution was promulgated in 1964, political power still tends to rest with army officers. Despite coups and countercoups, government policy has rapidly shifted leftward. The provisional constitution of April 1964 and the constitution issued May 1, 1969, emphasize the socialist policies of Syria by declaring that all wealth and resources now belong to "all of the people."

The government institutions of the sixties included the National Council of the Revolutionary Command (NCRC), which was made up of seventeen military officers. Later in 1965 the NCRC was renamed the National Revolutionary Council (NRC) and was expanded to include close to a hundred members, mostly civilians who were willing to accept military hegemony. As a new national parliament, the NRC could enact laws, amend the provisional constitution when necessary, supervise all referendums, determine the budget, and elect a Presidential Council, which was to formulate the policy and programs necessary for the development of Syria. The Presidential Council was to appoint a cabinet (including a prime minister) to coordinate all government activities. In fact, however, both the cabinet and the NRC were responsible to the Presidential Council, which included a president, a vice-president, and three others. The degree to which these institutions were controlled by one military leader is shown by the fact that in September 1965 General Amin al Hafiz was simultaneously elected prime minister, chairman of the Presidential Council, and president of the NRC.

In early 1966, the veteran Baathist leader Salah al-Din al-Bitar agreed to form a new cabinet if the army would allow civilians to reassume control of the governmental process. The National Revolutionary Council was then enlarged from 95 to 134 and all military officers were excluded. This new attempt at civilian rule was shattered only two weeks later when Major General Salah al-Jadid, the recently dismissed Alawi chief of staff, staged a countercoup with the help of radical leftist military officers, including many from the Alawi sect. Although General al-Jadid was the real man in power, Nur al-Din al-Atasi, a member of one of the leading Sunni families, was invited to be chairman of the Presidential Council.

By mid-1970 General al-Jadid had been gradually dislodged from his position of primacy in the government structure by another Alawi officer, General Hafiz al-Assad, minister of defense. Because al-Jadid was able to maintain his position as leader of the civilian wing of the Baath party, he sought to undermine General al-Assad's influence by using the Baath party's structure to champion a militant approach against Israel, to support various guerrilla forces operating in Lebanon and Jordan, and to insist that a more radical form of socialism be implemented in Syria.

This competition for power was resolved on November 13, 1970, when General al-Assad, with the help of his chief of staff, Major-General Mustafa Tlas, instigated a bloodless coup d'état, in which al-Jadid and many of his supporters were forced into exile. Al-Assad appointed himself secretary-general of the Baath party, selected a relative unknown, Ahmad al-Khatib, to succeed al-Atasi as acting president, promised that his new government would form a "people's assembly" to draw up a new constitution, and announced his support of the proposed federation of Egypt, Libya, and Sudan. On March 12, 1971, General al-Assad was elected president for a seven-year term by 99.2 percent of the vote, and a new civilian cabinet that includes a wider base of moderates and independents has been formed. Under the amended provisional constitution of 1971, legislative power rests with a People's Council of 173 members. According to the constitution, the president can object to any law passed by the People's Council, but such an objection can be overruled by a two-thirds vote. The president may dissolve the council at any time but must appoint a new council within sixty days. These formal civilian institutions suggest the military desire to maintain an appearance of civilian rule.

President al-Assad's new government appears bent on following a relatively moderate course—one that seeks to mitigate the Baath's ideological fervor with pragmatism and greater cooperation with Syria's Arab neighbors. Working closely with the presidents of Egypt and Libya, President al-Assad signed an agreement on August 20, 1971, to establish the Federation of Arab Republics, joining the three countries. There is hope that this new manifestation of Arab unity will increase the growth and prosperity of Syria. What impact this tristate federation will have on Syrian politics is difficult to predict, yet as long as President al-Assad's government rests largely on the support of the military wing of the Baath party and the minority Alawi community, the military government of Syria will continue to be vulnerable to the cross pressures of foreign and domestic intrigues.

Political Processes

Although a general outline of the political institutions can be helpful in understanding the politics of Syria, full comprehension of the political system also requires an analysis of the processes, groups, and individuals that make up the political system.

The Politics of Instability

The chief characteristic of Syrian politics has been instability, although this might not have been foreseen. Syria, like many new states of Africa and Asia, inherited a form of democracy. Among the conservative elite the general assumption prevailed that only through a working constitutional system would their claim to equal status with former colonial powers be recognized, and most of these Western-educated nationalist leaders recognized the value of democratic institutions. In the era of a newly won independence there was no appeal to the traditional political system; by temperament, philosophy, and experience Syrian leaders were committed to some type of parliamentary democracy. Yet in spite of this stimulus, the dream has faded, the elaborate framework of constitutional democracy has been dismantled or at least robbed of its content, and the politics of Syria has been dominated by authoritarian rule, widespread instability, and chronic military intervention. An analysis of Syria's political processes requires the answers to three questions: (1) What are the causes of instability? (2) What are the causes of the failure of democracy? and (3) What explains the growth of army influence?

Antipathy to government, an attitude born of untold centuries of fear and resentment of authority, is traditional. Syria's peasants and lower classes have long identified government with the tax collector and the oppressor, friend and protector of the money lender and the landlord. Regimes come and go, but government remains; foreign or native, it performs the same functions, makes the same demands, imposes the same onerous obligations. Since conditions of life have not changed appreciably, Syria's masses have found it difficult to differentiate one set of rulers from another. When independence came, it brought another change of tax collector, but in most regions of Syria it did not bring perceptible improvement in the peasant's standard of living. Why, then, should he change his distrust of and antipathy to those in power? The new regimes thus tended to lack a broad base of support in the crucial early years.

Even within the political elite (including the major groups in Syria) hostility to government is widespread—a legacy of the struggle for independence, when almost everything done by the French rulers was resisted—and opposition persists especially among the young elites who are out of power. Obstruction, suspicion, and hostility, reinforced by economic, religious, and ethnic differences, are the norm of political behavior; the idea of a loyal opposition, one of the most significant in the democratic process, is completely unknown. Groups in power tend to find the idea of a legitimate opposition unappealing; all opposition is construed as treason. In most elections the results have been manipulated and farcical, which has tended to place a premium on extraconstitutional means of achieving power—the coup d'état. Instability thus has become the rule and democracy an illusion.

There was too an unreal quality to Syria's initial experiment in constitutional democracy. Middle Eastern politics has a long tradition of autocracy, whether monarchical or military, indigenous or foreign. Government was stern, distant, and unused to criticism; government by decree and fiat, by political power and threat of punishment was the recognized pattern. This is perhaps another way of saying that the peoples of Syria have had limited experience in democracy. The elites and the upper middle class in Damascus and Aleppo were familiar with its form and substance, though, it has been noted, few were allowed to hold positions of responsibility before independence. But to the lower classes and peasantry, the ideas and the institutions of democracy were alien; their contact with government was limited to the local bureaucrat and an occasional glimpse of a visiting dignitary. There was also a lack of trained civil servants to fill the needs of a newly independent state. The newly created bureaucracy floundered under the enormous strain of transition—building a welfare state, planning the economy, and maintaining law and order in the face of dissension, rebellion, and violence.

Political Parties

Syrian political parties have contributed to instability through their behavior. The traditional Nationalist party and the People's party generally ceased to aggregate and articulate popular interests after independence; rather, they degenerated into factional strife and corruption. The desire for power overcame scruples; politicians switched loyalties frequently and lost touch with the masses, with the result that the political process became divorced from society and devoid of motivation other than personal ambition.

Until the first major military coup in 1949, the National party dominated the Chamber of Deputies. The leading businessmen and landowners living in Damascus who made up the party nominally advocated republicanism, Pan-Arabism, and the economic development of Syria, primarily Damascus. Equally traditional and conservative were the leaders of the People's party, who represented the merchant and landowning elites of Aleppo and northern Syria. In contrast to the business and industrial interests of the Damascus-based Nationalist party, however, the People's party concerned itself with the agricultural interests of the large landowning classes. Divisions between these two parties were also evident in foreign policy: the People's party championed the Greater Syria scheme, which advocated unification with the Hashimite kingdoms of Iraq and Jordan.

Because both parties tended to exclude the young, aspiring, middle-class intellectuals, military officers, and professional groups, several new political groups began to emerge. Three such groups were the Syrian Social Nationalist party, which was founded by a Lebanese Christian, Antun Saadah, and which advocated the unity of Lebanon and Syria, the establishment of a centralized socialist state, and cooperation with the West; the Baath party and the Arab Socialist party (founded by Akram Hawrani), joined to spread the doctrines of Arab socialism and Pan-Arabism; and the Syrian Communist party, a small but extremely well organized party guided and directed by Khalid Bakdash, a capable, Moscow-trained Syrian Kurd from Damascus.

Role of the Baath Party: Initially the Baath party was comprised of teachers, students, large groups of urban laborers, some intellectuals, and a few members of the army officers' corps, all of whom were committed to secularism, the unifying concept of Pan-Arabism, and economic and social reform. However, several characteristics have hindered the party's move to unify and to emerge as the dominant political force in Syria. First, many of the early members among both the urban middle-class groups and the military groups were attracted by the reform programs and policies, which would fulfill their personal aspiration for improved social and economic status. There was especially a tendency for young military graduates to join the Baath party for practical rather than ideological reasons. Second, the Baath party, which is mainly concerned with gaining political power, has often employed the political technique of a "united front," a broad-based program of indoctrination, to gain large numbers of adherents. Third, the party has carefully organized plans for the recruitment of new members in ethnic and religious groups, the government bureaucracy, and the armed forces.

Utilizing the tactic of short-term alliances with various nationalist, socialist, and even Communist groups, the Baathists have been able to play a significant role in Syrian politics since 1954. An understanding of how the Baath party has gradually been superseded by

the military establishment requires an analysis of two broad characteristics of its internal structure.

First, the Baath Party, which should have a dominant position
because of its broad following in Syria and abroad, has been fractured
by divisive elements. One group, the older moderates headed by Aflaq
and al-Bitar, has been arguing for the reestablishment of parliamentary
government, whereas the leftist radicals (civilian wing) of the party
insist on absolute control of the government so that the necessary
reforms can be achieved. Also, large numbers of military officers in the
party reject civilian control and thus create a major obstacle to unified
organization. Equally divisive has been the conflict over Syria's
relationship with Nasser; some minority groups championed close
relations and others were less willing to accept collective leadership
sponsored by Nasser.

The second characteristic is a result of the Arab-Israeli
confrontation. Probably no single issue has played a greater role in
radicalizing the political process of Syria. The frustrations and
humiliation of the Israeli victory in June 1967 fomented a demand for
revenge and the recapture of lost territory and a general tendency
toward a military-oriented economy, although the events in late 1970
under the government of General al-Assad suggest a moderating
influence—removal of the more radical elements of the Baath party and
a greater concern to pursue policies structured to achieve internal
stability, economic growth, and political development. The unstable
Arab-Israeli situation, however, tends to encourage the civilian elements
of society in general and the Baath party in particular to allow the
military to assume greater control.

The Politics of Military Intervention

Crucial to an understanding of Syrian politics is comprehension
of the role and self-image of the Syrian military establishment. Young
military officers came to see themselves as the only disciplined,
organized group capable of ensuring stability and continuity. Democratic decision making is slow, but for many of these younger Syrian
officers time was short; a strong government to achieve unity and to
modernize their antiquated social and economic infrastructure was
needed immediately. Also, the military does not foster the ideas of free
opposition and compromise, both crucial to democracy.

In general terms, Syrian politics have been a function of
democracy's retreat and the rise of the military to power. These
developments should not occasion surprise in the light of the foregoing
analysis; indeed, similar developments have been part of a sweeping
process embracing much of the Middle East, Africa, Asia, and Latin
America. The Syrian experience, however, although similar to many
states plagued with recurring coups d'état, is unique in the way that
political institutions have developed. In modern Syria politics have
centered on the collision not only of two major institutions, the Baath

party and the military establishment, but also on the ethnic and religious diversity in the army itself.

With the establishment of the mandate system, the French immediately organized an indigenous military force, the Troupes Spéciales, largely recruited from the minority groups in Syria and Lebanon. The French never allowed this force to increase greatly in number; even three years after independence the number of Syrian officers was still less than eight thousand, and most had either Ottoman or French training. The tendency for the French to utilize non-Arabs in the Troupes Spéciales partly explains why most of the officers who precipitated the early military coups were not Arab (al-Zaim and al-Shishakli were both Kurds). Following the downfall of al-Shishakli, however, large numbers of Kurdish and other non-Arab minority officers were forced to resign from military service.

By the end of the 1950s and early 1960s large numbers of Alawi Muslims, especially from the lower-middle-class families, were graduating from the military academy at Homs, and some estimates suggest that over 50 percent of the military officers in Syria are Alawis. The Alawis' minority position in Syria helps to explain their reluctance to seek unification with Arab states dominated by the Sunnis. Much of this government's willingness to accept Soviet aid can also be understood in terms of its vulnerability to local and regional groups that oppose the leadership. Competing groups of intellectuals, technocrats, and military officers; religious, ethnic, and social differences; and regional feuds between the elite in Damascus and those in Aleppo and Homs create shifting alignments and realignments in the military and the national bureaucracy, which undermines the military clique in power. For the time being, the army dominates Syria, and Alawi officers dominate the army, but this state of affairs will no doubt be ephemeral.

Foreign Policy

Syrian foreign policy is largely a function of nationalism, Zionism, and neutralism. Syria has long been the seat of Arab nationalism. As early as the 1830s the Egyptian occupation of Syria under Muhammad Ali and his son Ibrahim gently stirred the Syrian sense of national consciousness. With the establishment of schools by American, French, and British missionaries, the introduction of an Arabic press, and the establishment of literary, scientific, and political societies and secret clubs, Beirut and Damascus became the centers of nascent Arab nationalism. Yet this early nationalism contained two conflicting ideas—Syrian nationalism and Pan-Arabism.

Syrian nationalism is largely championed by the now outlawed Syrian Social Nationalist party and by ethnic and religious minorities who fear a large, unified Arab state dominated by Sunni Muslims. This scheme for a Greater Syria is based on the fact that historically—under the Ottomans and before—Syria, Lebanon, and Palestine were united with Damascus as their capital. And even though Lebanon was separated by an Ottoman decree in 1861 and Palestine was separated as a British mandate in 1920, these Syrian nationalists look to the time when Greater Syria will be reunited.

Far more significant in Syria today is the concept of Pan-Arabism. Not since the time of the Crusades have the Arab states been politically united, and their internal weaknesses greatly facilitated the imposition of colonial domination. Pan-Arabism is a reaction against former colonial subjection and, in the minds of many Syrian leaders, the necessary preliminary to restoration of the greatness that once belonged to the Umayyad dynasty. Syria's initial demand for the creation of the United Arab Republic and the disintegration of this manifestation of Pan-Arabism three years later should be recognized as the result of these two forms of nationalism clashing within Syria's boundaries.

The creation of Israel must be seen as the key factor shaping present-day foreign policy in Syria. Israel is seen as an "insidious plot" and a tool of Western imperialism. The catastrophic Arab defeat in 1948 bred a lingering sense of frustration that generates a demand for action generally more virulent in Syria than in other Arab states. Analysis of this hostility must include several factors: the historical deception of the Sykes-Picot Agreement perpetuated by the Western powers after World War I, the general failure of independence to bring about the expected prosperity and progress, and the continuous bitter reminder of thousands of Palestinian refugees living in Syria that the present divided Arab nation is incapable of achieving her national destiny. Recent policy statements of Syria's present government, however, indicate greater flexibility about the Arab-Israeli conflict. General al-Assad appears much less willing to support unconditionally the Palestinian guerrilla forces, and he has even suggested that some type of political solution may be possible.

A central corollary of Syrian foreign policy has been the acceptance and advocacy of neutralism, or nonalignment. Neutralism is perceived as a visible symbol and a necessary consequence of the gaining and maintenance of Syrian independence. During the past two decades the basic essentials of the neutralist creed implied Syria's complete unwillingness to join any foreign-sponsored military pact, such as the Baghdad Pact. It also implied diplomatic freedom of action in which Syria would be free to evolve policies, programs, ideologies, and institutions in accordance with her own interests and not after consultation with one of the major powers. A neutralist policy, on the other hand, did not preclude temporary diplomatic, economic, or military association with either the East or the West. Thus Syria welcomed American aid during the late 1940s and the early 1950s, and even as late as 1964 Syria was receiving Food for Peace shipments and small development loans.

Far more significant has been the gradual increase of the influence of the Soviet Union. Although trade agreements were signed with various Communist satellites as early as 1952, 1956 saw the first major shipment of Soviet arms and economic aid to Syria. Except for the period of 1958-61, when Syria was part of the United Arab Republic, Communist influence has increased dramatically. By carefully identifying with the foreign policy aspirations of the Syrian people, the Soviet Union has gradually emerged as "a true friend" of Syria. Yet today Russia's stand on Israel influences Syria more than Soviet economic aid. Since the 1967 War, the Soviet Union has supported the Arabs against Israel, condemning the "expansionist policies" of Zionism and U.S. support of Israeli policies. The Arab-Israeli conflict will continue to shape both the foreign and domestic policies of Syria far into the future.

Political Prospects

The prospects for stability and political development in Syria are similar to those for many newly emerging nations. Plagued with a history of conquest, invasion, colonialism, and open exploitation; divided by cultural, social, and economic differences; and confronted by the Arab-Israeli conflicts, Syria's political future is difficult to determine.

Syria is faced with the dual challenge of creating a new political identity and establishing political institutions that have legitimacy. Political identity implies that a nation knows what it is, what it wants, and where it is going. Just as people face the challenge of discovering themselves, so nations too are often forced to evaluate their identities and destinies. Political cohesion and common purpose require a commitment to commonly accepted goals and ideals. Syria's political identity is thus still open to question; the social division, the political quarrels, and the cultural cleavages apparent in Syrian history challenge all attempts at creating a common set of goals and ideals. The internal struggles and international problems that Syria must face give room neither for optimism nor euphoria; a successful solution entails the difficult task of generating a new basis of allegiance among the masses to a new set of symbols of national unity and solidarity.

Equally challenging is the problem of establishing political institutions that are considered legitimate. Few would deny that Syria's political history since World War II has been one of constant change, a general disregard for the established constitutions, and a complete lack of faith in the institutions created by these constitutions. Also, the attempts by the Syrian military to establish a monolithic hierarchy of power and prestige have impeded the development of autonomous groups and organizations in society that could counterbalance the pressures for authoritarian centralism.

The process of modernization implies the popular acceptance of institutions, procedures, and legal structures that are capable of meeting the challenges of stability and progress. The process by which people come to accept their government, their constitution, and the procedures by which their political system functions requires time, experience, and experimentation. The history of the Syrian people has not been easy. Those willing to look beyond the rough outlines of instability and uncertainty find a people desirous of obtaining justice and progress. Few who know Syria well deny the genius and great national heritage of this people of al-Shams—together these suggest a bright future.

     To the west of Syria is Lebanon. Historically and culturally these two countries have much in common—both were part of the Umayyad and Abbasid empires and later the Ottoman Empire; both were under the French mandate system; both gained their independence after World War II and sought political development and modernization. Yet Lebanon has been relatively free of political instability, has developed a fairly pro-Western system, and has experienced substantial economic growth.

Selected Bibliography

Hitti, Philip K. *History of Syria*. New York: Macmillan Co., 1951.
A standard history of Syria by one of the leading Arab scholars.

Hourani, A. H. *Syria and Lebanon*. London: Oxford University Press, 1946.
Generally considered the best description and analysis of Syrian politics prior to World War II.

Longrigg, Stephen. *Syria and Lebanon under French Mandate*. London: Oxford University Press, 1958.
A very scholarly and complete history of Syria from the late Ottoman period to Syrian independence.

Seale, Patrick. *The Struggle for Syria*. London: Oxford University Press, 1965.
A carefully written analysis of Syrian politics in the late 1950s and early 1960s.

Torrey, Gordon H. *Syrian Politics and the Military: 1945-58*. Columbus, Ohio: Ohio State University Press, 1964.
An excellent introduction into the role of the army in Syrian politics, especially during the early years of Syria's independence.

Ziadeh, Nicola A. *Syria and Lebanon*. New York: Frederick A. Praeger, 1957.
Provides an excellent summary of the political events in the post-World War II periods.

Republic of Lebanon

The development of Lebanon as an independent political entity is a unique experiment in nation building by traditional means. Composed of competing small majorities and large minorities, Lebanon often seems impossible to govern. However, this small country has achieved an enviably high level of prosperity without having a solid economic base and has managed to have a relatively stable political system despite frequent near breakdowns. Lebanon has established a firm administrative structure and workable constitutional procedures.

Prosperity, stability, and constitutionalism are for the most part the results of constant adjustment and balancing of the interests of the various Lebanese communities, which is essentially a reconciliation process among leaders who often represent feuding blood relations, antagonistic families, or rival religious communities. When constitutional political structures grind to a halt, the community leaders search for solutions through their intermediaries. Traditional, intermittent, and inefficient as this process may be, it has helped the Lebanese live through an important stage in their political development.

Historical Background

The history of Lebanon begins with Mount Lebanon, a small, rugged mountainous area largely inaccessible to invading armies of the Ottoman Empire that became the abode of disaffected minorities—Christians, Druze, and Sunni and Shii Muslims. Mount Lebanon maintained a semiautonomous existence within the Ottoman state; local government was in the hands of Druze chiefs and amirs. In 1756 government of the Mount passed to the house of Shihab, whose members adopted the faith of the Maronite Christians, then a majority sect. The importance of the Maronite patriarch was thus increased, and French influence also increased through strong support to the Shihabi rulers. French diplomacy in the area was focused on protecting the Maronites and sustaining French influence. The British were linked with the Druze and were primarily interested in frustrating French influence. Foreign connections with these minority groups were maintained despite the Ottoman government and sometimes with its acquiescence.

Under pressure from the great powers, the Ottoman governor of Beirut set up a local council for Mount Lebanon in September 1841, the first legislative body in the history of Lebanon. The council was to hear complaints about taxes and to prepare new tax schedules, but its most interesting feature was its membership—three Druze, three Maronites, one Sunni, one Shii, one Greek Catholic, and one Greek Orthodox. The council collapsed immediately after a small Druze revolt during which the town of Deir Quamar was sacked and many Maronites were killed.

Between 1841 and 1860 several attempts were made under British and French pressure to divide Mount Lebanon into two districts, one Druze and the other Christian, each to be governed by an official chosen from the inhabitants by the Ottoman governor of the coastal city of Sidon. These attempts culminated in the Statute of 1845, which established in each district representative councils whose membership was apportioned among the communities. The new system broke down in 1859, however, and during the civil war of 1860 that ensued many Christians were massacred by some Druze groups. This time Britain and France interfered militarily.

Meanwhile, representatives of the great powers met to deliberate on the "Lebanon question" with representatives of the Ottoman government. The result was the Statute of 1861, according to which Mount Lebanon was to be governed by a non-Lebanese Christian appointed by the Ottoman government with the approval of the interested great powers. The statute also provided for the establishment of an administrative council with membership allotted among the religious communities. With slight modifications, the administrative council remained in power until World War I, when it was dismissed by Ottoman authorities. It was reestablished by the French for a short period, only to be dissolved to make way for direct French mandate in 1922.

Under French rule Lebanon was enlarged to its present borders in response to demands by the Maronite community. The enlargement of Lebanon complicated the existing problem by adding regionalism and stronger Pan-Arab sentiments. Additions to the Mountain included the coastal cities of Tripoli in the north and Sidon and Tyre in the south. These cities were predominantly Muslim, and their sympathy with Lebanon as a separate entity from geographic Syria was minimal.

In an attempt to integrate the new territories, the French divided the country into districts calculated to maintain a balance among various communities. Their efforts, reflected in the electoral laws of 1922, perpetuated old political arrangements, and it may be argued that by means of these electoral laws, the French revived the influence of feudalist elements in the country. Each district had its own established families and propertied, semifeudal notables. Most of the districts, however, were polycommunal—that is, they were composed of many semiautonomous communities. Candidates running for office could join a list, or slate, which would reflect the nature of the district and would compete with another similarly apportioned list. This practice brought forward established feudal families of long standing, who usually defeated lists of less well known notables. These arrangements intentionally or unintentionally strengthened the French rule in Lebanon by fractionalizing the country into jealous minorities.

Most Lebanese political structures were built with French assistance between 1926 and 1943. In 1926 a constitution suitable to the country was promulgated, and other administrative, judicial, and legislative structures began to take shape. The French interfered in constitutional life, however, at times suspending the constitution and at other times manipulating elections and suppressing dissident elements. Pan-Arab and nationalist sentiments became more intense, and political associations and parties also emerged during this period, some of which supported Arab unity and almost all of which demanded an end to French tutelage. Developments on the international scene, especially the Anglo-French rivalry in the region, created a favorable situation in which the Lebanese could press their demands for political independence.

After Lebanon was promised independence by the Free French in 1941, the British publicly urged immediate and complete independence. Strong British endorsement encouraged the Constitutional bloc, one of two coalitions that had emerged by this time, to press more vigorously its demands for an independent Lebanon. The leading personalities in this bloc were Bisharah al-Khuri and Kamil Shamun, both Maronites with strong connections with Muslim communities and the British and Arab leaders. The opposing coalition, the National bloc led by Emile Eddé, a Maronite, was supported by the French authorities. National bloc leaders believed in the "separateness" of Lebanon from the Arab world and the necessity of French protection.

The National Pact

The labors for independence were complicated by continuing conflicts between the two major communities, the Maronite Christians and the Sunni Muslims. The conflicts first arose over the separation of Lebanon from other Arab states, which the Christians promoted and the Muslims resisted. On the eve of independence a conflict arose over the identity of the new state: After independence, would Lebanon be an end in itself or a step toward a larger Arab unity? Would Lebanon be a nation or an Arab state constituting an integral part of a larger Arab nation?

The intercommunal conflicts were partially mitigated by other developments, the most important of which was the division of labor that gave form to Lebanese administrative and political institutions. The system set in motion under the French mandate was expanding and in the process was creating political and administrative careers. These were being filled by members of all communities, but Christians gained a dominant influence. The Maronites and middle-of-the-road politicians had greater access to the government than the Sunnis, who refused to cooperate and hence were at a disadvantage, although many Muslim leaders were persuaded to share the benefits. Dealing with the problem of rivalry over the distribution of political positions was relatively easy and was aided by the regional division of Lebanon into administrative and electoral districts that cut across community lines. Also, the proportional representation of the communities (i.e., the balanced ticket) was attractive to the semifeudal leaders and was not viewed as unfair.

The controversy over the identity of Lebanon was not easy to resolve. The Muslims feared that Lebanese nationalism meant a Christian nation associated with the West and separated from the Arab world. Christians saw Arab nationalism as ultimate incorporation into a larger Muslim nation away from the West. Secularism, toward which Christians leaned, was not fully appreciated by many Muslims. Yet Lebanon, independent or not, could not remain viable if half of its inhabitants insisted on being part of a larger political entity. These dialectics led to an interesting synthesis—the National Pact, which was a verbal agreement between the followers of the prominent Sunni Riyadh al-Sulh and those of the Maronite Bisharah al-Khuri early in 1943, and which was an understanding whereby Christians would cease to demand protection from abroad and Muslims would not press for incorporation into a larger entity.

Since its inception the National Pact has been subject to various interpretations. Some praise it as a holy covenant ushering in an era of communal cooperation. Others criticize it because it seems to consecrate confessionalism, or emphasis on religious differences, and the status quo without resolving the basic conflicts. Statements by al-Khuri and al-Sulh invited more speculation about what was implied by the pact. While on a visit to Egypt in the summer of 1943, al-Khuri said that Lebanon wants its "complete independence" and wants "to cooperate with the Arab states to the greatest possible extent." Al-Sulh said to parliament in the course of his first policy statement that Lebanon has an "Arab face" but would partake of what was good in the Western culture; Lebanon would be "neither a station nor a pathway for imperialism" in the Arab world. These are reassuring statements for those concerned, both in Lebanon and for the neighboring Arabs, and they give some indication of the content of the National Pact, but they do not clarify it.

Some claim that the pact was not only a political formula but also an approximation of Rousseau's *Social Contract*. That the agreement founded and perpetuated an association of Lebanese communities cannot be doubted. It cannot be doubted either that each community, while uniting itself with the rest, may remain as free as before. Partisans could read into the pact whatever they wished, and perhaps this was precisely the intention of its architects—to leave the door open for accommodation. Yet this open door would have serious consequences for governance and for the integration of the Lebanese political system.

The constitutional bloc adopted the National Pact and demanded independence more vigorously. The French had no other alternative, and they bowed to the increasing pressures from the Constitutional bloc, the British, and the Arab States and on March 25, 1943, declared that suspended constitutional life would be restored. Preparations for an election, set for the summer of 1943, started immediately. After considerable intercommunal wrangling, a formula for the apportionment of seats in Parliament was reached—of fifty-five seats, thirty would be for Christian and twenty-five for Muslim communities. The six-to-five ratio has been maintained, and ever since the total has been a multiple of eleven. This step signaled the beginning of a relatively workable accommodation and reflected the spirit of the National Pact.

The results of the 1943 elections were decisive: Bisharah al-Khuri and his Constitutional bloc won a resounding victory, and Parliament elected him president of the republic by forty-four votes, with eleven abstentions. The new president requested Riyadh al-Sulh to form the first cabinet, in which all six major communities were represented. The new Lebanese government amended the constitution, revoking restrictions applicable under the French rule and thus consolidating the power of the national government. The French responded by arresting the president and the prime minister. Other members of the cabinet withdrew to a small village where they established themselves as a temporary government. The Lebanese, both Muslim and Christian, called for a strike, which paralyzed the country. The British encouraged the national government to persist in its demands for independence, and with the United States, they advised the French to reverse their policy. On November 22, 1943, Independence Day, the president and the other national leaders were released. The atmosphere of that day had the air of a revolutionary triumph, which enhanced the legitimacy of the new regime and the polycommunal balance it seemed to have achieved.

Political Environment

The People

Polycommunalism: Lebanese society is a mosaic of separate communities that are not assimilated into a national culture. Loyalty is given instead to different religious faiths and schismatic movements, and each group practices its religious tenets, at least formally, with sanguine fervor.

These communities are Christian, Muslim, Druze, and other splinter minorities. The Maronites (Lebanese Catholics, also known as Uniate Catholics), who now constitute approximately 30 percent of the population, are an old Christian community that fled from persecution in neighboring countries and inhabited the mountain areas. The Greek Orthodox, 10 percent of the population, live in various parts of Lebanon and are descendants of old Christian Arabian tribes and the Byzantines. The Greek Catholics, 6 percent, have a similar long history. Sunni Orthodox Muslims constitute about 20 percent of the population. Shiis, 18 percent, are also a sect of Islam. The Druze, 6 percent, were among the early minorities that found refuge in the Lebanon. Originally Muslim, they deviated from Islam early in the eleventh century. Other religious and ethnic minorities include Protestants, Chaldeans, Armenians, Latins, and Jews.

The divisions between the various communities became more distinct in the mid-nineteenth century when feudalism was being shaken, and after 1861 each community started its own school system. Foreign missionary schools—French, British, Russian, and American—also began to have an impact among the Christian communities at this time, and they indirectly helped to increase existing intercommunal rivalries and jealousies. Since that time the communities have become even more distant from one another, and today each community has its educational system and its peculiar socialization norms and agents. The result has been a culture that orients youth in different political directions and delays the emergence of the shared culture that is necessary for social integration.

This socialization process has tended to reinforce traditional loyalties to different reference groups within and outside Lebanon. The immediate reference groups are the family and the community; the distant reference groups are different "mother worlds" with which the communities identify. The majority of Christians, particularly the Maronites, look to Western states for inspiration and possible protection. The Muslim Sunnis identify with the prominent Arab states, especially Egypt and Syria. Both communities recognize the educational contributions of the West, but events in the twentieth century brought doubt and suspicion about the West's political designs. These different orientations of the various communities make their assimilation into a "Lebanese" civic culture difficult.

Polycommunalism in Lebanon cannot be attributed only to religious differences, of course. Feudal structures, religious leaders, and kinship and fealty groups have reinforced and helped perpetuate communal rivalries.

Social Structure: Free trade and commerce have led to inequalities among the segments of the population. In 1960 it was estimated that the poor and low-income families, constituting about 50 percent of the population, had the smallest share of the gross national product. The richest families, constituting only 4 percent, had the largest share, 32 percent. This inequitable distribution of wealth could lead to discontent.

Economic development in the outlying regions reflects serious gaps from one region to another. Mount Lebanon is highly urbanized and developed, whereas the Biqa region and South Lebanon are the least developed, which indicates the advantages Christians tend to have over Muslims (inhabitants of the Biqa and the South are predominantly Muslims working in agriculture rather than in the trade and tourist-related services common in the Mount). These economic differences affect political processes and compound intercommunal rivalries.

Economic and Social Conditions

Lebanon is not blessed with oil or significant mineral resources, but her location, connecting the continents of Africa, Asia, and Europe, has always been advantageous. Lebanon has a gentle climate, plenty of rain, and natural harbors, and her beaches, scenic terraced mountains, and historical sites make Lebanon a tourist attraction.

In addition to location, Lebanon's major assets are enterprising people and the freedoms engendered by the polycommunal political system. Scarcity of mineral resources and dependence on trade have taken the Lebanese to various parts of the world to do business. In the past half century over one million Lebanese have emigrated to Latin America, North America, and Africa, and thousands work in Kuwait and other oil-rich Arab countries. Emigrants contribute to Lebanon's economy by frequent visits and the remittances they send home to relatives. The Lebanese are highly literate and are generally masters of two or three languages. They love competition and thrive on bargaining and free trade.

The economy of Lebanon began to expand after independence. The Lebanese now have a service economy, as distinguished from agricultural and industrial economies. More than two-thirds of the gross national product is derived from trade, banking, insurance, and related services (income from agriculture and industry constitutes only 30 percent). Lebanese merchants thrive on import and reexport trade and free exchange transactions in gold and foreign currencies.

An interesting feature of the Lebanese economy is the relation of imports to exports—imports for 1966 were worth almost six times more than exports, but the large deficit was fully covered and the balance of payments remained favorable. The free nature of the expanding economy has helped increase its gold and foreign exchange reserves, and the country has no external debts except for a small loan from the International Bank. In spite of setbacks, particularly in 1958 and 1967, the Lebanese economy has shown continued growth. In 1969 the per capita income of the Lebanese reached $633, which was high compared to that of other developing countries.

The first serious attempt at economic planning began in 1961, when the government adopted a five-year plan aimed at improving the standard of living of the long-neglected villages. The government built an excellent road network, improved drinking water facilities, and brought electricity to almost all outlying areas. The most ambitious project is on the Litani, a major river in Lebanon. The first two stages are completed and include a complex of dams, generators, and irrigation canals. When finished, this project will increase irrigated land by 40 percent and will double electric power output. These projects should stimulate economic life in the villages and may help stem the flow of rural people to overcrowded cities.

In spite of the relative affluence of the country, however, the economy remains precarious. The inflow of capital and the import-reexport trade cannot serve as a firm basis for the Lebanese economy; capital can flow out as easily as it flows in, and import and reexport trade is increasingly subject to pressures resulting from competition of the newly developed ports in Syria and elsewhere on the Mediterranean and in the Persian Gulf states. These potential difficulties have spurred the government to invest more money in development plans and to encourage industrial expansion.

Free trade and other freedoms have helped the national income and strengthened private enterprise, Lebanese and foreign, in education also. Lebanon has four major universities and seven colleges that attract students and capital from throughout the world. In addition to the public school system, there are French, American, and British missionary schools and Armenian, Protestant, Catholic, and Islamic schools, all privately financed. The major colleges have similar arrangements; except for Lebanese University, all depend on foreign resources. The American University of Beirut depends on American resources, Saint Joseph on French, and Arab University on Egyptian. Aside from their political significance, these centers of higher learning provide Lebanon and other Arab countries with physicians, engineers, executives, and other trained personnel.

The Lebanese press and the publishing industry reflect similar outside influences. Despite its small size, Lebanon has 49 independent dailies—forty Arabic, four Armenian, four French, and one English—and 112 weekly magazines and many monthlies, and the reading public extends to all Arab countries. The television networks are mostly foreign-owned companies, French and British. The impact of this medium on the socialization of Lebanese children is just beginning to be felt, and consequences for the family, the religious communities, and the economic system have yet to be examined.

Political Structure and Processes

The basic rules of the game are laid out formally in the constitution of 1926 and informally in a series of precedents dating back to 1840. The National Pact of 1943 affirmed these precedents as a basis for a continuing consociation of the major communities of an independent political entity.

The present constitution, promulgated under the French mandate, set up a parliamentary form of government under the tutelage of the French high commissioner and included provisions that gave him the right to suspend the constitution and to supervise Lebanon's "experimental apprenticeship in democracy." This constitution, except for changes that revoked the powers of the high commissioner, has remained essentially intact. The document reflects a unique, formal dualism that accommodates particularistic-sacral and universalistic-secular influences. This dualism is deliberate, and it reflects political experiences and present realities.

The constitution recognizes and reconciles two separate realms. In the religious realm, the state guarantees the freedom of all communities to worship freely. The religious authorities of each community are completely free from interference by the state in matters directly connected with their faith and the organization of their communities. These matters mostly concern marriage and inheritance, commonly referred to in Lebanon as matters of personal status. Each community has its own religious courts, which are recognized and legitimized by the state and which resolve conflicts over matters of personal status. The state thus safeguards the independence and integrity of the religious communities.

The political realm represents the total space of activity in which the political system functions. In this realm the Lebanese political system, much like any other, is concerned with governance through maintenance of order, integration of its elements, and growth of the civil polity. The constitution provides for this purpose a modern, rational framework that allocates and defines the separate functions of the executive, legislative, and judicial structures. Secular norms such as equality before the law, individual property rights, and other freedoms are guaranteed, and the constitution also expressly refers to achievement and merit as the basis for government employment. However, these are provisions of mixed character that tend to reconcile the particularistic and universalistic influences, taming the former and tempering the latter.

Particularistic influences represented by confessional polycommunalism and dispersed semifeudal status groups are tamed by electoral laws, which give communities proportional representation in Parliament but prevent them from becoming states within the state. Universalistic norms, such as merit and achievement, are tempered by a temporary provision that has become a permanent principle. Article 95 states that "in order to promote harmony and justice, the communities will be equitably represented in government employment . . . without prejudicing the good of the State." Achievement norms are thus complemented by the ascriptive notion of proportional sharing in the bureaucratic structure. The principle of communal representation finds full-blown expression at the highest level, where by precedent the president of the republic must be a Maronite, the prime minister a Sunni, and the speaker of Parliament a Shii. The dualism referred to above is also reflected in the personalities of the incumbents of the higher and lower offices. These men are mostly modern, rational, and achievement oriented; nonetheless, they owe their political style and position to particularistic and ascriptive forces such as community affiliations, inherited family status, and the regions from which they come.

The Executive

The presidency is the keystone of the political process in Lebanon. The president is the chief executive and is responsible for making policy. He is elected by Parliament from the ranks of the Maronite community for a nonrenewable term of six years. The president rules through a cabinet of ministers formed by the prime minister, who is designated by the president and is almost always a Sunni. The members of the cabinet, who also represent the various communities, are selected on the basis of competence and political considerations and are appointed by the president at the recommendation of the prime minister. The cabinet is responsible to the president for carrying out the functions of administration, although its members are also individually and collectively accountable to Parliament, from which the cabinet must seek a vote of confidence on the basis of a prepared policy statement.

The formation of every cabinet is preceded by protracted consultation that cuts across the myriad competitive geographical, economic, religious, and secular ideological interests in the country. Other interests that must be taken into account are those established families whose exclusion could spell trouble, not only because of the family status but because the families often symbolize political tendencies and followings. In fact, the question of who gets what, when, and how cannot be understood without an understanding of the history of these families.

Formation of the cabinet is thus a continuous process of balancing varying interests. The pressures are constant and are reflected in the cabinet crises that affect Lebanon on the average of every seven or eight months. Conflicts in the form of open disagreements over patronage or unauthorized statements by ministers that prove embarrassing to the government lead to resignations, reshuffles, and often to the formation of new cabinets. The cabinet is a loose coalition of men who meet the approval of the lower-lying groups in Parliament or the country at large, not a team. The ministers are not joined by a political program and are not disciplined through party affiliation. They are partly ministers and partly ambitious political leaders who cultivate their own political followings by serving as their spokesmen. The fragile compromises on which the cabinet is often based make it weak, short-lived, and relatively ineffectual.

The status of the cabinet is also affected by the president, who has virtually all the powers necessary to stabilize it. Yet Lebanese politics seem to require the president to be impartial and "above politics," and especially above his own community. His behavior and attitudes in office are watched carefully. If he wishes to move the country, the chief executive cannot play the game of Lebanese politics with much zeal because it would make him a party to internal conflicts rather than the final arbiter.

Parliament

Legislative authority lies in a popularly elected Parliament that is vested with the authority to enact laws. Members of Parliament are elected for four years to seats allocated on the basis of proportional representation by a formula agreed upon on the eve of independence in 1943. Once elected, however, a member of Parliament speaks for the whole country rather than for his community, a norm intended to reduce confessional consciousness. This principle is enforced by laws that form electoral districts so that they cut across communal concentrations and thus make it necessary for the candidate to appeal to communities other than his own.

Parliament is quite representative of the Lebanese population and, like the cabinet, reflects the squabbles and undercurrents of daily political life. Its sessions are characterized by considerable feuding between blocs, which are coalitions of members of Parliament who follow well-known political figures, former presidents, and presidential contenders. The influence of organized political parties in Parliament is minimal; members of Parliament who are affiliated with political parties are very few, and their membership in Parliament is not necessarily explained by party membership.

The composition of Parliament since 1943 reflects the economic changes in Lebanese society and provides some hope of reducing the political feuding between the traditionalist families and personalities represented in Parliament. Landlords, or semifeudal oligarchs, and lawyers have a reduced role, and professionals and businessmen dominate. Competition for seats is high, and the financial cost of campaigning has increased considerably. In the absence of strong mass political parties, the intense electoral competition has made Parliament a political casino of the rich.

Beyond debates and often negative criticism of the cabinet, Parliament is weak. Bills are passed only after long delays and deadlocks. The president towers over most legislators, and no cabinet has lost a vote of confidence because of a majority opposition. The whole Parliament is at the mercy of the executive, who is the dispenser of patronage and who holds the power of dissolving Parliament. A president is nonetheless careful not to antagonize Parliament, for he is dependent on it for the legitimization of his activities. Since independence, however, all presidents have obtained decree powers from Parliament for a limited period to help them launch their programs without undue delay.

Like the cabinet, Parliament seems to be impotent in time of crisis over basic issues such as foreign policy, and Lebanese presidents often have to make serious policy decisions alone at such times. Members of Parliament, except those close to the president, hesitate to give open support because of pressures from their heterogeneous constituencies. The occasional deliberate indecision of the president is also due to cross pressures similar to those to which members of Parliament are subject.

The weak posture of the Lebanese Parliament, its fragmented character, and its subservience to the executive do not make it insignificant, however. Its major function—the nomination and election of Lebanon's presidents—remains effective and intact, and like legislative bodies in conventional democracies in the West, it is the major legitimizer of government actions and the guardian of the constitution.

Political Parties

Political parties in Lebanon reflect the country's fragmented culture and the ideological undercurrents and political movements in the Arab world. Parties that are strictly Lebanese in orientation are still minority parties and are few in number. The remaining parties in Lebanon are extraterritorial associations concerned with integrationist hopes and plans for a Greater Syria, one Arab nation, one Muslim nation, or international communism—Lebanese political life manages to have room for all.

Parties that accept the Lebanese political framework and are devoted to preserving it are the National bloc, the Constitutional bloc, the Kataib, Najjada, the Progressive Socialists, the National Liberals, and small active parties in the Armenian community. All except the Constitutionalists have a relatively stable organization. The National bloc and the Constitutionalists predate independence and are the followers of the Eddé and al-Khuri families respectively. Both are essentially parliamentary blocs, although the latter is now faded.

The Lebanese Kataib, formerly a youth organization, became an active political party after independence. Headed by Pierre al-Jamayel, this organization is characterized by a paramilitary discipline, and it stands for an independent Lebanon as a nation. Its leadership and the rank and file are almost exclusively Maronite Christians, who have representatives in Parliament and the cabinet. The Najjada was formed a few years after the Kataib, perhaps as a reaction to the latter. It is organized in similar fashion, but its membership is composed exclusively of Sunni Muslims. The two organizations cooperated in forcing the hand of the French in 1943 to grant complete independence to the country. Both parties depend on the support of their respective communities, and the leader of Najjada, Adnan Hakim, gained a seat in Parliament in 1964.

The Progressive Socialist party, led by Kemal Jumblat, is organized along the same lines as European parties. Its political thought is modernist and idealist; it believes in a socialist ideology that prepares the way for complete human universalism and believes in religion but rejects sectarianism. Jumblat, a Druze, was elected to Parliament by his predominantly Druze district, however. The Druze peasants and workers in the party are attracted by the leader's family history in the Druze community, and the party also finds support among intellectuals from other communities.

The National Liberal party was formed in 1958 by President Shamun at the close of his term. It insists on a sovereign Lebanon among Arab states. It is a vote-getting instrument, and possibly because of this, it is the first pragmatic party in Lebanon. It is represented in Parliament by Shamun himself and his supporters.

The character of these parties reflects both particularistic and modernist forces in Lebanon. The leaders are sophisticated modern men, but the appeal of these parties is to family status as a symbol of traditional communal interests. They fail to appeal to a larger membership that could cut across communal lines because parliamentary seats are assigned on a confessional basis, which reinforces communal separateness and hinders the emergence of modern political parties.

Beirut, the capital of Lebanon, has been the center for Arab integrationist thought since before independence. For this reason, integrationist Pan-Arabic political associations are natural in Lebanon. The Syrian Social Nationalist party, organized early in the 1930s, was the first integrationist group. It called for the unity of Greater Syria—that is, the geographic area commonly referred to as the Fertile Crescent. The party had a considerable following in the Syrian Arab Republic up to 1954 and in Lebanon up to 1960. In both states it was suppressed because of its ideology and its role in attempted coups. The party is significant because it was the first party in Lebanon and the Arab world whose support cut across religious communities. The party is not extinct, although it is now overshadowed by more significant movements such as the Arab Nationalist Movement (ANM) and the Baath party.

The Baath party, split between left and right, is the governing party in the Syrian Arab Republic and in Iraq. The ANM and the Baath both call for a union of all Arab states from the Gulf to the Atlantic. Their following is found primarily in the cities, and their appeal is limited to the intelligentsia, the Sunnis, and the Greek Orthodox. Their goals of Arab unity and the containment of Israel receive considerable support among the Lebanese, but their attitude toward Lebanon—at times they are willing to reconcile themselves to an independent Lebanon and at others they reject it—hinders their efforts in Lebanon. They are legally banned in Lebanon but have always operated openly without much interference by Lebanese authorities.

The Muslim Brotherhood, which calls for Islamic unity, represents the extreme brand of religious traditionalism. The Communists, with followers among all segments of the population, are a minority but are among the best organized of modernist parties. Like the Pan-Arab parties, their development in Lebanon has been delayed, partly because they are banned, but more importantly, perhaps, because of the intrenched influence of primordial ties and polycommunalism. Loyalty to family and community is still above loyalty to economic class or political ideology. Strictly Lebanese and extraterritorial parties represent the "mother worlds" of the citizens of this small country. These "mother worlds" do not overlap but coexist, and they sometimes provide incompatible frames of reference that are very much a part of the Lebanese culture.

Foreign Policy

Lebanon's foreign policy is an extension of its domestic policies. It is a subdued policy, predicated on little initiative. The cross pressures influencing policy choices are enormous, and making choices or avoiding them evokes a series of new conflicts that have unpredictable consequences. Making choices in the area of foreign affairs is indeed a difficult task that often exacts a heavy price in terms of insecurity, civil conflict, and sometimes direct foreign intervention. Lebanon's policy of neutrality in the politics of the Arab states and of nonalignment in the East-West cold war does not seem to spare it from hazardous involvement.

The location of Lebanon in the heart of the Arab world and its small size and delicate political system have made it very sensitive to external political influences. Its polycommunal composition makes it relatively easy for interested regional and international forces to promote their influences in the country. As a result, Lebanon today is the vortex of many diverse and conflicting forces. Beirut is the headquarters of a number of businesses and foreign concerns, including agents of intelligence services representing big and small powers.

International conflicts, especially those connected with the Arab world, are mirrored in the divisions they produce on the domestic scene. For this reason Lebanon often finds itself engrossed in conflicts not of its own making. The situation becomes particularly dangerous when conflicting international or regional parties choose Lebanon as the stage for power plays. Such situations have often driven Lebanon to the brink of civil war and threatened its survival as an independent political entity.

The problems encountered in foreign policy over the past years deteriorated into the violent civil crisis of 1958, and the dilemmas of 1969 precipitated by the 1967 Arab-Israeli War threatened a similar crisis. Such crises bring to the surface intercommunal antagonisms and thinly veiled hostilities, which if allowed to explode could assume regional dimensions.

The crisis of 1958, the bloodiest in Lebanon's recent history, divided the country into two warring camps. The pro-Arab, pro-Nasser, anti-West, anti-Baghdad Pact, and anti-Shamun groups represented one camp; anti-Arab, anti-Nasser, pro-West, and pro-Shamun factions represented the other camp. The former camp was predominantly Muslim but attracted Christians from the Maronite community. The latter was composed of Christian Maronites and a scatter from the other communities. Both camps were armed; they engaged in bloody skirmishes and brought the economic system to a standstill. Political parties also took sides, with the Kataib for Shamun and the Progressive Socialists on the side of the opposition with all extraterritorial parties except the Syrian Social Nationalists.

President Shamun was accused of partisanship in the elections of 1957 when he reduced his opposition in Parliament at the expense of entrenched leaders. He was also accused of partisanship in the Arab cold war because he did not oppose the Western-sponsored Baghdad Pact. His disregard for the sentiments of the Muslims was considered a violation of the National Pact. The army refused to quell rebellious groups and limited its role to keeping them apart. The leader of the army, General Fuad Shihab, apparently felt that the crisis was political and that the armed forces must be spared partisan activity. What started as internal rivalry soon assumed international dimensions and came to reflect the competing influences of the United States, the United Arab Republic, the Kingdom of Iraq, and others. The situation in the region led to the landing of U.S. Marines on July 15. The conflict lingered until September 22, the end of Shamun's term of office, when General Shihab was elected to fill the post of president. Under Shihab the slogan of national unity rather than the National Pact was stressed, and Lebanon's commitment to the Arab world became stronger.

Under Presidents Shihab, Helou, and now Franjieh, Lebanon's relations with the big powers have not changed. These relations are based on a policy of nonalignment, with a preference for the Western powers. Historically, Britain, France and the U.S. have shown considerable interest in preserving the integrity and independence of Lebanon. Although they may not always admit it, the Lebanese hold to these relations and cultivate them partly because they could not protect themselves against covetous neighbors.

The Soviet Union did not manifest active interest in Lebanon until recently. In 1970, and especially after repeated Israeli incursions into Lebanon, the Russians expressed their willingness to give Lebanon support and assistance. Soviet statements about possible help to Lebanon were stronger than any made by the Western powers, with the possible exception of France. Russian concern with the integrity of Lebanon is new and may signal a change in Soviet policy commensurate with their improved position in the Mediterranean. Although it welcomes Russian concern, Lebanon continues to maintain good relations with the West. These relations, including economic and cultural ties, are old, yet events in the area might interfere and force a change in Lebanon's foreign policy. In November 1971 Lebanon concluded an agreement to purchase arms from the Soviet Union. Lebanon also recognized Communist China immediately after the Peking government was admitted to the United Nations.

Palestine Liberation Movement

The second major crisis that divided the people began in the aftermath of the Arab-Israeli War of 1967. The solidarity achieved by the Lebanese was threatened in 1969 by the entry of the fedayeen, the Palestine Liberation Organizations, into south Lebanon without the sanction of Lebanese authorities. The Lebanese are sympathetic toward the Palestinians, but they are not in agreement as to whether the Palestinians should operate from Lebanese frontiers. In April 1969 Prime Minister Rashid Karami and his cabinet resigned in protest over police tactics used in quelling the mounting pro-Palestinian demonstrations, but he was asked by President Charles Helou to form the cabinet anew.

In the early stages of the crisis the president led an open discussion of the issues in a manner unmatched by the most democratic societies. On the home front the participants included the various parliamentary blocs, the clergy, the army, and representatives of the two hundred thousand Palestinians camped in Lebanon. On the outside the ruling authorities of many Arab states, including Libya and Sudan, contributed their share to the discussion by supporting the fedayeen.

Generally "the establishment," including those who benefited from the Lebanese system, both Christian and Muslim, seemed to agree that the cause of the Palestinians should not endanger Lebanon or threaten its political balance. The president called for the withdrawal of the fedayeen but did not close the door to a negotiated settlement. In Parliament the Nahjist bloc, followers of former President Shihab, and the Progressive Socialists were in favor of permitting the fedayeen to operate from Lebanon but preferred a negotiated settlement. The electoral constituencies of members of this bloc, mostly Sunni Muslims, Arab nationalists, Orthodox Christians, and leftists, were strong supporters of the fedayeen and against any restriction of their movements in Lebanon. The Triple Alliance, composed of Eddé of the National bloc, al-Jamayel of the Kataib, and Shamun of the National Liberals, were opposed to the fedayeen because their actions would endanger the territorial integrity of Lebanon and compromise its sovereignty. A third cluster of legislators, the Center Group led by Sulayman Franjieh, were middle-of-the-road Christian and Shii Muslim politicians with some connections with President Helou.

The crisis was complicated by the presidential elections, which were less than a year away, and growing popular support for the fedayeen among many segments of the people, including workers, intellectuals, and various extraterritorial parties. Leaders of the Triple Alliance and those of the Center Group, who were themselves presidential contenders, seemed to relish the opportunity to embarrass the Nahjists by speaking against the fedayeen in order to consolidate the support of some segments of the Christian communities. The Nahjists could not openly oppose the fedayeen, even if they wished to do so, because this would further remove them from their Muslim electorate, pro-Arab nationalists, and leftists. To many segments of the populace, including intellectuals and students, Lebanon must stand up and be counted as an Arab state fully committed to Arab causes. The controversy on higher levels debated by old politicians was viewed as needless and perhaps harmful because it set Lebanon apart from the rest of the Arab world and put it again in the position of a "scab."

Later stages of the crisis developed with considerable rapidity and threatened to spill over to the international level. The fedayeen took positions in the southeastern frontiers, and pro-Palestinians took to arms in Tripoli and to a lesser extent in Beirut and Sidon. The situation became very ominous when the army repeatedly clashed with the fedayeen in late October. Other bloody clashes, reminiscent of 1958, occurred in Tripoli and near the Lebanese-Syrian border in the north. Syria closed her border to transit and other commercial traffic, threatening to cripple the Lebanese economy. The Israelis raided fedayeen strongholds in Lebanon and made public threats. The United States also expressed concern over the crisis and alluded to possible intervention.

Further deterioration, especially on the home front, was averted when President Nasser helped achieve a compromise accord between the Palestinians and the Lebanese government on November 3, 1969. Only after this accord was reached could Lebanon form a cabinet peaceably. On November 25, 1969, Karami succeeded in forming a coalition government representing the various parliamentary blocs, with the exception of the National bloc. President Franjieh is expected to honor the agreements reached with the fedayeen partly because he was a member of the cabinet that sanctioned them, and the Palestinians also are not anxious to provoke a crisis.

Political Prospects

The quizzical nature of Lebanon's political life, the collapse of one cabinet after another, the seemingly endless wrangling of politicians, and the crises that turn bloody make a casual spectator wonder what the Lebanese are up to. These are the Lebanese governing themselves Lebanese style, and how they weather bloody crises is something the Lebanese themselves wonder about. In the aftermath of every crisis a "reconciliation" cabinet is formed to calm tempers, and the Lebanese congratulate themselves on pulling through rather well this time. Despairing observers say, "God takes care of drunkards, of little children, and of the Lebanese," and others speak of "success by failure" or "Lebanese genius."

In a polycommunal system in which separate communities jealously guard their autonomy, the government has a limited role. Under such a system a call by any group or community for integration and unity through the promotion of "national unity" symbols may produce the opposite results—it may alarm other communities and threaten to undermine already existing solidarity. Attempts by the government to unify educational programs, reform the courts, or amend the constitution are carefully watched and resisted. The communities are sometimes apprehensive even over the government's economic policies, with which they agree, because change caused by economic development may spell danger to the traditional ties on which the communities are based. But by far the most decisive issues remain in the area of foreign policy.

Despite the lack of a concerted common will, the Lebanese have made forward strides. By assuming a subdued role in the process of governance, governments have made progress in promoting the constitutional framework and the electoral process as the basic legitimate avenues for political change and resolving conflicts. The level of prosperity attained by the Lebanese economy is partly the result of government encouragement and the relative stability of the country. The government has also succeeded in unifying primary and secondary education programs without nationalizing the various private institutions of learning. Many other projects initiated by private groups, especially in the cultural fields, have contributed to a developing Lebanese character. Basic obstacles to national integration do not seem to lend themselves to reconciliation at this time and are therefore deferred or avoided.

It is difficult to ponder the prospects of this small country. Lebanese politics and the future of Lebanon are linked with developments in the Arab world. The success of the system in the future will depend on its ability to absorb the effects of change generated by its economic policies and on its ability to foster genuine cooperation with the Arab states.

Socioeconomic changes caused by industrialization in the form of stronger labor unions and increasing urbanization, class consciousness, and education also provide a serious challenge to the traditional communal leadership and, indeed, to the structure of the community itself. The test for Lebanon comes at precisely the point at which the emerging interests threaten to clash with the communal arrangements. The ability to meet the challenge depends on the capacity of the system to adopt a basis for existence other than a strict confessional balance. A balance based on the common destiny of all Lebanese would take into account the emerging secular forces represented by political parties, labor, trade, and professional groups, but a balance of this kind cannot be achieved without some government initiatives and a conscious effort to promote national integration and cohesion. The alternative is continuing conflict with decreasing latitude for compromise.

The second serious challenge, tied inextricably to the first, arises from Lebanon's relationships with the Arab states. Pressures from these states increase whenever the Lebanese ruling authorities appear disinclined to cooperate fully with leaders of the Arab world. In recent years and especially since 1958, Arab leaders, who are significant figures in Lebanese politics, have shown considerable understanding of Lebanon's dilemmas. The Lebanese too have come to recognize the benefits of positive, active cooperation with the Arab states.

Selected Bibliography

Binder, Leonard, ed. *Politics in Lebanon*. New York: John Wiley and Sons, 1966.
A collection of seventeen articles analyzing politics in Lebanon.

Grassmuck, George, and Salibi, Kamal. *Reformed Administration in Lebanon*. Ann Arbor, Mich.: University of Michigan, 1964.
A detailed manual of the administrative structures of government in Lebanon.

Hitti, Philip K. *Lebanon in History*. New York: Macmillan Co., 1957.
The history of Lebanon from prehistoric to modern times.

Hudson, Michael C. *The Precarious Republic*. New York: Random House, 1968.
Political modernization and change in Lebanon.

Meo, L. M. T. *Lebanon: Improbable Nation*. Bloomington, Ind.: Indiana University Press, 1965.
How Lebanon was created and how it continued as a viable state.

Qubain, Fahim I. *Crisis in Lebanon*. Washington, D.C.: Middle East Institute, 1961.
A study of the 1958 crisis in Lebanon.

Salibi, Kamal S. *The Modern History of Lebanon*. London: Weidenfeld and Nicolson, 1965.
A historical survey of political developments in Lebanon since the Shihabi rule.

Suleiman, Michael W. *Political Parties in Lebanon*. Ithaca, N.Y.: Cornell University Press, 1967.
A study of political parties in a fragmented political culture.

Hashimite Kingdom of Jordan

Jordan is a state in crisis, and the linkage between international political factors and domestic conditions, which was important in the creation and development of the state, remains critical today. Transjordan, the precursor of Jordan, emerged as an entity not on the basis of demands by a politically conscious people who regarded themselves as a separate nationality but rather as an arrangement between the representatives of the British government, who ruled the area under a mandate after World War I, and Amir Abdullah, the second son of Sharif Husayn of Mecca (later the king of Hijaz). From the beginning the state lacked the requisites for self-sufficiency and depended to great extent on assistance from outside its borders.

The contemporary crisis results from many divisive elements. There are the usual conflicts between modern and traditional forces that characterize transitional societies and provide their mixed political culture, but in Jordan these conflicts are influenced and intensified by the peculiarities of the system. Three sets of divisions reflect numerous political, economic, and military conflicts. First, the Jordanian territory is divided between the West Bank of the Jordan River, occupied by Israeli forces since the War of June 1967, and the East Bank, which is free of foreign domination. This situation contributes greatly to the state of hostility between the two countries. Second, there is a general division of outlook and orientation between the Jordanians of Palestinian origin and the more traditional Transjordanians, who have so far supported the reigning monarch, King Husayn of the Hashimite dynasty. Third, there are the divisions between the neighboring Arab states and Israel, which are supported by different major powers, and there are divisions among the Arab states, and Jordan is caught in the middle. The combined disintegrative effect of these conditions may overwhelm Jordan.

Problems of this nature are not unique to Jordan, of course. The initial formation of many older states was not rooted in consciousness of a national identity, and the territories of many new states are products of administrative or colonial divisions that contain internal conflicts. None of the Middle Eastern states is capable of economic and military autarky; most have depended on large-scale foreign assistance. (In fact, compared to Israel, the per capita assistance received by Jordan from all external sources since 1948 has not been substantial.)

Some positive aspects help balance the negative conditions in Jordan. First, the great majority of the population is Arab and Muslim and shares a tradition of opposition to foreign dominance and to Israel. Second, the Palestinians have provided the state with skills and resources it lacked. Given the appropriate conditions, the Palestinians may well be the requisite for the state's viability and further development, whatever political form may emerge. Third, in spite of staggering internal and external problems, Jordan has managed to achieve some measure of economic development and political integration. Fourth, the conflicting aspirations of other states in the area may cancel each other and thus maintain a Jordanian entity. Finally, although the monarchy is in retreat everywhere in the Arab world, King Husayn has shown a good deal of resilience. He has survived several coups d'état and assassination attempts, a defeat at the hands of Israel, and civil upheavals. Further, he has shown some capacity for adaptation to change. Consequently, Jordan should not be hastily written off.

Historical Background

The present territory of Jordan was once the biblical home of the Samaritans and the early Israelites. During the sixth century B.C. the Nabataean Arabs, the ancestors of today's Palestinian Arabs, developed a culture around their capital at Petra. Despite foreign invasions they preserved their independence until the first century B.C., when their domain extended over most of present-day Jordan and Syria. The area was hellenized during the third and fourth centuries B.C., when northern Jordan was part of the Seleucid province of Syria and the cities of Amman and Jerash became prominent. The Romans and the Persians also ruled the territory before it was incorporated into the Islamic empire in the seventh century. The area was conquered by the Turks in the sixteenth century, and until World War I Jordan was a stagnant part of the Ottoman province of Damascus. As a political system, however, Jordan is a recent phenomenon with little continuity with the past, its creation dates from the period of settlement immediately following World War I.

The Amirate (Principality)
of Transjordan

During the war Britain, France, and Russia made a series of secret agreements to partition the Middle East, which was contrary to the policies of the United States, as expressed in Wilson's Fourteen Points and other public statements advocating self-determination of peoples. Further, Britain, the major foreign power in the Middle East at the time of the 1918 armistice, had made conflicting commitments to the Zionists through the Balfour Declaration and to the Arab nationalists through the Husayn-McMahon correspondence. The Arabs, who had fought on the side of Britain against the Turks, believed that the latter commitment bound Britain to support their freedom and independence.

In spite of the promises to the Arabs and the report of the King-Crane Commission, which stated the preference of the inhabitants of the Fertile Crescent for independence, Great Britain and France divided the area into separate mandates. Through the San Remo Conference and other agreements of 1920 France obtained mandates over Syria and Lebanon, and Britain acquired mandates over Palestine (to the satisfaction of the Zionists), Transjordan, and Iraq. The League of Nations, which was dominated by Britain and France, ratified these arrangements, including the British declaration on the subject of a Jewish national home in Palestine, despite the fact that the substantial Arab majority never consented to it.

Meanwhile, Amir Faysal, the third son of Husayn, had established an Arab kingdom at Damascus (1919-20). Transjordan, the area east of the Jordan River, was later to be included in his kingdom. In 1920 the French drove Faysal from Damascus, taking over their share of the bargain with Britain, and Transjordan was subsequently divided into four tribally based autonomous governments set up by the British high commissioner for Palestine. These republics were used by nationalists from Damascus for activities against France, which resulted in a French threat to invade Transjordan. The situation became serious when Faysal's brother, Amir Abdullah, who had been chosen for the throne of Iraq by the Arab National Conference of Damascus in 1920, arrived in Transjordan with a force of irregulars to attack the French. He was supported by the local Arabs.

The British did not want French forces in Transjordan or a war with Abdullah, who had been an effective ally during World War I, and they proposed a compromise, which was worked out by the colonial secretary, Winston Churchill; the high commissioner, Sir Herbert Samuel; and Colonel T. E. Lawrence. Abdullah was persuaded to abandon his campaign against France, to renounce his claims to Iraq, and to agree to the mandate provisions in return for a government under his leadership in Transjordan to be supported by British financial assistance and advisers. The new principality was officially created on May 26, 1923, with the provision that it would become independent at some future date.[1]

Development of Independent Transjordan

Transjordan occupied an area of 34,550 square miles and had an estimated population of 200,000, of whom over 90 percent were Muslim Arabs. Politically the amirate was semiautonomous, as Britain controlled its foreign affairs, defense, and finances. Its territory was exempt from the provisions of the mandate regarding a Jewish national home in Palestine.

Between 1924, when the country was virtually a British protectorate, and 1946, when it became more or less independent, a series of significant changes gradually occurred. The tribes were largely settled, and they achieved some unity as a result of efforts by Abdullah and the Arab Legion. Exposure to Western ideas and the beliefs of neighboring Arab nationalists caused greater political consciousness and the emergence of opposition to both Abdullah's autocracy and British domination. The first result was the convening of an Assembly of Notables by Abdullah in 1926 to draft a constitution, but no compromise was reached between the amir and the nationalists, who demanded the expulsion of the British and a representative assembly with control over the executive.

Nationalist pressures did result in a treaty with Britain in 1928, however. The treaty declared Transjordan "independent" and promised that it could control domestic legislation and administration. National sympathies for other Arab states were recognized through provision for future cooperation in customs and trade policy. Independence was nominal however; Britain retained control over foreign policy, financial administration, and the armed forces (the Arab Legion). Although the treaty provided for the promulgation of a constitution, which was drafted by British advisers and adopted by Jordan in April 1928, the constitution retained British supremacy in foreign affairs and defense and gave the amir considerably more power than the legislature.

The amir was authorized to appoint the executive council, whose members held six of the twenty seats in the legislative council, and the remaining members were to be elected through a two-stage election system. The legislature's authority was limited to discussing and delaying laws. Further, the amir was authorized to dissolve the legislature and to rule by martial law. The nationalists opposed the constitution, accusing the amir of autocracy under the guise of democracy and the British of domination under the guise of independence. They formed a congress in Amman and adopted a "national pact" that repudiated the mandate and declared Transjordan to be an independent and constitutional Arab state, and they boycotted the elections in 1928. Abdullah in turn declared martial law and arrested the influential members of the congress. The first election resulted in the supremacy of a small elite composed of local landowners and tribal leaders who were friendly to Abdullah, Circassian allies of the court, and friendly ulama. In spite of increased nationalist pressure, with minor modifications this constitution and the elite group remained dominant in the system until the end of World War II.

Throughout World War II Abdullah remained Britain's loyal ally. Early in the war he announced that he would send his troops anywhere in the world to support Britain's military efforts. His Arab Legion helped the British crush the nationalist uprising of Rashid Ali al-Gaylani in Iraq, and it later participated in the British campaigns against the Vichy government in Syria. At the end of the war the legion constituted the largest item in Transjordan's budget. These policies were well received in the West, but they did not accord with nationalist aspirations in the Arab world.

In 1946, in recognition of Abdullah's faithful service, Britain concluded a treaty of alliance declaring Transjordan a fully independent kingdom, but Britain still retained control over the Arab Legion through British officers "on leave." In 1948, before Britain ended her mandate over Palestine, another treaty authorized Britain to station troops in parts of Transjordan and to assist the latter in case of an attack, and Britain promised to continue her subsidy.

The Palestine War and the
Emergence of Jordan

During the Arab-Israeli War of 1948, which Abdullah had tried to avoid through secret negotiations with the Jewish Agency, the legion was the only Arab army that performed even moderately well, although it did so only in the early part of the war. In the middle of hostilities (May 30, 1948) British officers and financial support were withdrawn at the instruction of the British government,[2] and the legion lost its effectiveness. Awareness of the influence of the pro-Israeli groups in President Harry Truman's administration and reluctance to antagonize the United States, on which Britain depended for political and financial support during the critical period of the European Recovery Program (Marshall Plan), no doubt contributed to the British decision to abandon their faithful ally. By the end of the war Israel held possession of all the land, or 54 percent of Palestine, assigned to the Jewish state by the United Nations partition plan. It had also seized an additional 30 percent of the area, or most of the land assigned to the Palestinian Arabs. Only the fairly barren and hilly central region and the small Gaza Strip, 16 percent of the area, were held by the legion and Egypt respectively.

After the armistice Abdullah began a series of steps to incorporate the portions of Palestine he held into his state. The efforts of the Arab League, the Egyptians, and the Palestinians to block his plans were to no avail. He convened two Palestine refugee conferences in 1948, the second of which asked him to annex immediately the area west of the Jordan River. Following the wishes of the king, Parliament approved the merger. In 1949 civil government replaced the military in the West Bank and four Palestinians were added to the cabinet. Later the Palestinians were invited to vote in elections and the cabinet was increased to eleven members, five of whom were Palestinians. The union with the new territory was officially consummated in April 1950, and the state formally became the Hashimite Kingdom of Jordan. (The term *Jordan* was used in Transjordan to refer to the state even before this formal unification, however.)

Political Environment

The Arab-Israeli War of 1948 and the unification of Transjordan with parts of Palestine changed the character of the state—its territory increased by 2,165 square miles but its population tripled. The new population consisted of 400,000 West Bank Palestinians and 460,000 refugees who had lost much of their land and most sources of employment. Access to the Mediterranean routes, especially through the port of Haifa, and trade with the Mediterranean coast were lost.[3]

In spite of immense difficulties, Jordan, a country with few natural resources, had gone some distance toward improving her economic conditions before the 1967 War and Israel's occupation of the remainder of the West Bank. As a result of this war, Jordan lost some of its most productive agricultural land and its growing tourist industry, especially in Bethlehem and the old city of Jerusalem, which had earned a good portion of Jordan's foreign exchange.* Further, a quarter of a million new refugees were created almost overnight. As of January 1, 1969, 747,434 refugees were registered with the U.N. Relief and Works Agency, and an additional 100,000 were receiving some service but were not registered.† The problem of settling and integrating the refugees, which was beyond Jordan's capacity before, became even more acute.

The People

Ethnic and Religious Groups: Jordan's population, estimated at 2,145,000 in 1967, is 99 percent Arab and 93.5 percent Sunni Muslim, which is ethnically and religiously homogeneous compared to states such as Iraq, Syria, or even Israel. The non-Arabs consist of Circassian and Chechen Muslims who came to the area from Russia at the invitation of the Ottoman sultan in the nineteenth century. Although they have retained their own language, they are conversant in Arabic. The non-Muslim Arabs are mainly Orthodox Christians.

*See *The Middle East and North Africa: 1969-70*, 16th ed. (London: Europa Publications, 1969), pp. 387-97. This source includes data on the East and West banks and considers it "a serious understatement" to refer to the economic consequences of the 1967 War for Jordan merely as "a grave setback," p. 390.

†Of the total, 478,369 refugees were registered in the East Bank and 269,065 were registered in the West Bank. Under international pressure Israel readmitted a small number (fifteen to twenty thousand) of the refugees created as a result of the 1967 War into the occupied West Bank. See Ibid., p. 386; and Norman F. Howard, "Jordan: The Commando State," *Current History*, January 1970, pp. 16-20, 49.

Social Structure: Divisions between tribal, rural, and urban sectors of the population are evident. With the advance of modernization the center of political power has shifted from the traditional tribes and rural areas to the cities. The cities are centers of mobility, new ideologies, and movements for change, as are the refugee camps. Bedouin raids against sedentary agricultural regions and towns ended by 1933, and many bedouin became semisettled cultivators of the land. They still constitute one of the most traditional segments of the Jordanian society, however.

Although some Muslim-Christian and Arab-Circassian divisions are observable, they are not significant. The real division of outlook and orientation is between the Palestinians and the Transjordanians. This division is not ethnic, despite some difference in origin. Rather, it is the product of differences in literacy, unbanization, economic background, mobility, articulation, and acculturation.

In Transjordan the settlement of nomads is of recent origin, and tribal ways have thus influenced the internal structure and outlook of the villages and towns. West Bank villages and towns have not been influenced in this fashion, although families still play an important role. At the time of the union, Transjordan's towns resembled a group of adjoining villages and contained only 10 percent of the population, whereas 30 to 40 percent of the Palestinian population was urban. The population of Amman, which grew from 30,000 in 1947 to 450,000 in 1968, is a testimony to the change in population since the union. Further, 52 percent of Palestinian (more than twice as many as Transjordanian) school-aged children were in school before the 1948 War.

Economic differences at the time of the union also influenced the outlook of the two groups. Transjordan had a lower standard of living because of its lack of water and scarcity of natural resources. There were a few rich people, but many barely subsisted. In the West Bank, however, there was some industry and commercial agriculture and a small but growing urban middle class.

The refugee camps, where most of the Palestinians are located, add a dimension to social divisions. Whereas the refugees come from a more modernized background and are more mobile, their living conditions are worse than some of the most traditional segments of Jordan's population. Because they have lost their homes and means of livelihood, depend on international dole for the necessities of life, and are surrounded by a world they regard as mostly hostile or indifferent to their cause, the refugees have developed a political orientation that combines fatalism and despair on the one hand and self-reliance and a drive for effective political and military organization on the other hand.

Economic Conditions

Jordan is a predominantly agrarian society, but although a large part of its population depends on agriculture and stock raising, over 90 percent of the land was not cultivable before 1967 because of inadequate rainfall and characteristics of the terrain. East Jordan (94 percent of the entire area) is desert and barren hills with one major exception—a narrow fertile strip from the Syrian frontier south to Maan that includes the Jordan River valley. On the West Bank the land is poor but it is generally better cultivated.

Jordan's main winter crop is wheat, and in a good harvest year some surplus is available for export. As a rule, however, Jordan is not self-sufficient and must import part of its yearly consumption of grain. Fresh vegetables and fruits, grown mainly on the West Bank, accounted directly or indirectly for 39 percent of total exports in 1967. The raising of livestock, mainly by bedouin, is limited because of a shortage of water. The East Ghor Canal, completed in 1964, increased the irrigated land by 10 percent, but its utilization has been impeded by Israel's sabotage of its diversion system, ostensibly in retaliation against Arab guerrilla activities. Further irrigation projects, especially full use of the Jordan and Yarmuk rivers, are essential to the country's economic development, but so far conflicting Arab and Israeli claims have impeded such use, mostly to the detriment of Jordan. Israel, protected by military superiority, has implemented its plans for diversion of the waters of these rivers.

Jordan's mineral resources are small. No commercially profitable petroleum reserves have yet been found. Phosphate, produced from two rich deposits near Amman, is by far the most important mineral. In 1967 phosphate production was 1,255,000 tons, contributing 35 percent of the value of all exports. Useful but as yet undeveloped deposits of copper, iron ore, nickel, and manganese have also been found, and the Dead Sea has valuable deposits of potash and bromine. The Palestine Potash Company was destroyed in the War of 1948, but some production has continued.

Jordan's industry is small-scale and of recent origin and consists mainly of the manufacture of cigarettes, soap, cement, matches, sugar, beer, and vegetable oil. Lack of energy resources, insufficient capital and technical knowledge, poor transportation and communication networks, a restricted local market, and difficult economic conditions have hindered further industrialization. The Palestinians have contributed skills and have enlarged the domestic market, however, and foreign assistance and the efforts of the public sector have encouraged private investment and given some impetus to further development of mining and industry.

Jordan has also improved its transportation and communication networks. The repair of the Hijaz railroad, which runs from Damascus to the south of Jordan through Amman, was resumed in 1968. The extension of the facilities of Jordan's only port, Aqabah, and the opening of the Amman-Aqabah road in 1960 have been of great economic significance. Jordan continues to improve transportation and port facilities by devoting a good portion of economic development funds to this purpose.

Dependence on foreign assistance has been an almost permanent feature of the country's finances. This dependence was the main reason for Abdullah's reluctance to break with the British, who remained the major source of foreign aid until 1957. (Total British contribution for the 1946-56 period amounted to 80 million pounds.) In 1957, when Jordan again acquired a pro-Western posture, the United States became the main source of foreign assistance. (Total U.S. contributions for the 1946-67 period amounted to $600 million.) The War of 1967 created a new situation. As agreed by the Khartoum Conference of Arab heads of state (August 1967), Jordan's budget deficits ($106 million a year) and additional amounts for military purposes were covered by other Arab countries, including Saudi Arabia, Kuwait, and Libya. As a result, Jordan had managed to recuperate partially from the 1967 War when the nine-day civil war of 1970 again caused financial conditions to deteriorate.

Political Culture

Jordan's society and politics are characterized by a special mix of outlook and orientation in which traditional and so-called modern elements exist side by side and compete for acceptance and integration. Continued interaction between modern and traditional sectors usually results in modernization. This trend is influenced by the international environment, especially the emergence of the state of Israel, whose peculiar brand of religiopolitical nationalism, reliance on modern technology and organization, citizen army, efficiency, and territorial expansion have caused the people of Jordan to borrow and change even more rapidly to meet new situations. Some of the Jordanian government's efforts to respond to the needs of the society—the growth of secular education and cultural borrowing in the realms of technology, bureaucracy, and the armed forces—have also had modernizing consequences.

The Transjordanians have not been exposed to the internal and external influences that molded the Palestinian outlook, nor have they suffered as much at the hands of the Israelis. Transjordanian nationalism has been more traditional, regarding Islamic and tribal ways as the natural mode of life for Arabs. A large segment of Transjordanians still detest the modern values and manners that the Palestinians cherish and do not always agree with the latter's quest for more rationalization in the political and administrative apparatus, more democracy, and the curtailing of Western influence. Although opposition to monarchical autocracy and foreign domination also had a history in Transjordan, the majority of its people seem to have developed a loyalty to the Hashimite house and a sense of pride in their identity. The Palestinians, on the other hand, have no reason for loyalty to the Hashimites, especially in view of Abdullah's secret negotiations with Israel to consolidate his gains and King Husayn's attempts to curb the Palestinian national movement. To summarize, in the conflict between traditional and modern the Transjordanians are generally oriented toward the political status quo and the Palestinians are generally in favor of change.

There are also factors of unity: (1) Both groups are of Arab and Islamic background; (2) the spirit of nationalism, although based on somewhat different premises, prevailed in both Transjordan and Palestine before the union; (3) the presence of British authorities and ambivalent attitudes toward their role were common to both areas; (4) the Palestinians and Transjordanians share a feeling of hostility to Israel and Zionism: and (5) both have a general affinity with other Arab states and causes.

Political Structure

Political forms, especially as they appear in written constitutions, often do not reflect the dynamics of political life in developing areas. The gap between formal political patterns and the political process is clearly visible in Jordan, yet institutional developments have not been completely divorced from their social base. In fact, both formal and informal arrangements have been modified from time to time in response to the demands of the politically articulate population.

The 1946 constitution replaced the organic law of 1928, with only minor changes. The formal relationship of government institutions and the composition of the elite remained basically unaltered. The union with the West Bank, the assassination of Abdullah in 1951, and the emergence of King Talal changed the situation and resulted in the 1952 constitution, the only one Jordan has had since the union (except during the brief interlude of federation with Iraq in 1958). The new boundaries of the state were officially recognized and a number of modifications in the formal structure emerged. The elite structure was already being modified by the addition of the Palestinians to the cabinet and to Parliament, although the new members represented the king more than the electorate.

The basic departure in the 1952 constitution was the formal acceptance of the principle of executive responsibility to Parliament. Parliament consists of a senate (the Council of Notables) and the House of Representatives. The senate has thirty members, all appointed by the king. The membership in the past has come mostly from the former decision makers and other elder notables loyal to the king (minimum age requirement for membership is forty). The House has sixty members, and membership is equally divided between East and West Jordan and is elected by male citizens over eighteen years of age, except for nomads (minimum age requirement for membership is thirty). The cabinet is appointed by the king and must resign if it receives a vote of no confidence. Legislation is the function of Parliament, but legislation passed by Parliament can be vetoed by the king. Parliament can override a veto by a two-thirds majority of each house, however.

The constitutional powers of the king are extensive. In addition to the veto over legislative enactments, appointment of the members of the upper house, and nomination of the cabinet, the king is authorized to dissolve the House of Representatives, provided that a new House is elected within four months. The relationship between the monarch and Parliament has changed from time to time on the basis of variables other than the formal structure, however. The personality of the decision makers, their base of support and legitimacy among different segments of the population, and internal and external political circumstances have exerted an influence. There has been a long-term movement of modification of the formal structure toward more popular participation, however.

Jordan's legal system is based on civil and criminal codes that emerged in 1951 and 1952. The civil code was patterned after the Palestine Civil Procedure Rules and was thus influenced by English common law and the Shariah. The criminal code was based on the Syrian model and therefore was influenced by French judicial concepts and rules. The areas of personal status, such as marriage, divorce, and inheritance, are regulated by the Shariah. A judicial structure also established in 1951 consists of local courts for minor civil and criminal cases, courts of original jurisdiction for all major civil and criminal cases, two courts of appeal (one each for East and West Jordan), and the Court of Cassation (the Supreme Court).

Political Processes

The general conflicts of Jordan are between the forces of change and the resistance of the status quo, but this does not adequately explain the harsh realities of the state and the agonies, hopes, and problems of its people. Located in the center of the Arab lands, Jordan is a state in which the currents of this world crisscross. It is visibly scarred by crises of internal and external origin that hinder the effectiveness and legitimacy of the government. The crisis of effectiveness is evident in the government's incapacity to defend its territory and in its inability to accommodate popular demands. Nowhere are the consequences of the two defeats at the hands of Israel more readily felt than in Jordan. Part of the land, including one of the holiest cities of the Muslim world, is occupied by the enemy, and the unoccupied area is filled with refugees. Yet Jordan's government cannot repel Israel, nor can it succumb to Israel's terms without tearing itself asunder.

The rise of the Palestinian resistance movement among refugees has added a new dimension. Seeking to regain what they regard as their homeland, the members of the resistance engage in the only type of military action they regard as effective against Israel—guerrilla activities. Israel retaliates, and because Israel has command of the skies, she can bomb Jordanian towns, villages, and the countryside at will. Jordan's main Western friend, the United States, has been more sympathetic to

Israel than to Jordan; to protect Israel's security and in response to internal political pressures, the United States government has periodically provided Israel not only with diplomatic and moral support but also with additional funds and weapons, which, regardless of the intent, have helped Israel to retain the Arab lands annexed after the 1948 War and to continue the military occupation of the areas gained after the 1967 War.

The emotions, identifications, and loyalties of the people of Jordan are very much influenced by these conditions, and to understand Jordanian politics these issues will be discussed in terms of the significant individuals and groups that make up the political system.

Monarchy

An unmistakable trend toward republicanism has been a recent feature of the Arab world. In the case of such countries as Egypt and Iraq, however, the key factors in the emergence of republicanism may have been the fallen monarchs' behavior, internal and external policies, and divergence from nationalist feelings. With the exception of some of the Palestinian commando groups, Jordanians question not so much the legitimacy of the monarchy itself as the sphere of authority the monarch should have and, more importantly, the nature of the foreign and domestic policies he sponsors.

Abdullah's alienation from nationalist elements of liberal and extremist orientation, especially among the educated Palestinians, the refugees, and the Pan-Arabs, caused his unpopularity and death. His successor, Talal, who had a reputation for liberalism and who favored closer ties with the Arab world, was quite popular among the nationalists, and opposition to him came from the conservatives and pro-British forces. Before his short reign was ended, Jordan witnessed some diffusion of liberal and democratic ideas and more public participation in the government than ever before. Talal was mentally ill, however, and decision making was soon preempted by the conservative politicians of his father's vintage and orientation who controlled the regency council.

Husayn II, Talal's son, reached the age of eighteen and became king on May 2, 1953. At the age of sixteen he had witnessed the assassination of his grandfather and an unsuccessful attempt on his own life by a Palestinian nationalist while he was entering the al-Aksa mosque in Jerusalem, the third holiest shrine of Islam. The new monarch soon familiarized himself with the rules of the game and emerged as the major decision-making figure. In spite of his continued reliance on traditional leaders and his employment of some traditional techniques, King Husayn is more modernized, more flexible, and more successful in the art of negotiation and compromise than his grandfather, who was patriarchal, autocratic, and somewhat capricious in his style of governing. Husayn's popularity and effectiveness have fluctuated from time to time, depending on his internal and external policies.

On the whole, modern nationalists have opposed Jordan's links with the West because of the latter's support of Israel and the British legacy in the area. They have favored closer cooperation with Egypt, Syria, and the USSR. The Anglo-French-Israeli invasion of Egypt in 1956 increased nationalist pressure for solidarity with the "progressive" Arab states, but Husayn insisted (and still insists) on the necessity of cooperation with the West. The differences between the king and the modern nationalists came to a head on April 10, 1957, when Husayn demanded the resignation of the prime minister, Sulayman Nabulsi, who favored establishing diplomatic relations with the USSR and union with Syria. Public protests were complicated by reports of the discovery of a plan for coup d'état in which the chief of general staff and personal friend of the king, Abu Nuwar, and Nabulsi were supposed to have cooperated. Subsequently the king, with the help of the army and the traditional elite, suspended the constitution, proclaimed martial law, dissolved all political parties, and dismissed a number of Arab nationalists, Palestinians, and liberals from the government. The king has since then remained the dominant decision maker in spite of attempts at coups d'état, popular uprisings, and even the request for British troops to support his regime in 1958.

Ironically, Jordan's defeat in the 1967 War temporarily increased the legitimacy of Husayn. Having stood by the other Arab states he could not be credibly accused of "collusion" with Zionism or imperialism. Further, the war with Israel has continued, and Jordan has served as one of the main battlefields. However, the rise of the resistance movement among the Palestinians after the 1967 War and its enthusiastic support by the Arab masses increased the difficulties of the king, who tried to restrain guerrilla activities because of his fear of Israeli retaliation and the guerrilla challenges to his own powers.

The continuing occupation of the West Bank and the increasing strength of the resistance movement caused several armed conflicts between the king's supporters and the guerrillas, which culminated in the nine-day civil war of September 17-26, 1970. Although Husayn's military forces won the upper hand against the guerrillas in this war, his legitimacy suffered because of the harsh measures employed by the army against guerrilla forces and civilians and because of reports, not denied in Washington or Jerusalem, of the contingency plan for joint American-Israeli military operations in Jordan to save him.

The future of the monarchy in Jordan remains uncertain. Even if the Arab-Israeli conflict is resolved, the king's continued insistence on ruling rather than reigning may in the long run mean either monarchical absolutism or the abolition of the monarchy.

The Army

The army is by far the most important institution in Jordan. Knowledge of its recruitment patterns, internal structure, capability, and orientation is essential to understanding the country's internal and external politics.

Jordan's army, formerly known as the Arab Legion, was established in 1923 by G. F. Peake, a British officer, by merging a small local police force with a reserve force recruited mainly from the Egyptians, Sudanese, and Palestinians. Later Major John Bagot Glubb, the second in command, formed a desert patrol of bedouin to bring order to the tribes. By 1933 the bedouin no longer presented a major threat to the central government. Glubb became commander of the legion in 1939. Commanded by British officers, the army was the bulwark of support for the monarchy and traditional forces.

After Glubb's dismissal in 1956 the situation began to change. In fact, his dismissal reflected the emergence of a different orientation in the lower ranks of the officer corps, which consisted of the younger officers (especially Palestinians) recruited after the union. Abu Nuwar's attempted coup caused the king to try to further ensure the loyalty of the army by strengthening the bedouin units and special forces of the palace and by appointing to sensitive command and intelligence positions officers who were related to the royal house or who had a traditional background. (Because of tribal and Islamic orientation, the bedouin have been reluctant to oppose Husayn, who is regarded as a direct descendent of the Prophet.) Although these policies have not been entirely successful, the army is still the main bastion of support for the monarchy.

The defeat of 1967 caused a great deal of dissatisfaction with the army, especially among the people of the West Bank, who felt that the army did not engage in an effective fight against Israel. This resentment was caused mainly by the troops' withdrawal from a number of West Bank cities to fight in Jerusalem. The Israeli air force, which had practically destroyed the Egyptian air force, prevented the troops from reaching that city. Without air cover, supposed to be provided by Egypt, and without antiaircraft defenses, the Jordanian forces were badly defeated despite bitter fighting by the small Jerusalem garrison. Inadequate planning, preparation, and armaments characterized the armed forces. The young officers have since become still unhappier with the situation and on occasion voluntarily cooperate with the guerrillas. A notable example occurred in March 1968 at Karamah, when a sizable Israeli force that had crossed the Jordan River to "punish" the guerrillas was engaged in severe fighting. This incident increased the prestige of the guerrillas and temporarily improved strained relations between them and the army.

The duration and intensity of the conflict with Israel has caused increasing allocation of resources to military preparation, to the detriment of economic development programs. The Jordanian government has always relied on the West for arms, but immediately after the 1967 War the United States imposed an embargo on arms shipments to the Middle East. Although this embargo was impartial in the sense that it applied to all the belligerents, it actually hurt Jordan, the weaker and more vulnerable side. In 1968 the United States agreed to sell some small arms, a number of tanks, and a few F-104 Starfighters to Jordan, but these planes were no match for Israel's superior air force, recently well supplied with U.S. Phantoms and Skyhawks. A number of tanks, surface-to-air missiles, and obsolescent jetfighters were also purchased from Britain. After the nine-day civil war, the United States authorized $30 million for military assistance to Jordan in the same bill that granted Israel $500 million in military credit and loans. Although the Jordanian army is somewhat improved, its basic weaknesses remain, and its air-defense capabilities are still virtually nonexistent. Jordanians from all levels of leadership have criticized the country's dependence on the West for military aid.

The Jordanian army and the commandos have engaged in some tests of strength. A major incident occurred in November 1968, when a number of civilian and military personnel were killed or wounded. The result was an uneasy compromise between the king and the Palestinians. In the six-day civil strife of June 1970, in which nearly a thousand people were killed or wounded, there was some indication that not all the members of the armed forces supported the king. The strife was prolonged because some of the older officers and guerrilla extremists continued to fight after the initial ccasc-fire and preliminary compromises. A temporary peace was finally achieved after Husayn dismissed some of the high-ranking officers, including the army commander-in-chief, Sharif Nasser Ben Jamil (Husayn's uncle) and the commander of the Third Armored Division, General Zaid Ben Shaker (the king's cousin), who had ignored the king's order and fired on refugee camps. Afterwards the king made additional gestures that appeared to move him closer to the Palestinians and the younger officers. He appointed a new cabinet and publicly authorized a search for the purchase of arms from any source in order to strengthen Jordan's security.

These changes proved to be temporary, however. A cease-fire was subsequently arranged between Jordan (and the UAR) and Israel through the efforts of the United States, but the guerrilla organizations were not invited to participate and they refused to accept the cease-fire. After the hijacking and destruction of four Western commercial aircraft by one of the commando organizations, the Popular Front for the Liberation of Palestine, Husayn appointed Field Marshal Habis Majali, a bedouin, commander-in-chief of the armed forces and military governor of Jordan, with absolute power to quell the guerrillas. The king also formed a military cabinet on September 16, 1970. The government then ordered the guerrillas to lay down their arms and evacuate the cities. This action resulted in the bitter nine-day civil war, which caused enormous destruction, several thousand casualties, and the weakening of both the Jordanian government and the guerrilla forces. A great deal of effort by Gamal Abdul Nasser; Jaafar Numayri, the Sudanese president; and Bahi Ladgham, the Tunisian prime minister, was required to arrange a truce. A "comprehensive agreement" regulating the relationship between the Jordanian government agencies and guerrilla organizations was signed by King Husayn, Yasir Arafat of the Palestine Liberation Organization, and Ladgham on October 13, but this agreement did not prevent subsequent clashes, and the relationship between the army and the guerrilla organizations continues to be marked by bitterness and hostility.

Political Parties

The nature of the political environment, the role and orientation of institutions, and political movements in other Arab countries and those sponsored by the major powers influenced the development of political parties in Jordan.

Before the union with the West Bank, Abdullah generally pursued a policy of hampering the formation of independent political parties and creating his own parties from above. The most important independent party of this period was Istiqlal ("independence"), although the Baath and the Communist parties also had some support. The situation changed substantially during the 1948 Arab-Israeli war as the old parties of Palestine and Transjordan either disappeared or were radically transformed.

After the union political parties acquired a great deal of vitality. The new constitution recognized the right of the people to form political organizations, and this was followed by the emergence of representative government and an increasingly meaningful electoral process that lasted until 1957. But there were also some serious handicaps. Constitutional freedom was limited to organizations that pursued lawful objectives, resorted to peaceful means, and possessed constitutional regulations. Political groups were required to hold licenses from the Ministry of Interior according to a law passed in 1953. Moreover, in 1954 the cabinet was authorized to disband the existing parties.[4] Party development suffered from these restrictive laws, government discrimination, and the people's initial unfamiliarity with partisan politics.

Four types of parties developed. The Arab Revival, Baath, Liberal, National Socialist, and Arab Nationalist parties were unionist, or Pan-Arab. The National bloc, Constitutional bloc, the Ummah ("nation"), and the Arab Constitutional parties desired to maintain the status quo. The Communist and National Front parties were Marxist. The Muslim Brotherhood and Islamic Liberation parties were religio-political.

With the exception of the fourth group, these parties were secular, and all agreed, at least nominally, on anticolonialism and the emancipation of Jordan from British domination. Among the secular parties, the Baath and the Communist parties, whose members were predominantly Palestinian, were the most revolutionary and doctrinal, whereas the Arab Constitutional and Ummah parties, whose members were mostly Transjordanian, were more conservative in outlook and traditional in composition. Some parties supported the monarchy; others advocated republicanism. The Communists were openly republican, the Baath, Liberal, and Arab Nationalist parties tended to be republican, and the remainder were monarchists. Initially only the Communist party advocated forcible and violent change.

In the elections of 1956, the only free election Jordan has ever had, only three parties were licensed—the National Socialist, the Arab Baath, and the Arab Constitutional. Four others were also allowed to participate with unofficial government approval—the National Front

(Communist), Muslim Brotherhood, Islamic Liberation, and Ummah. Thirty of the forty seats in the House of Representatives were won by these parties, with the remainder going to independents. Supported by both the Palestinians and the Transjordanians, the National Socialists, who advocated closer ties with Syria and Egypt and opposed Jordan's treaty with Great Britain, received the largest number of votes and the largest number of seats (twelve) in the House. Their leader, Nabulsi, was invited by the king to become prime minister, a precedent that could have become significant had the parliamentary system survived. In general the result of the elections was favorable to Syria and Egypt and indicated large-scale support for them among the Jordanians. Under Nabulsi's leadership the 1948 treaty with Britain was abrogated and an agreement concluded with Egypt, Syria, and Saudi Arabia to grant Jordan $36 million annually to replace British aid. This agreement was implemented only partially, however, as the relationship among the signatories soon became strained.

The suspension of the constitution by the government in 1957 and the disintegration of the National Socialist party indicate that competitive-aggregative parties of the Western type can survive only in an atmosphere in which the electoral process is fair and constitutional guarantees are observed. Moreover, because such parties have not fared well in the Jordanian environment since 1957, the interaction between the government and the governed has been uneven and marked by a hiatus. The parties that have survived can muster only a limited following. The Arab Constitutional party now supports Arab unity through peaceful means and generally follows Egypt's leadership in Arab affairs. Others such as the Ummah and Muslim Brotherhood also continue but with little vitality.

The leftist-doctrinal parties, on the other hand, show some capacity to survive, partly because of their ideology and organization and partly because of support from external sources. The Baath party was accused of being involved in plans to overthrow King Husayn and was banned in 1957, but it continues to exist on the left of the political spectrum, and it cooperates with the Syrian Baath party. The Communist party has operated in one form or another since before the union. Until 1967 its support came mainly from the West Bank and the refugees. Soviet policies toward the Middle East have had a distinct effect on the fortunes of this party. Between the time of the creation of Israel, which was supported by the Soviet Union, and the Suez crisis of 1956 the party could not gain much support among the Arabs, but after the Suez crisis and the Soviet support of Arab nationalists against Israel, its popularity increased. The June War and the subsequent Soviet and American attitudes toward Arab-Israeli disputes also increased the strength of the party throughout Jordan. The Syrian Social Nationalist party is a relatively new doctrinal organization. It is well disciplined and has its own small militia, and it cooperates with its Lebanese parent party in calling for the unity of the Fertile Crescent (Syria, Lebanon, Iraq, Jordan, and Palestine). This party remains small, however, and is unlikely to become a major force in the internal politics of Jordan in the immediate future.

The Palestine Liberation Movement

An important outcome of the 1967 War was the rise of the Palestinian resistance movement. The guerrilla has become a symbol of self-respect not only for the refugees but also for other Jordanians who have been disillusioned with their government's inability to resist Israel. The guerrilla organizations now constitute the most significant political group in Jordan, and they can no longer be easily ignored by Israel, the Arab governments, or the major powers.

Despite differences in ideology and tactics (see chapter 21), the main guerrilla groups agree on the "liberation" of Palestine to make it a "democratic and nonsectarian" political system in which Arabs and Jews can live in equality, not an easy goal to achieve, especially as some members are either noncommital or in favor of an Arab Palestine. Most guerrillas maintain that their conflict is not with world Jewry, however, but rather with Zionism as embodied in Israel.

The guerrillas differ with the king over both foreign and domestic policies. They point out that the Jordan government's cooperation and friendship with the West, especially the United States, has not deterred the latter from tacitly recognizing Israel's territorial expansion substantially beyond the 1947 United Nations partition plan, and that this has been the case in spite of the fact that many in the West regard conquest as an illegal method of acquiring territory.

The resistance movement is not of one mind regarding internal politics. Al-Fatah and the Palestine Liberation Organization, the most important and largest groups even before the recent civil war, have not so far subscribed to a specific political ideology, nor have they as a rule taken sides in the conflicts between the "socialists" and the "pro-Western" governments of the Arab world. Consequently, they do not seek to overthrow the monarchy as long as their major goals are not opposed. Instead, they are attempting to acquire support abroad and to develop a mass movement among Palestinians through socialization and organization. Other groups, such as the Popular Front for the Liberation of Palestine and the Popular Democratic Front, advocate revolutionary and socialist programs supporting the overthrow of such conservative Arab regimes as the monarchy in Jordan. King Husayn has thus sought to deal mainly with Yasir Arafat, the leader of al-Fatah, and has raised questions regarding the loyalty of the latter groups to Arab causes.

The civil war weakened the guerrillas, especially the more revolutionary organizations. In the agreement that followed, the commandos accepted the unity and sovereignty of Jordan, undertook to conduct their military activities within prescribed rules and areas, and promised not to interfere with Jordanian military personnel. The king in turn agreed to recognize the right of the resistance movement to engage in guerrilla activity, to try guerrillas arrested for violating Jordanian law, and to publish a newspaper and operate a radio transmitter free of censorship. Whether the Jordanian government and the guerrilla organizations can operate according to this agreement remains doubtful. It is even more doubtful that the pre-1967 decision-making system and relationship between the East and West banks will reemerge without substantial modification.

Foreign Policy

The goals of Jordan's foreign policy have been to maintain the monarchy and ensure the security and economic development of the state. Several factors have influenced this policy: the emergence of Israel and its conquest of Arab lands, the plight of the Palestinians and their resistance movement, the orientation of the major powers, inter-Arab rivalry and cooperation, and Jordan's dependence on foreign assistance.

Despite increasing internal pressure and opposition from a number of Arab states, Jordan has so far followed a pro-Western course because of the orientation of its monarchs. In inter-Arab rivalries Jordan has followed a shifting course, depending on the government's evaluation of the situation. This flexible policy toward other Arab states emerged during Talal's reign, when the policies of Abdullah were modified, and it has been continued by King Husayn. In 1953 and 1954, when border clashes with Israel threatened a new Arab-Israeli war, Jordan improved relations with other Arab governments and received promises of military support. In 1955 relations with Egypt and Syria deteriorated because it seemed probable that Jordan would join the Baghdad Pact. However, due to internal and external opposition Jordan decided not to join the pact, and relations with Syria and Egypt improved as a result of the 1956 election, the dismissal of Glubb, and the abrogation of the 1948 pact with Britain.

In 1957 King Husayn's favorable attitude toward the Eisenhower Doctrine, which was opposed by the Nabulsi government, resulted in a cabinet crisis and demonstrations and riots that ended with the suspension of the constitution and the political parties. The United States airlifted arms and supplies to Jordan to counter Syria's developing friendship with the Soviet Union, and Syrian troops, stationed in Jordan according to a previous agreement between the two governments, were withdrawn at the request of King Husayn. Relations with the United States improved, whereas those with Syria and Egypt deteriorated.

In February 1958 Iraq and Jordan formed the Arab Federation in response to the formation of the United Arab Republic by Egypt and Syria, but the Iraqi government was overthrown and its monarchy ended in a coup on July 14, 1958. The Iraqi republic was immediately recognized by the UAR, which also denounced the "pro-imperialist" government of Jordan. Popular opposition to the government was followed by another report of armed conspiracy against Husayn and a parade of bedouin tribesmen in Amman supporting the king. After the United States landed troops in Lebanon, the British landed troops in Jordan at the request of King Husayn to bolster his regime. The development of discord between the new Iraqi government and the

UAR did not detract from continued enmity between King Husayn and President Nasser. The Jordanian government arrested a number of prominent political and military leaders on charges of plotting against the king in cooperation with the UAR or with the "Communist conspiracy" in Iraq.

When the UAR was dissolved in September 1961, Jordan was the first country to recognize Syria's secession. After a period of internal relaxation, stricter government controls reemerged in 1963 following a series of violent demonstrations by Jordanians in sympathy with the new Baathist-led coups in Syria and Iraq. Husayn soon came to regard the new Syrian regime as a greater threat than Egypt, and rapprochement with Egypt started at the first Arab summit conference on the issue of Israel's diversion of the waters of the Jordan River in 1964.

Relations with Egypt continued to improve, and those with Syria deteriorated. In 1966 Jordan and Syria accused each other of subversive plots. In July 1966 Jordan suspended support of the PLO and accused the chairman of the executive committee, Ahmad al-Shuqayri, of pro-Communist activity. An Israeli raid at Samu in November aroused bitter feelings in Jordan, and Syria and the PLO called on the Jordanians to revolt against Husayn. (The Samu raid reflects a curious relationship arising from Syria's sponsorship of some of the guerrilla organizations, their use of Jordanian territory, and Israel's retaliations against Jordan rather than Syria.) As the prospects of war with Israel grew, Jordan developed closer relations with the UAR, and tensions with Syria eased. A five-year defense pact was signed with Egypt before the Six-Day War, and Jordanian troops were placed under Egyptian command. Relations between the two countries have since continued to be cordial.

The 1967 War, Israeli occupation of the West Bank, and subsequent American policies have changed the picture. In 1956 the position of the United States in the Arab world was improved by President Eisenhower's response to the invasion of Egypt by France, Britain, and Israel. At that time the United States and the Soviet Union insisted on the withdrawal of the occupying forces from the Arab territories. In 1967, however, the United States did not insist on Israeli withdrawal, and in 1971 the prospects of peace or solution of the conflict remained remote.

After the war Husayn engaged in a diplomacy based on moderation. He sought diplomatic support from all possible sources and military support from the West to secure the withdrawal of Israeli troops. In the Khartoum Conference Jordan supported Egypt's proposal to seek the recovery of the land occupied after the June War rather than the destruction of the state of Israel. Jordan also accepted the United Nations Security Council resolution of November 22, 1967, and cooperated with Gunnar Jarring, the special envoy of the secretary-general.

The king also made several trips to Washington after June 1967, but verbal reaffirmations of the United States in favor of the "political independence and territorial integrity" of Jordan were not translated into deeds or meaningful pressure on Israel during Lyndon B. Johnson's administration. In January 1968 the United States Agency for International Development terminated all financial support to Jordan on the grounds that it was now receiving adequate aid from other Arab states. Further, the United States generally supported Israel's position in the United Nations. When the U.N. General Assembly voted overwhelmingly to prevent Israel from annexing Arab Jerusalem, the United States abstained, encouraging Israel's implementation of its plans and later denunciation of the United Nations. Although the United States opposed annexation, she also abstained on a Security Council resolution censuring Israel for her annexation of the city and seemed to have subsequently moved closer to the Israeli position on other issues.

Although Israel's greater Jerusalem policy and references to "de-Arabization" and colonization of some of the occupied lands did not cause an open change in the American direction, her deep-penetration raids into Egypt and the probability of larger scale hostilities and the involvement of major powers resulted in some modification of policy in Washington and a more ardent search for peace by the new administration of Richard M. Nixon. The United States began to vote for the Security Council resolutions that asked Israel to rescind measures designed to change the status of Arab Jerusalem (resolutions which Israel promptly rejected) and urged Israel to resolve her conflicts with the Arabs through negotiated measures designed to implement the 1967 Security Council resolution. Despite the fact that the U.S. is the main source of assistance and is presently the sole supplier of sophisticated weapons to Israel, however, the ability of the U.S. to influence her is limited as long as pro-Israeli groups* can muster substantial support from Congress against the administration in cases of disagreement between the two governments.

The hopelessness, frustration, and anger of the Jordanians with the earlier policies of the United States were reflected in demonstrations in Amman, grenade attacks against the American military attaché's residence, and bitter denunciations of policy before the United Nations. The feelings culminated during the six-day civil strife in which a United States attaché was killed and a number of Americans were molested by the guerrillas, who later hijacked and destroyed the Western commercial airplanes. Clearly the influence and prestige of the United States in Jordan was declining despite King Husayn's pro-Western orientation.

To counteract sagging American support, King Husayn visited Moscow in October 1967. This visit was followed by an agreement with

*For the role of pressure groups in American foreign policy in the Middle East see Ernest Haas and Allen Whiting, *Dynamics of International Relations* (New York: McGraw-Hill Book Co., 1956), pp. 283-84, and Harry B. Ellis, *The Dilemma of Israel* (Washington, D.C.: American Enterprise Institute, 1970), pp. 51-52. The importance of Zionists and other pro-Israeli groups in the electoral process is not limited to such states as New York, Illinois, and California, where large blocs of Jewish voters reside. In many other states and districts candidates for office are reluctant to alienate any organized group whose support may determine the outcome of a closely contested election.

the Soviets for cultural and scientific cooperation, increased trade, and economic assistance. The Jordanian government declined the offer of Soviet military aid, however. In November 1968 Jordan signed an agreement with Rumania for oil exploration and trade and technical assistance, and in 1969 and 1970 improved diplomatic and commercial relations with a number of other East European countries, including East Germany. Commercial relations have also begun to develop with the People's Republic of China, which has supported the Arab nationalists in general and the Palestinian movement in particular. China even accused the Soviet Union of betraying the Arabs in the June War by not providing meaningful support and by later engaging in "collusion" with the United States to adopt the November 22, 1967, U.N. resolution. However, it is unlikely that China's influence in Jordan will increase substantially in the immediate future, except among some of the guerrilla groups, because of China's limited resources, its distance from the area, and its conflicts with the Soviet Union, which has so far been the main supporter of the Arabs.

Western European governments are improving their relations with the Arabs in general and with Jordan in particular. France's abandonment of her pro-Israeli policy may make her the second most important foreign power in the Arab Middle East if present trends continue and peace is not achieved. Britain has a long history of association with Jordan, and her long-term economic interests in the area lie mainly with the Arabs. The future of Britain's relations with Jordan will depend to some extent on the government of Prime Minister Edward Heath and the extent to which it initiates new policies.

Secretary of Defense Melvin Laird visited Europe in 1970, just before the cease-fire between Jordan and Israel. His consultations with NATO members suggested that they did not perceive the Middle Eastern situation mainly as a conflict between the West and the Soviet Union. It was reported that NATO members did not favor the U.S. grant of the second Israeli request for a large number of sophisticated new fighter bombers, and at least some West European governments indicated readiness to supply the Arabs with the means to increase their defenses against Israel, emphasizing the necessity of Israeli withdrawal from the lands occupied since 1967.

Political Prospects

It is risky to speculate about the political prospects of any country in the Middle East, especially Jordan, whose future depends not only on the uncertain course of its own internal developments but also on external events over which it has little control. The biggest problems remain the Arab-Israeli conflict, the refugees, and the position of the major powers.

Present conditions may continue and the conflict with Israel may go on for many years, in which case it is probable that there will be an accelerated rate of integration in favor of the Palestinians, who now constitute a substantial majority of the population. Jordan's economic situation is difficult but not hopeless as long as support from outside sources continues. In fact, Jordan has managed to improve its economic picture to a limited extent in spite of the drains of the war.

In foreign affairs, the possibility that the government of Jordan may request military aid from the Soviet Union should no longer be discounted. The continuation of hostilities with Israel is likely to intensify their tempo, with further escalation and increased casualties on both sides. Jordan's attitude toward Israel has been moderate, but the longer the conflict continues the more remote are the prospects of reconciliation. It is still possible that a peaceful solution to the Arab-Israeli conflict may be reached, especially in view of the 1970 cease-fire. Jordan has accepted the principle of political independence and integrity of all states in the area and freedom of naval passage through international waterways, and Israel has acknowledged some responsibility for settling the refugee problem. The extent of this responsibility is not clear, however; the Israeli and Jordanian positions are far apart on the refugee issue, and Israel's new claims on occupied lands further complicate the situation.

It is possible that in the future a new state of Palestine (in addition to Israel) may be created from the West Bank area. Whether the political integration of Jordan has gone far enough for the state to remain unified if and when the Arabs regain the West Bank is difficult to say. As for monarchy, King Husayn may disappear from the scene overnight or it is equally possible that he will soon become the only secure monarch in Arab lands, depending on his legitimacy among the people and his willingness to accept fewer discretionary powers. It is also possible that Jordan will become part of a larger Arab state through some form of unification, which might offer economic advantages.

There are some similarities between the political systems of Jordan and Saudi Arabia, the focus of the following chapter. Both are monarchical, pro-Western, and transitional. Saudi Arabia's political elite is more patriarchal and its social base more traditional than that of Jordan, and Saudi Arabia does not have an internal social group comparable to the Palestinians, nor has it been in the forefront of the wars with Israel. Further, because of abundant oil resources, Saudi Arabia is not dependent on foreign economic assistance. Nevertheless, Saudi Arabia's political system and elite face some of the same long-term challenges of legitimacy and effectiveness that have been noted in Jordan, because such challenges are inherent in the process of modernization.

Footnotes

[1] See Morris, *Hashemite Kings*, pp. 93-97.

[2] Glubb, *Soldier with the Arabs*, pp. 135-36.

[3] Don Peretz, *The Middle East Today* (New York: Holt, Rinehart and Winston, 1963), pp. 309-11. See also his *Israel and the Palestine Arabs* (Washington, D.C.: Middle East Institute, 1958).

[4] For a discussion of political parties in this period see Abidi, *Jordan: A Political Study, 1948-51*, pp. 191-212.

Selected Bibliography

Abdullah, King of Jordan. *My Memoirs Completed.* Translated by Harold Glidden. Washington, D. C.: American Council of Learned Societies, 1954.
A personal account of Abdullah's rise in Jordan, with a favorable view of the monarchy.

Abidi, A. H. H. *Jordan: A Political Study, 1948-57.* London: Asia Publishing House, 1965.
A scholarly, well-documented account of the development of modern Jordan.

Glubb, John Bagot. *A Soldier with the Arabs.* London: Hodder and Stoughton, 1957.
Personal account of Glubb's experiences as commander of the Arab Legion.

———. *Syria, Lebanon, Jordan.* London: Thames and Hudson, 1967.
A survey of the history of Jordan and discussion of its tensions and role in the Middle East.

Harris, George L., ed. *Jordan: Its People, Its Society, Its Culture.* New Haven, Conn.: Human Relations Area Files Press, 1958.
A brief but comprehensive survey of culture, institutions, and politics in the Hashimite kingdom.

Howard, Norman F. "Jordan: The Commando State." *Current History,* January 1970.
A brief but excellent presentation of the current military and political conditions in Jordan.

Hussein, King of Jordan. *My War with Israel.* New York: Morrow, 1969.
Husayn's account of the events leading up to the 1967 War.

———. *Uneasy Lies the Head.* London: Heinemann, 1962.
Husayn's description of his regime during the 1950s.

Morris, James. *The Hashemite Kings.* New York: Pantheon, 1959.
Contains a great deal of useful information on the political history of Jordan.

Patai, Raphael. *The Kingdom of Jordan*. Princeton, N.J.: Princeton University Press, 1958.
An excellent study of Jordanian society and culture.

Shwadran, Benjamin. *Jordan: A State of Tension*. New York: Council for Middle Eastern Affairs, 1959.
An analysis of Jordan's tensions and its role in the Middle East.

Sparrow, Gerald. *Hussein of Jordan*. London: Harrings, 1961.
Official biography of King Husayn.

———. *Modern Jordan*. London: George Allen and Unwin, 1961.
General history.

Vatikiotis, P. J. *Politics and the Military in Jordan: A Study of the Arab Legion: 1921-57*. New York: Frederick A. Praeger, 1967.
A recent, useful account of the evolution of the military and its importance in the politics of modern Jordan.

Kingdom of Saudi Arabia*

Saudi Arabia brings together a modern economy based on oil and a traditional Arab social order based on strict interpretation of the teachings of Islam. As the cradle of Islam and the keeper of its two holiest cities, Mecca and Medina, Saudi Arabia's Islamic heritage transcends mere religious belief to encompass all aspects of human endeavor. The Saudi leaders, devout followers of the very conservative Wahhabi sect of Islam, consciously look back to Muhammad and his teachings. At the same time, the sizable oil income is rapidly transforming Saudi Arabia from a desert kingdom to a modern state.

Saudi Arabia's greatest long-term political challenge—one the regime must meet to survive—is to accommodate the rapidly changing political needs and aspirations of its people, induced by extensive programs in education, communications, transportation, health, and many other fields. David Howarth's description of the capital city, Riyadh, could as easily describe the entire country: "It is a meeting place of Western material technique and a strict Eastern moral code; it is more than a meeting place, it is the scene of a head-on collision between the two."[1]

Historical Background

The history of modern Saudi Arabia is essentially the history of the house of Saud, which dates from the time of the family's founder,

*The author is a foreign service officer. The views expressed are his own and do not reflect those of the U.S. Department of State.

Muhammad ibn Saud (1703/04-92), who was the hereditary amir of a small central Arabian oasis town, Diriyyah. The house of Saud set itself apart from other dynasties of Najd, as central Arabia is called, by its acquisition of a driving ideological force in the form of a religious revival.

Early Development of the Saudi State

In the year 1744/45, Muhammad ibn Saud became the patron of Shaykh Muhammad ibn Abd al-Wahhab, a zealous Najdi Sunni revivalist who was preaching strict adherence to the fundamentals of Islam. The Wahhabis,* as the followers of Muhammad ibn Abd al-Wahhab's teachings were called, abhorred any practice that denigrated total allegiance to God, particularly the common practice of seeking intercession through saints. Tombs were considered graven images, and to this day Wahhabi dead are buried in unmarked graves.

The Wahhabi revival went almost totally unnoticed by the outside world until 1801, when a Saudi-Wahhabi force sacked the Shiite holy city of Karbala, in what is now southern Iraq, and destroyed the tomb of the Prophet's grandson, Husayn. In 1806 they captured Mecca and Medina, defeating the Ottoman Turkish garrisons. In the east Saudi-Wahhabi armies were pushing into Oman, and the Saudi amirs exacted an annual tribute from the sultans of Muscat. Thus, in only a few years, a Saudi "empire" extended from Iraq south to Yemen and east to Oman.

The rapid Saudi-Wahhabi expansion was not unchallenged long. Roused to action by the loss of Mecca and Medina, the Ottoman sultan, Mahmud II, persuaded his Egyptian viceroy, Muhammad Ali, to recover the lost territories. Muhammad Ali sent his son Ibrahim Pasha with a large Turko-Egyptian force, which finally captured Diriyyah in 1818. The amir, Abdullah ibn Saud Al Saud, fourth in the Saudi line, was beheaded; Diriyyah was sacked and burned and was never again the Saudi capital; and the peoples of Najd were subjected to a cruel occupation for four years until the last of Ibrahim Pasha's troops were withdrawn. Thereafter, the Turks concentrated on western Arabia, which contains the Muslim holy cities of Mecca and Medina, the two points of primary interest to the Turks.

By the mid-nineteenth century, the Sauds had regained control of Najd, making Riyadh their new capital. Before the century was out, however, the Sauds again lost their entire patrimony and were forced into exile. Muhammad ibn Rashid, whose family had dominated the area around the north Arabian town of Hayil for centuries, took

---

*The term *Wahhabi*, after the name of the founder, was first used by opponents of the revival. Wahhabis usually prefer to be called Muwahadin, or Unitarians, a term that refers to their strict monotheism. Descendants of the founder, who comprise the religious leadership of the country, are known as Al al-Shaykh, or house of the Shaykh.

advantage of warring among the Saudi princes to displace them. Abd al-Rahman ibn Faysal Al Saud, grandfather of the present king, remained in Riyadh as governor under the Rashidis, but after an abortive revolt in 1891, he fled with his family to exile in Kuwait.

Creation of the Kingdom of Saudi Arabia

The creation of the Kingdom of Saudi Arabia was the accomplishment of one man, Abd al-Aziz ibn Abd al-Rahman Al Saud, known to the West as ibn Saud. A striking figure well over six feet tall, he was a master of tribal politics and warfare, and his many wives and scores of children attested to his prowess with the opposite sex in the best desert tradition. But what set Abd al-Aziz apart from his Arabian contemporaries was his breadth of vision. He saw beyond the confines of the central Arabian desert and dealt on equal terms with Western diplomats, soldiers, and oil men, although he did not fully comprehend the tremendous changes his dealings would bring to his country.

Abd al-Aziz's first accomplishment was to wrest the Saudi capital, Riyadh, from the Rashidis. In 1902 Abd al-Aziz and a band of forty men who had departed from Kuwait the previous year stole over the walls of Riyadh, killed the Rashidi governor, and captured the city. Yet the capture of Riyadh did not signal the immediate defeat of the Rashidis; it was twenty years before Abd al-Aziz finally defeated the last Rashidi amir and captured the Rashidi capital, Hayil. In the intervening period Abd al-Aziz consolidated his hold on the Najd, drove the Turks out of eastern Arabia, and created a powerful military force, the Ikhwan ("brotherhood"), composed of zealous bedouin tribesmen converted to Wahhabism.

World War I brought the Arabian peninsula temporarily to the attention of the great powers, and the British and the Turks competed for the loyalties of the area's three major leaders—Abd al-Aziz in Riyadh, Saud ibn Rashid in Hayil, and Sharif Husayn of Mecca. Ibn Rashid chose the Turks, and Abd al-Aziz and Sharif Husayn chose the British. The war also brought two famous Britons to the Arabian peninsula. With the consent of Sharif Husayn, T. E. Lawrence (Lawrence of Arabia) set out from Hijaz on raids against the Turks that have since become legendary. In 1917 the British sent a mission to urge Abd al-Aziz to attack the Rashidis and to cooperate more closely with Sharif Husayn. In this group was H. St. John B. Philby, who remained in the peninsula to become a major writer and explorer.

After the war Abd al-Aziz finally took Hayil, and Sharif Husayn proclaimed himself king of the Arabs. Relations between the sharif and Abd al-Aziz, never good despite British efforts, deteriorated. In 1919 an Ikhwan force wiped out an army under the sharif's son Abdullah in a border dispute. A survivor told the writer that only those with horses (about one hundred, including Abdullah) escaped. "Thank God I had a horse," he added, indicated for the first time which side he was on.

When the sharif claimed the title caliph of all Muslims after the dissolution of the Ottoman caliphate in 1924, it was more than the fanatical Ikhwan could accept, and they marched on Taif. The city did not resist, but a shot was fired as the Ikhwan entered the gates, and they sacked it. When the terrified Hijazis heard the news, they pressured the sharif to abdicate in favor of his son Ali. But Ali fared little better than his father, and in January 1926 he too sailed into exile, leaving all the Hijaz to the house of Saud. In a quarter of a century Abd al-Aziz created a kingdom. He claimed the title amir of Najd after the recapture of Riyadh, and when he conquered Hijaz he changed his title to king of Hijaz and Najd. In 1932 the country was renamed the Kingdom of Saudi Arabia.

Discovery of Oil

Saudi Arabia was created by the sword, but its economy was built by oil. The first oil exploration was begun in 1933, and five years later the first well, Damman number one, was spudded in by an American firm eventually (in 1946) named the Arabian American Oil Company* (ARAMCO). Revenues were small at first because of World War II, but thereafter oil money flowed into the government's coffers in such amounts that the kingdom was completely revolutionized. Abd al-Aziz devoted much of his new wealth to the welfare of his people, and by the time of his death in 1953 the Saudi Arabian government was heavily involved in economic and social development programs.

The Reign of King Saud

Abd al-Aziz was succeeded by his oldest surviving son, Saud, whose reign (1953-64) was characterized by palace intrigue and heavy spending. Even with the vast oil income, the Saudi treasury was almost empty at times. Unfortunately Saud was the product of an earlier time and was more at home dealing with tribal politics than trying to rule a twentieth century oil kingdom. In 1964 the royal family and religious leaders, acting in accordance with Islamic law, chose his brother Faysal, the crown prince, to succeed him. Another brother, Khalid, was then chosen crown prince. Saud went into exile and died in Athens on February 23, 1969.

The Reign of King Faysal

King Faysal ibn Abd al-Aziz Al Saud has been in public affairs longer than any other head of state. His public life began in 1919, when

*ARAMCO is wholly owned by Standard Oil of California, Texaco, Mobil, and Standard Oil of New Jersey.

at the age of fourteen he represented his father as the Versailles Peace Conference. He became viceroy of the Hijaz after it was conquered in 1926 and has held the office of foreign minister since 1930 (except between 1960 and 1962, when he retired to private life). His numerous international contacts, an advantage his brother Saud did not possess, have enabled Faysal to deal with confidence in world affairs. For much of King Saud's reign Faysal acted as president of the Council of Ministers, set up by Abd al-Aziz a month before his death. In this position Faysal expanded the administrative structure of the government and instituted austerity measures that successfully restored Saudi finances to a sound position.

As king, Faysal has spent much energy planning for the economic and social development of his people. Although he desires to provide the advantages of Western technology, he has also tried to preserve a social system based on a strict interpretation of Islam. Whether or not this dual purpose can succeed, King Faysal has assured for himself a place in history as a strong monarch, a leader of the moderate Arab states, and an influential Islamic figure.

Political Environment

Geographical, climatic, and religious factors have long been major determinants of political behavior in that part of the Arabian peninsula that is now Saudi Arabia. A hot desert land for the most part, it has produced a conservative, tribally oriented people. The acquisition of vast oil resources has greatly affected Saudi political behavior in the last generation.

Geographical Determinants

Saudi Arabia has a land area of about 830,000 square miles, almost four-fifths of the Arabian peninsula. It extends about 1,200 miles from north to south and about 1,000 miles from west to east at its farthest extremities. Although nearly all of Saudi Arabia is desert, there are wide variations in terrain and climate. For about four months during the winter the climate is generally balmy, often with cold nights in the interior desert. Summers are very hot, often exceeding 110 degrees and occasionally reaching 140 degrees in the interior. Coastal areas are quite humid, and although they are not so hot as the interior, they are more unpleasant.

Extending from the Red Sea inland 15 to 75 miles is a hot, humid (although desert) coastal plain called Tihamah. Rising abruptly from the plain for the entire length of western Saudi Arabia is a narrow escarpment range of mountains with heights ranging from 3,000 and 4,000 feet in the north to nearly 10,000 feet near the Yemen border. The northern segment of mountains and plain makes up the Hijaz, with its cities of Mecca, Taif, and Medina. The southern part is called Asir, and its most important town is Abha. To the east the mountains drop off quickly to between 2,000 and 4,000 feet, and the extending plains descend gradually to sea level at the Persian Gulf.

The center of the country is called Najd, and its most prominent land formation is Jabal Tuwaiq, a "Grand Canyon-esque escarpment" that extends in an arc some 600 miles from north to south. The major towns of Najd are Riyadh, the capital, and the twin (and rival) towns of Buraydah and Anayzah in the north. Al-Kharj, a short distance southeast of Riyadh, is a major oasis.

South of Najd is the Rub al-Khali, the Empty Quarter. Covering 250,000 square miles (almost the size of Texas), it is the largest body of sand in the world. Some of its sand mountains rise 800 feet. The few bedouin who traverse this forbidding place call it merely "the Sands." Much of the area is uninhabited and largely unexplored, although ARAMCO has recently discovered oil there.

North of Najd is a smaller sand desert, the Great Nafud, linked to the Rub al-Khali by a narrow sand strip, the Dahna, which more or less divides Najd from the Eastern Province. The Eastern Province is a low, barren plain dotted with rock formations. In it are several large oases, including Qatif, on the coast, and al-Hasa, which is farther inland (the entire region was formerly called al-Hasa). The major towns are al-Dammam, the province capital; Qatif town, Dhahran, al-Khubar, and Hufuf, the largest town in al-Hasa oasis. North of the Great Nafud is the Northern Frontiers Province, many of whose inhabitants migrate seasonally into Iraq, Jordan, and Syria.

The People

Population Structure: Saudi Arabia's four million or more people* are probably about equally divided among city and large town dwellers, villagers in scattered oases, and nomads. The nomads, although still important, are no longer the independently powerful political force they were during the early years of King Abd al-Aziz. In 1926, when he unified the Saudi legal system, he abolished tribal customary law. However, tribal and extended family ties remain strong in Saudi Arabia, linking all segments of the population through common ancestors. The small yeoman-farmers, the backbone of political support of the Saudi amirs in the nineteenth century, are still a major segment of the population, but movement to the cities and larger towns is increasing. Saudi Arabia still does not have a great city like Cairo, Beirut, or Baghdad; its three largest cities, Riyadh, Jiddah, and Mecca, each have populations of less than 300,000. Nevertheless, these and other towns are rapidly becoming major urban centers and focal points of political power.

*Although a census was taken in the early 1960s, no population figures were ever released, and estimates vary upward from four million people.

Cultural differences between Saudi Arabia's geographical regions are pronounced. Jiddah, the largest city and the country's major seaport, is also the diplomatic capital (rather than Riyadh in the more conservative Najdi heartland). The Hijaz, due to its position on historically important trade routes and because it is the site of the Hajj, has long been a cosmopolitan area, and it has also become the commercial center of the kingdom. Many of Saudi Arabia's leading technocrats, diplomats, and army officers are Hijazis. Because of their more cosmopolitan outlook, many Hijazis tend to be impatient with the traditional political structure largely dominated by the conservative Najdis.

Najd, the political and spiritual as well as the geographical center of the country, has an insular character reflecting its historical isolation. Many of its tribally oriented inhabitants consider themselves the only "racially pure" Arabs, and great Najdi families hold important positions in all branches of government. The al-Sudayris, for example, hold most of the provincial governorships not held by the royal family or its collateral branch, the bin Jiluwis. Unlike inhabitants of the coastal areas, the Najdis have never known more than temporary periods of foreign domination. They have therefore escaped the psychological scars of colonialism and exercise their political prerogatives with the easy authority of desert aristocrats.

The people of the mountain villages of Asir have been the most isolated inhabitants in the kingdom, although roads and airports are now being built there. The tribes of the Northern Frontiers, as mentioned above, have close blood ties in Jordan, Iraq, and Syria. Many bedouin from the north were Ikhwan in the early days of King Abd al-Aziz and are still recruited in the tribally oriented National Guard.

The Eastern Province is an amorphous area; its character is the hardest to define. Although one finds a large Shiite minority, their contribution to the character of the province has been overshadowed both by the Sunni-Wahhabi hegemony and by the oil industry, which is located mainly in the Eastern Province. The oil industry has drawn Saudis from every part of the country, third-country Arabs, and other nationals as well. This mix of people who work Western work shifts, have steady salaries, and own their own homes has created a middle class unlike Saudis in the rest of the kingdom. Contacts with Iran and the East, which were developed centuries ago by those living on the Persian Gulf, also give the area a slightly different character from the rest of the country. Politically and economically, however, Eastern Province is overshadowed by Najd and the Hijaz respectively.

Social Conditions: Great strides have been made in education, particularly in recent years (education is free to all Saudis). In 1968 there were 1,478 schools and 288,810 students compared to 1,071 schools and 164,730 students in 1966. The number of female students rose from 12,000 to 86,000 in the same two years, a major innovation in Saudi society. The country now has three institutions of higher learning: Riyadh University, the College of Petroleum and Minerals in Dhahran, and King Abd al-Aziz University in Jiddah. In 1968, 5,000

Saudis were enrolled in colleges and universities, about one-fifth of them abroad in Europe and the United States. The government has also established five vocational training schools and is planning others.

Welfare programs are also extensive. Medical services, although not yet of consistently high quality, are free, and Saudis are sent abroad at government expense for treatment unavailable in the kingdom. A program for drilling water wells for farmers and nomads has been instituted, and water desalination plants are being built for cities and towns on the Red Sea and Persian Gulf coasts.

The Impact of Islam

It is difficult for a Westerner to conceive of the impact of Islam in a Muslim country, particularly in Saudi Arabia. Islam has an influence over Saudi politics both as a way of life and as a "political" ideology. Under strict Wahhabi interpretation, there is no distinction between spiritual and temporal matters. The laws are Islamic and are administered by Islamic courts; time is computed by the sun, a system geared to the Muslim cycle of five daily prayers (each new "day" begins at sunset, the time of which varies each day); the lunar calendar is used because it marks Muslim holy days; and religious regulations are enforced by a religious police force, the Mutawwiin. A Saudi's attitudes toward politics, ethics, society, and law are inescapably molded by Islam.

Wahhabism has in addition assumed the role of a political ideology for the Saudi state. From the mid-eighteenth century it has been the glue that held together the disparate group of petty amirates and principalities that were conquered by succeeding generations of Saudi amirs, and to this day it sets Saudis apart from nearly all other Arab Muslims. The traditional Wahhabi social and political order is now threatened by the social changes created by modern economic and technological advances, yet the pull of Wahhabism in the land of Mecca and Medina is still very strong.

Economic Conditions

Prior to the discovery of oil, Saudi Arabia was a land of nomadic herdsmen and subsistence farmers; its principal sources of foreign exchange were the annual pilgrimage to Mecca and irregular foreign subsidies. The influx of oil revenues has therefore brought great wealth where previously there was great poverty. By 1969 annual oil income had reached $1.17 billion and the gross national product was $2.6 billion. Oil production rose to 3.9 million barrels a day in 1970 and was exceeding 4 million barrels a day by early 1971. Moreover, revenues are expected to rise substantially as a result of price increases obtained in agreements with the oil companies in early 1971.

The Saudi government has allocated a major portion of its revenues to economic development, the budget for which exceeded $.5 billion by 1968. Communications and education have received high priority. A national all-weather road system is being constructed; the national airline connects most towns with the larger cities; and national radio and television networks are being completed.

The Saudis are making efforts to diversify their single-commodity economy. A steel mill and a fertilizer plant have been built and other projects are being considered. Diversification is stressed in the First Five-Year Plan (1970-75), for which guidelines were set by the Saudi Central Planning Organization. However, it will be difficult to diversify much because Saudi Arabia has few natural resources other than oil. Nevertheless, with a relatively small population, the world's largest proven oil reserves (conservatively estimated at 92 billion barrels), and a projected steady increase in world demand for oil, the Saudi economy does not appear to face the uncertainties of many "one-crop" economies.

The effect of rapid economic and social development on the Saudi political process has been to create, at least temporarily, a relatively high degree of political stability by Middle Eastern standards. Material prosperity has minimized economic discontent and, for the present, has bought off the potential political discontent of a people with little or no participation in the political process. The full effect of economic and social changes on political attitudes cannot be gauged, however. An older generation who grew up in harsher times is in power and is often not receptive to new ideas. A new generation of educated, articulate, ambitious young people has arisen but has yet to be heard. Their time may not be far off, however.

Political Structure

The legal structure of Saudi Arabia is based on the Shariah, or Islamic law, according to the conservative Hanbali school of jurisprudence. Its primary sources are the Quran and the Sunnah, or Tradition of Muhammad. The king, as the imam, is the chief administrator of justice and hence the final court of appeal. According to Islamic legal theory, however, Shariah law operates independently of the king, and he himself is subject to it. Theoretically he can be sued in his own courts.

Disputes involving government decrees are adjudicated by the Board of Grievances, which serves as the principal administrative tribunal, or by administrative committees in the various ministries. Administrative decrees are considered legal regulations enacted to carry out Shariah law or to regulate areas not covered by it. All other cases, civil and criminal, are referred to the religious courts. The Ministry of Justice, created in September 1970, replaces the more traditional office of the chief qadi as the institution for supervising the national court system. The chief qadi had always been a member of the Al al-Shaykh until the death of the last chief qadi in 1969. The creation of a Ministry of Justice and the appointment of al-Harakan, not an al-Shaykh, as minister are significant steps toward the modernization of the Saudi legal system.

The king also has supreme executive and legislative powers, in consultation with the Council of Ministers, Royal Advisers, and the heads of the various independent agencies. Royal decrees, recorded in the official gazette, *Umm al Qura*, have the force of law.

Unlike Arab states in which the development of modern government institutions was guided by colonial governments, administrative development in Saudi Arabia evolved as it was needed, often in haphazard fashion. King Abd al-Aziz originally had no formal government machinery—his personal, patriarchal rule of the Najd of that day was adequate. When he conquered the Hijaz, however, he realized that this relatively more sophisticated area needed a more institutionalized form of government. Abd al-Aziz created a Hijazi government patterned after Sharif Husayn's Ottoman-style administration, with his son Faysal, the present king, as viceroy. Government consisted of a Consultative Assembly and later a ministerial body called the Council of Deputies, the precursor of the national Council of Ministers. The development of central government institutions came later, often as outgrowths of the Hijazi administration. As the country developed, the central government had to exercise increasing authority. Centralization was an uneven process, however, and was often delayed for years until the death of a strong regional personality.

The first national ministries to be established were Foreign Affairs, in 1930, under Prince Faysal; and Finance, in 1932, under Abd al-Aziz's legendary treasurer, Abdullah al-Sulayman. Most government functions were administered as departments of the Finance Ministry or as independent agencies before becoming ministries. In 1944 the Ministry of Defense (now Defense and Aviation) was created from the Agency of Defense. In 1951 the Ministry of Interior reappeared; earlier it was part of the Hijazi administration. Communications, Agriculture and Water Resources, Education, and Health were all organized in the 1950s. In the early 1960s Petroleum and Minerals, Labor and Social Affairs, Commerce and Industry, and Information were created, rounding out the present number of Saudi ministries at thirteen.

King Abd al-Aziz in October 1953 created the Council of Ministers to act as a cabinet and consultative body for enacting legislation as one of his last deeds (he died a month later), and over the years it has grown in influence and power. However, since the ministers (many of whose ministries predate the council) jealously guard their independent authority, the scope of collective action by this body remains limited. Moreover, council decisions must have the approval of the king.

Local government is still evolving. Due to a strong central government and vastly improved communications with the capital, provincial governors, or amirs, are greatly reduced in power from the days of King Abd al-Aziz, when they ruled almost autonomously in his name. The division of authority on the local level between the amir and the national ministries is still not precisely defined.

For administrative purposes there are eighteen provincial districts, or amirates, in Saudi Arabia, five of which—Riyadh, Eastern Province, Mecca (including Jiddah and Taif), Hayil, and Northern Frontiers—are considered major amirates. Medina and Qasim are administered like major amirates but are not so important. Amirs from these seven areas report directly to the minister of interior; the remaining amirs report to the deputy minister.

There are a number of independent or semi-independent agencies in the Saudi government. One of the oldest is the Consultative Council of Hijaz, now seldom convened. Another, the Central Planning Organization, has grown in importance in recent years. With the need for a more rational approach to economic planning, its head has been accorded the rank of minister. The Saudi Arabian Monetary Agency (SAMA) functions as a semiautonomous central banking institution under the Ministry of Finance. There are two public corporations— Saudi Arabian Airlines, the national carrier, and the General Petroleum and Minerals Organization (Petromin), which is charged with encouraging capital investment in Saudi mining and industry. There are also the General Personnel Bureau (a civil service bureau), the General Intelligence Directorate, the religious police (Mutawwiin, which are divided into two public morality committees), and the Technical Assistance Board to coordinate foreign technical assistance. The Royal Advisers give the king advice on both foreign and domestic problems.

Political Processes

A major characteristic of Saudi political behavior is the pronounced personalization of the political process. The political power that any Saudi, including the king, can wield is to a great degree the reflection of the personal allegiance he has been able to command. His successor, even with the same family or tribal standing and the same legal powers, is not guaranteed the same degree of political power unless he is able to build his own personal following.

The King

Political life in Saudi Arabia centers around the king, the supreme executive and legislative authority in the kingdom. Centralization of authority is accentuated by King Faysal's hesitance to delegate authority; he participates in the decision-making process at every level. For example, routine requests for entry visas by foreigners wishing to visit or work in the kingdom often go to the king for personal approval. The king's personal views thus help set the tone of government policy.

Faysal continues to hold a weekly public majlis, or court, in which any citizen can petition him about a personal grievance or can proffer advice. Although the king's advisers argue that he should discontinue this practice because of the press of business, the king refuses, feeling that the public majlis is a form of basic democracy.

The king draws on a wide variety of sources for advice in decision making, and rank and title often mean less than long-established personal relationships. In addition to his Royal Advisers and the more formal advisory bodies such as the Council of Ministers and lesser independent agencies and committees, the king is often guided by the informal advice of members of the royal family, religious leaders, old friends and long-time associates, technocrats, and even trusted expatriates.

To help meet his personal and official needs, the king maintains an entourage of advisers and retainers called the Royal Diwan. The present Royal Diwan probably has less political influence than those of King Saud and Abd al-Aziz, but it is an important link in the decision-making process of the king.

The Royal Family

The royal family, the Al Saud, numbering between 3,000 and 7,000, is the main political constituency of the kingdom. Although collectively it has no formal role in government, the king must maintain the confidence of the royal family to stay in power. Augmented by the Council of Ministers, the ulama, and other important dignitaries, the royal family constitutes what in Islamic law is called *ahl al-aqd wal-hall*, "the people who bind and loose." In 1964 this group exercised its authority to depose a ruler and name his successor by removing King Saud in favor of his brother Faysal.

The royal family is generally circumspect about its affairs and little is known of its internal dynamics. Apparently precedence is gauged by age and generation; occasionally an older, unknown prince takes precedence over politically more prominent princes at public family gatherings.

A number of royal princes, most of whom are sons of King Abd al-Aziz, play major political roles in Saudi government apart from royal family politics. Several political groupings, often based on full-brother relationships from among Abd al-Aziz's many wives, stand out among the brothers. One of the most important groupings is the Al Fahd, so-called after the eldest of seven sons whose mother was a member of the powerful al-Sudayri family (the brothers are also known as the al-Sudayri Seven). Prince Fahd is minister of interior and second deputy prime minister and is considered one of the most powerful men in the kingdom after the king. His brother, Sultan, is minister of defense and aviation, and two other brothers are deputy ministers to Fahd and Sultan. Many of the younger royal princes have studied in colleges and universities in the United

States and Europe and are entering government and military service, including Faysal's younger sons.

The Bureaucracy

The development of the bureaucracy has greatly affected the Saudi political process by channeling the exercise of political power into a relatively organized system of administration based on established procedures and regulations. Of course there is a gap between how the system appears on an organization chart and how it actually operates; in practice, government administration is still highly personalized with little or no delegation of authority by the ministers and agency heads beyond a few trusted lieutenants. Nevertheless, a start has been made and the advantages of efficient public administration are being recognized.

Of possibly more importance, the Saudi bureaucracy contains the country's heaviest concentration of young, educated Saudis. These young bureaucrats, many of whom hold degrees from Western universities, are articulate and ambitious and tend to be impatient with traditional administrative practices. They are placing pressure on the government for a greater role in the decision-making process, and this pressure will increase as more of them enter government service.

The Armed Forces

Saudi Arabia's armed forces have not played a major role in politics since the Ikhwan were disbanded in the late 1920s. (The Ikhwan had grown restless in peacetime, had revolted against Abd al-Aziz, and were defeated in the last great bedouin battle in 1929.) Not until after World War II were the first attempts made to create a modern professional military force. A small British training mission was set up shortly after the war, and in the early 1950s the United States became the principal adviser to the Saudi armed forces. More recently the Saudis have also retained a sizable number of Pakistani military advisers. In the last few years, especially since the June 1967 War, the Saudis have embarked on a number of ambitious programs to upgrade and modernize their armed forces in air defense, mobility, air transport, naval capabilities, and officer training. Saudi midshipmen now study in Pakistan and many officers receive advanced training in Europe and the United States.

Like their counterparts in the bureaucracy, the young military officers are seeking higher professional standards and more individual responsibility. Many are frustrated with the slow pace of change and are becoming restive. Moreover, the young officers tend to be more stirred by Arab nationalism and hence are more critical of the regime's close friendship with the United States, which they brand as a friend of the Arabs' enemy, Israel. Of all the armed forces, the junior officers felt the most humiliated over the Arab defeat in 1967 (even though no Saudi troops were engaged) and were the most bitter over what they considered Western support of Israel during the 1967 War.

Beginning in the summer of 1969, rather extensive political arrests were made in Saudi Arabia, and a large proportion of them were military officers. There has been no indication to date that Saudi authorities link the arrested officers with a specific plot or conspiracy to overthrow the regime, but the arrests do reflect a general rise in the level of restiveness among military personnel.

Other Groups

Business, religious, and tribal leaders, although influential in their own spheres, have little independent political power. Businessmen work through the king, the royal family, and the bureaucracy, especially to obtain government contracts and regulatory legislation favorable to their interests. Although religious leaders have a strong influence on the country, they must also work through the king to obtain their objectives, and they have had mixed results. For instance, they were successful in persuading the king to maintain a ban on commercial cinema, but they failed to persuade him not to introduce national television. (Many religious leaders are opposed to both on the grounds that the Quran forbids the reproduction of the human form.)

Tribal politics no longer occupy a central position in the political process but are still a force in Saudi politics. They are generally handled by the king and his provincial amirs in much the same personalized way as in King Abd al-Aziz's time. Tribal leaders are dependent on the king for their political authority and for the welfare of their tribes. One innovation in tribal politics is King Faysal's substitution on occasion of economic development projects for traditional tribal subsidies. The practice is not entirely popular with the tribal leaders, who cannot grant or withhold projects to political allies and rivals as they could the subsidies.

The Saudi labor force has never played an important role in politics. Almost no manual labor is performed by Saudis; most of it is done by Yemenis and other expatriates. With the exception of small (but growing) numbers in Najdi and Hijazi towns and cities, most Saudi skilled and semiskilled labor is employed by the petroleum industry in the Eastern Province. There have been occasional labor disturbances among the oil workers, but they were generally sparked by economic rather than political grievances.

The relatively insignificant role of labor in the Saudi political process can be attributed to a number of factors. First, the Saudi labor force is economically very well off by Middle Eastern standards. The Ministry of Labor takes an almost paternalistic interest in the welfare of Saudi workers, and ARAMCO, the largest employer in the kingdom, has instituted numerous plans such as low-interest, long-term home owners' loans for the benefit of its Saudi workers. Thus there are only rare economic grievances to spur political activism. A more important factor, however, is the prohibition of labor unions. Without a mass organization to mobilize the workers in a common cause, Saudi labor has thus far remained too disparate to make its voice felt. If economic conditions deteriorate or means other than a union can be found to organize and mobilize workers, they might be able to play a greater political role, particularly in the Eastern Province.

Special Problems

Two problems have major bearing on Saudi Arabian politics— the Hajj, or pilgrimage to Mecca, a unique annual undertaking that would tax even a highly developed industrial state, and a shortage of trained manpower.

More than 1,250,000 people, of whom over 375,000 were foreigners, attended the Hajj in 1971, and the number increases each year. The burden of administering an event of this magnitude is staggering. The traffic on Standing Day alone is equivalent to the traffic for a dozen Rose Bowl games at the same time in the same place, except at the Hajj the participants speak a dozen different languages. Every division of the Saudi government deals with some aspect of the Hajj, and the government as a whole is almost totally preoccupied with it for six to eight weeks each year. There are problems of transportation, housing, communications, security, traffic, currency, health, and even diplomacy. Teams of Foreign Office officials go abroad to help issue special Hajj visas, and the rest of the Foreign Office is preoccupied with protocol for important Hajjis (participants in the Hajj) such as Muslim heads of state. Administration is coordinated by the Ministry of Hajj and Waqf and the Higher Hajj Committee headed by Prince Fawwaz bin Abd al-Aziz, amir of Mecca. Mutawwafin, a special group of Hajj "travel agents" closely regulated by the government, are responsible for seeing that the personal needs of the Hajjis are met.

The Hajj has a major impact on the country's economy. Annual receipts reach an estimated $75 million, counting both the public and private sectors, and the government spends an estimated $60 million per year to administer the Hajj, much of which also enters the Saudi income stream.

The present regime's administration of the Hajj has shortcomings but the emphasis should be rather on how well it has done, considering the size of the task and the developing state of the Saudi bureaucracy. Moreover, since Mecca is in Saudi Arabia, any regime would have to cope with the Hajj and be influenced by it. For example, the Saudi fiscal year, which follows the lunar calendar, is eleven days shorter than the solar year and is therefore more costly in terms of "annual" contracts and wages. A practical reason for not converting to the solar year, however, is that eventually the Hajj would fall on the fiscal new year and the government does not have the resources to administer the Hajj and to prepare an annual budget at the same time.

The second problem, the shortage of trained manpower, is not unique to Saudi Arabia, but two factors set the Saudi problem slightly apart from the problems of other developing countries. Saudi Arabia's tremendous oil revenues enable it to develop at a faster pace than its other human and material resources would normally allow. The state therefore has a proportionately greater difficulty supplying trained manpower to staff development projects than countries with less income. Schools, training facilities, and other programs are being expanded, but the process of education takes time, and in the near future Saudi Arabia will have difficulty decreasing the shortage.

The second factor that distinguishes Saudi Arabia's problem is more political. To meet manpower requirements, Saudi Arabia has traditionally drawn on outside sources. King Abd al-Aziz gathered around him a remarkable group of expatriates, mostly Syrians and Egyptians, who served him (and his successors) in senior policy-making positions. In recent times the state has needed technocrats and teachers rather than political advisers, and except for highly qualified Westerners in senior advisory and managerial positions, most of the expatriate labor force has been drawn from other Arab states. As the number of radical Arab regimes whose political philosophies are inimical to the Saudis grows, expatriates from these radical Arab states have created an increasing internal security problem. To help alleviate the problem Saudi Arabia has turned to non-Arab neighbors like Pakistan, but language barriers often limit the number of men who can be used.

Foreign Policy

Saudi foreign policy can be characterized in general as pro-Western, anti-Communist, and anti-Zionist. The Saudi regime tends to view the world from a decidedly Islamic point of view, however; pro-Western attitudes are thus a reflection of mutual economic interests and mutual antipathy to communism rather than the result of Saudi affinity with Western political institutions or social values. In fact, Western social values are often castigated by Saudi religious leaders who wish to bar "corrupting Western influence" from the country. Saudi antipathy to communism and to socialism and Arab radicalism, which the Saudi leadership considers indistinguishable from communism, is basically aimed at what is seen as an atheist threat to Islamic society. Zionism (as differentiated from Judaism) is regarded in great measure as a threat to Muslim Palestinian Arabs.

The Saudi leadership, a product of the long-isolated Najd, also tends to take an insular and rather defensive view of the world. In the early 1920s it felt encircled by the Hashimite (the family of Sharif Husayn) states of Iraq, Transjordan, and Hijaz. Today it feels encircled by the threat of Zionism from Israel, Baathism from Syria and Iraq,

Arab socialism from Egypt, Sudan, and Libya, Marxism from Southern Yemen, and potential radical Arab insurgency in the Gulf states.

In the long run, Saudi Arabia's greatest foreign policy concern is the opposition, actual and potential, of the radical Arab states, which consider Saudi Arabia to be a reactionary feudal monarchy standing in the way of "progress" for the Arab people. Saudi Arabia has sustained propaganda campaigns, attempts at subversion, and other harassments from a growing number of Arab states, and although the Arab-Israeli conflict seems at present to overshadow the Arab radical-conservative confrontation, the latter remains the greater long-term external threat to the Saudi regime.

Since the Arab defeat in June 1967, the Arab-Israeli question has become the single foreign policy issue with which the Saudis are most preoccupied. Because of their Islamic point of view, the Saudis were opposed to the creation of Israel and were especially hostile to the Israeli occupation of the Old City of Jerusalem and the Muslim holy places after the 1967 War. Since the war Saudi Arabia has joined the other Arab states, radical and moderate, in a common cause against Israel. The Saudis have sent a detachment of troops to Jordan to occupy a position facing Israel, and they are giving an annual subsidy of $100 million to Egypt and $40 million to Jordan. Saudis also contribute to al-Fatah, the most prominent of the Palestinian commando groups. It is doubtful that Saudi Arabia would actively oppose a peaceful settlement with Israel, but Saudis believe this should be left exclusively to the states bordering Israel whose territories were occupied during the 1967 fighting.

A charter member of the Arab League, Saudi Arabia has consistently supported the idea of Arab unity. Saudi concepts of Arab unity and nationalism in general, although set in a more Islamic cast, are similar to those of other Arab states.

In bilateral Arab relations, Saudi Arabia is probably closest to her fellow monarchies, Jordan and Morocco, but relations are also close with Kuwait, Lebanon, and Tunisia. Relations with Algeria have also improved; King Faysal paid a state visit to Algeria in June 1970.

Prior to the 1967 War, the UAR was Saudi Arabia's greatest antagonist. During Yemeni civil war, which began in 1962, Saudi Arabia backed the Yemeni Royalists and the UAR backed the Republicans; Saudi-Egyptian relations reached a new low, and diplomatic relations were broken in 1962. Relations were restored in 1965, however, and after the Arab defeat in 1967 Egypt and Saudi Arabia left off their confrontation in their preoccupation with Israel. Since Anwar al-Sadat became president of Egypt in September 1970, Saudi-Egyptian relations have improved even further. In July 1970 Saudi Arabia finally recognized the Yemen Arab Republic, signaling the end of almost eight years of civil war.

Saudi opposition to the People's Democratic Republic of Yemen has remained unabated since that state's independence in 1967 and is likely to continue as long as the regime maintains its extreme Marxist posture. Relations with the lower Gulf states are generally cordial, and the Saudis have voiced support for the idea of a federation of Arab amirates among the Gulf amirates. Saudi Arabia has long had a territorial dispute with Abu Dhabi and Oman over the Buraymi Oasis—a dispute further complicated by the discovery of oil in the area.

Since the early 1960s the Saudis have been the main proponents of an Islamic summit. King Faysal believed that such a meeting would strengthen Islam and weaken the popular appeal of socialism, particularly Nasserism, in Arab and other Islamic states. After 1967, however, the king became more interested in enlisting non-Arab Islamic states in the cause against Israel and hoped that an Islamic summit could achieve that aim. He played a major role in convening such a summit in Rabat in late 1969 and a follow-up Islamic Foreign Ministers' Conference in Jiddah in March 1970.

Saudi Arabia also sponsors and largely finances the Mecca-based Muslim World League, which supports Muslim activities in Africa and Asia. Saudi Arabia probably has closer relations with Pakistan than with any other non-Arab Muslim state. Pakistan has a military advisory team in Saudi Arabia and has sent the Saudis many contract technicians, particularly doctors. Saudi Arabia in turn strongly supports Pakistan's position in its dispute with India over Kashmir.

Saudi Arabia has long been a friend of the West, particularly the United States. In addition to mutual oil interests, the United States plays a major military advisory role and provides (at Saudi expense) advisory services in many fields from airline operations to radio and television. Other Western states also have close political and economic relations and provide technical assistance to Saudi Arabia. The Arab-Israeli conflict, however, has made it increasingly difficult for Saudi Arabia to maintain friendly ties with the United States. In 1962 Saudi Arabia discontinued U.S. rights to a military base at what is now called Dhahran International Airport, and since 1967 Arab pressure on Saudi Arabia to loosen its ties with the United States has greatly increased. Although he may disagree with U.S. policy toward Israel, King Faysal has so far been able to resist that pressure.

Political Prospects

Since the rebellious Ikhwan were put down in the late 1920s, there has been no serious threat to the internal security of the country, and during the past two decades of growing turmoil in the Arab world, Saudi Arabia has been relatively tranquil. Under King Faysal the chances of continued stability appear to be fairly good, at least by Middle Eastern standards.

Important factors in Saudi stability have been the willingness of the regime to allocate a large proportion of the country's oil income to economic and social development projects and the maintenance of sound monetary and fiscal policies. Despite the Saudi regime's impressive achievements, however, and to a great extent because of their success, the regime will face growing domestic problems in the future. Economic and social development has greatly affected the nature of Saudi society. Traditional patterns are breaking down, including the traditional loyalty to the royal family based on religious zeal and tribal (in the broadest sense) identification. To the new class of young educated Saudis, traditional loyalty is not enough, and younger members of the bureaucracy and the military are pressing for more authority and responsibility. The continued loyalty of this group to the regime may depend on the degree to which the regime can accommodate the desire of the young for greater participation in the political decision-making process.

Given the growing general instability in the Middle East, Saudi Arabia will also have to face greater external problems. Opposition by radical Arab regimes to what they consider a reactionary feudal monarchy will certainly not abate, although it may be temporarily overshadowed by the Arab-Israeli conflict. In the wake of the British withdrawal from the Persian Gulf in 1971, Saudi relations with the Gulf states and with Iran are taking on a new dimension.

With the advent of mass communication, Saudi foreign policy determination must take public opinion into account. Close identification with the United States, even for national self-interest, will probably have to be tempered in view of public identification of the United States with Israel, and in the event of another Arab-Israeli war, the Saudi regime would probably find it impossible to maintain close relations with the United States.

King Faysal's successor will have to meet the demands of a modern society without the benefit of the considerable stature Faysal has attained in over fifty years of public life. Moreover, Faysal's successor will lack the unchallenged authority over the royal family, which during his reign has largely restrained the internecine quarreling that plagued the Al Saud family in the nineteenth century and which reappeared briefly in the reign of King Saud. Inability to maintain royal family unity could undermine the new regime's stability.

Because of their vast quantities of oil, large number of expatriate workers, and almost absolute rule by traditional Arab monarchs, Saudi Arabia and Kuwait are often viewed as similar. But although the regimes face similar challenges—the economics of oil and the politics of Arab conservatism in a tide of growing Arab radicalism—the internal problems of the two countries are actually rather different. Saudi Arabia is geographically large, historically venerable, and religiously and socially homogeneous to a much greater extent than Kuwait, which is essentially a small Gulf amirate whose many nationalities form a heterogenous and diffuse population.

Footnote

---

[1] Howarth, *Desert King*, p. 2.

Selected Bibliography

Arabian American Oil Company. *Aramco Handbook*. Rev. ed. Dhahran, Saudi Arabia: Arabian American Oil Company, 1968.
Presents a good survey of Saudi Arabia, its historical setting, and its oil industry; also has a good annotated bibliography.

Burton, Sir Richard F. *Personal Narrative of a Pilgrimage to Al-Madinah and Mecca*. London: Bell, 1898 and other editions.
A fascinating account of the pilgrimage by a famous nineteenth century British explorer.

De Gaury, Gerald. *Faisal, King of Saudi Arabia*. London: Arthur Barker, 1966.
Probably the best biography of King Faysal.

Howarth, David. *The Desert King: Ibn Saud and His Arabia*. New York: McGraw-Hill Book Co., 1964.
A popularly written biography of King Abd al-Aziz "ibn Saud." A particularly good account of the taking of Riyadh.

Lawrence, T. E. *Seven Pillars of Wisdom*. Garden City. N.Y.: Doubleday & Co., 1935.
The well-known work by Lawrence of Arabia.

Philby, H. St. John B. No study of Saudi Arabia would be complete without sampling the works of this fascinating explorer, writer, and self-appointed adviser to King Abd al-Aziz. The following three are suggested:
Arabian Jubilee. New York: Viking Press, 1946.
Arabian Oil Ventures. Washington, D.C.: Middle East Institute, 1946.
Saudi Arabia. London: Ernest Benn, 1955.

Thesiger, Wilfred. *Arabian Sands*. New York: E. P. Dutton & Co., 1959.
Experiences in the Empty Quarter of one of the foremost explorers of Saudi Arabia.

Winder, R. Bayly. *Saudi Arabia in the Nineteenth Century*. New York: St. Martin's Press, 1965.
Scholarly; the best published account in English on Saudi Arabia in the nineteenth century.

State of Kuwait

Early in the summer of 1946 Kuwait's venerable ruler, the late Shaykh Ahmad ibn Jabir Al Sabah, turned a silver valve wheel to start oil gushing into the bowels of the tanker *British Fusilier*, and the first fruits of Kuwait's oil fields began to flow into the commercial and industrial arteries of the world. The ceremony marked a turning point in the history of his people. In a speech to the foreign and local dignitaries gathered to witness the birth of Kuwait's oil age, Shaykh Ahmad, despite some twinges of doubt, accentuated the positive prospects of the wave of change he sensed was about to engulf his tidy little principality: "Undoubtedly every one of my people and my friends will rejoice with me in this happy event, which, by the grace of God, is for our future welfare.... I thank God for such an opportunity."[1] The pragmatic and guardedly optimistic stance assumed by Kuwait's ruler in 1946 continues to characterize his country's approach to its problems and the conduct of its affairs.

The name *Kuwait* evidently derives from the diminutive form of the Arabic word *kut*, "fort," and since oil profits began to pour into its coffers in the 1940s, Kuwait has indeed been a "small fortress" of prosperity among Middle Eastern states, most of which are racked with poverty. The average annual income for each Kuwaiti is now about $4,000, which closely resembles the U.S. average personal income, whereas most Middle Easterners exist on pittances of approximately $200 a year.

Economic prosperity gives Kuwait its present world importance and conditions the country's political life in domestic and foreign aspects. One of the few Arab states with a functioning parliamentary government, Kuwait has also raised a massive, complex bureaucratic structure to help its citizens enjoy the fruits of a modern, sophisticated, industrial welfare state. Vast sums of oil earnings have filtered through this bureaucratic apparatus into the hands of the populace. Nevertheless, the process of modernizing the country and its political life has brought frustration and danger as well as positive accomplishment.

A fundamental social-political split separated Kuwait's populace into two groups. Basically, the government is constructed to serve the interests of native-born Kuwaitis, the "citizens" who monopolize control of the political decision-making process and who channel most of the opportunities to amass wealth into their own hands. Yet over half of the inhabitants are recent immigrants, officially "temporary residents" who do not enjoy the privileges of Kuwaiti citizenship but possess skills that are vital to the principality's progress. Moreover, because the state is a tiny island of plenty in an ocean of scarcity, it has had to cope with a formidable array of foreign policy problems. By adopting a policy of cooperation with the world powers, careful neutrality among competing Arab states and ideologies, calculated dispensing of massive economic aid to other Arab countries, and financial underwriting of some of the costs of the Arab struggle against Israel, Kuwait has thus far managed to avoid the pitfalls that threaten its independent existence.

Kuwait has yet to ensure its ultimate survival as a separate political entity, but the state has coped with its problems imaginatively and with some success. In fact, Kuwait is looked to by some Arab states—particularly those on Arabia's Gulf coast—as something of a political model and a testing ground for institutions that may be copied by other states that face similar adjustment to rapid modernization.

Historical Background

Each period of Kuwait's evolution as a state has produced a peculiar legacy that is expressed in today's political environment. Kuwait's present territory, the composition of the population, the structure of society, the patterns of economic life, and even many of the religious and intellectual attitudes that undergird the state's present-day ideological outlook are endowments of the various stages in the country's development.

The Tribal Maritime City-State

The amirate of Kuwait is somewhat larger than the state of New Jersey. Its present territories consist of the compact, barren, gravel desert hinterland enclosing Kuwait Bay, an extensive indentation of eastern Arabia's coast situated at the northwest corner of the Persian Gulf. Founded by migrating Arab tribesmen during the early eighteenth century, the state originally encompassed little more than the immediate environs of the town of Kuwait itself, a site favored by shallow wells and a reef-protected anchorage. To this place, according to legend, several clans of the great Anaza tribe migrated in 1716 to escape the droughts and tribal upheavals that convulsed Arabia during the late seventeenth and early eighteenth centuries, and Kuwait has retained ties of blood and custom with the surrounding deserts from which the principality's founders sprang. The bedouin clans that settled Kuwait were collectively labeled the Bani Utub, "the people who migrated."

But although the neighborhood's water wells attracted the Utub herders to Kuwait in the first place, the harbor ultimately determined the main thrust of the community's development until the current oil age. By the middle of the eighteenth century most Kuwaitis were turning to the sea for their livelihoods, and they had begun to build a maritime oriented yet tribally organized city-state. Increasingly, they sustained themselves by such seafaring pursuits as pearl fishing, sailing trade vessels, and shipbuilding, and by commercial activities connected with a large merchant community, serving as a port for the caravans from interior Arabia and providing market services for surrounding tribes. The configuration of the peculiar maritime society that emerged in Kuwait during its first two centuries remains an important element in the modern state's social structure. Basically, this was a society dominated by a few great families—for the most part the same ones that retain so much influence in Kuwait today.

By the 1750s one of these families, the Al Sabah, was recognized by the remainder of the population as the senior spokesman, or ruling house. Whereas the right to govern was entrusted to the Al Sabah family collectively, actual executive authority was vested in the household's most generally acceptable adult male, who served as the shaykh, an office now dignified with the title *amir*. Succession to the office of shaykh did not pass necessarily from father to son but was determined by a conclave of the ruling family. Other important members of Al Sabah, especially close relatives of the ruling shaykh, provided the help that the ruler required to administer the realm, a practice that still prevails to a surprisingly large degree in the selection of the highest officers of Kuwait's government.

The amirate's traditional administrative apparatus was unsophisticated in design and informal in operation. Law was upheld by the shaykh, who sat as a chief magistrate dispensing justice according to Islamic, tribal, and local practice. All Kuwaitis held the right to approach the shaykh personally with complaints and opinions during weekly public audiences. A few of the ruler's armed retainers normally sufficed to keep peace in the town, and during the rare times of emergency a levy of able-bodied men defended the community. Most revenue came from customs duties, and although no distinction was observed between the ruler's personal expenses and public expenses, Kuwait's shaykhs enjoyed a reputation for sober frugality.

Al Sabah did not monopolize political decision making. Families such as Al Ghanim, Al Khalid, Janaat, and Al Salih constituted an oligarchy of merchant seafarers who controlled the town's economic and social life. The elders of these families were consulted and indeed often dominated policy deliberations, and they continue to play a significant role in modern Kuwaiti politics. Far less influential than the oligarchs was a middle group that included minor ship captains, small merchants, master craftsmen, and a handful of Muslim preachers and teachers. The mass of the populace, including wage-earning seamen, pearl divers, artisans, and day laborers, possessed little political leverage outside the right of direct access to the ruler. Today, however, their descendants enjoy full Kuwaiti citizenship, including the franchise and civil service job preference, and some have even been brought into the Kuwaiti cabinet.

Despite basic social solidarity among the populace, traditional Kuwait had splits and cliques, many of which revolved around personal feuds within the Al Sabah family. Others reflected competition among the merchant oligarchs, and a few focused on religious or ideological disputes, such as controversies instigated by the clash of a seafaring society's mores with the puritanical doctrines of Wahhabi Islam, which seeped into the city from interior Arabia. Some of these old rivalries and a tendency toward the coalescing of cliques around a dominating personality still animate modern Kuwaiti political behavior. Nevertheless, compared to many other traditional Arab politics, Kuwait was relatively united and free from factional strife during its first two and a half centuries.

The solidarity of the closely knit early Kuwait community was promoted by the adherence of most of the citizenry to a common set of values and behavior patterns which were an amalgam of the ethics of the desert tribesman, the seaport merchant, the seafaring man, and, of course, the Muslim believer. Kuwaitis were known for industry, enterprise, frugality, moderation, honesty, hospitality, and tolerance, all of which were nurtured by Kuwait's highly developed sense of communal autonomy and self-awareness. But although independence is still prized by Kuwaitis, other old virtues such as frugality have suffered since 1946.

Communal Independence

Kuwait's independent existence has faced a succession of threats. During its first century the autonomy of the city-state's evolving way of life was challenged by would-be tribal overlords—the Bani Khalid and Bani Kaab—and by the expansion of the Wahhabi-Saudi imperium in Arabia. After the Wahhabi tide receded, the ambitions of the Ottoman authorities in Iraq became a new danger. The Ottomans had always claimed Kuwait as a dependency of their southern Iraqi vilayet (province) of Basrah but took no steps to assert such pretentions before the late nineteenth century. These threats were ultimately blunted through imaginative, pragmatic diplomacy.

The strategems used by Kuwait's early shaykhs to ensure their independence still retain some validity in current Kuwaiti foreign policy. The first principle of foreign relations was to try to avoid trouble by assuming a posture of friendly neutrality. Second, the

Kuwaitis were more concerned with preserving the actual substance of independence than with asserting all the specific practices associated with the exercise of sovereignty. When the Ottomans seemed likely to occupy Kuwait in 1871, Shaykh Abdullah ibn Sabah recognized Ottoman suzerainty over his realm, agreed to fly the Ottoman flag, and accepted the title of district administrator under the Ottoman authorities in Iraq. This symbolic pledge of allegiance satisfied the Ottoman sense of empire, and Shaykh Abdullah was left to govern Kuwait without interference.

At other points in history Kuwait's rulers were willing to offer a de jure submission to an outside threat to preserve their de facto independence. A similar tactic was the payment of tribute to buy off potential tormentors such as the Wahhabis. A device that did not suggest the subservient status implied by tribute payments was the periodic dispatch of money to various bedouin tribes that inhabited Kuwait's hinterland to ensure their cooperation, or at least their benevolent neutrality. Finally, the shaykhs developed considerable facility in playing off competing foreign ambitions. Kuwait's foreign policy is still characterized by a predilection for prudence and discretion, the balancing of contending foreign interests, and the calculated use of the state's financial resources.

Shaykh Mubarak's Greater Kuwait

Only once did the state abandon its normal caution to embark upon an adventurous foreign policy, and this action had important political consequences. In 1896, following a violent coup d'état in which the reigning shaykh and his heir apparent were murdered in their beds, the ambitious Mubarak ibn Sabah took direction of Kuwait's affairs and held power until his own (natural) demise in 1915. Usually remembered as the prince who placed Kuwait under British protection in 1899, Shaykh Mubarak is less well known as the author of a political revolution inside his realm. He relied on his sons and close associates (many of them drawn from Kuwait's lower classes) to assume complete control of the state's government machinery, and his descendants subsequently monopolized not only the office of Shaykh but most other important positions in the government as well. Accompanying this intrafamily maneuvering was an increase in the power of the shaykh at the expense of the great merchant families, and since the time of Shaykh Mubarak the oligarchs have attempted, with varying success, to recapture their pre-1896 control of the state's councils and policies.

Perhaps even more vital to the state's long-term destiny was Shaykh Mubarak's success in enlarging Kuwait's territory. In 1896 the state consisted essentially of the districts that immediately surrounded the town of Kuwait, plus an indifferently exercised influence over a handful of nearby tribes. Profiting from the fluid political situation prevailing in northeastern Arabia, Shaykh Mubarak extended his sway among the region's tribes so that it existed on a fairly firm basis over a domain that stretched several hundred miles into the Arabian interior. By 1900 Mubarak was among the most influential of the peninsula's rulers, although ultimately his ambition led him to overextend his claims, and he suffered military defeats in the interior that were costly to his prestige and that halted Kuwaiti expansion. Nevertheless, by relying on the aid of his British protectors, the shaykh was able to consolidate his claim to an extensive Greater Kuwait, the boundaries of which received international recognition in the Anglo-Ottoman draft treaty of 1913. Several years after Mubarak's death the British dealt away half of this territory to Saudi Arabia, but the remainder of the shaykh's patrimony was large enough to include the sites of the great oil fields that are the source of modern Kuwait's wealth.

British Protectorate

Between 1899 and 1961 Kuwait was a British-protected state whose sovereignty was compromised in several respects. The relationship of the two states can be regarded as a marriage of convenience dominated by Britain. Shaykh Mubarak was anxious to gain British protection against the Ottomans, who displayed alarming signs of intending to convert their legal suzerainty over Kuwait into actual administrative control. For reasons of imperial defense strategy the British were receptive to the idea of assuming a protectorate. Both Britain and Kuwait thus gained their immediate objectives in the Anglo-Kuwait agreement of 1899, which forbade Kuwait to cede or mortgage any of its territory or to engage in diplomatic relations with any other powers without British permission. Consequently, until 1961 the British conducted Kuwait's foreign relations. Kuwait's ambiguous international status—being both an Ottoman and a British protected area—was clarified in 1914 when World War I erupted and Britain unilaterally declared Kuwait to be an "independent" state under British "protection."

Britain's presence in the principality had already been asserted in 1904, when a British political agent responsible to the British political resident in the Persian Gulf was appointed, and he set up an agency court that assumed legal jurisdiction over all Westerners resident in Kuwait. The British supplied military assistance to Kuwait on several occasions during the course of their protectorate, notably in 1902, 1921, and 1929/30, when external threats to the amirate occurred. Nevertheless, the Kuwaitis grew somewhat disenchanted with their protector when it appeared that Kuwaiti interests were being sacrificed. Discontent was particularly apparent after the Treaty of Uqayr of 1922, when the British handed over large slices of Kuwaiti-claimed territory to Saudi Arabia and Iraq. The Uqayr settlement also established the Kuwait-Saudi Arabia Neutral Zone along the Gulf coast, a jointly owned territory in which extensive petroleum deposits subsequently were developed and which was not finally partitioned between the two states until 1970.

The British never interfered in Kuwait's domestic affairs to the same extent that they did in some of their other Persian Gulf protectorates. Still, they exerted considerable, and at times decisive, influence in the amirate. Also, they backed the rationalization of Kuwait's administrative structure, which started in the late 1930s, a move that was the first step in the creation of Kuwait's present government apparatus. By the 1940s several British experts were employed by the ruler in his central administration; these men were among the earliest of the foreign administrators who currently fill key government posts.

Kuwait began its rapid development as an oil-powered welfare state under British tutelage. By the mid-1950s modernization was proceeding so rapidly that the traditional political machinery, including the British supervisory regime, was becoming obsolete. By 1961 the now wealthy shaykh of Kuwait held the largest block of investments in the London market and controlled a correspondingly large percentage of the sterling areas's finances. Clearly, the state of Kuwait had become too important in world economic affairs to be treated as less than fully sovereign, and in June 1961 the 1899 protectorate agreement was replaced by a military alliance. A last echo of the protectorate was sounded in the summer of 1961, when in response to a Kuwaiti request, British military force once more was made available, this time to counter an Iraqi threat to the newly free amirate. This crisis was overcome, however, and Kuwait was able to resume a fully independent, if somewhat perilous, existence.

Modern Welfare State

The 1950s saw Kuwait's transformation from an old-fashioned, mud-walled Persian Gulf seaport into a neon-lit, air-conditioned world of opulence surrounded by the rubble of demolition and the noise of construction. The 1950s were difficult years, as traditional certainties were uprooted to make way for a raw new reality. But the new Kuwait matured and by 1970 had apparently passed through the worst phases of adjusting to the trials of affluence. In the process, one of the most thoroughgoing welfare states in the world emerged.

Political Environment

The People

Population Structure: Modernization has produced major changes in the composition of Kuwait's population and the structure of its society. From somewhat fewer than 100,000 people in 1940, the amirate's population approached 730,000 in 1970. Since the early 1960s native-born Kuwaitis have been outnumbered by aliens because the oil boom has been accompanied by a massive immigration of foreign executives, technicians, and workers. Recently the population has been expanding at an annual rate of nearly 12 percent, which makes Kuwait the fastest-growing country in the world. The 55 percent of Kuwait's residents who are listed as foreigners are mainly Arabs of Palestinian, Iraqi, Lebanese, Syrian, and Egyptian origin, although some Iranians, Indians, Pakistanis, and Westerners have also been attracted.

Most of the newcomers are young, unmarried males and they form a rootless but highly competitive group. Almost without exception they come to Kuwait to make money. Some foreign laborers live a hand-to-mouth existence in the high-priced amirate, but other immigrants have made fortunes. Most important, the skills, energy, and modern attitudes of the newcomers have been an essential ingredient in Kuwait's modernization. The aliens dominate the vital middle management sector of business and government and provide a large majority of the professionals. In 1969, for example, only 33 of the 700 medical doctors who practiced in Kuwait were native-born.

Social Conditions: All Kuwaitis enjoy the blessings of a welfare system that is comprehensive to a degree unparalleled elsewhere in the Middle East and hardly equaled elsewhere in the world. Some benefits are reserved for citizens, but all residents enjoy free education and health care, no income taxes, and bonuses such as free telephone service. Low-income Kuwaitis are bolstered by a $2.25 daily minimum wage and generous family assistance grants that range up to $220 a month. For citizens, the purchase of a home is underwritten, and the more affluent can profit from the government policy of buying their land at high prices.

The educational establishment is Kuwait's special pride and is significant politically because it is expected to provide the state eventually with sufficient trained local talent to free it from dependence on alien experts and workers. Education is compulsory up to age sixteen. Over 200 new, well-equipped schools provide free education from kindergarten through the academic or technical-vocational secondary level. Almost 7,000 teachers, many of them Egyptian, instruct some 120,000 students. A tuition-free university has been opened, and government grants cover all the costs of sending Kuwaiti students abroad to study subjects not yet taught in Kuwait. Adult education is aimed at ending illiteracy, and the state television and radio network presents some educational programs. Within a few decades Kuwait could become a major educational center drawing students from the entire Arab world. The domestic political effects of this lavish welfare system, combined with the government's policy of ensuring jobs for all citizens, has been to undercut the potential appeal of revolutionary ideologies, at least among the native-born.

Economic Conditions

The legacy of Kuwait's most recent period of history is apparent everywhere, although the essence of the new Kuwait is

manifest particularly in the economic and social spheres. The effects of
the oil boom are all-pervasive. Including its half of the former Neutral
Zone, the amirate possesses almost 20 percent of the world's proven oil
reserves and is the sixth largest oil producer in the world. The five
companies that exploit Kuwaiti oil represent American, British, Dutch,
Japanese, Spanish, and Kuwaiti combines. The oil companies exert a
tremendous impact on the economy. The largest, the Kuwait Oil
Company, employs 5,000, has a payroll of $2 million a month, and
spends $20 million annually on local purchases. The indirect income
from oil is even larger; the Kuwait government received 83 cents for
each of the more than 900 million barrels pumped from its oil fields in
1969, which totaled over $800 million and made up over 90 percent of
the state revenues. Another source of government income is earnings
from investments of past oil profit accumulations.

Although petroleum will probably constitute the basis of
Kuwaiti economic activity for at least another century, the country is
taking steps to diversify its economy. An airline and an oil tanker
company were among the early fruits of this effort. A five-year
development plan (1966-71) and a second plan (1972-82) promise
generous financial support for new industry. A large petrochemical
complex and several smaller processing plants have already entered
production. However, Kuwait's prospects for industrial development
are hampered by a dearth of natural resources, except oil and natural
gas, and by less intrinsic handicaps such as shortages of skilled labor.
Accordingly, although 15 percent of the labor force works in nonoil
industry, these workers account for only 3 percent of the gross national
product.

Far more significant at this time are commercial activities
connected with expediting the thriving import trade, contracting the
conglomeration of private and publically financed construction
projects, and providing an array of services. The government has
stimulted private enterprise by participating in the establishment and
financing of new businesses. It has fueled Kuwait's extraordinary real
estate boom by purchasing privately owned land at highly inflated
prices and by selling off valuable city real estate at less than prevailing
market prices. Some 20,000 families have shared some $2.5 billion in
the land bonanza, which the government freely admits is administered
so that large amounts of its huge oil royalties can be diffused among the
citizenry. This does not mean that the wealth has been distributed
evenly. The scions of the old oligarchical families and some expatriates
with a smell for quick gain have garnered the bulk of the largess.
Eighteen of the great Kuwaiti families control 90 percent of Kuwait's
private foreign investment activity; the old oligarchy is more prosperous
than ever.

An unfortunate side affect of the new climate of easy wealth
has been the erosion of the old Kuwaiti virtues. The spirit of
enterprising self-reliance has been replaced among some citizens by
complacent indolence because they no longer have to work hard for
their livelihoods.

Political Structure

Since 1962 Kuwait has been a functioning constitutional state, if not fully democratic. Its present government structure does not represent a total departure from traditional political forms, however, for many of these forms are enshrined in the constitutional charter.

Antecedents to Constitutional Government

Kuwait's original government was patriarchal in character, but it was not an autocratic despotism. From the state's earliest days the shaykhs were limited both by custom and by the check posed by a strong oligarchy. The traditional decision-making apparatus employed a functional partnership between the Al Sabah skaykhs and the spokesmen of the great families, although the execution of policy normally was the exclusive province of the shaykh.

Only after Shaykh Mubarak came to power in 1896 did the rulers begin to escape traditional restraints and to assume a more autonomous policy-making role. Yet after his death in 1915 some oligarchs tried to reassert their customary consultative role. Their efforts bore fruit in 1921, when at the time of his accession Shaykh Ahmad ibn Jabir agreed to form a Consultative Assembly of twelve delegates selected by the notables. The assembly's members were too divided to face the shaykh as a united body, however, and after a time the meetings stopped.

But the idea of an assembly was not dead. After two abortive experiments in the 1930s with councils chosen by a small body of electors, a group of young, Iraqi-influenced Kuwaitis who called themselves the National bloc persuaded the ruler to form a second Consultative Assembly in 1938. The second assembly had an even stormier history than the first, although it did receive the shaykh's assent to a protoconstitutional Organic Law, which would have restricted the executive's prerogatives had it survived. (Several of the law's features were revived in Kuwait's present constitution, including the designation of the nation rather than the shaykh as the legitimate source of authority.) The second assembly outdistanced its support when it passed laws injurious to some merchants and called for union with Iraq. The resulting furor culminated in rioting, loss of life, and eventually the ruler's smashing of the would-be parliamentary movement.

A far milder form of consultative chamber—the Supreme Council—appeared in the 1950s. This group was essentially no more than a council of the Al Sabah family attended by those who supervised executive departments, so in the final analysis, Shaykh Mubarak's concept of a centralized ruling apparatus prevailed until 1961. Nevertheless, the idea of a formal institutionalization of the consultative and decision-making process was not foreign to Kuwait.

The Constitution of 1962

In 1961 Kuwait was reeling under the pressures of Iraq's threat to absorb the country, a rising flood of alien immigrants, and a constellation of difficulties that stemmed from rapid economic and social change. The ruling family became convinced that the country was in the midst of a serious political crisis and that the traditional solidarity of the native-born Kuwaitis must be mobilized in defense of their independence and self-identity. Consequently, in December 1961 the ruler called for the election of a Constituent Assembly to draft a constitution and to act as a temporary parliament for the amirate. Leaning heavily on the advice of Muhammad Sanhuri, an eminent Egyptian constitutional expert, the Constituent Assembly presented a draft constitution which was promulgated in November 1962 by the ruler.

The charter consists of five parts, the first of which details the nature of the state and declares that "sovereignty resides in the people," that the "people of Kuwait are part of the Arab nation," that the state religion is Islam, and that Islamic law should be the main source of legislation. Kuwait is a "hereditary amirate (principality)" to be ruled by descendants of Shaykh Mubarak; the ruler is empowered to indicate his own successor subject to the proviso that the heir must have attained his majority and must be approved by the national assembly.

The fundamental innovation in the constitution is the establishment of a National Assembly, a body that consists of fifty deputies popularly elected by Kuwait's eligible citizen electors for four-year terms. Five deputies represent each of the state's ten constituencies. Cabinet ministers, up to one-third the number of the elected members, may also sit in the assembly by virtue of office, and because many Al Sabah princes hold cabinet portfolios, the ruling house has had ample representation in the legislature. Legislative power is a dual function of the assembly and the amir. For instance, the ruler appoints the cabinet, but the assembly may override any veto invoked by the amir by a two-thirds majority vote. The amir must consider all legislation within thirty days or seven days in the case of emergencies. Deputies may question any minister, debate any policy question, and conduct confidence votes on the record of any individual minister, although confidence votes on the performance of the prime minister or the cabinet at large are not allowed. If the assembly believes that it cannot work with the prime minister, the issue can be presented to the amir, who may then either dismiss the prime minister or call for an election of a new assembly (the assembly cannot be dissolved two consecutive times on the same grounds). Deputies may debate the budget in detail and ratify or reject all important treaties, such as those pertaining to peace, alliances, natural wealth, residence status, and finance. The charter specifies that the amir is to exercise his executive powers through the medium of the prime minister and the cabinet. Up to now the office of prime minister has been filled by the heir apparent to the throne and has served as a link between the amir and the assembly.

The constitution also promises that Kuwaiti society will be based on social justice, that the right to private property will be protected, and that old virtues such as the sanctity of the family and the Islamic and Arab heritage will be upheld. The constitution may be amended if the amir and two-thirds of the assembly agree on a proposal, but amendments that question the validity of the royal regime or the basic liberties of the people may not be entertained.

The Ministries and Other Executive Departments

The promulgation of the constitution facilitated the consolidation of Kuwait's expanding central administration by designating the prime minister's office a coordinating agency. Today fourteen ministries supervise most of the specialized functions of the government—Foreign Affairs, Defense, Interior, Finance and Oil, Public Works, Guidance and Information, Education, Social Affairs and Labor, Health, Islamic Affairs, Electricity and Water, Justice, Trade and Industry, and Posts and Telephones and Telegraphs. The ministers are appointed by the amir, but they are responsible to the National Assembly. The ministries are the direct institutional descendants of the executive departments established in the late 1930s, and they therefore predate the constitution. Other offices exercise executive functions, although they do not have the status of ministries. These include the quasi-independent Kuwait Fund for Arab Economic Development, the amirate's regional agency for dispensing foreign aid.

The Municipalities

Local government in the urban areas of Kuwait is the province of three central-government-dominated municipalities: Kuwait city, Ahmadi, and Jahra. Many tasks of the municipalities involve welfare functions, such as overseeing housing allowances, and there is considerable overlapping of the responsibilities of central and municipal authorities, as might be expected in a small state. In rural areas tribes still retain considerable autonomy.

The Judicial System

As in many other Middle Eastern countries, Kuwait's courts are not a separate branch of government but are functions of the Ministry of Justice. Although the theoretical supremacy of Islamic law is constitutionally recognized, in practice a codified law based on the Egyptian system is applied. The police investigate minor crimes and present them in magistrates' court. The attorney general looks into major felonies and prosecutes them in criminal assize court. Civil cases are tried in general court, which has sections for commercial, civil, and personal status cases. A hierarchy of appeals courts also exists. Most lawyers are aliens, including a large contingent of Egyptians.

Political Processes

Much of Kuwait's political life revolves around issues that are tied to the state's affluence—how to protect it, how to increase it, how to control it, how to distribute it.

Kuwait for the Kuwaitis

Kuwait's populace is split into two legally distinct classes. The citizens, the native-born Kuwaitis whose family roots can be traced to the days of the old maritime city-state, monopolize control and participation in the state's legal political processes. The immigrants, who provide 70 percent of Kuwait's working force—the experts, technocrats, and workers whose enterprise and modern skills are converting the amirate's resources into a bonanza—are barred from participation in the state's constitutional political life and are denied the full benefits of the lavish welfare system.

The split originated in the 1950s, when Kuwait's need for trained manpower to staff its burgeoning economy and government bureaucracy attracted tens of thousands of educated, or at least industrious, immigrants from surrounding countries. Soon native Kuwaitis began to fear that they would lose control of their own country and ultimately their distinctiveness as a result of the inundation of foreigners, and in the late 1950s the government adopted a defensive posture. In 1959 the landmark Naturalization Decree limited Kuwaiti citizenship to those residents (and their heirs) who had lived in the state continuously since 1920. The decree was amended in 1960 to allow fifty aliens to be naturalized each year after ten years residence if they were of Arab blood or fifteen years if they were non-Arab. The effect of the naturalization laws was reinforced by the Electoral Law of 1962, which disqualified non-native-born citizens who had been naturalized since 1952 from voting in national elections. In effect, only literate, native-born Kuwaiti males twenty-one years old and older can vote. The electorate now consists of about 40,000 Kuwaiti citizens.

Kuwaiti defensiveness was also manifest in the regulations that reserved all senior civil service posts, civil service tenure, and exemption from civil service examinations to citizens. Only citizens can own or trade land, and in business the regulations are such that most commercial dealings must be officially carried on through Kuwaiti citizens.

Many aliens are envious and bitter. With few exceptions they are psychologically estranged from the citizenry; they have little sense of permanent identification with the country or allegiance to the government and are motivated mainly by self-interest. Some are apostles of one or another version of revolutionary Pan-Arab nationalism. Their frustrations constitute an obvious threat to political stability, yet by and large, the foreigners are the most modern and dynamic elements in Kuwait's population.

Native Kuwaitis show few signs that they will alter their self-protective policies. Indeed, now that a generation of modern, educated native-born Kuwaitis is emerging from local and foreign schools, things may get worse for foreigners as they lose their occupational leverage. The assembly has also begun to tighten the laws governing the entry of foreigners into the amirate.

Constitutionalism

For the most part, the native citizenry seems ready to stand together to prevent their community from being overwhelmed by foreigners. Yet they also display diversity in their specific approaches to coping with their country's problems and energy in pursuing their own intramural political ambitions.

Constitutional politics is played in two arenas—the cabinet and the National Assembly. Because political parties are illegal, much political activity seems to be devoted to seeing which cliques and individuals among the small, clublike groups that constitute the Kuwaiti political elite will control the political apparatus and thus the distribution of state wealth and favor. The political factions to a large extent reflect the traditional structure of society—the Al Sabah princes, the merchant oligarchs, and the middle and lower classes. These groups are fragmented, however, so politics often consists of constructing alliances that cut across and through the main divisions. These alliances shift according to the specific issue being considered. In general, the Al Sabah have been able to control cabinet politics and to hold their own in the assembly, but they have not totally dominated decision making by any means. On occasion, Al Sabah prince-ministers have been sharply questioned by legislators, draft treaties have been turned down, and budget items have been slashed. The National Assembly has not performed merely as a rubber stamp for the amir and the prime minister.

One reason for this is that the Al Sabah themselves are divided into personality-oriented cliques. After the death of Amir Abdullah in 1965, his brother, Sabah, became ruler, which broke a tradition whereby two branches of the family, the Al Jabir and the Al Salim, had alternated in supplying the shaykh. With Sabah's accession as amir, two Al Salims had possessed the title in succession, and loud grumbling was heard among the Al Jabir and their political allies. A cabinet and parliamentary crisis quieted only after an Al Jabir prince was selected as heir apparent and prime minister. Accompanying this settlement was a redistribution of cabinet posts in which several middle-class allies of the

Al Jabir faction were given posts at the expense of some of the oligarch allies of the Al Salim group.

Most political confrontations have been carried on by conservatives acting within the accepted political context. Political contests often seem grounded on old feuds between or within families; other eruptions reflect the strivings of ambitious individuals or cliques anxious to safeguard or capture competitive advantages. These rivalries are fought in contests for assembly seats, in parliamentary jousting within the assembly, and in the maneuverings of cliques for power in the cabinet. The major exception to this cozy situation has been provided by the activities of a loose coalition of Pan-Arab nationalist reformists that has captured occasional election victories and influenced some parliamentary decisions. Their parliamentary leader is Ahmad al-Khatib, and the group has a following among the growing ranks of middle-class Kuwaiti citizens and has forged some tentative links with the alien technocrats who reside in Kuwait. Small as its parliamentary strength is, this bloc may play a pivotal role in Kuwait's future in avoiding a serious confrontation between the citizens and the expatriates. The government has displayed increasing wariness over the group's apparently growing influence, however, and has been invoking censorship and other restrictions to combat so-called threats to internal order and national security.

Social Organizations

An increasingly significant, if indirect, role in Kuwait's political life is being played by numerous organized clubs, societies, institutions, recreational associations, and less formal groupings. Most of Kuwait's adult male population—native-born and recent immigrant alike—participate in such organizations, which serve as focal points for the social, cultural, and professional activities of the many subcommunities within the amirate.

Ostensibly, none of these associations is organized for political purposes, because political parties and similar organizations are barred from functioning openly in Kuwait. But because of the absence of legal vehicles for carrying on party politics or related dealings, considerable activity that is political in nature takes place within these organizations. Much of this activity consists of little more than gossiping about the political issues of the day, but significant are disguised campaigning for political candidates, lobbying for legislation and administrative proposals, and even clandestine organizing of demonstrations.

A few "social clubs" actually are fronts behind which ideological political groups—including those that are potentially revolutionary—carry on their affairs. Indeed, virtually all the political creeds that are important in the Arab world are nurtured somewhere within the network of Kuwaiti social, cultural, or professional organizations. The organizations that have arisen within Kuwait's large community of expatriate Palestinians have been especially active and successful in influencing the foreign policies of the Kuwaiti government. Nevertheless, although these groups may be the seeds from which major political movements may spring eventually, so far they have been too fragmented and too closely watched by the government to play more than a secondary part in political processes.

Administrative Decision Making

In many ways the decisions of administrators are more influential than legislative maneuverings in determining the policies and actions of the government. In old Kuwait, policy as well as routine business was conducted face to face in a system conditioned by personal relationships, and today, despite an elaborate facade of offices and operational directives, many important decisions and ordinary procedures demonstrate the continuing vitality of traditional modes of administrative deliberation.

The decision makers are of two varieties—overtly political appointees, such as cabinet ministers, and ostensibly professional civil servants. The influence of the politicians is obvious; most of the assembly's legislation is initiated in the cabinet, as most legislators have been content to react to matters presented to them rather than to initiate bills themselves.

But the cabinet politicians depend increasingly on the professional civil servants who staff their ministries to prepare legislation and to execute laws. The concept of a professional civil service is quite new to Kuwait—it was established firmly only in the 1950s. The civil service does not yet function smoothly because of the persistence of traditional, personality-oriented practices and the difficulties rooted in the explosive expansion of the civil service apparatus. Still, even if it is inefficient, the bureaucracy is an important cog in Kuwaiti political life.

Some of the inefficiency is deliberate, because civil service appointments are viewed as a vehicle for distributing oil wealth among the citizenry and as a means of giving idle Kuwaitis a job. (Almost one person in ten in Kuwait has a government job.) Consequently, most offices are grossly overstaffed; five people are commonly employed to do work that one could perform. Paper pushing and snarls of red tape are endemic, and influence peddling prevails because the distinction between private or family interests and public duty is not finely drawn. Despite regulations to the contrary, civil servants of all ranks commonly hold second jobs, often in businesses operated by close relatives. Ironically, some senior officials are overburdened with work because few people will accept a decision as final until the top man has personally approved it.

The highest civil service posts are reserved for Kuwait citizens, but because a minority of these senior appointees possess modern educational qualifications, most depend heavily on expert advice. Much of this advice must come from expatriates, who fill over 50 percent of the civil service posts and dominate the middle ranks of the bureaucracy. In truth, the wheels of government (and private business as well) are turned by the labors of the aliens. The massive presence of non-Kuwaitis within the civil service provides the chief vehicle whereby the majority of the state's population—the noncitizens—can exert practical influence on government actions. Nevertheless, noncitizens are still barred from the highest jobs, from permanent job tenure, and from the higher pensions, which adversely affects the morale and performance of many civil servants.

The Armed Forces

Although they number but 10,000 men, the armed forces are a significant quantity in the Kuwaiti political equation. So far, the military has played a role somewhat analogous to that of the Jordanian army, in that it has supported the political status quo rather than revolution. The amir takes his title of commander-in-chief seriously because in an internal upheaval the armed services could become the ultimate prop to his rule. The services are a particular interest of all the Al Sabah, and most leading officers, including those in the national police, are members of the clan. Also, only native-born Kuwaitis are recruited as soldiers. Both officers and men are well trained, well equipped with the latest arms and aircraft, and better paid than any other troops in the Middle East, and they enjoy considerable prestige. Some combat exposure has been gained by those who have passed through the Kuwaiti contingent that serves on the Egyptian-Israeli Suez Canal battle line.

Foreign Policy

Most native Kuwaitis, while they consider themselves part of the greater Arab nation, do not want to lose their present privileges or their chance for an even brighter future. Consequently, Arab nationalism is a popular creed, but the practical enthusiasm of the average native-born Kuwaiti for its doctrines is qualified in important respects. Just as this attitude is a touchstone of Kuwaiti domestic politics, so too it conditions the conduct of Kuwait's foreign policy.

In foreign dealings Kuwait has tried to be the friend of all or failing this, at least to balance the ambitions of competing political interests and states against each other. The latter technique was used in surmounting Kuwait's first great crisis as an independent state. In 1961 Iraq revived an old claim that the amirate was an integral part of her southern province of Basrah. The Iraqi move was evidently prompted by a combination of domestic political pressures on the Baghdad regime and its desire to forestall a possible Egyptian push into the Gulf. The Kuwaitis asked for and received immediate British military aid under the terms of the alliance that had replaced their old protectorate relationship, but they balanced this request with a similar one to Saudi Arabia, and in addition, they asked the United Nations to consider the Iraqi threat to their independence. However, a Soviet confrontation with the Western powers prevented an effective U.N. response, and the scene of diplomacy shifted to the Arab League, where Egypt pushed Kuwait's successful application for league membership and proposed a formula whereby a 3,300-man Arab League force, jointly raised by Egypt, Saudi Arabia, Sudan, Jordan, and Tunisia, would replace the British as Kuwait's protectors. The issue was finally settled in 1963 in the wake of a change of regime in Baghdad, and in October 1963 a Kuwait-Iraq accord recognized the "independence and full sovereignty of Kuwait." The price of this peace to Kuwait was revealed a week later when Kuwait approved an $84 million interest-free "loan" to Iraq; for its benevolent aid in the crisis, Egypt was forwarded a $70 million grant.

By 1963 then Kuwait had established its essential relationship to the Arab states. Kuwait accepts the general validity of Arab nationalism and its overall aims but avoids specific commitments to any Arab camp by assuming a position of friendly, impartial neutrality toward Arab ideological rivalries. This posture was emphasized by the creation in 1962 of the Kuwait Fund for Arab Economic Development, which was founded as a testament to Kuwaiti philanthropic instincts and, even more, to its pragmatic political sense. Kuwait promised that the Arab states could expect financial aid no matter what their ideological stance might be, so long as they were willing to uphold the amirate's independence. Drawing on capital that approaches a billion dollars, the fund has granted several low-interest development loans to Arab states; a $20 million loan enabled Sudan to modernize a creaking railway system, for example. Happily, the massive aid effort is well administered, and it contributes much to Kuwaiti prestige among Arabs everywhere. By steering a neutral course among the ideological rivalries that divide the Arabs, the Kuwaitis have earned a reputation as generous providers of precious financial aid. This service has made Kuwait's continuing existence useful to other Arab states and has thus strengthened the state's changes to lead an independent existence in the future.

Kuwait has given strong backing to the Arab cause in its confrontation with Israel, expressed symbolically by the small Kuwaiti army contingent stationed on the Suez battle front and more weightily by massive financial grants to Jordan, Egypt, and the Palestine Liberation Organization since the 1967 Arab-Israeli War. In 1970 Kuwait increased its annual contributions to Egypt and Jordan to $182 million—almost a quarter of its budget. During the aftermath of the 1967 War Kuwait temporarily cut oil sales to states—the United States and Britain particularly—accused of backing Israel's cause. The amirate's relationship to the Palestinian Liberation Organization is friendly and cooperative. However, the presence of 150,000 expatriate Palestinians causes many Kuwaitis to view with some wariness the potential political influence that this large minority could wield in a political crisis.

Kuwait is playing an important role as a mediating political influence and as a supplier of aid and advice in Gulf affairs. It enjoys good relations with all the Gulf powers, including Iran, Saudi Arabia, and Iraq. It has encouraged the small Arab states in the Gulf in their federation effort and enjoys particularly close relations with Bahrayn, whose rulers share close kinship ties with the Al Sabah family.

In its dealings with the world at large Kuwait's preference for nonaligned neutrality again is manifest. It maintains correct relations with the world's major power blocs. Its economic relations with the West, especially the United States, Britain, and West Germany, are intimate and mutually profitable. Nevertheless, in cooperation with most of the Afro-Asian and Arab blocs, it has condemned American involvement in Southeast Asia and the lingering British presence in southeastern Arabia. It profits from mutually beneficial oil marketing arrangements with the Soviet Union and backed Communist China's candidacy for a U.N. seat. In short, Kuwait has revived many of the principles that used to characterize its cautious approach to foreign relationships before the 1899-1961 interlude of Britain's protectorate.

Political Prospects

The long-term permanence of Kuwait as an independent entity is in doubt, for although it is rich, it is also small and vulnerable. It is not immune to internal revolution or foreign conquest. Overturning of the present regime is conceivable in a number of situations, particularly if the alien population were allowed to unite into a cohesive force or if a younger, more modern body of native Kuwaitis grew tired of the pace of evolutionary change and toppled their fathers from power. Already there are ample signs of generation differences among Kuwaiti citizens.

But in a sense the Kuwaiti revolution is already well under way. For twenty years the country has been experiencing a cultural upheaval, the effects of which are surely more profound than those that could be produced by overturning today's political structure. Moreover, even should the city-state be absorbed into a larger political entity, or if it should join such a unit voluntarily, Kuwait will doubtless survive as a dynamic center from which modernizing impulses will radiate into the surrounding region. Kuwait's record of pragmatic adaptation to changing circumstances shows that there is an excellent chance that an independent or at least a self-governing, autonomous Kuwait will continue to exist and that it will continue to exert an influence far greater than its small size would seem to warrant.

Kuwait and the Gulf states emerged out of the same eastern Arabian cultural and historical tradition. Presently all the states of that area have monarchical-patriarchal governments; they tend to be moderately pro-Western; and they are in the midst of transforming themselves from medieval to modern societies. Eastern Arabia is blessed with abundant oil reserves that are providing the means to pay for rapid economic and social transformation, although the process of modernization has generally been carried further in Kuwait than in the Gulf states. Nevertheless, behind the facade of opulence and rapid social change, severe strain threatens to rip apart eastern Arabia's existing political fabric.

Footnote

[1] Dickson, *Kuwait and Her Neighbors,* p. 656.

Selected Bibliography

Abu Hakima, Ahmad. *History of Eastern Arabia, 1750-1800: The Rise and Development of Bahrain and Kuwait.* Beirut: Khayats, 1965.
Draws extensively from Arabic sources and describes the early development of Kuwait as a city-state.

Al-Marayati, Abid A. "The Question of Kuwait." *Foreign Affairs Reports* 15 (July 1966).
An in-depth analysis of Kuwaiti-Iraqi relations with special emphasis on the 1961 crisis.

Dickson,   H. R. P. *Kuwait and Her Neighbors.* London: George Allen and Unwin, 1956.
One of the most important studies of twentieth century Kuwait.

El Mallakh, Ragaei. *Economic Development and Regional Cooperation: Kuwait.* Chicago: University of Chicago Press, 1968.
A detailed study of Kuwait's economic development and the influence of its financial assistance policies within the Arab world.

Holden, David. *Farewell to Arabia.* New York: Walker & Co., 1966.
A perceptive journalistic account of Kuwait's political role as an affluent oil state.

International Bank for Reconstruction and Development. *The Economic Development of Kuwait.* Baltimore: Johns Hopkins Press, 1965.
Includes massive amounts of economic data and much practical information on the Kuwaiti political structure and processes.

Monroe, Elizabeth. "Kuwayt and Aden: A Contrast in British Politics." *Middle East Journal* 18 (Winter 1964): 63-74.
Explores the smooth exit of British political power from Kuwait and the resulting benefits that accrued to both countries.

Shehab, Fakhri. "Kuwait: A Super-Affluent Society." *Foreign Affairs* 43 (April 1964): 461-74.
An insightful, well-presented, still valid portrait of Kuwaiti political realities.

Gulf States

(Bahrayn, Qatar, Abu Dhabi, Dubai,
Sharjah, Ajman, Umm al-Qaywayn,
Ras al-Khaymah, Al-Fujayrah,
Oman)

An incident that occurred in July 1970 in an isolated seaside palace of the sultans of Oman tells much about the current political scene in the Gulf states. Oman's British-educated crown prince, Qabus ibn Said, engineered a palace coup that ended the thirty-eight-year reign of his tradition-bound father and sent the old man into exile. Supported by Britain and most of the ruling family, the new young sultan called for wholesale changes in his realm and announced: "I have watched with growing dismay and increasing anger the inability of my father to use the new-found wealth of this country for the good of the country."

Feuding within royal houses is an ancient Middle Eastern practice, and although modernizing revolutions and generation gap conflicts are newer aspects of Middle Eastern life, they are common now in most parts of the region. Still, it is unusual in this day to see a monarch overturned by a Western-oriented prince rather than by a zealously idealistic junior army officer of middle-class origins and socialist leanings. The source of the leadership that led Oman's modernizing coup d'état of 1970 indicates the nature of the prevailing stage of political evolution in the Gulf states.

There is considerable variation in definitions of the term *the Gulf*. In some situations the label is used in a restrictive, literal sense to refer only to the body of water in the region's center. At other times *Gulf region* is used in a broad sense to include virtually all of Iran, Iraq, and the Arabian penisula. Moreover, the region carries several titles: in the West and in modern Iran it has generally been called the Persian Gulf; Arabs, on the other hand, are conscious of their nationalism and now speak of the Arabian Gulf. In current usage the term *Gulf states* is a narrower concept than *Gulf region*, and it usually refers to a number of small eastern Arabian principalities—Bahrayn, Qatar, Abu Dhabi, Dubai, Sharjah, Ajman, Umm al-Qaywayn, Ras al-Khaymah, Al-Fujayrah, and Oman.

A complex of geographic, cultural, and historical factors implies that there is an identifiable, distinct Gulf region that cuts across the borders of several Middle Eastern states. This region includes two separate but connecting bodies of water—the landlocked Persian or Arabian Gulf and the Gulf of Oman—and the shore districts immediately surrounding these two gulfs. Together these inlets of the Indian Ocean form a corridor linking the Middle East heartland with the seaward approaches to southern Asia and eastern Africa. Some of the oldest, most important communications routes in the Eastern Hemisphere converge here, and today great oil ports and international jetports testify to the area's renewed importance in the world's transport network.

Although the Gulf states lie in the center of the Islamic world, they were relatively isolated from the currents of change that began to alter the political consciousness of the Middle East during the nineteenth and early twentieth centuries. Since World War II, however, traditional modes in the region have been yielding to modernization because the Gulf area contains over half of the world's proven petroleum reserves. Tapping this vast energy source has transformed a parched, poor backwater of the earth into a locale of worldwide political and economic significance.

Unlike most other parts of the Middle East, which have adopted at least the facade of modern government, the Gulf states are characterized by the vitality of political attitudes and practices that are rooted in the traditions of the premodern era and the all-but-dead age of European world empire. Some approaches to modern political life have been made and many more are planned for the near future, but one can understand the contemporary political scene in the region only if he realizes that government is still conducted within a context that remains largely traditional. In practice, political modernization has often meant that new bureaus and offices operate alongside still functioning traditional institutions, producing a peculiar coexistence of old and new political structures and procedures.

Historical Background

Political institutions and processes in the Gulf—perhaps even more strikingly than in other parts of the Middle East—are conditioned by geographic and historical factors.

The Traditional Political Environment

Before Europeans began to penetrate the Gulf in the sixteenth century, distinctive versions of Middle Eastern civilization had evolved

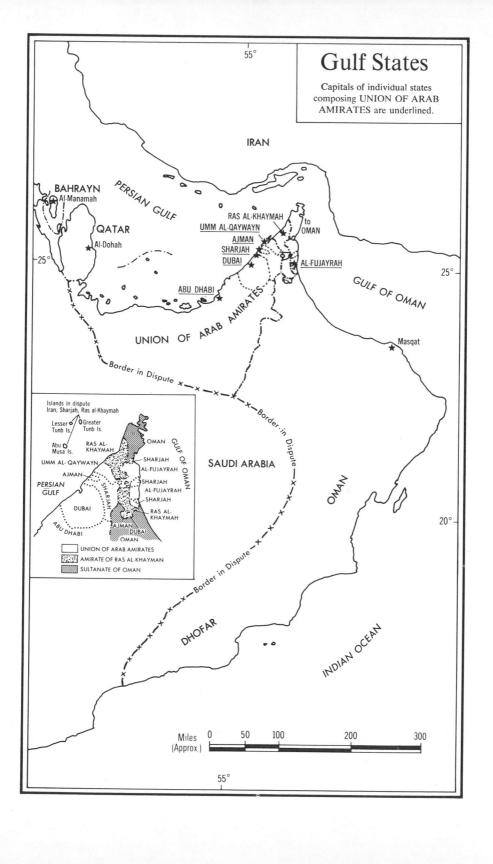

Gulf States

Capitals of individual states composing UNION OF ARAB AMIRATES are underlined.

IRAN

PERSIAN GULF

BAHRAYN
Al-Manamah

QATAR
Al-Dohah

RAS AL-KHAYMAH
UMM AL-QAYWAYN
AJMAN
SHARJAH
DUBAI
to
OMAN

AL-FUJAYRAH

GULF OF OMAN

ABU DHABI

UNION OF ARAB AMIRATES

Masqat

Border in Dispute

Border in Dispute

SAUDI ARABIA

OMAN

Islands in dispute
Iran, Sharjah, Ras al-Khaymah

Lesser Tunb Is. / Greater Tunb Is.

Abu Musa Is.

RAS-AL-KHAYMAH

OMAN

GULF OF OMAN

UMM AL-QAYWAYN

SHARJAH
AL-FUJAYRAH

AJMAN

SHARJAH
AL-FUJAYRAH

PERSIAN GULF

SHARJAH

SHARJAH

RAS AL-KHAYMAH

DUBAI

AJMAN
DUBAI
OMAN

ABU DHABI

☐ UNION OF ARAB AMIRATES
▨ AMIRATE OF RAS AL-KHAYMAN
▨ SULTANATE OF OMAN

Border in Dispute

DHOFAR

INDIAN OCEAN

Miles
(Approx.)

0   50   100   200   300

along the Gulf coast. Until the oil age dawned the region was poorly endowed with the resources to support a high level of civilization; fish, pearls, dates, and camels were the principal products of the area. The prevailing poverty was mitigated somewhat by the Gulf's strategic location athwart communications routes. To serve and to exploit traffic passing along these trade lines and to harvest profits from local products, a number of maritime city-states grew up in the region. Probably the most characteristic elements of premodern Gulf civilization were the activities of its maritime society—commerce, transport, shipbuilding and provisioning, fishing, and pearl diving.

In the seaports the goal of political administration was to create a maritime-economic situation conducive to profit making and to preserve enough internal order so that business could thrive and government revenues could increase. Most seaport towns formed separate city-states and derived their revenues from customs, fees from trade and pearl fishing, other taxes such as those on date palm trees, and particularly on profits from the local ruler's commercial ventures, because a town's ruler was often its largest trader as well. Money was expended to maintain the ruler's military-commercial establishment, to subsidize allies, to bribe potential troublemakers, and to provide tribute to greater powers that might claim rights of suzerainty. No distinction was made between the ruler's public and private spending.

Most city-states emerged from tribal origins, and traditional political organization in the Gulf was based on a comparatively uncomplicated patriarchal-tribal concept. In small city-states the shaykh-patriarch of the dominant local tribe also served as the town's ruler. In larger seaports, although the ruler often had tribal connections of note, his influence depended to a greater extent on his leadership of the local merchant-tribal oligarchy. Also, in larger centers the significance of tribal-oriented political and social attitudes was somewhat blurred because such places housed a conglomeration of peoples.

Yet kinship units of various sizes and forms afforded (and still afford) the organizational context of the area. A large proportion of the town inhabitants hailed from neighboring rural tribes, and it was common for rural dwellers to take seasonal jobs in the towns. Large city-states' authority over nearby tribes seldom was more than nominal. Settled tribes supported themselves by raising crops and fishing (if they were located close to the sea), and nomad tribes raised animals and provided caravan drivers. The rural inhabitants of the region, particularly the nomad bedouin, had a more primitive existence regulated by a less developed, less cosmopolitan system of values than that of the urban dwellers.

Interstate relationships in the Gulf were traditionally marked by frequent outbreaks of violence, so political configurations were constantly in flux. Much of the disorder was produced by the tribal and religious particularism characteristic of the premodern Middle East (factionalism was the norm, not the exception), but aggressive drives to rise above a bare subsistence level of living also provoked trouble. Fluctuations in the level of regional trade or maritime activity were frequent and caused political repercussions by triggering intense competition among port cities. Violence, commerce raiding, and tribal disorder on land and sea accompanied the rise and decline of states.

Many Gulf principalities owed their rise to marauders who in time became patriarchal leaders and state builders. Because traditional political machinery was weak and a state's well-being depended much on the ability of its leader, few states remained long without rivals after the demise of the strong personalities who first led them to regional greatness. Moreover, although larger towns almost always enjoyed de facto independence, it was not unusual for them to recognize the formal supremacy of some greater political power (which might be located either outside or within the region) so long as the local state's essential autonomy and urban interests were preserved.

The Founding of the Modern Gulf States

Most of the existing Gulf states emerged as distinct polities during the eighteenth century. Direct descendants of the traditional city-states of the area, they still display several of their peculiar characteristics, and their foundation and early growth followed the traditional pattern of state-building in the Gulf.

Migrations have long been prime causes of political change in the region, but the late seventeenth and early eighteenth centuries were particularly vexed by tribal movements, which were probably triggered by an unusually long drought in Arabia's interior. The migrations of one tribal group, the Utub, were especially important. The Utub moved out of central Arabia during the seventeenth century to settle in Qatar, where they were introduced to maritime life. Contined pressure stimulated more movement, and they occupied Kuwait about 1716. One of the branches of the tribe, Al Sabah, settled in Kuwait and rules to this day. Other divisions of the Utub moved back to Qatar in the 1760s and founded the short-lived, pearl-fishing city-state Zubarah. In 1782 the Sunni Al Khalifah branch moved on to occupy the wealthy oasis and pearling islands of Bahrayn, where they lived as a warrior-merchant elite holding a tight rein over the archipelago's indigenous agricultural and fishing population. Al Khalifah still provides Bahrayn's ruling house, although their title was disputed by Iran until 1970, when the Persians finally agreed to recognize Bahrayn's independence.

Abu Dhabi was founded in the 1760s on that part of Arabia's east coast later known as the Trucial Coast (after the mid-nineteenth century treaties, or truces, imposed by Britain that forbade local principalities from making war upon each other at sea). The town of Abu Dhabi was established at a coastal point where Bani Yas tribesmen from the interior could obtain fresh water convenient to the offshore pearl-oyster banks they wished to exploit. Most Bani Yas clung to nomadic life, but by the 1790s the shaykh of the tribe's paramount branch, the Al Bu Falah, moved his seat to the town of Abu Dhabi. Later another branch of Bani Yas, the Al Bu Falasa, founded the pearling port of Dubai, which by 1834 had become an independent rival to its mother town.

The secession of a dependent town from its mother city-state because of tribal politics or economic necessity was a common phenomenon in the Gulf, and many of today's seven Trucial States owe their independent existence to such splits. During the late eighteenth century the long-established Qawasim tribe dominated much of the Gulf coast east of Abu Dhabi from their seat at Ras al-Khaymah. However, in subsequent years Ras al-Khaymah was eclipsed by another Qawasim seaport, Sharjah; by 1910 the two towns had split into two states. Between 1936 and 1952 still another Qawasim town, Kalba, enjoyed independence until it was reunited with Sharjah. Two other independent principalities had emerged in 1820, the Nuaym tribal port of Ajman and the Al Ali tribe's port of Umm al-Qaywayn. Even as late as 1952, the separation of the Al-Sharqiyyin tribal state of Al-Fujayrah from Sharjah was recognized. Many of the political problems that still divide the Gulf states can be traced directly to old tribal animosities.

Eighteenth century tribal movements and the reorienting of political entities that were already in existence created a significant political legacy for today's Gulf states. The alliance of the Saudi rulers of a small central Arabian oasis city-state with the revolutionary Wahhabi version of Islam gave birth to an aggressively expansionist state that united much of Arabia—the direct precursor of today's Saudi Arabian monarchy. Oman also experienced political reconstruction during the period under the leadership of the Al Bu Said family, which still provides the sultanate's ruler.

The tumult of the Gulf in the eighteenth century also led to war—a free-for-all struggle among the new political creations of the region for local supremacy. The implications of this contest—so characteristic of the premodern Gulf in causes and form—were destined to draw Britain into the political affairs of the region, a political connection that lasted until 1971.

Britain and the Transitional Order

Western involvement in Gulf affairs began in the sixteenth century with the imposition of loose Portuguese political control. After Portugal's grip relaxed, Britain, the Netherlands, and France established commercial presences in the region, but this European interest weakened during the eighteenth century as trade profits dipped, and only the British were still active in the Gulf by the end of the century.

Britain's interest in the Gulf revived during the first decade of the nineteenth century as an indirect consequence of her rise to supremacy in India and the resulting need to protect India's frontiers. The British recognized that the seaward approaches to India must remain in friendly hands. This interest evolved into an active supervisory role between 1806 and 1820, when British shipping became involved in the general maritime warfare that had broken out in the Gulf in the eighteenth century. The British authorities in India viewed attacks on her shipping as a serious threat to imperial communications, and naval-amphibious expeditions to the Gulf ultimately neutralized the naval power of several regional groups, especially the Qawasim. To safeguard their victory the British forced several of the polities to sign the General Treaty for Suppressing Piracy and Slave Traffic.

This 1820 engagement was the legal foundation on which the structure of British political dominance in the Gulf was built. It was followed in the next three decades by other treaties and policies that curtailed the old free-wheeling practices of interstate relations and placed the local rulers under a tacit British protectorate, although they retained titular sovereignty. Once Britain's supremacy was established, the chief concern of the imperial administration was to ensure the peace of the Gulf's waters. This strategic concern meant that British policy tended to preserve the political status quo and other features of the region's traditional civilization that promoted peaceful occupations. The British discouraged changes that could cause tumult. The period of British dominance thus created a transitional order in which the states and peoples of the Gulf neither abandoned traditionalism—although they moved away from it—nor realized modernism—although they approached it in some limited instances.

The British established the *residency system* based on institutions developed during their political control of India. There had been a British *resident* in the Gulf since the seventeenth century (between 1763 and 1946 he was stationed at Bushire on the Iranian coast, after that at Bahrayn), but his functions were more economic than political. After 1820 the office was redefined so that it became primarily concerned with political affairs, especially with preventing outbreaks of maritime disorder. To accomplish this aim, an almost exclusive reliance was placed on naval patrol by gunboats. (Only in the twentieth century, especially after World War II when safeguarding oil fields on the Gulf's shores became a major concern, were extensive British land forces deployed in the Gulf.) In addition, Britain installed an extraterritorial regime in the region whereby British subjects and Westerners in general were placed under the legal charge of the British resident. The apparatus of extraterritoriality evolved steadily over the years. Until it was virtually scrapped in 1971 it operated through a well-developed hierarchy of British courts that functions throughout the Gulf states.

The initial British impact on the Gulf states stabilized the volatile international environment, but between 1860 and World War I the region's ancient maritime culture was altered profoundly. During the late nineteenth century modern, European-directed communications ventures—steamship lines particularly—and accompanying technological paraphernalia intruded into the Gulf. This invasion undermined much of the Gulf's traditional maritime-oriented economy and seriously dislocated established social and political organization within the local polities. The local maritime communities, especially those connected with commerce and shipping, were disastrously affected by the economic upheaval following the 1860s, and the Gulf was thrown back on its meager resources and became a virtual economic backwater until the oil age. Accompanying these catastrophic developments was growing political impotence within the internal administrations of the Gulf states and increasing political subjugation of those states to extraregional powers. Eastern Arabia came more under British control, and by World War I Britain's supremacy in the Gulf seemed virtually unassailable.

The steady growth of British power meant that the Gulf's potentates had to contend with a political environment of tightening guidelines and restrictions. In 1891 and 1892 a series of so-called exclusive and nonalienation treaties gave Britain explicit control over the foreign relations of several eastern Arabian states (a control that she had already exercised for several decades) and solidified the protectorate there. At the height of Britain's power her position in the Gulf did not depend essentially on formally drawn legal engagements, however. More significant was the evolving corpus of precedents, unofficial understanding, and mutually accepted usages that regulated practical relations between the British and local rulers.

Most rulers became resigned to the fact that the British resident's advice could not be ignored in basic matters. Local political leaders who sought to defy Britain had to contend with sanctions that might take the form of exile for an offender or even a gunboat bombardment. On the other hand, the British often afforded military assistance to loyal princes who were threatened with internal subversion or external dangers. By the early twentieth century British support had become a more important prerequisite for a ruler's continuance in power than his government's popularity among his own subjects. As late as 1970 such modes of indirect rule remained valid; for instance, the British played a large role in overthrowing the rulers of Sharjah in 1965, Abu Dhabi in 1966, and Oman in 1970.

The low point in the disintegration of the efficiency of the eastern Arabian governments was World War I, when only British grants, loans, and subsidies kept several bankrupt local governments afloat. Administrative chaos and internal dissension were widespread. In Oman civil war broke out and a conservative, religion-inspired separatist movement succeeded in maintaining an independent hermit state, the Imamate of Oman, in the country's interior from 1913 until the mid-1950s. To avoid the trouble and expense of assuming direct administrative control of the Gulf states, the British moved to halt the process of political decay and during the 1920s convinced some Gulf rulers to adopt procedures that would inject the germs of modern political practice and curb the most flagrant administrative anachronisms and abuses.

Most noteworthy of the new procedures was the *adviser system*, which called for the employment of a person familiar with modern administrative techniques—invariably a Britisher—to serve a Gulf prince as head of his administration. As the system matured, other European, Indian, or Middle Eastern experts were hired to set up and supervise subsidiary government departments. Initially the most urgent attention was given to reforming finance, public security, and legal justice. Later health, education, and economic development became concerns of

the advisorate. The advisers were not British government officials but
foreign experts officially answerable to and salaried by the local ruler.
Charles Belgrave, who served Bahrayn's ruler between 1926 and 1957,
was the most famous of the advisers. The system was instituted in
Oman in 1920 when a British "prime minister" initiated financial
modernization and legal reforms and recruited a British-officered
mercenary internal security force, the Muscat Levies, the first of several
similar formations that were mustered in the region. After World War II
the adviser system was adopted throughout the Gulf states and remains
the foundation of modern administrative structure and procedure and
the base on which the several state bureaucracies of the region are built.

The coming of the oil age began to erode Britain's supremacy in
the Gulf. By the 1930s American oil interests were undermining
Britain's monopoly over the modern sector of the economy, and the rise
of independent-minded governments in Saudi Arabia, Iraq, and Iran
threatened her political hegemony. The oil era revived the Gulf's
importance in the world economy and ultimately increased its political
significance. Moreover, unlike the economic upheaval of the post-1860
era, the changes brought by oil tended to be constructive. Until the late
1940s the impact of oil exploitation was limited to Iran and Iraq,
eastern Saudi Arabia, and Bahrayn, but since that time much of the rest
of eastern Arabia—most noticeably Kuwait—has also experienced the
varied effects of oil-powered modernization.

Since the late 1940s the course of events in the Gulf has been
determined largely by the interaction of four movements: (1) the
reorientation and redefinition of British interests; (2) the initiation of
genuine indigenous political and social modernization within the Gulf
states—a movement that started in Iran and Iraq before World War II;
(3) the phenomenal expansion of the oil industry in the region; and
(4) the search for new interstate relationships among the Gulf countries
and between these states and extraregional powers interested in the
region.

After World War II Britain began to lay down the burdens of her
worldwide empire, and when the British quit India in 1947, the strategic
concern for the Gulf as part of the Indian empire's frontier screen was
abandoned, although remnants of the old imperial attitudes and a
considerable part of the old political structure in the Gulf remained until
1971. The first apparent change was the switch of the headquarters of the
British residency from Bushire to Bahrayn. In the early 1950s the
residents began to encourage political innovations, but more important
was the manner in which the British began to treat the local rulers. Before
World War II British officialdom often treated the Gulf princelings in the
Indian fashion as so many feudatories, but the postwar breed of officer
tried to avoid overt interference in the internal affairs of the amirates
by building personal ties of friendship and confidence. As one British
resident put it: "A hint dropped here and there in the course of a casual
conversation is often more effective than formal advice."

The waning of the defense-of-India-oriented British policy did
not mean that the Gulf was less important to British interests. Rather,

Britain remained preoccupied with the region's affairs because Gulf-produced oil had become the leading source of Western European and British energy resources and because Gulf oil earnings became a key element in the sterling area's monetary system. Indeed, by the late 1950s the British were maintaining several battalions of troops and naval and air forces at Bahrayn, Sharjah, and Oman to protect their political-economic stake in Gulf oil.

During the 1960s, however, Britain began to doubt the necessity for the hard-line military stance that characterized her Gulf policy in the 1950s. An early manifestation of this change in outlook was Britain's grant of complete independence to Kuwait in 1961. The tremendous cost of maintaining a watch on the Gulf, the resulting drain on Britain's balance of payments, and the belief that this political stance in the Gulf was becoming an anachronism that contributed little to Britain's genuine interests prompted the Labour government to announce in January 1968 that it would surrender Britain's de facto protectorate over the Gulf states by the end of 1971. During the summer of 1971 Bahrayn and Qatar declared themselves fully independent and together with Oman joined the Arab League and the United Nations. Although Britain continued to maintain bases and some air and land forces in Oman, the bulk of her forces finally withdrew from the Gulf on December 2, 1971. She recognized the complete independence of the seven Trucial States, and treaties of friendship replaced the early nineteenth century truce agreements upon which Britain's protectorate regime had been legally founded. In any event, it would be misleading to say that Britain "left" the Gulf when she withdrew most of her military contingents and recognized the unconditional independence of the Gulf states, because she retains important economic interests and political influence there.

Economic and Social Environment

When they gained complete independence in 1971, the Gulf states were undergoing the strains of profound economic and social change. The cause of this movement was the accelerating pace of oil development in the region, which began in the mid-1930s, when Bahrayn's small oil field was brought into production and a large refinery that processes local and Saudi Arabian oil was constructed there. In the 1940s Qatar began to pump oil from its fields, and in the 1960s Oman, Abu Dhabi, and Dubai each brought major new fields into production. The oil reserves of the Gulf states are immense, and especially since the early 1960s the development of both land and offshore deposits has proceeded at a rapid pace. By 1972 over $500 million was being earned by the Gulf states from oil-related activities; the oil revenues of both Oman and Qatar were approaching $80 million; and Abu Dhabi's income exceeded $350 million, and this amirate's per capita income—estimated at $6,500—was the highest in the world.

Most of the region's oil wealth, however, is being exploited by Western and Japanese companies, and royalties and other oil-related income are concentrated in the hands of a small oligarchy of local political leaders and local or foreign businessmen. Extreme poverty exists in some areas among groups that have not yet been touched by the oil bonanza—herding, date growing, pearling, fishing, and trading still sustain the essentially premodern subsistence level of many who dwell in eastern Arabia. However, considerable portions of oil income are beginning to be diverted into new public social welfare and private business operations to benefit the masses. The governments of the Gulf states are developing educational systems that will supply a literate labor pool with the technical skills necessary to operate a modern economy. Public health and housing facilities and communications, including roads, airports, and port facilities, are being pushed, and this development will accelerate as the Gulf states' oil revenues continue to escalate. Such development will also stimulate a more modern political outlook in the populace.

The most obvious social consequence of the Gulf state oil boom is a population explosion. Until the 1950s the total population of the region was considerably less than one million. During the 1960s massive immigration into the Gulf states—chiefly from other Arab states but also from Iran, Pakistan, India, and even East Africa and the West—began to push the population up to an estimated total of 1.3 million in 1972. Bahrayn's population is close to 200,000; Qatar's approximates 100,000; the seven Trucial States have witnessed a rapid rise to nearly 300,000 people; Oman, including its dependency of Dhofar, probably exceeds 700,000. All the Gulf states are overwhelmingly Arab, but growing foreign minority concentrations are present in the larger towns and oil centers.

Political Structure

Although the governments of all the Gulf states are basically patriarchial monarchies, political structures of individual states vary according to the degree of formal institutionalization of consultative legislative procedures and the sophistication of the bureaucratic apparatus. Political structures are thus most complex in the established oil-producing states of Bahrayn and Qatar, are somewhat sophisticated in the new oil states of Abu Dhabi, Dubai, and Oman, and are least changed from traditional forms in the relatively undeveloped states of the eastern Trucial Coast—Sharjah, Ajman, Umm al-Qaywayn, Ras al-Khaymah, and Al-Fujayrah.

The Ruling Families

Political power as exercised by all the Gulf state rulers is an extension of family power defined within a tribal context. The

monarch derives his title from the fact that he was born into the
particular branch of the ruling tribe from which rulers are chosen, and
he is selected ostensibly because of his superior ability to lead and to
represent the ruling family's interest. Succession does not pass
according to primogeniture. Rather, the privilege of exercising sovereignty belongs to the ruling family collectively, and the actual ruler is
the designated leader of a particular household who is vested with the
responsibility of providing political leadership. Thus, succession often
passes from brother to brother, uncle to nephew, or father to younger
(instead of eldest) son, a situation that encourages family factionalism,
and succession struggles, common in the past, are still encountered.
Under British urging, the rulers of several Gulf states have therefore
adopted the practice of naming (after due family consultation) their
successors in an attempt to head off succession disputes.

Family ties and personal alliances remain a key factor in public
affairs and frequently play a determining role in the ruler's selection of his
top aides and advisers. Indeed, until recently it was common to see all the
chief posts of government filled by members of the ruler's family.

Law

Islamic law still plays an important role in all the Gulf states.
The rulers are advised by judges who are specialists in religious law,
although the ruler himself generally serves as final arbiter. In the past
few years the trend in the more developed states has been to place the
administration of justice on a more formal and modern footing. The
present legal apparatus in Qatar exemplifies this trend. The ruling
shaykh has appointed the deputy ruler as a chief justice and has set up
three types of courts: Islamic religious courts, which rule on matters of
personal status and morals; civil courts, which apply a codified civil law
according to published rules of civil and criminal procedure; and labor
and traffic courts, which attempt to order some of the problems that
have attended Qatar's oil boom.

In Oman, which is dominated by the relatively puritanical Ibadi
version of Islam, the traditional religious jurist class still forms an
influential element courted by the ruling sultan; indeed, these specialists in traditional law formed a major bulwark of the conservative,
isolationist Imamate of Oman, an autonomous regime in Oman's
interior provinces until the mid-1950s which still maintains itself as a
government in exile. Modernization of the Gulf states' legal machinery
will be a major concern during the next few years because of the
probable need to erect a substitute for the preindependence British-
administered court system, which has largely regulated the administration of justice among resident Westerners, oil men in particular.

The Bureaucracy

A chief factor differentiating the governments of the Gulf states
is the degree of formal bureaucratization. In undeveloped political

structures, such as those in Al-Fujayrah, Umm al-Qaywayn, Ajman, Ras al-Khaymah, and Sharjah, there is little administrative specialization; the ruling shaykh and a few trusted subordinates can oversee the details of government because the societies are relatively simple and the populations are small. Judicial proceedings are conducted by the rulers themselves in accordance with Islamic law and local custom, and the rulers personally conduct a weekly public majlis, or assembly, at which subjects may present petitions or opinions.

Bahrayn is the most bureaucratized of the Gulf states; development of a modernized political structure started in the 1920s. Bahrayn's population is larger than that of any Gulf state save Oman, the principality has long been a regionally important commercial center, and oil production began in the archipelago in the 1930s, all of which contributed to the evolution of Bahrayn's relatively sophisticated political structure. The ruling amir is assisted in policy-making tasks by a crown prince and an appointed Council of Administration, which consists of a president, eleven members, and a secretary. Presently the council is staffed by members of the ruling Al Khalifah family and the heads of some administrative departments. Administrative tasks are overseen by a secretary of government and conducted in several administrative departments, all of which are headed by Bahraynis (including some princes of the royal house), although several employ foreign experts in responsible positions. The most influential departments are those of Health, Education, Ports and Customs, Information, Police and Public Security, Finance, Oil Affairs, and Law. The Law Department supervises the Bahrayn courts, which administer codes for criminal, pearl-fishing, commercial, and personal status cases. A gendarmerie type of police force is responsible for internal security.

Bahrayn's patriarchal political structure is being modified. Basic constitutional reform, which apparently drew heavily on Kuwaiti precedents, was announced in 1970 and will establish an elected legislature and cabinet government. Bahrayn has conducted cautious experiments with elected bodies since the late 1950s. For instance, local affairs are conducted by four urban municipalities and two rural municipalities administered by municipal councils, half of whose members are elected by male and female taxpayers and half are appointed by the ruler. The government was a pioneer in the Middle East in providing welfare services. Free education and health care have been available in Bahrayn since the 1930s, although not on the lavish scale encountered today in Kuwait. A peculiarity of Bahrayn's political structure is that it is geared to solve municipal problems as well as "national" problems, which underlines the ministate or city-state character Bahrayn shares with most of the Gulf states.

Qatar's ruler also announced in 1970 that he was promulgating a Kuwaiti-style constitutional regime, including a cabinet and a thirty-three-member consultative assembly. Until this development Qatar's government modernization aimed mainly at coping with the practical problems of oil exploitation.

At an intermediate stage of development are the political structures of the newer oil states—Abu Dhabi, Dubai, and Oman. The government apparatus of Abu Dhabi (whose estimated per capita income of $6,500 makes it one of the richest states in the world) is expanding the most rapidly and in the direction of a full-scale welfare state, with twenty-eight administrative departments. Meanwhile, tiny, free-wheeling, business-oriented Dubai's reorganization is aimed at facilitating commercial exchange and carrying out the tasks of municipal government in the city of Dubai itself.

Oman faces a different kind of administrative situation from the other Gulf states because it covers a large habitable land area. Up to this point, however, most of the apparent activity in updating the government of Oman has taken place at the central level, where a new Petroleum Affairs and Development Department and a well-established Military Affairs Office, both of which employ many foreign advisers, are especially active. The several Omani provinces are still regulated by walis (governors) in the traditional manner, but in July 1970 a palace revolution unseated Oman's isolationist ruler in favor of his British-educated, modern son. Comprehensive administrative changes followed; for instance, Oman's south Arabian dependency of Dhofar was no longer treated virtually as the ruler's personal estate, divorced from the regular administration. The expansion of the sultanate's military forces has already extended the central power's influence in the isolated tribal districts of the provinces, most of which were traditionally virtually autonomous.

If the Gulf princes can maintain themselves in power in the post-British years, development of the individual political structures will probably follow either the Saudi Arabian or the Kuwaiti example, at least initially. In Saudi Arabia the ruling family has tried to increase the effectiveness of its bureaucracy but to retain essential power, whereas Kuwait has moved partially away from patriarchal rule toward democratization.

The Union of Arab Amirates

The Union of Arab Amirates—a confederation of Abu Dhabi, Dubai, Sharjah, Umm al-Qaywayn, Ajman, and Al-Fujayrah—came into formal existence in December 1971, when the Trucial States gained final independence from Britain. These states retain their independent identities and control over their own domestic political affairs but agreed to coordinate their foreign, economic, and defense policies.

The idea of federation had been under consideration since the early 1950s, when the British persuaded the quarrelsome shaykhs of the Trucial States to form the Trucial States Council to discuss mutual problems. The confederation concept received renewed impetus when the British announced early in 1968 that they were going to withdraw military protection from the Gulf states in 1971. Most of the region's rulers decided that they had to act together or face an uncertain future separately. Originally the union was envisioned as a link among all the small eastern Arabian principalities. However, after two years of wrangling the large amirates of Bahrayn and Qatar opted for separate independence—a status they achieved in the summer of 1971—and a small Trucial State, Ras al-Khaymah, decided to remain independent. It is possible that in the future Bahrayn, Qatar, Ras al-Khaymah, and possibly even the large Sultanate of Oman may elect to join the union.

The union's highest authority is the Supreme Council, which consists of the six rulers. The decisions of this body are binding only if they are unanimously approved. A legislature of thirty-four members will be elected; Abu Dhabi and Dubai will each hold eight seats; Sharjah, six seats; and Ajman, Umm al-Qaywayn, and Al-Fujayrah, four seats each. The first president of the union, who will serve a five-year term, is Shaykh Zayid of Abu Dhabi; the first vice-president is Shaykh Rashid of Dubai, and his son and heir, Shaykh Makhtum, is the first prime minister. A fifteen-man cabinet will perform the technical executive functions of the union. Initially the union's capital will be Abu Dhabi, but a new capital will be built on the border between Abu Dhabi and Dubai by 1977.

The rulers have evolved plans for mutual defense that involve the use of the present 1,500-man, British-officered Trucial Oman Scouts as a nucleus from which a mobile, armor-equipped, federal army of brigade strength can be formed. A small flotilla of patrol ships and a forty-plane air force, including fighter bombers, transports, and helicopters, is also being planned. Seasoned British officers will provide leadership and technical advice for several years. The chief mission of the federal armed forces is to blunt a threat of destruction by internal subversion of any member government and to provide some deterrent against invasion. In addition, the individual principalities will continue to increase their own internal security forces.

All the union's members see association as an uneasy marriage of convenience. Alliance groups asserted themselves in the bargaining that accompanied the birth of the federation. One group that has tended to follow the lead of Abu Dhabi includes Sharjah, Ajman, and Umm al-Qaywayn. Dubai has the support of Al-Fujayrah. The cement that binds the union's members together is their need to defend their independence, sovereignty, and security.

Political Processes

Political decisions in the Gulf states revolve increasingly around the rapid economic and social development that has accompanied the rise of the regional oil industry. Encouragement of an environment conducive to continued economic growth is considered more important by local governments than establishment of broadly based participation in political processes or political safeguards for civil rights, and the peculiar blend of paternalistic traditionalism and free-spending welfare statism characteristic of the present political situation will probably continue for several years.

Despite the recent proliferation of administrative bureaus, the mechanics of most political processes are still quite traditional. Theoretically most Gulf state governments are absolute, but in actuality a ruler is bound not only by the strictures of Islamic law and local tradition but also by public opinion. Generally, no significant matters are settled by the ruler without consulton with other important members of his family and the prestigious elders of the community. In Bahrayn and Qatar this consultation process was formalized by the creation of advisory councils, and it is being extended as newly established parliaments begin their deliberations. Other Gulf states will probably follow this precedent.

In addition to the ruler and his family, the traditional oligarchy—a mixture of the tribal elite, the established local commercial leaders, and the major religious figures—also participates in political policy formation. This leadership group increasingly includes men with modern educations, advanced technical skills, and modern attitudes, a group that is growing in number and significance, that is active in both private enterprise and the government bureaucracy, and that in many cases, particularly in Bahrayn, includes sons of the old oligarchs who have received a modern education. Some senior foreign experts also participate in policy making; some of these men are salaried advisers of the ruler and others are private consultants or employees of foreign companies.

Political organizations are still unsophisticated in most of the Gulf states. No recognized political parties exist, although in the 1950s a group called the Committee of National Union, a Pan-Arab alliance of students, intellectuals, oil laborers, and town artisans and tradesmen, was active in Bahrayn. The ruler cracked down severely on the committee, however, and with the help of British troops he scattered its leaders, some of whom were jailed or exiled. This group has recently shown signs of reconstituting itself and will undoubtedly play a large role in Bahrayn's new parliament under one guise or another. Labor unions as such are not allowed to operate in any of the Gulf states.

Political life in most Gulf states is being increasingly affected by the activities of social, professional, and community "clubs." In Bahrayn, for example, virtually the entire urban and rural population is included in such organizations. Club leaders are coming to be regarded as the membership's spokesmen in dealings with the government, and they are thus assuming a role in political life, albeit an unofficial one. Some clubs are adopting ideological stances, especially those with large numbers of educated, young members, and these clubs may well become the focus of important political action in the future.

Citizens who are most disaffected with political trends bided their time until the British troops left, but after this occurred more serious opposition to government and political processes began. With the exception of the ultraconservative traditionalists who support the theocratic imam in Oman or disgruntled members of various ruling families, most of the opposition is oriented toward revolutionary Arab socialism inspired by the Pan-Arab Baath party, especially its Iraqi branch. Radical sentiment is particularly apparent among the large number of migrants—many of them of Palestinian origin—who have been recruited to fill new jobs created by oil exploitation. One revolutionary group, the National Front for the Liberation of the Occupied Arabian Gulf under the direction of Muhammad Ahmad Ghassani with headquarters in Aden, is an outgrowth of the Dhofar Liberation Front. The National Front for the Liberation of the Occupied Arabian Gulf, which has received aid from the People's Democratic Republic of Yemen and from Communist China, is currently directing most of its efforts at toppling the royal regime in Oman, but it has also presented a program calling for the armed overthrow of all the present regimes in the Gulf states, removal of all vestiges of British political influence, and elimination of Western oil monopolies.

Although the number who favor revolution in the Gulf states is small, the possibility of an upheaval is probably highest in Bahrayn, which contains a large, politically aware indigenous group. If a truly revolutionary regime were to come to power in one or more of the Gulf states, it would doubtless be dominated by a faction drawn from the ranks of the young, educated, modern men, and it would probably concern itself largely with increasing the capabilities of the existing political apparatus and attempting to remove the elements of traditionalism that still characterize political structures and processes.

Oil-Related Problems

Three interrelated problems currently vex the political climate in the Gulf states: the relationship between the local governments and the foreign oil companies that operate within their territories, the status of migrants and minorities within the states, and the borders between the states.

When the oil companies first began operating in the Gulf they found that the local population was almost totally devoid of modern knowledge, and they thus had to provide education and social welfare services to develop modern skills. In effect, the oil companies had the status of autonomous economic-political units operating within the state. Although a close partnership between oil companies and the local ruling elite continues, the recent progress of the Gulf states in providing their own education, health, welfare, and economic development projects has lessened the influence of the oil companies.

Company-government relations have not always run smoothly despite their common interest in maintaining the flow of oil. The states naturally seek to increase their share of oil profits, and they press for increased oil production at every opportunity, although this attitude is less characteristic of the Gulf states than of more politically

sophisticated parts of the Middle East. In addition, the states seek
increased control over company policies by increasing national representation on boards of directors and among the companies' top
management. To accomplish these goals, the Gulf states that produce
oil have government departments that deal with the oil companies, and
these departments are among the most important of all government
offices.

Oil production and the accompanying economic boom have
attracted a large number of migrant laborers into the oil-producing Gulf
states from other parts of the Gulf region, other Arab countries, India,
and Pakistan, and in some states the migrants threaten to swamp the
indigenous population. Politically they are a disturbing element no
matter how necessary they may be economically, for they are a rootless
proletariat with little stake in their adopted, often temporary,
homelands. There is considerable defensive agitation among the
long-established residents of several of the Gulf states to deny the
migrants permanent residence or citizenship. The problem is made even
more complicated because an estimated 75 percent of the migrants are
young, unmarried males—a particularly volatile group that could
become a decisive element in a situation of political revolution or rapid
modernization.

Another oil-related problem concerns the borders of the states.
Traditionally the Gulf states were content to recognize the fuzziest of
frontiers, but with the coming of oil exploitation it became necessary
to draw more exact borders, a process that began in the Gulf in the
1920s and continues today. Border disputes reached their peak in the
1950s in the so-called Buraymi dispute, which produced violent
confrontations involving the armed forces of a number of regional
states, Saudi Arabia, and Britain. Border disputes are currently focusing
on rival claims to small islands and the seabed of the Gulf itself. Most of
these disagreements are being negotiated successfully, with the exception of the violent dispute between Iran and several Gulf states over the
ownership of three small islands in the lower Gulf.

Foreign Policy

Foreign policy questions may well determine the future for the
Gulf states. The individual states cannot generate enough political and
military power by themselves to counter efforts by strong outside
forces to overthrow them or to cripple their independence.

Until recently Britain supervised the foreign relations of all the
Gulf states. But since full independence was achieved in 1971 the Gulf
states, both individually and collectively, have been focusing attention
on problems of foreign relations. Most of these problems revolve
around three questions: What will be the future structure of interregional relationships? What will be the nature of their relations with
the other Arab states? and What will be the nature of their relations

with the great powers, especially Britain, the United States, the Soviet Union, Japan, and Communist China, who have shown interest in the region?

The birth of the Union of Arab Amirates is, of course, one response to the need for the Gulf states to define their foreign relationships. If the union is successful, it will allow the member states to solve the problem of their relations with other member states and will allow them to deal with outside powers as a united bloc. Kuwait and Oman appear ready to form a close, cooperative relationships with the union states. Also, the union, like Bahrayn, Oman, and Qatar, has joined the Arab League and the United Nations. These actions will involve the Gulf states more intimately in the politics of the Arab-Israeli confrontation, even if their contribution to the Arab cause is only financial and moral support.

Of more immediate significance will be the relationship of the Gulf states with Iran and Saudi Arabia. Iran is fearful of a radical Arab nationalist overthrow of the status quo in the Gulf after 1971. Initially she was not enthusiastic about the union, mainly because of the projected membership of Bahrayn, but since the Iranians agreed in 1970 to the principle of Bahrayni independence outside the union, they have seemed willing to accept the idea. Tehran's occupation of Gulf islands which may contain oil and that are also claimed by three small Trucial States continues to irritate Iranian-Gulf state relations.

Saudi Arabia's attitude toward the Gulf states, as well as the course of its own modernization effort, will affect profoundly the future of the small states clinging to its eastern borders. In the past Saudi Arabia has claimed large tracts of the territory of individual Gulf States, particularly Abu Dhabi and Oman; however, the Saudis have indicated that they intend to support the integrity of the Gulf states in the future. Also, late in 1968 Iran and Saudi Arabia agreed to mount a joint surveillance over the Gulf, to respect each other's rights and the political status quo in the region, and to cooperate in blunting revolutionary activity there. By renouncing ambitions to dominate the area individually, Saudi Arabia and Iran have enhanced prospects for the continued existence of the present regimes in the Gulf states.

On the other side of the political spectrum, Iraq, because of its revolutionary domestic program and its foreign policy of cooperation with the Soviet Union, is viewed with wary suspicion by other Gulf countries. Nevertheless, the Gulf states—Bahrayn and some of the Trucial States especially—have shown a willingness to cultivate good relations with Baghdad as insurance against Iranian moves to extend its influence.

Oman is a special case, because it is not contemplating membership in the union at the present time. Until recently Oman has held a more or less isolationist position, although it has maintained a close de facto alliance with Britain. Now that Oman has a relatively forward-looking government and has joined the ranks of oil producers, however, the old isolationism is being replaced by a more open foreign policy, a tendency that will be encouraged by the sultanate's need to cultivate friends to offset the uncertainties of having the unfriendly People's Democratic Republic of Yemen pushing against its western borders.

Events in the Gulf states will continue to reflect the pressures of outside powers interested in the area. Considerable investment capital will doubtless have to be channeled from oil earnings into less wealthy but more populous Arab states in order to retain their goodwill. The Soviets are evidencing considerable interest in increasing their role in the area; Communist China is becoming interested in the Gulf as a potential source of oil to power its industry; the United States has immense oil investments in the region and has an obvious interest in seeing the Gulf states progress toward modernity within an environment of political stability; and Britain remains an especially significant factor in Gulf politics. With the exception of some contingents that will remain in Oman, British military forces have been evacuated, but Britain's political and economic influence will remain as long as the Gulf states seek her advice and technical aid.

Political Prospects

It is an open question whether the Gulf states can survive as separate, independent entities in the rapidly changing political environment of the Middle East. With the exception of Oman, which is based on an extensive territory and a distinct Ibadi Islamic subculture, the other Gulf states originally were little more than the political expression of various tribal particularisms. Most of these states would have disappeared during the course of the nineteenth or twentieth century without the prop provided by the British protectorate regime. Their continued existence is being upheld by their rapidly expanding role as suppliers of petroleum and their consequent importance to the world's economy and by the fact that many other countries have political or economic interests in the Gulf states that they do not wish to abandon. If the Gulf states survive, it will probably be the result of a policy of prudent balancing of conflicting foreign ambitions against one another. Certainly the Gulf states cannot develop—at least not in the near future—the raw power that would enable them to trust their own intrinsic political strength as the ultimate guarantee of their endurance.

But will the Gulf states have the desire to maintain their independence in the future? The present generation of leaders is derived mainly from the aristocratic and oligarchical families that always have been closely identified with the preservation of the separate principalities' identities. But the older generation of leaders is being replaced by rulers and administrators who wish to encourage large-scale modernization in at least the economic and social spheres and who are willing to engage in some political cooperation with neighboring Gulf states. Such was the case in Abu Dhabi in 1966 when tight-fisted old Shaykh Shakhbut was replaced by development-minded Shaykh Zayid; such

was the case in Oman in 1970 when the wily hermit sultan, Said ibn
Taymur, was toppled by his son Qabus.

Generally the new breed of forward-looking, albeit aristo-
cratically sired Gulf state rulers is willing to use the services of young
technocrats to rationalize the structure of their administrative apparatus; they also display a cautious readiness to allow a formal sharing of
policy-making power by approving the establishment of legislative
bodies. The Union of Arab Amirates is to have a "national assembly."
Bahrayn and Qatar are initiating legislatures and a version of cabinet
rule, and other states doubtless will follow these precedents. Nevertheless, initially these legislatures will probably be dominated by the
ruling families and scions of the local tribal oligarchy, and these people
are committed to preserving their countries' separate identities.
Lower-class voices will make themselves heard to the point where they
may assume essential control of political life, however. Forty years of
modern-style education in Bahrayn have produced a generation that is
familiar with the Pan-Arab ideals of various nationalist ideologies, and
perhaps such ideas will erode the devotion of the emerging educated
masses to the idea of preserving the separate independence of a group
of tiny, vulnerable states. In short, the validity of the Gulf states
separateness must be reasserted or they may simply be absorbed into
larger entities.

A factor that might discourage such a withering away of
internal allegiance to these ministates is the increasing attractiveness of
local economic opportunities and welfare services that are accompanying the rise of a wealthy, oil-based economy in the Gulf. As in Kuwait,
it is doubtful if the Gulf states' peoples—although they will give
theoretical approval to Arab national aims—will in practice wish to
surrender their present chances for an affluent life by voluntarily
submerging their interests and standard of living.

This does not mean that the politically weak but economically
rich Gulf states will be allowed to settle their own fate. The future of
eastern Arabia is tied to the course of external events and ambitions
over which it has little control. Considerable skill will be necessary if
the small but very rich states are to preserve their independence in an
environment in which they are ringed by larger, more powerful
neighbors. It is apparent that the ability of Britain or other outside
powers to guarantee a peaceful status quo in the Gulf is decreasing; no
outside power can hold back or channel the tide of change that is
overtaking the Gulf. Undoubtedly some sort of regional understanding
among the Gulf states and Saudi Arabia, Iraq, and Iran will have to be
reached if the area is to avoid constant crises and perhaps serious armed
conflicts.

The tide of change that now surges through the Gulf will
determine its future. The prospects of the region will therefore involve
four major problems: What will be the nature of the economic, social,
and intellectual forces that operate in the Gulf? How will the system of
internal order within the Gulf states adapt to the increasing strains that
result from rapid and pervasive modernization? How will the claims of

regional and Pan-Arab nationalisms be accommodated to the still parochial tribal and family loyalties that undergird the political life of all the Gulf states? What posture will the Gulf states assume toward the powerful foreign countries that retain significant interests in the region?

The approach that the Gulf states will adopt to cope with their problems is indicated by Kuwait, a country that has experienced nearly identical pressures to those that now vex the Gulf states. Many observers in eastern Arabia consider Kuwait a model that can provide useful precedents for their own confrontation with modernity. In many ways the Gulf states today are similar to southwest Arabia at the time of Britain's withdrawal from that region. It is an open question whether the ruling princes of the Gulf states will be able to avoid the fate of their erstwhile southwest Arabian counterparts now that Britain no longer protect them. However, the Gulf states possess advantages not present in southwest Arabia, the most notable of which is the great wealth the Gulf's oil resources provide and the resulting rapid economic and social change in the region. Also, the rulers of the Gulf states have had more time to prepare to meet the political uncertainties that full independence will bring.

Selected Bibligraphy

Adamiyat, Fereydoun. *Bahrein Islands: A Legal and Diplomatic Study of the British-Iranian Controversy*. New York: Frederick A. Praeger, 1955.
A basic study of the Bahrayn dispute presented from the Iranian point of view.

Arabian American Oil Company. *Oman and the Southern Shore of the Persian Gulf*. Haarlem (no date).
An excellent study of recent events in the Trucial States and Oman; devotes much attention to tribal affairs.

Busch, Brinton C. *Britain and the Persian Gulf: 1894-1914*. Berkeley and Los Angeles: University of California Press, 1967.
A scholarly treatment of Britain's imperial involvement in the Gulf area.

Hay, Sir Rupert. *The Persian Gulf States*. Washington, D.C.: Middle East Institute, 1959.
A standard description of the Gulf states in the post-World War II period by a former British political resident in the area.

Hazard, Harry, ed. *Eastern Arabia*. New Haven, Conn.: Human Relations Area File Press, 1956.
An interesting compendium of information drawn from a myriad of sources; excellent bibliography attached.

Human Relations Area File. New Haven, Conn.
An archive of photocopied articles concerning the Gulf states; additions to the file made periodically; organized topically and geographically.

Kelly, J. B. "The Legal and Historical Basis of the British Position in the Persian Gulf." *St. Antony's Papers*, no. 4, *Middle Eastern Affairs*. London: St. Antony's College, 1958.
A statement of the growth of British political power in the Gulf in the nineteenth century.

Landen, Robert G. *Oman since 1856: Disruptive Modernization in a Traditional Arab Society*. Princeton, N.J.: Princeton University Press, 1967.
A political and economic history of modern Oman; concentrates on the breakdown of the traditional maritime society of the Gulf under the pressures of modernization.

Lorimer, J. G. *Gazetteer of the Persian Gulf, Oman, and Central Arabia*. Calcutta: Government of India, 1908-15.
A monumental, encyclopedic, four-volume study of the Persian Gulf in early modern times.

Mann, Clarence. *Abu Dhabi: Birth of an Oil Sheikdom*. Beirut: Khayats, 1964.
A straightforward history drawn very largely from Lorimer.

Marlowe, John. *The Persian Gulf in the Twentieth Century*. London: Cresset, 1962.
The standard account of the recent history of the Gulf region; devotes at least as much attention to Iraqi, Saudi Arabian, and Iranian history as it does to events in the Gulf states.

Middle East Economic Digest and *Arab Report and Record*. London, current.
Up-to-date information about political and economic events in the Gulf states; indispensable for the student who wishes current data. These publications issued four special reports on various Gulf states in 1969, each about twenty pages long:
> *Abu Dhabi.* June 1969.
> *Dubai.* July 1969.
> *Qatar.* October 1969.
> *Bahrain.* December 1969.

Princeton University Conference. *Middle East Focus: The Persian Gulf.* Princeton, N.J.: Princeton University Press, 1969.
The proceedings of a conference. Valuable contributions from many of the world's leading students of the Gulf concerned with everything from political prospects to the Gulf's fisheries.

Qubain, Fahim J. "Social Classes and Tensions in Bahrain."*Middle East Journal* 9 (1955): 269-80.
One of the few readily available discussions on the topic.

Wilson, A. T. *The Persian Gulf: An Historical Sketch from Earliest Times to the Beginning of the Twentieth Century*. London: George Allen and Unwin, 1928.
A classic presented from a pro-British imperial perspective.

Yemen Arab Republic*

Part of the area known to the Romans as *Arabia felix*, or fortunate Arabia, Yemen has been a home for people, governments, and perhaps more than its share of politics for several thousand years. Whatever its relative fame in ancient times, there is no doubt that this land has been consigned to obscurity for well over a millenium. In 1962, literally overnight, Yemen became the scene of a civil war, which brought the inevitable foreign intervention, world attention, the United Nations, nationalistic slogans, a new government, new institutions, international conferences, truces, and more conferences. This obscure land is no longer quite so remote, but neither is it yet understood by the outside world. In Yemen, as in so many parts of the Arab world, history and tradition strongly shape the new political institutions and processes.

Historical Background

Ancient Yemen was dominated by a succession of South Arabian dynasties centered in and south of the present republic's boundaries, the most famous of which were the Minaean and Sabaean (Queen Bilqis of the Sabaeans is better known to English-speaking readers as the Queen of Sheba). Here the peninsula's earliest civilizations took root and flourished as a result of a favorable climate and their location astride important trade routes. Local rulers extracted heavy tolls from northbound caravans bearing South Arabian frankincense, a rare product that was highly prized in the Mediterranean

*The author is a foreign service officer. The views expressed are his own and do not reflect those of the U.S. Department of State.

world, where it was consumed in the fires of Greek and Roman temples. However, following the development of seaborne trade by the Romans, the regional economy withered, and with the collapse of the famed earthen dam at Marib in the fifth century A.D., Yemen entered an epoch of poverty from which it has yet to emerge.

For several centuries before the Islamic conquest in 631 A.D., Yemeni and South Arabian kingdoms alternately conquered or were conquered by rival African dynasties in Abyssinia, and during this period Christianity and Judaism took root and enjoyed fluctuating strength. The pattern by which Islam supplanted these religions resulted in a factionalism that remains politically significant. Sunni Muslims, who subscribed to the Shafai school of interpretation, established themselves in Yemen's southern highlands and coastal plains at an early date. By the end of the ninth century rival Shia peoples had settled in the northern mountain areas. The Shiites were adherents of the Zaydi sect, named for Zayid, the great-grandson of Ali (the son-in-law of the Prophet). The Zaydis reached Yemen in 893 under the leadership of Hadi Yahya, a grandson of the philosopher al-Qasim al-Rassi, who in turn was a direct descendant of the Prophet's daughter Fatimah. Zaydi kings henceforth exercised varying degrees of hegemony over the lowland Sunnis for a period of ten and one-half centuries, until the Republican revolution of 1962. These kings were imams—religious chiefs—who used their theocratic power to build a tightly knit oligarchic society, the territorial limits of which were determined by shifting tribal allegiances and by what military power the imams could muster.

During the two periods of Ottoman occupation—from 1568 to 1630 and from 1849 to 1904—the power of the Zaydi imams was often eclipsed by that of Turkish governors. Ottoman suzerainty was tenuous at best, however, and was usually limited to major towns and the coast.

Yemen had become isolated from regional trade and communications long before the Ottoman era, but the Western European voyages of discovery stirred these regional backwaters. Portugal's discovery of the Cape route to India and the subsequent growth of Portuguese, British, and Dutch seaborne trade brought merchants from these and other nations to trade at the Yemeni ports of Hodeida and Mocha. The latter name became synonymous with coffee, which was grown in the mountains and loaded at this port for Europe.

By occupying Aden in 1839, Britain established a military presence in South Arabia, which limited the southern expansion of Turkish and Yemeni influence and encouraged rival territorial claims by South Arabian sultans. When the Turks strengthened their hold over Yemen in the second half of the nineteenth century, they faced increased internal dissidence and a hostile British presence in Aden.

Imam Yahya obtained significant concessions from the Ottomans after 1904 by carrying on a revolt begun by his grandfather in 1891, and Turkey finally evacuated Yemen after the Ottoman defeat in World War I. Yahya then came into conflict over his southern frontiers with the British-backed sultans of the Aden Protectorate, with

King Abd al-Aziz ibn Saud, and with the independent Idrisi ruler of Asir on his northern border. These latter disputes led in 1934 to a war with Saudi Arabia, which the Saudis quickly won. However, ibn Saud returned captured Yemeni territory without delay or punitive demands and concluded a treaty with Yahya that allowed demarcation of their common frontier.

As World War II approached, Mussolini made considerable diplomatic efforts to win Yahya over to the Fascist cause and to thus improve Italy's strategic position vis-à-vis Britain at the southern entrance to the Red Sea. Despite his dispute with Britain over the Aden Protectorate frontier, however, the imam remained uncommitted.

In the mid-1940s dissident Yemeni exiles in Aden and elsewhere in the Arab world formed a "Free Yemeni" organization to mount a revolution, and in 1948 followers of Abdullah al-Wazir assassinated Yahya but were in turn overpowered by the imam's son and heir apparent, Ahmad. Ahmad reigned from 1948 until 1962, during which time he made Taiz the national capital for fear of living amid the intrigues of Sanaa.

In 1958 Ahmad's son, Crown Prince Muhammad al-Badr, was influential in bringing Yemen into the short-lived United Arab States, a loose, three-way confederation with the newly formed United Arab Republic that had joined Egypt with Syria, and also obtained extensive military and technical assistance from Eastern Europe. Ahmad became increasingly uneasy with a subsequent growth in Egyptian influence, which worked against his traditionalist regime and exacerbated his relations with South Arabia's anti-Nasserist sultans, and Nasser dissolved the United Arab States in late 1961 following Syria's secession from the UAR. However, by then the neighboring South Arabian sultans had become sufficiently suspicious of Ahmad's intentions to give serious thought to creating an anti-Yemeni federation (which is explained in more detail in the following chapter).

Despite these increasing brushes with the outside world, Ahmad managed to keep Yemen more or less in its traditional state of isolation throughout his reign, and after surviving numerous assassination attempts by domestic enemies, he died of natural causes in September 1962. His son, al-Badr, succeeded him immediately and announced his intention of promulgating some modernizing measures, but his rule ended within a week—on September 26—when Colonel Abdullah al-Sallal led the Sanaa garrison in a revolt. Al-Badr and his followers escaped from Sanaa to the northern mountains and from there engaged in a long and bloody conflict with the revolutionaries.

Al-Sallal proclaimed a republic and received immediate military and technical support from Egypt, whereas al-Badr received help from Saudi Arabia, Iran, and initially Jordan. The Egyptian-backed Republicans were able to control most urban areas and communications routes from the outset, but al-Badr's Royalists occupied a considerable area of the northern highlands and managed to tie down a large Egyptian expeditionary force that at times included well over fifty thousand men. Ostensibly a Yemeni civil conflict, the hostilities soon pitted Saudi Arabia against Egypt and became a focal point for broader monarchist-revolutionist Arab tensions and a concern to the great powers. To encourage withdrawal of Egyptian and Saudi support to the warring factions, the United Nations established an observer mission in 1963; however, due to its limited mandate and modest resources this mission was unable to effect a disengagement. Later moderate Republicans banded together as the Third Force to reconcile the two sides, but this effort also failed.

Despite his leading role in the 1962 insurgency, President al-Sallal failed to provide the charismatic leadership that he and Egypt needed to uphold the revolutionary republic against al-Badr's Royalists and the increasingly hostile Republican moderates. Accordingly, al-Sallal left Sanaa for Cairo in mid-1965 for extended "consultations." The prime ministry briefly passed to the moderate Ahmad Numan and then to Lieutenant General Hassan al-Amri, who became increasingly defiant of Cairo. In a surprise move, al-Sallal returned to Sanaa in mid-1966 and reimposed a vigorously pro-Egypt regime. Al-Amri and a number of other prominent politicians journeyed to Cairo to protest al-Sallal's return and found themselves under house arrest. Meanwhile, the UAR continued to face strong Royalist guerrilla actions over vast and forbidding terrain.

The Arab-Israeli War in June 1967 rendered Egypt's difficult military situation in Yemen even more untenable, and at the same time it provided an unexpected opportunity for disengagement and rapprochement with Saudi Arabia. President Nasser and King Faysal agreed that Egyptian forces would be shifted from Yemen to the northern front in exchange for withdrawal of Saudi aid to the Royalists, and the UAR evacuation began without delay and was completed by mid-December 1967.

Al-Sallal left Yemen in October to find alternative sources of support in the Arab world, but shortly after his departure pro-al-Amri nationalists seized control of the government. Back in power, al-Amri found himself under Royalist siege as the last Egyptian troops departed, but he was aided by an eleventh-hour airlift of Soviet weapons and dissension within Royalist ranks and was able to hold out and eventually to regain a major portion of Republican territory. With support from the powerful Hashid tribal confederation, al-Amri also managed to turn back several subsequent Royalist offensives and to frustrate an attempted coup by leftist army officers in August 1968. However, he resigned the premiership in July 1969 following a series of intragovernmental disputes, although he retained his seat on the influential Republican Council. Al-Amri's resignation and the resultant confusion in Republican ranks failed to benefit the Royalists because al-Badr's ill health, waning Saudi support, and the assassination of Prince Abdullah bin Hassan presented them with a leadership crisis at the same time.

The next government, which lasted until February 1970, was headed by Abdullah Kurshumi, an engineer by profession and a former minister of public works, and it was followed by the government of

Muhsin al-Ayni, who had served previously as Yemeni ambassador to Washington, the U.N., and Moscow. Throughout the last half of 1969 and into the beginning of 1970, Republican-Royalist hostilities continued on a sporadic basis, particularly around the northern city of Saada, which fell to the Royalists in February. During the Islamic Foreign Ministers' Conference in late March in Jiddah, al-Ayni (who was serving concurrently as foreign minister) conferred with Saudi officials about a peace settlement.

The talks were successful and resulted in an immediate cease-fire between the Republicans and Royalists and a series of moves toward rapprochement between Sanaa and Jiddah. The Saudis withdrew support from the Royalists, and the Yemeni government announced its willingness to accept the return of all Yemeni exiles (except the imam and members of his immediate family). On May 23 a number of Royalist and dissident Republican exiles reached Sanaa. Three ministerial portfolios, twelve seats on the newly expanded National Council, two added seats on the Republican Council, and two governorships were offered to the returnees. By mid-1970 the first tangible steps toward meaningful resolution of the long civil war had taken place.

Yemen's first permanent constitution was promulgated on December 30, 1970. This constitution provided for a three-to-five-man plural executive, the Republican Council, but various leaders called for abolition of the council and urged al-Iryani to become president. A compromise was reached by installing a three-man council, the smallest permitted by the new constitution. Muhsin al-Ayni resigned in February 1971 to allow elections for the new Majlis al-Shura and formation of a new government. The aging "Free Yemeni" leader and political moderate, Ahmad Numan, assumed the premiership under council chairman al-Iryani in May, but he resigned in August in the face of a budget crisis. Following a brief but frantic search for a successor, General Hassan al-Amri formed a new government on August 23; however, he was forced into exile only two weeks later after a bizarre episode in which he shot and killed a Sanaa photographer. Al-Iryani then summoned Muhsin al-Ayni from his ambassadorial post in Paris to form yet another government in mid-September. Al-Ayni inherited a more troubled Yemen than he had left seven months earlier. Relations with the neighboring People's Republic had deteriorated, budget problems had become more acute, and hinterland tribes were becoming more vocal in their demands on the central government. Yemen had found peace, but not respite from its myriad problems.

Political Environment

Yemen is a land of contrasts and paradoxes. Its forbidding mountains and inaccessible valleys form an agricultural zone that perhaps could feed the entire peninsula. Until recently Yemen was a hermit kingdom, yet its emigrants were found in Arabia, East Africa, and even in the United States. Orthodox and heterodox Islam exist side by side. The country is inhabited by both nomadic tribesmen and sedentary villagers. The imam was rich and the masses were poor; Republican government finances are austere, whereas private capital is increasingly bountiful.

Geographical Determinants

The present Yemen Arab Republic covers about 75,000 square miles and is bounded on the west by the Red Sea, on the south by the Peoples' Democratic Republic of Yemen, and on the north by the Kingdom of Saudi Arabia. To the east Yemen's terrain becomes less inhabited and less fertile and eventually blends into the trackless Rub al-Khali (Empty Quarter); despite the imaginative lines drawn by some map makers, no eastern frontier has ever been demarcated.

The Tihama Desert plain, varying in width from twenty to fifty miles, parallels the Red Sea coast. The Tihama ends abruptly in a series of rugged mountain ranges running in a general north-south direction, which are bisected transversely by deep *wadis* (valleys containing rivers subject to alternating seasonal dryness and torrential flows). These mountains form the highest part of the Arabian peninsula and Yemen's intermountain plateaus contain the peninsula's best agricultural land. Seasonal monsoon clouds strike the upper mountain areas and in most years precipitate generous rains that make much of the countryside green. Some rainfall is captured for hillside agriculture by a network of ancient terraces; the voluminous remainder rushes seaward through the fertile wadis and eventually under the sands of the Tihama. By diverting seasonal floods or drilling to the fairly shallow water table, Tihama farmers can produce impressive crops in most years.

Despite a triangular road network that connects the three major cities—Sanaa, Hodeida, and Taiz—the country's mountainous terrain is a formidable obstacle to communications. Internal and external air services are minimal, and sea transport is limited to one modern port—Hodeida—which unfortunately is too small and too shallow to operate efficiently. Climatic conditions are related to altitude; the Tihama is swelteringly hot for half the year, whereas the mountains and plateaus are perennially temperate.

Geography has been a strong determining factor in the evolution of Yemen's political, economic, and social systems. Mountainous terrain has impeded communications and has thus reinforced particularism. Ample rainfall (by regional standards) has facilitated the growth of an agricultural economy and a sedentary population, and a lack of oil or other exportable raw materials has left Yemen's approximately 5.5 million inhabitants among the poorer Arabs. Although political processes have been modernized since the revolution, the Yemeni social system is essentially a product of physical remoteness and resultant ideological isolation.

The People

Tribal and Religious Groups: Throughout its prerevolutionary stages Yemeni society remained highly divisive, a result of the rugged physical terrain, poor communications, and historical religious differences that made adversaries out of the northern highland Zaydis and the peripheral Shafais. The society was organized by clans, tribes, and tribal confederations. Leadership from the tribal level to the Zaydi imams was by ascription—that is, primarily according to heredity and lineage. With infinite numbers of mutually defensive or hostile elements, Yemeni society existed in a constant state of fission—neither disintegrating nor coalescing.

The long-dominant Zaydis have probably been no more numerous than their Shafai neighbors, although approximately two-thirds of Yemen's tribes are Zaydi, indicating that tribalism is more predominant in the northern highlands than elsewhere. Tribalism in Yemen is not synonymous with nomadism, however; in both the Zaydi and Shafai areas people lead generally sedentary lives in permanent villages, although sedentarization has not inhibited the far-ranging movement of northern tribesmen for purposes of intertribal warfare. The durable stone dwellings of the Zaydis tend to be clustered together near cultivable lands, and in some cases elaborate fortifications give these settlements a medieval European appearance.

In the south the Shafais pursue a similar, village-oriented existence, although they are even more firmly linked to their agricultural economy. Because they have a less pronounced tribal organization, they are also less prone to engage in the feuds and skirmishes that have long occupied their northern neighbors. Shafais of the mountainous southern region of Hujariyah are renowned for their willingness to leave home in search of lucrative jobs, and their remittances from abroad continue to be economically significant. The Shafais and other Sunni lowlanders have also tended to be Yemen's merchants and traders, and from handling Yemen's foreign trade—first at Mocha and now at Hodeida—they have developed broader contacts with the outside world than many of their Zaydi compatriots.

A large Ismaili population remains in the Zaydi highlands in and around Manakha. The Ismailis, who by doctrine are Shia dissenters, are securely situated in their rugged mountain homeland and in their relative wealth from fertile land. Approximately 50,000 Jews lived in Yemen before their evacuation to Israel in 1949. Because of the imam's protection and an intricately codified system of mutual tolerance developed with the Zaydis, they lived mainly in the northern highland areas. Only a handful remain today in and around the northern town of Saada.

These tribal and religious divisions are complicated by other factors. The Zaydi-Shafai division mirrors the fundamental split between Shia and Sunni Islam, but societal organization also differs to some extent between north and south and between the highlands and lowlands. Because of the heavy admixture of negroid stock in the

Tihama region there is even a longitudinal racial division between the cool uplands and the torrid coast. To make this picture even more confusing, almost eight years of civil war have imposed—at least for the short run—differences in political philosophies. In addition, rapidly expanding contacts with the outside world have spurred modernization in urban centers while leaving hinterland regions and their peoples untouched.

Social Conditions: Yemen's standard of living and level of literacy (10 percent) are among the lowest in the Arab world. Education still consists mainly of traditional Islamic pedagogy (at religious colleges in the mosques), although a modern school system has been introduced, providing a thirteen-year course through the secondary level, and there are several vocational schools. There are no universities in Yemen; however, a number of Yemeni students are enrolled in higher education abroad, mostly in Egypt, Communist China, and other Communist countries. Health care is limited; there is only one physician per 50,000 people.

Economic Conditions

One of the most impoverished states in natural resources and per capita income, Yemen has little to export and can thus ill afford the products it needs. The European-run coffee trade at Mocha was lucrative during the eighteenth century, but it declined afterwards as production shifted to more accessible parts of the world. Modest amounts of coffee are still exported, along with cotton, hides, salt, and garden products for the Aden market. Qat, a mild narcotic leaf that is chewed as a stimulant, is widely consumed in the domestic market and is also exported to neighboring countries. Unfortunately the profitability of qat as domestic trade discourages the cultivation of coffee, which thrives at the same altitudes and terrace locations, and qat is therefore effectively preventing the aquisition of much-needed foreign exchange that could be earned by the substitution of coffee. In addition, qat-chewing is a costly and debilitating habit that diverts money and energy from development.

Large-scale foreign aid projects began during the imamate and are continuing. The USSR, Communist China, and the United States each built intercity motor roads, and other projects include the Sanaa airport and a new harbor at Hodeida (USSR), the Taiz water system (United States), the Sanaa textile mill (China), and several telecommunications projects (West and East Germany). Help from Egypt ended with the evacuation in December 1967. Many countries, including the United States, responded to Yemen's appeal for famine aid in mid-1970. If the Jiddah Agreement leads to resolution of the Republican-Royalist conflict and the disappearance of the tensions that were its byproduct, as appears to be the case, Yemen's wealthy neighbor Saudi Arabia could become another source of development aid. The United Nations has completed or planned numerous

development projects and should play an increasingly important role by
coordinating and possibly inheriting some of the heretofore poorly
integrated foreign aid projects.

Under the imamate the monetary system was based on the
Maria Theresa thaler, which had an intrinsic value in relation to world
silver prices. Shortly after the revolution the regime shifted to the paper
riyal, which soon became unconvertible. The military costs of the civil
conflict fell mainly on Egyptian shoulders, but after the 1967
evacuation the Republicans had to rely largely on their own meager
financial resources. The republic survived, but the riyal eventually
declined to a sixth of its original value. The prospect of permanent
peace is now at hand, and so is the possibility of inflation.

Petroleum explorations have yielded negative results to date,
and unless foreign aid is dramatically increased—an unlikely event—
there is little promise in Yemen's economic future, and limitations will
thus be imposed on reform and modernization.

Political Structure

Despite the fact that Zaydi rule did not extend to all areas at all
times, the Zaydi theocracy constituted Yemen's prerevolutionary
political structure. According to Zaydi doctrine any free male citizen of
good character and other prescribed attributes could become imam
through "popular acclamation." In practice, however, the office was
the preserve of an inner circle of the noble *sayyid* class* and was
inherited or usurped according to the twists and turns of palace
intrigues. As tax collectors, judges, and governors, the sayyids monopolized all aspects of government authority except the military, and the
imam enjoyed absolute power by channeling his orders through this
caste hierarchy and enforcing compliance with military levies drawn
strictly from Zaydi tribes. Authority was further ensured by a system
whereby the imam would hold the sons of key tribal leaders as
hostages. As crown prince and briefly as imam, Muhammad al-Badr
promised to reform this anachronistic government system; events
proved that this promise was too little too late. When the revolution
occurred in 1962, the sayyid bureaucrats found themselves jobless—and
in some cases headless!

Yemen's imams exercised their powers without the impedi-
ments of written constitutions, restricted only by the Shariah as
interpreted by the ulama. To fill the vacuum left by the ousted sayyids,
revolutionary legal structures had to be established. Since at the outset
the republic was financially as well as militarily dependent on the UAR,
this task was performed under Egyptian guidance. The emerging

*Technically, the term *sayyid* means a descendant of the Prophet; in Yemen it can apply as
well to illustrious persons of southern Arabian descent, who are also known as *qadis*. Literally,
a *qadi* is a judge who is well versed in traditional Islamic jurisprudence.

institutional structures have closely resembled those of other Arab socialist polities in which military leadership predominates. According to the constitutional proclamation issued by President al-Sallal on November 2, 1962, supreme authority rested with the Revolutionary Command Council, composed of key military and civilian revolutionary leaders; executive authority was to be exercised through a cabinet and various ministries; and security affairs were to be the responsibility of the Higher Defense Council.

The provisional constitution published on April 27, 1964, stipulated that the president was to preside over a Presidential Council, the membership and tenure of which were decided jointly by the president and incumbent council members. One or more vice-presidents were selected from the council's ranks on nomination of the president and with the council's approval. The president also appointed the chairman of a subordinate Executive Council, composed of the several ministers. The Executive Council was charged with preparing draft laws and the state budget for submission to the Presidential Council and with issuing administrative decisions to the ministries. The judiciary was to be independent and subject to secular regulations. Laws have tended to evolve according to basic Islamic principles, but the fledgling court system is in the process of secularizing the Shariah system used during the imamate.

Following the exile of President al-Sallal in 1967, Qadi Abdul Rahman al-Iryani became the titular chief of state, Although the 1964 provisional constitution remained in force, the structures described did not develop. Rather, al-Iryani became chairman of a three-man Republican Council, and in March 1969 a forty-five-member National Council was also inaugurated. The latter organization has drawn its membership from the tribal shaykhs and therefore has remained conservative. It has been an essentially consultative body and has enjoyed only nominal parliamentary functions. When the Royalist and other exiles rejoined the Republican government in May 1970, the Republican Council was expanded to five seats and the National Council to sixty-three.

Yemen's new constitution, promulgated on December 30, 1970, should bring significant changes to the structure of postrevolutionary institutions. This document substitutes an elected 159-member Majlis al-Shura (consultative council) for the National Council; the Republican Council will consist of three to five members, who will choose among themselves a "chairman" to serve as chief of state. Majlis members are to be elected for five years and council members for three. The chairman will have the right to nominate one-fifth of the Majlis membership, to appoint the prime minister, and to act as commander-in-chief of the armed forces.

The new constitution paves the way for a more powerful presidency at the expense of the prime ministry, although this theoretical change will be subject to an important and unpredictable variable—the personalities of future council chairmen and prime ministers. As Yemen's first permanent constitution, the 1970 document appears to be a bridge between already modern-minded urbanite leaders and the cautious, conservative tribes. Significantly, the constitution describes Yemen as an "Arab Islamic state" and looks to the Shariah as the source of all laws and the sanctity of private property. Membership in foreign political parties or their branches is specifically forbidden.

Yemen's government structures have evolved along the pattern of centralization that is in vogue in more advanced Arab socialist polities, but there are problems adapting modern political devices to a basically tribal, particularistic society. Sanaa authorities have only been able to implement government decrees in urban centers and in areas under the control of friendly shaykhs, and the government must find the means of gaining cooperation from the other tribal areas.

Political Processes

Yemeni political processes since the revolution differ from those of the past because of changes in leadership patterns and types of constituencies.

Leadership

The first factor, leadership, involves more than factional competition at the top. The sayyid oligarchy was destroyed; Yemen's elite must therefore be recruited from new sources, and because only a relatively small number of Yemenis have more than an elementary education, recruitment is difficult. A few dozen youths received foreign university or military training during the imamate,* and many of these men sided with the republic and functioned as an administrative cadre within key ministries. More recently, additional hundreds of youths have received technical training abroad—especially in the USSR, Czechoslovakia, Lebanon, Egypt, and China—through foreign scholarship programs. (It is too early to determine what political influences will result from their varied, primarily Eastern, ideological encounters.) The Republican officer corps, like that in most Middle Eastern states, is also a training area for the new elite.

Because no thorough study of Yemen's changing elite has been made, it is difficult to know exactly how leaders are recruited and how they rise and fall within the new "establishment." There are still paradoxes, however; members of old, aristocratic families who have embraced the republic hold important positions beside self-made young men who have found room at the top. Political power obviously increases or solidifies the social and economic status of Yemen's new leaders, but social and economic credentials are not necessarily passports to political power.

*Al-Sallal was a member of a small cadet contingent that trained in Iraq in the 1930s.

Among the tribes authority patterns remain much as before. Tribal leadership is transmitted hereditarily if a shaykh's son is capable; if he is not, a nonhereditary leader appears according to the age-old workings of "tribal democracy." For centuries the Zaydi tribes have aligned themselves within two large confederations, the Hashid and Bakil. Although forever feuding among themselves, the two groups usually have been allied in times of external trouble. The major tribal shaykhs continue to exercise strong influence over the course of government decision, and support from the tribes is as important to Republican Yemen as it was to the imams. Premier al-Amri's appreciation of this fact won support from the Hashids in his 1968 confrontation with the leftist army dissidents.

The ideological coloration of the political leadership is far from homogeneous. Despite their common allegiance to Arab nationalism, Republican leaders have embraced Baathist, Nasserist, tribal-traditionalist, pro-Western liberal, and other dissimilar doctrines. These differences add to their personal leadership rivalries to impede cohesion at the decision-making level.

In the al-Sallal era ultimate decision-making powers alternated between the president and various prime ministers or ministerial groups according to a shifting pattern of allegiances within the revolutionary leadership stratum. On the basis of this uneven pattern, presidential powers ranged from nominal to extensive. In the post-al-Sallal era, the premiership has gained decisive influence at the expense of the presidency, although implementation of the new constitution may reverse this trend. Until the entire political system takes firm root, however, leadership patterns probably will continue to be determined by the appearance of charismatic personalities or shifting coalitions within the top military and civilian strata rather than according to legislated rules of succession.

Constituencies

Yemen has several distinct political constituencies, although none can be described as a pressure group in the usual sense. The army is an important constituency because of the weakness of civilian institutions and the unique leadership role of military officers. The support of individual military units for their commanders has already resolved some intra-army leadership rivalries and probably will do so in the future. The military role in domestic political processes is still evolving and cannot be defined with accuracy. Sanaa, Taiz, and Hodeida, Yemen's only towns of significant size, reflect rival urban constituencies, and popular reaction to Republican rule making in these urban centers is important. As yet there is no sizable distinctive middle class in these urban elements. As noted before, Yemen's tribes remain organized on traditional lines; because each shaykh must receive total support from his followers or step down, tribal chiefs personify the "opinion" of their followers and thus collectively form yet another constituency. Youths, primarily in urban areas, form a fourth and potentially vocal group that could wield great influence in the future. Several patriotic youth organizations have been formed by the government since the revolution, and more are likely to appear.

Republican processes resemble those of the imamate to the extent that the flow of rules from the top is considerably stronger than the voicing of demands from below. Yemen's masses have just emerged from an epoch of theocratic-authoritarian rule and are unaccustomed to articulating their demands in a manner short of rebellion. The new order therefore involves applying unfamiliar institutions in an anachronistic environment.

Foreign Policy

Although Yemen was a hermit kingdom in its prerevolutionary days, its isolation lessened considerably during Imam Ahmad's final years. Then, as before, foreign policy was determined by the need for outside support to counter Britain's presence in South Arabia. Although ibn Saud's lenient terms for settling the Saudi-Yemeni war of 1934 more or less resolved the northern frontier problem, the southern boundary dispute with Britain and her sultan protegés extended from Turkish times into the revolutionary era. This boundary had been demarcated by an Anglo-Turkish commission between 1901 and 1907 and was the subject of an Anglo-Turkish convention in 1914; however, after Turkey's defeat in 1918 the issue brought Yemen and Britain into conflict. Despite a 1934 treaty generally recognizing the status quo, numerous incidents before and after clouded Anglo-Yemeni relations. Yahya flirted with Italy on the eve of World War II in an effort to give Yemen a better bargaining hand, and Ahmad's romance with the UAR and Eastern Europe in the 1950s was similarly motivated.

In a move that was to have ironic consequences, Ahmad eventually joined the Jiddah Pact (between the then-friendly Saudis and Egyptians) in 1956, and through his son al-Badr opened Yemen's doors to the Egyptian influences that later undermined his dynasty. Inheriting a revolution along with the imamate, al-Badr suddenly found himself relying on the Saudis and fighting against Egyptians bearing Czech and Soviet arms similar to those he had bought for his father in the 1950s. After occupying most of Yemen's southern and central areas at al-Badr's expense, the Republicans inherited Ahmad's border feud with Britain. Although Republican-British diplomatic ties were soon severed, Sanaa sought to retain relations with both East and West and welcomed needed aid from both camps. Sanaa-Cairo relations were warm at the outset but cooled as domestic opposition to al-Sallal increased, and they turned even cooler when the UAR terminated its military support. At that time, a massive airlift of weapons and supplies by the USSR saved the incumbent anti-al-Sallal Republican regime, a gesture that may have continuing foreign policy implications.

Postrevolutionary Yemen's links with the non-Arab world have been forged mainly through foreign aid projects. Principal contributors have been the United States, West Germany, East Germany, the USSR, and Communist China. Although Sanaa severed relations with Bonn in 1965 and with Washington in 1967, and Western influence all but disappeared, Yemen reestablished full diplomatic relations with West Germany in mid-1969 and welcomed the opening of an American interests section in the Italian embassy in 1970. Considering Yemen's announced neutralist policy and continuing need for assistance from all willing sources, it is likely that Sanaa governments will continue to look both eastward and westward for needed assistance. The recent renaissance in Yemen's relations with the West and the Jiddah Agreement (1970) should mark the beginning of a new positive era in Saudi-Yemeni relations.

It remains to be seen how China and the USSR will react to changes following the 1970 internal peace settlement; their influence has been significant to date, and it could remain so in the future. However, both the USSR and China have new options in the neighboring People's Democratic Republic of Yemen and will probably reconsider the costs of remaining influential in Yemen. Due to the religious conservatism of tribal and other traditionalist elements in Yemeni society, Islam represents an inhibiting factor to the development of broader popular ties with the USSR and China, although this religious impediment would not necessarily prevent closer political ties if an incumbent regime desired to implement them.

Despite the often-discussed goal of a Greater Yemen that would encompass all of southwestern Arabia, relations between Sanaa and the postindependence regime in the neighboring People's Republic have varied from cautious to hostile. Both Sanaa and Aden established prestigious ministerial offices for the conduct of "unity affairs," but the increasingly doctrinaire-leftist posture of the Aden regime has prevented cooperation in this area and has soured relations on all levels. The People's Republic refused to occupy twelve seats reserved for it in the National Assembly that was inaugurated in Sanaa in March 1969. It is difficult to see how integration could proceed even under more propitious circumstances, because integration would certainly involve economic and political sacrifices that one or both partners would scarcely be willing to make.

Yemen is somewhat uniquely involved in the Arab-Israeli conflict, because the mass emigration of its Jewish citizenry in 1949 injected a significant oriental element into the ethnic makeup of the new Israeli state. However, after this event, Yemen's geographical remoteness and preoccupation with internal problems have tended to make the conflict seem rather distant, despite Yemen's loyalty to the Arab League. Although the postrevolutionary republic has been firmly committed to the Arab cause—both in spirit and official pronouncement—the civil war and the problems of adapting to peace have provided more tangible objects for the concern of Yemeni decision makers. At the height of the civil war, preoccupation with Arab unity contributed to local political change, yet today the new Yemeni leadership is preoccupied with internal problems and can do little more than render moral and political support to Palestinianism.

Political Prospects

Yemen is beset with an extraordinary range of problems, and it is useful to determine whether these problems are new or inherited, soluble or insoluble.

Enduring throughout Yemen's Islamic history, Zaydi-Shafai divisiveness is obviously an inherited problem. By destroying the imamate, the Republicans have dismantled the government structure by which the Zaydis legitimized their hegemony over the Shafais. The problem could have been acute had the Zaydis embraced more extreme Shia tenets; however, hostility appears to have resulted from mundane political frictions rather than from mutually intolerable beliefs. Although these frictions undoubtedly persist in the Republican era, both on a popular level and within elite circles, the evolving Republican political system at least provides an arena in which the Shafais can compete for a fair share of power.

Competition within leadership circles will be difficult to resolve and political energies will continue to be absorbed in intraelite maneuvering. Because revolutionary political institutions as yet have only shallow roots, the government process probably will continue to involve a heavy output of partially enforceable decrees, and correspondingly minimal demands will be heard from below. The mechanisms of a truly modern republican system will probably develop slowly under the weight of traditional political processes. Factionalism is an established fact of national political life, and the road to national unity will be long and difficult.

If Yemen's civil war has been extinguished as a result of the Jiddah Agreement, problems that have arisen from foreign involvement and the fuel that these have added to the fires of internal dissension should begin to diminish. Peace does bring a new problem: because subsidies paid to the tribes by the UAR and Saudi Arabia turned the fighting into a mercenary struggle from which the tribes profited, Sanaa will have to convince the tribes that peace too has rewards.

Poverty has shadowed Yemen's past and present, and it would be unrealistic to predict its rapid disappearance. Although the imam's stultifying economic policies have been abandoned, the revolutionary regime cannot decree prosperity with the stroke of a pen. Indeed, the new government may have to face new problems of inflation. By following a neutralist course and accepting aid from every quarter, Yemen has embarked on development projects well beyond its financial resources or repayment capabilities. These projects have hastened modernization in many areas, but the resultant debts through long-term credits and gaps in coordination and planning could generate a financial crisis.

Yemen has rejected its hermit past and elected to join the modern world, which in itself ensures a multiplication of national problems, because the modern world is hardly a serene place for a traditional society. But a decision of this type is irrevocable, and Yemen has been caught in the stream of modernization, which will doubtless involve many lessons and perhaps unpleasant experiences. To date, foreign assistance has provided a cushion against some of the more painful problems, but the Yemenis themselves will eventually have to bear large burdens. Despite its reputation in Roman times as *Arabia felix*, Yemen has not enjoyed a blissful history. And although its past troubles were of little interest or importance to the world, its political future in this age of Middle Eastern tensions is bound to have significance for neighbors in the Arabian peninsula and for distant polities.

A study of the neighboring People's Democratic Republic of Yemen is appropriate when considering the political prospects for Yemen and adjacent parts of Arabia, because developments are keyed to local political forces that cross the border between the two Yemens.

Selected Bibliography

Brown, William R. "The Yemeni Dilemma." *Middle East Journal* 27, no. 4 (Autumn 1963): 349-67.
An excellent description of Yemen's deposed sayyid oligarchy and of the social and economic aspects of the 1962 revolution.

Ingrams, Harold. *The Yemen: Imams, Rulers, and Revolutions*. London: John Murray, 1963.
An excellent overview of modern Yemen's political history and a helpful explanation of the complex relations between imamate Yemen and British South Arabia.

Macro, Eric. *Yemen and the Western World since 1571*. New York: Frederick A. Praeger, 1968.
An interesting perspective of Yemen in its relations with the Ottoman and Western worlds.

Schmidt, Dana Adams. *Yemen: The Unknown War*. New York: Holt, Rinehart and Winston, 1968.
A journalistic study of the civil war; difficult English rendering of Arab names but extensive treatment of events on both the Republican and Royalist sides.

Somerville-Large, Peter. *Tribes and Tribulations: A Journey in Republican Yemen*. London: Robert Hale, 1967.
An impressionistic, descriptive work about postrevolutionary Yemen.

Wenner, Manfred. *Modern Yemen: 1918-66*. Baltimore: Johns Hopkins Press, 1967.
A scholarly and extraordinarily comprehensive treatment of the final stages of the imamate and the advent of Republican rule.

People's Democratic Republic of Yemen *

The People's Democratic Republic of Yemen seems to be an almost perverse name for this recently independent state, because it inevitably leads most non-Arabs (and perhaps some Arabs as well) to confuse the state with its immediate neighbor to the north—the Yemen Arab Republic. The territory encompassed by the People's Republic was known throughout much of history as South Arabia; under Britain in the nineteenth and twentieth centuries, the region coincided with Aden and the Western and Eastern Aden Protectorates; immediately preceding independence, it became the ill-fated South Arabian Federation. With the Yemen Arab Republic, the People's Republic† constitutes the lower half of the southwestern corner of Arabia—a region that in many ways is unique from other parts of the peninsula. Despite geographical similarities and historical ties, however, the two states differ politically.

In the Yemen Arab Republic, revolutionaries overthrew a long-established, reasonably unified theocratic state and have since attempted to construct a modernist state along moderate lines. In Southern Yemen, one of several competing anticolonialist groups vanquished its rivals by force on the eve of independence and fell heir to a far-from-unified excolonial domain. This group has since attempted to construct a modern state along extremist lines. Both regimes are

---

*The author is a foreign service officer. The views expressed are his own and do not reflect those of the U.S. Department of State.

†On November 30, 1970, the state's official name was changed from the People's Republic of Southern Yemen to the People's Democratic Republic of Yemen; however, the two Yemens are still popularly identified as *northern* and *southern*. In this chapter the terms *Southern Yemen, People's Democratic Republic of Yemen*, and *People's Republic* are used interchangeably to describe the postindependence state; applicable names are used for the various preindependence entities.

committed to the establishment of a Greater Yemen and thus to regional political integration, but each insists that integration take place on its own terms, and the goal is perhaps more elusive than ever as relations become increasingly marred by suspicion. The politics of the Yemen Arab Republic can be described as traditionalism in a new guise; the politics of the People's Republic involves a single doctrinaire party that has thus far retained its monopoly of power.

Historical Background

The ancient Arabian people comprised two major groups—the Adnanis in the north and the Qahtanis in the south. Qahtani civilization reached remarkable heights, even by contemporary standards. The name *South Arabia* brings to mind the first great civilizations of the Arabian peninsula—the Himyarite, the Minaean, and the Sabaean—whose peoples were sedentary Arabians of Qahtani stock who spoke an ancient Semitic tongue related to the Amhara language of Ethiopia. (These kingdoms, which flourished between 1200 B.C. and the sixth century A.D., also appeared in Yemeni history because their domains overlapped present political boundaries.)

The Incense Route provided an economic base for these early dynasties. Originating on the South Arabian coast a few hundred miles east of Aden, this wealth-bringing route passed through the Wadi Hadhramawt, a long, oasislike valley, and then northward across the Yemen highlands. Like Yemen, South Arabia faded into obscurity after incessant interdynastic wars, conquest by the Persians in 575 A.D., and the advent of Islam fifty years later. Highland Yemen—from early Islamic times a Zaydi stronghold—retained a semblance of nationhood, and the name Yemen thus survived, whereas the names of South Arabia's several kingdoms did not.

The next important stopping points in local history do not occur for a number of centuries. Although Aden had flourished in antiquity, the port fell into disuse for more than a millennium. The Ottoman Turks fortified it in the mid-sixteenth century but did not accord it special strategic interest. In the next century, however, Britain, Portugal, and Holland began to recognize Aden's potential value as a way station en route to the Indies. Muhammad Ali's conquests in Arabia in 1818 and his rising challenge to imperial Ottoman authority caused the British government—particularly the India Office—to fear that Aden would fall under Egyptian control, and a British force under Captain Haines therefore seized the port in 1839 on orders of the Bombay presidency. This act planted the Union Jack in South Arabia and linked control of Aden and adjacent territories to Britain's "imperial lifeline" strategy for the next one and a quarter centuries. After the opening of Suez, Aden became one of the world's great bunkering ports and enjoyed a prosperity that contrasted markedly with the poverty of the petty kingdoms in the interior.

Thirty-seven years before the annexation of Aden, Britain signed a friendship treaty with the Sultan of Lahej, who controlled a large territory to the northwest. Throughout the nineteenth century similar treaties · were concluded with the remaining South Arabian potentates—more than twenty in number—offering them military protection in return for British control of their external affairs. As a result, Britain not only exercised sovereignty over Aden but gradually came to exercise de facto control over much larger adjacent areas, which eventually came to be known as the Western and Eastern Aden Protectorates.

Technically a "settlement" of the Bombay presidency, Aden was transferred to Colonial Office jurisdiction in 1937. The port and its environs were subject to close economic and political controls before and after this date, but the sultanates in the Western and Eastern Protectorates amounted to a *cordon sanitaire* between Aden and Yemen, with the result that Aden developed and modernized, whereas the interior remained poor and backward. Aden had little to do with the back country, and the rural people distrusted the cosmopolitan Adenis.

The Yemeni-South Arabian frontier problem, the evolution of which was described in the preceding chapter, grew as Britain's influence in South Arabian affairs increased, and as Arab nationalism and traditionalism collided in the 1950s, this frontier problem generated side issues of incredible complexity that persist today in different guises. South Arabia's Shafai sultans had ample reason to fear the intentions of Yemen's Zaydi imams. For example, Imam Yahya refused to accept the frontier as defined by the Anglo-Turkish convention of 1914, and in the 1920s he occupied territories in several sultanates, which he relinquished in 1934 only after coming to grief with the Saudis on his northern flank. In the Anglo-Yemeni Treaty of Sanaa signed in the same year, he agreed finally to respect the status quo pending settlement of the border problem. Meanwhile, the Royal Air Force had come to the aid of threatened border sultanates and had learned to use aircraft against dissident tribes and sultans who disrupted South Arabia's internal security in other areas. By the late 1930s, mainly through the efforts of a British political agent, Harold Ingrams, aerial policing had pacified even the notoriously feud-ridden Hadhramawt. This success led to the posting of political advisers in the hinterland, through whom Britain assumed greater responsibility—and blame—for regional political developments.

The hostility of Yemen's Imam Ahmad and the collective weakness of the twenty-odd protectorate sultans eventually encouraged the Colonial Office to embark on a federation scheme that, it was hoped, would provide greater regional economic and political viability. The initial plan was drafted by Kennedy Trevaskis, political agent for the Western Protectorate, and was submitted for consideration by the sultans in early 1954. Most were lukewarm at the outset and even less enthusiastic when the plan was attacked by the Cairo and Sanaa radio stations. Imam Ahmad feared that a unified Shafai state on his southern border would weaken the loyalty of his own Shafai subjects. While the unification scheme remained dormant, Yemeni-British relations took a turn for the worse in 1956 as a result of the Suez invasion, Crown Prince al-Badr's increased influence with his father, Ahmad, and Yemen's growing ties with the Communist world.

Formation of the United Arab States (the new UAR plus Yemen) in 1958 produced mixed reactions in South Arabia. This new involvement of Cairo in peninsula affairs encouraged nationalist elements in Aden to work more actively against Britain and her federation scheme. The Western Protectorate sultans became alarmed and consequently were more eager to reconsider the idea of unity. The Eastern Protectorate rulers, although hardly comforted by Ahmad's flirtation with Nasser, remained cool toward federation because they anticipated petroleum discoveries in their area which they had no desire to share with their western neighbors. Nevertheless, the first step toward unity took place in February 1959, when six Western Protectorate sultans joined the Federation of the Amirates of the South. Over the next four years British and Adeni leaders wrangled over when and how to bring Aden into this scheme, and the merger was finally accomplished in January 1963, and the Federation of Amirates became the South Arabian Federation. Unfortunately for Britain and the pro-British sultans, Yemen had plunged into civil war four months earlier and was now host to a large Egyptian expeditionary force. The southwestern Arabian political game was no longer a local affair.

In the mid-1950s South Arabia's political factions began organizing numerous political groups, a majority of which would serve as focal points for nationalist independence agitation and thus as vehicles for undermining the federation. Among them were the Lahej-based South Arabian League (SAL); the People's Socialist party (PSP), a political arm of Abdullah al-Asnaj's Aden Trades Union Congress (ATUC); the United National party (UNP), a moderate probusiness group; and the National Liberation Front (NLF), originally a Yemen-based guerrilla group. During the federation's chaotic infancy especially virulent clashes occurred between the federation government and the PSP-ATUC, whose membership included many disenfranchised Yemeni immigrants. By 1964 South Arabia's future president Qahtan al-Shabi deserted the SAL to lead the NLF, which at that time was the UAR's chosen instrument for anti-British nationalist agitation. In 1964 the NLF sparked a serious revolt by tribesmen in the Radfan district and thus gave the independence struggle a forceful push.

Although the Radfan revolt was the most violent anti-British action to this time, it was by no means the first externally inspired problem for London decision makers. During the preceding decade Britain's policies in the protectorates and the evolving South Arabian Federation had attracted increasingly critical attention from the Afro-Asian states, both within and outside the United Nations. As early as 1955 the "Aden question" was raised at the Bandung Conference, which endorsed the anti-British position of its Arab members.

More nettling problems arose in the United Nations, first through efforts of the Special Committee on Information from Non-Self-Governing Territories (established in 1948), and more specifically through the work of its successor, the Special Committee on the Implementation of the Declaration on the Granting of Independence to Colonial Countries and Peoples (established in 1961). The latter special committee directed its attention to Aden between April and July of 1963, during which time it attempted unsuccessfully to gain permission for a subcommittee to visit South Arabia. Britain refused entry to the subcommittee on the grounds that its activities would constitute interference in the internal affairs of the territory. In December 1963 the U.N. General Assembly adopted a resolution "regretting" Britain's refusal to cooperate and accepting the special committee's allegations that removal of the Aden base was desirable for reasons of regional security. Britain's position was that she was attempting to grant independence at the earliest possible date, but that she was not accountable to the special committee as if it were a court of law. The committee again considered Aden in 1964 and appealed once more for permission for a subcommittee visit and for representation at a South Arabian constitutional conference to be held in London in June 1964; it was rebuffed on both requests.

An additional problem arose in the U.N. at this time when Yemen complained to the Security Council about a Royal Air Force raid on the border village of Harib on March 28, 1964. This raid had been in retaliation for an earlier Yemeni raid and other incursions into South Arabian territory; however, the Security Council allowed debate of the Yemeni charges and on April 9, 1964, adopted a resolution expressing concern over the situation and "deploring" various incidents in the area—including the attack on Harib. Despite her efforts to defuse the situation and lead South Arabia to independence, Britain was fighting a losing battle because of the adverse international publicity that the Afro-Arab nations were generating.

After the election victory of a Labour government in 1964, London policy makers inclined toward creation of a unitary independent state in lieu of the federation, which had been a Tory idea. The value of Aden as a military base was also debated. In September 1965 two British legal experts were dispatched to Aden to draft a constitution for the coming independent state. However, this gesture was nullified by a sudden rise in terrorism that forced Britain to suspend the existing Aden constitution and to impose stronger military controls. In a dramatic policy reversal, London next decided (in February 1966) to withdraw all British armed forces from South Arabia by December 1968. South Arabia's moderates became disenchanted, and nationalist extremists began to compete in earnest to see who could deal the federation its deathblow.

In early 1966 the NLF merged with another radical group, the Organization for the Liberation of the Occupied South (OLOS), and this composite organization was named the Front for the Liberation of Occupied South Yemen (FLOSY). The merger was unsatisfactory for both parties, and in late 1966 the NLF withdrew. FLOSY then formed a commando unit known as the People's Organization of Revolutionary Forces (PORF) to compete with the NLF. A U.N. fact-finding mission finally visited Aden in April 1967 but was unable to communicate with any of the competing factions. Britain's final withdrawal date had by then been moved forward to late 1967, and troops evacuated the interior in June and Aden in August. While the British-equipped South Arabian army cautiously attempted to fill the resultant vacuum, FLOSY (including PORF) and the NLF girded themselves for a final contest. The storm broke in November 1967, when the NLF, with tacit support from the South Arabian army, defeated FLOSY in a series of bloody encounters. The NLF made last-minute takeover arrangements with Britain, and on November 30, 1967, an NLF government under Qahtan al-Shabi inherited an independent South Arabia. The country was immediately renamed the People's Republic of Southern Yemen, and the NLF dropped its middle initial and came to be known simply as the National Front (NF).

Although the NF's victory over FLOSY left it in complete control of the newly independent polity, intra-NF factionalism soon perpetuated many of the uncertainties of the preindependence era. In early 1968 a clash developed between a doctrinaire left-wing faction centered in the Hadhramawt and a more pragmatic group linked to al-Shabi. After resolving this disagreement in the moderates' favor, the regime continued to grapple with budget problems, to search for aid in a rather disinterested outside world, and to bicker with London over short-term financial support. Despite this chaotic environment, the People's Republic remained unexpectedly stable during the ensuing year. In April 1969, however, fighting within the NF General Command forced President al-Shabi to appoint his cousin, Faysal Abd al-Latif al-Shabi, premier. In June the General Command forced both to step down and in their place appointed a "more revolutionary" five-man Presidential Council.

In 1968 and 1969 the NF's relations with the Western world were marked by bitter harangues from Aden's press and radio, although the regime cultivated broader ties with Eastern Europe, China, and other Arab nationalist governments. Intraparty disputes continued unabated, and in December Faysal al-Shabi was placed under house arrest. Although the NF secretary-general, Abd al-Fatah Ismael, appeared to be winning, no single faction in the mystery-shrouded General Command could be assured of its position. This instability manifested itself in the continuing aggressive attitude of the People's Republic toward its neighbors—the revolutionary Yemen Arab Republic as well as conservative Saudi Arabia and Oman (then the Sultanate of Muscat and Oman). In December 1969 Southern Yemeni forces penetrated Saudi territory in the area of al-Wadiyah but were driven back by Saudi air action.

In March 1970 Aden boycotted the Jiddah Foreign Ministers Conference, which Yemen's premier al-Ayni attended and used to negotiate a rapprochement with the Saudis. During the same month the

NF claimed that it had foiled an attempted coup, and reports from Aden indicated that perhaps as many as twelve hundred suspects— many of them alleged supporters of Faysal al-Shabi—were arrested as a result. On April 3, 1970, Aden radio announced that former premier Faysal Abd al-Latif al-Shabi had been shot "while escaping" detention. Throughout the remainder of the year, the faction-ridden party managed to retain its political grip under the joint leadership of Premier Muhammad Ali Haytham and the Presidential Council chairman, Salim Rubai Ali.

President Rubai Ali astounded neighboring Yemen, foreign observers, and perhaps many Southern Yemenis as well when he announced during the November 30, 1970, independence celebrations that the country would henceforth be known as the People's Democratic Republic of Yemen (PDRY). This gesture followed increased tensions between Aden and Sanaa and accompanied the announcement of a new national constitution. Although the Southern Yemeni and Yemeni prime ministers had met a few days earlier and had issued statements reasserting their adherence to the idea of a unified Greater Yemen, the choice of this new national name revealed the increasing ideological distance between the two governments and the NF's desire for political integration on its own terms.

Political Environment

The political environment of Yemen was described in terms of several contrasts and paradoxes. The People's Republic milieu can be introduced in terms of a single phenomenon: the political, social, and economic gulf that separates modern Aden from the undeveloped hinterland. Economic development has put Aden in tune with region-wide Arab politics; but backwardness has shielded the former protectorate areas from modernist influences. The NF, which has a radical but doctrinaire approach to political, social, and economic reform, thus has been confronted with two operational worlds.

Geographical Determinants

Whereas the Red Sea coast, the adjacent Tihama Desert, and longitudinal mountain ranges give a north-south orientation to the geography of the Yemen Arab Republic, the People's Republic extends in an east-west direction along the Indian Ocean shore of the Arabian peninsula. As in northern Yemen, geography imposes communications barriers, but here the similarity ends. Although the mountains of the Yemeni Hujariyah extend southward into the western portions of the People's Republic and low mountain ranges are found throughout national territory to the east, the overall terrain is more desertlike and formidable. The Wadi Hadhramawt is an exception to this picture; it is green and fertile from abundant underground water and age-old cultivation. The hinterland remains backward and remote, and the total national population of only 1,200,000 is spread thinly over 111,000 square miles of territory.

Aden, which has a present-day population of 150,000, is also a product of geography; the port was a natural way station on the route to British India after the opening of the Suez Canal, and it grew rapidly as shipping companies found that it was a convenient bunkering station. As a result of Britain's nineteenth and twentieth century strategies for defending the empire "lifeline," Aden also grew as a naval base and communications center. After the closure of the Suez Canal in 1967, however, port activities declined sharply almost overnight because ships following the route around Africa to the Far East required bunkering facilities at locations farther south.

The People

Rural-Urban Division: Religion is an important social determinant in the political environment of the Yemen Arab Republic, but because the Shafai sect is predominant in the People's Republic, this source of divisiveness is absent. Nevertheless, another schism has arisen from wide disparities between Adenis and their hinterland neighbors and has provided the nation with analogous problems. Because Aden's economy evolved around the port and an adjacent oil refinery, its work force became technically skilled by regional standards, which meant higher wages, better living standards, and more advanced education. As a result, Adenis developed a degree of cosmopolitanism and political sophistication not found upcountry or in neighboring Yemen, and before the NF's rural campaigns, at least, Aden's environment was more favorable for political recruitment. The growth of a strong trade union movement provided the means for the politcally aware populace to articulate its demands.

Although they are "country cousins" in every sense, the protectorate peoples by no means constitute a homogeneous rural society. Inhabitants of the former Western Protectorate area display social organization patterns resembling those of Yemen; peoples of the former Eastern Protectorate area vary from nomads to completely sedentarized Hadhramis. Most of the sultans and their retainers in the former protectorates fled to Saudi territory; the few who remained were brought to trial, imprisoned, or otherwise persecuted by the NF. Despite the disestablishment of the hereditary ruling class, however, the PDRY's rural peoples remain as particularistic and segmented as before. Like their Yemeni corevolutionaries, Aden's present leaders must politicize a backward rural population in order to substitute their own authority for that of the traditionalists.

The Wadi Hadhramawt poses unusual problems. Because the area is a fertile island in the barren hinterland, the Hadhramis are agriculturally richer than their western neighbors. They have ethnic and cultural ties with the East Indies, where many of their people emigrated in times past and earned sizable fortunes. The Hadhramis are proud and aloof and feel superior to tribesmen on both flanks, especially to the "untrustworthy" Aden urbanites. The wadi has long been a scene of tribal feuding, and only the skillful truce making by Political Agent Ingrams and threats of punitive bombing by the RAF effected the relative peace that prevailed during the immediate preindependence years. After the NF takeover an ultraradical faction was able to entrench itself in Mukalla, the port and traditional gateway to the Hadhramawt, and the result of this bizarre mixture of revolutionary influences and conservatism are not yet apparent.

Ethnic Groups: Aden's ethnic makeup is far from homogeneous. A large number—perhaps half—of its employed male population has traditionally been of Yemeni origin. For these Yemenis, Aden employment meant an income that would have been impossible at home. Until their exodus in late 1967 and early 1968, Somalis constituted the second largest immigrant work force. There are also some Pakistanis and Indians and a very small community of Jews. The country is predominantly Muslim Arab, however.

Class Conflict: Antagonisms between the sayyids and commoners, which have existed in the Yemeni and the People's Republic hinterlands since prerevolutionary times, complicate the already complex ethnic situation. This class conflict is sufficiently strong to have manifested itself in feuds within South Arabian (particularly Hadhrami) emigrant communities as far away as Java. In the revolutionary NF era a dispute of this nature presumably would be dismissed as irrelevant; however, Southern Yemen's rural peoples are unlikely to forget their ancient prejudices and class distinctions.

Economic Conditions

Of the NF's many problems, economic ones appear to be the most persistent and insoluble. Other states have embarked on independence with minimal exploitable resources and empty treasuries, but few have had such poor long-term growth prospects as the PDRY.

The economic forces that affect Southern Yemen's political environment are interrelated with social factors; the polity is not socially homogeneous or economically integrated. The interior is poor, whereas Aden was not only self-sufficient but genuinely prosperous, although this relative wealth disappeared in the preindependence turmoil. The radical economic and political policies of the NF also discouraged potential private investors, and later nationalizations—particularly during the first half of 1970—all but eliminated private enterprise. Many Aden trading firms were owned by Yemenis; as business declined, their proprietors relocated in Hodeida, Yemen, and Hodeida and nearby Djibouti on the African shore now enjoy new prosperity at Aden's expense.

The first economic disaster occurred before independence, however, when the closure of the Suez Canal diverted world shipping around Africa and cost Aden its sizable bunkering trade. Britain's military pullout a few months later was the second major blow, because air and naval bases in the Aden area had pumped large sums of money into the local economy. The closure of Suez and withdrawal of British forces turned the preindependence recession into a depression. In addition, Britain understandably failed to deliver expected budget support once the new regime had taken over.

Despite this reversal of fortune, Aden's economic environment still has a modernist outlook and retains the permanent stamp of contact with the outside world. The NF has gone on a nationalization spree, and modernist influences now are distinctly socialist. In a manner indicative of its internal discipline, the NF faced its bleak income situation by imposing heavy cuts in public spending. Public servants' salaries were reduced on several occasions, and employees were exhorted to contribute portions of their monthly salaries to regime-sponsored causes. Having committed itself to austerity, the NF thus far has managed to preserve 100 percent hard-currency backing for the PDRY dinar, which has retained its par value. Although this effort reflects a somewhat unexpected display of fiscal responsibility, it is undoubtedly adding to the regime's unpopularity. The effects of the economic crisis are felt primarily in Aden and its environs, however; the hinterland is insulated by its own primitiveness.

With the exception of Lahej and some isolated cotton-growing areas, the western rural areas have little potential for agricultural development. Poor and mountainous, they are underdeveloped and probably will remain so. In the absence of petroleum discoveries, the former Eastern Protectorate area is even more devoid of development potential; however, its seminomadic inhabitants are self-sufficient at a subsistence level and thus are able—and inclined—to remain aloof from the nation-building process.

As is customary in the case of anti-Western fledgling socialist regimes, the USSR and Communist China have demonstrated interest in the People's Republic, although they have offered loans and development aid programs at a slower rate and in smaller amounts than might have been expected. This circumstance is partly explained by the fact that the two rivals have extensive aid commitments and corresponding political interests in neighboring Yemen and are undoubtedly aware that excessive support for Aden would cause unfavorable reactions in Sanaa. Also, the decline of Western influence in the PDRY probably makes the question of aid less urgent in Soviet and Chinese eyes.

The NF's internal factionalism appears to be a far more serious malady than the factional disputes in neighboring Yemen. In Sanaa, intragovernmental conflicts more often involve pragmatic issues than fundamental splits over political philosophy; in the People's Republic, the latter is the rule. Not only does this emphasis on ideology perpetuate infighting but it also detracts from the regime's ability to deal with the PDRY's economic challenges.

In assessing these economic determinants it is necessary to look to questions of balance. Regional economic and social disparities are obvious. In the federation era political unity proved to be a difficult goal to achieve, and unity in fact never proceeded far enough to include the Eastern Protectorate. Under these circumstances British South Arabia could not approach economic integration. The NF has now imposed an external shell of unity, and the party probably hopes to consolidate its position by unifying actions in both the political and economic spheres. However, in the absence of sufficient trade, aid, and natural resources, economic development will likely remain an elusive goal.

Political Structure

The task of describing the PDRY's political structure is rendered difficult by the fact that until its takeover the NF operated as a secret underground organization. Before independence, outside observers mistakenly assumed that FLOSY—organized along lines resulting from its association with UAR political advisers—was heir apparent to South Arabian leadership. The NF was a surprise in terms of its military effectiveness and its discipline and organization. NF leaders are well versed in revolutionary doctrines and have appeared determined to build a radical socialist system without making concessions to local traditionalism. Admittedly, they have had less government structure to dismantle than their fellow revolutionaries in Yemen.

As noted previously, Britain concentrated on governing and modernizing Aden, and the hinterland sultans were left mainly to their own devices. The "Ingrams peace" brought order to the tribes but no change in government organization. Unification began in the 1950s, but by the mid-1960s this effort was a shambles. Aden's urban institutions facilitated takeover by the NF, and the exodus of the sultans created a helpful vacuum upcountry. What the NF inherited was not a nation but rather an area of former British hegemony, demarcated to exclude the interference of neighboring states.

The NF has used a time-tested method of applying geography to the cause of politics—divide and rule. In an early decree the regime abolished the sultanate boundaries and substituted a system of six governorates, which were designed to cut across the traditional administrative areas of the sultanates. To date there is little evidence that the new governorates will enjoy effective political autonomy from Aden. On the other hand, anti-NF dissidents began a series of military actions in several governorates in mid-1971; these could conceivably lead to loss of NF authority in some areas.

Although little is known about the inner workings of the NF, some information is available about its main structural features. The party's supreme decision-making body is the General Command, which at present has forty-one members. An elite Executive Committee, composed exclusively of General Command members, functions as an inner directorate for this policy-making body. Formerly consisting of nine members, the Executive Committee was reorganized and reduced to seven members in January 1970. Due to the NF's chronic difficulties in resolving internal factionalism, the PDRY is at present governed by a Presidential Council rather than a single executive. This council, the chairman of which is the titular chief of state, was reduced from five to three members in December 1969.

According to the new constitution announced on November 30, 1970, legislative power was transferred from the NF General Command to a 101-member People's Supreme Council, which was elected in July 1971. According to the promise of President Rubai Ali, in the interim the NF formed a Provisional Council to make arrangements for these elections. The People's Supreme Council will add a novel feature to the PDRY political landscape, but it remains to be seen whether this parliamentary body will amount to more than a bureaucratic extension of the NF General Command.

In sum, the People's Republic is a single-party state, the structure of which resembles a giant pyramid. Control emanates downward and outward from the central command structure in Aden to party members spread geographically and functionally throughout the national domain. It is believed that as a general rule the regime has tended to substitute party loyalists for professionally competent public servants, both in the civil and military sectors.

Political Processes

The NF has disestablished the PDRY's traditional leaders and has gathered all government authority under its own wing. What has resulted is not only a one-party state, but a state in which political processes are evolving according to an extremely doctrinaire pattern. The NF has made no effort to disguise its radical socialist philosophy and appears inclined to apply this philosophy to urban Aden and the backward hinterland without distinction.

The NF's constituencies are fairly well defined. Aden provides a ready-made target for political recruitment because its citizenry, which has been exposed to political action by rival labor unions and anti-British independence groups, is conditioned to slogans and modern methods of political recruitment. By contrast, the hinterland peoples have only recently been exposed to revolutionary concepts and are considerably less inclined to grasp—let alone embrace—the NF's appeal. The party appears to comprehend this obstacle and is accordingly focusing its main efforts on youths. Indeed, the curious spectacle of leftist youth demonstrations in such a remote, traditionally conservative site as Mukalla early in the postindependence era illustrates that transistor radios and skillful propaganda can perform remarkable politicizing functions in a short time. The more isolated and diffident tribesmen and the remaining sayyids can be expected at best to form a reluctant constituency or—more likely—a passive opposition. Present NF efforts to distribute sequestered land to the landless in each governorate illustrate the party's ideology and its desire to penetrate these strongholds of traditionalism. As in Republican Yemen, the task of political consolidation is a formidable one for the regime.

In addition to the PDRY army and public security forces, the NF has at its disposal a paramilitary force known as the Popular Guard. Relations between the party's civilian leadership and the army's officer corps were marked from the beginning by distrust, especially since the army remained neutral during the height of the NLF-FLOSY struggle and cooperated with the winning NF side only at the last moment. By carrying out a continuing purge of suspect officers and by substituting party-affiliated replacements of known loyalty, the NF has built a more trustworthy army; however, the distrust that exists between the civilians and the officers reportedly also exists among the officers as well.

Single-party polities are by no means unusual or unworkable entities in the present age. However, in the People's Republic the one party that has a monopoly of power is endeavoring to rule and to survive in the face of unusually limited national economic resources. The party's greatest dilemma is that it has so little with which to reward participants within or outside its ranks.

Foreign Policy

With its pressing economic needs and few means for resolving them, the NF at first looked in all directions for foreign aid. What little came was for the most part from the Communist countries and Arab nationalist regimes, notably Syria and Iraq. The subsequent development of economic relations in these directions coincided with the NF's political inclinations, and thus the overall orientation of the PDRY's foreign policy is now eastward and toward the radical Arab regimes. This means that two Arab states with great resources for extending aid—Saudi Arabia and Kuwait—are the least likely to respond to NF overtures. Saudi Arabia is a special object of Aden wrath because of its alleged support for the exiled sultans. As noted previously, PDRY forces perpetrated an incident on Saudi territory at the oasis of Wadiyah in December 1969 but were driven back by Saudi air action.

Aden's policy toward its eastern neighbor, Oman, is similarly hostile. Although the archconservative sultan of Muscat and Oman was overthrown by his more liberal son, Qabus, in July 1970, the Omani regime remains a target for PDRY subversion; and because of Omani military and organizational weaknesses, these subversive efforts pose a tangible threat. Reportedly with Chinese help, the NF is actively supporting the Popular Front for the Liberation of the Occupied Arab Gulf (PFLOAG) and the Dhofar Liberation Front (DLF), which operate against the Omani gendarmerie in the adjacent region of Dhofar. Like the PFLOAG, the NF seeks to undermine the established regimes in the Gulf, which it regards as being under British control. It is therefore safe to assume that the present regime will continue to support—by moral if not material means—future regional insurgency movements as they arise.

The NF's relations with the nationalist, revolutionary regime in Yemen are scarcely better than with its natural conservative adversaries. Although the party's choice of the names *Southern Yemen* and *People's Democratic Republic of Yemen* for the post independence state have implied an eagerness to proceed with political integration, the Aden regime has consistently antagonized Sanaa and therefore rendered cooperation in unity affairs impossible. Serious doctrinal differences exist between the two governments, and it is natural that each would be disinclined to proceed except on its own terms. This quest for Yemeni unity is comparable to the region-wide search for Arab unity: its proponents agree on the desirability of the goal but are unwilling to subordinate themselves to one another in order to achieve it. Whatever course Aden-Sanaa relations may take, Sanaa constitutes a political and perhaps even a military force that cannot be readily dismissed. By contrast, Oman is weaker and in NF eyes undoubtedly "overdue" for a political change considerably more drastic than that which occurred with the ouster of the sultan. Since the concept of a Greater Yemen could include all of southern Arabia as far as the Gulf of Oman, frustrated unity plans in the north could easily impel the NF to try its luck with more aggressive policies against Oman in the east.

The People's Republic, a member of the League of Arab States, condemns Zionism in most vociferous rhetoric. However, its geographical remoteness and economic and military weakness render the PDRY generally incapable of contributing to the Arabs' confrontation with Israel.

Political Prospects

The current domestic and external problems of the People's Republic will not be resolved easily, and the future therefore will probably resemble the present. Because the need for economic viability is the most pervasive of the regime's challenges, the NF will have to continue its frustrating search for outside help, and judging by the results to date, this search will continue to focus primarily on the Eastern world. Responsiveness of the USSR and China will be determined to some extent by Soviet strategic interests in air and naval facilities in the Indian Ocean and by the twists and turns of Sino-Soviet competition. One or both powers could exhibit a greater interest in southwestern Arabia if developments elsewhere in the Middle East are perceived as warranting an increased presence on the southern flank. The continued influence of the USSR and China of course would leave a distinctive political stamp.

In addition to its economic problems, the NF will continue to face serious problems in the political sphere. Its leaders will have to resolve their factional disputes and attempt to politicize the PDRY's rural peoples and to build broader bases of support for the party's narrowly defined brand of revolution. The highly politicized Adenis will not be long tolerant of inaction or failure, nor will the ousted traditional leaders of the hinterland be oblivious to opportunities for reestablishing themselves. Although they are not a serious threat to the regime at the moment, the deposed sultans—with outside help—could take advantage of popular dissatisfaction in the hinterlands to reestablish themselves, particularly in Beihan and in areas to the east. Tribal revolts did occur in July and December 1968, and there were reports of dissidence in northern border areas in late 1970. The NF's present policies of restricting the travel of foreigners and resident diplomats in these potentially troublesome areas may indicate that its control over the countryside is less than complete. There are many clouds on the PDRY's political horizons, and these appear to cast their heaviest shadows on the incumbent rulers themselves.

In the event that adverse pressures lead to the NF's demise, several disparate groups can be expected to rush to fill the resultant political vacuum. Waiting in the wings are such inherently incompatible factions as the strongly Arab nationalist FLOSY, the more moderate SAL, and the conservative ex-sultans and their traditionalist followers. Wedged between these power seekers at various points on the political spectrum would be NF defectors, Baathists, and many politically indifferent hinterland inhabitants. Those who disagree with the NF have a common complaint for the present, but it is unlikely that this shared attitude would provide the basis for national unit if the NF loses its power, indeed, it would be safer to predict keen factional rivalries and bitter infighting as an aftermath. Although the NF has manufactured some of its own troubles by its doctrinaire approaches to government, it should be noted that any successor group or coalition would face almost the same problems, because the PDRY has a shortage of economic resources.

The preceding chapters have carried the reader from the vortex of Middle Eastern politics—the eastern Mediterranean—southward through the Arabian peninsula to the two Yemens. As the last two chapters often suggest, this literary journey has not only been southward but backward in time as well. Remote and poor, the two polities in southwestern Arabia appear quite distinctive when compared to their more fortunate oil-rich Arab neighbors. The environment, the problems, and the hopes for Yemen were seen as quite different from those of the PDRY, although common threads of urban-rural rivalries, of modernizing challenges, and of dedication to common Arab goals were encountered. Whether in relatively obscure southwestern Arabia or in the Arab world as a whole, diversity becomes apparent when we delve into details, and unity—or at least similarities—appear when we step back for longer views. In the next chapters the reader will step into a distinctively different world comprising Israel, Turkey, and Iran. This step should not be too disconcerting if the concepts of distance and focus—and hence unity and diversity—have become familiar ideas along the way.

Selected Bibliography

Al-Marayati, Abid A. "United Nations and the Problem of Aden." *India Quarterly* 22, no. 3 (July-September 1966): 257-78.
Discusses the evolution of Afro-Asian attitudes toward the "Aden question" and provides a chronology of U.N. involvement in the issue during the early and mid-1960s.

Ingrams, Harold. *Arabia and the Isles*. 3d ed. New York: Frederick A. Praeger, 1966.
By one of the foremost authorities on South Arabia's tribes and the problems of pacifying and governing them, the man who engineered peace in the Hadhramawt.

Little, Tom. *South Arabia: Arena of Conflict.* London: Pall Mall Press, 1968.
Balanced treatment of historical and contemporary development; an admirable job of sorting out the complex events that preceded independence.

Trevaskis, Sir Kennedy. *Shades of Amber: A South Arabian Episode.* London: Hutchinson, 1968.
Authoritative discussion of the federation scheme by a principal architect.

Waterfield, Gordon. *Sultans of Aden*. London: John Murray, 1968.
A detailed and scholarly review of recent South Arabian history.

State of Israel

Israel is a small country of 7,992 square miles situated on the eastern edge of the Mediterranean Sea; as a result of the June 1967 War, in which Egypt, Jordan, and Syria were defeated, it occupies an additional 26,500 square miles. According to the Jerusalem Program adopted at the 1968 Zionist Congress, Israel's fundamental aims as a Jewish and Zionist state are to effect the unity of the Jewish people, to promote Israel as the focus of Jewish life, to "ingather" the Jewish people to Israel through immigration (*aliyah*) from other countries, to maintain the Jewish identity through education, and to protect Jews living outside Israel. Except for the fact that statehood has been achieved, these goals have not changed since the foundation of the Zionist movement at Basel in 1897.

For ideological inspiration Israel draws on a 3,000-year-old religious heritage and the socialist principles of modern Zionism. The country abounds in religionational symbols—archaeological digs emphasizing Israel's connection with the ancient Jewish kingdoms in Palestine, Bible contests, and the Star of David on the national flag. Memories of the Jewish holocaust during World War II are reinforced by museum displays, literary works, and concentration camp survivors who live in Israel.

The religious and national themes are skillfully woven throughout Israeli life and have helped to unite a heterogeneous population drawn from scores of countries and cultures. Although the Israeli is an ardent nationalist, nationalism has not prevented the emergence of tenaciously held minority views or guaranteed the efficient operation of the political system. Political disputes in Israel are often bitter, and the government is occasionally reluctant to make basic decisions for fear of provoking divisive party struggles. However, despite frequent disagreements over tactics and differences in ideological emphasis, Zionists have generally agreed that Israel must be maintained as a physical refuge and as a spiritual and cultural homeland for Jews.

Establishment of Israel

Israel became an independent state as the result of an intense pioneering effort that began in Palestine in the 1880s, skillful international diplomacy sponsored by the World Zionist Organization (WZO), and military victory over the Arab states, a process that took little more than fifty years. On November 2, 1917, a year before the end of World War I, the British gave the Zionists an invaluable assist by issuing the Balfour Declaration, which emphasized the British government's willingness to help create a Jewish national home in Palestine. Shortly afterward British troops drove the Turks from Palestine and established military rule over the former Ottoman province. A civilian government headed by a British high commissioner and under the general supervision of the Colonial Office was set up in 1920. British control was further strengthened by the allocation of the Palestine mandate by the League of Nations. Under the terms of the mandate, which became effective in 1923, Britain was made responsible for securing the establishment of the Jewish national home and the development of self-governing institutions in Palestine.

The British were interested in Palestine mainly for strategic reasons, and they found themselves caught between irreconcilable Arab and Jewish pressures. The Zionist purpose, although often obscured by intra-Zionist divisions and disagreements between Zionist and non-Zionist Jews, was to acquire by purchase as much land as possible from the Arabs, to become a majority of the population, and to create a Jewish state.

As the Zionists established political parties, labor unions, schools, and an underground army (the Haganah) during the interwar period, the outlines of postindependence Jewish political life began to take shape. The main governing authorities were the National Council of the Yishuv (Jewish community in Palestine), the WZO, and the Jewish Agency, each of which had an executive body to direct daily business. By 1930 the National Council had become responsible for education and health as well as for social and religious welfare. The Zionist executive managed the internal affairs of the Zionist movement and administered the Jewish National Fund, a land-purchase agency. In effect, the WZO and the Jewish Agency developed into a single quasi-governmental organization. The Jewish population, about 85,000 in 1914, was augmented by a steady flow of immigrants and reached 650,000 in 1948.

By the 1930s the Arabs had come to view the Zionists as outsiders determined to oust them from their lands, but the Zionists, concerned with their own plans for a national state and with the fate of their coreligionists in Hitler's Europe, continued to build a quasi-governmental apparatus in anticipation of independence. Sporadic Arab-Jewish friction, occasional Arab attacks against Jewish settlements, and the Arab revolt of 1936-39 failed to halt the development of the Jewish community. The Yishuv had to contend not only with the Arabs but with the British mandatory authorities as well. British policy was inconsistent and confusing to both Jews and Arabs. As early as 1923 the British government angered the Zionists by removing Transjordan from the scope of the Jewish national home. The Peel Commission report of July 1937 described the mandate as unworkable and the Arab and Jewish positions as incompatible; it recommended partitioning the country. Later that year another British commission contradicted Peel and reported that partition was infeasible. A White Paper of 1939 proposed the creation of a unitary Palestinian government within ten years, the restriction of Jewish land purchases, and the limitation of Jewish immigration to 75,000 over the next five years, with further immigration subject to Arab agreement. Had this latter proposal been fully implemented, it would have effectively throttled the movement for a Jewish state.

World War II and the postwar exhaustion of Britain radically transformed the prospects of the Palestinian Jewish community and once again changed British policy. In 1942 the WZO adopted as its official policy the Biltmore Resolution, drafted by David Ben-Gurion, which favored unlimited Jewish immigration and Jewish statehood in the whole of Palestine. Revelations of Nazi Germany's slaughter of European Jewry created widespread international sympathy for the Zionist program. A Jewish terrorist campaign against the British, conducted mainly by the Irgun and the Stern Gang, combined with Arab hostility, further undermined British determination to remain in Palestine. In early 1947 the British took the problem to the United Nations, and on November 29 the U.N. General Assembly, subject to strong and probably decisive pressure from the United States, voted to partition Palestine into a Jewish and an Arab state, with an international enclave comprising the holy city of Jerusalem.

Although the Zionists reluctantly accepted partition, it was rejected by the Arab states, and civil war between Jews and Arabs in Palestine immediately ensued. On May 14, 1948, following the withdrawal of the last British troops, the Israelis declared their independence, which was recognized on a de facto basis within nine minutes by the United States; the Soviets followed several days later. In startling contrast to their future policies, the Soviets allowed the shipment of substantial quantities of needed Czech arms to the Israeli army.

After the Israeli declaration, armies from Egypt, Iraq, Lebanon, Syria, and Transjordan moved across the Palestinian frontiers to thwart Jewish statehood and to occupy territories allotted to the Palestinian Arabs. Badly led, poorly equipped, and eventually outnumbered, the Arabs proved no match for the Israelis, who occupied about 2,000 square miles of land that had been granted to the Palestinian Arabs under the Partition Resolution. Armistice agreements were concluded with Egypt, Transjordan, Lebanon, and Syria in 1948 and 1949, leaving

Israel with jagged cease-fire lines for borders and a bitter legacy of fear and suspicion that has yet to be dispelled. The semipermanent confrontation with the Arab states and since 1967 with the Palestinian guerrilla forces (fedayeen) has colored virtually every aspect of Israeli national life.

Political Environment

Despite continued warfare, Israel is rapidly becoming an affluent and industrialized society whose living standards, culture patterns, and values resemble, at least superficially, those of Europe rather than those of its Arab neighbors.

The People

Population Structure: The Israeli population is divided into three broad groups—European Jews, Oriental Jews,* and Palestinian Arabs. At the beginning of 1972 the population was estimated at 3,013,000, of whom 12.7 percent were non-Jewish. About 70 percent of the 383,000 Arab citizens were Muslims, another 20 percent were Christians, and most of the rest were Druzes. An additional one million Arabs, including 70,000 in occupied East Jerusalem, were living in land occupied by Israel since the 1967 War.

Israel is a nation of immigrants; more than 1.3 million have come since 1948, the majority arriving during the late 1940s and early 1950s. About 90 percent of the immigrants from 1882 to 1948 were born in Europe, mostly in Poland and Russia, they and their Israeli-born children constituted 30 to 40 percent of the total population in 1971. The largest non-European Jewish communities came originally from Iraq, Yemen, and Morocco, with several other Arab countries contributing substantial numbers. Government authorities predict a continuing influx of 30,000 immigrants per year, and some 100,000 persons arrived between June 1967 and the summer of 1970. At least 230,000 Jews emigrated between 1948 and 1970, many left because of inadequate housing and a lack of job opportunities. The number of Jews has almost quadrupled since 1948, and this rapid increase in population constitutes a serious burden on the economy in general and the welfare services in particular. In 1970, for example, about 120,000 families, mostly Oriental Jews, were on relief, including 18,000 families totally supported by the Ministry of Social Welfare, and up to 20 percent of the population is classified as poor. Despite these

---

*In common parlance, the Europeans, including Americans and South Africans, are known as Ashkenazim; the Orientals, mostly Arabic-speaking Jews from the Middle East and North Africa, as Sephardim. Technically, both terms refer to European groups, the Sephardim being Jews who were forced to leave Spain in the fifteenth century.

problems, government policy is to increase the Jewish population by
further immigration and by encouraging large families.

About 80 percent of the population is urban, with 55 percent
situated in Tel Aviv, Jerusalem, and Haifa. The government hopes to
disperse these heavy urban concentrations, partly for reasons of
defense, and to encourage sizable numbers of Jewish families to move
to Jerusalem in order to strengthen Israel's claims to the occupied Arab
part of the city.

Ethnic Divisions: Israeli society is partly stratified along ethnic
lines. The main divisions are between Europeans and Orientals and
between Jews and Arabs. The European group is still dominant, because
of its early colonization of the land, its superior technical skills, and its
political sophistication. The Europeans and their children occupy the
best jobs and control the highest political posts. Orientals tend to be
poorer, not so well educated, and less adequately housed than the
Europeans; in addition, they often have larger families and maintain
more traditional family and kinship relationships than their European
neighbors. Until immigration to Israel, the Orientals were almost totally
unaware of European culture and technology, and they remained
outside the Zionist movement. They had also generally escaped the
waves of anti-Semitism that characterized recent European history.

The government has undertaken many programs to alleviate the
Orientals' plight, but these efforts have not yet bridged the communal
gap. Although Orientals constitute 60 percent of the total primary
school population, in 1970 only 35 percent of secondary school and
14 percent of university students were Orientals. Overt ethnic hostility
appears to have subsided since 1967 in the face of the Arab threat,
although the Isareli-Egyptian truce arranged in August 1970 appears to
have intensified social stresses in Israel, and rioting and demonstrations
by Oriental youths throughout the spring and summer of 1971 have
served to reemphasize questions of poverty and discrimination. Premier
Golda Meir has stated on several occasions that internal disunity poses a
greater potential danger to Israel than the Arab threat.

The position of the Israeli Arabs is anomalous. In theory
they possess equal rights with Jewish citizens, but they have been
subject to overt discrimination at both private and government
levels. This situation results from the bitter Arab-Israel struggle,
which has domestic repercussions in Israel as well as in the Arab
states, and from the fact that Israel is officially a Jewish state.
Much of the land owned by Israeli Arabs was expropriated after
1948, often without adequate compensation, and until 1966 the
Arab community lived under military government. Although
attempts have been made by Jewish groups to win the friendship of the
Israeli Arabs, Arab-Jewish social contacts are minimal, and even
educated Arabs have limited occupational opportunities. In 1966, for
example, only three Arabs were reported to be employed among 2,000
senior Israeli civil servants. Most Arabs still live in rural villages; only a
few reside in the Jewish cities. About 30,000 Israeli Arabs are nomads
(bedouin) or seminomads.

Modernization of Israeli Arab society and more frequent contacts with other Arabs since the June War have increased the appeal of radical ideologies among the Arab population. Friction between the Arab and Jewish communities is therefore growing, and several hundred Israeli Arabs have been sentenced to prison for collaboration with the fedayeen. In November 1969 serious communal clashes in Acre were only narrowly averted after the discovery of a guerrilla cell in the town.

Social Conditions: The average life expectancy in Israel is seventy-two years, which is comparable to that of the most developed nations. Medical services are highly developed, and in 1967 there was one physician for every 430 people. The Jewish literacy rate is about 90 percent. Western mass culture has had a major impact on Israel through radio, television, films, and tourists. Nonetheless, it would be a mistake to view Israel as a European state or an outpost of Western culture; the country has its own unique political structures, ideologies, and problems.

Economic Conditions

The Israeli economy is characterized by a low resource base, high productivity, a decline in manpower devoted to agriculture, and increasing industrialization, particularly in defense-related industries. Economic underdevelopment has been largely overcome by an efficient and technologically skilled labor force and massive inputs of capital from both foreign and domestic sources. A short-term recession in 1966/67, with 12 percent of the labor force unemployed (unemployment among Israeli Arabs was about twice as high), has been replaced by a booming economy, and unemployment declined to 3.3 percent in 1971. Israel's GNP increased by 40 percent between 1967 and 1970; per capita annual income, almost comparable to European levels, stood at about $1,560 in 1970.

Despite favorable trends, however, Israel's economy is beset by grave problems. Water resources are inadequate, and the diversion of the Jordan River through the National Water Carrier Project is proving to be only a temporary solution. Although Israel possesses some of the best agricultural land in the area, much of it is of marginal quality, and it is insufficient to produce enough food for the population; in 1968 $83 million in agricultural products had to be imported.

Continued high standards of living will depend on large foreign capital imports, substantial increases in production, and stabilization of the defense budget, the latter threatened by the rapid momentum of the Middle Eastern arms race. Private consumption has been expanding by 7 to 8 percent a year, a rate deemed excessive by Israel's economic planners, but the rate of increase dropped considerably during 1970. General economic policy, therefore, is geared to the reduction of imports and a rise in exports and personal savings.

The burden of defense is staggering. In 1970 security expenditures represented 45 percent (about $1.26 billion) of the entire government budget; hidden costs—shelters, security roads, border settlements—raised the total to about 50 percent of the budget, or nearly 30 percent of GNP, compared with 12 percent of GNP in 1966. In fact, Israel spent more on defense in 1968, 1969, and 1970 combined than during the entire 1948-67 period, including the June War. Moreover, costs are expected to rise substantially in 1971/72 and to continue at these high levels at least until the mid-1970s. About one-fourth of the entire labor force, some 220,000 persons, were engaged in the defense effort in 1970. The net cost of administering the occupied territories in 1969/70 was about $35 million.

The foreign currency cost of defense has also risen dramatically, from about $160 million in 1966 to about $800 million in 1970. According to the director-general of the Israeli Finance Ministry, about 88 percent of the large balance of payments deficit in recent years was related to military imports. Israel's external account deficit showed a rapid progression from $530 million in 1967 to $1.3 billion in 1970. The total foreign debt in 1970 was about $2.8 billion and was expected to rise to about $3.5 billion by the end of 1971.

In order to finance spiraling defense costs and to maintain the high level of services for an expanding population, Israel has had to rely heavily on foreign capital; since independence Israel has received more aid on a per capita basis than any other country in the world. As of 1970 the cumulative total amounted to at least $10 billion, including government grants and loans, private contributions, remittances, and business investments. Between 1950 and 1967 Israel received $9,267,000,000 in capital imports, of which $1.9 billion in loans was repaid.[1] The major grant contributors during this period were world Jewry ($4.9 billion) and the West German government ($1.96 billion), including reparations from 1953 to 1965 and restitution payments to private individuals, which are still continuing. Israel bond campaigns provided another $1.26 billion in loans. From 1948 to 1971 the United States contributed more than $1.2 billion in economic loans and grants and as much as $1 billion in military loans.

Israel's primary overseas fund-raising instrument, Keren Hayesod, raised an average of about $70 million per year in the first twenty-two years of Israel's existence; 75 percent of these funds originated in gifts to the American United Jewish Appeal (UJA) and 25 percent from collections in fifty-four other countries. In May 1967 alone, in anticipation of the June emergency, Keren Hayesod collected $400 million. The monies raised by this organization were used to establish 257 Jewish agricultural settlements from 1920 to 1948 and 490 agricultural settlements and 27 new towns from 1948 to 1970. Continuing large contributions are viewed by the government as of critical importance. Premier Golda Meir has stated that in 1971, for example, Israel would require $1 billion from world Jewry—$400 million from the UJA, $200 million in gifts from other countries, and $400 million in Israel bonds. In fact, the government hopes to receive a total of about $104 billion in capital imports in fiscal year 1971/72, but collections often fall short of goals.

Political Culture

The political culture is the environment, including national values and beliefs, in which political action takes place. The Israeli political environment has been strongly influenced by the democratic values of modern Judaism and by the socialist-egalitarian ethic of Labor Zionism. The pioneers, attracted to socialism and concerned with establishing a full Jewish life in a Jewish land, attempted to build an agrarian-based labor common-wealth; their goal was to redeem the Jew through manual labor and work on the soil. Exploitation of man by man was to be ended. The Labor Zionists were only partly successful, however, and in many respects the Jewish occupational structure of the diaspora was duplicated in Israel; in 1967, for example, only about 3.5 percent of the Jewish population lived in kibbutzim (agricultural collectives), down from 7.5 percent twenty years earlier. As of 1971 only about 10 percent of the working population was engaged in agriculture; most Israelis worked in industry, the professions, commerce, finance, and public services.

Although kibbutz origins are still useful to an aspiring Israeli politician, the agrarian ideal seems to be dying, and many young people do not return to the kibbutz after military service. The decline of the kibbutz is related to the growth of affluence, a weakening of national idealism, the growth of social and economic complexity on a national level, and the development of bureau-cratic state institutions at the expense of voluntary associations. Moreover, the decline of European immigration has dried up most sources of manpower for the kibbutz; Oriental Jews find the kibbutz way of life alien to their traditional customs and they seldom join.

A kind of class consciousness based on professional status is developing in Israel as more people enter scientific and white-collar jobs. The farmer-pioneer is even being replaced by the military man as the new cultural hero. A loosening of ideological rigidity can also be seen in the decline of doctrinaire socialism and in the growth of capitalistic, middle-class values among the younger generation. Nonetheless, the strength of Labor Zionism is still great, as manifested in the continued electoral success of old-line political parties and the dominance of Israel's political life by a European-oriented elite.

The image of the Jewish holocaust in World War II has exerted an unseen but profound influence on Israeli political life. It has shaped the government's relationship to the Arab states and has determined the policy of unrestricted Jewish immigration to Israel. To many Israelis, however, particularly Orientals and those born in Israel (sabras), the European conflagration is not a graphic reality. The trial of Adolf Eichmann in 1961 was in large measure an effort by Premier Ben-Gurion to instruct Israeli youth (and the world community) in the lessons of the Jewish experience in World War II.

Political Structure

Israel is a democratic, parliamentary republic with a cabinet form of government. Its political system, in contrast to those of many Middle Eastern states, is efficient and generally responsive to the popular will. The main instruments in the formulation of national policy are the cabinet, the Knesset (legislative assembly), the Histadrut (General Federation of Labor), and the Jewish Agency. At the local level government is exercised through a system of elective councils, including municipal councils, town councils, and regional village councils, all under the supervision of the Ministry of Interior. However, these councils are overshadowed in power and importance by the institutions of the national government.

The functions of Israel's president, who is elected by the Knesset for a five-year renewable term, are largely ceremonial, although potentially important in a few areas. The president signs laws and treaties, receives foreign ambassadors, serves as a goodwill emissary on diplomatic missions, and when the occasion requires, formally asks the appropriate political leader to form a government. In contrast, the prime minister has extensive powers to determine policy, allocate resources under existing law, propose new legislation, and direct the operations of government. The prime minister must be a member of the Knesset; cabinet ministers are usually party leaders and members of the Knesset but need not be. The cabinet normally meets once a week for general discussions; detailed work is accomplished through special cabinet committees. The cabinet committee on security is an exclusive inner group in which crucial decisions affecting national security are made. Cabinets may be dissolved by a vote of no confidence in the Knesset; expiry of the Knesset term; resignation of the cabinet; and resignation or death of a prime minister. Some seventeen cabinets held office from 1948 to 1970.

Israel's supreme legislative authority is the Knesset, a 120-member body; elections are held at least once every four years on the basis of proportional representation in a single national constituency. In theory the Knesset is considerably more powerful than the United States Congress. It operates without formal constitutional restraint or threat of executive veto, and it can be dissolved only after the expiry of its term of office or by its own collective decision, but not by the prime minister. In practice its powers are more circumscribed than theory would suggest, and the subordination of legislative to executive authority is pronounced. Cabinet ministers, in fact, have more authority in initiating legislation than the Knesset. Draft legislation is usually proposed in the appropriate ministry, approved by the cabinet, and then sent for consideration to the Knesset.

The major feature of Knesset operation is an entrenched multiparty system. Party discipline is strictly enforced, although party lines are apparently less rigidly drawn in standing committees of the parliament than in the full Knesset. Because the Knesset member in effect owes his job to the party, which places him in a winning position on the electoral list, rather than to the voter, he has little flexibility in adopting positions independent of his party.

The Knesset is required to be in session no less than eight months per year. The most important item on its agenda is the budget. In most cases bills are passed after three plenary readings by simple majority of those present and voting. The basic work is done in nine committees of nineteen members each, including finance, foreign affairs and security, public services, education and culture, and labor. In addition to no confidence votes, Knesset influences over government policy is exercised during frequent question periods, in which cabinet ministers are required to reply orally or in writing to questions from the floor. Although the Knesset is an important national forum for the discussion of public issues, interest in its activities seems to have waned as a result of the formation of the "unity" government in 1967, the June War, and the desire to close ranks in a time of prolonged crisis. It is not a major power center, and political reputations are usually made elsewhere.

Although not formally part of the government structure, the Histadrut is a quasi-governmental labor federation that some have termed a state within a state. Its widespread activities have been steadily cut back since independence as the government assumed many of its functions, but it still retains considerable power. The Histadrut is composed of thirty-eight national unions, whose basic unit is the workers' committee elected by office or plant workers. In 1969 membership totaled 1,080,000, including housewives, and represented almost 90 percent of all wage earners. Histadrut enterprises account for about 25 percent of total industrial output and more than 50 percent of heavy industry. It is still the country's main agency in the social welfare field, and its medical organization provides comprehensive health insurance for a majority of the population.

Elections for the Histadrut's governing body are held every four years. These elections are second in importance only to those for the Knesset and are held on the same partisan and electoral basis. As a result, many Histadrut managers belong to the same party as that of the prime minister, thereby automatically endowing the government with the major voice in labor legislation, wage policy, and other economic questions. Nonetheless, friction between government and labor is frequently intense, as underlined by the wave of strikes in 1970 and 1971.

Another quasi-governmental organization is the Jewish Agency of the WZO, which operates under a covenant signed with the government in 1954. Under the terms of this covenant, the Jewish Agency is responsible for promoting immigration to Israel, organizing immigrant health and welfare services, establishing agricultural settlements, and aiding higher education and research. Its budget for fiscal year 1970/71 was $356 million, and this increased in 1971/72 to over $400 million. Both the Jewish Agency and the WZO, which, among other things, is responsible for Jewish educational work in the diaspora and public information, are controlled by the Zionist parties in Israel.

Israel has no formal written constitution, partly because of disagreement between religious and secular parties over the nature of religious authority in the new state. A main issue was whether Israel would be a theocracy or a secular republic. Nonetheless, a series of basic laws adopted by the Knesset serves as the outline of a constitution. The legal system is based on British mandatory law, Knesset legislation, and court jurisprudence. Ottoman law has been virtually eliminated, although Jewish, Muslim, and Christian religious authorities retain control in matters of personal status (marriage, divorce, inheritance). The judicial system is composed of civil, religious, and military courts under the general supervision of the Ministry of Justice. The Supreme Court stands at the apex of this system, but it does not possess the power of judicial review over Knesset legislation.

Political Processes

Political Leadership

Israeli political life has been directed since independence by an aging,* European-oriented elite possessed of a common cultural outlook and background. Most members of the Knesset come from Eastern Europe, although the proportion of Israeli-born members has been increasing in recent elections. In the 1969 Knesset, sixty-eight members were born in Eastern Europe, fifteen were born in Arab countries, twenty-one were sabras, and seven were Israeli Arabs; several others were born in Western or Central Europe. Some changes in political attitudes and processes are to be expected as the sabra and Oriental Jew gain more influence; relatively young leaders such as Yigal Alon and Moshe Dayan (both sabras) already occupy positions of considerable importance.

The continuity of political leadership is striking. Although the old Labor Zionist veterans are dwindling in number, they or their ideological descendants have generally managed to retain control of key political posts. Frequent changes in government have not been matched by a comparable turnover in personnel, and the number of new ministers filling cabinet posts is relatively small. Only four persons have served as premier, and only three as foreign minister, including Golda

*David Ben-Gurion was seventy-six when he retired in 1963; the late premier Levi Eshkol died in office in 1969 at the age of seventy-three; Golda Meir was seventy-one when she assumed the premiership following Eshkol's death; and Zalman Shazar was seventy-three when he became president in 1963. The youngest member of the Israeli cabinet in 1971 was forty-seven.

Meir, who held the office from 1956 to 1966. David Ben-Gurion served as prime minister for thirteen of Israel's first fifteen years, and Levi Eshkol was minister of finance for eleven years before succeeding Ben-Gurion as premier. Moreover, the major cabinet posts and the ministries responsible to them have been controlled by a single party—MAPAI (Israel Workers' party). These positions include the premiership, the Ministry of Defense (until Moshe Dayan became defense minister in 1967), the Ministry of Finance, the Ministry of Foreign Affairs, and several others. The broadening of the governing coalition in response to the Arab threat in 1967 and the formation of the Israel Labor party (ILP) in 1968 have tended to reduce MAPAI's commanding influence.

Israel's European leaders, many of whom were born or reared in the kibbutzim, derive their authority and political legitimacy as the country's founding fathers. As the archetypal representatives of the new Israeli and as military defenders of the community, the kibbutzniks attained an elite status in the new state. They occupy many of the higher ranks in the army and in the government, and their proportion in the Knesset usually ranges from 10 to 15 percent. Virtually every kibbutz is affiliated with a political party; when the kibbutz membership divides over political loyalties it also separates into different units. MAPAM (United Workers' party of Israel) ranks first in the number of kibbutzim attached to it, MAPAI is second, and Ahdut Avodah (Unity of Labor) is third. Each of these parties has over 20,000 kibbutz members.

If the Europeans and particularly the kibbutzniks have been overrepresented, the Orientals, reflecting their lesser economic and educational position, are underrepresented in political life, not only in the Knesset but also in the cabinet, the civil service, the Jewish Agency, and the Histadrut. Nonetheless, their numbers in the Knesset (and doubtless elsewhere as well) are slowly increasing, from nine in the first Knesset to fifteen in the seventh, and one or two ministerial posts are usually reserved for Orientals. Despite the Orientals' potential group strength, their voting patterns do not appear to be substantially different from the more established segments of the population, and bloc voting is not popular. Communal tickets have not been successful in national elections since 1955, partly because of a lack of campaign funds, but Orientals have fared somewhat better on the municipal level. Sephardi rioting in 1959 impelled MAPAI and other parties to add Orientals to their electoral lists, a policy that lessened the desire of the Orientals to organize on their own.

Political Parties and the
Electoral System

The Israeli political system is composed of a bewildering array of parties and factions characterized by frequent splits, coalitions, and shifting alignments (see table 8 for a list of parties and election results

Table 8

Israeli Political Parties and Recent Knesset Election Results

	Number of Votes	Percentage of Votes	Members in Knesset	
	1969	1969	1965	1969
The Alignment (Israel Labor party and MAPAM)	632,035	46.22	63	56
GAHAL bloc	296,294	21.67	22	26
MAFDAL	133,238	9.74	11	12
Alignment Arab parties	47,989	3.51	4	4
Agudat Israel	44,002	3.22	4	4
Independent Liberal party	43,933	3.21	4	4
State list	42,654	3.11	1	4
New Communist party	38,827	2.84	3	3
Poalei Agudat Israel	24,968	1.83	2	2
Ha' olam Hazeh	16,853	1.23	1	2
Free Center party	16,393	1.20	4	2
Israel Communist party	15,752	1.15	1	1
Land of Israel movement	7,591	0.55	–	–
Peace list (Abbie Nathan)	5,138	0.37	–	–
Sephardi list	2,116	0.15	–	–

Source: Adapted from Israel Economist, November 1969, p. 297.

in 1969). The main parties are basically ideological coalitions whose various beliefs and positions have been shaped over the past seventy years. Although a number of parties contest for office (twenty-one in the Knesset elections of 1949, twenty-four in 1959, and sixteen in 1969), most, except for the Arab and Communist organizations, are agreed on Zionist fundamentals. Political instability is thus not so great as these numbers might suggest; moreover, the dominance of a central coalition of parties and the homogeneity of the elite narrow the opportunities for radical political change. Although the 1965 elections were perhaps the most bitterly contested in the nation's history, many observers considered the campaign relatively superficial in that the parties failed to present the voter with clear choices on the issues. A distinct shift away from the socialist-labor parties was apparent on domestic issues during the 1969 elections, but there were few interparty differences on security and foreign policy.

About one-third of the electorate are registered party members, and the so-called floating vote is relatively small, although evidently increasing. One reason for the low independent vote is the socioeconomic controls the parties exercise over their members and supporters. Parties are not only vote-getting institutions but also ideological and subcultural groups. Many parties that began in the mandatory period founded their own housing developments, labor exchanges, trade unions, youth groups, newspapers, and credit bureaus. Many also operate business enterprises, insurance companies, theaters, and recreation centers. Voter political consciousness is high; more than 80 percent of the 1,750,000 registered voters cast ballots in the 1969 Knesset elections. Interest in elections for the Histadrut is less intense; the lowest percentage in fifty years voted in 1969.

Electioneering is intense. Campaigning ordinarily takes place in private clubs or apartments, but the introduction of television seems to have inaugurated a new era in campaigning. Campaign spending is high; each party is permitted by law to spend from public funds about $35,000 for every seat held in the outgoing Knesset and up to one-third of the public allotment from private sources, an arrangement that tends to perpetuate the strength of the old, established, wealthy groups. Private campaign funds are raised abroad from the United Jewish Appeal and by independent party fund drives. Most Zionist parties have affiliates in the United States and Great Britain to aid in these drives; for example, there are seventeen branches of the Poale Zion (United Labor Zionist Organization) in New York City alone. Contributions from Histadrut enterprises are also significant. It was estimated that in the 1965 campaign political advertisements alone accounted for as much as $1.3 million in expenses and party administrative costs for ten times that amount.

Candidates are chosen by party caucus or in small committees without voter participation. In theory a party list could include 120 candidates for Knesset elections, but only the largest parties ever run a complete slate; if the party receives 1 percent of the vote, it will have one representative in parliament. The party campaigns for a list as a whole rather for individual candidates; voters must choose the entire list—split-ticket voting is impossible. Since only a percentage of the list will win election, the party makes an effort to place the candidates it wants to win at the top of the list where their success will be virtually assured. This is possible because the party managers have a fairly good idea how the vote will turn out—the vote received by each party has not fluctuated widely since 1948. As a result, there is considerable party infighting for the select positions on the electoral list. In 1969, for example, twenty-four of the ILP's "safe" seats were given to new candidates, resulting in the displacement of several veteran members of the Knesset. Although it is not essential to the party's success, some effort is made to balance geographic and group interests in the selection of candidates. This system has been criticized because it does not permit representation of citizens by voter district.

MAPAI and the Israel Labor Party: Despite the fragmented multiparty character of the system, governments always reflect the dominant position of MAPAI, a moderate, socialist party, and until his retirement in 1963, that of its leader David Ben-Gurion. All prime ministers have belonged to MAPAI, but although it is the largest single party, it has never attained a Knesset majority. At the local level MAPAI's dominance is less pronounced.

MAPAI's fortunes in recent years illustrate the tendency toward fission and fusion in the Israeli political system. In 1965 MAPAI joined with Ahdut Avodah to form a larger grouping known as the Alignment for the Unity of Israel's Workers. The MAPAI-Ahdut alignment was part of an attempt by MAPAI's leaders, increasingly pressured by young members of the party who were demanding their fair share of the political fruits, to ensure the continuity of the country's leadership and the continued development of the Zionist welfare state. Ben-Gurion opposed the alignment and led his followers, including Moshe Dayan, out of the party to form RAFI (Israel Workers' list), which claimed to represent the younger generation Israelis.

RAFI's defection threw MAPAI into internal disarray and forced it to reorganize down to the grass-roots level. Many Israelis welcomed Ben-Gurion's failure to stage a comeback during the 1965 elections under the RAFI label. Ben-Gurion had been frequently criticized by intellectuals for his autocratic methods, his hard-line foreign policies, his apparent indifference to Israel's structural economic problems, and the personality cult he fostered. In 1968 RAFI, along with Dayan, rejoined MAPAI and Ahdut Avodah to establish the Israel Labor party. Ben-Gurion, however, long antagonistic to Levi Eshkol, then premier and head of the ILP, remained out of the new party as head of the State list, a rump faction of RAFI. Ben-Gurion has since resigned his seat in the Knesset, and the prospects of his State list are in doubt.

During the ILP's preconvention elections in December 1970, MAPAI elected 70 percent of the delegates; the Ahdut Avodah faction, about 17 percent; and RAFI, about 13 percent. As the smallest faction in the ILP, RAFI's future is uncertain and probably depends on the political fortunes of Moshe Dayan. The combined party has about 300,000 registered members, representing one-sixth of the electorate. They include many wealthy businessmen, professionals, and other middle-class citizens, as well as workers. Along with MAPAM, a Marxist-oriented socialist party which combined with ILP to contest the 1969 elections, it represents the broadest political force in Israel's history, with fifty-six members in the seventh Knesset.

The Religious Parties: Though frequently in coalition with MAPAI or ILP, the Orthodox religious parties are generally opposed to the secularizing trends represented by their coalition partners. The religious parties constitute perhaps 12 to 16 percent of the electorate and draw much of their strength from nonsocialist, religious Polish and German immigrants from the 1930s and from their children. However, these parties did not appeal to an earlier generation of agnostic or even atheistic Russian and Polish Jews who were primarily interested in a secular version of Zionism. In addition to the Europeans, the parties also appeal to religious traditionalists among Oriental Jews, although many Orthodox Jews regularly vote for the secular parties.

Ultra-Orthodox Jews are represented by the small Agudat Israel (Association of Israel) and its labor arm Poalei Agudat Israel. The Agudat program is to transform Israel into a traditional Jewish state, one that is administered by rabbinical authorities and based on scripture. The much larger MAFDAL (National Religious party) demands greater rabbinical influence in the shaping of secular law than presently exists, but it does not call for the establishment of a theocratic state. MAFDAL's strength has remained relatively constant for many years, and it has been a coalition partner in every government through 1971. All three parties, which incidentally compete against one another at the polls, have exerted strong pressures to maintain the purity of the Sabbath and at least some of the external forms of Orthodox Judaism, including the institution of *kashrut*, ritual slaughter of meat, and the traditional interpretation of who is a Jew.

As frequent holders of the balance of political power in the cabinet or Knesset, the religious parties have been able to maintain considerable control over religious life and in matters of personal status. Although they are interested in other issues, they are often willing to trade votes in return for government concessions to their views or for government support for religious institutions. In 1971 MAFDAL ministers threatened to resign unless their demands for a greater religious voice in educational policy were met. Although the government refused on this occasion, such political maneuvering serves as a restraint on secular decision making.

The Opposition: In recent years GAHAL (Freedom-Liberal bloc), composed of the Herut and Liberal parties, has been the main opposition to the government, with twenty-six members in the 1969 Knesset. GAHAL served in the government from 1967 to mid-1970; it left the coalition after the government accepted the U.S.-sponsored cease-fire along the Suez Canal. GAHAL advocates "free enterprise," is adamantly opposed to the politicoeconomic dominance of the Histadrut, and favors retention of all occupied Arab territories. As a strong opposition party, it has an appeal for discontented Oriental voters who, partly because of their experience in Arab countries, may also be responding to GAHAL's anti-Arab platform. GAHAL also appeals to many lower income workers. The Herut wing of GAHAL has strong ties to the prestate Irgun Zvai Leumi terrorist organization. Like that of so many other Israeli parties, its leadership is composed primarily of Eastern European immigrants, especially those of Polish background. The Independent Liberal party, which describes itself as a progressive centrist party concerned with constitutional, economic, and social reforms, remained outside GAHAL when the Herut-Liberal merger took place in 1965.

Other, much smaller Knesset parties that are usually in opposition include the Free Center party, which splintered from GAHAL, although it entertains similar views; RAKAH, the Moscow-oriented, predominantly Arab, New Communist party; MAKI, the

Jewish Israeli Communist party, which broke with Moscow over its support for the Arab position; and Ha' olam Hazeh (This World), a Jewish, non-Zionist group that emphasizes neutralism in foreign affairs, separation of state and religion, and complete equality between Arab and Jew. In addition, several political associations, each with probably less than 1,000 adherents and operating on the fringes of national life, have sprung up in recent years. These include MATZPEN (Israel Socialist Organization), a group of Peking-oriented Communists and al-Fatah sympathizers who split with the old Communist party in 1962, and SIAH (Israeli New Left), a vaguely Zionist group that left MAPAM in 1969. SIAH advocates the evacuation of all occupied territories, the creation of a Palestinian state on the West Bank, and the "reestablishment" of social justice in Israel. Brit Shalom (Brotherhood of Peace), founded before independence by the late Judah Magnes, continues to favor the establishment of a binational Jewish-Arab state in Palestine.

Coalition Government

The process of forming a government is often tedious, usually lasting at least six weeks and occasionally longer. According to law the leader of the largest Knesset party is asked by the president to form a government, which is then formally approved by the Knesset. However, since no single party has ever attained a Knesset majority, the major party (formerly MAPAI, now the ILP) must seek coalition partners from among the smaller groups. The most frequent coalition members have been the religious parties and the small socialist workers' parties. Until May 1967 MAPAI refused to enter into coalition with Herut (Freedom), a right-wing opposition party, and the Communists are still excluded. A basic principle governing the formation of a coalition is to admit a fairly large number of partners in order to provide as much flexibility as possible and to reduce the likelihood of government dissolution. By tradition, the coalition members accept collective responsibility for government decisions; failure to do so would very likely lead to the government's downfall. A vote of no confidence by the Knesset usually registers internal cabinet disagreements rather than an opposition attempt to bring down the government.

As the price for participation in the government, a party is forced to compromise on some issues and ideals; in return it receives control over one or more ministries and a share in government patronage. An interesting case in which the selection of a minister was not the result of interparty bargaining or compromise was the appointment of Moshe Dayan as defense minister in 1967. A leader of RAFI, a small party which left MAPAI in 1965, Dayan was literally forced upon a reluctant Prime Minister Eshkol, who was also defense minister at the time, by a worried public anticipating war with the Arabs.

The head of government (the premier) is the leader of the major party and is in effect selected by party caucus. After the death of Levi

Eshkol in 1969, the nomination of Golda Meir as premier was recommended unanimously by the Israel Labor party's leadership bureau, whose decision was later ratified by the ILP's central committee. In theory the Knesset could refuse to confirm the nomination, but in practice such an eventuality is almost nil.

Israeli Arabs in Politics

The Israeli Arabs are on the margins of Israeli politics. Many Jews do not fully trust them, and their loyalty to the state, especially in times of war with Israel's Arab neighbors, is often questioned. Although they are permitted to sit in the Knesset, they are barred from appointment to the cabinet or from sitting in the Knesset foreign affairs and defense committee. Only after the 1969 elections was an Arab elected to the largely honorific post of deputy speaker of the Knesset, and in 1971 an Arab was elevated to the rank of deputy minister. Although they constitute a potential bloc of more than 150,000 voters, the Arabs remain basically unorganized. The Jewish parties campaign for Arab votes, but large political meetings are rarely held in Arab areas. The Israeli leadership began to court the Israeli Arabs more intensively after 1967 because of their great potential for disruption in the aftermath of the June War. In 1969 the Alignment platform called for increased efforts to integrate the Arabs into Israeli cultural and social life. In order to reduce what was expected to be a heavy Arab vote for RAKAH, the ILP campaigned hard for its satellite Arab parties, and Golda Meir warned that a RAKAH victory would prejudice the opportunities for Jewish-Arab cooperation in Israel.

Until 1969 the Arabs generally split their votes between MAPAI and its two Arab lists, the Communists (now primarily RAKAH), and MAPAM. The Arab lists are conservative and not highly structured organizations. They rely on traditional community leaders and patterns of family loyalty to deliver the vote. MAPAM, the only Jewish party that accepts Arab members on an equal basis, has long championed the cause of Arab civil and political rights in Israel and pressured the government to abolish military rule over the Arabs. Nonetheless, MAPAM has never had the appeal of the Arab parties, which many young Israeli Arabs charge with ineffectiveness, or of the Communists. In 1969 RAKAH won 30 percent of the Arab vote, compared to 22.6 percent in 1965, and supplanted the MAPAI-sponsored lists from first place. RAKAH's margin in Nazareth—the largest Arab urban center in Israel—was even greater (40 percent of the vote). This relatively large Communist vote is not an expression of strict ideological leanings but an Arab nationalist protest against the Jewish state, and much of it comes from younger Arabs who have been educated entirely in the Israeli educational system. A few Arabs vote for the Jewish religious parties whose leaders, as cabinet members, are thought to have some influence on the status of Arabs in Israel. At the same time, several thousand Jews may vote for the Arab lists, probably because of lack of political sophistication or confusion at the polls.

The Jerusalem Arabs occupy a special position in Israeli Arab politics. Officially they are still Jordanian citizens and retain Jordanian passports; some remain in the service of Jerusalem's municipal adminis-tration. They were not allowed to vote in the 1969 Knesset elections but were permitted to vote in the Jerusalem city council elections. (About 4,000 of 35,000 eligibles cast ballots in Jerusalem in 1969.) Theoretically, Jerusalem Arabs who apply for Israeli nationality will be permitted to vote in national elections, but none had applied by 1969.

The Military in Politics

The role of the military in political life, although somewhat indirect, is nonetheless an influential one. Most observers agree that civilian control over military policy is unquestioned. Although many chiefs of staff have belonged to MAPAI, the army itself is not associated with any particular political philosophy, and few officers express strong interest in politics. The armed forces have served as a primary instrument of immigrant socialization, providing general education to the equivalent of eighth grade, teaching Hebrew to immigrant recruits, and imparting skills to the untrained.

Over the years, however, the Ministry of Defense has developed a kind of self-generating momentum. Military leaders have been able to define issues in such a way that it is difficult for civilians of independent views to adopt a contrary course. Some Israelis believe that Israel is developing a military-industrial complex that may have undesirable consequences for civilian control. For many years before the June War, the role of the Defense Ministry and basic strategy in the Arab-Israeli conflict were central themes in the struggle for political power. For a time it even seemed that the civilian authorities might lose control of the ministry.

Difficulties between civilians and the military became acute during the Lavon Affair, which originated in an attempt in 1954 by Israeli intelligence to sabotage Western installations in Egypt, to effect a break in U.S.-Egyptian relations, and to disrupt negotiations between Great Britain and Egypt over the status of British forces in the Suez Canal Zone. This episode remained a volatile issue in Israeli politics until about 1963 and prompted charges that the Defense Ministry's extracurricular activities were a threat to Israel's democratic traditions. It led ultimately to a curtailment of the army's political activities and closer civilian supervision of the intelligence services.

State and Ideology

One of the most perplexing issues confronting Israelis since independence is the kind of society Israel is to be. Is it to continue as a democratic Jewish state and, if so, what will its ideological posture be? These are not merely academic questions. The Jewish character of Israel is threatened by the high birth rate of Israel's Arab citizens and by the inexorable demographic pressures of Arabs living in the occupied zones, and there is also some question as to the loyalty of native-born Israelis to classic Zionist concepts. Many question the basic assumptions of Zionism, and Zionist leaders themselves repeatedly demand a rejuvenation of the movement. Although the Law of Return (July 5, 1950) specifies that every Jew has a right to immediate Israeli citizenship upon arriving in the country, less than 20 percent of world Jewry have actually moved to Israel. If Israeli Jews will for a long time remain only a small part of the Jewish people, will the Zionist claim that Israel is *the* Jewish state, rather than simply a country inhabited primarily by Jews, retain its force?

Although Zionist officials have frequently argued that the Jewish people cannot survive without Israel and that diaspora Jews, especially the young, are ignorant of their heritage, there is considerable evidence that many Israelis do not feel strongly about Judaism as a religion. Perhaps 70 percent of the Jewish population are basically nonobservant, and many complain about the restrictions over everyday life exercised by the Orthodox religious establishment. An opinion poll in 1968 disclosed that 59 percent of those questioned favored separating Jewish nationality and religion. This does not mean that Israeli Jews reject their religion, but it does indicate that many are becoming Israeli or Hebrew nationalists, as opposed to Zionists (i.e., Jewish nationalists) who believe that Jewish people everywhere are or should be immutably linked together.

Moreover, many Israelis of European origin are concerned over the prospect of Israel's "Levantinization," by which they mean the normalization of the country as a Middle Eastern state without worldwide Jewish ties. These fears are fueled by an awareness that the Orientals, who constitute a majority of the population, will before long play a much more significant political and social role in Israeli life. A few Orientals have been integrated into the European elite, but many others have been left behind, and some are disillusioned with the Israeli experience. They are not separatists, and most simply demand full equality with the Europeans. However, they do not share classical Zionist views regarding the role of the state, and their differing cultural standards and perceptions are transforming Israel into a society quite different from that of 1948.

Equally difficult questions are posed by the rapid growth of the Arab population. If the occupied territories are retained, the Israeli Jews could be outnumbered in their own state by 1990. Such a development could lead either to the rapid dissolution of the Jewish state if the Arabs were granted full political equality or to the adoption of authoritarian controls over the Arab majority if the Arabs were denied political rights. In either case the essential features of present Israeli life would be undermined.

Foreign Policy

The basic aim of Israel's foreign policy is to ensure the country's security by diplomatic means; a secondary and related goal is to encourage large-scale Jewish immigration, both to increase manpower and to fulfill the Zionist dream. In pursuit of these goals, Israel maintains diplomatic relations with some one hundred countries. The Ministry of Foreign Affairs is an outgrowth of the political department of the Jewish Agency for Palestine, established in 1929; its permanent staff of about one thousand persons is well trained in the arts of diplomacy. Abba Eban, foreign minister since 1966, when his predecessor, Golda Meir, stepped down, is known for his effective presentation of the Israeli case. On the semiofficial level, the World Zionist Organization and its many affiliates are concerned with maintaining a favorable image of Israel in foreign countries, promoting immigration, and raising funds. At present it has formal organizations in more than forty countries and undertakes fund drives in fifty-five countries.

Israel's international position will be determined over the long term by its relationships with the great powers, primarily the United States and the Soviet Union, and by the outcome of the struggle with the Arab states. As a small country with a limited manpower base and an economy that is unable to manufacture the major weapons systems required for defense despite recent advances in production, Israel is absolutely dependent on the diplomatic and military support of outside powers. Despite its substantial qualitative military superiority over the Arabs, which has enabled it to win three wars in twenty years, Israel feels that its very survival is threatened by the hostile neighbors which encircle it. These fears are heightened by the knowledge that Israel is not formally allied with any country and by a painful awareness of the fate of European Jewry during the Nazi era.

Relations with World Jewry

Although Israel has no formal allies, it does have a close relationship with diaspora Jews, whom many Israelis regard as their country's only "firm and constant friends." Indeed, the support of world Jewry has at times been critical for Israel. Zionists believe that the survival of Israel is essential for the survival, at least in the religious sense, of Jews everywhere, and this belief has led many to give willing help when needed. In 1970 the chairman of the Jewish Agency executive defined the ideal role of diaspora Jewry in Israel's struggle as not just financial largesse, but "an absolute commitment to help Israel with whatever she needed; active defense of Israel's policy and assistance in the creation of a favorable image for Israel; ... [and support of] Israel's policies even if they run counter to the positions taken by one government or another of the countries where Jews live."[2]

Israel and the World Community

Israel's posture in the international community is one of self-reliance and independence. Although it initially attempted to avoid involvement in cold war disputes, this has proved impossible. The country prides itself on its ability to defend itself without foreign troops, and its leaders strongly assert the right to determine the country's course without outside interference. As Prime Minister Meir and others have often stated, neither the United Nations nor the great powers will be permitted to adjudicate what Israel considers to be its vital interests. Thus, Israel has refused to allow United Nations forces (e.g., the U.N. Emergency Force) to be stationed on its side of the armistice lines; it has disregarded numerous U.N. resolutions concerning the status of Jerusalem, military raids into neighboring countries, and the Palestine refugees; and it has failed to sign the nonnuclear proliferation treaty (NPT), sponsored by the United States and the Soviet Union. The U.N. itself, many of whose members take outspoken anti-Israel positions, has been accused of being biased against Israel, and the actions of the Security Council and the General Assembly regarding Israel are said to have no moral authority. This assertive stance is partly related to the historical perceptions of the European-oriented Zionist—after centuries of submission to and humiliation by the Gentile majority in the countries where Jews lived, it is thought that no one can defend the Jews but themselves.

As an Asian country, Israel has made considerable effort to expand its relationships with the Afro-Asian world, particularly since the Bandung Conference of 1955, when Israel began to realize the extent of its isolation in the non-Western world. A relatively large technical assistance program was established, and Israeli military and agricultural experts were sent abroad. Part of this continuing effort is related to a desire to counteract the strong pro-Arab position among many former colonial states, which tend to view Israel as an outpost of Western imperialism. Some prominent Israelis feel that Israel still neglects Asia, however, and that it should pay more attention to such countries as Japan, South Vietnam, and Taiwan.

Israel and the Great Powers

Despite Israel's desire to be free of foreign constraints, it needs a steady supply of arms from outside and therefore requires a reliable friend capable of delivering them. This axiom led former premier David Ben-Gurion to tie his country to France in 1954—an understanding that lasted until 1967, when President Charles de Gaulle declared Israel to be the aggressor in the June War and placed an embargo on arms to

Israel. The same consideration since that war has prompted the Israeli government to focus its diplomatic attention on the United States. As Defense Minister Dayan declared in November 1970, the U.S. is Israel's "only friend," and as the main supplier of modern arms to Israel its goodwill is crucial: ". . . when the U.S. appeals to us, we must think seventy-seven times before refusing, although we must insist on our vital interests."[3]

Israel's relations with the United States have always been close, despite difficulties and disagreements, notably in the 1950s, and differences in perspective on Middle East issues. The United States was instrumental in securing Israel's independence in 1947 and 1948, and the American Jewish community has been a constant source of funds and political support. Since 1967 Israel has become almost totally dependent on the United States for major weapons supplies. Israeli policy is thus directed toward maximizing U.S. diplomatic and military support and minimizing restrictions on Israel's freedom of action. The four-month delay in returning to the peace talks in the autumn of 1970 was a calculated protest against alleged Egyptian and Soviet cease-fire violations; it was also designed to produce a strong American commitment to Israel—ideally, an open-ended arms pipeline and acceptance of Israel's demands for major territorial revisions in its favor. Much of Israel's diplomacy in 1971 was focused on efforts to obtain new military aircraft (F-4 Phantoms) from the U.S.

Israel's relations with the other great powers are less intense. The tacit understanding with France proved essential during the 1950s, but since 1967 France has been in official disfavor because of the arms embargo and French courtship of the Arabs. Great Britain has played a more marginal role, although Israel expressed concern in 1970 because the United Kingdom did not favor Israel's territorial demands. The initially euphoric relationship with the Soviet Union, which stemmed from Soviet recognition of Israel within days after independence, has progressively deteriorated. Diplomatic relations were severed during the June War, and in 1970 Israel nearly found itself in armed confrontation with Soviet pilots and missile crews stationed in the UAR. The USSR's strong support for the Arabs, and the alleged Soviet mistreatment of Russian Jews are irritants in Soviet-Israeli relations.

The Arab-Israeli Conflict

Israel's relations with the Arabs have been troubled since the beginning of Jewish settlement in Palestine. Since the establishment of the state, Israeli policy has been characterized as active self-defense. Large-scale retaliatory raids, both before and after the 1967 War, have been undertaken in response to Arab guerrilla incursions and terrorist attacks. Underlying this policy is the belief that demonstrations of superior military force will ensure tranquility along the cease-fire lines. The small size of the country makes it difficult for military planners to defend in depth—at its narrowest point before 1967 Israel was only twelve miles wide—and this has also encouraged military activism. Territorial gains made during Israel's war for independence were never given up, and the Palestinian refugees created by that war were not compensated or allowed to return. Israel argues that because the Arabs attacked and lost in 1948 they have no right to expect favors from the victor. Further, Arab threats to destroy Israel were not conducive to negotiations in good faith. With regard to the refugees, Israel has insisted that it must remain a Jewish state and that, in any case, the Arab "expulsion" of Jews from their countries constituted a de facto exchange of populations.

Israel's attempt to break out of the ring of Arab hostility by attacking Egypt in 1956 in conjunction with Britain and France failed because of international, mainly American, pressures. After a four-month occupation, Israel was forced to withdraw from the Sinai peninsula and the Gaza Strip. The Arab states were no more willing to recognize Israel or sign a permanent peace treaty after the Suez campaign than they had been in 1948. This humiliating and disappointing experience has colored Israel's policies since the June War.

In the spring of 1967 tensions began to increase once again along the armistice lines, and profound concerns for the physical safety of the country led to Israel's preemptive strike against the UAR. As in 1956, the Israelis hoped to defeat the Arabs decisively and to demonstrate the futility of further Arab military encounters. Many expected the Arabs to make peace after their disastrous defeat; when it became clear that they would not, the Israeli position progressively hardened. In contrast to 1956 and 1957, the U.S. has supported Israel's quest for a permanent peace settlement, and Israel has been able to sustain a long-term occupation. Israel vows not to withdraw from Arab lands until a final peace settlement encompassing "a permanent, contractual, reciprocal agreement" has been achieved, and then only to "secure and defensible boundaries," not to the pre-June 5, 1967, armistice lines. Israel is adamantly opposed to the so-called Rogers Plan, detailed in the U.S. secretary of state's December 1969 speech, which calls for only minor border rectifications.

There are powerful political pressures within Israel for absorbing all or large parts of the occupied territories. Menahem Begin, leader of the GAHAL bloc, believes in retaining and colonizing all "liberated" territories. Ezer Weizmann, son of Israel's first president and another GAHAL leader, declared in 1970 that occupied Hebron on Jordan's West Bank "was, is and will be part of Israel. King David was crowned there and reigned there for seven years and six months. It is part of Israel."[4] Although he does not lay claim to the Sinai peninsula on nationalist or historical grounds, Weizmann wants to retain it for security reasons. The Land of Israel movement, a nonpartisan group with some 100,000 members, including many retired generals and relatives of soldiers killed in action, also resists any Israeli withdrawal and opposed returning to the Jarring talks in the winter of 1971. The movement does not consider the Sinai peninsula to be part of "historic Israel," but it believes that the Suez Canal represents Israel's best defense frontier with Egypt. According to the Free Center's 1969

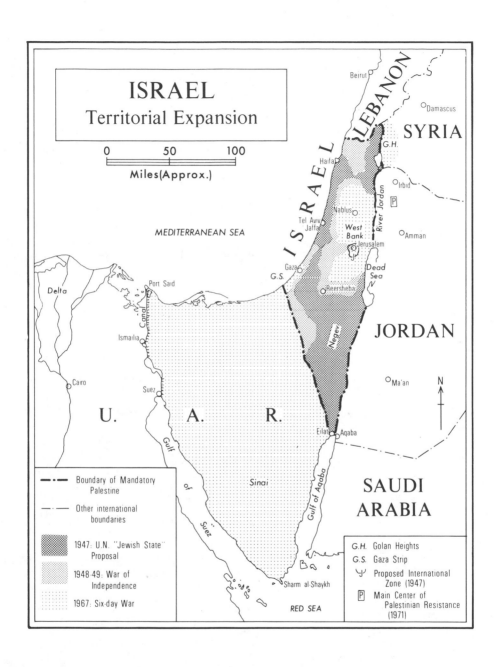

ISRAEL

Territorial Expansion

0   50   100

Miles(Approx.)

MEDITERRANEAN SEA

Beirut

LEBANON

Damascus

SYRIA

G.H.

Haifa

ISRAEL

Irbid

P

Nablus

Tel Aviv
Jaffa

River Jordan

West
Bank

Amman

Jerusalem

Gaza

G.S.

Dead
Sea

Port Said

Delta

Canal

Ismailia

Cairo

Suez

U.   A.   R.

Gulf of Suez

Beersheba

Negev

JORDAN

Ma'an

N

Eilat   Aqaba

Sinai

Gulf of Aqaba

SAUDI
ARABIA

Sharm al-Shaykh

RED SEA

- ·- ·-   Boundary of Mandatory
          Palestine

- · —   Other international
          boundaries

          1947: U.N. "Jewish State"
          Proposal

          1948-49: War of
          Independence

          1967: Six-day War

G.H. Golan Heights

G.S. Gaza Strip

ᴪ   Proposed International
      Zone (1947)

P   Main Center of
      Palestinian Resistance
      (1971)

election platform, Israel is advised to create "an established fact" by populating all "liberated" territories with Jewish civilian settlements and by completely integrating the occupied lands into Israel. In a similar vein, RAFI is in favor of establishing permanent settlements in all territories.

The Jewish religious interest in the territories is intense. As the chief Sephardic rabbi stated shortly after the war: "The land was promised to us by the Almighty, and all the prophets foretold its return to us. Therefore, it is forbidden to any Jew ever to consider returning any part whatsoever of the land of our forefathers."[5] Major General Shlome Goren, former chief rabbi of the Israel defense forces, views Israel's occupation of the Arab lands as the realization of biblical prophecy; according to Rabbi Goren, the 1967 victory "must be the result of a divine plan which history has forced upon us in order to fulfill what God told his prophets."[6] Religious sentiment is not limited to verbal posturing; the three cabinet members who belong to MAFDAL, for example, frequently threaten to withdraw from the government coalition in order to prevent it from adopting a more conciliatory territorial position.

The less extreme territorial program is represented by those who are motivated more by security considerations than by religious or historical factors. Moreover, the Israeli military's assessment of what constitutes defensible borders may be more realistic than that of some annexationist-minded civilians. Government officials have stated that the Jordan River must henceforth be Israel's "eastern defense border," an idea that was originally conceived by Deputy Premier Allon, who believes that no foreign (Arab) army should be allowed to enter the West Bank, even though substantial parts of the territory may be returned to Jordan. Both the Golan Heights of Syria and the Gaza Strip are expected to remain under permanent Israeli control, while a strip of land connecting Sharm al-Shaykh in the Sinai with the Israeli port of Eilat will be retained to ensure Israeli passage through the Straits of Tiran. Jerusalem is considered nonnegotiable by most Israeli Jews; historical and religious associations with the Western (Wailing) Wall and other shrines make it unthinkable for them to return the Arab sector to Jordan or to consider plans for the city's internationalization.

On the other hand, several Israeli political and intellectual figures have opposed the drift of Israeli policy since 1967. Popular reaction to the government's refusal to allow Nahum Goldmann, president of the World Jewish Congress, to visit Cairo in the spring of 1970, indicates some movement in favor of compromise with the Arabs. Many are fearful that permanent occupation will eventually lead to the creation of an Arab majority in the Jewish state. MAPAM has opposed the annexationist campaign and Jewish settlement in Hebron but favors continued military occupation until peace is attained. Ben-Gurion recommends withdrawal from all territories except Jordanian Jerusalem and the Golan Heights.

As for the occupation itself, it has been relatively mild. The basic policy is one of indirect rule with a minimum of interference in Arab life. The occupied lands are divided into several military districts headed by Israeli military governors, but Arab officials have been retained where possible. Jordanian civil law remains in effect on the West Bank and Palestine mandatory laws in the Gaza Strip, supplemented in both places by Israeli military regulations; Israeli law has been introduced into the Golan Heights. Jordanian Jerusalem and neighboring villages were annexed outright on June 27 and 28, 1967, and are not considered by most Israelis as occupied territory.

Israeli security interests are ensured by swift punishment for collaborators in the Palestine guerrilla movement, destruction of houses of suspected guerrillas or their supporters, and banishment of opposition Arab notables and officials. As the occupation has progressed such measures have become harsher and more arbitrary. In early 1971 the Arab mayor of Gaza and the municipal council were removed from office in response to continual agitation and difficulties in the Strip. By the end of February 1971 at least thirty-six Israeli military and civilian agricultural settlements had been established in the occupied territories, with several more planned. To soften these negative aspects of occupation, the government has formulated an open bridges policy whereby non-Israeli Arabs are allowed to visit Israeli-held territory; about 107,000 Arabs visited occupied Jordan during the summer of 1971. In addition, Arabs from the Gaza Strip and the West Bank are encouraged to seek employment in Israel. They are paid relatively high wages, and in mid-1971 there were 40,000 foreign Arab workers in the country, the government's established ceiling.

The shape of a final settlement to the Arab-Israeli conflict is unclear. Israel has adhered to a firm negotiating stance and seems fairly secure in the knowledge of strong U.S. support and continuing arms supplies. Another round of fighting is always possible, but skillful diplomacy can be counted on to exploit the already substantial international sympathy for Israel's beleaguered position.

Political Prospects

To a large extent the future of Israel depends on forces outside its control—the position of the Soviet Union, the military skill of the Arab states, and the policies of the United States. Continued warfare would result in even more severe casualties for Israel than in the past, and it is questionable how long Israel could withstand the strain or could refrain from extreme solutions. Nahum Goldmann has already pointed to Israel's failure as a military state: the Zionist dream of a physical refuge for Jews and a Jewish cultural flowering cannot be secured in conditions approaching permanent war. Israel's elder statesman, David Ben-Gurion, appears to share this belief.

The nature of Israeli politics is, of course, more dependent on the decisions of Israeli leaders; however, it is unlikely that the government was aware of the profound social changes that would occur when unrestricted Jewish immigration was instituted after independence. Moreover, the democratic framework of the state and the diversity of the Jewish population have encouraged the emergence of minority factions that frequently disrupt the political system's smooth operation. Nonetheless, the Israeli is generally a cautious citizen and voter, and radical experiments are not likely unless military disaster or diplomatic defeat transforms the situation. Most groups accept the political rules of the game and are content to discuss the issues in recognized forums instead of taking to the street. As long as the Arab threat remains, and it has so far been a constant factor in Israeli life, the underlying divisions of Israeli society may be partially submerged. The challenge for Israel is to achieve an accommodation with the Arab states while maintaining basic agreement on the fundamentals of the Israeli body politic.

Israel and Turkey, the subject of the following chapter, are very different in demographic composition, social system, and political structure. Israel is a small, predominantly Jewish state, urban, relatively industrialized, and sophisticated in Western technology. Turkey is a large Muslim country, still mostly rural and agricultural. A few similarities also merit comment, however. Both countries are in but not of the Middle East, because Turkey prefers to view itself as a European state with few ties to its southern neighbors, and Israel emphasizes its Western character and links to world Jewry. Moreover, both countries maintain a generally pro-Western outlook: Turkey is formally tied to the West in the NATO alliance, and Israel has a special diplomatic and military relationship with the United States. Finally, both countries have functioning multiparty systems, in contrast to many other Middle Eastern states.

Footnotes

[1] Oded Remba, "The Dilemmas of Israel's Economy," *Midstream* 15 (February 1969): 50-62.
[2] *Israel Digest* 13 (March 6, 1970): 1.
[3] *Israel Digest* 13 (November 13, 1970): 1-2.
[4] *Jerusalem Post*, March 13, 1970, p. 8.
[5] Quoted in Don Peretz, "Israel's New Arab Dilemma," *Middle East Journal* 22 (Winter 1968): 50.
[6] *Bahamaneh*, October 1970.

Selected Bibliography

Arian, Alan. *Ideological Change in Israel.* Cleveland, Ohio: Case Western Reserve University Press, 1968.

Badi, Joseph. *The Government of the State of Israel: A Critical Account of Its Parliament, Executive, and Judiciary.* New York: Twayne Publishers, 1963.

Bernstein, Marver. *The Politics of Israel: The First Decade of Statehood*. Princeton, N.J.: Princeton University Press, 1957.

Dror, Yehezkel, and Gutmann, Emanuel, eds. *The Government of Israel*. Jerusalem: Hebrew University, 1961.
A documentary collection relating to the mandatory and statehood periods.

Fein, Leonard. *Israel: Politics and People*. Boston: Little, Brown & Co., 1968.
An excellent study emphasizing parties and political culture.

Friedmann, Georges. *The End of the Jewish People?* Translated from the French by Eric Mosbacher. Garden City: Doubleday & Co., 1967.
An excellent discussion of Israeli religious, political, economic, and social life, with emphasis on social and ideological change.

Halevi, N., and Klinov-Malul, R. *The Economic Development of Israel*. New York: Frederick A. Praeger, 1968.

Halpern, Ben. *The Idea of the Jewish State*. Cambridge, Mass.: Harvard University Press, 1969.
The best one-volume intellectual history of Zionism.

Kanovsky, E. *The Economy of the Israeli Kibbutz*. Cambridge, Mass.: Harvard University Press, 1966.

Kraines, Oscar. *Government and Politics in Israel*. Boston: Houghton Mifflin Co., 1961.

Landau, Jacob. *The Arabs in Israel: A Political Study*. London: Oxford University Press, 1969.

Perlmutter, Amos. *Military and Politics in Israel: Nation Building and Role Expansion*. London: Frank Cass and Co., 1969.
A study of civilian-military relationships.

Rackman, Emanuel. *Israel's Emerging Constitution: 1948-51*. New York: Columbia University Press, 1955.

Seligman, Lester. *Leadership in a New Nation: Political Development in Israel*. New York: Atherton Press, 1964.
A discussion of political recruitment and attitudes.

Zidon, Asher. *Knesset: The Parliament of Israel*. New York: Herzl Press, 1967.

Zweig, Ferdynand. *Israel: The Sword and the Harp; the Mystique of Violence and the Mystique of Redemption: Controversial Themes in Israeli Society*. Rutherford, Madison, and Teaneck, N.J.: Fairleigh Dickinson University Press, 1969.
An excellent sociological study.

Republic of Turkey

The Republic of Turkey is different in many respects from the other countries of the Middle East. It is one of the largest countries in area, the most populous country, and one of only three whose population is not predominantly Arab. As the prime political heir of the Ottoman Empire, it has a claim to a long history of political independence that is equaled or surpassed only by its eastern neighbor, Iran. Its political transformation from multinational empire to charismatic leadership under a one-party dictatorship to multiparty competition is unique in the Middle East and perhaps the world.

Turkey's character as a border country is emphasized by its physical and diplomatic position. It is the only Middle Eastern country that has territory on the continent of Europe and one of only two that has a common boundary with the Soviet Union. During the years of the cold war Turkey was the first in the region to firmly commit itself to the Western cause. It is a member of the North Atlantic Treaty Organization (NATO) and has the largest standing army in the Middle East. History, size, and strategic position give Turkey a crucial place in the affairs of the Middle East, and the unique changes in the Turkish political system since World War I are worthy of detailed study.

Historical Background

The Turkish political system has undergone a series of radical changes. These can best be understood in terms of four major traditions: the pre-Islamic, Islamic, Ottoman imperial, and Republican.

Four Traditions

The pre-Islamic tradition of the Turks links them with their ancestral home. Before their conversion to Islam the Turks were a series of loosely knit tribal peoples on the steppes of central Asia. They were renowned horsemen and soldiers, qualities that brought them to the attention of Islamic rulers, who hired them as bodyguards and soldiers. More and more Turks adopted Islam and moved into the Middle East, and these soldiers gradually achieved prominence and political power, partly because they displayed tenacious loyalty in protecting the frontiers of the Islamic world. The central Asian origins of the Turks and the role they played in the world of Islam constitutes what may be called the heroic image in the Turkish historical experience.

The Turks were relative latecomers to Islam; their conversion took place between the ninth and eleventh centuries A.D. In their role as soldiers and government officials, particularly in border provinces, they assumed the primary responsibility for defending the faith, and this combination of devout belief, military prowess, and political dominance firmly fixed the Muslim faith in the Turkish national identity. Unlike the Arabs and the Persians, the Turks submerged their pre-Islamic history. The most glorious chapters in their history were written during their leadership of the community of the faithful, and in turn they gave Islam some of its greatest earthly successes (much as the Arabs and Persians had in an earlier day).

The Ottoman Turks are perhaps best known in the West for their conquest of Istanbul (Constantinople) in 1453, and this is not altogether inappropriate. When they took over the seat of the Eastern Roman Empire, the Turks absorbed some of the imperial traditions and created an empire that exceeded ancient Rome in size, power, and wealth. It was without doubt the greatest state in the Western world between the fifteenth and eighteenth centuries, and despite the empire's later decline and fall, the Turks have not forgotten their role as world leaders.

The causes of the decline of the Ottoman Empire have been traced elsewhere. Here we need only note that the dissolution of the Ottoman state was spurred by the expansionist ambitions of the European great powers and by the demands for political independence of the subject nationalities in the Balkans. When the Muslim Arabs joined the nationalist bandwagon during World War I, the Turks concluded that the multinational empire was beyond salvation. At war's end, even Anatolia (Asia Minor)—the heartland of the empire and the only territory inhabited predominantly by ethnic Turks—was threatened with partition among the European powers. In May of 1919 Greek troops landed in the Aegean port city of Izmir (Smyrna) to claim large portions of western Asia Minor, but this landing and the three-year war that followed inspired a strong nationalist reaction in the Turkish population. Mustafa Kemal Ataturk, a flamboyant military officer, organized a popular nationalist resistance army which he led to victory over the Greeks. He then capitalized on the revolutionary situation to undermine and destroy the discredited Ottoman dynasty and most of the institutions of the empire.

Ataturk was also freed of the problem of ethnic rivalry and conflict. The threat of an independent Armenian state in Asia Minor had been eliminated by deportation and voluntary migration before World War I. The large Greek minority, with the exception of residents of Istanbul, was required to emigrate to Greece under a treaty concluded between the new Turkish Republican government and Greece. By the mid-1920s the only significant ethnic minority that remained under Turkish rule was the Kurds, who inhabited the eastern and southern border areas of the new Turkish state.

The Republican tradition in Turkish political culture is largely the creation of Mustafa Kemal Ataturk, and it stems from his attempts to remold the communal sense of identity and the basic institutions of society and government. Charging that the religious values and dynastic loyalties of the Ottoman Empire had caused the Turks to fall, Ataturk promulgated such modern concepts as secularism, nationalism, and republicanism. Against stiff opposition he insisted that some of the chief institutions of the old regime be abolished, including the sultanate and the caliphate, the office of shaykhulislam (highest religious functionary in the Ottoman system), the Ministry of the Sheriat (Shariah), religious courts of law, religious schools and colleges, mystical dervish societies, and even such seemingly mundane and personal items as the fez, a brimless hat that had become traditional.

Sultanate and caliphate were replaced by republican political institutions, including an elected president and the Grand National Assembly, or parliament. Religious courts and laws were replaced by secular courts and legal codes modeled on European patterns. Schools and colleges were brought under the unified control of a new Ministry of Education; religious instruction was prohibited, and institutions such as mosques and pious foundations which could not be abolished were put under the direct control of the secular government. There was a new emphasis on the ethnic Turkish character of the state, as opposed to the Ottoman-Islamic character of the old system.

Perhaps the most dramatic symbol of change was the 1928 alphabet reform under which the Arabic script was abandoned in favor of the European or Latin alphabet. By changing their system of writing, Ataturk profoundly influenced the intellectual resources of his people. Within a generation only a relatively small minority would be able to read the classic Ottoman-Islamic literature in the original, and unless these classics were transliterated into the new script—the only legal script—they would be lost. Nor did Ataturk encourage widespread transliteration. His main object was to deemphasize the Ottoman cultural tradition and to focus the attention of the new Turk on his more limited homeland and on the development of a new nationalist culture.

The alphabet reform pointed up the heavy infiltration of the Turkish language by Arabic and Persian terms and expressions, which when transliterated into a latinized script adapted to the sound system of the Turkish language (a system liguistically unrelated to either of the two), appeared woefully out of place. Within a few years of the alphabet reform, a major effort was launched to nationalize the language by purging it of all foreign (i.e., Arabic and Persian) forms and expressions. And because Arabic and Persian had served as the chief carriers of Islamic culture and tradition, the effect was not only to heighten Turkish national consciousness but to cut one more tie to the Ottoman-Islamic tradition.

Ataturk thus sought to restructure completely the cultural and national as well as the political identity of the people of contemporary Turkey.

> The subsequent rise of military regimes in other Muslim countries in the Middle East has led some observers to see Ataturk and his revolution as the prototype of these later movements. There is, however, very little resemblance between them. Ataturk was not a revolutionary junior officer seizing power by coup d'état but a general and a pasha, taking control by gradual, almost reluctant steps in a moment of profound national crisis. He and his associates, though imbued with new ideas, were by status and habit men of the old Ottoman ruling elite, with centuries of military and imperial experience. Even after the destruction of the empire and the banishment of the dynasty, they still had the assurance and authority to demand—and receive—obedience, not needing either to court popularity or enforce submission.[1]

In short, Ataturk used radical and even revolutionary means to reach an essentially conservative end. He abolished hallowed institutions and prescribed traditional ideas in order to preserve the political independence and territorial integrity of the state. In this process of revolution for the sake of conservation, Ataturk on the one hand left the basic social structure of the Ottoman-Turkish polity untouched and on the other hand sowed the seeds for basic changes in that social structure, although these seeds were not to bear fruit until several decades later, long after the charismatic leader had passed from the scene. A prominent theme in the evolution of the Turkish political system has been the incorporation of an ever-widening circle of social groups.

The First Republic

First Phase: The so-called Struggle for Independence lasted from 1919 to 1923. During this phase Ataturk used the authority and prestige of his status as a military officer to establish a base of political power independent of the legal Ottoman government. He gained the support of military commanders throughout Anatolia and of such key civil service groups as the telegraph operators. Local nationalist societies, which had been formed to resist the imposition of foreign authority, also rallied to Ataturk's cause. Nationalists dominated the parliament elected in 1920, but the British forced the Ottoman sultan to dissolve it. Ataturk then called for new elections and convened a new legislative body in the interior town of Ankara, where he had earlier established his headquarters.

The new body titled itself the Grand National Assembly and became the source of legitimacy for the Kemalist regime. Ataturk was careful to obtain the approval of this body for all major policy initiatives, and although he was usually able to dominate the assembly by the sheer force of his personality, there were long and acrimonious debates. As long as the issue was nationalist resistance against foreign invaders, the members of the assembly were united, but religious functionaries and other conservatives were suspicious of Ataturk's intentions and were not mollified by his protestations of loyalty to the sultanate and to traditional religious values.

Their suspicions were well founded. Ataturk justified his major policy proposals with the argument that they were necessary for the preservation of the independence and integrity of the state. Soon after the successful conclusion of the war against Greek occupation forces, however, he extended this argument onto entirely new ground by using it to persuade a reluctant assembly to abolish the Ottoman sultanate. The opposition of the sultan's government to the national struggle for liberation had undermined popular belief in that government's legitimacy sufficiently to enable Ataturk to carry the day. If those who remained loyal to traditional institutions did not yet understand the sharp break with the past that this move represented, that meaning was brought home even more forcefully during the following two years. On October 29, 1923, the assembly declared Turkey a republic and elected Ataturk its first president. In March of 1924 the last vestige of traditional legitimacy was removed with the abolition of the caliphate.

Second Phase: The political system that emerged after the declaration of the republic was tailored to the leadership style of Ataturk. In many respects it resembled the parliamentary pattern common in Western Europe. There was an elected parliament, the Council of Ministers headed by a prime minister, and an elected president. Some features were unique, however. All legal power was concentrated in the parliament, or Grand National Assembly, which was "the sole rightful representative of the nation and exercised the right of sovereignty in its name." The members of the assembly were popularly elected, and they in turn elected the president of the republic from among themselves to serve a term of four years concurrent with the term of the assembly. Neither the president nor the prime minister nor the Council of Ministers was empowered to dissolve the assembly and call for new elections, as is the practice in most parliamentary systems, but the Council of Ministers depended on the confidence of the assembly and could be ousted from office by its vote.

It is an elementary rule of politics that when large bodies of people attempt to form a collective will, power inevitably tends to flow into the hands of a few leaders of cliques. The Turkish Grand National Assembly was no exception. It was, in fact, dominated from its first day until his death in 1938 by the energetic and domineering nationalist leader, Kemal Ataturk. His domination was not always complete, but the assembly never rejected an important measure sponsored by him.

Ataturk's domination of the assembly after 1925 was assured by outlawing organized political opposition and carefully handpicking candidates for membership in the parliament. His instrument for this purpose was the Republican People's party (RPP). The system thus came to resemble the single-party dictatorships of Western Europe; in some respects it was, in fact, modeled on the pattern of Mussolini's Fascist system, although it never developed into full totalitarianism. Yet the prime minister and other members of the cabinet could not be independent political leaders; like the rest of the Grand National Assembly, they were at the leader's beck and call.

This system survived for some time after the death of the leader. It was carried on through the difficult years of World War II by his closest associate, Ismet Inonu, who succeeded him in the presidency. Inonu lacked Ataturk's flamboyance but was able to maintain his dominance through the machinery of the political party.

Third Phase: In 1946, however, Inonu engaged in a major departure by allowing the formation of opposition parties. A previous attempt in this direction (during Ataturk's lifetime) had revealed a degree of latent opposition that was so disturbing it led to cancellation of the experiment after only a few months, but in the late 1940s there was no turning back. The culminanation came in 1950 when the opposition Democratic party won a landslide victory in the general election. Inonu chose to honor the openly proclaimed will of the electorate and voluntarily relinquished power. Turkey thus became perhaps the only country in modern history in which an autocratic regime peacefully gave up the reins of government.

Why Inonu and the Republican party chose this unusual alternative is not entirely clear. Part of the explanation undoubtedly lies in a genuine commitment to democratic principles of government, which was always implicit in the officially promulgated ideology of the republic. The example of the Western democracies also played a role, particularly in the aftermath of their overwhelming victory in World War II. In addition, Turkey was under heavy diplomatic pressure from the Soviet Union; it is likely that the Inonu government thought that Western support would be more readily available if Turkey adopted a political system in the Western mode. It is an open question whether the decision would have been the same if the reaction of the Turkish electorate had been accurately foreseen.

The Democratic party made no formal changes in government structure, but the effective center of power shifted from the president to the prime minister. Celal Bayar, elected president by the Democratic assembly in 1950, functioned primarily as ceremonial head of state, whereas the real political boss during the 1950s was Adnan Menderes, prime minister and general chairman of the party. Bayar and Menderes were the first two occupants of their respective offices who had never been professional army officers. This simple fact, largely unnoticed when they assumed power, was to play a major role in their downfall ten years later.

The Democratic party was organized as the result of a split in Republican ranks in 1946. Although its leaders had served loyally in the Republican hierarchy during most of the Ataturk-Inonu years (1923-45), they had been involved in some oppositionism. Celal Bayar, for example, had been a rival of Inonu, succeeding him as prime minister on one occasion. One of the chief areas of disagreement between the two men was economic policy: Inonu favored heavy government involvement and Bayar advocated reliance on private enterprise.

Perhaps of greater significance is the fact that several of the founders of the Democratic party had been prominent critics of a land-reform law proposed by the Inonu government and debated during the year before the formation of the new party. Menderes, one of the critics, represented one of the most prominent and wealthy landowning families in the Meander River valley in western Turkey, an area that was about to emerge as a prosperous cotton-growing region. This affiliation suggests that with the rise of the opposition, support of the Republican party by local notables was giving way. Their support weakened precisely when the party began moving against their interests. The alienation of many rural and provincial notable families from the Republican party has deepened in the years since this initial split.

When the Democratic party first came to power in 1950, however, it was not greatly different from the Republican party. It had the support of a wide variety of groups who had for a number of reasons been alienated by the long period of RPP rule. But the Democratic regime coincided with the beginnings of rapid and profound social and economic change in Turkey. In order to properly understand these changes, it is necessary to study the social and economic environment of the Turkish political system.

Political Environment

The People

Ethnic and Religious Groups: By contrast with the multiethnic Ottoman Empire, the Turkish Republic is a relatively homogeneous society. Major ethnic groups in the Balkan peninsula, primarily Christian, were separated from the empire before the First World War, and the largest single ethnic group, the Arabs, withdrew during the course of that war. A serious confrontation with the Armenians, who demanded the right to establish a separate state in the Caucasus region, resulted in the deportation or voluntary emigration of large numbers of this unfortunate group. The contemporary Armenian Soviet Socialist Republic, one of the constituent units of the Soviet Union, is the only reminder of the once extensive Armenian population of this general region.

The population remaining within the territorial confines of the modern Republic of Turkey is not so homogeneous or undifferentiated as might be supposed. The Kurds are the largest ethnic group after the Turks. Concentrated primarily in the relatively poor provinces of southeastern Turkey—the region adjacent to the borders with Iraq and Iran, where many of their ethnic cohorts reside—the Kurds of Turkey number approximately 2.5 million, or less than 10 percent of the population.[2] Although they have been largely quiescent during most of the years since the formation of the republic, there have been occasional flare-ups. Insurrections occurred in 1925 and 1935, apparently motivated by a combination of ethnic and religious factors. During the extended civil war across the border in Iraq in the 1960s there were reports of gunrunning and other types of smuggling across the Turkish border. Turkish officialdom has been sensitive to suggestions of separatist sentiment among the Kurds of the southeastern provinces. In general, the government has applied a policy of assimilation, implemented through the extension of educational facilities and plans for basic economic development in the affected provinces. Many Kurds have chosen to pursue social and economic opportunities in the larger cities of Turkey.

Other ethnic groups are far less numerous; none account for more than 50,000 persons each, except for the Greeks of Istanbul and the Arabic-speaking inhabitants of several provinces along the Mediterranean coast and the Syrian border. The greatest concentration of Arabs has been in the Hatay province, an area ceded to Turkey in 1939 by France, which then held the mandate over Syria. Other ethnic groups include Circassians, concentrated around the city of Adapazari, east of the Sea of Marmara; the Armenians of Istanbul; and the Laz, who live primarily along the Black Sea coast near the Russian border. None of these groups has played a significant role in Turkey's internal politics since 1923. The Greeks of Istanbul became the target of official hostility in the wake of the Cyprus dispute of the 1960s, and several thousand of those who had elected not to become Turkish citizens under a treaty ratified in 1930 were forced to emigrate to Greece.

Turkey also presents a superficial impression of homogeneity in terms of religious identity. Close to 99 percent of the population is identified as Muslim. Among this massive Muslim majority, however, there are an indeterminate number of Shiites, known in Turkey as *Alevis*. Concentrated primarily in the north central Anatolian plateau (in the provinces of Sivas, Tokat, and Amasya), this group is less prominent today than in the heyday of the Ottoman Empire, when it comprised one of the most prominent of the dervish orders, the Bektashis. The group has occasionally sought political expression, notably through the formation of the short-lived Unity party, which competed in the election of 1969, winning eight seats in the national parliament. The Alevis have been particularly conscious of their religious differences with the Sunni majority, and they therefore favored Ataturk's secularizing reforms, which they believed would prevent the use of the power of the state for the support of the rival sect.

Social Structure: Without doubt the single dominant fact of Turkish society has been the gap between the urban sector and the rural hinterland. An explication of this gap and the changes it has undergone during the past quarter century is essential to an understanding of contemporary Turkish politics. Nearly three-fourths of the population has lived in the countryside and has depended on agriculture for its livelihood. Until 1950, however, the urban minority—better educated, cosmopolitan, and politically conscious—dominated society and politics without serious challenge from the rural majority. Ataturk's regime rested on a political base made up of an alliance between the urban elite, particularly the civil bureaucracy and the military officers' corps, and prominent local notables, particularly large landowners.* The local notables supported the national, or urban, elite so long as their domination of their local areas was not disturbed. Since the end of World War II, however, this alliance has broken down, and Turkish politics has shown increasing signs of instability as a result.

The breakdown of the alliance between the national elite and local notables was foreshadowed by the persistent narrowing of the social and economic gap between major urban centers and rural areas. One of the most important instruments of this change was the rapid expansion of the highway system. Between 1950 and 1961 all-weather roads more than doubled in mileage, and most of the expansion was in the provincial rather than the national trunk system. The social and economic effects of the new roads cannot be overemphasized. By breaking down the physical isolation of the village and the small town, the roads provided inhabitants with unprecedented opportunities for physical and social mobility and a correspondingly higher standard of living. For example, a village fifty miles from the national capital had been effectively isolated from the outside world until construction of a major asphalt highway within a few miles of it. Subsequently, regularly scheduled bus service was inaugurated both to the local government center and to Ankara, now scarcely an hour's drive away. Milk was now picked up daily by truck, allowing an increase in production and providing a reliable source of income. A villager with a debilitating disease was no longer dependent on the ministrations of the local soothsayer; he was now but an hour's ride from modern medical facilities.

Highways also give villagers a heightened awareness of the larger society of which they are a part. With the transistor radio and the newspaper, roads make possible the establishment of a national network of mass communications, a necessary prerequisite for a national political system that has true mass participation. There were 131 daily newspapers in 1950; by 1955 the number had grown to 278; and in 1962 there were over 400. Significantly, most of these were published in small towns and provincial centers rather than in major cities.[3] The number of radios has shown a similar increase.

*Although there has been no class of large landowners in Turkey comparable to that of Egypt before 1952 or that of Iran, a small group of such landlords, centered primarily in the western (Aegean), southern (Mediterranean), and eastern parts of the country, has retained considerable political, social, and economic power.

One of the most dramatic results of these developments in transportation and communications was the movement of villagers and small townsmen to larger cities. Between 1945 and 1965 the proportion of Turks living in cities of more than 20,000 increased from 14 to 25 percent. Another explanation for this movement is dissatisfaction in the traditional community, which may be attributed in part to the increasing pressure of population on available land. Most land belonged to peasant families, who owned modest plots they worked themselves. But there is no longer enough arable land to accommodate all those who depend on agriculture for a livelihood. Moreover, as standards of living rise, people find it more difficult to eke out a living in the village. Added to these factors is a sharp increase in the use of tractors and other agricultural machines during the past twenty years. These machines are of little help to small farmers who have tiny plots, but they are of great economic benefit to large-scale operators, who previously employed large numbers of sharecroppers or landless peasants. The substitution of machine power for human labor threw many peasants out of work and forced them to seek their fortunes elsewhere—precisely when the roads to the cities opened.

Unfortunately, the displaced rural villager usually arrives in the town or city without the skills that are in demand in an urban environment. Even if he had marketable skills there would not be enough jobs; although industry in Turkey expanded rapidly during the 1950s, the rate of expansion was not enough to accommodate the influx of ex-villagers. The result is now visible in every major Turkish city—unsightly, crowded shantytowns which, like slums the world over, have created serious problems of social dislocation and economic and administrative problems for already overburdened municipal authorities.

The flow of villagers to the city and the simultaneous development of industry and commerce had a profound impact on the social structure of urban centers. Up to the end of World War II, cities were dominated by notable families and government officials. With the rise of industry and commerce after the war, these groups found themselves challenged by an emerging group of entrepreneurs and merchants, most of whom operated on a small scale and kept personal control of their businesses. As these men gained wealth and status, the prestige of the civil servant and the army officer correspondingly declined. The prestigious skills and callings in the government bureaucracy also began to change, and the scientific and engineering skills essential to an industrial economy came to be valued. The road to success began to run through technical schools and universities in Istanbul and Ankara rather than through the traditional route of the military staff college or schools of medicine and law.

Industrialization should also create a working class, although the rise of such a class in Turkey has been hampered by the predominance of relatively small-scale enterprise, the shortage of skilled workers, and a negative attitude toward labor organization by the government—the right to strike was not enacted until 1963.

To sum up, in place of the traditional gap between the urban-educated, professional and official elite on the one hand and the impoverished, uneducated rural peasantry on the other, groups of professionals, merchants, and industrialists, both large and small, emerged in the cities and challenged the long-standing dominance of the elite. In addition, the peasants themselves became more involved in the affairs of the nation. Coinciding with these developments was a hearty economic boom during the first half of the 1950s, which resulted in sudden wealth for some and a higher standard of living for many. Significantly, military and civil officials failed to benefit from this economic boom as much as the newly rising groups; in fact, the accompanying inflation cut deeply into their fixed salaries and aroused resentment among them.

Economic Conditions

The Turkish economy is an active one by Middle Eastern standards, due in part to the relative fertility of the soil and variations in climatic conditions, which permit cultivation of a wide variety of crops, some of them (e.g., tobacco, nuts, raisins) in heavy demand on the international market. It is also due partly to the relatively rich variety of mineral resources in the country.

Agricultural products range from cotton, tobacco, and cereals (especially wheat) through such specialized products as figs, silk, olives and olive oil, dried fruits, and licorice roots, to nuts, mohair, skins and hides, furs, wool, linseed, and sesame. Two-thirds of exported leaf tobacco is sold to the United States each year, providing a fairly constant though inadequate source of foreign hard currency. Mineral products include chrome (of which Turkey is among the four main producers in the world), coal, lignite, sulfur, manganese, iron ore, copper, and oil. Although Turkey does not compete with the major oil producers of the Middle East, domestic wells produced 2.7 million tons of crude petroleum in 1967, which at least represents a significant saving in foreign currency.

Like many developing nations, Turkey is plagued by a gap in its foreign trade and payments balances. Its primary trading partners have been the United States and West Germany, both hard-currency states. Although Turkey has been accepted as an associate member of the European Common Market, it will not be able to participate on an equal basis for some years. The greatest hope for closing the gap in foreign exchange lies in tourism; in 1969 Turkey attracted some 500,000 travelers, primarily to the picturesque Aegean coastal area. A second major source of foreign exchange earnings has been remittances from Turkish laborers who have found work in European, especially German, industries. In addition, the workers have learned skills that enable them to upgrade their standard of living when they return to Turkey. Several hundred thousand have gone to Europe over the past decade, but not enough have yet returned for their impact to be strongly felt.

The Turkish commitment to economic development has been strong, shown by the adoption of five-year plans since 1963. This commitment is not new; it received major impetus in the 1930s, when the government embarked on a large-scale program of investment in heavy industry. Today industrial investments continue to grow under both private and government auspices. Major establishments exist in such industries as cotton and wool textiles, cement, paper, and iron and steel. Sugar, refined from beets grown domestically, is produced in sufficient quantities to satisfy the national demand. Electric power production has increased to a level of 56 billion kilowatt hours.

Per capita income in 1968 stood at approximately $200 at the prevailing rate of exchange. As part of a plan to upgrade the standard of living of Turkish citizens, the government is allocating considerable funds (10 percent of official expenditures, second only to the budget for defense) to extend the education system, and literacy had risen to 49 percent by 1970.

Political Effects of Changing
Socioeconomic Conditions

These developments help to explain the politics of the 1950s. Initially the Democratic party had broad support from a wide variety of groups that had been antagonized by the Republican regime. As the partiality of the Democratic regime for agriculturists, entrepreneurs, and industrialists became apparent, and as its policies of vigorous economic development resulted in increasing inflation, support among urban groups began to wane. Civil servants were especially alarmed by the ability of those with partisan connections to escape or circumvent official regulations, including criminal prosecutions in some cases. Moreover, after 1955 economic conditions in general worsened seriously. World prices for agricultural products dropped and government subsidies within the country consequently became more costly (these subsidies were derived largely from tax revenues collected from city dwellers). A severe shortage of foreign exhange even resulted in a total ban on the importation of coffee, a singularly important ingredient of Turkish social life.

Although these conditions eroded support for the government in the cities, the Democratic party remained popular in smaller towns and villages. Inflation undoubtedly produced an adverse reaction there too, but the peasants were still generally better off than they had been before the economic boom. Moreover, government agents such as the gendarmerie and local civil officials were no longer as peremptory, arbitrary, or haughty as they had been during the Republican era. And if they proved exceptionally zealous in enforcing unpleasant laws or regulations, there was now the possibility of using the influence of the local party organization, particularly on the Democratic side, to bypass the official bureaucracy. Thus, the peasants and small townsmen, who had been subject to harsh treatment at the hands of the governments before 1950 and who had gained a measure of influence over that same government machinery under the Democrats, were unimpressed by the outcry of the urban groups against violations of democratic rights and liberties, which became increasingly common in the late 1950s.

Those in smaller towns and villages who supported the Democratic party had one other major feature in common. Although the leading groups among them were the products of the modern educational system of the republic and often had technical training at the university, they retained great respect and affection for traditional values and ideas, especially in religious matters. The national leaders of the Democratic party were well aware of this tendency among their followers and were therefore receptive to demands for the introduction of religious instruction into the public schools, for example, and for expanding preachers' training institutes, which had been opened a few years before the Democrats came to power. To an extent these measures and the pressures that produced them indicated a survival of the opposition to the basic reforms of the 1920s and 1930s, and they aroused the intense suspicion and hostility of educated, urbanized groups, including military officers.

Not only did the officers share a common social background with the other urbanized groups in the elite, but they too were adversely affected by the economic developments of the 1950s. They also shared the modernistic outlook of the rest of the urban elite, and they identified with Ataturk, a highly successful officer himself, like his cohort and successor, Ismet Inonu. Indeed, since the Democratic regime of the 1950s was the first government of the Turkish Republic whose leaders had had no connection with the military, it was not surprising that the military should look upon Menderes and his party with deepening suspicion and mistrust.

These social tensions sought political expression, but the political system the Democratic party had inherited from the Kemalist regime proved unsuited to such expression. Thus, although the electoral strength of the Democratic party began to erode in the late 1950s, the electoral law guaranteed it a large majority in the Grand National Assembly, where Democratic members were as loyal to their leaders, Bayar and Menderes, as their Republican predecessors had been to Ataturk and Inonu. There was one crucial difference, however. The Republican regime had enjoyed the confidence of the military and the Democratic regime did not. Early in 1960, when the Menderes government attempted to stifle the opposition with increasingly repressive measures, the opposition took to the streets. Protest demonstrations in the cities became a daily occurrence, and the threat of violence increased. Finally, Menderes fell back on the army and ordered troops to move against those who were opposed to the government. This order subjected the military to an intolerable tension that they could only resolve by overthrowing the government itself.

Political Structure

The military junta arrested all the leading officials of the Democratic regime, including President Bayar, Prime Minister Menderes, all cabinet ministers, and all the Democratic members of parliament. Provincial governors were replaced by military officers, and in some provinces large numbers of locally elected officials and civil bureaucrats were also arrested. Judicial trials were arranged for those arrested; after more than a year of litigation, prison terms of varying lengths were meted out. Fifteen death sentences were also handed down, but the junta commuted all but three of these to life imprisonment. Thus, the only lives claimed by the 1960 coup in Turkey were those of the deposed prime minister, Menderes, and two of his closest associates.* Most of the prison sentences were reduced by amnesties enacted after the resumption of civilian government, and by the late 1960s none of the former Democratic officials remained in jail.

One of the first acts of the military junta was to commission a group of legal experts to write a new constitution. As a reaction against the partisan excesses of the Menderes regime, there was a general determination to incorporate more reliable safeguards against abuse of government power in the new document. The days of unlimited parliamentary supremacy were over.

The new constitution provides for a bicameral legislature in place of the unicameral Grand National Assembly. The lower house, or National Assembly, is the more powerful of the two chambers and has 450 members elected for four-year terms. Legislative proposals are initiated here and may be debated and voted upon in the Senate only after the National Assembly has completed its deliberations. No bill becomes law without the assent of the National Assembly; however, bills rejected by the Senate may be enacted into law by the National Assembly.

The Senate is thus intended to act as a brake on hasty or partisan legislation that might emerge from the National Assembly, as was the case during the closing days of the first republic. Several instrumentalities enable the Senate to perform this function. Its composition and mode of selection differ from those of the National Assembly. Its 150 popularly elected members serve six-year staggered terms, on the model of the U.S. Senate, and an additional fifteen members are appointed by the president of the republic "from among people distinguished for their service in various fields." At least ten of these appointees cannot be members of any political party. Finally, the remaining members of the Committee of National Unity—the official

---

*The former minister of the interior allegedly took his own life in the immediate aftermath of the coup. He had become the object of particular fear and hatred because of his prominent role in the increasingly repressive tactics the Menderes government had adopted.

name of the military junta of 1960 and 1961—are entitled to permanent or life membership in the Senate, so long as they do not join any political party.*

Relations between the executive and the legislature are fully spelled out in the new constitution. The president of the republic is elected to a seven-year term by a two-thirds majority of the National Assembly and the Senate from among their own members. He is not eligible for reelection and must disassociate himself from political party affiliation upon election. Under the first republic the president was elected to a term concurrent with that of the assembly, and he tended to remain closely tied to a partisan majority of that body. The president appoints the prime minister, who in turn nominates the ministers and presents them and the government's program to both the National Assembly and the Senate. Only the National Assembly is required to give a vote of confidence, however, and it may also vote no confidence in the government, forcing its resignation. Under specified conditions the prime minister may ask the president to dissolve the National Assembly and call for new elections. These provisions, which are quite similar to the procedures prevailing in Western European countries such as France and Italy, are in sharp contrast to the simpler arrangements of the Turkish system before 1960. The obvious purpose is to give the assembly leverage against a headstrong prime minister and cabinet.

These arrangements will not be effective in a situation in which the prime minister and the cabinet have strong support in the assembly, however, as was the case with the Menderes regime of the late 1950s. To prevent the recurrence of such a situation there is now a system of proportional representation, which makes it unlikely that a political party can win overwhelming numbers of parliamentary seats on the basis of bare majorities or pluralities in the popular voting. As a further guarantee against the abuse of government power, there is now a constitutional court that has the power of invalidating legislative acts that contravene the constitution. The court also has the function of trying the president, prime minister, and other high judicial and administrative officials in cases of malfeasance.

Political Processes

One source of tension between the national urban elite, including the military, and the supporters of the Democratic party before 1960 was the official sanction of religious training and observance, which was interpreted by the elite as a potential threat to the modernizing reforms instituted by Ataturk. These suspicions were embodied in the new constitution in the form of a ban on the repeal or

*Less than twenty senators remain in this category. Several have died, one was elected president of the republic, and a few resigned to run for elective office.

revocation of those reform laws "which aim at raising the Turkish society to the level of contemporary civilization and at safeguarding the secular character of the Republic. . . ." The laws thus protected include the hat and alphabet reforms and laws abolishing or closing religious dervish orders, tombs and shrines, and religious control over education and civil law. Nothing more clearly illustrates the divisions that still permeate Turkish politics and society.

Some of the junior officers in the military junta of 1960 and 1961 felt so strongly about these matters that they were willing to sacrifice democratic procedures and to establish a new authoritarian regime of their own. They were overruled by more moderate senior officers who were willing to rely on the constitutional and political safeguards outlined. The peaceful retirement of the junta in 1961 did not signify an end to the political involvement of the military, however. There were two attempted coups d'état in the first two years under the new constitution, both of which were narrowly defeated by the circumspect action of senior commanders, particularly in the air force, who remained loyal to civil authorities. Nevertheless, rumors of military plotting against the government continued to crop up with each new political crisis. Early in 1971 these rumors were substantiated when a strongly worded public statement by the top commanders of the armed forces led to the resignation of the government. This unusual development was wryly referred to as a "coup by communiqué" by some observers. Also, the first two presidents of the second republic have been military officers; one was the leader of the junta itself, and the other resigned the office of chief of the general staff and was appointed to the Senate in order to be elected. In addition to his position as head of state, the president is designated by the constitution as presiding officer of the National Security Council, which includes members of the cabinet and the chief of the general staff and commanding officers of the armed forces. Although this body has only advisory functions in matters of national security, it is significant that it has frequently met in secret session during periods of political crisis since 1961. It appears to be a channel through which the military can exert direct influence on the civilian government.

Political Parties

One of the results of the new constitutional and legal system of the second republic was the growth of a wider variety of political parties. During the first election under the new system the major question was how the voters who had supported the outlawed Democratic party would cast their ballots. Several parties competed, but the Justice party emerged with the bulk of this support (35 percent of all votes cast), which established the group as the heir of the old Democratic party. In the elections of 1965 and 1969 the Justice party captured a majority of the seats in the National Assembly. Most of its leaders are former Democrats who had served as mayors or provincial leaders of the earlier party and who rose to the top when the national Democratic leadership was imprisoned by the military regime. Unlike the former Democratic leaders, however, the new group is not composed of oppositionist members of the old elite; on the contrary, these are men who have risen from lower social echelons. Suleyman Demirel, leader of the Justice party since late 1964 and prime minister from 1965 to 1971, typifies the new group. He was born in 1924 in a small town in a conservative section of southwestern Anatolia, and he is an engineer and a graduate of Istanbul Technical University. When he became leader of the party he was new to partisan politics and had never before held an elective office. However, he had served in the Menderes government as director of the important State Water Administration, the agency entrusted with the construction and operation of some of the regime's favored projects, chiefly dams.

Like the Democratic party before it, the Justice party favors less government restriction in religious matters and less government interference in economic affairs. The nature of Turkish politics in the early years of the second republic is perhaps best illustrated by the campaign symbol first adopted by the Justice party*—the letters *A.P.* (for the Turkish *Adalet Partisi*) set below an open book (representing the law) topped by the semicircle of the rising sum. This symbol was an open bid to identify the party with the outlawed Democratic party; its very name was meant to suggest justice for the fallen leaders, who were awaiting judgment before a special court. But there was another, unofficial, interpretation of the Justice party symbol that was the subject of a whispered campaign. According to this rumored version, the letters *A.P.* stood for *Allah* (God) and *Peygamber* (Prophet); the open book was the Quran; and the semicircle represented the light of religious inspiration. The significance of this interpretation is that it was suggested at all. It served to confirm the fears of many of the urban elite that the new party was even more openly opposed to Ataturk's secularizing reforms than the Democrats had been. Elect the Justice party, they believed, and Turkish modernization will come to a grinding halt; indeed, the country may be dragged back into the Middle Ages. Although Justice party rule after 1965 assuaged these exaggerated fears, they indicate the extent to which consensus on basic values in Turkey had suffered.[4]

The Justice party is thus regarded by both supporters and opponents as representative of the group typified by Suleyman Demirel—that is, members of a rising middle class from smaller towns who have achieved a degree of success and wealth by taking advantage of the educational and economic opportunities afforded by the Republican regime. The popularity of this party has prompted one observer to label it the first true grass-roots party in the Middle East.[5]

---

*The Justice party subsequently abandoned this symbol and adopted a gray horse instead. This too was designed to remind voters of the connection with the Democrats, as the words *demir kirat* (iron or gray horse) closely resemble the name *Democrat*.

The Republican party, by contrast, has been a minority party since the election of 1950—that is, since the introduction of competitive party politics. It retains the support of such urban groups as civil servants. In an effort to make headway against the Justice party, the RPP has moved to the left ideologically. It has advocated the kind of land reform that over twenty years ago helped propel the Democratic party into being, and in addition it now favors nationalization of major industries such as petroleum and steel; it has remained intensely suspicious and intolerant of public displays of religious piety.

The Republican party's leftward trend has alienated an important segment of its former support, particularly that of the local notable families, which may explain the sharp drop in its share of the vote in the 1965 general election. It was certainly a major factor in the split the party suffered during the spring of 1967, when about one-third of its more conservative parliamentary representatives broke away to form a new party, the Reliance party. In the general election of 1969, however, this new party won only a dozen seats in the National Assembly, against more than 140 for the RPP.

Of the other minor parties competing in Turkish politics today the most noteworthy is the Turkish Workers (or Labor) party. An outgrowth of socialist thought which merged in the aftermath of the 1960 military coup, this party was the first serious Marxist political organization in Turkish history. It appealed for social justice and equity on behalf of workers and peasants, particularly the unemployed, unskilled, and landless. Paradoxically, its greatest electoral support has come from urban intellectuals who have lost faith in the ability of the larger parties to solve Turkey's social and economic problems. The party has polled as much as 18 percent of the vote in localities where the split between rich and poor is particularly wide. Nationally, however, it has polled no more than 3.5 percent of the vote, although it managed to seat fifteen members in the 1965 National Assembly. In 1969 it won only two seats in the parliament. In the summer of 1971, a large proportion of the party's leadership was arrested and imprisoned as part of a general antileftist campaign directed by the military authorities. The party's image had been blemished by widespread outbreaks of violence between extremists of right and left on university campuses, and by the appearance of groups of urban guerrillas in the largest cities, although the party's connection with these groups was not clearly established.

At the opposite end of the political spectrum stands the National Action party under the leadership of a former colonel, Alpaslan Turkes. The protofascist character of this party is indicated by the fact that it conducted a program of training in guerrilla tactics during the summer of 1969. Turkes was a prominent figure in the 1960 military coup and a strong advocate of extended military rule at that time. He is staunchly anti-Communist and anti-Soviet and has professed pannationalist ideas that include vague suggestions of ultimate political union with the numerous Turkic groups located in Soviet central Asia. These ideas are not new, but they have been discouraged by governments and most political leaders since the early 1920s. In the election of 1969, the National Action party polled about 2 percent of the vote and gained only one seat in the National Assembly. It is therefore significant not because of its political strength but because it represents an extreme ideological position now more openly expressed than before.

Although the Justice party won a majority of the seats in parliament for the second consecutive time in the 1969 election, political stability failed to materialize. Factionalism led to a split similar to that which occurred in the Republican party. The result was that the Demirel government was left with only a razor-thin parliamentary majority. It was thus in a poor position to stem the rising tide of violence noted above. Finally, in the spring of 1971 the military officers, as noted previously, demanded the resignation of the Demirel regime and its replacement by a nonpartisan government committed to undertake economic and social reform and to reestablish the sagging authority of the state.

It remains to be seen whether such an accommodation between the military and the political parties can last. It was clear by the early 1970s, however, that the Turkish political system had over a period of two decades demonstrated that the expansion of political participation in a system of competitive political parties is a hazardous undertaking.

Foreign Policy

Ataturk's essentially placid foreign policy was summarized in his motto "Peace in the world, peace in the homeland." He rejected such adventurist programs as Pan-Turkism, which aimed at building a new empire out of a union of the Anatolian Turks with the Turkic peoples of central Asia. Instead, he preferred to avoid foreign entanglements and to reform and rebuild the Turkish state at home.

Ataturk departed from a passive foreign policy only twice during his presidency. In 1936 he took advantage of the crisis generated by Hitler's remilitarization of the Rhineland to persuade a specially convened diplomatic conference to restore Turkish sovereignty over the straits of the Dardanelles and the Bosporus,* a diplomatic coup for the conflicting interests of Great Britain and Soviet Russia, which were centered on the disposition of the Turkish straits. The British favored opening the straits to all ships at all times to enable the British navy to extend its power into the Black Sea. Soviet Russia, like the previous czarist regime, was diametrically opposed to this view and was anxious to keep the straits closed to all but naval fleets of the Black Sea powers in order to exclude the British. The result was a compromise that allowed limited access to the Black Sea for the British and other outside navies.

*The straits had been demilitarized and placed under international administration by the Lausanne Conference of 1923, which produced the treaty that finally settled the First World War for Turkey.

The second diplomatic initiative under Ataturk, not fulfilled until after his death, was the annexation by Turkey of the territory of the Hatay, including the port city of Alexandretta (Iskenderun). This area was, in effect, ceded by France, which held the mandate over Syria. The Turkish case was based on the allegedly Turkish character of the population (actually mixed Turkish and Arab), but the desire to gain control of the port facilities of Alexandretta was undoubtedly the real motive. This represents the only territorial acquisition Turkey has made since the formation of the republic in 1923.

Although Turkey signed a mutual defense pact with Britain and France shortly after the outbreak of the Second World War, the German invasion of the Balkans was so swift and overwhelming that neither of the Western Allies opposed the maintenance of a strictly correct policy of neutrality by the Inonu regime—a policy that lasted throughout the war, despite appeals for cooperation by both the Axis and the Allies. Finally, in February 1945 Turkey declared war on Germany, which entitled her to charter membership in the United Nations.

No sooner had the war ended than Turkey became the subject of a concerted campaign of diplomatic pressure from the Soviet Union. The Soviets demanded the right to establish a naval base in the Dardanelles and asked for the cession of certain territories in the Caucasus border areas. In response, Turkey abandoned her World War II neutrality and established a new friendship with the West, particularly the United States. In March of 1947 the Truman Doctrine promised aid to Greece and Turkey to bolster their resistance against Soviet pressures. Massive amounts of American military and economic aid began to flow into the hitherto impoverished Turkish economy, and it helped generate the economic boom of the 1950s. In 1950 the new Democratic regime reciprocated by sending Turkish volunteer troops to fight in the Korean War. In 1952 the relationship was further cemented when Turkey was admitted to full membership in NATO.

In 1955 Turkey took the first step in a major extension of the Western alliance system in the Middle East by signing the Baghdad Pact with Iraq. Later Iran, Pakistan, and the United Kingdom joined the pact to link it more closely with both NATO and SEATO. This intrusion of the Western alliance system into the Middle East was strongly resented by some Arab regimes, especially that of Egypt's President Nasser. Egypt's proclaimed policy of cold war neutrality, on the other hand, was anathema to the Turks, for whom Soviet expansionism was the prime danger to be resisted at all cost.

The Baghdad Pact suffered a serious blow when Iraq withdrew after undergoing a revolution in 1958. Renamed the Central Treaty Organization (CENTO), its headquarters was moved to Ankara. CENTO's greatest achievements have been the development of communication and transportation links between Turkey, Iran, and Pakistan. Turkey's relations with the West have been further strengthened by its admission to associate membership in the European Common Market, with the ultimate prospect of full membership when its economy reaches a sufficiently high level of development.

In late 1963 the Turkish people began to have second thoughts about Turkey's place in international politics, and within six months the country was rife with anti-American sentiment and there was talk of greater neutralism in foreign policy and even possible withdrawal from NATO. The cause of this apparently sudden shift was the outbreak of severe communal fighting between Greeks and Turks on the island of Cyprus. A hopelessly outnumbered Turkish minority was completely reliant on support from mainland Turkey, but when Turkey threatened to move militarily against the island, it was restrained by its Western allies. The United States was particularly anxious to prevent the outbreak of war between Greece and Turkey, both members of NATO. The Turkish reaction to the lack of American support in the Cyprus crisis was sharp. In effect, many Turks said: "We helped you fight your war in Korea, now that we need your help, where are you?"

One result of this crisis was a new rapproachement between Turkey and the Soviet Union, which lead to a number of economic and technical assistance agreements (although the Turks remain intensely suspicious of their colossal northern neighbor). Another result was a concerted diplomatic effort by the Turks to mend their fences with governments of Third World countries, especially their Arab neighbors. In particular, Turkey assumed a more pro-Arab position in the Arab-Israeli conflict: the government gave cautious support to the Arabs, although it generally maintains correct relations with Israel. The official policy reflects a shift in public opinion; cultural affinity with the predominantly Muslim Arabs now appears to have become significant in the public mind.

Relations with the United States have remained strained. Turkey's insistence on control of its own affairs and recognition of its complete territorial sovereignty were recognized in new status-of-forces agreements that extend Turkish jurisdiction over the thousands of American military and civilian personnel still in the country. The hostility and suspicion that have seeped into Turkish-American relations are not caused only the the Cyprus problem but also by resentment of the affluence and general lack of sensitivity toward Turks on the part of the thousands of American military personnel stationed in the country since 1952. Leftists charge that this situation is comparable to colonialism and is an insult to Turkey, and this charge initially evoked a positive public response. From this point of view, violent extremist attacks on American institutions and symbols, including the kidnapping of American servicemen early in 1971, are not as senseless as they might appear.

Political Prospects

The Turkish political system has run the gamut of forms from a comprehensive nationalist movement aiming at national liberation to a one-party dictatorial phase under a charismatic leader to a competitive political stage interrupted by a military coup d'état.

The present system is based on an uneasy balance among forces including rising groups from smaller towns backed by the hitherto inert peasantry and the old Ottoman official and military elite, which survices primarily in the form of the Republican party and the officer corps. The new groups that now challenge the older Ottoman elite are themselves the product of the modern facilities and opportunities established under the republic.

Greater pluralism and wider participation have led to increased social and ideological tensions, which appear in the form of a dilemma confronting the older elite. Committed to democratic practices and progressive reform and development, the members of this group seem unable to acquire the majority support they must have to accomplish their goals by democratic means. Alternative methods of seizing power require the active collaboration of the armed forces, but the eighteen-month period of military rule in 1960 and 1961 indicated that the higher ranks of the officer corps had no particular desire for overt control over government and society. These senior officers have so far had sufficient power to prevent younger, more radical officers from taking over.

Continued political stability is threatened by the progressive weakening of the ideological consensus underlying the Republican political culture. As the decade of the 1970s opened, the political scene was marked by labor strikes, boycotts, and demonstrations, fractionalism in the dominant Justice party, and finally, as we have seen, renewed intervention by the military. None of these were harbingers of optimism for the future.

The case of Iran, Turkey's eastern neighbor, which is discussed in the following chapter, provides some interesting comparisons and contrasts. Like Turkey, Iran experienced a period of liberal constitutionalism followed by a period of reaction and ultimately the seizure of power by a charismatic military leader. There the similarity ends, however; unlike Ataturk, Reza Khan did not successfully pursue his commitment to modernization.

Footnotes

[1] Lewis, *Emergence of Modern Turkey,* p. 285.

[2] *Statesman's Yearbook, 1971-72* (London: Macmillan & Co., 1971), pp. 1384ff. This figure is based on official census data, which classifies the population according to "mother tongue." It is possible that the actual number of Kurds is greater than this, as some live in other parts of the country and not all report Kurdish as their native language. No other reliable statistics are available, however.

[3] See *Turkiyede Cikan Gazete ve Dergiler* [Newspapers and Magazines Published in Turkey], (Ministry of Press and Tourism, Directorate of the Domestic Press Division, June 1963).

[4] See F. Tachau and A. H. Ulman, "Dilemmas of Turkish Politics," *Turkish Yearbook of International Relations, 1962* (Ankara, 1964), p. 1.

[5] W. B. Sherwood, "The Justice Party of Turkey," *World Politics* 20, no. 1 (October 1967).

Selected Bibliography

Cohn, Edwin J. *Turkish Economic, Social, and Political Change.* New York: Frederick A. Praeger, 1970.
An analysis of various aspects of Turkish development.

Dodd, C. H. *Politics and Government in Turkey.* Berkeley and Los Angeles: University of California Press, 1969.
A comprehensive review of the contemporary Turkish political system.

Frey, Frederick W. *The Turkish Political Elite.* Cambridge, Mass.: Massachusetts Institute of Technology Press, 1965.
Analysis of social backgrounds of members of Turkish parliaments from 1920 through 1957 with insights into the relation between social changes and politics.

Heyd, Uriel. *Foundations of Turkish Nationalism: The Life and Teachings of Ziya Gokalp.* London: Luzac, 1950.
An account of the life and thought of a prominent Turkish nationalist of the early twentieth century.

Karpat, Kemal H. *Turkey's Politics: The Transition to a Multiparty System.* Princeton, N.J.: Princeton University Press, 1959.
A detailed account of Turkish politics with emphasis on the origins of the multiparty system.

Kinross, Lord (Patrick Balfour). *Ataturk: A Biography of Mustafa Kemal, Father of Modern Turkey.* New York: William Morrow and Co., 1965.
The most complete and objective biography available.

Lewis, Bernard. *The Emergence of Modern Turkey.* New York: Oxford University Press, 1961.
A highly readable and authoritative study of the historical background of the modern Turkish Republic.

Lewis, G. L. *Turkey.* 3d ed. New York: Frederick A. Praeger, 1965.
A compact history of the Turkish Republic.

Mardin, Serif. *The Genesis of Young Ottoman Thought.* Princeton, N.J.: Princeton University Press, 1962.
An account of the first evidences of modern political thought among the intellectuals of the late Ottoman Empire.

Ozbudun, Ergun. *The Role of the Military in Recent Turkish Politics.* Harvard University Center for International Affairs, Occasional Paper no. 14.
Analysis of the political involvement of the Turkish army in recent years.

Rivkin, Malcolm D. *Area Development for National Growth: The Turkish Precedent.* New York: Frederick A. Praeger, 1965.
Analysis of economic development policies.

Robinson, Richard D. *The First Turkish Republic: A Case Study in National Development.* Cambridge, Mass.: Harvard University Press, 1963.
Knowledgeable account of Turkish politics and economic developments, especially during the 1950s.

Roos, L. L., Jr., and Roos, N. P. *Managers of Modernization: Organizations and Elites in Turkey (1950-69).* Cambridge, Mass.: Harvard University Press, 1971.
A careful study of changes in the personnel of key segments of Turkish bureaucracy as reflective of socioeconomic and political changes.

Szyliowicz, Joseph S. *Political Change in Rural Turkey: Erdemli.* The Hague: Mouton, 1966.
A rare case study of politics in a small provincial town in southern Turkey.

Weiker, Walter F. *The Turkish Revolution, 1960-61.* Washington, D.C.: Brookings Institution, 1963.
An account of the 1960 military coup, its background, and its impact on Turkish politics and society.

Iran

Geographical, historical, and cultural features distinguish Iran from the other countries in the Middle East. The country is the second largest in territory (after Saudi Arabia) and the third largest in population (after Turkey and Egypt). It has the longest frontier with the Soviet Union (1200 miles) and borders on the warm waters of the Persian Gulf and the Gulf of Oman. Iran, Turkey, and Israel are the only three non-Arab countries in the region. Iran's racial and cultural identities are Aryan and Iranian, and its national language is Persian, an Indo-European language.* The state religion is Shia Islam, a minority sect in the predominantly Sunni Middle East.

Iran faces formidable problems in the construction of a modern nation-state: ethnic, tribal, social, and ideological divisions, and the absence of genuinely representative political institutions. The transformation of the Iranian political system from a traditional absolutist monarchy to a modern constitutional one is continuing. Since the constitutional revolution of 1905, the country has twice alternated between parliamentary democracy and dictatorship. Constitutional forms have not been abandoned, but the position of the shah has fluctuated between that of a reigning monarch and that of a ruling dictator. Democratic institutions and constitutional practices have not developed sufficiently to guarantee long-term political stability.

Iran's social and economic modernization has been largely accomplished from above by the state under the dictatorial leadership of the country's two most recent rulers, Reza Shah and his son, Muhammad Reza Shah, although the resulting social and political

---

*Farsi, or modern Persian, is one of the Indo-Iranian languages. It developed from middle Persian during the ninth century, contains many words derived from Arabic, and is written in a modified Arabic script.

tensions remain unresolved. A social revolution has so far been averted
by the maintenance of a strong army and repressive measures and by
extending some of the benefits of economic growth to the potential
forces of dissent. The preservation of this precarious balance depends
on three factors: the continuing effective leadership of the shah, the
loyalty of the army and the police apparatus, and a sufficiently high
rate of economic growth to satisfy the rising expectations of the
increasing number of politically conscious citizens.

Historical Background

Iran's unique civilization constitutes a cultural and historical
bridge between the predominantly Semitic Middle East and the Indian
subcontinent. The country boasts of a glorious past that dates back to
at least 550 B.C., when the Persian Achaemenid Empire was established
by King Cyrus. Iran's diverse population (including Persians, Turks,
Kurds, and others) shares a rich, continuous cultural heritage that is
mainly Iranian-Islamic but that has absorbed and integrated influences
from central Asia, ancient Greece, the Arab world, India, China, and
the West. Like Turkey but unlike most of the Arab world, Iran
remained formally independent under the impact of the West, and the
country thus escaped the psychological and political fetters of
colonialism and maintained a proud and distinct sense of national
identity.

Contemporary Iran is heir to four political traditions: the
pre-Islamic imperial tradition, the Islamic tradition, the semicolonial
tradition, and the constitutional tradition. The multinational bureaucratic empires of the pre-Islamic era gave Iran the monarchical system,
which rests on the authority of a "king of kings," the shahanshah. They
also provided the tradition of a state religion—Zoroastrianism—before
the Arab conquest in the seventh century.

The Arabs brought Islam to Iran, the Iranians passed on to the
Arabs their imperial tradition, and from the blending of these two
traditions the multinational bureaucratic Muslim empires were established. The Iranians played an important part in the organization and
management of these imperial systems, but they also maintained their
separate cultural identity, language, and national traditions. Shia Islam,
the country's state religion since the sixteenth century, synthesizes
many Islamic and pre-Islamic traditions into a distinctly Iranian mold.

The increasing Anglo-Russian rivalry in Iran during the nineteenth century gradually reduced the country to semicolonial status,
and the secret Anglo-Russian treaty of 1907 divided it into three zones:
a Russian sphere of influence in the north, a British sphere in the south,
and a buffer zone between for the Iranians. The country thus escaped
formal colonization and some of its crippling effects, but continuing
interference in its affairs by Western powers has caused anti Western
sentiments.

Constitutionalism in Iran has been accompanied by anti-imperialism and Iranian nationalism. The constitutional revolution of 1905 brought these three movements together and provided the country with the basis for the adoption of Western political institutions of parliamentary democracy. This process contrasts with the adoption of a constitutional form of government in developing countries in which the system was primarily introduced and sponsored by Western powers, and constitutionalism has shown greater resiliency in Iran than in many countries.

Parliamentary Democracy and Political Fragmentation: First Phase (1905-25)

Increasing Western penetration, the inability of the inept monarchs of the Qajar dynasty (1794-1924) to meet this challenge, and a rising nationalist and modernist movement prepared the way for the constitutional revolution. The ulama, the merchants, and the liberal intellectuals formed the three main elements of the constitutional revolutionary movement. The ulama provided the necessary mass support for the alien political idea of constitutional democracy, the merchant class contributed the funds, and the intellectuals gave the movement ideological shape and direction. This unlikely alliance was made possible by common nationalist and anti-imperialist sentiments and the coming together at this time of their previously divergent interests. The ulama feared a weakening of traditional Islam under the impact of the West and thus a loss of their positions of prominence. The interests of the merchant class were threatened with the grant of numerous concessions that robbed them of their traditional sources of revenue. And the liberal intellectuals could not gain an opportunity to experiment with their political ideas as long as the autocratic shahs remained in power.

The constitutional regime was achieved in 1905 in a relatively bloodless revolution, but the young regime faced nearly insurmountable problems. The weakness of the government had led to a series of power struggles by local potentates; the Russians and the British were active in their respective northern and southern spheres of influence; and the constitutional government in Tehran was rife with dissension. The first Majlis (the lower house of Parliament) was representative of the three constitutional middle-class sources of support, but thereafter the traditional landed aristocracy reasserted itself through rigged elections. Although the country enjoyed unprecedented political freedom, the new middle-class elements had proved too divided and inexperienced to assume effective power.

When World War I broke out Iran declared its neutrality. The country was on the brink of disintegration: German agents had penetrated the south, the Russians were advancing in the north, the Turks had occupied parts of the northwestern provinces, and the British were raising a local army, the South Persia Rifles, against the Germans, and the Bolshevik Revolution of 1917 in Russia probably saved Iran's independence. Anglo-Russian rivalry had so far saved Iran from colonization, but an Anglo-Iranian agreement in 1919 proposed to reduce the country to a protectorate. In a display of nationalist resurgence, however, the Majlis rejected the treaty. Political fragmentation, blatant foreign interference, and the ineffectiveness of the constitutional regime paved the way for a military coup and another era of strong central government.

Monarchical Dictatorship and Modernization:
First Phase (1925-41)

The bloodless coup d'état on February 26, 1921, was led by Colonel Reza Khan, the commander of the Persian Cossack Brigade, and it met with tacit British and domestic political approval. This military takeover differed fundamentally from previous takeovers in Iranian history: it was led by an indigenous modern army trained by the Russians and staffed after their departure, by young Iranian officers. Reza Khan also represented a new social figure: he came from the lower middle class, was an intense nationalist, had risen to the top through the army, and was imbued with ideas for the modernization of the country.

Nevertheless, traditional patterns reasserted themselves once again. Because Reza Khan modeled himself after Mustafa Kemal Ataturk in neighboring Turkey, he initially sponsored plans for the establishment of a republic. But the abolition of the caliphate in the Turkish Republic and the secularizing trend of the Kemalist reforms turned the Iranian ulama against such plans. With consummate political shrewdness, Reza Khan turned the tables and became the chief opponent of the agitators for a republic. To assure everyone of his piety, he also made a pilgrimage to the holy Shia shrines. His military successes in asserting central government authority, his political appeasement of traditional elements, and his espousal of nationalist goals pushed the last Qajar shah into political exile and paved the way for his own ascendance to the throne. In February 1925 the Majlis deposed Ahmad Shah and the Qajar dynasty, and in December a Constituent Assembly elected Reza the new shah.

Reza Shah's monarchical dictatorship was characterized by both tradition and modernity. In the beginning of his rule he was supported by the growing nationalist and modernist middle classes, and his chief advisers came from these social ranks. As the basis of his internal policies shifted from reform to self-aggrandizement, however, he fell into the mold of traditional Iranian rulers by becoming the country's largest landowner and by assuming nearly all the prerogatives of an absolute monarch. The liberal nationalism of the parliamentary era also gave way to an authoritarian nationalism that exploited the imperial symbols of pre Islamic Iran. Zoroastrianism, pre-Islamic imperial architecture, and national epic poetry were revived; Muslim religious manifestations were suppressed.

Under Reza Shah's leadership, the bases of a modern secular state were built, however. A vigorous program of modernization in the army, the government bureaucracy, the judicial system, and the educational system, and construction of an economic infrastructure (including roads, cross-country railroads, public finance, banking, and public health) was undertaken. Even compared to the achievements of the Kemalist regime in Turkey, Reza Shah's accomplishments were impressive. He had less to start with than Ataturk, he faced greater religious and political opposition to his programs of centralization and secularization of the state, and he tried to accomplish both of these aims primarily through the army and the police without the aid of a political party.

In foreign policy also Reza Shah worked from a weaker position than Ataturk. He felt dependent on the British in the first half of his rule, but in the second half he tried to assert his independence by increasing economic collaboration with the Germans. But the presence of many German advisers provided the Allies with the pretext to occupy Iran in September 1941 and to demand Reza Shah's abdication in favor of his eighteen-year-old son.

Parliamentary Democracy and Political Fragmentation: Second Phase (1941-53)

The Allied occupation of Iran, the abdication of Reza Shah, and the liberation of political prisoners and parties in 1941 unleashed the political forces that had been dormant for fifteen years. In the absence of a dominant political force, the Majlis became once again the arena for political struggle. From the beginning four main political forces were discernible: the court, the aristocracy, the Tudeh (Communist) party, and an assortment of liberal and religious nationalists, later organized into the National Front. The presence of foreign troops during the war and the subsequent great power rivalries also affected the outcome of the political struggles, but the pervasive Iranian belief in the myth of the omnipotence of the great powers has often had the effect of self-fulfilling prophecy.

The court, headed by the young Muhammad Reza Shah, was at first on the defensive. Its sources of political power consisted of Allied support for the monarchy, the demoralized Iranian armed forces, and whatever popular support the shah could personally muster. Very early the shah recognized in the armed forces his main autonomous base of power, and with the exception of a few passing challenges from within and without the armed forces, the alliance of the court and the army has been a continuous political force in Iran since 1941.

The traditional Iranian aristocracy consisted of heterogeneous, overlapping elements: the powerful landlords, the Qajar princes, the tribal chiefs, and some prominent members of the Iranian civil and military bureaucracy who had been co-opted into the elite. Together these diverse elements were popularly referred to as the *hezar famil* (the "thousand families"). In the face of the revolutionary threat from below and the possibility of another prolonged period of royal dictatorship, the aristocracy acted with some political cohesiveness in this period. However, it was weakened by considerable factionalism and ambivalence toward the court. To retain its privileges, an alliance with the court seemed necessary, but the temptation of absolute power was as strong for the dominant politicians of the aristocracy. The result was a pattern of shifting alliances between the court and different factions of the aristocracy; the shah played his part according to the classic maxim of divide and rule in a succession of changing governments. Parliament served as the main instrument of intraelite struggles.

The outs who were challenging the ins consisted mainly of the Communists and the nationalists. In its earliest appearances, communism in Iran was tied to the Bolshevik Revolution, and Communist and Marxist leaders were exiled or imprisoned by Reza Shah. They reappeared in 1941 to establish the Tudeh party, however. As the only political party that had a coherent doctrine and organizational cadre, the Tudeh's success was assured during this period of relative freedom. The presence of Soviet troops in the northern provinces between 1941 and 1946 provided the party with additional political support. In a relatively short time the party achieved the status of a mass political organization by appealing to Iran's working class, establishing an extensive network of party cadres in the provinces, undertaking a vast program of political propaganda and agitation, and forming a number of front organizations.

The nationalist forces represented a wide ideological spectrum and found their organized expression in an assortment of short-lived political parties that ranged from the Right to the Left. Some of these parties were led by well-known politicians and primarily served their political ambitions; others had a wider base of support but lacked lustre and political power. Sayyed Zia's National Will party and Qavam's Democratic party were the chief examples of the former type; both parties were primarily organized around a coalition of incompatible political forces to oppose the growing strength of the Tudeh party, but they declined with the demise of their political chieftains. Others, such as the Iran party and the Niruye Sevvum ("third force") party, had a relatively homogeneous structure but lacked the resources and organizational talents to make an impact.

Despite its organizational weaknesses the nationalist movement had developed into a powerful force by the late forties, a force that both the Tudeh and the ruling oligarchy had to reckon with. Much of the political orientation of the movement was determined by the forceful character of its charismatic leader, Muhammad Musaddiq. By his liberalism, anti-imperialism, and the gifts of a consummate politician, Musaddiq formed a coalition of some contradictory nationalist forces into the National Front, which brought him to power in March 1951 and kept him there until August 1953.

Musaddiq's two-and-a-half-year premiership was the climax of a three cornered power struggle among the Iranian ruling oligarchy (consisting of the court and the aristocracy), the Communists, and the nationalists. The struggle was waged in the context of an emerging cold war among the great powers, in which Iran served as an important theater. With the exception of a few important setbacks, the Tudeh party was in the ascendancy during this period, but because of their collaboration with the separatist movements in Azarbayjan and Kurdistan, their identification with Soviet foreign policy objectives, and their ideological antipathy to nationalism, the Tudeh failed to capture the nationalist movement. Moreover, the party was declared illegal in 1949 and had to go underground.

Having rid itself momentarily of the Communist offensive, the oligarchy now faced a nationalist upsurge. Anti-British feelings had gathered momentum in a movement for the nationalization of the oil industry, and it was to the leader of this movement, Musaddiq, that the conservative Majlis had to turn for leadership in 1951. Musaddiq's policies soon alienated the ruling oligarchy and the United States, however. Although he was a member of the Qajar aristocracy, he showed thorough contempt for the traditional methods of political bargaining by appealing to mass support outside the Majlis. Although he was not a Communist, his liberalism permitted the banned Tudeh party to engage in open activity along with an assortment of other political parties. Although he was a monarchist, his interpretation of the constitution called on the shah to reign and not to rule, and to give up his control of the army. Although he was friendly to the United States, he was uncompromising in his nationalization policy and would not accept an Anglo-American formula for a solution to the oil dispute.

Musaddiq resigned in July of 1952 in a struggle with the shah over the control of the army but was reinstated after massive demonstrations in his support. During the following year, however, further attempts at a settlement of the oil dispute failed, economic conditions deteriorated, and Musaddiq's sources of middle-class support consequently dissipated. The Tudeh party was now calling for a united anti-imperialist front with the National Front forces, but the latter persistently refused.

In the meantime, a group of retired army officers under the leadership of General Zahedi and in collusion with the court and the American Central Intelligence Agency were preparing for a coup d'état.[1] A first attempt at a coup failed on August 15, 1953, however. The shah fled the country, and for four days the Tudeh and some National Front forces took over the streets in jubilant demonstrations and called for the establishment of a republic. But by August 19 the situation had reversed itself. Alarmed by the Tudeh's revolutionary slogans, the moderate nationalists assumed a passive but watchful attitude and the government ordered security forces to disband the demonstrators. A small band of professional toughs reversed the situation and brought all of the King's Men into the open. By the end of the day, General Zahedi had emerged from hiding, Musaddiq's residence had been sacked by royalist forces, and the pro-shah factions of the army were in control. A few days later the shah victoriously returned to the capital.

Although it took the army, the CIA, and the prestige of the monarchy to unseat Musaddiq, the failure of the nationalists and the Communists should be primarily attributed to the confusion and disarray of their own forces. Musaddiq had no political or military organization of his own; the Tudeh leadership lacked the will, and was reportedly forbidden by Moscow, to attempt a unilateral seizure of power. Parliamentary democracy and a multiparty political system had failed once again, mainly because of the absence of political consensus about national goals and rules of conduct of the power struggle.

Political Environment

In its twenty-five hundred years of recorded history, Iranian society has fluctuated between centralization achieved by powerful kings and political fragmentation. The construction of a modern nation-state out of a traditional corporate society has demanded both bureaucratic centralization and national integration. The bureaucratic traditions of imperial Iran and a well-integrated national cultural tradition have, on the whole, supported the state and nation-building aspects of political modernization. By contrast, the monarchical and semicolonial traditions have come into conflict with constitutionalism and nationalism. Both bureaucratic centralization and national integration have been severely impeded by the decentralizing pressures of geography, ethnic and tribal sectionalism, social and economic dualism, and Iran's traditional political culture of cynicism.

Geographical Determinants

Iran's geography has played an important part in her history and politics. The vast Iranian plateau has historically been a crossroads of great population movements. The Indo-European tribes are believed to have passed through this plateau into Europe and India in prehistoric times, and the Aryan tribes made the plateau their homeland. However, the country has been successively invaded by the Greeks, the Arabs, the Mongols, the Turks, the Afghans, and the Westerners. The conquerors were often absorbed culturally, but the resulting political fragmentation and social instability have created political insecurity.

The size of the country (628,000 square miles) and the presence of natural barriers (three high mountain ranges and two vast deserts) have made the establishment of central authority difficult to achieve, although modern methods of transport and communication make increasing political centralization possible, if not inevitable.

In foreign relations, geography seems to have played a dual role in Iran's modern history. As a strategic crossroads between Europe and India, the country has generated rivalry for control among the European powers. The French, the Germans, the Russians, and the

British all recognized that access to Iran and the warm waters of the Persian Gulf was the key to the control of India, but because the power of Russia and Britain balanced each other, the country's formal independence was guaranteed during the nineteenth century. In self-defense, Iranian diplomacy has developed a tradition of playing the great powers against one another to its own advantage.

The People

Ethnic and Tribal Groups: Of the twenty-eight million Iranians, one-half to two-thirds belong to the largest ethnic groups—the Persians. The rest belong to a variety of other Iranian, Turkish, and Arab ethnic groups. The Kurds, the Lurs, and the Baluchis are the main Iranian minorities. The Azari Turks, who inhabit the Azarbayjan provinces, the Bakhtiari, the Qashqai, and the Khamseh tribes constitute the main Turkish minority groups. The Arab minorities are concentrated in the Khuzistan province and in the islands of the Persian Gulf. An estimated 15 percent of the population belongs to the tribes.

Despite considerable ethnic diversity, Iran has minimized its minority problems through a large measure of cultural integration. The minorities' identification with Iranian nationalism has been facilitiated by such factors as the dominance of Persian as the national language, a common Islamic-Iranian cultural tradition, substantial religious homogeneity, the absence of race consciousness, and a relatively high degree of individual social mobility. The fact that during Iran's long history the largest and culturally dominant ethnic group (the Persians) have often been the ruled rather than the rulers has also blurred ethnic distinctions. Intermarriage between ethnic groups, particularly in the cities, has also had an effect.

Nevertheless, modern nationalism has made an impact among some ethnic groups. The Azari Turks, the Kurds, and the Arabs have each expressed their nationalism in political terms. The establishment of the twin Soviet republics of Azarbayjan and Kurdistan in 1945 was, among other things, a manifestation of sectional nationalism. As a result of internal weakness and military operation by the central government, both of these republics collapsed after a year of existence. But both regimes owed their short lives to some legitimate grievances and to demands for cultural autonomy in addition to Russian support. In contrast, the Arab population in Khuzistan constitutes a diminishing minority that is affected by the increasing clashes of Iranian and Arab nationalisms.

The problem of tribal sectionalism is essentially a traditional phenomenon, and the tribes in Iran have gradually lost their autonomy as a result of the increasing power of the central government. Reza Shah (1925-41) pursued a policy of forcing sedentarization of the tribes, which had demoralizing effects on the tribes and contributed to considerable social and economic dislocation. The process of modernization has had a more serious and lasting effect, however. Traditional authority in the tribal social structures has been greatly weakened by the education, urbanization, and alienation of the younger generations. Tribal loyalty is too parochial for the young to accept; modern political ideologies are gradually taking its place.

Social Structure and Conditions: Iran has the dualistic social and economic life—traditional versus modern—that is characteristic of a developing country. Low productivity, low income, a low level of savings and investment, and a generally low level of education and social mobility characterize the traditional—basically the rural—sector, whereas the modern—essentially the urban—sector is dynamic and growing. This dualism is strikingly apparent in technology, in standards of living, in cultural values, and in life styles.

More than 60 percent of the population lives in the rural sector, but no more than 12 percent of the country's territory is under cultivation. Because of the shortage of water, low levels of technology, the low area of cultivable land per man, and a backward land tenure system, yields have been traditionally low. Modern communications media have made the rural population increasingly aware, and migration to the cities has progressively increased, but urban unemployment and slums have sharpened the social class antagonisms, the conflict between modernity and tradition, and the public consciousness for reform.

In response to political pressures the government has had to undertake dramatic social reforms in the sixties, collectively labeled the White Revolution. Land reform was the most significant reform, but it has been supplemented by a worker's profit-sharing scheme, legal reforms to grant equal rights to women, and the formulation of several revolutionary corps—literacy corps, development corps, health corps, and women's corps. The revolutionary corps have absorbed the surplus of those eligible for military service and have provided Iranian villages with essential social services at minimal cost to the government. They have also established a channel of contact and communication between urban youth and the rural population.

Under the impact of more than a decade of oil revenues and rapid economic growth, social conditions have changed—dramatically in the cities and visibly in the countryside—and a new and growing salaried middle class is heavily dependent on the momentum of this growth. In contrast to the small traditional middle class that was largely independent of government largess, the new middle class looks to government spending both in the public and private sectors for the sources of its income. On the other hand, the amassing of fortunes on the top of social hierarchy—achieved primarily through urban land speculation—and the establishment of financial and industrial enterprises has widened the gap between the very rich and the very poor. As long as the momentum of this growth can be maintained and increasing numbers of aspirants to higher social and economic status are co-opted, status politics will prevail over interest politics, but failure on either of these two grounds will open the present regime to serious challenges from the Left.

Economic Conditions

The land tenure system in Iran was traditionally characterized by overconcentration and absentee landownership. A proverbial one thousand (extended) families owned most of the agricultural land and enjoyed its fruits in luxurious urban living. Except for local variations, farm crops were generally divided between the peasant and the lord on the basis of their respective contributions to the five factors of rural production: land, labor, oxen, water, and seed. The peasant often provided only the labor and therefore received no more than one-fifth of the crop. He was plagued by periodic crop failures, indebtedness, and increasing government taxation.

However, rural conditions have been changed by land reform inaugurated in 1962. The reforms at first aimed at undermining the political power of the landed aristocracy and decreasing leftist opposition to the shah's government, but the reform measures were gradual enough to prevent serious antagonism from the landlords. In the first stage of the reform holdings were reduced to one village, prices were determined according to property tax statements filed by the landlords (who had invariably underestimated the value), and the measures were enforced vigorously and with dispatch.

In the second stage, however, landlords were given a choice of five alternatives—tenancy, sale to the peasants, division of the land, formation of a joint enterprise, purchase of the peasant rights by the landlord—and the results often did not favor the peasants. The third stage, which commenced in 1966, has emphasized production maximization through formation of rural cooperatives and farm corporations. As a result of the reforms, some 700,000 rural households own land, 1.3 million are tenants, and 795,792 remain small holders unaffected by the reform laws. By 1969, 8,388 rural cooperatives, with a membership of 1,260,420 farmers, and some fifteen farm corporations had also been established. Domestic and foreign investors are also being encouraged to establish farm corporations to cultivate the land reclamated by the new dams.

The reforms have led to increasing mechanization and commercialization of Iranian agriculture. They have also appreciably improved the standard of living of the new peasant landowners and thus created considerable social stratification and conflict in Iranian villages between the new rural bourgeoisie and the agricultural workers. Despite the reforms, however, two-thirds of Iran's rural population still have no land or less than ten acres. It therefore falls to the industrial sector to absorb Iran's surplus labor in rural areas, but aside from oil, industrialization of the country did not begin until Reza Shah's rule. Of the traditional crafts, only rug weaving has been encouraged on a large scale for purposes of export; most other manufacturing industries have been of a light, import-substituting variety.

In the absence of an integrated national market, most efforts thus far have had to go into construction of roads, railroads, airports,

high dams, irrigation facilities, public utilities, education, and public
health. Since 1949 a series of national economic plans has set forth
projects and targets for economic development. The first two plans
(1949-61) concentrated mainly on building an economic infrastructure,
and the following two (1962-72) have moved toward industrialization.
Heavy industries are represented now by a steel mill complex in
Isfahan, constructed by the Soviets, and petrochemical plants in the
south, constructed in cooperation with private Western firms. The
development plans have been almost entirely financed by oil revenues.

The oil industry has thus provided the country with its major
source of savings and foreign exchange earnings. Before its nationalization in 1951 the industry was run by the British-owned Anglo-Iranian
Oil Company, and Iran received less in revenues than the British
government received in taxes on the company. After three and a half
years of sharply reduced oil exports imposed by the boycott of
nationalized Iranian oil from the international markets, production
resumed in 1954 under the auspices of a consortium principally made
up of the eight major international oil companies. Payments to Iran
during this period have increased from nearly $9 million in 1954 to
over $1 billion in 1970. Total oil revenues today account for about 17
percent of Iran's gross national product, more than 80 percent of the
country's annual foreign exchange earnings, and about 55 percent of
government revenues.

Political Culture

The political culture of contemporary Iran is characterized by
the Iranians' dual response to their historical political, social, and
psychological insecurity caused by centuries of political instability born
of successive foreign invasions and internal upheavals. The elite's
response to political insecurity has largely been cynical opportunism
combined with a mystical reliance on the individual's secretly-held
beliefs.* The masses, on the other hand, have defended themselves
against political change by apathy, fatalism, a cynical mistrust of those
in power, a mystical veneration of "legitimate" power, and a pragmatic
tolerance of "illegitimate" power. Cynicism has defended the individual
against the unreliable tides of fortune, and mysticism has provided the
subtle, deep ties of personal loyalty that are necessary for social life.
Many ordinary and politically prominent Iranians belong to sufi
(mystic) orders, although they are sceptics in thought and behavior.

Iranian society today is far more dynamic, stratified, and
acquisitive than it has ever been, however, and as a result, traditional
corporate values—allegiance to the religious order, the tribe, the guild,
the extended family—have been seriously undermined. But no sense of
national community has yet commanded personal loyalty, and in the

*The traditional Shia practice of taqiyah (dissimulation) allows for false representation of one's
beliefs to protect one's physical safety.

absence of a charismatic leadership to inspire or party leadership to discipline, the traditional political culture has persisted. In times of national crisis (as the constitutional revolution and the oil nationalization movement), however, cynicism may be replaced by a spirit of mystical dedication and national struggle.

The dominant leadership styles that have emerged from this culture and political setting range from traditional uses of power (e.g., Reza Shah and the present monarch) to unsuccessful attempts at charismatic leadership, of which Musaddiq, the revered nationalist leader of early fifties, is the best example. It took Musaddiq a long time to establish his reputation for political integrity, but when he assumed power he could no longer command the loyalty of his supporters except by appearing to be powerless in the face of his enemies. He acted with a deep but possibly unconscious understanding of what might be called the Persian martyrdom complex. He shed tears, took refuge in the Majlis for a while, and stayed in bed as a patient for long periods of time while he conducted the affairs of state. Nevertheless, he was constantly accused of possible betrayal of the nationalist cause by one or the other of his supporters. Once he was ousted politically, however, in part because of the public's failure to support him actively, he achieved the status of a political martyr beyond blame.*

The shah's political style is of an entirely different kind. He divides and rules, but he is respected for his successful manipulation of the political forces. In the absence of mass political parties, the shah has skillfully kept the Iranian political elite sufficiently divided to assert his own unquestioned authority. Alliances have formed around traditional interest groups and informal cliques. The present politically dominant group, the Iran-Novin party, represents one such informal clique. Aside from their government posts, however, members of the clique have no autonomous base of power. The shah could replace them with an alternative group without fear of significant undesirable consequences. There is, in fact, a whole complex of such groups and individuals awaiting their turn in a shifting pattern of alliances. Family ties, membership in such informal institutions as the *dowreh* (which brings individuals of the same class, professional, or ideological interests together in periodic social gatherings), and increasing professionalization play important parts in the formation of such alliances. Common ideologies or political programs play a minimal role, and individual or clique interests assume dominance.

The authority of the shah depends on his traditional patrimonial-monarchical legitimacy. The legitimacy of his subordinates among the political elite are simply emanations of his power and authority. Increasing political participation, development of subsystems such as political parties and trade unions, and a declining sense of

---

*The veneration of Imam Husayn, the Prophet's grandson and the Shia's martyred saint in Iran, is another historical example. To claim the caliphate, he came from Medina to Kufa, in Iraq, on the promise of support from followers in that city. But he faced a cruel death with his family, beseiged by enemies and unaided by friends. The episode has been annually reenacted in Iran and by the Shiites in Iraq in passion plays and religious processions.

powerlessness will undoubtedly cause fundamental changes in the
Iranian political culture. In the meantime, however, the patterns
present a serious barrier to effective political organization.

Political Structure and Processes

In transitional societies there is often a sharp discontinuity
between political structures and processes, and Iran is no exception to
this general rule. Government structures are those of a liberal,
democratic, constitutional monarchy. They have been kept relatively
intact since the constitutional revolution, although the underlying
political reality has changed considerably. In contrast to transitional
societies which have undergone structural reorganization from monarchy to republic or from one constitution to another, Iran has
maintained the constitutional forms. Even Reza Shah could not
dispense with either the monarchy or the constitution. The strengths of
both institutions, one traditional and one modern, have frustrated other
attempts at fundamental changes in the political structures. As was
noted earlier, the recurrent fragmentation and centralization in Iran
have reasserted themselves in modern times in two alternating periods
of parliamentary democracy (1905-25 and 1941-53) and monarchical
dictatorship (1925-41 and 1953 to the present).

The constitution of Iran consists of two parts: the fundamental
laws, ratified on December 30, 1906, and their supplement, ratified on
October 7, 1907. Patterned after the Belgian constitution, the fundamental laws declare the regime of Iran a constitutional monarchy with
the shah as the chief of state. He is the commander-in-chief of the
armed forces, he ratifies laws, inaugurates the Houses of Parliament, is
empowered to dissolve them, appoints half of the senators, and signs
the treaties. All powers of the realm are declared by the constitution to
emanate from the people. The legislative branch of the government is
composed of a Majlis and a Senate. The Majlis consists of two hundred
deputies, elected every four years; the Senate is composed of sixty
members.

Executive power is held by the cabinet. The prime minister and
cabinet members are appointed and dismissed by royal decree, but they
are individually and collectively responsible to the Parliament, which is
entitled to remove them by a vote of no confidence.

The 1953 coup brought the traditional ruling oligarchy back to
power and gave the United States a preponderant position in Iran. With
the active support of the United States, the Zahedi government set out
to consolidate its power by a crackdown on the Tudeh and the National
Front, the settlement of the oil dispute, and a campaign of anti-
Communist propaganda and terror. The chief instruments of government power were the army and an emerging secret police, the SAVAK;
together they managed to dismantle much of the apparatus of the
parties of the Left.

The position of the shah in the new regime had also undergone a fundamental change. The shah had decided to become his own prime minister, and by 1955 he had concentrated sufficient power into his own hands to relieve General Zahedi of this position. Since then his appointees to this position have generally been technocrats who were subservient to his will. The single exception was Ali Amini, who became prime minister in 1961 in another crisis. The economic bonanza of the late fifties had led to a period of overspending by the government and the private sector, to an inflationary spiral, and to an exhaustion of the country's foreign exchange reserves. Under these conditions of economic crisis, the old and new political forces of the Left were once again coming to the surface.

The elections of the twentieth Majlis in 1959/60 provided the occasion for another round of political confrontations. The first elections had been so rigged by Prime Minister Iqbal's Milliyun party that the Loyal Opposition, the Mardom party, and the real opposition were insisting on its cancellation. Under these pressures the shah was persuaded to accept Iqbal's resignation and to call for another round of elections, in which a moderate leader of the National Front was allowed to be elected. In May 1961, under pressure from the opposition forces and from the John F. Kennedy administration, the shah called on Ali Amini—a politician of the oligarchy known for his liberalism and independence—to form a new government.

Amini came to power with a reformist program. Parliament was dissolved, fairer elections were promised, an economic stabilization program was vigorously implemented, a number of corrupt government and military officials were prosecuted, and land reform was inaugurated. However, the prime minister was caught between two uncompromising forces: he depended on the shah, whose control of the armed forces was essential to the survival of his government, and he was seeking a coalition with the National Front, which demanded immediate free elections. In the end he was forced to postpone the elections, rule by decree, and concentrate on social and economic reforms, and under the pressure of political failure he had to resign in July 1962.

The new government under Prime Minister Asadullah Alam, a close adviser to the shah, pursued Amini's social and economic reforms. However, a persistent economic recession and the social dislocation produced by the land-distribution program continued to create an unstable political situation. The government had nearly lost the support of its traditional sources of social support, the landlords, without gaining support from the new urban and rural middle classes. A series of tribal uprisings in the south and massive demonstrations by the religious opposition in the cities during March and June of 1963 were branded as "black reaction" and brutally crushed by the government's security forces.

The survival of the regime was primarily guaranteed by mounting oil revenues. The crop failures of 1963/64 were largely offset by imports of foodstuff from abroad, and the rising expectations of the politically articulate sectors of the population were absorbed by the spending and employment opportunities made available to them by the government. By 1964 massive government spending had turned the economic recession of the early sixties into another period of economic growth.

In the meantime, the transformation of traditional Iranian society into an acquisitive social order had paved the way for the emergence of a new ruling elite. Earlier experiments with "democracy from above" had completely failed. The Milliyun and Mardom parties, which had been organized in 1957 to form respectively His Majesty's Government and the Loyal Opposition, had turned out to be no more than the same old faces. Both sessions of the twentieth Majlis, dominated by their members, still represented the conservative interests of the traditional oligarchy, and on Amini's recommendation, the Majlis was dissolved by the shah in May 1961.

The elections of the twenty-first Majlis were carefully managed to exclude the older politicians and to include a new breed. The overwhelming number of the new deputies were relatively young (80 percent between the ages of thirty and fifty), were serving in the Majlis for the first time (81 percent), had a record of government service (69 percent), and held a university degree (67 percent).

Out of these elections emerged also a new political party which still holds the majority of the Majlis seats and of the cabinet portfolios. The Iran-Novin party was officially proclaimed in 1963 to fill the vacuum left by the Milliyun and Mardom parties. On March 7, 1964, Prime Minister Alam was replaced by Mansur, Iran-Novin's leader, and when Prime Minister Mansur was assassinated in January 1965, his vice-chairman in the party, Amir Abbas Hoveyda, was appointed to replace him.

Hoveyda has continued in the position of the prime minister until the present time, an unprecedented tenure of office. He has reshuffled the cabinet several times, but the profile of his ministers has remained basically unchanged. The cabinet draws members from an elite group of young, Western-educated technocrats who have proved loyal to the shah and are pragmatic in outlook. This group and its counterpart in the private sector have headed Iran's social and economic development in the direction of "guided capitalism." The government has undertaken the responsibilities for the development of Iran's economic infrastructure and heavy industry, but private investors, both foreign and domestic, have been encouraged to develop the other sectors of the economy. In the upsurge of many joint enterprises in banking and consumer industries Iran has been increasingly drawn into the orbit of international capitalist development.

Organized opposition to the government has appreciably declined since 1965. The Tudeh and the National Front organizations have been largely transferred to Europe and the United States. Domestic support for their cause appears amorphous, and the extent of their organized activities in Iran is obscure. Student opposition to the government is still lively and embarrassing, however, particularly outside the country, where the government cannot impose silence. Religious opposition to the regime is perhaps the strongest continuing force.

Although the forms of constitutional monarchy have been kept intact, neither the Parliament nor the existing political parties are important loci of power. The shah has used the existing structures to legitimize his rule, although he has provided political access to the loyalist interest groups. Serious challenges are prevented by a ban on all opposition political parties, however.

Foreign Policy

Iran's geographic position at a crossroads of great power rivalries has played a decisive role in the country's efforts to maintain its precarious independence while advancing its national interests. Three different doctrines have been proposed and put into practice by different Iranian political leaderships—positive equilibrium, negative equilibrium, and positive nationalism.

Before the Bolshevik Revolution of 1917, when Iran was subject to the intense rivalries of Great Britain and imperial Russia, the Iranian oligarchy was equally divided between the anglophiles and the russophiles. Each side tried to advance its own fortunes and to maintain a precarious equilibrium by offering positive privileges to its own favorite great power. German activities in Iran before and during World War I also provided some Iranians with the short-lived opportunity of seeking the protection of a third great power. After the Bolshevik Revolution, however, Russia substantially withdrew from the scene, and Iran was exclusively dominated by Britain. Following an unsuccessful attempt in 1919 to reduce Iran to a protectorate, the British were satisfied to leave Iran in the strong hands of Reza Shah. Iran's relations with the Soviet Union were also put on a friendly basis by the Treaty of 1921, which renounced all former Russian privileges in Iran but permitted Russian military intervention if Iran became a base of operation against the new Soviet regime.

In the thirties, however, Reza Shah's internal position was strong enough to challenge—somewhat fruitlessly—the prerogatives of the two great powers. In 1933 he unilaterally cancelled the British-held oil concession in Iran, but after complaints to the League of Nations and some British show of force he had to accept their modified terms for a new agreement. In the late thirties Germany once again reasserted its influence, which was welcomed by Reza Shah, but the Allied occupation in 1941 put an end to the German influence.

Allied cooperative relations in the early part of the war left little room for the Iranians to maneuver. In the 1943 Tehran Declaration, however, Iran obtained from the Allies a pledge to respect its territorial integrity and a promise of evacuation following the war. Iran declared war on Germany and made a contribution toward the war effort by providing a transit route for the Anglo-American supplies to Russia. The Russian and British occupation of the northern and southern provinces, however, provided each power with important diplomatic leverage to influence the central government. It was in this context that the Tudeh party leaders advanced their doctrine of positive equilibrium, maintaining that the Soviet Union, a socialist power with no exploitative designs, should enjoy at least as many rights in Iran as Britain. During the parliamentary debates on the proposed Soviet oil concession Musaddiq and other nationalists proposed a doctrine of negative equilibrium, maintaining that Iran should assert its national independence by denying all privileges to foreign powers. The rejection of the Soviet proposals for an oil concession and the nationalization of the British-owned oil industry was an outgrowth of this doctrine.

The outbreak of the cold war brought the United States on to the Iranian scene. The U.S. role during the Azarbayjani crisis was marginal but important, and nationalists began to look to the United States as a source of possible deliverance from traditional Anglo-Russian domination. Their hopes were dashed by hysterical anti-Communism in the United States and by American commitments to Britain. Moreover, Musaddiq's intransigence in his nationalization policy also threatened the mutual Anglo-American interests in the Middle Eastern petroleum industry. The United States therefore cast off her earlier courting of the nationalists to side with the shah and the traditional Iranian ruling oligarchy in the coup d'état of 1953.

To ensure internal and external security, the new regime broke away from traditional Iranian neutrality and joined the Western-sponsored Baghdad Pact in 1955. In view of the continued U.S. refusal to commit herself fully to the alliance, the shah persuaded the United States in 1959 to enter into a mutual security agreement.

In the sixties the shah's government has shown increasing independence from reliance on U.S. economic and military aid. The shah called his own foreign policy positive nationalism, and since the early 1960s this label has been changed to independent national policy. In practice the doctine has meant an effort to maximize Iran's power and prestige by diversifying her relations with the great powers. The thaw in the cold war and the shah's consolidation of his internal power have helped him in the pursuit of these goals. In 1962 Iran reached an understanding with the Soviet Union that resulted in Iranian pledges not to grant military bases to any foreign power. Since then, relations with the West have been cordial, but cultural and trade relations with the socialist countries have also greatly increased. Socialist countries have become the single most important sources for Iran's non-oil exports, and many bilateral trade agreements have made it possible for Iran to export crude oil to Eastern Europe in exchange for industrial equipment. The most significant departure from Iran's Western orientation was the conclusion of an agreement with the Soviet Union (in January 1961) for the construction of a steel mill in Isfahan in exchange for the export of Iranian gas to the Caucasus.

The shah's positive nationalism also envisages an important role for Iran in the regional politics of the Middle East. Through membership in the Organization of the Petroleum Exporting Countries (OPEC) Iran has joined the other major oil-producing countries in defense of collective interests. Early in 1971 Iran successfully led the six Persian Gulf member states of OPEC in collective bargaining against the Western oil companies. A five-year agreement was finally reached to raise posted prices by twenty cents per barrel. Since payments to the exporting countries are calculated on the basis of posted rather than realized prices, the agreement has increased government oil revenues considerably.

Through membership in the CENTO and Regional Cooperation for Development (RCO) Iran is allied with Turkey and Pakistan. Agreement has been reached between Iran and Turkey for the construction of an oil pipeline from western Iran to the Mediterranean coast of Turkey; another agreement was concluded between Iran and Pakistan for the joint production, refining, transport, and marketing of Iranian oil on a monopoly basis in Pakistan; negotiations have been also undertaken between the three countries to combine their national airlines. Iran's relations with the Arab countries have not been without friction, however. By maintaining de facto trade relations with Israel Iran has antagonized Arab states. Diplomatic relations with Egypt were ruptured in 1960 but were reestablished in 1970. In October 1971 President al-Sadat visited Iran and met the shah, underlining further improvement in relations. Iran has provided diplomatic support to the Arabs in their confrontation with Israel and this has somewhat ameliorated the effects of relations with Israel. Moreover, Iran's diplomatic support to the Arabs is also due to cultural and religious affinity, which is strong in the public mind.

The shah views Iran's position as pivotal in the Persian Gulf. British withdrawal from the Gulf in 1971 and from the east of the Suez generally, American preoccupation with Vietnam, the Nixon Doctrine for a general retrenchment, and U.S. commitment to Israel which resulted in the weakening of its position in the Arab world all are creating a power vacuum in the area. In the aftermath of the 1967 Arab-Israeli War, the Soviet Union has substantially filled this vacuum in some of the Arab countries and is now moving in the direction of the Persian Gulf, and China is also making a bid for entry into the Arab world. The shah believes that as the strongest power bordering on the Persian Gulf, Iran should assume the leadership role in the security of the Gulf and protection of the weaker oil-producing Arab states against possible encroachments by the Arab revolutionaries. In this task Iran has common interests with the West and the monarchical Arab states. As a prelude to this tacit alliance the shah agreed to settle his differences with the British and the Arabs on Bahrayn, and after a U.N. team found that the people of Bahrayn desired independence, Iran forfeited its claim to the island.

Iranian relations with Iraq, another Persian Gulf power, have been complicated by several other factors. The shah and the republican regime in Iraq have viewed each other with mutual suspicion. The dispute over the control of the Shatt al-Arab at the mouth of the Gulf, the Kurdish guerrillas in Iraq who have used Iran as a sanctuary across the border, the presence of large number of Iranians in the Shia holy cities of southern Iraq, and the nationalist unrest of the Arab minority in Khuzistan have also contributed to strained relations between the two neighboring states. Culturally, however, the two countries have strong ties because about half of Iraq's population are Shia Muslims and a substantial number have Iranian origins.

Iran's foreign policy has evolved from that of a weak power that is experimenting with different strategies for security to one of a growing state that is able to take some advantage of the rivalries of the great powers to assert itself regionally. In the foreseeable future, however, the country will continue to depend on the great powers—and particularly on the West—for military hardware. The Iranian armed forces have so far successfully contained internal challenges to the government, but their external periphery of action will be limited by the deterrence provided by the great powers and by other regional powers.

Political Prospects

Despite the country's external and internal successes, no lasting political institutions have yet emerged to guarantee long-term political stability in Iran, and another severe economic crisis similar to that of the early sixties could upset the present unstable equilibrium. The shah has personally shown greater self-confidence since his successful battle against Musaddiq, but between the shah, who holds most of the power, and a repressed body politic there lies no organized institution of importance except the army and the SAVAK. The internal politics of both of these institutions remain largely unknown, but in a situation of crisis it is probable that the competing factions within these organizations would take different sides.

The rapid economic growth of Iran during the past decade has seriously undermined the traditional social and political systems, although it has also paved the way for the emergence of a modern system. Economic modernization is taking place under essentially traditional social and political relations, however. As increasing numbers of people receive secondary and higher education, as large numbers of graduates of Western universities return to the country, and as expectations of an increasing number of politically conscious citizens rise, demands for political freedom and participation will become more insistent. The articulation of group interests has appreciably increased in recent years in the press. Student opposition is subdued at the home universities but extremely vocal abroad, where it has organized in a worldwide Confederation of Iranian Students. The organization of these interests will have to be realized in the establishment of genuinely representative trade unions, political parties, and other voluntary associations. Barring intervention by revolutionary violence of the army, therefore, another era of parliamentary democracy may follow the present monarchical dictatorship. In any case, the growing pains of political development will remain.

Parts 1 and 2 of this volume have dealt with the Middle East primarily from the point of view of its internal dynamics. Part 1 viewed the area as a whole from the perspectives of geography, history, social and economic life, ideological trends, and the challenge of political modernization. The second part dealt with the political configuration of the individual Middle Eastern states. Despite some historical and cultural unity, the contemporary Middle East is characterized by considerable national and political diversity. The political systems of the Arab states (Egypt, Iraq, Syria, Lebanon, Jordan, Saudi Arabia, Kuwait, the Gulf states, Yemen, and the People's Democratic Republic of Yemen) range from traditional amirates and monarchies to single-party and multiparty republics, and the political systems of the non-Arab states (Israel, Turkey, and Iran) are as diverse. Nationalism and the struggle for modernization are traits common to all, however.

Part 3 will deal with the Middle East from the perspective of its international position. The following chapter underlines the centrality of Middle East's position and shows how internal and external factors make this area one of the world's most explosive. Internal revolutionary turmoil, inter-Arab rivalry, and the Arab-Israeli conflict have combined with competition between the great powers to undermine the purposes and principles of the United Nations Charter.

Footnote

---

[1] The most complete published account of this episode is still the article by Richard and Gladys Harkness, "The Mysterious Doings of CIA," *The Saturday Evening Post*, November 6, 1954, pp. 66-68.

Selected Bibliography

Arasteh, Reza. *Education and Social Awakening in Iran, 1850-1960.* Leiden: E. J. Brill, 1962.
Survey of a subject important to problems of political development.

Arberry, A. J., ed. chairman. *The Cambridge History of Iran.* Cambridge: Cambridge University Press, 1968.
A survey in the distinguished Cambridge series to be published in eight volumes; volumes 1 and 5, already published, are *Land of Iran* and *The Saljuq and Mongol Period*

Avery, Peter. *Modern Iran.* New York: Frederick A. Praeger, 1965.
The only up-to-date history of modern Iran available.

Baldwin, George B. *Planning and Development in Iran*. Baltimore: Johns Hopkins Press, 1967.
The best single-volume introduction to the economic development of Iran. (On land reform, however, consult Lambton.)

Banani, Amin. *The Modernization of Iran, 1921-1941*. Stanford, Calif.: Stanford University Press, 1961.
A good analysis of the social and economic changes under Reza Shah.

Brown, E. G. *The Persian Revolution of 1905-09*. London: Cambridge University Press, 1910.
A classic account.

Binder, Leonard. *Iran: Political Development in a Changing Society*. Berkeley and Los Angeles: University of California Press, 1962.
A sophisticated structural and functional analysis of Iran's political development.

Cottam, Richard W. *Nationalism in Iran*. Pittsburgh: University of Pittsburgh Press, 1964.
An excellent and sympathetic analysis of the phenomenon of Iranian nationalism with an emphasis on the Musaddiq era.

Elwell-Sutton, L. P. *Persian Oil: A Study in Power Politics*. London: Lawrence & Wishart, 1955.
Lively account of oil, imperialism, and nationalism in political conflict.

English, Paul Ward. *City and Village in Iran: Settlement and Economy in Kirman Basin*. Madison, Wis.: University of Wisconsin Press, 1966.
Relations between rural and urban populations in a section of Iran analyzed by a social geographer.

Esfandiary, F. M. *The Identity Card*. New York: Grove Press, 1966.
A Kafkaesque novel about the search for personal identity in the setting of today's Iran.

Iran Almanac. Tehran: Echo of Iran, annual since 1961.
An excellent publication that includes a myriad of information on contemporary Iran from telephone numbers of the ministries to Iran's balance of payments.

Journal of the Society for Iranian Studies.
A quarterly journal that contains many articles pertinent to this chapter.

Keddie, Nikki. *Religion and Rebellion in Iran: The Iranian Tobacco Revolt, 1891-92*. London: Frank Cass and Co., 1966.
A detailed and scholarly analysis of the dress rehearsal for the Persian constitutional revolution.

Lambton, A. K. S. *The Persian Land Reform, 1962-66*. Oxford: Clarendon Press, 1969.
A thorough and extremely informative analysis of Iran's agrarian problems and recent changes.

Mohammad Reza Shah Pahlavi. *Mission for My Country*. London: Hutchinson, 1960.
The shah's revealing account of his own political mission.

Nirumand, Bahman. *Iran: The New Imperialism in Action*. New York: Monthly Review Press, 1969.
Analysis of Iran's problems from the point of view of the New Left.

Ramazani, R. K. *The Foreign Policy of Iran, 1500-1941: A Developing Nation in World Affairs*. Charlottesville, Va.: University Press of Virginia, 1966.
A thorough account of Iran's foreign relations to 1941 (to be followed by another volume to cover the period since then).

Tehranian, Majid "Iran: Politics of Anti-Americanism." *Nation,* October 24, 1966, pp. 415-18.

Upton, Joseph M. *The History of Modern Iran: An Interpretation.* Cambridge, Mass.: Harvard University Press, 1960.
A short but insightful and balanced analysis of Iran's modern history with an emphasis on the decentralizing pressures on the government.

Wilber, Donald N. *Iran: Past and Present.* 6th ed. Princeton, N.J.: Princeton University Press, 1968.
A useful compendium of background facts.

Zabih, Sepehr. *The Communist Movement in Iran.* Berkeley and Los Angeles: University of California Press, 1966.
A good history.

111

International Perspectives

The location of the Middle East, which makes it an essential trade and communications link between Europe, Asia, and Africa and a strategic military position, and the area's immense oil reserves (over 60 percent of the world's known reserves) ensure a pivotal position in world affairs for the Middle East. This chapter examines the elements of Middle Eastern international politics—inter-Arab relations, relations between the Arabs and Israel, and relations between the Middle Eastern countries and the United Nations, the Third World, and the big powers—and the factors that influence these relations.

Inter-Arab Relations

Inter-Arab relations have long been characterized by disagreement, rivalry, and shifting temporary alliances. The Arab people desire unity, but whether they can overcome dynastic ambitions, power struggles, ideological conflicts, differing foreign policy objectives, and differing policies toward Israel to achieve concerted political, economic, and military action remains to be seen.

The center of inter-Arab rivalry has shifted several times since the 1920s, when it originated with a dynastic quarrel between the Hashimites and the Saudis over the latter's claim to most of the Arabian peninsula at the expense of the Hashimites and their kingdom of Hijaz. In this political contest, which lasted until the early 1950s, Saudi Arabia was supported by Egypt, Syria, and occasionally Yemen against the Hashimite monarchies of Jordan and Iraq. The rivalry ended when the Arab factions reestablished a united stand on the Israeli problem resulting from the Palestine War of 1948 and because threats to the monarchical system in the Middle East, especially since 1952, drew them together.

The focus of Arab rivalry shifted to Egypt immediately after Egypt reached an agreement with Britain over the evacuation of the Suez Canal Zone in October 1954. Gamal Abdul Nasser reactivated the anti-Hashimite campaign to discourage Iraq from participating in cold war alliances and from becoming a founding memeber of the Baghdad Pact and to prevent Jordan from joining the pact. Nasser's first objective failed—the Iraqi goverment joined the Baghdad Pact, disregarding opposition within Iraq and in other Arab countries—but the second succeeded. The pact polarized Arab governments and severely shook their solidarity. The revolution in 1958 ended the rule of the Hashimite dynasty in Iraq and was followed by Iraq's withdrawal from the Baghdad Pact and a temporary accord between Egypt and Iraq. However, an anti-Egyptian attitude was revived under the rule of Abd al-Karim Qasim, who refused to acknowledge Nasser as the leader of the Arab world and further limited Nasser's influence in Iraq by imprisoning his supporters. Qasim's challenge to Egypt forced Nasser to adjust his position toward conservative Arab states such as Jordan and Saudi Arabia; through alignment with them Nasser aimed at isolating Iraq within the Arab League. The shift in alignments drew severe criticism from the extreme revolutionaries in the Middle East, especially from the Baathists in Syria, who felt that Nasser had betrayed the revolutionary cause by befriending the hereditary monarchs.

Nasser's rapport with the conservatives soon ended, and a confrontation between revolutionary and conservative elements came with the overthrow of the monarchy in Yemen on September 26, 1962, and the proclamation of the Yemeni Republic. Egypt viewed the change as favorable to the revolutionary socialist cause and quickly moved in to support the new regime with more than 50,000 troops. Saudi Arabia saw the change and Egyptian presence in Yemen as a direct threat to its system and security and supported the Royalists with weapons, supplies, and money. The entrance of Egypt and Saudi Arabia into the conflict polarized Arab politics—revolutionary Arab states supported Egypt and conservative states supported Saudi Arabia—and made it virtually impossible for the Republicans and the Royalists to conclude a peaceful settlement.

Arab rivalry in Yemen and other areas (between Egypt and Jordan and between Syria and Iraq, for example) was acute until May 1967, when the Arab countries, faced by a major crisis with Israel, temporarily overlooked their differences and achieved a degree of unity. Immediately preceding the 1967 Arab-Israeli War, Arab ministers of oil convened in Baghdad and decided to stop the flow of oil to foreign powers that took a stand against the Arabs. The Arabs also sought to implement past military pacts in order to revive the unified Arab command that had been planned after the establishment of the state of Israel.* Iraq dispatched troops into Jordan on May 31 to take up positions beside Jordanian troops on Israel's border; Kuwait dispatched troops into Egypt; and Jordan and Egypt concluded a military agreement whereby Jordan agreed to engage Israel in battle in the event of an outbreak of hostilities between Israel and Egypt.

The Arab states made serious efforts to implement the agreements: a selective oil embargo was instituted against Britain, the United States, and West Germany by Algeria, Iraq, Kuwait, Lebanon, Libya, Saudi Arabia, and Syria immediately following the 1967 Arab-Israeli War, and Jordan honored its pledge to fight Israel and did engage in battle once Egypt was attacked. There is no evidence, however, that realistic training took place among the armed forces of the Arab countries. The joint Arab command did not act as an administrative coordinating agency for the Arab armies, and no joint binational or multilateral field exercises were inaugurated before or during the crisis that culminated in the 1967 War.

At the Khartoum (Sudan) Conference in September 1967, the Arab countries set a policy toward Israel that permitted no formal peace, no direct negotiations, and no diplomatic recognition. They also decided that Libya, Kuwait, and Saudi Arabia would grant annual subsidies to Egypt and Jordan to offset the economic loss of closure of the Suez Canal and Jordan's loss of the West Bank. Further, Saudi Arabia and Egypt decided to settle long-standing differences, and King Faysal and President Nasser agreed to withdraw all Egyptian troops and support from Yemen by mid-December of that year. Egypt evacuated all its forces on schedule (within three months of the agreement) and Saudi Arabia withheld its support to the Royalist forces (resuming it in November 1969, however).

Although the Arab leaders presented a common front that lasted from May to September 1967, efforts at unity were partly offset by differences over foreign policies, the issue of economic sanctions, and coordination of military activities against Israel. The Arab countries' relations with Britain, the United States, and the Soviet Union are of special interest. The revolutionary states—Algeria, Iraq, Syria, Egypt, Sudan, and Yemen—severed diplomatic relations with Britain and the United States over their alleged collaboration with Israel during the 1967 War, but the conservative and moderate states— Kuwait, Lebanon, Saudi Arabia, Tunisia, Morocco, Jordan, and Libya†—did not follow suit, although some of them recalled their ambassadors.

Arab policy toward the Soviet Union was also diverse. The countries in the revolutionary camp sought to strengthen their ties with

*The Arab Collective Security Pact was signed by the members of the Arab League in June 1950 and was implemented in 1953. This pact was revived in 1961 in order to solve the Kuwaiti conflict with Iraq. The January 1964 Cairo summit conference held by the heads of the Arab League member states established a joint Arab command under the Egyptian General Ali Ali Amer and allocated an annual defense budget of $42 million to strengthen the armed forces of Jordan, Lebanon, and Syria.
†Libya joined the revolutionary ranks after the overthrow of the conservative regime on September 1, 1969.

the Soviet Union after the war, but those in the conservative and moderate camps, with the exception of Jordan and Kuwait, had no desire to develop a close relationship with the Russians. Kuwaiti and Soviet high officials exchanged friendly visits late in the summer of 1967 and Husayn of Jordan visited Moscow in the fall of that year. This contact led to the signing of cultural and commercial agreements with the Russians, but Jordan did not accept Russia's repeated offers of arms, instead preferring to depend on traditional friends, Britain and the United States.

With regard to economic sanctions, Saudi Arabia and other conservative oil-producing Arab countries considered the recommendations of the Baghdad Conference (an indefinite oil embargo and a complete trade boycott against Britain, the U.S., and West Germany, and the nationalization of American and British oil interests in the Middle East) too severe, and they decided at the Khartoum Conference to lift the selective oil embargo. This moderate policy was determined by the need for oil revenues and the desire not to close the channels of communication with the West.

Later evidence of Arab differences was reflected in divergent military policies toward the state of Israel. The Rabat Conference of 1969 broke down in a quarrel over objectives and financing of military preparations. Egypt submitted a military report (the details of which have not been made public) outlining contributions of troops, weapons, and money to be provided by each Arab country for a war with Israel. Iraq, Syria, and Southern Yemen protested that Egypt's proposals did not set the destruction of the state of Israel as the ultimate goal but were limited to the recovery of the lands occupied by Israel since June 1967; Morocco and Algeria referred the whole matter to the Palestinians; Kuwait and Saudi Arabia refused to increase their support for the strengthening of Arab armies; Libya, Sudan, Jordan, and Lebanon supported the Egyptian proposal; Tunisia advocated the use of arms only by Palestinians and recommended that the Arabs seek a political solution to the Arab-Israeli conflict.

Since the failure of the Rabat Conference two developments of considerable significance have occurred: the emergence of a new alliance among three Arab countries—Libya, Egypt, and Syria—and the end of civil war in Yemen. The future of these developments is unpredictable.

The Federation of Arab Republics formed between Egypt, Libya, and Syria in August 1971 and aimed at the coordination and integration of the three countries. Observers have noted that Egypt, Libya, and Syria have complementary ideologies and economic resources and requirements, and they foresee a pooling of Syria's great agricultural potential, Egypt's surplus of labor and talent, and Libya's oil revenues. Militarily, the planned federation could mean a widening of the Arab western front against Israel, extending from Libya through Egypt. The federation could also mean intensification of Syria's military commitment on the eastern front against Israel. (The eastern front of Syria, Jordan, and Iraq has been unsuccessful in coordinating military activities against Israel.) Syria might strengthen Egypt's position in future peace negotiations with Israel. Until November 1970 Syria had rejected the November 22, 1967, United Nations Security Council resoltuion and had opposed a peaceful solution to the Arab-Israeli dilemma, but Syria's new alliance with Egypt suggests a change in Syria's policy.

The second development—an agreement signed in the summer of 1970 between Yemeni Republicans and Royalists that provided for representation of Royalists at all levels of government—was made possible by the realization of both Yemeni factions that neither side had any hope of winning, by King Faysal's belief that the leaders of the Republican regime are not radicals and extremists but moderate men, and by Nasser's preoccupation with Egypt's problems.

The Arab-Israeli Dilemma

Arab-Israeli relations are one of the most important elements of Middle Eastern international politics, and the Arab-Israeli conflict also strongly influences the relationships of Middle Eastern states with other states of the world.

Sources of conflict are the seizure by the Zionists of territorial rights and resources controlled by the Palestinian Arabs before 1948; Israel's effort to exercise military, political, and economic control over the territories occupied in the 1967 War until a settlement is negotiated (the settlement would terminate the state of war, formally acknowledge Israel's existence, and provide for new Israeli frontiers); and the Arabs' insistence on Israel's withdrawal from all Arab territories occupied since June 1967, their request for what they consider to be a just solution to the Palestinian refugee problem, and the reluctance of some Arab states to recognize Israel.

Theoretically, the Arab-Israeli conflict could be ended by compromises in which both sides would modify their objectives and positions, but there are a number of obstacles to a compromise agreement. Both Arabs and Israelis attach symbolic value to the conflict, and as the issues become identified with nationalistic and sacred causes, they become more difficult to resolve through political compromise, because government officials and the masses alike come to regard any reduction of demands or change in objectives as the sacrifice of national or religious integrity. On both sides this symbolism is evident: the Arabs regard their conflict with Israel as "the defense of justice," a defense against "imperialist aggression," a defense against "attempts to destroy Arab revolution," and the "vindication of national honor." The Israelis symbolize their conflict with the Arabs as a "defense of national sovereignty," and a "fight for survival." This technique of escalating issues into principles undermines the bargaining flexibility of the two sides.

The outbreak of violence is another bar to an Arab-Israeli compromise. The use of violence by both sides prior to the 1967 War made it impossible to resolve earlier disputes through diplomatic and political negotiations. In addition, the Israeli military victory in June 1967 and the controlled display and use of force since then have not convinced the Arabs that a reduction of their demands for justice and the liberation of occupied territories is preferable to continued violence. Similarly, the military activities of the Palestinian guerrillas and the Arab states' military preparedness have not helped persuade Israel to change its demand for security.

The absence of direct, purposeful communication between the Arabs and the Israelis is also an impediment to a compromise settlement. Both sides communicate their objectives through the use and display of military force, and one of the consequences of this violence was the breakdown of the Armistice Agreements (see the Glossary), which marked the end of formal communication between them. The only important channels of communication now open to the parties in the Arab-Israeli conflict are the United Nations and the big powers.

The emergence of the Palestinian resistance movement after the 1967 War has become another obstacle to agreement between the Arab states and Israel. The guiding principles of the movement are that Palestine must be liberated, which means the eradication of Zionist society in Israel and the emergence of a new society in which both Jews and Palestinians would live, and that liberation can only be accomplished through armed struggle. In the present political climate of the Middle East, which is heated by the resistance movement's activities and objectives, any Arab country that has a large Palestinian population and that shows a willingness to compromise or directly negotiate with Israel has reason to fear grave internal disorder.

The availability of arms for Israel and the Arab states is the final obstacle to a compromise settlement. The big powers aggravate the situation in the Middle East by arming the two camps in violation of their international obligations to preserve peace in the area. To underline this problem, it is only necessary to recall the French, British, and American concern about an Arab-Israeli arms race, which resulted in the Tripartite Declaration of 1950. According to that declaration, the three nations undertook to intervene against any party seeking to change boundaries set by the Armistice Agreements between Israel and her four Arab neighbors—Egypt, Jordan, Lebanon, and Syria—in 1949. Since 1950, however, all three powers have provided arms to both sides in the Middle East. In addition, Britain, France, and Israel collaborated against Egypt in 1956, and the U.S. government has done little to implement President Johnson's policy statement of May 23, 1967, which said that the United States is firmly committed to the support of territorial integrity of all nations in the Middle East.

In 1955 the Soviet Union entered the arms race in the Middle East by negotiating an arms agreement with Egypt, which broke the Western monopoly over arms supplies to Middle Eastern countries. Consequently, France, Britain, and the United States decided to help Israel maintain a superiority over the Arabs, claiming that armaments were necessary to Israel's survival. They also continued to supply arms to some Arab states (such as Lebanon, Morocco, Tunisia, Saudi Arabia, Libya, Jordan) to preserve these states' influence in the Arab world and to secure British, U.S., and French oil interests.

The flow of jets, missiles, sophisticated electronic equipment, and small arms into the Middle East since 1967 from the big powers, particularly from the Soviet Union and the United States, has encouraged the combatants to think that they can achieve their objectives through force. The Israelis talk of forcibly defending the occupied lands until a final settlement is reached with the Arabs. Some Arabs talk of forcibly liberating these lost territories if the Israelis do not agree to a complete withdrawal. The United States reaffirms her intention to maintain careful watch on the balance of power in the Middle East and to provide arms to friendly states as the need arises. The Soviet Union assures some Arab countries that they will receive extensive aid to defend their legitimate national rights. If these factors remain in balance, the conflict will certainly continue. Only if one or more variables change can the conflict subside and a compromise settlement between the contestants be reached.

The United Nations

The involvement of the United Nations is another major element in the international politics of the Middle East. For over twenty years the United Nations has been occupied with disputes in this region. The activities of the United Nations in the Middle East have included the establishment of the following: United Nations Special Committee on Palestine (1947), United Nations Partition Plan (1947), United Nations Truce Supervision Organization in Palestine (UNTSO) (1948), the Armistice Agreements (1949), United Nations Emergency Force (UNEF) (1956), the United Nations Observation Group in Lebanon (UNOGIL) (1958), the United Nations Yemen Observation Mission (UNYOM) (1963), and the Gunnar Jarring mission since 1967.

U.N. involvement in the Middle East, particularly since the 1950s, has centered around two basic issues*—inter-Arab rivalry and the Arab-Israeli conflict—and in both areas the U.N. has had successes and failures.

Inter-Arab Rivalries

On May 22, 1958, Lebanon requested the United Nations Security Council to consider the Lebanese civil war crisis, and the

*The United Nations also dealt with the following complaints: Lebanon and Syria against the continued presence of French and British troops on their soil in 1946, Iran against the USSR concerning the presence of Soviet troops in her territory in 1946, Syria against Turkish troop concentrations along her borders in 1957, Britain against Iran concerning the nationalization of the Anglo-Iranian oil company, Egypt against the presence of British troops on Egyptian territories in 1947, the questions of independence of Libya and the problem of Muscat and Oman, and the questions of Southern Yemen and Bahrayn.

council adopted a Swedish proposal that called for an observation group to check infiltration of arms, supplies, and personnel across the Lebanese border from Syria. The resolution gave a limited mandate to the U.N. Observation Group in Lebanon—it could take no police action and it operated directly under the supervision of the secretary-general. The group noted limited infiltration of small arms and armed men across the Lebanese border but could not determine their source.

American intervention also influenced the Lebanese crisis. On July 15, acting on a request from Lebanese President Kamil Shamun, United States Marines landed in Lebanon in an attempt to support Shamun and stabilize the situation. This willingness to intervene militarily was probably linked to the overthrow of the pro-American regime in Iraq, which had occurred the day before, and to the political crisis in Jordan, which threatened to end the rule of King Husayn.

In the Security Council, American and Soviet representatives engaged in heated debate over the U.S. intervention. However, international tensions were eased when the moderate General Shihab was elected president and fighting between factions in Lebanon ended. On August 21 the General Assembly unanimously adopted an Arab resolution requesting the secretary-general to consult with governments concerned and to make practical arrangements that could help uphold the principles of the U.N. Charter in Lebanon and thereby facilitate the withdrawal of U.S. forces. The UNOGIL mandate ended on December 10, but U.N. observers remained—not to observe infiltration but to provide the international presence that would enable American troops to withdraw without losing prestige.

Another example of United Nations involvement in inter-Arab rivalry is the Yemen dispute. Following the eruption of the conflict, Secretary-General U Thant made his office available to Yemen, Saudi Arabia, and Egypt for assistance that might encourage peace in the area. The United Nations became more actively involved after the disputants accepted disengagement proposals made by the United States. The terms of the agreement provided for termination of Saudi Arabian aid to the Royalists, withdrawal of Egyptian troops from Yemen, the establishment of a demilitarized zone on the Saudi Arabia-Yemen borders, and the stationing of United Nations observers to supervise implementation of the agreement.

The Security Council endorsed the creation of UNYOM in June 1963, and the mission became operational the following month. The function of UNYOM was limited to supervision of the implementation of the terms of the disengagement, and it had neither the power nor the authority to effect disengagement in any way. Like its predecessor in Lebanon, this group was not concerned with altering domestic affairs in Yemen or with influencing Yemen's behavior toward other states. The mission did exercise its limited authority, and it reported that there were indications that the Yemeni Royalists continued to receive military supplies from external sources, and that there was no reduction of Egyptian forces in Yemen. The group's responsibility was discontinued in 1964. Examination of the Lebanon and the Yemen cases shows that in a civil war situation it is difficult for U.N. observers to establish cooperative relations with warring factions and their supporters.

The Arab-Israeli Conflict

The United Nations first became involved in the Arab-Israeli conflict in 1947, when the British government submitted the Palestine question to the U.N. General Assembly. The Palestine question has since proved to be one of the most severe tests of the United Nations. It is beyond the scope of this chapter to review all the efforts made by the United Nations to de-escalate the Arab-Israeli conflict. The important question we ask is, To what extent do the parties to the conflict consider U.N. involvement to be in their national interests?

Israel's Position: Israel has had serious reservations about the ability of the United Nations to settle the conflict or to secure its national interests. In the course of the prolonged General Assembly proceedings on the last phase of Israeli withdrawal from the Gaza Strip in 1957, the Canadian representative proposed that withdrawal be contingent on an agreement between Israel and Egypt to let the United Nations assume administrative responsibilities during a transitional period, as had been suggested by Secretary-General Dag Hammarskjold. The extent of international administration was still undecided when the Israeli troops withdrew from the strip, however.

The United Nations Emergency Force in the Gaza Strip encountered resistance from Palestinians, who demanded immediate return to Egyptian control. In response to the demand of the Gaza population, a governor was appointed by authorities in Cairo to administer the strip. Hammarskjold tried to persuade President Nasser not to send troops into Gaza or to permit the resumption of commando activities, but the Egyptian president made it clear that the return of the governor to Gaza was imperative. Israel protested that it had been deceived into believing Egyptian administration would not be restored to Gaza. UNEF's ability to control this situation was limited by its lack of police authority, an ambiguous policy toward infiltrators who attempted to cross the armistice demarcation line, and the general problem of maintaining order.

Egypt maintained its blockade of the Suez Canal to Israeli shipping after the execution of the Egyptian-Israeli General Armistice Agreement. Israel complained to the Security Council that the Armistice Agreement had terminated the state of war between the belligerent parties. Egypt contended that according to international law the state of war continued despite the Armistice Agreement and that the blockade was legal. On September 1, 1951, the Security Council asked Egypt to lift its blockade. The Soviet Union did not veto this resolution, but the recommendation was never implemented.

On May 22, 1967, Egypt announced its intention to again close the Gulf of Aqabah. The gulf had been closed by Egypt from 1949 to

1956, but from 1956 to 1967 the gulf was open to Israel under United Nations supervision. The UAR argued that the gulf had always been a national inland waterway and that Israel's presence on the gulf lacked legitimacy. Israel's occupation of Port Eilat had been established in 1948 after the Egyptian-Israeli Armistice Agreement was signed, and according to international law, annnexation of a territory occupied by military force could have legal effect only if the state of war had ended by the signing of a peace treaty. Egypt claimed that the conclusion of the Armistice Agreement did not end the state of war.

Israel maintained that the state of belligerency proclaimed by Egypt was a violation of the Armistice Agreements and insisted that the Gulf of Aqabah was an international waterway in which Israel had the right to free navigation. As for the United Nations role in the gulf's blockade, Israel asked: Why did the Security Council fail to act and to inquire into guarantees of freedom of passage? The closure of the Suez Canal to Israeli shipping from 1948 to 1967 and the blockade of the Gulf of Aqabah in 1967 reinforced Israel's doubts about the U.N.'s ability to secure Israel's national interests.

Israel also contends that its conflict is not with the United Nations but with the Arab states. Consequently, until July 1970 Israel insisted that the conflict must be solved directly with the states concerned and that United Nations presence during the negotiations was unnecessary. Nevertheless, Israel has shown willingness to use the United Nations mechanism to implement foreign policy objectives when other means fail. Thus, Israel's endorsement and implementation of negotiations based on the Rhodes formula* since August 1970 indicates that Israel has eased its unequivocal demand for direct talks with the Arabs. When negotiations moved into a new phase in February 1971, Israel expressed readiness for meaningful negotiations on all subjects relevant to a peace agreement.

The Arab Position: The Arabs have fluctuated from resentment and disappointment to acceptance of the United Nations' role in the Arab-Israeli conflict. The Arabs strongly resented the General Assembly's adoption of the Partition Resolution of November 29, 1947, which called for the establishment of a Jewish state, an Arab state, and an international area around Jerusalem. For part of an Arab country to become subject to alien authority without the consent of the majority of its population and against its will, they added, violated the principle of national self-determination.

Although the Arabs do not always consider the action of the United Nations in their interest, they have frequently cooperated with the world organization and have used it as one means to implement

---

*This formula was used to bring Israel, Lebanon, Egypt, Syria, and Jordan to sign the Armistice Agreements of 1949 under the auspices of the U.N. In 1949 Arab and Israeli delegations met separately on the island of Rhodes with the United Nations mediator, Ralph Bunche of the U.S. Bunche carried proposals and counter proposals between the two sides, and the talks eventually produced the Arab-Israeli Armistice Agreements. The latest indirect negotiations are under the auspices of Gunnar V. Jarring of Sweden, Secretary-General Thant's special representative to the Middle East, and involve Israel, Jordan, and Egypt.

their policy objectives. Unlike Israel, for example, Egypt accepted the stationing of United Nations forces on its territory in 1957 to ensure the withdrawal of French, British, and Israeli forces, to allow Egypt to neutralize its conflict with Israel and to pay more attention to domestic problems. Moreover, immediately following the 1967 Arab-Israeli War, the helpless Arabs appealed to the United Nations to repel Israeli "aggression." Their hopes were disappointed, however; the General Assembly and the Security Council were stalemated. Nonetheless, both organs adopted resolutions calling for cease-fires and humanitarian treatment of Palestinian refugees, condemning Israel for violating the U.N. Human Rights Declaration, and demanding that Israel rescind its measures for annexing the old city of Jerusalem. The Arabs, particularly Jordan and Egypt, welcomed the November 22, 1967, U.N. resolution.

Finally, Arab states have supported U.N. involvement because of Israel's military superiority. Egypt, for example, remains opposed to direct talks with Israel but accepts Jarring to promote a settlement in the Middle East. Egypt and Jordan accepted the Rhodes formula for negotiating a settlement with Israel and have been participating in the talks since August 1970. Egypt's expressed willingness to sign a peace treaty with Israel is extremely significant; it marks a concession to Israel's most crucial demand in the Arab-Israeli talks. But despite progress, concrete differences still exist between Egypt's position and that of Israel on major issues.

The Issues: On withdrawal, Egypt insists that Israel should withdraw from all Arab territories occupied in 1967—the Arab sector of Jerusalem, Golan Heights in Syria, the West Bank of Jordan, the Gaza Strip, and the Sinai peninsula. Israel agrees to withdraw only to new, secure, recognized boundaries, not to the lines that existed before June 5, 1967. Egypt wants a settlement guaranteed by the United States, the Soviet Union, France, and Britain and enforced by a United Nations peace-keeping force on both the Israeli and Arab sides of the borders. Israel opposes imposition of a solution by a third party and the stationing of United Nations forces on its side of the borders. Egypt still demands a just settlement of the Palestine refugee problem and insists on repatriation or compensation, according to numerous U.N. General Assembly resolutions, for all Palestinians who left Israel or Israeli-occupied territories in the wars of 1948 and 1967. (On December 11, 1948, the United Nations General Assembly adopted Resolution 194, which specifically stated that "the refugees wishing to return to their homes and live in peace with their neighbors should be permitted to do so at the earliest practicable date, and that compensation should be paid for the property of those choosing not to return and for loss of or damage to property." This resolution has been recalled often by the General Assembly but has not been implemented.) Israel is willing to offer some compensation and limited resettlement aid but insists on Jewish exclusiveness—that is, Israel wishes to remain exclusively Jewish in structure and function as a state. Egypt is willing to guarantee freedom of navigation in the Gulf of Aqabah and to reopen the Suez Canal to all shipping, including Israeli shipping, once Israel fulfills its obligations under the November 22, 1967, United Nations Security Council resolution. Israel insists on retaining the Sharm al-Shaykh area to ensure access to the Gulf of Aqabah.

The indirect talks under Jarring will probably continue as long as both Israelis and Arabs view the use of the United Nations as in their national interest. Israel hopes that these talks will eventually lead to direct negotiations with the Arabs. Egypt, Jordan, and most Arab states would prefer to keep the talks indirect.

The Third World

Israel has established diplomatic relations with Cambodia, the Congo Democratic Republic, Nigeria, Senegal, Tanzania, Thailand, Zambia, and others and also provides technical and military assistance to these countries. In 1966 Israeli Premier Levi Eshkol visited seven African states and stated his hopes for strengthening relations, but Israel has failed to win the sympathy of the Afro-Asian states. Evidence of this was seen at the conferences held in African and Asian capitals during the sixties, where resolutions critical of Israel were often passed by large majorities.

Because of their nationalist aspirations, their psychological complexes, and their experience with foreign domination, the Arabs strongly identify with Afro-Asian nations and their nonalignment policy. As early as 1954 the Arab League members resolved that the Arab states should strengthen their diplomatic representation with Afro-Asian countries and exchange political missions to promote political, cultural, and economic cooperation. To this end, Egypt assumed leadership and played a significant role in the evaluation of nonalignment policy.

Nonalignment—that is, the policy of not aligning with the U.S., the USSR, or Communist China—springs from the continuing struggle against colonialism, which reached its peak in the 1950s, when more than twenty African and Asian countries gained their independence from Western powers. Its ultimate objective is the attainment of a state of freedom from foreign determinants of domestic and foreign policies. Despite ideological, semantic, and philosophical diversities and con- fusion, there is an underlying consensus among nonaligned countries that (1) nonalignment ensures political freedom and contributes to national self-respect and moral integrity; (2) in contrast to alliance membership, which serves as a restraint, nonalignment permits freedom of expression and action; (3) nonalignment keeps a small nation from getting involved in conflicts of no concern to it; (4) alignment would make local problems more difficult to solve; (5) alliances involve military obligations that divert scarce resources from the urgent needs of economic development; and (6) nonaligned nations are in a position to accept aid—indeed, to bid for economic aid—from both sides in the cold war.*

The two most important landmarks in the series of conferences that helped to clarify these nations' policies are the Bandung Conference of 1955 and the Belgrade Conference of 1961.

The Bandung Conference was a gathering of Afro-Asian nations rather than nonaligned countries. North and South Korea, Nationalist China, Australia, New Zealand, and Israel were not invited; neither were Britain, France, the United States, and the Soviet Union. Although the nations at Bandung represented a variety of political views and cultural backgrounds, they shared a fundamental unity on the following issues: (1) the necessity of maintaining independence against colonialism, (2) the principle of racial equality, (3) the fear of nuclear weapons, and (4) the need for economic development.

Egypt played a leading role at the conference. Nasser called for an end to the game of power politics in which small powers are used as tools by the big powers. He urged the big powers to recognize and respect the right of small states to pursue their own domestic policy and to let them act in the international system without outside pressure or interference. He added that small nations are bound to play a constructive role in improving international relations and easing international tension. World peace, he stated, would be attainable if the United Nations regulated, limited, and reduced armed forces and armaments and if nations adhered to the United Nations Charter and carried out their international obligations.

Nasser's influence was also manifest in the final Bandung Conference communiqué, which denounced all forms of colonialism and imperialism stressed the importance of economic cooperation between Asian and African nations, supported fully the Declaration of Human Rights set forth in the United Nations Charter, declared support for the principle of self-determination of peoples and nations, declared its support for the Arab peoples in Palestine, called for revision of the United Nations Charter to provide a more equitable representation of Afro-Asian countries in the Security Council, and called for effective international control of nuclear and atomic weapons.

The conference failed to create a permanent organization to complement these proposals and decisions because many of the nonaligned nations did not want to set up machinery that would bypass the United Nations. The conference also failed to give new peace-making directions. The real significance of the conference was perhaps the fact that it was held. For the first time Asian and African leaders conferred among themselves on matters of interest to their own people. Prior to this, Asian and African affairs had been determined by Western powers.

Following the Bandung Conference, the big three of the Arab world—President Nasser, President al-Quwatli, and King ibn Saud—met

*For more details see Laurence Martin, *Neutralism and Nonalignment* (New York: Frederick A. Praeger, 1962).

in Cairo and declared their adherence to the principles advanced at Bandung. In a joint communiqué they stated their determination to safeguard the Arab world against what they called the evils of the cold war and to resist foreign alliances. This statement was aimed especially at the Baghdad Pact, which Nasser regarded as a disruptive factor in the common front of the Arab League.

Nasser's next conference was at Bironi, Yugoslavia, where he met with Nehru and Tito in July 1956. As three pillars of nonalignment, they assessed the world situation and suggested that the following measures would reduce world tension: peaceful coexistence, end to power camps, development of backward economies, removal of embargoes on the normal flow of trade, recognition of the Peoples' Republic of China, and support for self-determination of all peoples and nations.

In 1958 Egypt cooperated with its neighbors in the first Conference of Independent African States in Accra. Later this group split into two camps, the Brazzaville and the Casablanca groups. The Casablanca group, Egypt, Ghana, Guinea, Mali, and Morocco, supported the Lumumbist faction in the Congo and were generally militant anticolonialists. (Patrice Lumumba, the ousted premier of the Republic of the Congo, was murdered in the Congo's secessionist province of Katanga January 17, 1961, an act that was regarded by many nations in the Third World as part of an imperialist conspiracy.)

The most important meeting held by the nonaligned nations since Bandung was the Belgrade Conference of September 1961. A preparatory conference held at Cairo established qualifications for attendance: a policy of independence, peaceful coexistence with states with different social systems, support for the national liberation of still dependent peoples, abstention from military blocs, and for members with military alliances, evidence of being free from involvement.

World peace was to be first on the agenda, but anticolonialism was the dominant theme. President Sukarno of Indonesia attacked the Dutch over the status of West Irian; the Arab states deplored the existence of Israel; Tunisia was critical of France; and Cuba attacked the United States. There seemed to be a split between militant nonaligned nations (Indonesia, Guinea, Mali, and Cuba), which favored vocal condemnation of Western colonialism and neocolonialism, and a group including Burma, Ceylon, Cambodia, Egypt, and Yugoslavia, which advocated the global character of nonalignment and a focus on world peace. The prime achievement of Belgrade was the attempt to induce the big powers to prevent war, to demand disarmament with controls and inspections, and to suggest a special disarmament session of the United Nations General Assembly or a world conference under the auspices of the United Nations. Since the Belgrade Conference, however, three pillars of nonalignment—Nasser, Nehru, and Sukarno—have died; new problems have arisen in many countries of the Third World; and Arab countries such as Egypt and Syria have become more dependent on the Soviet Union, especially since 1967.

In summation, most Middle Eastern states have followed a policy sympathetic to the principle of self-determination, to the United Nations Charter, and to Afro-Asian cooperation for peace and development. Israel has made limited economic and diplomatic gains in many Asian and African countries, and the Arab states, led by Egypt, have made impressive gains in world public opinion and have manipulated Afro-Asian conferences, which focused not only on Arab problems and Afro-Asian concerns over colonialism and racial discrimination but also on a wide range of international problems resulting directly or indirectly from East-West confrontation in the cold war.

The Big Powers

The big powers have played a dynamic role in the evolution of the events in the Middle East and still greatly influence its international politics. All of the big powers have foreign policy objectives in the region that are determined by strategic, economic, and political considerations.

The United States

Major U.S. foreign policy objectives in the Middle East appear to be to avoid direct military confrontation with the Soviet Union, to minimize Soviet influence and maintain the balance of power, to protect U.S. oil interests (see table 9), and to maintain the existence of the state of Israel. The United States has used economic, military, and political instruments to implement these policies. Economic assistance has taken many forms—nonrepayable grants (not offered in Soviet aid programs), provision of food under the 1954 Public Law 480,* development loans dispersed through the export-import bank and the Agency for International Development (AID), technical cooperation, and development grants—and has gone to every country in the Middle East (see table 10).

Throughout the last two decades the United States has also provided large amounts of military assistance to Middle Eastern countries. The major recipients of American military aid from 1946 to 1969 were Iran and Turkey, and since 1967 the U.S. has become a major supplier of arms to Israel. Both Iran and Turkey joined military alliances with the United States. American objectives were to improve

*This food provision of Public Law 480 has made it possible for many Middle Eastern countries to buy U.S. surplus agricultural commodities—primarily wheat. The terms of the law allow for payment in the buyer's national currency rather than in dollars or gold. Public Law 480 activities were called "Food for Peace" by President Kennedy and "Food for Freedom" by President Johnson.

the capability of Iranian and Turkish armed forces to contain the Soviet Union, to provide domestic stability in these countries, and to provide the United States with military bases (in Turkey) for stationing bombers and missiles. (The military sites were considered necessary to ensure the effectiveness of the U.S. deterrent system, but the system later became obsolete and was replaced by submarines in the Mediterranean.)

Despite economic and military aid given to Middle Eastern countries, American objectives in the region have not met with much success due to the desire of Turkey and Iran to improve their relations with the Soviets, thereby minimizing the Soviet threat against them and decreasing their dependence on Western powers for protection; the U.S. rejection of the Egyptian request for aid to build the Aswan Dam; American support for conservative Arab countries against the revolutionary states in order to maintain the status quo, implementation of the Eisenhower Doctrine in 1957, which was aimed at isolating Nasser and his Syrian allies and building a strong anti-Communist alliance without them; the landing of U.S. Marines in Lebanon in 1958 (looked upon by the revolutionary Arab states as aggression and manipulated by the Chinese and Soviets for anti-American propaganda in the Arab world); and the strong American support of Israel.

The existence of the state of Israel and the Arab-Israeli conflict are certainly stumbling blocks in the path of American diplomacy in the Middle East. The United States cannot assume a policy of neutrality in the region nor can she appease simultaneously both Israel and the Arab states. The aftermath of the 1967 War demonstrates that many Arab states have, for the most part, lost faith in the United States. They feel that the United States has failed to force Israel to evacuate the occupied territories in spite of President Johnson's promise in 1967 to guarantee the territorial integrity of all nations in the Middle East. Also, President Nixon's promise to watch the balance of power in the area, to supply friendly states with arms when the need arises, to sell American jets to Israel, and to increase financial support to Israel has led some Arab states to believe that the United States condones, if not actually subsidizes, Israeli expansion.

The Nixon administration's Middle East policy seems to operate on three levels: to prevent the United States from being drawn directly into the conflict; to confirm the U.S. commitment to the maintenance not only of the state of Israel but also of Israel's military superiority over the Arab states; and to avoid a military confrontation with the Soviet Union. The United States has apparently succeeded thus far in maintaining the existence of Israel, in avoiding a military confrontation with the Soviet Union, and in protecting oil interests. However, the continuation of this success is uncertain because of instability in the region and the emergence of extreme nationalism and new governments. Further, weariness of world power, a reaction to the apparently endless struggle in Vietnam, and the growing consciousness of domestic problems have built up a high level of popular resistance to steps that might lead to new and costly military commitments. The United States has failed to eradicate Soviet influence in the Middle East, a failure that worries America, her NATO allies, Israel, and conservative Middle Eastern governments.

The Soviet Union

Soviet involvement in the Middle East has historically been determined by strategic considerations—the security of Russia's southern flank and an open passage to the Mediterranean through the Bosporus and the Dardanelles—and Soviet interest has thus traditionally focused on Iran and Turkey. Immediately after World War II, Stalin attempted to gain a foothold in the Middle East. He applied pressure on Turkey to give the Soviets two northern provinces and demanded the right to protect the Bosporus and the Dardanelles and delayed withdrawal of Soviet forces from Iran in an attempt to gain oil concessions. Met by opposition from Turkey, Iran, Britain, and the United States, Stalin abandoned these two efforts but later tried to penetrate to the Middle East through Israel. He urged Eastern European countries to give military aid to the Zionists in Palestine to undermine the British position, endorsed the United Nations' partition plan in November 1947, and extended recognition to Israel in May 1948. However, Soviet-Israeli relations cooled in the early fifties as Israel became more closely identified with the Western countries. The Soviet Union's failure to further her objectives through Turkey, Iran, or Israel in the 1940s may have led to Soviet support of the Arabs in the 1950s.

Until the mid-1950s the Soviet Union did not wield significant political, economic, or military power in the Middle East. The change dates from the controversy over the Suez Canal and the subsequent Egyptian victory and British withdrawal that allowed Soviet power to replace British influence in the eastern Mediterranean. Since the Soviet Union's important decision to finance the Aswan Dam, Soviet influence has penetrated Egypt, Syria, Iraq, Algeria, Sudan, and the People's Democratic Republic of Yemen. The Soviets have also slightly changed the balance of power in the Mediterranean region by increasing their naval presence and by aiding the Arab countries against Israel.

The Soviet Union's basic strategic interest in the Middle East is defense. Shortly after the United States began deploying submarines to the Mediterranean, Soviet naval vessels began to appear more frequently in that sea. In the summer of 1964 Soviet naval units were a common sight in the Mediterranean, and in the fall of 1965 a group of Soviet destroyers and submarines called at Port Said in Egypt. During 1966 more ships, including a guided missile cruiser, visited the same port, and Russian naval vessels also docked at Algiers. When the Arab-Israeli crisis of 1967 escalated, the Soviet Union sent ten additional ships to join the forces of about twenty already present in the Mediterranean. Since the 1967 War, the Soviet fleet has continually been expanding in the Mediterranean. This fleet uses Port Said and Alexandria in Egypt, Latakia and Tartus in Syria, and Algiers in Algeria.

The Soviet buildup in naval power is as yet no match for the United States Sixth Fleet in the Mediterranean,* which together with the fleets of its NATO allies maintains a three-to-one superiority over the Soviet fleet. The Sixth fleet is thus a deterrent to the Soviet Union in the Middle East. Further, the Soviet Union does not have control over the Straits of Gibraltar, the Dardanelles, or the Bosporus, so that even if Soviet ships are present in the Mediterranean, Soviet supply lines remain vulnerable and could be closed off at these points. But by developing a counterforce to American and NATO capability, the Soviets have achieved one strategic objective—increasing Soviet prestige and influence. It is also significant that Soviet naval units were used to demonstrate Soviet commitment to the Arabs for the first time during the Arab-Israeli crisis of 1967, an action that reaped political dividends in the Middle East.

Naval supremacy and operational capability in the Mediterranean will depend on the continuing presence of the Sixth Fleet and fleets of NATO allies, the Soviet Union's ability to secure communication lines between the Black and Mediterranean seas through the Bosporus and Dardanelles, the establishment of permanent naval bases in the Arab states, and the opening of the Suez Canal.

The Soviet Union also provides economic assistance to Middle Eastern countries in the form of loans, credits, and investments in long-term projects such as the Aswan Dam (see table 11). The amount of trade between the USSR and Middle Eastern countries has increased over the last two years; for example, total Soviet trade with Egypt rose from $369 million in 1968 to $460 million in 1969, and trade with Iran increased from $126 million to more than $220 million.

The military aid the Soviets offer the Arab countries includes grants, barter deals (that is, an exchange of commodities), involvement of Soviet military experts, and the training of military personnel (see table 12). The introduction of Soviet antiaircraft missiles and pilots into Egypt in the spring of 1970, probably prompted by Israel's deep-penetration raids into Egypt, indicates that the Soviets have decided to escalate their involvement in the Middle East. Soviet increases in the supply of arms to some Arab states have been a response to the U.S. policy of denying arms to nonaligned states and the full support of Israel. By contrast, the Soviets cooperate not only with nonaligned countries but also with U.S. allies such as Iran and Turkey.

---

*At this time the Soviet Mediterranean fleet consists of a minimum of thirty and a maximum of sixty-five ships, among them missile cruisers, submarines, a helicopter carrier, and marines. NATO intelligence estimates that the Soviet force in the Mediterranean consists of ten to twelve submarines, one with nuclear missile launching capacity; one helicopter carrier with about twenty helicopters; two cruisers, one with guided missiles; seven destroyers, six with missiles; five destroyer escorts; three minesweepers; four amphibious vessels, including one capable of landing tanks and five hundred men; and twenty auxiliary craft. The U.S. Sixth Fleet in the Mediterranean consists of forty-eight to fifty combat ships, including two large carriers; two heavy cruisers; two hundred aircraft; and twenty-five thousand men. For more information on both fleets, see Alex Douglas-Home, "Red Fleet Off Suez: Mediterranean Challenge" (*Atlantic Community Quarterly* 7, no. 1 [Spring 1968] : 78-89).

Although Soviet policy in the Middle East has paid strategic and political dividends, the ideology of the Communist party has not taken root in the Middle East—indeed, the Communist party is banned in all Middle Eastern countries except Israel. Some Arab states share Soviet views about anticapitalism and anti-imperialism, but these states maintain ideological independence. The Soviets have failed ideologically in the Middle East because of the existence and strength of Arab nationalism, the split in Middle Eastern Communist parties, Turkish and Iranian fear of communism, condemnation of Soviet occupation in Czechoslovakia, and the existence of the ruling Baath party in Syria and Iraq and the Arab Socialist Union in Egypt.

To sum up, the Soviet Union has spread her influence in the Middle East by using economic, military, and political approaches and has thereby accentuated the failures of Western powers, gradually eroding U.S. influence in the region. The USSR has also succeeded in increasing the operational mobility of her navy in the Mediterranean, which jeopardizes the U.S. Sixth Fleet and NATO forces.

France

French policy toward the Middle East today is largely determined by France's colonial heritage in the region and her desire to secure a favorable strategic position in the Mediterranean to bolster Europe's southern flank and to ensure the flow of Arab oil.

For many years de Gaulle was thought to be pro-Israel because of France's involvement in the 1956 Suez war against Egypt and France's close political, economic, and military ties with Israel. In 1958 de Gaulle met some Arab demands to save France's interests in the Middle East, but between 1958 and 1962 de Gaulle concentrated on French cultural and economic interests and made no attempt to renew political relations with the Arab states. At the same time, Israel strengthened relations with France because she feared Arab solidarity caused by the Algerian War.

Algeria's independence in July 1962 further improved Arab-French relations. Jordan, Saudi Arabia, and Syria reestablished diplomatic relations with France, and Iraq and Egypt followed suit shortly thereafter. But France did not limit herself to an exclusive Arab alliance; when Egypt requested that France stop sending arms to Israel, France made it clear that she would maintain a free hand in Middle Eastern concerns. France also tried to ignore inter-Arab rivalries; for example, she supplied arms to Saudi Arabia, Egypt's primary rival in the Arab world, and despite Egypt's pleas (and to the great satisfaction of the Saudi Arabian government), France did not recognize the revolutionary Yemeni Republic declared in 1962.

During the crisis that led to the 1967 Arab-Israeli War, de Gaulle felt that he could take a neutral position, but the outbreak of hostilities forced France to take sides, and de Gaulle released a statement declaring Israel a "warring state." Since the 1967 War there has been a significant change in French policy. Immediately after the war de Gaulle placed an embargo on aircraft to Israel and the three Arab countries most directly involved in the fighting—Jordan, Egypt, and Syria. In reaction to the Israeli raid of December 28, 1968, which destroyed the bulk of Lebanon's commercial fleet, de Gaulle also placed an embargo on the supply of all military material, including spare parts, to Israel. The Arab reaction was favorable to de Gaulle's embargo decision, but Israel believed that the new French policy created a strategic imbalance, because Israel was the only major purchaser of arms from France. (All these countries have since received large amounts of arms from other sources.)

French-Israeli relations further deteriorated when French authorities terminated the French Renault auto company's activities in Israel (which brought the Arab countries' boycott of this industry to a halt) and ended French collaboration with Israel in the fields of intelligence and nuclear research. Israel felt that France was sentimentally obliged to her and that France would not take sides with the Arabs, but Israel has been established for twenty-two years and France apparently no longer feels bound to her. The French vote in the United Nations now concurs more frequently with that of the Arab states and that of the Soviet Union.

De Gaulle's middle-of-the-road policy toward the Arab-Israeli dilemma was based, according to some opinions, on the assumption that France would thus eventually be in a position to mediate in the conflict, and certainly such a role would enhance the international prestige of France. De Gaulle consistently followed a policy in the Middle East that put highest priority on France's national interests, and his successor, Georges Pompidou, has respected this legacy. At present, it appears that French policy favors the Arab countries because they represent more economic and strategic potential for France than does Israel. The policy seems to assume that a coalition with Israel is increasingly less to France's advantage, while a coalition with the Arabs would enable France to implement her objectives in the Middle East.

Britain

Britain was the dominating foreign power in the Middle East from World War I until the end of the Suez Canal crisis in 1956. Her strength began to decrease in 1947, when she gave up mandatory rule over Palestine, and in 1954, under the pressure of Arab nationalism, Britain abandoned her military bases at Suez. Two years later a significant development further eroded British position and prestige in the Middle East. The British invaded Egypt with the collaboration of France and Israel to end Egypt's threat to the remaining British position in the region and to end the Egyptian claim to sovereignty over the Suez Canal Company, thereby reestablishing British and French ownership of the Canal. Britain and France argued that the 1888 Constantinople Convention had internationalized the Suez Canal

Company; Egypt maintained that the company was Egyptian and that therefore its nationalization was a prerogative of the sovereign state of Egypt.

The invasion of Egypt occurred when Britain was suffering from an identity crisis and when the forces of nationalism and anticolonialism were emerging full-blown on the world stage. To the emerging states the dispute over the Suez Canal was a conflict between imperialism and nationalism. From the start the United States was against the use of force to resolve the Suez dispute, and Soviet and U.S. opposition plus pressure from the world community forced Britain and her collaborators to withdraw their forces from Egypt. The Suez episode marked the end of British dominance in the Middle East, and both the Conservative and Labour governments in Britain have since shared a mutual desire to eschew the Suez episode and to consider it the last imperial experience in British history. British objectives in the Middle East now appear to be the protection of oil interests—more than two-thirds of British oil comes from the Middle East—and disengagement from the Persian Gulf area.

Initial British commitment to the Gulf derives from a series of treaties signed in the latter part of the nineteenth century between Britain and the semitribal states and townships on the south side of the Gulf. These treaties were intended to end piracy against British or British-Indian merchants and to guarantee Kuwait's territorial integrity to prevent Russia and Germany from turning it into a naval station. Since the discovery of oil in southern Persia in 1908, the exploration for and exploitation of oil in the Gulf has made the area of utmost importance to British interests, which include direct British investment in the production of oil (British Royal Dutch Shell Group in the Iranian Oil Operating Consortium, Iraqi Petroleum Company, Qatar Petroleum Company, Abu Dhabi Petroleum Marine Areas Oil Company, and others invest British capital in Middle East oil), the earnings from these companies, which amount to billions of dollars, and banking of these funds.

These British interests have been subject to threats of nationalization of capital assets by revolutionary or anti-Western governments and of the breakdown of stability in the area caused by the emergence of strong nationalism or by claims such as that of Iraq to Kuwait, of Saudi Arabia to the Buraymi Oasis, and of Iran to Bahrayn. In this confusion of rivalries and sovereignties the presence of British military forces once served to maintain the status quo. On three occasions British forces were deployed in the Gulf area: in 1959 they expelled Saudi troops from the Buraymi Oasis and came to the aid of the sultan of Muscat and Oman against the Egyptian-supported movement led by the imam of Oman; in 1961, British forces protected Kuwait against Iraq until replaced by an Arab peace-keeping force.

A major decision concerning the Middle East was made by the Labour government in January 1968: Britain was committed to withdraw her military forces from the Gulf by the end of 1971. The outgoing Labour government based its position on Britain's need to restrict government expenditures because of a balance of payments deficit, on the belief that the presence of British troops increased instability and promoted rather than restrained Arab nationalism, and on the decision that British presence in the Gulf ran counter to British interests in the Middle East because it aligned Britain with conservative feudalists rather than with progressive nationalists.

The opposition, which included Prime Minister Edward Heath and Foreign Minister Sir Alex Douglas-Home, feared that withdrawal of all British forces from the Gulf area might lead to expropriation and interruption of trade and oil exploitation, increased Soviet influence, revival of inter-Arab rivalries and territorial claims, and greater instability in the area. Despite these fears, however, the Conservative government adopted the Labour government's policy and decided to withdraw British forces on schedule.

China

The interest of the People's Republic of China in the Middle East began in 1954 and has since increased. China today has diplomatic relations with Algeria, Egypt, Morocco, Kuwait, Sudan, Syria, Iraq, Iran, Tunisia, Libya, Yemen, and the People's Democratic Republic of Yemen. (Israel recognized Communist China in January 1950, but China did not recognize Israel.) China also seeks to open relations with the Arab countries that maintain diplomatic relations with Nationalist China—Jordan and Lebanon.

China's basic objectives in the Middle East appear to be to gain the acceptance and support of the Arab states as the only legitimate Chinese government; to use the Middle East as a revolutionary front against the Western powers, the United States in particular; and to enlist Arab support for China's policies toward the Soviet Union. China has employed economic, cultural, political, and military means to implement these objectives.

China began competing with the big powers by pledging hundreds of millions of dollars in loans to countries in the Middle East. Chinese economic relations with Egypt, for example, have taken many forms: lines of credits, grants-in-aid, trade agreements, and the promotion of scientific cooperation. On June 11, 1967, China diverted large amounts of wheat purchased from Australia to Egypt and donated $10 million in cash, claiming that Egypt needed the aid to resist the aggression of American imperialists.

Yemen is another recipient of Chinese aid and trade. In 1958 Yemen and China signed a treaty that provided for commercial, technical, and cultural cooperation. Yemen agreed to export agricultural and mineral products to China; in return, China agreed to extend to Yemen $16.4 million in interest-free loans, repayable in ten years in commodities, Swiss francs, or sterling. Under the provisions of the treaty, Chinese technicians and workers were dispatched to Yemen to build a road from Sanaa, the capital, to Hodeida, a commercial center on the Red Sea. In 1964 the countries signed the Sino-Yemeni Economic-Technical Cooperation Agreement, in accordance with which the Chinese helped Yemen build a textile plant in Sanaa and similar projects.

China has also signed economic and cultural agreements with Algeria, Iraq, Lebanon, Morocco, Tunisia, Sudan, and Syria; however, all of the agreements were challenged by Russian, European, and American aid, which was better in quality and quantity. Disillusionment with economic aid as an instrument of foreign policy implementation and internal turmoil during the Cultural Revolution probably prompted the Chinese to decide in February 1966 to reduce economic aid to the Middle East. Chinese assistance to Middle Eastern countries since 1956 has totaled $300 million; aid from the USSR and its satellites has exceeded $5 billion.

China uses the struggles between the Arabs and the West and between the Arabs and Israel to further her foreign policy objectives. For example, China supported the Algerian Liberation Front beginning in November 1954, and since the front had been organized to end French colonialism, support by the Chinese furthered China's influence not only in Algeria but in the entire Arab world and Africa as well. On September 22, 1958, China was the first country in the Communist bloc to recognize the Algerian provisional government, a decision considered by the Arab countries as proof of sympathy and support of the Chinese people for the liberation movement in the Middle East. China's support to Algeria continued after Algeria's independence was proclaimed in 1962, and in February 1965 a military agreement was signed between the two countries to provide Chinese arms to the new Algerian government.

Similarly, China considered the nationalization of the Suez Canal by Egypt as an inspiration to all who opposed colonialism. When Egypt was attacked by Britain, France, and Israel in 1956, China offered moral and material support, but it is questionable whether the offer to send volunteers to help Egypt in battle was serious.

China escalated aid to the Palestinian Arabs in 1965. In March of that year the leader of the Palestine Liberation Organization (PLO) was invited to Peking, and the signing of a pact with China for military aid and training culminated his visit. This training program continues to date. A permanent PLO representative in Peking supervises the training of members of the various Palestinian resistance movements and the shipments of small arms to these groups. China also trains leaders of the Dhofar Liberation Front—a Marxist group seeking to gain independence for the Province of Dhofar from the British-protected sultan of Muscat and Oman—and supplies them with arms.

By fully endorsing the Palestine resistance movements and by publicly denouncing the Soviet Union's support of the U.N. November 22, 1967, resolution as an example of Soviet alliance with the United States against the revolutionary movements in the Middle East, China has probably contributed to the emergence of a Soviet policy that provides more backing to resistance movements. Thus, in early

1970 a delegation of resistance movements led by Yasir Arafat went to Moscow and was encouraged to cooperate with Arab Communist guerrilla forces. Officially, however, the Soviet Union still advocates a peaceful political solution to the Arab-Israeli impasse in accordance with the November 22, 1967, resolution.

China's relations with many Middle Eastern countries have paid dividends to both sides. She has furthered her war against colonialism and imperialism by supporting the Arab cause in Algeria and Palestine and the Dhofar Liberation Front in the Arabian peninsula; in return, the Peking regime has been diplomatically recognized by many Middle Eastern countries, thus achieving two foreign policy objectives. But China's third foreign policy objective—eradicating Soviet influence in the Middle East—has failed. The Arab countries that have diplomatic relations with China have refused to support her against the Soviet Union, because these states believe that the USSR is a major force in the struggle against imperialism, and weakening the relations between them and the Soviets would lessen the effectiveness of the anti-imperialist front.

Table 9

**Value of Direct American Investment and Income
in Middle East Oil
(Millions of Dollars)**

Year	Direct Investment	Income
1960	1,119	698
1961	1,191	755
1962	1,148	846
1963	1,206	825
1964	1,240	893
1965	1,436	813
1966	1,557	852
1967	1,608	1,010
1968	1,654	1,069

Source: Adapted from United States Department of Commerce, *Survey of Current Business,* 1961 to 1969 issues.

Table 10

Cumulative U.S. Economic and Military Aid
to Middle Eastern Countries, 1946-69
(In Millions of U.S. Dollars)

	Loans	Grants	Total Economic	Military	Total Military & Economic
Iran	549.7	453.9	1,003.6	1,332.4	2,336.0
Iraq	26.9	28.4	55.3	46.7	102.0
Israel	856.5	369.6	1,226.1	_a	_b
Jordan	23.1	566.7	589.9	_a	_b
Lebanon	11.5	72.5	84.0	9.0	93.0
Saudi Arabia	31.1	27.5	58.6	_a	_b
Syria	24.0	36.3	60.4	0.1	60.5
Turkey	1,370.6	1,184.7	2,555.3	3,045.1	5,600.4
Egypt	619.1	293.0	912.2	−	912.2
Yemen		42.6	42.6	−	42.6
Total	3,512.5	3,075.2	6,588.0	_b	_b

Source: U.S. Overseas Loans and Grants and Assistance from International Organizations, July 1, 1945-June 30, 1969. The table was set in its present form in Lee E. Preston and Karim A. Nashashibi, *Trade Patterns in the Middle East* (Washington, D.C.: American Enterprise Institute, October 1970).

[a]Classified.

[b]Totals cannot be computed because classified figures are not available.

Table 11

Major Middle Eastern Recipients of
Soviet Economic Aid[a] 1954-68
(In Millions of U.S. Dollars)

Country	Amount
Egypt	1,011
Iran	508
Iraq	184
Syria	233
Turkey	210
Yemen	92

[a]For more detailed information see U.S. Department of State, Bureau of Intelligence and Research, *Communist Governments and Developing Nations: Aid and Trade in 1968.* Research Memorandum RSF-65, September 5, 1969.

Table 12

**Middle Eastern Recipients of Soviet Military Aid
1955 to June 1967
(In Millions of U.S. Dollars)**

Country	Amount
Egypt	1,500[a]
Iran	100
Iraq	500
Syria	300
Yemen	100

Source: Wynfred Joshua and Stephen P. Gibert, *Arms for the Third World: Soviet Military Aid Diplomacy* (Baltimore: Johns Hopkins Press, 1969), pp. 23, 73.

[a]It is estimated that the Soviets have supplied Egypt with $2.5 billion worth of military equipment since 1967.

Selected Bibliography

Hunter, Robert E. *The Soviet Dilemma in the Middle East: Problems of Commitment.* Adelphi Papers, no. 59. London: Institute for Strategic Studies, September 1969.
A comprehensive study of the Soviet role in Middle Eastern politics.

————. *The Soviet Dilemma in the Middle East: Oil and the Persian Gulf.* Adelphi Papers, no. 60. London: Institute for Strategic Studies, October 1969.
A good study of Soviet oil interest in the Persian Gulf.

Hurewitz, J. C., ed. *Soviet-American Rivalry in the Middle East.* New York: Columbia University Press, 1969.
Soviet-American economic, cultural, and military rivalry in the Middle East.

Kerr, Malcolm. *The Arab Cold War, 1958-1967.* New York: Oxford University Press, 1967.
An account of inter-Arab rivalry.

Khouri, Fred J. *The Arab-Israeli Dilemma.* New York: Syracuse University Press, 1968.
An excellent, objective study of the Arab-Israeli conflict since its beginning.

Klieman, Aaron S. *Soviet Russia and the Middle East.* Baltimore: John Hopkins Press, 1970.
Soviet policies and objectives in the Middle East.

Lall, Arthur. *The United Nations and the Middle East Crisis, 1967.* New York: Columbia University Press, 1968.
An extensive study of United Nations involvement in the Arab-Israeli conflict in 1967.

Lenczowski, George. "Arab Bloc Realignments of Revolutionary and Conservative Factions in Arab Politics since June 1967." *Current History* 53 (December 1967): 345-51.
Inter-Arab rivalry with emphasis on Arab realignment in 1967.

Miksche, Ferdinand O. "The Soviet Union as a Mediterranean Power." *Military Review* 48, no. 7 (July 1968): 32-36.
An account of Soviet naval strength in the Mediterranean and the strategic reasons behind it.

Polk, William R. *The United States and the Arab World*. Cambridge, Mass.: Harvard University Press, 1969.
American-Arab relations in the twentieth century.

Rouleau, E. "French Policy in the Middle East." *World Today* 24, no. 5 (May 1969): 209-18.
French policy objectives in the Middle East and the means France uses to implement her policies.

Safran, Nadav. *The United States and Israel*. Cambridge, Mass.: Harvard University Press, 1963.
A thorough account of Israel's emergence as an independent state and the role of the United States in supporting Israel's existence.

Wheeler, G. "Soviet and Chinese Policies in the Middle East." *World Today* 22, no. 2 (Fall 1969): 64-78.
The nature of Soviet and Chinese policies in the Middle East, with assessment of the success and failures of their policies.

Palestinian Nationalism

The crushing military defeat that Israel inflicted on three Arab states in June 1967 was seen by the leaders of the Palestinian Arab nationalist movement as a fundamental step toward their own victory, a starting point for their efforts to build a new nation independent of Arab governments as well as of Zionism. The subsequent growth of armed Palestinian resistance to Israel has transformed the entire Middle East situation.

Palestinian resistance was not a major military threat to Israel at the start of the 1970s, but the guerrillas, or *fedayeen* (literally "men of sacrifice"), made the Palestinian Arab people into a major factor in Middle Eastern power politics. Skyjackings by one group, the Popular Front for the Liberation of Palestine (PFLP), in which Western and Israeli hostages were used to gain the release of PFLP prisoners, helped gain world attention. The Arab governments, Israel, and the big powers can no longer ignore them. The bloody civil war of September 1970 and later encounters between the guerrillas and King Husayn's forces in Jordan wore down the guerrillas' political and military strength, however, and by 1971 they were moving back into the underground existence they had known before the War of 1967, but they remain a political factor nonetheless.

Torn by factionalism, the guerrilla organizations tried to develop a unified program. Their stated purpose was destruction of the Zionist state structure of Israel—though not of the Israeli or Jewish people themselves—and replacement of Israel by a secular state in which Muslims, Jews, and Christians could live together on equal terms. To implement this goal the guerrilla leaders ultimately hope to mobilize not only more than one million Palestinians living since July 1967 under Israeli military occupation in West Jordan, Israeli-annexed East

Jerusalem, and the Gaza Strip but also more than one and a half million Palestinians in the diaspora of the Arab world, including 800,000 in refugee camps and settlements and leaders of Arab business and intellectual life.

Palestinians compare their experiences with Algerians, Cubans, Vietnamese, and other colonized peoples; they regard the Israeli immigrants as foreign colonizers who established themselves on the Palestinians' land with the aid of Western technology, capital, and military power. Moreover, they reject the interference of the Arab governments and the intervention of the big powers, but they accept aid from any state as long as it is unconditional. The spearhead of the Palestine revolution is the armed resistance movement, whose leaders studied the methods of Mao Tse-tung, Che Guevara, Ho Chi Minh, and the Zionist guerrillas who fought the British and the Arabs under the pre-1948 mandate. Rejecting compromise political settlements of the Middle East crisis like the one envisaged under the U.N. Security Council resolution of November 1967, the guerrillas hold only the bitter prospect of a struggle that will last for generations if necessary.

Historical Background

Palestinian Arab nationalism as it has emerged in the 1970s is a late example of the general awakening of Arab nationalism in the last century. Most of the former Arab provinces of the Ottoman Empire first achieved national identity in the mandates and protectorates controlled by Britain, France, and Italy; the exception was Arab Palestine.

In 1917, when Britain was still locked in war with Turkey and her European allies, the British foreign secretary, Lord Balfour, promised Zionist leaders that the Jews would have a "national home" in Palestine, without prejudice to the non-Jewish communities living there. At the same time, Britain and her allies promised the Arab rulers, who had joined them against the Turks, that they would have independent states, including an Arab Palestine. The incompatibility of the Zionist and Arab claims during the British mandate in Palestine (1920-48) led to friction and growing warfare. The Jews in Palestine, with the moral and financial support of the world Zionist movement, finally defeated the Arabs, despite the tardy support of the postcolonial Arab governments, and the creation of the state of Israel and the 1947-49 Arab exodus temporarily ended the Palestinian Arabs' hope that they too would have a state of their own.

The roots of the Arab failure in Palestine, as the Palestinians themselves have eloquently explained, lay in the essentially feudal structure of their society, with its inequalities and apparent incapacity to use the tools and techniques of modern technology, economy, and organization. The Zionists had superior resources, motivation, determination, and skill in statecraft, shown by the fact that Israel won and retained extensive international support.

Political Fragmentation in
Pre-1948 Palestine

Although relations between the Arab majority and the Jewish minority were generally good before World War I, the conflicting commitments made by Great Britain to the Arabs and the Jews soon caused rapid deterioration. It was clear that there were basic contradictions between the Balfour promise of a Jewish national home and a series of messages and pledges to the Arabs in which

> Palestine had not been excepted by the British government from the area in which they had pledged themselves to King Husayn [formerly Sharif Husayn of Mecca] to recognize and support Arab independence. The Palestinian Arabs could therefore reasonably assume that Britain was pledged to prepare Palestine for becoming an independent Arab state. On the other side, the Zionists naturally saw, in the British promise of a "national home" in Palestine, the entering wedge for the insertion into Palestine of the Jewish state of Israel which was in fact inserted there in 1948.[1]

Rioting erupted between Arabs and Jews at frequent intervals in the 1920s and 1930s. An Arab strike movement that began in 1933 included demonstrations and uprisings against British authorities in Jaffa, Nablus, Haifa, and Jerusalem. One of these strikes, aimed at securing a halt to all Jewish immigration, was accompanied by the first guerrilla warfare, which was carried on in the Judean hills of Jordan's West Bank, where al-Fatah and the other guerrilla organizations tried to establish permanent bases after the 1967 War. During the Arab general strikes the Zionist labor organizations moved their men into the controlling positions in the economy and the public services, hitherto held by Arabs.

The armed revolt of November 1935 was led by Izz al-Din al-Qasim, an Arab revolutionary of peasant origin sentenced by the French for his resistance activity in Syria in the 1920s. This first recognized leader of fedayeen and a number of his followers were killed in a major battle with British forces. Some of al-Qasim's followers regrouped and led a more violent revolutionary effort in 1936-39, which the British put down only with great difficulty. A series of British commissions during this period first proposed and then rejected the partition of Palestine into Arab and Jewish states.

In 1939 some leading Palestinian Arab notables, such as Jamal al-Husayni, the Muslim mufti of Jerusalem, despaired of obtaining satisfaction for Arab aspirations from the British and communicated with the Axis Powers—Germany and Italy. The Zionists, on the other hand, strengthened their ties with the British and geared their efforts to prospects of an Allied victory in World War II. The economy and the political and social structure of Palestine moved into separate Jewish and Arab compartments. The new Jewish immigrants, who poured in as refugees from Nazi terror and extermination in Europe, brought the skills and the knowledge to cope with modern life that was lacked by all but the relatively small upper class of Arabs.

The Arab revolt of the 1930s and its sporadic extension through the World War II years, when Palestine became a military base for Great Britain and the Allied war effort, lacked effective leaders. Rival families such as the al-Husayni and Nashashibi occasionally fought each other as well as the British and the Zionists. The National Freedom League, founded in 1943/44, became the only effective non-Communist Arab workers' organization. Upper-class and middle-class Arab interests were represented by the Istiqlal ("independence") party led by several prominent Palestinian families. The Communist party of Palestine (which also had branches in Syria and Lebanon) split into a Jewish and an Arab branch, corresponding roughly to the 1965 split between today's two Israeli Communist parties (MAKI and RAKAH).

In 1947 came the unsuccessful United Nations partition resolution and the end of the British mandate (see the chapter on Israel for a more complete explanation). The Arab-Zionist fighting that attended the proclamation of the state of Israel in May 1948 found about 700,000 Jews and 1,350,000 Arabs in Palestine. The fast-growing Jewish population was a relatively well-organized and homogeneous group sharing common ideals and a nationalistic fervor. The Arab population, on the other hand, was socially and politically fragmented with few dynamic leaders and a confusion of social and political ideals. The ill-conceived and badly organized military intervention of the Arab regular armies in Palestine helped set the stage for the dark years the Palestinians were soon to know as refugees living on international charity, barely tolerated by many Arab governments, and largely ignored by the rest of the world.

Arab-Zionist Fighting

Palestinians took only a small part in the Arab-Zionist fighting of 1947-49 for many reasons. The number of armed, trained, and organized Palenstinian fighters was small; their leaders did not coordinate among themselves or with the regular Arab armies; and they lacked weapons, supplies, and financial resources. Palestinian volunteers were among the seven thousand men of the "Arab Liberation Army" commanded by Fawzi al-Kawukji, who had also led some of the resistance to the British in 1936-39. Another small Palestinian armed group under Abd al-Qadir al-Husayni, a cousin of the mufti, operated against Jewish settlements and communications.

In March 1948 Abd al-Qadir al-Husayni's forces drove the Palmach, the armed militia of the Jewish kibbutzim, out of the village of Qastal, which had been reserved for the Arab state in the unimplemented partition plan of 1947. But the Palmach attacked, overcame al-Husayni's forces, and killed him. After this Arab defeat, the Haganah, which had become the regular Zionist army, rolled from victory to victory. Meanwhile, the Arab Legion of King Abdullah of Transjordan, commanded by Sir John Bagot Glubb ("Glubb Pasha"), was invading the West Bank, which Abdullah annexed to his kingdom in 1950. In the Gaza Strip, during the September 1948 truce period the mufti proclaimed a Pan-Arab Palestinian government under the protection of King Faruq of Egypt, whose troops, including Captain Gamal Abdul Nasser, were fighting the Israelis in the area.

As the Jewish forces advanced, the Arabs of Palestine fled. In some cases, Jewish regular or irregular military units destroyed their homes and forced the Arabs to flee at gunpoint. In other cases, savage acts (by both Zionists and Arabs) against civilians, such as the unprovoked massacre of 254 inhabitants, including women and children, of the Arab village of Dayr Yasin by Jewish guerrillas of the Irgun Zvai Leumi and Stern Gang,[2] caused Arabs to leave. Even more often, towns and rural areas were emptied of their Arab population when mere reports of atrocities and massacres by Zionist forces, true or false, spread among them.

The Refugees

An official report by the United Nations Economic Survey Mission for the Middle East in 1949 found that by the summer of that year only 133,000 out of the original estimated 859,000 Arab residents remained in Israel. Of those who fled, 545,000 went to Jordan, 188,000 to Gaza, 100,000 to Lebanon, 70,000 to Syria, and 4,000 to Iraq. Jordan granted full citizenship and working rights to the refugees, and many Palestinians achieved economic and social integration in Jordan. Syria tended to limit the refugees' economic—though not their political—rights. In Lebanon perhaps as many as 40,000 refugees were able to buy or otherwise obtain work permits and foreign passports, usually Jordanian. A considerably smaller number obtained Lebanese citizenship.

By April 1950, 960,021 Palestinian Arab refugees were receiving emergency aid from what came to be known as the United Nations Relief and Works Agency for Palestine Refugees (UNRWA), according to official figures. The Clapp mission, sent by the United Nations Palestine Conciliation Commission, estimated the 1947-49 refugees at 710,000 persons. After the new exodus of Palestinians following the 1967 War, the number of refugees registered with UNRWA rose to 1,425,019 (June 1970).

The majority of refugees have little but the UNRWA ration, which is worth about ten cents a day. (Babies and small children receive special rations.) Through the years since 1948 UNRWA has provided an ambitious program of schooling and medical services in the refugees' host countries, although the failure of more than twenty contributing governments to help meet additional costs threatened to curtail UNRWA's services severely in 1971/72. UNRWA sources estimate its total expenditure since 1948 as about $500 million, and UNRWA and other sources have estimated the additional aid given by Arab governments and private Arab welfare and social services for subsistence, housing, medical care, schooling, and resettlement as close to $100 million.

Confiscation of Arab Property

Palestinian poetry and fiction disclose deep bitterness over the evictions and the confiscation of Arab property inside Israel. The Israeli government promulgated a series of laws and ordinances, some of which were based on British military legislation of the mandate and some of which were new, such as the Absentee Property Law of March 1950, which provided the framework for the gradual Israeli expropriation of the best property. Many frontier incidents were caused by the "infiltration" of Arabs returning clandestinely to see what had become of their lost homes or farmlands and sometimes to take fruit, vegetables, or livestock back to the other side of the 1949 armistice line.

The Resistance

The decision of exiled Palestinians to begin armed resistance independent of the Arab governments can be traced to 1952. A group composed mainly of students at the American University of Beirut founded a committee to oppose all peace plans aimed at "absorbing" or "resettling" the Palestinian Arab refugees. Some of the same students, including George Habbash, a Palestinian medical student, and Hanni al-Hindi, a Syrian, formed the Arab Nationalist Movement (ANM) in Beirut as a rival to the Syrian Baath party. The ANM called for the armed liberation of Palestine and held the Arab governments responsible for the 1948 defeat. It advocated a strong Pan-Arab, socialist state system that could eventually confront Israel.

In the Gaza Strip Egyptian military intelligence helped organize the first groups of fedayeen. From here, from Jordan's West Bank, and from Syria the fedayeen operated deep inside Israel on sabotage and reconnaissance missions. Their leaders, two Egyptian intelligence officers, were assassinated by the Shin Beth, the Israeli Secret Service, however. This early fedayeen activity prompted the Israeli army's raid on Egyptian troops and police in Gaza in February 1955, which inspired President Nasser's request for heavy arms from the U.S. and Britain. When he was unable to obtain them he concluded the first deal with the Soviet Union for the purchase of arms through Czechoslovakia in 1955.

In 1959 another group of Palestinians, including Yasir Arafat, began publishing a secret resistance magazine, *Our Palestine*, which called on Arab governments to give Palestinians a free hand in organizing their resistance movement. Arafat (code name Abu Amar) was first a refugee in Gaza, then a civil engineering student at Cairo University, where he became chairman of the Palestinian Student Federation and a leader and trainer of the Palestinian and Egyptian fedayeen who fought the British army in the Suez Canal Zone in the early 1950s. He next fought against the Anglo-French expeditionary force in the Suez invasion of Egypt in November 1956. Between 1957 and 1965, as an engineer based in Kuwait, he helped organize the first secret cells of al-Fatah.

The Arab governments feared the developing resistance, especially King Husayn's monarchy in Jordan, where more than half the population was Palestinian. Husayn, Nasser, and the other Arab chiefs of state decided that if official channels were created for the Palestinian resistance, the political threat to their regimes would be minimized. Therefore, in 1964 the Palestine Liberation Organization (PLO) was created as the official Arab Palestine "entity," military training camps were opened, Arab governments were asked to admit Palestinians to their military academies, and Ahmad al-Shuqayri was elected the first chairman of the PLO executive committee. The PLO opened offices for recruiting, propaganda, and fund raising in most Arab capitals, although its offices in Jordan were subject to occasional harassment and closure by King Husayn's security forces. However, Ahmad al-Shuqayri's talent for lengthy, fiery oratory soon established an unfavorable image for the PLO in the world at large and in many Arab circles.

In September 1964 the Arab Nationalist Movement led by George Habbash resolved in a conference that armed struggle was the only way to liberate Palestine; that "secondary conflicts should be shelved in favor of the main battle with imperialism and Zionism," and that all the revolutionary groups should be unified. On November 2, 1964, the ANM lost its first member in an unplanned clash with Israeli troops, but it suppressed the news to avoid disclosing its clandestine operations. Its military branch was named Abtal al-Audeh ("heros of the return").

Meanwhile, support from the Baathist regime and the army in Syria had enabled al-Fatah to begin reconnaissance operations inside Israel, and the organization was secretly planning organized armed resistance. On January 1, 1965, al-Fatah's first communiqué announced an attack with explosives on the Israeli national water carrier. This announcement was ignored by Arab and world public opinion, and Arab security forces hunted down and arrested fedayeen. Al-Fatah raids from Syria led in 1966 to a sizable Israeli operation against the West Jordanian town of Samua, which in turn touched off anti-Husayn riots throughout the West Bank and in Jerusalem by bitter Palestinians who resented the lack of defenses in the villages near the truce line with Israel. PLO leadership was accused of helping to foment the trouble, and PLO operations were suspended in Jordan, but al-Fatah continued its attacks from Syria. Israeli officials, including the chief of staff, General Itzhak Rabin, publicly threatened reprisals against Syria for protecting the guerrillas, which, coupled with unverified Soviet and other intelligence reports of Israeli preparations for a large-scale operation against Syria in May 1967, contributed to President Nasser's decision to mobilize the Egyptian army in Sinai in support of Egypt's mutual defense pact with Syria.

Guerrillas played little part in the 1967 War, although some Egyptian commandos did penetrate Israel nearly as far as the Lydda airport before the Israelis detected and destroyed them. Units of the

Palestine Liberation Army (PLA), military wing of the PLO, were stationed in Egypt, Gaza, Iraq, and southern Syria when war broke out, and those in Gaza fought stubbornly with light arms against the invading Israeli armored forces, but they were soon overrun.

In the shock of defeat, the Arab people realized that their governments and regular armies had failed them catastrophically, and the clandestine Palestinian leadership resolved to organize rapidly for resistance in the newly conquered territories and toward mobilization of the Palestinians in the diaspora. Immediately after the war, al-Fatah and three smaller groups, the Youth Organization, Abtal al-Audeh, and the Palestine Liberation Front, secretly agreed on the need for armed struggle but failed to reach unity, and al-Fatah unilaterally resumed its own operations in August 1967. The other three groups merged into the Popular Front for the Liberation of Palestine under George Habbash, which began military operations on October 6, 1967.

The national congress of the Palestine National Council ousted al-Shuqayri before its meeting in July 1968 and in his place elected Yahya Hammudah, an Amman attorney earlier barred from Jordan because of his antiregime nationalist activity. (Al-Shuqayri had drawn criticism for his inflammatory, irresponsible statements about the destruction of Israel, which were used in Israeli propaganda and which were judged helpful to Israel. He was also accused of poor planning and organizing.) A newcomer at this congress was al-Saiqah ("thunderbolt"), a Palestinian organization created by the doctrinaire Marxist "civilian" wing of the Syrian Baath and controlled by the military committee of the Damascus branch of the Baath party. When Syrian Defense Minister Hafiz Assad ousted this wing from power and formed a new government in November 1970, he placed al-Saiqah under his personal control. In April 1969 Syria's Iraqi Baathist rivals had created their own guerrilla group, the Arab Liberation Front (ALF), which also suffered an eclipse during the Jordan civil war in September 1970 when Iraqi troops stationed in Jordan failed to aid the Palestinians.

The guerrilla leaders groped their way toward a politicomilitary strategy for the long war ahead, but the Palestinian movement at the beginning of the 1970s lacked a unified military, political, and ideological program. The emergence of many small groups, some created deliberately by Arab governments to cause confusion and disarray in Palestinian ranks, sharpened competion. The most powerful group was the combined PLO-al-Fatah organization (they merged in 1969), but two Marxist groups, George Habbash's PFLP and the Popular Democratic Front (PDF) of Nayef Hawatmeh, became serious challengers for leadership and attracted from al-Fatah many of its younger followers, especially after the PFLP successfully wrung concessions from King Husayn after fighting his forces during June 1970 and then emerged on the world scene with the hijacking and destruction of four airliners in September 1970.

The skyjackings helped to detonate the Jordanian civil war of September 17-27, 1970, in which the Palestinians lost thousands of men on account of the superior fire power of King Husayn's army. In a

series of new cease-fire agreements and "peace accords," at first
supervised by an inter-Arab officers' commission headed by the former
prime minister of Tunisia, Bahi Laghdam, and an Egyptian brigadier
general, the guerrillas gradually lost the freedom to operate openly in
Jordan as King Husayn's men wore down their forces, confiscated their
arms, and kept them on the defensive.

The fedayeen fought to keep their bases in the Ghor Mountains
of East Jordan, however, and they maintained some supporting
services—clinics, orphanages for the children of commandos killed in
action (the *shuhadah*, "martyrs"), and schools and other social
services—in the refugee camps, often near those maintained by
UNRWA. In Jordan and later in Lebanon the Palestinian guerrilla power
structure had begun to resemble a state within a state.

The Guerrilla Organizations

Structure

The internal structure of most guerrilla organizations closely
parallels that of al-Fatah. Outside the occupied areas, in every
Palestinian community of any size there is a regional al-Fatah
committee, which includes political, information, and military bureaus.
Cells in each refugee camp, university, or place of work keep in contact
with the regional committee through small delegations or individuals.
The regional committees together constitute the central committee of·
al-Fatah, the executive branch of which is composed of a secret
political bureau that, like the regional committees, always includes
delegates of al-Assifa, the military branch. In January 1968 al-Fatah
established the Palestine Armed Struggle Command (PASC), which
comprised eight smaller groups in addition to al-Fatah. PASC's political
activity was slight and was confined mainly to issuing communiqués on
behalf of its various members. In addition to the PLA conventional
forces, which had fought the Israelis and been defeated in the Gaza
Strip in 1967, the PLA in 1968 formed its own guerrilla force, the
Popular Liberation Forces.

Political and Military Programs

All the principal guerrilla groups support a democratic and
secular Palestinian state, and the PDF and al-Fatah place emphasis on
the role of the Jews. Al-Fatah insists that it welcomes anti-Zionist Jews
into the organization, claims that several serve in responsible posts, and
points out that some of its founders, including Kamal al-Nimri and
William Nassar, both of whom are serving long terms in Israeli prisons,
had one Jewish parent.

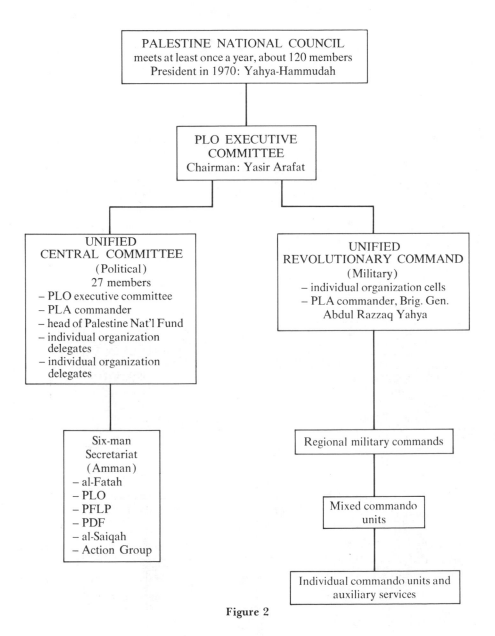

Figure 2

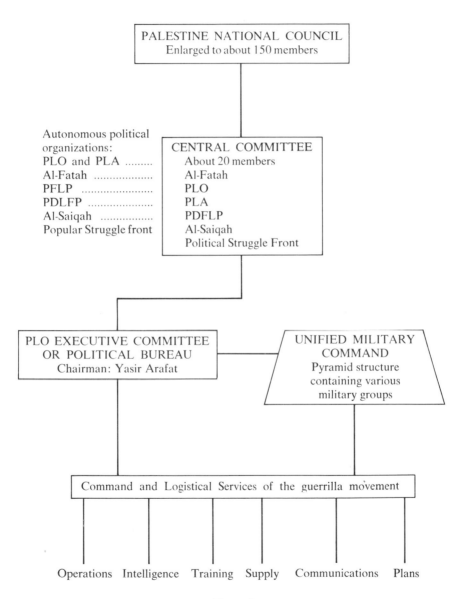

Figure 3

Al-Fatah acknowledges criticism from Israel and the West that, like other Palestinian groups, it has not formulated a detailed political program and counters: "It is quite difficult and risky at this early stage to make a clear definitive statement about the new liberated Palestine. Realism rather than romantic day dreaming should be the basic revolutionary approach. We do not believe that victory is around the corner."[3] Al-Fatah has also preferred to avoid ideology and political interference in its host countries. Whereas the PFLP and other groups hijacked aircraft and made other attacks on objectives outside Israel, including American-owned oil installations, al-Fatah rejected and disapproved of such attacks, demanding that the war effort concentrate on the Israeli military machine and the economy of Israel alone.

For the war effort, an al-Fatah pamphlet calls Lebanon a key base. Galilee, adjoining the Lebanese frontier,

> is the heart of Palestine and Israel's Achilles' heel. In it are the state's water and power sources, and all the heavy industries are centralized there. Its topographical nature is ideal, for in it the mountains, which are an extension of the mountains of Lebanon, are covered with trees (the friends and protectors of the fighter) and penetrate deep into the area. In addition, 40 percent of Galilee's population is Arab; natural water barriers do not exist there; nonhuman barriers are difficult to set up there because of the population density in the area.[4]

Al-Fatah's announced purpose is to build gradually toward a full-scale mobile war in which larger units, perhaps reaching conventional battalion size, would gradually engage the Israelis.

The more leftist organizations agree with al-Fatah on military strategy but not on military tactics or ideology. The PDF and PFLP especially think in terms of a revolution to transform the society and the politics of the entire Arab world as a prerequisite to the struggle for Palestine, and they state that their aim is to build a Marxist-Leninist society.

The PFLP says in its platform, published in 1969: "Israel is the prime opponent; she is trying to defend her aggressive expansionist racial structure and prevent us from regaining our land, our freedom, and our rights." The second enemy is world Zionism, which "as a racial religious movement is trying to organize and recruit 14 million Jews in all parts of the world to support Israel, protect its aggressive existence, and consolidate and expand this existence." "World imperialism" is the third enemy of the PFLP, notably the United States, which "through Israel is able to fight the Arab revolutionary movement." A fourth main enemy for the PFLP is "Arab reaction represented by feudalism and capitalism," which exists, the PFLP contends, because of Arab alliances with the West. The rulers of Kuwait, Saudi Arabia, and the oil-producing Gulf states are meant, according to the PFLP, for they do not serve the interests of the masses.

The PFLP analyzes the relative merits of the "revolutionary roles" of the Palestinian social classes—a factor al-Fatah passes over. "The revolutionary classes on the Palestinian battlefield are the workers and peasants," according to the PFLP. However, the Palestinian "petite bourgeoisie" can be won as an ally by an effective political leadership drawn from the working class.

In this connection, the PFLP says that President Nasser's regime in Egypt was the most "national" because of its anti-imperialist successes and its socialist reforms. Next in line are Syria, Iraq, Algeria, and the People's Democratic Republic of Yemen (in the latter country a regime closely linked to both the PFLP and the PDF took power in 1969). "Except for Southern Yemen, however, these regimes preserved the petite bourgeoisie and its interests in the industrial, agricultural, and commercial sectors. At the same time they produced a new class of military men, politicians, and administrative personnel whose interests became interlocked with the petite bourgeoisie, thus forming the upper class in these communities." Realizing a true "war of national liberation" against Israel and imperialism would mean loss of their privileges, this new upper class is not a reliable ally of the Palestinian revolution, according to PFLP. Therefore, "relations with these regimes must be both of alliance and conflict, ... alliance because they are antagonistic to imperialism and Israel and conflict over their strategy in the struggle."

However, much of the strategy has been formulated by upper-middle-class Palestinians such as Yusuf Sayegh, professor at the American University of Beirut and president of the PLO's inner planning group. With him, the PFLP insists that the liberation struggle will transform the very nature of Arab society and bring it into touch with "the requirements of modern life":

> The habits of underdevelopment, represented by submission, dependence, individualism, tribalism, laziness, anarchy, and impulsiveness, will change through the struggle into recognition of the value of the order, accuracy, objective thought, collective action, planning, comprehensive mobilization, the pursuit of learning and the acquisition of all its weapons, the value of man, the impulsiveness of women—who constitute half of our society—from the servitude of outworn customs and traditions, the fundamental importance of the national bond in facing danger and the supremacy of this bond over clan, tribal, and regional bonds.[5]

The other main leftist guerrilla group is the Popular Democratic Front, a 1969 offshoot of the PFLP led by Nayef Hawatmeh, a Jordanian-born former ANM revolutionary. Dedicated to bringing about total change in the social and political life of the Arab world, the PDF has been the only fedayeen organization that strongly emphasizes the political training and indoctrination of its recruits. It rejects recognition of Israel but also rejects the idea of slaughtering the Jews and throwing them into the sea, to the approval of Western leftist circles. Contacts with MATZPEN ("the compass") and other Jewish far left groups in Israel have been possible because the PDF favors a revolutionary Judeo-Arab democratic state that would liberate "the Arab from reactionary culture and the Jew from Zionist culture."[6]

Palestinian leaders have never admitted publicly that religious differences affect the fedayeen movement, but the main leaders, except George Habbash of the PFLP, are Muslim, and Arab sympathizers with the PFLP observe that Habbash's support would be greater if he were not Christian, although this would be difficult to prove. Conversely, Arab leftist critics of al-Fatah, including Communists, often use the past affiliation of Arafat and others with the Muslim Brotherhood to charge them with being "rightist and clerical," which is a principal reason why Saudi Arabia, self-styled champion of Muslim orthodoxy, supports al-Fatah financially. Thus, in a small way sectarian factors have divided fedayeen ranks at times.

All the guerrilla groups operate both with other politicomilitary organizations and with clandestine cells for intelligence, counterintelligence, and organizational work inside the occupied territories. All are committed to support equality for Jews in their projected democratic Palestinian state, although only al-Fatah and the PDF have sought Jewish support for their struggle. In terms of numbers, finances, weapons, and organizational structure, al-Fatah had a clear edge, although struggles with Arab regimes, especially the bad military mauling the smaller fedayeen groups took from King Husayn's forces in September 1970, pressured the guerrilla leaders to form a united front.

Training and Recruitment

An advanced training school for personnel, part of which is attached to the Algerian military academy at Cherchell, west of Algiers, provides political and military indoctrination. Basic training consists of six to eight weeks of physical training, including jujitsu and karate, and obstacle course, knife, and basic light weapons instruction, with stress on the Kalashnikov and the AK-47 Chinese assault rifle, the RBJ light antitank rocket launcher, bazooka, and 103-MM recoilless rifle. Al-Fatah and PLO weapons experts developed together several new types of rockets and launchers, which by 1970 were being built in their own secret workshops. There is also advanced training in heavier weapons, the Hebrew language, map work, demolition, methods of penetrating the Israeli electronic defenses in the Jordan valley and on the Lebanese frontier, and antiaircraft techniques. Political instruction takes place at both the basic and advanced training levels and discussion groups continue at the advanced operational bases near the frontier.

Recruiting and reception centers operate mainly in Jordan, Syria, and Lebanon. At first al-Fatah and the other groups took mainly Palestinian recruits, but other Arabs came to be accepted. Volunteers from Turkey, Pakistan, Iran and other Muslim countries, European countries, Canada, the United States, and Latin America are now found in al-Fatah, the PFLP, and the PDF.

The Impact of Palestinian Nationalism

Palestinian nationalism has generated shock waves throughout the world. In the Arab countries, where the Palestinians have their bases of political, military, and economic support, governments and societies have been shaken and may yet undergo drastic change, although by 1971 the movement's challenge to King Husayn had contributed greatly to its decline. Israel has awakened to the realization that the Palestinian Arabs they knew mainly as refugees or as docile neighbors have become a threat to Zionism in thought and action. The big powers also face the power of Palestinian nationalism as they attempt to keep peace, to defend their Middle Eastern friends in war, and to achieve their political and economic objectives.

The Arab World

Palestinian Arab nationalism has a double impact in Arab societies: it acts as a galvanizing force, especially among political radicals and the younger people, and it has an increasingly disruptive impact on the conservative Arab governments and societies.

The Palestinian freedom fighter became a hero in the Arab world's arts, entertainment, and information media, and most of the dissatisfied movements and people in the Arab world can gather around this image. "The Palestinians," one frequently hears in Arab cities from Casablanca to Baghdad, "are the only people really doing something about Israel. What is more, they are the only movement capable of modernizing Arab society." The death of President Nasser in September 1970 left the Arab masses without a charismatic leader, and some Palestinians hope that the fedayeen movement can unite and capture this leadership role.

Some guerrilla movements are openly committed to the overthrow of "reactionary" regimes, including Saudi Arabia, Kuwait, Jordan, and Lebanon. Until the 1970s at least, Syria, Egypt, and Iraq managed to neutralize or minimize this impact. Syria and Iraq attached guerrilla units composed of Palestinians and some of their own nationals to their regular military establishments and severely controlled—in the case of Syria, at least, even imprisoned—others. Both also created their own Palestinian organizations. In Egypt, which has a small Palestinian population, the guerrilla organizations were permitted to provide support and information but not to conduct operational activities. The Palestine Liberation Organization and its military branch, the Palestine Liberation Army, enjoyed official status but were subordinated to the Egyptian regular forces. In September 1970, during the Jordan civil war, the last PLA unit was moved from the Suez Canal front to Jordan. Egypt sponsored its own Arab Sinai Organization for operations within Israeli-held Sinai. When President Nasser accepted the U.S. peace initiative of June 1970 he closed the guerrilla radio broadcasting facilities in Cairo because the guerrillas had been attacking his policies, but the government of President Anwar al-Sadat partially restored these facilities in 1971.

Jordan felt the shock of Palestinian nationalism most keenly. The guerrillas in Jordan gained power and prestige from the tough resistance that al-Fatah and the Jordan army offered against a major Israeli attack on Karamah in the Jordan valley on March 21, 1968. However, King Husayn's ruling East Jordan establishment felt that the guerrillas' policy of provoking Israel into reprisal attacks might lead to the Israeli conquest of the rest of Jordan. Successive confrontations with King Husayn's security forces, culminating in 1970 in civil war, hampered guerrilla operations against Israel and weakened the guerrillas militarily. Some guerrilla leaders were tempted by Western-sponsored proposals to establish a new Palestinian Arab state outside Israel, either on the West Bank or on both the East and West banks of Jordan, supplanting the Hashimite kingdom with a new republic of Arab Palestine, but the idea found no official backing from the guerrilla movement or from Israel.

Lebanon stayed out of the 1967 War and consequently lost no territory to Israel. Lebanon also tried to avoid involvement with fedayeen, because its affluent and predominantly Christian trading classes worried that Lebanon might follow the course of Jordan and disturbance and conflict would harm business. However, guerrilla bands used the rugged slopes of the Arkub, the Lebanese side of Mount Hermon, as a transit base; its caves, valleys, and villages afforded shelter for crossings from unoccupied Syria into the Golan Heights, as Syria severely restricted operations from its own territory. Israel sent a number of warnings to Lebanon about the fedayeen presence. Then in December 1968, after an attack by Popular Front guerrillas on an Israeli airliner at the Athens airport, Israeli helicopters ferried in commandos who destroyed thirteen Lebanese civil airliners on the ground.

The Beirut airport raid marked the beginning of Lebanon's involvement with Palestinian nationalism. The guerrilla groups, until then severely restricted, began to emerge into the open. Clashes between the guerrillas and security forces caused demonstrations in Beirut, Saidah, and other Lebanese cities in favor of the guerrillas, and civil war threatened in October 1969. But confrontations between the Lebanese army and the guerrillas were settled mainly by al-Fatah leader Yasir Arafat, General Emile Bustani (then the Lebanese army commander), and the mediation of Egypt's President Nasser. On November 3, 1969, General Bustani and Arafat signed the so-called Cairo Agreement, by which Lebanon recognized the right of al-Fatah and the Palestine Liberation Organization to be present in Lebanon, in return for which they were supposed to respect Lebanese sovereignty and territorial integrity.*

Although often breached, the agreement became the basis for the guerrilla presence in Lebanon. In May 1970 the Lebanese army and the guerrillas fought against an attempt by Israeli armed forces to eradicate the guerrillas in the Arkub. An Arab guerrilla rocket attack on an Israeli school bus on May 21 brought Israeli reprisal shelling of Lebanese border villages, with a resulting exodus of Lebanese refugees. However, leaders such as President Sulayman Franjieh, Pierre Jemayel, and former president Kamil Shamun saw the Palestinians as potential allies of traditional Lebanese leftist foes, and these members of the Lebanese establishment were prepared to fight against internal sub-version by the guerrillas and their supporters or against external invasion from either Syria or Israel. In Lebanon, as in Jordan, domestic politics polarized over the Palestinian issue.

Israel

Before the 1967 War, Israel rarely felt guerrilla armed resistance activity because Arabs in Israel, although they did not enjoy equal civic, educational, and political rights with Jews, did have a higher average living standard than most inhabitants of the Arab countries. By 1970, however, the Israeli military victory and conquest of 30,000 additional square miles of Arab land had altered the situation. Another 300,000 Palestinian Arabs had been displaced eastward, and 1.4 million Arabs and 2.5 million Israelis found themselves living together under Israeli rule,** and some Israeli intellectuals realized that from being the oppressed and persecuted under Nazi Germany in the 1930s and 1940s, they had become the occupiers of conquered land themselves.

At first, the appeals of the guerrilla leadership had little impact on the people of the occupied lands. The Israeli military administration proclaimed that it would be liberal and would allow Arabs to govern themselves except in security matters. Considerable liberty of expression was permitted. Defense Minister Moshe Dayan's "open bridges" policy permitted some West Bank farmers and merchants to ship their products to their usual East Bank outlets, and East and West Bank residents were sometimes able to visit relatives. At the same time, al-Fatah's early cells in the West Bank and Gaza were quickly detected and smashed.

---

*The fedayeen were not to carry arms in public without license, use towns and villages as bases, fire from Lebanese territory across the border into Israel, plant mines near the border, or operate in the immediate area of the Beirut-Haifa highway, which crosses the Israeli border at Ras Naqqurah. In return, the guerrillas were granted use of "access corridors" in southern Lebanon for infiltration operations. They were supposed to coordinate operations with local Lebanese army commanders.

**Since the 1967 War, just under 600,000 Arabs live in West Jordan (excluding East Jerusalem), about 356,000 in the Gaza Strip, 68,000 in East Jerusalem (as enlarged when Israel annexed it in June 1967), 65,000 in Sinai, and about 6,500 in the Golan Heights, where Israel moved in Israeli settlers to replace many of the Muslim Syrians who had fled or been expelled.

As the occupation grew more oppressive, however, resistance increased. Several thousand homes of those who helped, or were suspected of helping, the fedayeen were blown up or confiscated by Israeli military authorities. Curfews, mass arrests and house searches, the deportation of civic and intellectual leaders of the West Bank and Jerusalem Arab community, reports of torture in Israeli prison camps, the settling of Jews on confiscated Arab land, and subtler forms of economic and psychological pressure evoked protests even from such Israelis as Knesset deputy Uri Avnery, as well as from the Israeli Communists and the far left MATZPEN group.

The military impact of the guerrillas on Israel remained relatively small, but beginning in the summer of 1968, the fact of their presence began to penetrate the Israeli population's consciousness. Sabotage and terrorist acts in the cities and the civilian casualties they occasionally caused had more psychological impact than attacks on military camps, sniping, the mining of roads, or even the shelling of border settlements. But exaggerated guerrilla claims lowered whatever credibility the guerrilla communiqués might have had among the Israeli population.

By October 1969 it was clear that some of the Arabs inside pre-1967 Israel were cooperating with the guerrilla movement. In that month, for example, one commando group carried out several sabotage acts on vital communications and industrial supply centers. By the summer of 1970, a new front for guerrilla activity had been opened on the Israeli-Lebanese border, causing some Israelis to recognize Palestinian Arab nationalism as a force that Israel and the Zionist movement would ultimately have to destroy or accept.

The Great Powers

Before the War of 1967, the world rarely took notice of the Palestinian national resistance movement. The first recognition by a non-Arab government came in March 1965, when the first PLO chairman, Ahmad al-Shuqayri, was ceremoniously received by Chinese leaders. The Soviet Union, in contrast, was slow to give support to the Palestinians. Even after Yasir Arafat's first visit to Moscow in 1968 as part of President Nasser's delegation, the Soviet media carried a statement attacking what they called "the romantic and reckless course" of the Palestinians. The first purely Communist fedayeen organization, the Ansar ("partisans"), created in March 1970 by Jordanian, Syrian, Iraqi, and Lebanese Communists, was not admitted to the unified command structure under the leadership of al-Fatah and the Palestine Liberation Organization. Consistent with Soviet foreign policy, the Arab Communists did not support Palestinian insistence on armed struggle and rejection of the U.N. Security Council resolution of November 1967 calling for a peaceful settlement. Moscow gradually accepted Palestinian nationalism as part of the Arab cause to which it was committed, but the Russians preferred to deal with established

Arab governments, which they influenced through economic and military commitments, rather than with guerrilla movements that tried to assert their independence.

The United States government is identified by all the guerrilla leaders and organizations as the "main enemy of the Palestinian revolution." Yasir Arafat, Nayef Hawatmeh, and George Habbash speak repeatedly of Israel as an "extension" or "colony" of the United States. "We know the United States is against us and is trying to crush our revolution," George Habbash told a group of Westerners, including the author, who were held hostage in an Amman hotel in order that the PFLP could wrest concessions from King Husayn in June 1970. Arafat and others also accused the U.S. of helping the Jordan army prepare new antiguerrilla action. Nevertheless, the PLO and al-Fatah opened permanent information offices in the United States (as well as Western Europe).

In the United States, sympathy for the Palestinians comes from a mixed group. Because the vast majority of the one million Arab-Americans in the United States have been politically inactive and not much interested in Palestine, the New Left and part of the protest movement carries the weight of support for the Palestinian cause. The New Left opposes the Israeli and Arab governments as part of the world capitalist establishment; groups like the Black Panthers and the Black Power movement declared themselves in favor of the Palestinians, and spokesmen like Stokely Carmichael contacted the Palestinians. Anti-Zionist Jewish groups and individuals, like the American Council for Judaism and the American Jewish Alternatives to Zionism of Rabbi Elmer Berger, expressed sympathy for the idea of a secular Palestine state. Another group of allies comes from the small but vocal radical white Right in the United States, including the old Klu Klux Klan, the Minutemen, and other groups that tinge their anti Zionism with downright anti-Semitism, forgetting that Arabs are also Semites.

Intellectuals such as I. F. Stone and Noam Chomsky raised the issue of Israel's future in terms of militarism and expansionism. In the *Columbia Forum* of March 1970 Chomsky criticized the "nationalist extremism of the American Zionists," maintaining that it had contributed to creating "an atmosphere in the United States in which discussion of the basic issues is at best difficult." Like Nathan Weinstock, another writer with socialist views, Chomsky suggested that "only a democratic and socialist revolution in the Middle East ... would move both Arab and Jewish societies in these directions and "would serve the vital interest of the great majority of the people in Palestine, as elsewhere,"

Such ideas and a long series of U.N. resolutions calling for repatriation or compensation of the Palestinians have seemingly exercised little influence on American policy. In April 1970, the U.S. assistant secretary of state for Near East affairs, Joseph J. Sisco, defined American policy toward Palestinian nationalism for this writer as follows: Any Palestinian Arab role in an Arab-Israeli peace settlement is "critical," and "had been taken into consideration all along. A just, honorable, and durable peace is not possible unless it meets the legitimate concerns of the many people whose lives are touched daily by the so-called Palestinian question.'' Sisco and the U.S. secretary of state, William Rogers, in June 1970 mentioned Palestinians only in terms of the rights of refugees. However, in his foreign policy message to Congress of February 1971 President Nixon said: "No lasting settlement can be achieved in the Middle East without addressing the legitimate aspirations of the Palestinian people. For over two decades they have been the victims of conditions that command sympathy. Peace requires fruitful lives for them and their children, and a just settlement of their claims.''[7]

Political Prospects

After twenty-three years of suppression by Israel and its neighbor, the Hashimite Kingdom of Jordan, the Palestinians have emerged as a nation seeking statehood. They have succeeded in mobilizing financial, intellectual, and military resources behind an armed resistance movement, the political impact of which has grown beyond its actual military effectiveness against Israel.

The Palestinians reason that their best prospects lie in generating world political and diplomatic pressures like those that helped bring independence to Algeria despite the military defeat of the guerrillas by France. They also count on expoiting the differences and weaknesses of present Israeli society and of eventually winning wide sympathy among Jewish intellectuals, leftists, and Oriental Jews for the idea of a non-Zionist secular state in Palestine. Although this idea has no appeal for the older generation of Russian and East European Jews now ruling Israel, the Palestinians hope that the rising generation of young sabras and other Jews who did not experience the ghettos and persecutions of Europe may eventually come to feel differently.

In their diaspora world, the Palestinians' "refugee mentality" is being replaced by militant nationalism that demands the birth of a new Palestine, no matter what the price, and this militancy has emerged in such acts as the PFLP's hijacking of airplanes and taking of hostages. With this state of mind the Palestinians might conceivably touch off a new world war. With the waning of the refugee mentality comes also the end of Palestinian moral, if not material, subservience to and dependence on the established Arab governments, which the Palestinians feel have failed to understand or to solve the Palestine problem. The Palestinian revolutionary movement will behave more and more like an established nation, whether or not it soon acquires a territorial base of its own.

The Palestinians are also certain to act as a modernizing force in the Arab world. Members of the Palestinian professional classes are already sought after by governments, business firms, and armies as advisers and instructors. The growing literature and legend of the resistance movement contributes to the modernizing, secularizing trends in the Arab world. It is no accident that the officers who overthrew the post-1967 regimes in Libya, Sudan, and Iraq insisted that the liberation of Palestine must go hand in hand with the remaking of their own societies. Similar slogans will undoubtedly be heard tomorrow in the monarchies of Saudi Arabia, Kuwait, and the Gulf states.

The negative factors in the Palestinians' prospects are, first of all, their lack of a territorial base. This fact had led some Israeli planners, Westerners, Egyptians, and members of King Husayn's ruling establishment to approach older-generation Palestinian leaders living under Israeli occupation with the idea of a buffer Palestinian state, composed of the West Bank and probably Gaza, that would have privileged links to both East Jordan and to Israel—a neutralized mini-Palestine acting as an economic and diplomatic transition zone between Israel and the Arab world. But what slight support might have existed for this idea was buried in the general Arab resentment and resistance toward Israeli occupation, the suspicion of anything suggested by the West, and most of all, by the implacable opposition of the guerrilla leadership. Many schemes for a future Palestinian territorial base involve the eventual disappearance of the Hashimite Kingdom of Jordan and its replacement by a new Palestine entity, probably through violent revolution. This entity would likely enter into war with Israel, but it might also provide the nucleus of a state with which Israeli leaders would some day find themselves negotiating peace. Diplomats and statesmen of the big powers who are trying to plan for peace in the Middle East and who forget that the West Bank, Jerusalem, Gaza, and the little al-Himma area were all once parts of pre-1948 Palestine, with Jerusalem its heart, would be unable to arrive at any plan that made sense to the Palestinians.

The second serious deficiency, which guerrilla leaders are unwilling to remedy until they win a secure territorial base, is the lack of a government-in-exile. Arab heads of state especially have urged the creation of a provisional Palestine regime, and although many Palestinians fear that this bureaucratization would slow down their movement, others feel that it is a needed prerequisite to expected statehood.

The proliferation of fedayeen organizations and their differences over ideology and tactics are another serious defect. Each of the major groups has its own plans; each began in the early 1970s to take on some of the attributes of a political party. In the terms of President Nasser, the guerrillas lack "unity of ranks." More serious are ideological differences between al-Fatah and the PLO and the Marxist-inclined movements and groups that depend on Arab governments, which might even lead to internecine warfare.

The Palestinians' desire of total independence from Arab governments and big powers, even if partially achieved, may turn out to be a mixed blessing. The strategy of al-Fatah and even of the PFLP includes a showdown that would involve the regular Arab armies in a "popular liberation war" against Israel. If the Palestinians cut their links with these governments, they would find themselves in a crucial battle period without allies, except perhaps for distant Communist China. Such isolation could lead to a Palestinian defeat far exceeding those of 1948 and 1967. Their leaders are mindful of these contradictions as they face their unknown destiny.

Table 13

The Principal Palestinian Guerrilla Groups

Name and Initials	Estimated Fighting Strength	Main Leaders	Arms Sources	Income Sources	Ideology
Al-Fatah, The Palestine National Liberation Movement	15,000	Yasir Arafat Salah Khalif Khalid al-Hasan Muhammad Najjar Hanni al-Hasan Zuhayr al-Alami	China open market, captured Israeli arms, rockets of own manufacture	Mainly Palestinian private individuals channeling payments through governments of Saudi Arabia, Kuwait, Libya, Abu Dhabi	No political ideology except liberation of Palestine through armed struggle and creation of democratic, secular Palestinian state
Palestine Liberation Organization (PLO); Palestine Liberation Army (PLA); Popular Liberation Forces (PLF)	10,000	Yasir Arafat Brig. Gen. Abdul Razzaq Yahya Shafiq al-Howt Abu Mahmud	Same as al-Fatah, East Europe and Arab governments	Same as al-Fatah, plus Arab govt. subsidies decided by Arab League	Same as al-Fatah
Popular Front for the Liberation of Palestine (PFLP)	4,000	George Habbash Ahmad al-Yamani Haytam Ayubi	East Europe, Iraq, open market, captured Israeli arms	Iraq Private	Marxist-Leninist in sense similar to Asian parties
Popular Democratic Front for the Liberation of Palestine (PDF)	1,000	Nayef Hawatmeh Salah Raafat Adib abd Rabu Bilaad al-Hasan	Syria, East Europe, open market, captured Israeli arms	East Europe Private	Trotskyist; committed to total revolution in Arab politics and society
Popular Front for the Liberation of Palestine - General Command	500	Ahmad Jabril Fadil Chrorou	Miscellaneous	Miscellaneous	None except military struggle

Table 13 (Continued)

Name and Initials	Estimated Fighting Strength	Main Leaders	Arms Sources	Income Sources	Ideology
Al-Saiqah (Thunderbolt)	7,000	Zuhayr Muhsin, Dafi Jamani, Ahmad Shahabi, Yusuf al-Berji	Syria, USSR, open market, Captured Israeli arms	Syria	Baathist (Syrian branch)
Arab Liberation Front (ALF)	3,000	Zayd Haydar, Munif al-Razzaz	Iraq	Iraq	Baathist (Iraqi branch)
Popular Organization for the Liberation of Palestine (POLP)	100	Not available	China	Mainly refugees in camps in Syria	Maoist
Popular Struggle Front (PSF)	200	Bajat abu Gharbiya	Private	Private	Formerly Baathist; now devoted entirely to clandestine action inside Israeli-occupied lands
Arab Palestine Organization (APO)	100	Ahmad Zarur	Miscellaneous	Miscellaneous	Unknown
Action Group	50	Isam Sartawi	Iraq, Egypt	Egypt	Unknown
Ansar (Partisans)	50	Fuad Nasr, Khalid Bagdash	USSR	USSR	Soviet Communist

---

Footnotes

---

[1] Arnold Toynbee's introduction to *Palestine Diary*, 2 vols., by John and Hadawi, 1:xii-xiv.

[2] Cf. *New York Times*, April 10, 1948; Jon Kimche, *The Seven Fallen Pillars* (New York: Frederick A. Praeger, 1953), pp. 228-29; address by the commander of the Jewish attacking force to an audience of New York Jews in *New York Times*, November 30, 1948.

[3] Palestine National Liberation Movement, *Dialogue with Fateh* (Beirut: al-Fatah, 1969), p. 15.

[4] Palestine National Liberation Movement, *Political and Armed Struggle*, p. 43.

[5] Popular Front for the Liberation of Palestine, *Strategy for the Liberation of Palestine* (Amman: Information Department, 1969). The foregoing quotations of PFLP doctrine are also from this text.

[6] Popular Front for the Liberation of Palestine, *The Palestinian Resistance Movement: A Critical Study* (Beirut: Dar al-Talia, 1969), pp. 163-67; translated in Laila Kadi, *Basic Political Documents of the Armed Palestinian Resistance Movement* (Beirut: Palestine Research Center, 1969), pp. 173-74.

[7] U.S. Information Service news release, February 25, 1971.

Selected Bibliography

Aims of the Palestinian Resistance Movement with Regard to the Jews: Quotations from Resistance Leaders and Documents. Beirut: Palestine Research Center and Fifth of June Society, 1970.
Supports the statements of Palestinian resistance groups for the creation of a secular, democratic state.

Barbour, Nevill. *Nisi Dominus*. 1946. Reprint. Beirut: Institute for Palestine Studies, 1969.
A valuable work on the background of the present phase of Palestinian history; a thorough study of Palestine under the British mandate; thoughtful, well documented, reliable.

Childers, Erskine B. *The Other Exodus. Spectator*, May 12, 1961. Reprint. Beirut: Fifth of June Society.
A study of the flight of Palestinians following the 1948 war and analysis of Israeli methods and tactics in creating the refugee crisis by an expert on Arab affairs and East-West relations. Includes letters written to *The Spectator* in response to the article.

Davis, John. *The Evasive Peace*. London: John Murray, 1968.
An account of the Palestinian refugees with close insight and sympathetic familiarity by a former U.N. official and director of UNRWA in the Middle East, who sees no solution to the problem except the dissolution of the present Israeli political entity.

Dodd, Peter, and Barakat, Halim. *River without Bridges: A Study of the Exodus of the 1967 Palestinian Arab Refugees*. Beirut: Institute for Palestine Studies, 1969.
The reasons for the flight of the Palestinians at the outbreak of the war by sociologists who conducted field studies in the refugee camps in Jordan following the 1967 War.

Gaspard, J. "Palestine: Who's Who among the Guerrillas." *New Middle East*, no. 18 (March 1970): 12-16.
A timely and clear analysis of the different groups of the Palestinian resistance.

Hadawi, Sami. *Bitter Harvest: Palestine between 1914 and 1967*. New York: New World Press, 1967.
Historical and analytical presentation of Palestinian nationalism that increases understanding of Arab views and reactions by a Palestinian who held office under the British mandate.

Harkabi, Yehoshafat. *Fedayin Action and Arab Strategy*. Adelphi Papers, no. 53. London: Institute for Strategic Studies, December 1968.
An interpretation of Palestinian resistance within the framework of official Israeli views by a former head of Israeli intelligence.

Hudson, Michael. "The Palestinian Arab Resistance Movement: Its Significance in the Middle East Crisis." *Middle East Journal* 23, no. 3, (Summer 1969): 291-307.
A major document on Palestinian resistance; a lucid, comprehensive, and accurate account of the different groups (primarily al-Fatah) and the awakening of strong nationalistic consciousness among the Palestinian refugees.

Jiryis, Sabri. *The Arabs in Israel*. Monograph Series, no. 16. Beirut: Institute for Palestine Studies, 1969.
A work based on extensive research in legal and official documents; the most thorough and authoritative study of the legal and social position of the Arab minority in Israel. Written by an Arab lawyer in Israel.

John, Robert, and Hadawi, Sami. *The Palestine Diary*. 2 vols. Beirut: Palestine Research Center, 1970.
Valuable historical study of the Palestine problem; accurate, well documented, scholarly. Volume 1 (1914-45), British involvement in Palestine; volume 2 (1945-48), big power and U.N. intervention.

Kadi, Leila S. *Basic Political Documents of the Armed Palestinian Resistance Movement*. Beirut: Palestine Research Center, 1969.
A useful reference work on the Palestinian resistance groups; includes historical background, documents published by various groups, and interviews with some leaders. Also valuable for discussions of the ideological differences among the resistance organizations.

Palestine National Liberation Movement, al-Fatah. *Revolution until' Victory*. Beirut: al-Fatah, 1970.
Al-Fatah's strategy, aims, and achievements reviewed in this official statement; includes excerpts from the Western press on the subject of the guerrillas.

Palestine National Liberation Movement, al-Fatah. *Political and Armed Struggle*. Beirut: al-Fatah, 1970.
Explains the movement's aims and policies and reviews its political and military accomplishments and objectives.

Rodinson, Maxime. *The Arabs and Israel*. Marmonsworth, Middlesex (England): Penguin Books, 1968.
Analysis of the Arab-Israeli conflict following the 1967 War; an in-depth study of the area's problems, especially in terms of international implications.

Sharabi, Hisham. *Palestine Guerrillas: Their Credibility and Effectiveness*. Washington, D.C.: Institute for Strategic and International Studies, Georgetown University Press, 1970.
An analysis of the Palestinian resistance groups: military effectiveness, ideological interpretations, and future prospects.

————. *Palestine and Israel: The Lethal Dilemma*. New York: Pegasus, 1969.
A timely study of the problems faced by the Palestinian resistance groups, covering Israeli policy and aims regarding the Arab states and American intervention and its aims and consequences.

Sources in Arabic

Among the background works written by Palestinians, the most useful brought to this writer's attention include the studies by Naji Alloush—*Al-Thawra wal-Jamaheer* [Revolution and the Masses: 1948-61] (Beirut: Dar al-Talia, 1963) and the newer and more analytical *Al-Thawra al-Filistiniya: Ab-adaha wa Qadayaha* [The Palestinian Revolution: Its Aims and Problems] (Beirut: Dar al-Talia, 1970). Alloush has been close to Arafat and the al-Fatah leadership since the early days of the movement, and his viewpoint is essentially that of al-Fatah. Perhaps the most scholarly and thorough historical study in Arabic is Saleh Mas'oud Abu-Ysir's *Jihad Shaab Filistin* [The Struggle of the People of Palestine] (Beirut: Dar al-Fath, 1968). A basic text used by all the resistance groups is Youssef Sayegh's *Stratagiya al-Tahrir al-Filistiniya* (Beirut: Dar al-Talia, 1969), which is a recipe for the remaking of Arab society.

A few of the innumerable pamphlets and periodicals are prime sources for the serious, Arabic-reading student. *Filistinuna*, appearing irregularly between 1959 and 1965, was the pioneer publication of al-Fatah and shows the development of its ideas. *Al-Hadaf*, a weekly magazine that first appeared in Beirut in July 1969, is the organ of the PFLP edited by Ghassan Khanafani. *Al-Horriya*, also a weekly, was established in 1959 by Habbash and Mohsin Ibrahim, who is still the owner, as the organ of the ANM. When the PDF broke away from the PFLP, the magazine remained with the PDF and usually expressed the views of its leader, Nayef Hawatmeh. However, since 1969 its owners have formed the Organization of Lebanese Socialists, which is influenced by New Left and Trotskyist ideas. Also useful for following the thought and political operations of the PDF is a collection of its papers presented to the Sixth Palestinian National Council in September 1969, *Harakat al-Muqawama al-Filistiniya fi Waqi'ha ar-Rahen* [The Present State of the Palestinian Resistance Movement: A Critical Study] (Beirut: Dar al-Talia, 1969). Al-Fatah published first weekly then daily its *Fateh* in Amman and a popular monthly magazine, *Al-Thawra al-Filistiniya* [The Palestine Revolution]. It also issues pamphlets and brochures regularly and sporadic publications for students, women, and the *Ashbal*, "Lion Cubs," the junior al-Fatah organization.

Glossary

Abbasid [ab-BASS-id]. Arab dynasty, descended from Abbas (an uncle of Muhammad), which ruled from Baghdad over some parts of the Muslim community from A.D. 750 to 1258.

absolute monarchy. A political system headed by a hereditary ruler whose authority is not limited by any other individual or governmental body in that country.

Aden [AH-den]. (1) Port city situated on the Gulf of Aden, between the Red Sea and the Indian Ocean; (2) former British colony surrounding the city of Aden; (3) former British protectorate surrounding Aden colony, now officially called the People's Democratic Republic of Yemen.

Ahali [a-HA-lee]. Political group that emerged in Iraq in the 1930s and whose pioneering efforts at formulating a democratic socialist ideology appealed to many intellectuals. Members of this group later formed the National Democratic party, which emerged in Iraq after World War II.

Ahdut Avodah [ah-DOOT ah-vo-DAH]. An Israeli political party aligned since 1965 with MAPAI.

Alawi [AH-la-wee]. A Shiite Muslim sect, also sometimes called Nusayri [noo-SAY-ree], that has adherents in Syria, Turkey, and other Middle Eastern countries. Also Alawite.

al-Fatah [al-FET-ah]. A popular revolutionary group of Palestinian Arabs that seeks the eradication of Israel's Zionist character and the establishment of a secular, democratic Palestinian republic. The name is a pun on the Arabic word *fath*, "victory," and the reversal of the initials for *harakat tahrir Filistin*, the "movement for the liberation of Palestine."

aliyah [ah-lee-YAH]. Hebrew word for the immigration of Jews into Palestine (since 1948, Israel).

amir [ah-MEER]. Title for the head of state in some Middle Eastern countries, translated as "ruler," "prince," or "nobleman." Also spelled emir.

amirate. (1) A country ruled by an amir, or a principality; (2) in Saudi Arabia, a province. Also spelled emirate.

Anatolia. The peninsula comprising the Asiatic part of Turkey; also called Asia Minor.

Arab. (1) A native speaker of the Arabic language; (2) a person who identifies with the Arabic cultural tradition; (3) a bedouin, or camel nomad; (4) a citizen of a country in which the predominant language and culture are Arabic.

Arab League. An association of Arab Middle Eastern and North African states formed in 1945 to encourage cooperation in political, military, economic, social, and cultural matters among its members. The original members—Egypt, Iraq, Jordan, Lebanon, Saudi Arabia, Syria, and Yemen—have since been joined by the People's Democratic Republic of Yemen, Qatar, Bahrayn, Oman, the Union of Arab Amirates, Kuwait, Algeria, Libya, Morocco, Sudan, and Tunisia.

Arab Legion. Former name of the army of Jordan (before 1949, Transjordan).

Arab nationalism. A movement advocating the unification of all Arabs and their independence from non-Arab control. *See also* Pan-Arabism.

Arab socialism. An ideology calling for state ownership of the means of economic production in the Arab countries and for the eradication of "feudalism," "capitalism," and other socioeconomic systems thought to favor foreign or traditionalist political influences in the Arab world.

Arab Socialist Union. The only legal political party in Egypt. It serves to mobilize popular support for the government's modernization programs and for Arab socialism.

Arabia. The Arabian peninsula, currently comprising Saudi Arabia, Yemen, the People's Democratic Republic of Yemen, and the Gulf states.

Arabian. (1) Pertaining to the Arabian peninsula; (2) pertaining to nomadic Arabs.

Arabic. A Semitic language originating in Arabia. The written (classical) Arabic is based on the language of the Quran and early Arab writers, whereas the spoken (vernacular or colloquial) language varies from one region to another and diverges somewhat from written Arabic in its pronunciation, vocabulary, and grammar.

Arabism. The feeling of being an Arab by language or culture, often equated with Arab nationalism or Pan-Arabism. The Arabic word *urubah* is also used.

Armenia. (1) The region of eastern Anatolia between the Caucasus mountains and Lake Van; (2) a kingdom in that region that lasted from the fourth century B.C. to the eleventh century A.D.; (3) an independent republic in that region, 1918-21; (4) a Communist state, part of the Union of Soviet Socialist Republics since 1921.

Armenian. (1) Anyone descended from inhabitants of Armenia or identified with that region; (2) a subject or citizen of Armenia; (3) a member of the Armenian millet within the Ottoman Empire; (4) an adherent of one of the Armenian Christian sects; (5) the language of Armenia, which belongs to the Indo-European language family and which has a distinctive alphabet; (6) a native speaker of the Armenian language.

Armenian Catholic. Pertaining to an offshoot of the Orthodox Armenian (Gregorian) church that has entered into communion with the Roman Catholic church while retaining many traditional Armenian rites.

Armistice Agreements. Agreements signed between Israel and its four neighbors—Egypt, Jordan, Lebanon, and Syria—in 1949 under the auspices of the United Nations acting mediator, Ralph J. Bunche. Each of the four Armistice Agreements established a Mixed Armistice Commission (MAC) that provided a meeting place for personnel of the parties and the United Nations to deal with armistice problems. The commissions consisted of two representatives of each of the parties of the respective agreements and the chief of staff of the United Nations Truce Supervision Organization or his deputy—a total of five in each MAC. Israel declared the Armistice Agreements invalid after the 1967 War.

asabiyyah [aw-saw-BEE-yah]. The feeling of group loyalty toward a particular state or community.

Assyrian. A religious-cultural group in Syria and Iraq. *See* Nestorian.

Aswan [ass-WAHN]. Upper Egyptian site of the High Dam, built during the Nasser regime with Soviet aid after the United States and the United Kingdom withdrew their support.

Azarbayjan [ah-zer-bye-JOHN]. (1) The mountainous region west of the Caspian Sea; (2) a Communist state, part of the USSR since 1920; (3) the northwestern-most province of Iran. Also spelled Azerbaijan and Adharbayjan.

Azari [AH-ze-ree]. Pertaining to the region or people of Azarbayjan, as in Azari Turkish, the Turkic dialect spoken in that area.

Baath [BAHTH]. An Arab socialist party now ruling in Syria and Iraq.

Baghdad Pact. *See* Central Treaty Organization.

Balfour Declaration. Official statement by Britain's foreign minister in 1917 that supported the establishment of a Jewish national home in Palestine.

Balkans. The mountainous region of southeastern Europe formerly ruled by the Ottoman Empire, now comprising Yugoslavia, Albania, Greece, Bulgaria, Rumania, and European Turkey.

Bahai [ba-HYE]. Originally a mystical offshoot of Shiite Islam in nineteenth century Persia, now a distinct religion that stresses toleration of all faiths.

Bandung [ban-DOONG]. An Indonesian city, site of the 1955 conference of leaders representing Asian and African states, including Egyptian President Nasser. Also spelled Bandoeng.

bedouin [BED-a-win]. Collective term for Arab camel nomads.

Byzantine Empire. The Roman Empire of the East (A.D. 330-1453), which had its capital at Constantinople (originally named Byzantium, now Istanbul) and which upheld Greek Orthodox Christianity.

caliph. Successor to Muhammad as head of the Islamic community.

caliphate. The office of caliph.

Capitulations. Treaties between the Ottoman Empire and various Western countries that gave Westerners living in Ottoman territory immunity from local laws and taxation.

Catholic. (1) Pertaining to the ancient, undivided Christian church or to any group of Christians that claims descent from that church through an uninterrupted line of bishops going back to St. Peter, the first pope or bishop of Rome; (2) pertaining in the West to the Roman Catholic church, which in the Middle East is called the Latin rite; (3) pertaining to any one of several Middle Eastern rites now in communion with the Roman Catholic church that have broken off from Orthodox, Nestorian, or Monophysite churches, such as Armenian Catholic, Chaldean Catholic, Coptic Catholic, Greek Catholic (also called Melchite or Melkite), and Syrian Catholic.

Central Treaty Organization (CENTO). A regional military alliance formed in 1955 by Britain, Turkey, Iraq, Iran, and Pakistan to contain Soviet penetration into the Middle East. Originally called the Baghdad Pact, its name was changed when Iraq withdrew following a revolution in 1958.

Chaldean. Pertaining to the kingdom of Chaldea (626-539 B.C.), the last of the ancient Mesopotamian empires.

Chaldean Catholic. Pertaining to an offshoot of the Nestorian church that has entered into communion with the Roman Catholic church while retaining much of the Syriac liturgy and many other Nestorian practices.

Circassian. (1) A native of Circassia, the region on the northeastern coast of the Black Sea; (2) a descendant of an emigrant from that region. Circassians now are found in Syria, Jordan, Egypt, and other Middle Eastern countries.

Committee of Union and Progress (CUP). A party of Turkish army officers and intellectuals that demanded constitutional government in the Ottoman Empire. The party seized power in 1908 and began a program of Westernization, but it was discredited for bringing the country into World War I on the German side. Also called Young Turks.

Constantinople Convention. Treaty signed by the Ottoman Empire and the leading European powers in 1888 that declared the Suez Canal open to merchant vessels and warships of all powers during times of war as well as peace.

Constitutional bloc. A political party in Lebanon that favored independence from France before 1943.

constitutionalist. Any person or group favoring limitations on the power of governments or rulers by a popularly elected body, guaranteed by law.

constitutional monarchy. A political system headed by a hereditary ruler whose powers are restricted by law, precedent, or other constituent government bodies within the country.

Copt. A Christian who recognizes the patriarch of Alexandria and believes in the single nature of Jesus Christ. Most Copts are in Egypt and Ethiopia.

Crusades. European Christian military expeditions against Muslims (or sometimes against Orthodox Christians), especially between the eleventh and the fifteenth centuries.

Democratic party. A Turkish political party formed in opposition to the Republican People's party during the 1940s. It came to power in the 1950 elections, was ousted by a military coup in 1960, and was later outlawed.

dervish. Muslim mystic, or sufi.

devshirme [dev-sheer-MAY]. (1) The system of recruiting Christian boys and training them, following their conversion to Islam, for service in the Ottoman army and bureaucracy; (2) the class of soldiers and bureaucrats produced by that system.

diaspora [dye-ASS-po-ra]. Collective term for the Jews outside of Palestine (since 1948, Israel), now sometimes applied also to displaced Palestinian Arabs.

dowreh [dow-RAH]. Persian word denoting a social gathering.

Druze [DROOZ]. Member of an independent religious sect, originally an offshoot of Ismaili Shiite Islam, that believes in the divinity of al-Hakim, a Fatimid caliph who disappeared in 1021. This sect is now concentrated in some of the mountainous areas of Israel, Syria, and Lebanon.

Eisenhower Doctrine. An official U.S. policy statement, adopted in 1957 and directed mainly at the Arab world, that offered Middle Eastern states economic and military assistance, including the use of U.S. military forces to "protect the territorial integrity and political independence" of states requesting aid against "armed aggression from any nation controlled by international communism." The Arabs, preoccupied with their problems with Israel, predominantly denounced this doctrine, considering it an attempt to provide pretexts for intervention in the internal affairs of the Arab states.

emirate. *See* amirate.

→ **etatism.** The doctrine that the state should play a major role in economic development. It was one of the basic principles expounded by Mustafa Kemal Ataturk in Turkey.

etesian winds. Mediterranean winds that recur annually.

ethneme. The minimum distinctive political "organism" in its sociocultural setting, not necessarily coincident with existing states.

European Economic Community (EEC). A regional organization, established in 1958, that has developed a common market among its members, Belgium, France, Germany, Italy, Luxembourg, and the Netherlands, and since January 1972, Britain, Denmark, Norway, and Ireland. Other states such as Turkey have established an associate relationship with the community.

Farsi [far-SEE]. *See* Persian.

fedayeen [fed-ah-YEEN]. Arabic word for heroes who sacrifice themselves for a noble cause, now often applied to Palestinian guerrillas fighting against Israel.

feddan [fed-DAN]. Egyptian unit of land area equal to 1.038 acres.

Federation of Arab Republics. The federation formed in August 1971 of Egypt, Libya, and Syria.

fellaheen [fel-lah-HEEN]. Arabic for "peasants"; singular: *fellah* [fel-LAH].

Fertile Crescent. The cultivated areas of present-day Israel, Syria, Lebanon, and Iraq.

Front for the Liberation of Occupied South Yemen (FLOSY). Arab nationalist organization working for the independence of Aden and South Arabia from Britain, superseded in 1967 by the National Liberation Front (now the National Front).

GAHAL [ga-HAL]. Israel's most militant and conservative political party.

Gaza Strip. Portion of Palestine adjacent to Sinai, held by Arab armies at the end of the 1948 Arab-Israeli War, captured by Israel in 1956 and in 1967, and under Israeli occupation since 1967.

ghazi [GHAH-zee]. Muslim military adventurer or border warrior.

Grand National Assembly. Turkey's parliament, established in 1920 at Ankara.

Greek Catholic. Pertaining to any Uniate offshoot of the Greek Orthodox church that has entered into communion with the Roman Catholic church while retaining many traditional Byzantine (Greek) rites; sometimes also called Melchite or Melkite.

Greek Orthodox. Pertaining to the Christian sect, widespread in Lebanon and Syria and formerly in Turkey, which recognizes the spiritual authority of the patriarch of Constantinople (now Istanbul) and which was the official religion of the Byzantine Empire.

gross domestic product (GDP). The monetary value of all production that occurs within a country, regardless of whether its owners are citizens or foreigners.

gross national product (GNP). The monetary value of all production in a country, including net income earned by citizens' foreign investment and excluding net earnings of foreigners' investments in that country. In many Middle Eastern countries, especially large oil exporters, GDP is substantially greater than GNP.

guerrilla. Member of a small independent army that harasses the enemy by surprise attacks.

Hadhramawt [hod-ra-MOWT]. The southern coast of the Arabian peninsula.

Haganah [HAW-ga-nah]. The army of Israel; before 1948, the chief self-defense force of the Jewish settlers in Palestine.

Hajj [HODGE]. The pilgrimage to Mecca and Medina, obligatory for Muslims who are physically and financially able to make it.

Hashimite [HASH-i-mite]. A descendant of Hashim, an uncle of Muhammad, and especially a member of the dynasty ruling in the Hijaz (1916-25), Syria (1918-20), Iraq (1921-58), and Jordan (1921-). Also spelled Hashemite.

Hebrew. (1) The Semitic language of ancient and modern Israel, sacred to the Jews; (2) an ancient tribe regarded as the ancestor of the Jews.

Herut [hay-ROOT]. Formerly Israel's right-wing political party, which merged with the Liberal party to form GAHAL.

high commissioner. Title of the chief political officer of the ruling country in most of the Middle Eastern mandates and also in Egypt from 1914 to 1936.

Hijaz [he-JAZZ]. (1) Mountainous region in western Arabia; (2) former kingdom ruled by the Hashimite family (1916-25).

Hijrah [HIJ-rah]. The emigration of Muhammad and his followers from Mecca to Medina in A.D. 622 (year 1 in the Muslim calendar).

Histadrut [hiss-ta-DROOT]. Israel's main labor union, which also owns and operates many business enterprises in the country.

Ibadi [ee-BAH-dee]. A strict, puritanical sect of Muslims who profess a version of Islam that is distinct from the Sunni and Shia branches. The Ibadis are a branch of Khawarij Islam, and today they are concentrated in Oman and in a few isolated North African oasis towns.

Ikhwan [ikh-WAHN]. The name of a bedouin army in Saudi Arabia, disbanded in 1929; literally, "brothers." *See also* Muslim Brotherhood.

imam [ee-MAM]. (1) Muslim religious or political leader; (2) member of the line of Muslim leaders, beginning with Muhammad's cousin Ali, regarded by Shiites as legitimate; (3) title of the rulers of Yemen until 1962; (4) leader of Muslim congregational prayers.

Iran [ee-RAWN]. The official name of Persia since 1935.

Iran-Novin [ee-RAWN no-VEEN]. A political party in modern Iran.

Iraq [ee-ROCK]. The Republic of Iraq, which includes Mesopotamia.

Irgun Zvai Leumi [eer-GOON tsvay le-OO-mee]. A Jewish guerrilla group in Palestine before 1948 that believed in using military means to force immediate Israeli independence. *See also* Stern Gang.

Islam [iss-LAWM]. A monotheistic religion, predominant in the Middle East, which is distinguished by its belief that God revealed himself to a succession of human messengers, the last of whom was Muhammad (d. 632), and provided a detailed set of rules by which men should live in anticipation of a day of judgment.

Islamic [iss-LAW-mik]. Pertaining to Islam.

Ismaili [iss-ma-EE-lee]. A Shiite Muslim sect which believes that there were seven legitimate leaders (imams) of the Muslim community after the death of Muhammad and that certain truths were vouchsafed to them and their followers but concealed from other Muslims.

Israel [IZ-re-al, iss-raw-EL]. (1) The ancient Jewish kingdom in Palestine; (2) the modern Jewish state; (3) pertaining to Israel.

Israeli [iz-RAY-lee]. A citizen of Israel.

Israel Labor party (ILP). Official name of MAPAI since 1968.

Jacobite. Member of a Syrian Christian sect that rejected the authority of the patriarch of Constantinople in the seventh century and that believes in the single, divine nature of Christ.

janissary [JAN-is-se-ree]. A Christian conscript foot soldier in the Ottoman army who was converted to Islam and trained to use gunpowder weapons.

Jazirah [ja-ZEE-rah]. Region comprising northeastern Syria and northwestern Iraq.

Jewish Agency (for Palestine). Political organization established by the British mandatory government of Palestine for the purpose of representing the Jewish settlers; it became the basis for the government of Israel.

Jewish National Fund. Organization for raising money to buy land for Jewish settlers in Palestine.

Jiddah [JID-dah] Agreement. Settlement between Yemeni Royalist and Republican forces, negotiated during a meeting of the foreign ministers of Muslim countries held in Jiddah in 1970.

jihad [jee-HAD]. Arabic for "struggle," often translated as "holy war," considered by many Muslims to be a religious obligation in defense of the Islamic community by peaceful as well as military means.

Jordan. (1) A river; (2) the Hashimite Kingdom of Jordan, consisting of what until 1949 was Transjordan and portions of Arab Palestine on the Jordan River's west bank, under Israeli military occupation since 1967.

junta [HOON-ta]. Term applied to a group of military officers who have seized control of a national government.

Justice party. A Turkish political party formed in 1961 by members of the outlawed Democratic party and holding power since 1965.

Kaabah [KAW-bah]. Sacred Muslim shrine in Mecca.

Kataib [ka-TA-ib]. A Lebanese nationalist group dominated by Maronite Christians.

Kemalism. Mustafa Kemal Ataturk's program of nationalism and rapid Westernization, implemented in Turkey between 1923 and 1938 and imitated then and later in many other Middle Eastern countries.

Kharijite [KHA-ri-jite]. A member of a Muslim sect which believes that any righteous man can become the leader of the Muslim community, regardless of his descent. The plural of this word in Arabic is *Khawarij.*

Khartoum [khar-TOOM] Conference. Meeting of Arab heads of state following their countries' defeat by Israel in 1967. At the conference they decided to seek a political settlement without direct negotiations with Israel, agreed that Libya,

Saudi Arabia, and Kuwait should subsidize Egypt and Jordan, and settled the Yemeni civil war by the withdrawal of Egyptian forces from that country.

khedive [khe-DEEV]. Title of Egypt's ruler from 1867 to 1914.

kibbutz [kib-BOOTS]. A Jewish settlement in Israel characterized by collective ownership of property and (usually) a communal living arrangement, sometimes established for defense purposes near Arab borders.

King-Crane Commission. Commission of inquiry sent by President Wilson in 1919 to ascertain the political aspirations of Syria and Palestine. The matter of governance of non-Turkish former Ottoman provinces was under discussion at the Paris Peace Conference after World War I. Wilson supported the concept of self-determination of peoples, as outlined in his Fourteen Points, and refused even to consider the wartime agreements concluded by Britain and France. To settle the question of governance, he proposed to send a commission of inquiry composed of American, British, French, and Italian representatives, but the Europeans refused to cooperate. Wilson therefore sent the American representatives, Henry C. King, president of Oberlin College, and businessman Charles R. Crane, with a staff of experts.

King and Crane found an almost unaminous desire for full independence in the Arab centers they visited. Syrians insisted on a united, independent state composed of Syria, Lebanon, and Palestine, and Zionism was opposed by both Muslim and Christian Arabs. If they could not achieve full independence, the Syrians would prefer an American mandate, with Britain as second choice. France was not acceptable.

On the basis of their investigation, King and Crane recommended an American mandate for Syria, or a British mandate as an alternative. They favored the establishment of constitutional Arab monarchies under the mandate system and opposed the establishment of a Zionist state in Palestine. The commission's report was ignored at the Paris Peace Conference, however, and as President Wilson had problems at home and could himself no longer crusade for self-determination, the British and the French divided the Arab provinces according to their interests and previous agreements. (Based on a discussion by George Lenczowski, *The Middle East in World Affairs*, 3d ed. [Ithaca, N.Y.: Cornell University Press, 1962], pp. 87-91). *See also* mandate system.

Knesset [KNES-set]. Israel's parliament.

Kurd. A person who belongs to a linguistic-cultural group concentrated in the mountainous region of eastern Turkey and Syria, northern Iraq, and northwestern Iran, and who aspires to political unity and autonomy.

Kurdish. The Indo-European language, related to Persian, spoken by the Kurds.

Latin. Pertaining to the Roman Catholic church in the Middle East.

League of Nations. Organization of countries established after World War I to promote international peace and cooperation, superseded by the United Nations in 1945.

Levant. The lands bordering on the eastern Mediterranean, roughly corresponding to western Turkey, Syria, Lebanon, and Israel.

Liberation Rally. Political group established by the Egyptian government after the 1952 revolution to replace the outlawed political parties and to mobilize popular support for the revolutionary regime.

MAFDAL [maf-DAHL]. Israel's national religous party.

Maghrib [MAW-ghreb, maw-GHREB]. Arabic word for northwestern Africa (Morocco, Algeria, Tunisia, and sometimes Libya).

Mahdist. Pertaining to the revolutionary movement or ideology of the self-styled Mahdi [MAH-dee] of the Sudan (d. 1885); the movement calls for a restoration of Islam to its original purity.

Majlis [MAJ-liss]. The parliament of Iran and of some Arab states.

MAKI [MA-kee]. Israel's Jewish Communist party.

Mamluk [mam-LOOK]. (1) A Turkish or Circassian slave soldier; (2) a member of the military oligarchy that controlled Egypt and Syria from 1250 to 1517 and retained local power in some parts of the Arab world until the nineteenth century.

mandate system. The method of governance adopted after World War I for the non-Turkish former Ottoman provinces and the German colonies. Various plans were proposed at the Paris Peace Conference; some Allied leaders supported outright annexation, and others favored some form of international administration. Previously made pledges and counterpledges further complicated arrangements.

Finally the delegates to the peace conference accepted a compromise that became the mandate system. Article 22 of the League of Nations Covenant specified that "the character of the mandate must differ according to the stage of the development of the people, the geographical situation of the territory, its economic conditions, and other similar circumstances." The article stated further that "certain communities formerly belonging to the Turkish Empire have reached a stage of development where their existence as independent nations can be provisionally recognized subject to the rendering of administrative advice and assistance by a mandatory until such time as they are able to stand alone. The wishes of these communities must be a principal consideration in the selection of the mandatory." Three types of mandates were prepared—A, B, and C. Iraq, Palestine, Jordan, Syria, and Lebanon were all designated Class A mandates and were entrusted to Britain (Iraq, Palestine, Jordan) and France (Syria and Lebanon). *See also* King-Crane Commission.

MAPAI [ma-PIE]. The Israel Labor party, predominant in the politics of Israel since 1948. The party espouses a socialist economy and democratic political procedures.

MAPAM [ma-PAWM]. The United Workers' party of Israel, smaller and farther to the left than MAPAI.

Mardom [mar-DOME]. Iran's "loyal opposition" party, founded by the shah in 1957.

Maronite. Member of a Christian sect, concentrated in Lebanon, which split from the Orthodox church in the seventh century because of its belief that Jesus Christ had two natures but only one will. The sect has been in communion with the Roman Catholic church since the seventeenth century.

MATZPEN [mots-PEN]. A small Israel group favoring a revolutionary Jewish-Arab state in Palestine.

Mecca. West Arabian city, the birthplace of Muhammad and site of the Kaabah.

Melchite, Melkite. *See* Greek Catholic.

millet [mil-LET]. Political-social community based on religious membership, involving non-Muslim subjects of the Ottoman Empire. The heads of the chief millets (Greek Orthodox, Armenian, and Jewish) were appointed by and responsible to the Ottoman sultan, but in most respects they had local autonomy.

Milliyun [mil-lee-YOON]. Iran's progovernment party, established by the shah in 1957.

monarchy. A political system in which power is held by a hereditary ruler, at least in theory.

Monophysite. Pertaining to the doctrine held by Copts, Jacobites, and Armenians that Jesus Christ possessed only one nature, wholly divine.

mufti [MOOF-tee]. A Sunni Muslim legal consultant; in modern times, the chief Islamic legal official in most Middle Eastern countries.

muhtar [mookh-TAR]. Chief officer of a village or a city district. Also spelled mukhtar.

Muslim [MOOSS-lim] . (1) Adherent of Islam; (2) pertaining to Islam.

Muslim Brotherhood. A political association, founded in Egypt in 1929 as a religious revivalist movement, that sought by revolutionary means to reestablish Islam as the basis for government and social behavior. Branches of the Muslim Brotherhood were established in Syria, Jordan, Lebanon, and other Arab countries. Now outlawed in most countries, the movement reportedly still exists underground.

Nahjist. Pertaining to a coalition of Lebanese political parties and leaders that are united in support of Palestinian guerrilla activities in Lebanon.

Najd [NEJD] . Desert region in north central Arabia, from which came the Saud family and Wahhabi Islam.

Najjadah [naj-JAD-dah] . Arab nationalist political group in Lebanon, in which Sunni Muslims predominate.

Nasserism [NAW-sir-izm] . Policy of Arab nationalism, rapid and government-enforced modernization, and resistance to foreign attempts at domination named for the late Egyptian President Gamal Abdul Nasser.

nation. A community based on strong cultural affinity that is the object of a group's political loyalty. This may be an independent country or a territory ruled by a government that the inhabitants of that territory regard as foreign.

National Assembly. The representative body or the legislature in several Middle Eastern countries.

National bloc. A political party in Lebanon which tends to stress that country's political distinctness from the rest of the Arab world.

National Charter. Egyptian document issued in 1962 that sets forth an Arab socialist ideology and program.

National Front. (1) Coalition of Iranian political parties supporting the nationalist policies of Muhammad Musaddiq, Iran's prime minister (1951-53), and opposing the shah; (2) the dominant political party in the People's Democratic Republic of Yemen (formerly the National Liberation Front).

National Front for the Liberation of the Occupied Arabian Gulf. *See* Popular Front for the Liberation of the Occupied Arabian Gulf.

nationalism. (1) Feeling of individual or group loyalty to a political community that is (or aspires to become) a nation-state; (2) the desire of a group for independence from foreign domination.

National Liberation Front. Aden-based, Marxist political movement formed in 1963 and directed against British rule and the traditional Arab leadership in South Arabia, now (as the National Front) the dominant political party in the People's Democratic Republic of Yemen (Southern Yemen).

National Pact. Unwritten agreement among Lebanon's Christian and Muslim leaders in 1943, in which Christians pledged not to demand Western protection if Muslims would not try to incorporate Lebanon into an Arab union.

National party. (1) Name of two movements in Egypt (1879-82 and 1907-52) which demanded that country's independence from foreign control; (2) an Arab nationalist group, based in Damascus, that opposes Syria's unification with Jordan and Iraq except as part of a larger unity scheme including Egypt; also called the Nationalist bloc or the National Syrian party.

National Union. Political organization formed in the United Arab Republic in 1958 to increase its citizens' participation in the conduct of government and other political processes. This was the successor to the Liberation Rally and the precursor of the Arab Socialist Union.

nation-state. A political entity that has its own government and commands the political loyalty of its citizens. This can also be called a state, but not in the sense used in the American federal system.

North Atlantic Treaty Organization (NATO). A regional group formed in 1949 to contain Soviet expansion, especially in Europe. Turkey has been a member since 1952.

Nestorian. Member of a Christian sect that believes that Jesus Christ has two distinct natures and that has adherents in Syria and Iraq. Also called Assyrian.

New Ottomans. Turkish political movement in the 1870s that demanded a constitution, parliamentary government, and other Westernizing reforms for the Ottoman Empire. Also called Young Ottomans.

OPEC. *See* Organization of the Petroleum Exporting Countries.

Organization of the Petroleum Exporting Countries (OPEC). Organization established in 1960 to safeguard the interests and coordinate the petroleum policies of member countries (Abu Dhabi, Algeria, Indonesia, Iran, Iraq, Kuwait, Libya, Qatar, Saudi Arabia, Venezuela).

Orthodox. Pertaining to any Christian sect that recognizes the authority of the patriarchs of Constantinople, Alexandria, Antioch, and Jerusalem.

Ottoman. (1) Member of a Turkish family, descended from Osman (d. 1326), that ruled over a multinational Islamic state called the Ottoman Empire, which at its height (sixteenth to seventeenth centuries) controlled the Balkans, Anatolia, the Fertile Crescent, western Arabia, and most of northern Africa; (2) any member of the ruling class of that empire; (3) a subject of that empire.

Ottomanism. The movement, prevalent in the Ottoman Empire in the late nineteenth century, that tried to hinder the growth of divisive nationalist movements by granting equal rights to all Ottoman subjects.

Pahlavi [PAH-le-vee]. (1) The language of ancient Persia; (2) name of the ruling dynasty of Iran since 1925.

Palestine. The traditional name of south Syria, also called the Holy Land. Since the seventh century and until 1948 it was mostly inhabited by Palestinian Arabs, and between 1921 and 1948 it was a British mandated territory. At present the area is part of the state of Israel or is under Israeli military occupation.

Palestine Liberation Organization (PLO). Arab Palestine entity established by the Arab heads of state in 1964.

Palestinian. A native of Palestine or a descendant of a native, especially if Arabic-speaking and non-Jewish.

Palmach [pal-MAKH]. Armed militia of the kibbutzim in Palestine before 1948.

Pan-Arabism. Movement or doctrine calling for the unification of all Arabs in a single state. Also called Arab nationalism.

Pan-Islam. Movement to unite all Muslims in one state, especially the late nineteenth and early twentieth century movement led by the Ottoman sultan.

Pan-Turkism. Movement to unite all Turkish-speaking peoples of the Middle East and central Asia in one state, especially popular among the Turks in Russia and the Ottoman Empire in the early twentieth century. Also called Pan-Turanism.

Parthian. Pertaining to the region from which came the rulers of Persia bearing this name (248 B.C.-A.D. 227).

pasha [PAH-shah; pa-SHAH]. High military or administrative title, often honorific, used in the Ottoman Empire and (until recently) in some of its successor states. Corresponds roughly to the English *lord.*

People's party. Syrian political group that urges unification with Iraq and Jordan.

Persia. Traditional name for the country that has been called Iran since 1935.

Persian. (1) A subject of Persia (or Iran); (2) the national language of Iran, which belongs to the Indo-European language group, is written in a modified Arabic script, and is spoken in some parts of Afghanistan and the USSR as well as Iran. The language is also called Farsi.

political modernization. The process by which a political system develops the effectiveness in its political structures and institutions that is essential to the achievement of its nation-building goals.

polycommunalism. Situation in which three or more religious or ethnic communities coexist within a single state, as in Lebanon.

Popular Front for the Liberation of the Occupied Arabian Gulf (PFLOAG). Nationalist group that calls for the revolutionary overthrow of existing Gulf state regimes, removal of all British influence, and elimination of Western oil monopolies; supported by Communist China and the People's Democratic Republic of Yemen.

Popular Front for the Liberation of Palestine (PFLP). Marxist guerrilla organization of Palestinian Arabs.

Progressive Socialist party. A nonsectarian Lebanese political party.

Qajar [KAW-jar]. (1) Turkish dynasty ruling in Persia (1794-1925); (2) a descendant of that dynasty.

Quran [koor-AWN]. The holy book of Islam. It contains revelations that Muslims believe Muhammad received from God and is one of the main sources of Islamic law and of Arabic language, literature, and culture.

Quraysh [koo-RAYSH]. Leading Arab tribe in northwestern Arabia, especially Mecca, in the seventh century.

RAFI [RAH-fee]. Israeli political party centered around the personal following of David Ben Gurion and Moshe Dayan.

RAKAH [RAH-kah]. The Arab Communist party of Israel.

republic. A political system in which power theoretically belongs to the people but is delegated to their elected leaders or representatives. In the Middle East any state not headed by a hereditary ruler is called a republic.

Republican People's party. Turkish political party founded by Mustafa Kemal Ataturk. It dominated Turkey's politics from 1923 to 1950 and from 1960 to 1965.

Revolutionary Command Council (RCC). Temporary executive committee established by the Egyptian army officers who seized power in 1952.

Rhodes formula. Series of indirect negotiations held on the island of Rhodes under U.N. mediation to end the 1948 Arab-Israeli War. The formula is sometimes proposed as the format for settling the current dispute; it has been implemented in the indirect talks between Jordan and Egypt and Israel through Gunnar Jarring, the special representative of the U.N. secretary-general.

Rub al-Khali [ROOB al-KHA-lee]. The extremely arid desert region of southeastern Arabia, literally the "Empty Quarter."

sabra [SAWB-rah]. Native-born Israeli Jew.

Safavid [SAW-fa-vid]. Turkish dynasty that ruled Persia from 1501 to 1736.

San Remo [san RAY-mo]. Site of the 1920 conference that divided the Arab Fertile Crescent into British and French mandates.

Sassanid [sa-SAW-nid]. Dynasty that ruled Persia from A.D. 227 to 637-41.

Saudi [sa-OO-dee] **Arabia.** The portions of the Arabian peninsula ruled by the Saud dynasty.

Savak [sa-VAWK]. Iran's secret police organization, which is responsible for maintaining internal security.

sayyid [SAY-yid]. (1) Descendant of the Prophet Muhammad; (2) Arabic title corresponding to *sir* or *mister*; (3) in Yemen, any person of South Arabian descent who exercised power before the 1962 revolution.

Seljuk [SEL-juk, sel-JOOK]. Turkish dynasty that conquered and ruled parts of Iran, the Fertile Crescent, and Anatolia between the eleventh and the fourteenth centuries.

Semitic. Near Eastern language group characterized by consonantal writing systems, highly inflected grammars, and structured morphologies, including Hebrew, Arabic, Aramaic, and Syriac; sometimes regarded (erroneously) as a racial group or applied exclusively to Jews.

Shafai [SHAF-a-ee]. (1) One of the four recognized legal schools in Sunni Islam; (2) in Yemen, a Sunni (as opposed to a Zaydi Shii) Muslim.

shah. Title of the ruler of Iran. Also shahanshah, "king of kings."

Shariah [sha-REE-ah]. The holy law of Islam, which purports to govern all aspects of behavior and is based mainly on the Quran and the recorded sayings and practices of Muhammad and his companions. In Turkish, *Sheriat.*

sharif [sha-REEF]. (1) Descendant of Muhammad; (2) provincial governor.

Shatt al-Arab [SHOT el-AH-rab]. Confluence of the Tigris and Euphrates rivers, which flows into the Persian (or Arabian) Gulf.

shaykh [SHAKE]. (1) Ruler; (2) tribal leader; (3) head of a village; (4) highly learned Muslim.

shaykhdom. A country ruled by a shaykh.

sheyhulislam [SHAY-hul-iss-LAWM]. Highest Muslim official in the Ottoman Empire and in some Middle Eastern successor states. Also called shaykh al-Islam.

Shiah [SHEE-ah]. Collective term for Muslims who believe that the leadership of the Islamic community should have passed from Muhammad, through his cousin Ali, to their descendants.

Shii [SHEE-ee]. Pertaining to the Shiah. Also Shiite.

Shuubiyyah [shoo-oo-BEE-yah]. Political movement, especially in the eighth and ninth centuries, of non-Arab Muslims seeking equality of power and status with Arabs.

SIAH [SEE-ah]. Left-wing party in Israel that advocates evacuation of occupied Arab territories.

South Arabian League (SAL). One of the earliest nationalist parties opposed to the British-dominated South Arabian Federation.

Southern Yemen. Common name for the People's Democratic Republic of Yemen, which was the People's Republic of Southern Yemen (1967-70), formerly the South Arabian Federation (1963-67), and previously comprising Aden Crown Colony and Aden Protectorate, both under British control.

Stern Gang. A Jewish guerrilla group in Palestine before 1948 that believed in using military means to force immediate Israeli independence. *See also* Irgun Zvai Leumi.

Straits. The Bosporus and Dardanelles, which link the Black Sea to the Mediterranean.

Suez [SOO-ez, su-WEZ]. (1) Egypt's chief Red Sea port; (2) the canal that links the Red Sea to the Mediterranean; (3) pertaining to the 1956 crisis between Egypt and Britain, France, and Israel following Nasser's nationalization of the Suez Canal Company.

sufism [SOO-fizm]. Body of Islamic beliefs and practices that seek to create a mystical communion between Muslims and God.

sultan [SUL-tan, sool-TAWN]. Title used by some Muslim heads of state, as in the Ottoman Empire.

sultanate. (1) A country ruled by a sultan; (2) the office of sultan.

Sunni [SOON-nee]. (1) A Muslim who accepts the legitimacy of the caliphs who succeeded Muhammad and the legal systems developed during the early caliphates; (2) a conscientious follower of Muhammad's recorded teachings and practices.

Sykes-Picot [pee-KOE] **Agreement.** Treaty between Britain and France in 1916 that proposed a division of the Arabic-speaking provinces of the Ottoman Empire following World War I.

Syria. (1) The Syrian Arab Republic; (2) general name for the lands bordering the eastern Mediterranean; also called the Levant.

Syrian Catholic. Pertaining to an offshoot of the Syrian Orthodox (Jacobite) church that has entered into communion with the Roman Catholic church while retaining many traditional Syrian rites.

Syrian Orthodox. (1) Pertaining to the Christian church of Syria, often called Jacobite, which broke away from the Greek Orthodox church in the fifth century by embracing the Monophysite doctrine of the wholly divine nature of Christ; (2) in popular Western usage, pertaining to the Greek Orthodox Syrians and Lebanese, even if they reject the Monophysite doctrine.

Syrian Social Nationalist party. Syrian nationalist group in Syria and Lebanon (now outlawed in both countries) that calls for a union of the Fertile Crescent countries.

Tanzimat [tan-zee-MAT]. The program of intensive Westernization enforced by the Ottoman government during the nineteenth century.

Third World. A group of states especially in Africa and Asia that are not aligned with either the Communist or the non-Communist blocs.

Tihamah [tee-HAM-ah]. Arid coastal regions of western Arabia.

Transjordan. The amirate (principality) taken from Britain's Palestine mandate east of the Jordan River in 1921 and awarded to Abdullah. Officially independent after 1923, it was renamed the Hashimite Kingdom of Jordan in 1949, after Transjordan had annexed the remnants of Arab Palestine west of the Jordan River (the West Bank).

Tripartite Declaration. Statement by Britain, France, and the U.S. in 1950 that upheld the 1949 armistice lines between Israel and its Arab neighbors.

Tudeh [too-DAY]. The Communist party of Iran (1941-53).

Turk. (1) Descendant of central Asian nomads who entered the Middle East from the eighth to the sixteenth centuries; (2) any speaking Turkish or a related language; (3) a citizen of the Republic of Turkey.

Turkey. Since 1923, the Republic of Turkey; formerly applied to the Ottoman Empire.

Turkish. (1) The national language of Turkey, which belongs to the Ural-Altaic language group, written since 1928 in a modified Roman alphabet and previously in Arabic script; (2) generic term for several languages spoken in Azarbayjan and central Asia.

Turkoman. Term applied to the Turks who live in countries other than Turkey, such as Iraq, Iran, and the USSR.

ulama [OO-le-mah]. Collective term for the body of Islamic scholars.

Umayyad [um-MYE-yad] **dynasty.** Arab family of the Quraysh tribe that ruled the entire Islamic community from A.D. 661 to 750 and over Spain until 1031.

umdah [OOM-dah]. Chief village official.

ummah [OOM-mah]. (1) The Muslim community, originally the state founded by Muhammad at Medina in A.D. 622, sometimes translated as "nation"; (2) the name of political parties in several Arab states, including Jordan.

Union of Arab Amirates (Emirates). Political confederation, formed in 1971, of several small Persian Gulf states (Abu Dhabi, Dubai, Sharjah, Ajman, Umm al-Qaywayn, Al-Fujayrah) formerly under British control.

United Arab Republic. (1) The state formed by the political unification of Egypt and Syria in 1958; (2) the name of Egypt from Syria's secession in 1961 until the formation of the Federation of Arab Republics in 1971, when Egypt readopted the name Arab Republic of Egypt.

United Arab States. Loose association of Yemen with the United Arab Republic (1958-61).

United Nations Emergency Force (UNEF). Multinational police force sent (after the Anglo-French-Israeli withdrawal from Egypt following the 1956 war) by the United Nations to supervise strategic points on the Egyptian side of the 1949 Israeli-Egyptian armistice line.

United Nations Observer Group in Lebanon (UNOGIL). Team of supervisors sent to check alleged Syrian infiltration of arms and personnel during the 1958 civil war in Lebanon.

United Nations Relief and Works Agency (UNRWA). A subsidiary organ of the United Nations established by the General Assembly in 1949 to support and train displaced Palestinian Arabs.

urubah [u-ROO-bah]. *See* Arabism.

wadi [WAH-dee]. Valley.

Wafd [WAHFT]. Unofficial Egyptian delegation that attended the 1919 Paris Peace Conference to present Egypt's case for independence from Britain, and which later became Egypt's most popular political party (1923-52).

Wahhabi [wah-HAW-bee]. Fundamentalist Muslim sect, predominant in Saudi Arabia.

waqf [WAHKF]. A Muslim endowment established for a pious purpose, or sometimes to evade Islamic laws governing inheritance of property.

West Bank. Term applied to the portion of Arab Palestine annexed by Jordan in 1949 and captured by Israel in 1967.

World Zionist Organization (WZO). Political group founded in 1897 that aimed at establishing a Jewish state in Palestine.

Yazidi [ya-ZEE-dee]. A small religious sect in northern Iraq and Iran that combines elements of Islam and Christianity.

Yemen [YEM-en]. (1) The Yemen Arab Republic (Kingdom of Yemen until 1962); (2) the mountainous region of southwestern Arabia. *See also* Southern Yemen.

→ **Yishuv** [ye-SHOOV]. The Jewish community in Palestine before 1948.

Young Turks. *See* Committee of Union and Progress.

Zaydi [ZAY-dee]. Member of a Shiite sect, predominant in the mountainous areas of northern Yemen, that recognizes a succession of leaders following Zayd, a descendant of Ali.

Zionism. Any movement that stresses the link between the Jewish people and the land of Israel, especially (since 1897) the political movement to return Jews to Palestine and to establish and maintain a Jewish state there.

Zoroastrianism. The national religion of pre-Islamic Persia. Its principal beliefs were in a supreme being and in a cosmic struggle between the forces of good and evil. There are still some Zoroastrians in Iran and in India (where they are called Parsees).

INDEX

Munqabad, Egypt 150
Musaddiq, Muhammad 406-408, 413,
    418, 420
Muscat 256
Muscat and Oman 338, 345, 431,
    445, 447
Muscat Levies 302
Mushaa 75
Muslim Brotherhood (Ikhwan al-
    Muslimin) (Jordan) 111, 118, 130,
    149, 157, 223, 245, 246, 464
Muslim World League 272
Muslim, Muslims 2, 15, 16, 31, 33,
    34, 35, 36, 37, 38, 39, 40, 41, 42,
    43, 46, 47, 53, 54, 56, 57, 58, 59,
    64, 65, 72n, 102, 108, 110, 111,
    114, 129, 170, 176, 179, 181, 184,
    191, 196, 207, 211, 213, 214, 215,
    216, 217, 222, 225, 226, 231, 233,
    235, 236, 240, 256, 258, 262, 269,
    270, 271, 272, 278, 318, 341, 352,
    359, 375, 378, 380, 384, 397, 402,
    404, 452, 454, 464-465, 468
Mussolini, Benito 140, 148, 319, 382
Mutawwafin 269
Mutawwiun (those who compel
    obedience) 130, 262, 265
Muwahadin 256

N

Nabateans 231
Nablus 454
Nabulsi, Sulayman 242, 246, 248
Nadir, Shah 42
Naguib, Muhammad 148, 151
Nahjist Bloc (Lebanon) 226
Najd, Saudi Arabia 256, 257, 258,
    260, 261, 264, 270
Najdi 268
Najjada, the (Lebanon) 222
Napoleon (see Bonaparte, Napoleon)
Nashashibi family 455
Nassar, William 460
Nasser Al-Din, Shah (Persia) 40, 42
Nasser, Gamal Abdul 63, 86, 111,
    112, 113, 114, 125, 133, 134, 138,
    140, 146, 148, 150-152, 153, 154,
    156-157, 159, 160, 161, 162, 163,
    164, 165, 166, 167, 172, 173, 182,
    194, 206, 224, 225, 227, 244, 249,
    319, 320, 336, 396, 426, 427, 429,
    433, 437-438, 440, 456, 457, 458,
    464, 466, 467, 472
Nasser, Lake 10
Nasserism 110, 111, 115, 118, 121,
    131, 187, 328
Nasserites 174
National Action party (Turkey) 394,
    395
National Bloc (Jordan) 245
National Bloc (Kuwait) 284
National Bloc (Lebanon) 213, 222,
    226, 227
National Congress of Asu (Egypt) 161
National Congress of Popular Forces
    (Egypt) 159
National Council of the Revolutionary
    Command (Iraq) 180
National Council of the Revolutionary
    Command (NCRC) (Syria) 201
National Council of the Yishuv (Israel)
    350
National Democratic party (Iraq) 175,
    182
National Freedom League 455
National Front (Iran) 405, 406, 407,
    414, 415, 416
National Front (Leftist Faction of
    Baath party) (Iraq) 175
National Front (NF) (PDRY) 338,
    339, 340, 341, 342, 343-345, 346,
    347
National Front for the Liberation of
    the Occupied Arabian Gulf 310
National Front party (Jordan) 245-
    246
National Liberal party (Lebanon)
    222, 223, 226
National Liberation Front (NLF)
    (PDRY) 336, 337, 338, 345
National Liberation party (Iraq) 182
National Pact of 1943 (Lebanon) 214-
    215, 218, 225
National Progressive party (Iraq)
    182